*Genders and Sexualities in History*

Series Editors: **John H. Arnold, Joanna Bou**...

Palgrave Macmillan's series, *Genders and Se*... ...foster new approaches to historical research i... ...d will promote world-class scholarship that co... ...es ...enes of genders, sexualities, religions/religiosity, civil ...ations, politics and war.

Historical studies of gender and sexuality have often been treated as disconnected fields, while in recent years historical analyses in these two areas have synthesised, creating new departures in historiography. By linking genders and sexualities with questions of religion, civil society, politics and the contexts of war and conflict, this series will reflect recent developments in scholarship, moving away from the previously dominant and narrow histories of science, scientific thought, and legal processes. The result brings together scholarship from contemporary, modern, early modern, medieval, classical and non-Western history to provide a diachronic forum for scholarship that incorporates new approaches to genders and sexualities in history

The essays comprising *Intersections of Gender, Religion and Ethnicity in the Middle Ages* pursue the interrogation of interlocking discourses in a medieval setting; in so doing, they demonstrate not simply that 'gender' needs to be thought about in conjunction with other categories of identity, but that the nature of the categories and the nature of the intersections has its own history. For the middle ages in particular, what constitutes 'ethnicity' is very clearly in question; but so too, in fact, are 'gender' and 'religion'. The cultural processes, social practices and representational habits of the period differ from that of the modern world. Through investigation of that difference, both the texture of the medieval past and the construction of the modern period are thrown into important relief. The book is of considerable importance to current discussions in medieval studies over the construction and negotiation of identities but, through its collective methodological and interpretive insights, it will also provide provocative and interesting reading for historians of gender and ethnicity in later periods.

*Titles include:*

John H. Arnold and Sean Brady (*editors*)
WHAT IS MASCULINITY?
Historical Dynamics from Antiquity to the Contemporary World

Heike Bauer and Matthew Cook (*editors*)
QUEER 1950S

Cordelia Beattie and Kirsten A Fenton (*editors*)
INTERSECTIONS OF GENDER, RELIGION AND ETHNICITY IN THE MIDDLE AGES

Chiara Beccalossi
FEMALE SEXUAL INVERSION
Same-Sex Desires in Italian and British Sexology, c. 1870–1920

Raphaëlle Branche and Fabrice Virgili (*editors*)
RAPE IN WARTIME

Peter Cryle and Alison Moore
FRIGIDITY
An Intellectual History

Jennifer V. Evans
LIFE AMONG THE RUINS
Cityscape and Sexuality in Cold War Berlin

Kate Fisher and Sarah Toulalan (*editors*)
BODIES, SEX AND DESIRE FROM THE RENAISSANCE TO THE PRESENT

Christopher E. Forth and Elinor Accampo (*editors*)
CONFRONTING MODERNITY IN FIN-DE-SIÈCLE FRANCE
Bodies, Minds and Gender

Rebecca Fraser
GENDER, RACE AND FAMILY IN NINETEENTH CENTURY AMERICA
From Northern Woman to Plantation Mistress

Dagmar Herzog (*editor*)
BRUTALITY AND DESIRE
War and Sexuality in Europe's Twentieth Century

Robert Hogg
MEN AND MANLINESS ON THE FRONTIER
Queensland and British Columbia in the Mid-Nineteenth Century

Julia Laite
COMMON PROSTITUTES AND ORDINARY CITIZENS
Commercial Sex in London, 1885–1960

Andrea Mansker
SEX, HONOR AND CITIZENSHIP IN EARLY THIRD REPUBLIC FRANCE

Jessica Meyer
MEN OF WAR
Masculinity and the First World War in Britain

Meredith Nash
MAKING 'POSTMODERN' MOTHERS
Pregnant Embodiment, Baby Bumps and Body Image

Jennifer D. Thibodeaux (*editor*)
NEGOTIATING CLERICAL IDENTITIES
Priests, Monks and Masculinity in the Middle Ages

Hester Vaizey
SURVIVING HITLER'S WAR
Family Life in Germany, 1939–48

Clayton J. Whisnant
MALE HOMOSEXUALITY IN WEST GERMANY
Between Persecution and Freedom, 1945–69

*Forthcoming titles*

Matthew Cook
QUEER DOMESTICITIES
Homosexuality and Home Life in Twentieth-Century London

Melissa Hollander
SEX IN TWO CITIES
The Negotiation of Sexual Relationships in Early Modern England and Scotland

---

**Genders and Sexualities in History Series**
**Series Standing Order 978–0–230–55185–5 Hardback**
         978–0–230–55186–2 **Paperback**
(*outside North America only*)

You can receive future titles in this series as they are published by placing a standing order. Please contact your bookseller or, in case of difficulty, write to us at the address below with your name and address, the title of the series and one of the ISBNs quoted above.

Customer Services Department, Macmillan Distribution Ltd, Houndmills, Basingstoke, Hampshire RG21 6XS, England

# What is Masculinity?

## Historical Dynamics from Antiquity to the Contemporary World

Edited by

John H. Arnold
*Professor of Medieval History, Department of History, Classics and Archaeology, Birkbeck College, University of London, UK*

and

Sean Brady
*Lecturer in Modern British History, Department of History, Classics and Archaeology, Birkbeck College, University of London, UK*

palgrave
macmillan

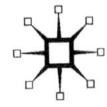

Editorial matter, selection and introduction © John H. Arnold and Sean Brady 2011, 2013
All remaining chapters © their respective authors 2011, 2013

All rights reserved. No reproduction, copy or transmission of this publication may be made without written permission.

No portion of this publication may be reproduced, copied or transmitted save with written permission or in accordance with the provisions of the Copyright, Designs and Patents Act 1988, or under the terms of any licence permitting limited copying issued by the Copyright Licensing Agency, Saffron House, 6–10 Kirby Street, London EC1N 8TS.

Any person who does any unauthorized act in relation to this publication may be liable to criminal prosecution and civil claims for damages.

The authors have asserted their rights to be identified as the authors of this work in accordance with the Copyright, Designs and Patents Act 1988.

First published in 2011
First published in paperback 2013 by
PALGRAVE MACMILLAN

Palgrave Macmillan in the UK is an imprint of Macmillan Publishers Limited, registered in England, company number 785998, of Houndmills, Basingstoke, Hampshire RG21 6XS.

Palgrave Macmillan in the US is a division of St Martin's Press LLC, 175 Fifth Avenue, New York, NY 10010.

Palgrave Macmillan is the global academic imprint of the above companies and has companies and representatives throughout the world.

Palgrave® and Macmillan® are registered trademarks in the United States, the United Kingdom, Europe and other countries.

ISBN: 978–0–230–27813–4 hardback
ISBN: 978–1–137–30560–2 paperback

A catalogue record for this book is available from the British Library.

A catalog record for this book is available from the Library of Congress.

10  9  8  7  6  5  4  3  2  1
22 21 20 19 18 17 16 15 14 13

# Contents

*List of Illustrations* — viii

*Acknowledgements* — ix

*Notes on Contributors* — x

1 Introduction — 1
  *John H. Arnold and Sean Brady*

## Part I  Paradigms and Nomenclature

2 The History of Masculinity: An Outdated Concept? — 17
  *John Tosh*

3 Can the Hegemon Speak? Reading Masculinity through Anthropology — 35
  *Diederik F. Janssen*

4 The Whig Interpretation of Masculinity? Honour and Sexuality in Late Medieval Manhood — 57
  *Christopher Fletcher*

5 Masculinity without Conflict: Noblemen in Eighth- and Ninth-Century Francia — 76
  *Rachel Stone*

## Part II  Masculinity and Hegemony

6 Masculinities in Early Hellenistic Athens — 97
  *Henrik Berg*

7 Masculinity As a World Historical Category of Analysis — 114
  *Simon Yarrow*

8 Hegemonic Masculinities? Assessing Change and Processes of Change in Elite Masculinity, 1700–1900 — 139
  *Henry French and Mark Rothery*

9 Masculinity and Fatherhood in England c. 1760–1830 — 167
  *Joanne Bailey*

## Part III  Maturing and Adulthood

10  Athenian Pederasty and the Construction of Masculinity    189
    *Thomas K. Hubbard*

11  An Orchard, a Love Letter and Three Bastards:
    The Formation of Adult Male Identity in a
    Fifteenth-Century Family    226
    *Rachel E. Moss*

12  'To Make a Man Without Reason': Examining Manhood
    and Manliness in Early Modern England    245
    *Jennifer Jordan*

13  'Boys, Semi-Men and Bearded Scholars': Maturity and
    Manliness in Early Nineteenth-Century Oxford    263
    *Heather Ellis*

## Part IV  Domesticities

14  St Francis of Assisi and the Making of Settlement
    Masculinity, 1883–1914    285
    *Lucinda Matthews-Jones*

15  Homes Fit for Homos: Joe Orton, Masculinity and
    the Domesticated Queer    303
    *Matt Cook*

16  Three Faces of Fatherhood As a Masculine Category:
    Tyrants, Teachers, and Workaholics As 'Responsible
    Family Men' during Canada's Baby Boom    323
    *Robert Rutherdale*

## Part V  Modern Frontiers

17  Cow Boys, Cattle Men and Competing Masculinities
    on the Texas Frontier    349
    *Jacqueline M. Moore*

18  Valorising Samurai Masculinity through Biblical Language:
    Christianity, Oscar Wilde and Natsume Soseki's Novel *Kokoro*    370
    *Kasumi Miyazaki*

19  'Proper Government and Discipline': Family Religion and
    Masculine Authority in Nineteenth-Century Canada    389
    *Nancy Christie*

20  Punters and Their Prostitutes: British Soldiers, Masculinity
    and *Maisons Tolérées* in the First World War                    413
    *Clare Makepeace*

## Conclusion

21  Masculinities, Histories and Memories                             433
    *Victor Jeleniewski Seidler*

*Index*                                                               453

# Illustrations

| | | |
|---|---|---|
| 1 | Red-figured ceramic fragment attributed to Onesimus (c. 490 BCE) | 193 |
| 2 | Red-figured krater attributed to Douris (c. 470 BCE) | 194 |
| 3 | Red-figured psykter attributed to Smikros (c. 510 BCE) | 195 |
| 4 | Red-figured pelike attributed to the Aegisthus Painter (c. 465 BCE) | 196 |
| 5 | Black-figured cup (c. 520 BCE). Gift of E.P. and Fiske Warren, 1908 | 197 |
| 6 | Red-figured kylix interior attributed to the Brygos Painter (c. 475 BCE) | 198 |
| 7 | Red-figured kylix attributed to Makron (c. 480 BCE) | 199 |
| 8 | Red-figured pelike attributed to the Calliope Painter (c. 430 BCE) | 201 |
| 9 | Black-figured amphora (c. 530 BCE) | 203 |
| 10 | Red-figured kylix interior attributed to the Briseis Painter (c. 475 BCE) | 204 |
| 11 | Red-figured kylix interior attributed to the Eretria Painter (c. 430 BCE) | 205 |
| 12 | Red-figured pelike attributed to Hermonax (c. 465 BCE) | 206 |
| 13 | Red-figured amphora attributed to the Dikaios Painter (c. 510 BCE) | 207 |
| 14 | Black-figured kotyle attributed to Amasis (c. 550 BCE) | 208 |
| 15 | Black-figured kylix attributed to the Painter of Louvre F51 (c. 530 BCE) | 208 |
| 16 | Red-figured kylix attributed to Douris (c. 485 BCE) | 210 |
| 17 | Red-figured kylix attributed to the Pedieus Painter (c. 510 BCE) | 211 |
| 18 | Red-figured kylix signed by Douris (c. 485 BCE) | 212 |
| 19 | Roman copy of the Diadoumenos of Polyclitus (original c. 420 BCE) | 214 |
| 20 | Red-figured kylix attributed to the Eretria Painter (c. 430 BCE) | 216 |
| 21 | Red-figured kylix attributed to the Eretria Painter (c. 430 BCE) | 217 |

# Acknowledgements

This book developed out of a conference held at Birkbeck College, University of London in May 2008. The editors would like to thank the many participants involved with 'What is Masculinity? How useful is it as a Historical Category?', without whom this collection of essays would not have been possible. The conference brought together for the first time scholars working in contemporary, modern, early modern, medieval, ancient and non-Western research fields to question the resonance and dissonances in recent scholarship that questions masculinities in history. It also aimed to discuss the similarities and profound differences in contexts and approaches to questions of masculinity across time and space in *la longue durée*, and involved scholars from the broad areas of history, philosophy, sociology, literary criticism, anthropology and art history. By necessity, this required all the delegates to think and discuss far outside their intellectual comfort zones. The editors would like to thank the delegates for taking this risk, and for making the conference such a stimulating and resounding success. This book brings together these disparate discussions, and aims to foster future scholarship and discussion on questions of masculinity across time-period disciplines. The authors in this collection have thanked individuals and sponsors in their chapters, and the editors extend thanks to them for enabling authors' contributions to this book. The editors would also like to thank the Leverhulme Trust and Birkbeck College, University of London, for their sponsorship of the conference. The collection has been awarded funding to support the reproduction of its images by the Scouloudi Foundation in association with the Institute of Historical Research, UK.

# Contributors

**John H. Arnold** is Professor of Medieval History at Birkbeck College, University of London. He has published various books and articles on the Middle Ages, and on the philosophy and practice of history, including *History: A Very Short Introduction* (2000), *Inquisition and Power* (2001), *Belief and Unbelief in Medieval Europe* (2005) and most recently *What is Medieval History?* (2008).

**Joanne Bailey** is Senior Lecturer in History at Oxford Brookes University. She has published *Unquiet Lives: Marriage and Marriage Breakdown in England 1660–1800* (2003), and articles on marital violence (*Social History*, 2006) and married women's legal status (*Continuity and Change*, 2002). Her current research explores parenting, and she has published articles on aspects of this topic in H. Berry and E. Foyster (eds), *The Family in Early Modern England* (2007), *History: The Journal of the Historical Association* (2010), *Family and Community History* (2010) and *Journal of Family History* (2010). She is completing a book titled *Parenting in England, 1760–1830: Emotions, Identities and Generations*, to be published in 2012.

**Henrik Berg** completed his PhD in Ancient History in 2010 at Uppsala University, Sweden, where he also lectures in Gender Studies, primarily critical theory on men and masculinities. He is also currently involved in a research project about the Swedish rescue service, masculinities and risk.

**Sean Brady** is Lecturer in Modern British and Irish History at Birkbeck College, University of London. His research interest focuses on gender, sexuality, politics and religion in nineteenth- and twentieth-century Britain and Ireland. His publications include *Masculinity and Male Homosexuality in Britain, 1861–1913* (2005; pbk 2009), and *John Addington Symonds (1840–1893) and Homosexuality: a Critical Edition of Sources* (ed. forthcoming 2011). He is currently working on a forthcoming monograph, *Religion in Society and Politics: Britain and Ireland 1801–2001*.

**Nancy Christie** presently teaches at McGill University in Montreal, Canada, and previously held the J.B. Smallman Chair at the University of Western Ontario. She has written two prize-winning monographs: *Engendering the State: Family, Work and Welfare in Canada* (2000) and *A Full-Orbed Christianity: the Protestant Churches and Social Welfare in Canada* (1996). She has edited several volumes, including *Households of Faith* (2002), *Mapping the Margins: the Family and Social Discipline in Canada* (2004), *Cultures of Citizenship in Postwar Canada* (2005) and *Transatlantic Subjects* (2008). Most recently she has published

*Churches and Their Peoples in Canada, 1840–1945* and is writing a two-volume history to mark Canada at 150.

**Matt Cook** is Senior Lecturer in History and Gender Studies at Birkbeck College, University of London. His publications include *London and the Culture of Homosexuality* (2003) and *A Gay History of Britain* (ed. and contributor, 2007). He is currently working on a monograph on queer home life in the twentieth century and two edited collections on post-war European sexualities and the queer 1950s.

**Heather Ellis** is Lecturer and Researcher in British History at the Centre for British Studies, Humboldt-Universität zu Berlin. Her doctoral project investigated the importance of generational conflict in the process of university reform in eighteenth- and nineteenth-century Oxford. She is the co-editor of *Masculinity and the Other: Historical Perspectives* (2009) and guest editor of a special issue of *Thymos: Journal of Boyhood Studies* (Fall, 2008) on the theme 'Boys, Boyhood and the Construction of Masculinity'. She has published widely on the importance of age in the construction of masculine identity, the history of the English public school system and Oxbridge, and the reception of classical scholarship. She is currently working on her postdoctoral project, which seeks to investigate the relationship between transnational scholarly networks and national identity in British universities between 1870 and 1945.

**Christopher Fletcher** is Chargé de Recherche at the Laboratoire de Médiévistique Occidentale, University of Paris I (Panthéon-Sorbonne). His first book was *Richard II: Manhood, Youth, and Politics, 1377–99* (2008). He has taught in London, Cambridge, Oxford and the University of Kent.

**Henry French** is Professor of Social History at the University of Exeter. He has published a number of studies of social identity, including *The Middle-Sort of People in Provincial England, c. 1620–1750* (2007). Since then he has been engaged on a three-year research project with Dr Mark Rothery and Dr Jennifer Jordan into gender identity over the *longue durée*, focusing on masculine identities among the English landed elite. This will result in a monograph entitled *Man's Estate: Masculinity and the English Landed Elite, 1680–1900*, due to be published in 2011.

**Thomas K. Hubbard** is Professor of Classics at the University of Texas, Austin. He is the author or editor of five books on Greco-Roman literature and history, including, most recently, *Homosexuality in Greece and Rome: a Sourcebook of Basic Documents* (2003). He is currently working on a book concerned with competition and Greek masculinity.

**Diederik F. Janssen** is an independent scholar residing in the Netherlands. He is editor of *Culture, Society & Masculinities* and of *Thymos: Journal of Boyhood*

*Studies*. He holds a Medical Doctorate and Bachelor of Cultural Anthropology, both from the Radboud University, Nijmegen.

**Jennifer Jordan** is a Postdoctoral Research Fellow at the University of Plymouth, working on the project 'Fatherhood and Masculinity in England c.1580–1720'. She has published articles in *Journal of Cultural and Social History* and the *Transactions of the Thoroton Society* and has also edited a collection of essays, *Desperate Housewives: Politics, Propriety and Pornography, Three Centuries of Women in England*, which is currently in press.

**Clare Makepeace** is currently a doctoral candidate in Modern British History at Birkbeck College, University of London. She holds a Master's in Historical Research from Birkbeck, University of London, and a Bachelor of Arts (Honours) in Modern History from the University of Oxford. She has articles forthcoming in *Cultural and Social History* and in the *Journal of International Women's Studies*.

**Lucinda Matthews-Jones** is Lecturer in Modern British History at Queen's University, Belfast. She holds a PhD in History from the University of Manchester (2010); her thesis was entitled 'Centres of Brightness: The Spiritual Imagination of Toynbee Hall and Oxford House, 1880–1914.'

**Kasumi Miyazaki** is Professor of Comparative Literature and History at Wako University, Japan. She is the author of *Reading Soseki after One Hundred Years* (2009) and is currently working on a critical biography of Oscar Wilde. She is convenor of the research consortium 'Masculinity and Friendship', Japan, fostering new developments in the study of nineteenth-century English literature and British history.

**Jacqueline M. Moore** is Professor of History at Austin College in Sherman, Texas. She is the author of several books including *Cow Boys and Cattle Men: Class and Masculinities on the Texas Frontier, 1865–1900* (2010) and *Booker T. Washington, W.E.B. Du Bois, and the Struggle for Racial Uplift* (2003). She is also co-editor of 'African American History Series'. In the course of researching the history of the Texas cattle industry she drove over 4000 miles without leaving the state.

**Rachel E. Moss** completed her PhD in Medieval Studies at the University of York in 2009, and in 2010 commenced as Chargé de Recherche at the Laboratoire de Médiévistique Occidentale, University of Paris I (Panthéon-Sorbonne) on the European Research Council Project 'Signs and States'. She is currently adapting her doctoral thesis into a monograph provisionally titled *Fictions of Fatherhood: Fathers in Late Medieval English Letters and Romances*. Her current research interests include adolescence, homosociality, male sexualities, patronage and gentry and mercantile reading cultures in the Middle Ages.

## Notes on Contributors xiii

**Mark Rothery** is currently a Postdoctoral Research Assistant on the project 'Consumption and the Country House, 1730–1800', funded by the Arts and Humanities Research Council and based at Northampton University, UK. He completed PhD at the University of Exeter in 2004 and was awarded the Postan Postdoctoral Research Fellowship by the Economic History Society, during which time he was based at the Cambridge Group for the Study of Population and Social Structure at the University of Cambridge. This was followed by a teaching fellowship and a lectureship at the University of Exeter, a Research Fellowship on a British Academy pilot research project 'Practices of Politeness' and a Research Fellowship on the project 'Man's Estate: Landed Gentility and Masculinity in England, 1660–1914', funded by the Arts and Humanities Research Council. He is the author of several articles, a co-author of a forthcoming book (with Henry French), *Man's Estate: Landed Gentility and Masculinity in England, 1660–1914*, and the author of *The English Landed Gentry, 1870–1939*, forthcoming.

**Robert Rutherdale** teaches in the Department of History and Philosophy at Algoma University in Sault Ste Marie, Ontario, Canada. He is the author of *Hometown Horizons: Local Responses to Canada's Great War* (2004) and has co-edited with Magda Fahrni *Creating Postwar Canada: Community, Diversity, and Dissent, 1945–1975* (2008). He is currently completing a book on fatherhood in Canada during the baby boom era.

**Victor Jeleniewski Seidler** is Professor of Social Theory in the Department of Sociology at Goldsmiths College, University of London. He has written widely in the areas of social theory, philosophy and ethics and has had a particular interest in gender, especially in relation to the critical studies of men and masculinities. His recent publications include *Transforming Masculinities: Men, Bodies, Cultures, Power, Sex and Love* (2005), *Young Men and Masculinities: Global Cultures and Intimate Lives* (2006), *Urban Fears and Global Terrors: Citizenship, Multicultures and Belongings* (2007), *Jewish Philosophy and Western Culture* (2008) and most recently *Embodying Identities: Culture, Differences and Social Theory* (2010). He is also the author of *Shadows of the Shoah: Jewish Identity and Belonging* (2000), *Man Enough: Embodying Masculinities* (1997), *Recovering the Self: Morality and Social Theory* (1994) and *Unreasonable Men: Masculinity and Social Theory* (1993).

**Rachel Stone** is an independent scholar and is currently Departmental Library Cataloguer in the Department of Coins and Medals, Fitzwilliam Museum, Cambridge. She has published several articles and chapters on Carolingian marriage, religion and gender history, and her book *Morality and Masculinity in the Carolingian Empire* will be published in 2011. She is currently translating Hincmar of Rheims's *De divortio Lotharii regis et Theutbergae reginae* with Dr Charles West (Sheffield University).

**John Tosh** is Professor of History at Roehampton University, London. He began writing about the history of masculinities in the early 1990s. His principal publications are *A Man's Place: Masculinity and the Middle-Class Home in Victorian England* (1999) and *Manliness and Masculinities in Nineteenth-Century Britain* (2005). More recently he has turned his attention to the relationship between masculinity and imperialism in nineteenth-century Britain.

**Simon Yarrow** is Lecturer in Medieval History in the School of History and Cultures at the University of Birmingham, UK. He is author of *Saints and Their Communities: Miracle Stories in Twelfth-Century England* (2006) and is interested in religious cultures and practices in the central Middle Ages, with a current focus on the materiality and narratives of relic practices. He is also interested in the gendering of historical and hagiographical narratives in twelfth-century England, and more broadly in the comparison of religious practices in the pre-modern world.

# 1
# Introduction

*John H. Arnold and Sean Brady*

> This primordial investment in the social games (*illusio*) which make a man a real man – the sense of honour, virility, 'manliness', or, as the Kabyles say, 'Kabylness' (*thakbaylith*) – is the undisputed principle of all the duties towards oneself, the motor or motive of all that a man 'owes to himself', in other words what he must do in order to live up, in his own eyes, to a certain idea of manhood.
>
> Pierre Bourdieu, *Masculine Domination*[1]

What is masculinity? It's a question to which various answers have been proffered, not only in the analytical confines of academia, but both explicitly and implicitly in self-help manuals, popular culture, feminism, governmental legislation, psychoanalytic theory, and in various quotidian interactions between boys and their fathers, husbands and wives, children and teachers, and so on and so forth. And indeed, as the chapters of this book demonstrate, it is a question which has been posed in a variety of earlier forms through a variety of historical media, from ancient theatre to medieval chronicles, from early modern letters to nineteenth-century pedagogic tracts. Pierre Bourdieu's attempt to outline the nature of masculinity is one notable response, perhaps helpful to us most particularly in his insistence upon the deep-rooted character of patriarchy, which he sees as producing and reproducing itself not only via social relations and cultural media but also through the embodied habits and practices of everyday experience. In his account, masculinity – and particularly the habit of masculine domination – has been very hard to challenge, because it has bound itself so very closely both to social power and to 'just how things are': a primary example of 'history turned into nature', of an ideological practice cloaking itself in the guise of inescapable necessity. We are thus reminded that the analysis of gender is at the heart of the analysis of power relations and politics in general.

The above quotation is helpful not only in what it elucidates, but also in what it tends to elide. In Bourdieu's view, what matters is the likeness and the structural similarity between various cultural patterns of male behaviour and ideology, from Kabyle tribesmen to modern French academics. However, as various authors in this book explore, there are important nuances, at the very least, to what we choose to term 'masculinity' as it is viewed across time; and, as several (though not all) of the authors here suggest, we may in fact be studying different phenomena, arising from different systems of power and gender, rather than anything which tidily coheres to one core of 'masculinity'. That is to say that honour, virility, manliness or 'Kabylness', and so forth, might as fruitfully be studied for how they differ as for how they converge. This, it seems to us, lies at the heart of the particular contribution which historians can make to the wider discussion: not simply 'what is masculinity?', but what has masculinity *been*?

Bound up in that question – how to write the history of masculinity – are in fact a variety of further issues; we would like here briefly to outline four, which we think have a particular bearing on scholarship in this area. First, as is ever the case when looking across *la longue durée*, we are confronted by substantial changes in the nature of the available sources. For example, whilst letters exist for most of the periods discussed in the following essays (and are indeed used by several of our authors), they only become something we might see as 'personal' documents in the later medieval period; before that, conformity to inherited rhetorical models, and expectations of a degree of public circulation, make letters a rather different form of material. Other kinds of documents do not exist in earlier periods: manuals advising the reader on social behaviour do not appear before the late Middle Ages, and only become a reasonably well-circulated medium in the seventeenth century. Trial records, of the kind which reveal something of the texture of everyday life, again tend only to appear in the late Middle Ages and after. And, of course, oral history – as pursued below by Robert Rutherdale – is simply impossible for anything but contemporary history. The variations in the available archives present us again with the question of comparability: are we actually looking at the same 'thing' across time? And does absence of a certain aspect of what we later perceive in masculinity indicate a real difference over time, or a difference over what our sources will reveal to us? One might also think of the changes in the sources not simply as a general hazard in the data, but as intimately connected (as Michel Foucault suggested in regard to the concept of 'man') with changing configurations of power/knowledge, and hence different ideological patterns within which various ideas of gender identity gain greater or lesser weight. Thus, perhaps, the greater ubiquity of advice manuals in the early modern period in Europe is not simply a neutral by-product of the rise of print publishing, but part also of the changed ideological position of the domestic household and its governance within the wider conceptions of the early modern polity. In short, the archive is not neutral, but is itself bound up with changing configurations of power and identity.

Second, it is apparent in various studies of gender that masculine identity is often figured relationally and/or comparatively, as frequently between men as between men and women. Here there are important sociological changes to be considered. Whilst certain elements of male–female relations have arguably remained broadly comparable over historical time (children in regard to mothers and fathers, husbands in regard to wives, even if the precise nature of those relations has varied considerably), the social practices and institutions through which men come into contact with, and are encouraged to regard themselves in relation to, other men have taken extremely different historical forms. For example, a key context for the formation of contemporary gendered identity is surely the classroom (whether co-educational or single-sex). But, as a general frame of gender experience, this is a product of late modernity, and, although educational contexts of course existed in preceding periods, they were never the general norm. In one chapter below, Clare Makepeace discusses conscripted soldiers in the First World War; again, whilst armies have existed throughout history, only in modern times has 'army life' been a widely shared homosocial context, and only in modern times has 'the army' been presented as a core part of national identity. Conversely, the elite warrior class of a much earlier era expected to live in a 'household' which included various men of a lower rank, who hovered between the position of servant and that of comrade; and the ideological mystification of 'chivalry' surrounding such elite social formations exercised, in those earlier periods, a wider attraction, such that elite merchants and the like aspired to similar social and affective relations. We are not suggesting that these different social forms are somehow too disparate for meaningful comparison, or refute any historical continuities ('chivalry', after all, had a resurgent attraction in Western modernity, and the affective notion of something like 'comradeship' can be found in various times and places, from ancient Sparta to contemporary youth gangs). Our point, rather, is that, while there may be shared and relatively continuous processes in the formation and maintenance of masculine identity, these have nonetheless occurred in radically disparate contexts, and are not evenly distributed across society. 'Being a man' has some universal, albeit notional, address in contemporary culture; but in previous times the arrangement of the whole social fabric may have made such an appeal more localised, or necessarily plural (as medieval historians have pointed out, a study of 'masculinity' in medieval Europe has to deal with the fact that knights, clergy and peasants were thought of as very different kinds of men). Moreover, in much of the pre-modern era, dominant ideologies saw hierarchy and inequality as inevitable or even God-given. Thus social difference and potential social tensions, which we might expect to feed into particular notions and experiences of masculinity, were positioned within wider ideologies and *mentalités*.

This raises the issue, thirdly, of gender in relation to other constructions of identity – most obviously race, class and sexuality, but also (as we look across the broader historical landscape) with regard to status, age, profession, religion, ethnicity and national identity. A key shared development in gender studies of all kinds in the last decade or so has been the recognition that gender rarely, if ever, stands alone in the formation of human subjectivity; rather, gender is one set of cultural codes which usually enmesh with other important aspects, such as notions of race or the hierarchies of class. As importantly, what comes most to *matter* in a society may differ over time. For some historians, gender – or, more precisely, some form of patriarchy – has always been the predominant code from which all other inequalities follow. But others have suggested greater variation – that in a particular period and context 'race', for example, might be the key issue (though, of course, still entwined with concepts of masculinity and femininity). More complex still, it has been suggested that in some early societies the strength (*virilitas*) associated with warrior masculinity operated as the principal factor, paradoxically somewhat independently of actual men: thus, as Rachel Stone demonstrates below, notions of being 'virile' could be applied to early medieval women.[2] There is a general question here of whether we are thinking of 'gender' particularly in terms of individual subjective experience, or (as Joan Scott also encouraged us to do) as part of the ideological representational fabric of society – of how relations of power were conceived and represented at a given historical moment.[3] In the latter case, in modern times it is likely that 'national identity' would be a key and recurrent accompaniment to ideas of masculinity, both within a European context of competing nation states, and (with added racial aspects) in a colonial context. Once again these present important issues of change over time, not specific to the issue of gender, but extremely important when coming to study it (if indeed it is a singular 'it') across *la longue durée*.

This leads us to our fourth point, as briefly touched upon above: the relationship between representation and experience. As John Tosh suggests in the following chapter, some cultural approaches to gender have been all representation and no experience, producing analyses only of the media of a period, and ignoring or taking for granted the lived reality experienced by historical subjects. Not that such 'experience' is accessible in some transparent or *a priori* state; we would tend to agree with Joan Scott's suspicion that a somehow unmediated lived 'reality' is but a phantasm, an impossible idea of pristine subjectivity which is in fact not only unavailable to the historian looking back, but equally unavailable to the historical subject himself or herself.[4] There is in this sense no dichotomy between 'discourse' and 'reality'; the point of a properly post-structuralist approach is to note that dominant modes of representing the world inform our own experience of that world. But it is thus important to explore the experience of culturally mediated reality, and to look to sources which bring a greater sense of the complex texture of everyday life; the historian should not simply listen to the prescriptive voice of a period's dominant ideology, but delve into its reception and interpretation. Moreover, as our earlier points make clear, histories of gender identity must pay attention to social, economic and political formations, which can change radically over time.

Of course, historians of masculinity have rightly drawn upon cultural representations of manhood, masculinity, honour and the like, as these provide such seductively informative perspectives. When considered over the whole period, from antiquity to modernity, some issues of comparability and interpretation again make themselves plain. Several of the authors in this book raise issues concerning the vocabulary of their sources – the keywords of masculinity for a given period, or perhaps (since part of the issue is whether 'masculinity' really is a trans-historical category of analysis) the keywords associated in particular with the legitimation of male power. For much of the pre-modern period, language itself is bound up with issues of ethnicity and hierarchy: the Latin of the church and the French of the Western European upper classes, for example. For all prescriptive sources, there are questions to be asked regarding circulation and readership, and we need to remember that the date of a given publication does not necessarily correspond to its period of maximum audience. As literary critics would, of course, remind us, with any kind of cultural production, the audience is actively engaged in the meaning of the work; and here, again, we perhaps need to spend more time considering how different accounts of masculinity are situated culturally, socially and politically. Would sermons heard in the nave on Sundays carry greater or lesser weight than printed advice manuals read at home alone? Did people respond to governmental propaganda in the dutiful fashion expected, or (as some recent work tends to suggest) could the most 'authoritative' cultural productions in fact prompt some elements of counter-reaction?[5] What, in any case, actually makes a cultural text 'authoritative', particularly with regard to something like masculinity? The latter point carries with it a particular issue when one thinks of masculinity within narrative rather than as an abstract set of prescribed norms; it is important to consider, for example, how an audience receives and interprets the potentially complex movements of narrative. One can see a fairly obvious match between abstract discussions of steadfast late-Victorian manliness and a succession of rather dull, Bulldog Drummond-style heroes; but what of more complex stories, such as the sexually enraptured hero of H. Rider Haggard's *She* (1887)? Can one simply 'read' masculinity from the tensions, reversals, surprises and closures of narrative, or are more diverse issues at play?

There are undoubtedly further issues to be considered; these are just those thoughts which have occurred to us through the process of organising the original conference on masculinity, and subsequently editing this collection of essays. Part of our desire in organising that conference was to prompt a broader discussion than is sometimes possible within the confines of our increasingly specialised historiographies. The study of masculinity calls out for interdisciplinary approaches (and we have indeed included one chapter on anthropology, and Victor Seidler's concluding chapter, which arises from a sociological perspective). But, perhaps even more pressingly, it calls out for more discussion within the historical profession, between our period boundaries. Only through greater discussion of this kind can we discern where there may be continuity and where there may be change, and whether the topic under discussion is 'masculinity' in all times and places, or something more protean and even more ideological. This book does not attempt to write 'a history of masculinity', and for that reason we have not arranged the chapters which follow in a chronological order. Our desire to elucidate 'historical dynamics' is, rather, to pose a number of thematic issues, and to juxtapose differing historical pictures and perspectives.

Part I of this collection explores issues of nomenclature in analysing masculinities, and identifies paradigms through which masculinities operate. In the first chapter John Tosh takes an overview of the recent explosion in masculinities in historiography. He questions, however, whether this burgeoning scholarship can be called 'the History of Masculinity', because of the variety of historiographical perspectives from which masculinity is questioned and analysed. Tracing the roots of historical questions of masculinity from the late 1980s, Tosh examines the original political project of questioning masculinity in history. In spite of burgeoning scholarship, historical practice has been sidelined by cultural interpretations, which emphasise meaning and representation. Tosh calls for a revitalised historical approach, re-engaging with agency, behaviour and experience. Diederik Janssen's chapter questions the use of anthropology, as a late arrival in the range of approaches to masculinities in gender studies. Janssen scrutinises and historicises the inherent problems in ethnography in relation to gender theory over the last 20 years. Taking Gayatri Chakravorty Spivak's famous question, 'can the subaltern (as woman) speak?', Janssen asks whether 'the hegemon (as man)' can speak, and looks closely and comparatively across a wide terrain, examining different anthropological perspectives, and noting the differently inflected lexicons within which male identity is expressed in a range of cultures, including Mexico, China, India, Africa and the US. In conclusion, Janssen argues that anthropologists and historians should not settle for a simple evocation of 'variety', but should see that there are various comparative conclusions that can tentatively be drawn when taking a broader cultural perspective.

Christopher Fletcher's chapter questions how historians can study past societies without reducing the society in question to 'a mere illustration of our own pre-existing categories of analysis'. Fletcher reminds us of the development of English constitutional historiography in the nineteenth and twentieth centuries, arguing that it holds lessons for the historicisation of masculinity. Both historiographies are set by the interests of their day; and Fletcher highlights not only the anachronism of 'masculinity' as a term prior to the eighteenth century, but the problems that it can unwittingly introduce into the attempt to historicise gender. He also argues, however, that medieval 'manhood' was at least as complex and ramified as modern masculinity, built upon issues of strength, vigour, steadfastness and concerns with honour and status, including conspicuous display – though sexuality, he argues, was a secondary consideration, unlike in modern masculinity. Rachel Stone, like Fletcher, challenges the direct applicability of modern conceptions of masculinity back into the distant past in her chapter on ninth-century noble masculinity in Francia. But her approach is not so much to stress the different priorities emphasised by a medieval male identity as to note that core notions of (male) strength and vigour – being 'virile' – can also be found, in the early medieval context, applied to some women, and to some men who in other senses clearly had been emasculated. As she argues, 'to Carolingian authors, therefore, "manly" behaviour encompassed an enormous range, from boldness in battle to persistence in faith and humble supplication.' This chapter points to a series of key shifts in male ideologies in the early Middle Ages, linked to changes in ecclesiastical and secular politics, and, through a mixture of close reading and broad perspective, Stone demonstrates the interrelationship of 'masculine' identity with other relational factors – and troublingly asks, in conclusion, whether pre-modern and modern masculinity, in this sense, really share anything in common.

In Part II of this book, the contributors explore hegemonies, a crucial theme in the analysis of masculinities since R.W. Connell's groundbreaking work in the 1980s, which adapted Antonio Gramsci's concept of hegemony to the social being and social statuses of gender. Henrik Berg, who examines masculinities in early Hellenistic Athens, works primarily from the literary sources of this very early period, in an attempt to reconstruct different inflections of masculine identity among the male elite. Berg analyses how elite male identity was positioned with regard to citizens, slaves, foreigners and women. Issues of ethnicity (above all) and social status are thus key determinants of masculine identity in this time and place. Within the literary genre, a figure emerges of ideal masculinity, as a responsible Athenian citizen who can support himself and his family and who never loses his self-control. As Berg notes, however, it is not clear whether other figures in these texts – women and slaves in particular – are in any sense understood to possess a comparative or negative *gender* identity.

Simon Yarrow's chapter explores masculinity as a category of world historical analysis through the prism of the medieval world. This chapter addresses what happens to the concept of masculinity when placed within the very broad span of world history (the focus here being 500–1500 CE, but with a still broader ambit kept in view), emphasising the dangers of working within 'the parochiality of [Western] modernity'. Yarrow argues that world history has thus far made little headway in the analysis of gender, and points out some key methodological stumbling blocks. But he demonstrates how useful the large historical canvas can be, if we are truly interested in thinking about issues of change and continuity, similarity and difference. By thinking beyond the abstracted claims for masculine identity made by literate cultural elites, we may consider how masculinity, as an embodied subjectivity, involves a variety of complex processes: labelling, imitation, the association of masculine traits with other categories of difference, performance, reflection, acts of subversion and divergence, and ultimately violence. As a way of thinking across cultures, Yarrow offers the notion of 'iconic masculinity', as a specifically embodied and culturally valued 'performance' of ideal male identity, experienced both within and between (in a colonial context) various cultures.

Henry French and Mark Rothery's co-authored chapter 'Hegemonic Masculinities? Assessing Change and Processes of Change in Elite Masculinity, 1700–1900' arises from the authors' larger project on male identity in early modern and modern England. Through using a modified Braudelian perspective, they criticise Connell's influential theory of hegemonic masculinities, arguing that Connell and others have conflated 'transient and changeable social stereotypes' with elements in 'deep seated and enduring' forms of hegemony. They regard hegemony as a useful interpretative concept, but criticise the interpretations and attributes given to masculine hegemony by scholars in recent years. In effect, this has exaggerated in scholarship the degree of change detectable in 'fundamental norms of masculine behaviour and attitude'. French and Rothery identify these deep-seated norms beneath changeable stereotypes, such as the fop or the polite gentleman. They locate the cultural changes in stereotype within perennial conditions of male self-valorisation – virtue, honour, self-control, independence – through evidence from families of the English gentry from the seventeenth to the twentieth centuries. In doing so, French and Rothery contribute significantly to a reassessment of historical change in masculinity, with a greater emphasis on continuity than on transformation.

Joanne Bailey's chapter examines how a research agenda defined by concerns with gender and identity furthers the history of men as fathers. Through a focus on gender, questions of fatherhood in the late eighteenth and nineteenth centuries in Britain are moved from 'father' as a biological category to the notion of social fathering, differentiating fathers from mothers in their social being. Bailey thus investigates masculinity in relationship to fatherhood, rather than subsuming fathers as a symbol or subcategory of masculinity. Approaching fatherhood through masculinity helps historians to recognise 'diversity, fluidity and potential gaps' between ideals, aspirations and actualities. This approach also questions notions of rapid change over time, challenging the dichotomy between early modern and modern fatherhood and masculinity. By concentrating upon the relationship between representation and experience, evolving codes of manhood and fathering styles can be contextualised with more analytical precision than has hitherto been the case.

Part III of this book focuses upon male maturation and adulthood across time and space, in profoundly differing social and cultural contexts. Thomas K. Hubbard examines Athenian pederasty and the construction of masculinity in Classical Athens. Hubbard notes that, although, on a theoretical level, historians have acknowledged the multiplicity, contingency and social constructedness of masculinities, in practice a focus upon certain themes (male sexual domination, violence, militarism, imperialism and oppression of minorities) has been so pervasive that they almost re-essentialise the concept of masculinity. He argues that more interesting than the fact of male dominance are its gaps, discontinuities and vulnerabilities: those points where masculine performance diverges the most from our stereotypical expectations. One such area is the sexual relationship between men and boys in ancient Athens. Using a wide variety of sources, Hubbard brings considerable nuance into the analysis of this area, setting the sexual element within a much wider range of social practices, and suggesting some degree of agency on the part of the youths involved.

Rachel Moss, through the use of fifteenth-century letter collections, focuses on the affective and social relations between older and younger men – 'adolescents' in medieval terms, but in fact usually including men in their twenties and even early thirties. Moss finds that 'maleness is not synonymous with manliness, and that hypermasculine, life stage-specific behaviours are features of late medieval adolescence.' What is tracked here is a particular passage from 'boys' to 'men', as the younger members of the Celys family balance a 'youthful' desire for unattached sexual encounters with women with the growing need to identify a suitable future wife. Through the correspondence, we see how fathers and other older men regulated, reproved and tacitly tolerated this dance of desire, honour and parental authority. Masculine identity for the medieval adolescent thus emerges through a social triangulation between sexually desired women and their own male relatives.

Jennifer Jordan's chapter notes that most work on early modern manhood – and, indeed, on masculinity and patriarchy in general – has focussed upon the adult male who has 'achieved' manhood, and has been less able to think about patriarchy in terms of youths and old men. This chapter focuses upon the former, looking particularly at 'the varied ways in which boys were encouraged to learn and display attributes of manliness from a young age', primarily via conduct literature. Moralists and parents wished to ensure that boys would turn into men; and thus, Jordan argues, although boys were dependents and hence lacking full 'manhood', they were nonetheless 'encouraged to achieve traits of manliness making them entirely male-gendered despite their sexual immaturity'. Thus, there is an important distinction between 'manhood' – as a state achieved – and 'manliness' – as a set of practices and qualities related to a gendered identity. As with Jordan's chapter, Heather Ellis is concerned to move beyond clear-cut distinctions between 'men' and 'Others', and argues that, even when gender is seen as intersecting with other discourses such as race and class, there is a tendency to simplify power relations, and read all categories of difference back into a too-simple male/female binary. She thus focuses in her chapter on maturity and age, as another way in which ideas of 'manliness' can be complicated. Following the lead of medievalist and early modern studies of universities, this chapter uses Oxford and Cambridge as a case study for the transition 'from boys to men', a process complicated in this period by the rising age of students. Ellis argues that manliness read as 'maturity' was a far more common preoccupation in this period than previous studies have recognised.

Part IV of this book focuses upon domesticities, the implications of domestic arrangements for masculinity, and men's attitudes towards domesticity. Domesticity has been central to questions of gender (and Women's Studies) since their inception. However, few studies have concentrated on domesticity and masculinity in all-male situations, particularly for the modern period and outside the university or monastic setting. In addition, the father's own sense of domesticity and changing role in the family unit since the Second World War is only beginning to be questioned by historians. In Lucinda Matthews-Jones's chapter, the nineteenth-century homosocial experiments of Toynbee Hall and Oxford House, establishments of the University Settlement Movement in London's East End, are examined for the culture of masculinity created there, and the specificity of the influence of St Francis of Assisi in these Protestant organisations. Although crucial to historiographical debates on outcast London, no attention has been paid to Christian spirituality and imagination in this area. For the men involved with the movement, many of whom went on to occupy positions of secular importance and prominence, the movement gave them a masculine identity that broke with the ideals of the previous generation. As Matthews-Jones states, 'this imaginary allowed settlers to be active, social and public men who lived in a space that was neither [traditionally] domestic nor straightforwardly ascetic.' Space, religion and a reworked sense of public and private duty and morality configure in this particular context to produce a different notion of masculine identity.

In 'Homes Fit for Homos', Matt Cook examines male queer 'at home', through the life of the controversial British homosexual playwright, Joe Orton. Cook analyses the problems posed by the figure of Orton for commentators both in the 1960s and in the 1980s. Orton's sexual promiscuity, amply demonstrated in his famous diaries, conflicts with the prevailing notion of the restrained middle-class homosexual of the homophile campaigns. According to his critics, Orton, who was murdered by his lover in 1967, would have been bemused and amused by the 'loony left' attempt in the 1980s to enfold gay men 'within the culturally central realms of home and family'. Cook argues, however, that Orton's supposed oppositional status is not this clear-cut, and examines his negotiation of the intersections of home, homosexuality and masculinity. That there *is* a 'queer domesticity' unsettles various assumptions about homosexual identity, but also the wider issue of masculinity with regard to gay sexuality.

Robert Rutherdale's chapter provides one of the first uses of oral history in the study of masculinity, being based upon a series of interviews with Canadian men of an earlier generation. It focuses upon their ideas about, and ways of recounting the experiences of, fatherhood: as tyrants, teachers and workaholics, and as 'Responsible Family Men'. In this way, Rutherdale demonstrates the different ways in which men attempted to master this normative domestic role, and how personal life paths and memories intersect with much wider social and historical forces. He argues that the paradigm of a post-war 'crisis' in masculine identity is highly problematic, and that a focus on 'responsible family men' demonstrates instead a spectrum of more-or-less effective male identities and social practices.

Part V of this book examines frontiers in the modern period – frontiers in space, and frontiers in the mind – and the effect that they had upon masculinities in various regions. Jacqueline M. Moore's chapter on the Texas frontier in the nineteenth century challenges the stereotype of the American cowboy, beloved in film and television (and concomitant scholarship) as the hero figure of manhood, straddling the frontier between civilisation and wilderness in the nineteenth century. Moore argues instead that, to contemporaries in nineteenth-century Texas, the birthplace of the American cowboy, cattlemen, townspeople and the settled people of the countryside did not at all regard the cowboy as 'manly'. He was, rather, unsettled and misgoverned; and cowboys essentially were regarded as permanent adolescents. They posed no threat to the class structure, and the myth of the masculine cowboy who answers to no man was predominantly a fiction. The cowboy earned his manly hero reputation outside the American West, by those who were worried by 'over-civilisation' creating emasculated men. The 'frontier' was a place of the imagination more than socio-economic fact: the imagined cowboy who tames the frontier played a very different cultural role from the actual cowboy in real frontier society.

Kasumi Miyasaki's chapter addresses the cultural encounter between East and West in the twentieth century, with regard to masculine identities, via a close reading of the most important novel in modern Japanese literature, Soseki Natsume's *Kokoro* (1914). *Kokoro* has been understood as a work of nostalgic praise for a lost, noble masculinity, more in tune with the feudal Edo period (1603–1867) than the capitalist and westernised nation born after the Meiji restoration. As a key cultural work, it sits at an important moment in the remaking of modern Japanese culture and society, articulating fraught cultural shifts, particularly in the realm of masculinity, from past to present. Mayasaki argues that the novel in fact connects the narrative of Samurai self-immolation to the spirituality of the Passion in Oscar Wilde's essay *De Profundis* (1905): the heroic act of committing suicide following one's lord is suffused with homoeroticism. The meaning of blood in *Kokoro* is subverted from the traditional sense of 'kinship' to a connection with Christian symbolism. Through this reworking, a wholly different sense of Japanese male–male relations, and past–present transitions, is given form.

In her chapter on family religion and masculine authority in nineteenth-century Canada, Nancy Christie argues that spirituality was central to frontier concepts of masculinity and fatherhood. The cultural status, and in particular the spiritual status, of fatherhood began to decline in the United States and Britain between the 1790s and the 1830s. But in the British North American colonies that became Canada the opposite process occurred, fostering instead the continuance of a much older patriarchalism, which presented the power of men as descending directly from God to the monarch and the fatherly magistrates in the home. Beyond the republican influences of the US and France, with their new emphases upon the moral mother, frontier Canadian society created a stronger patriarchal role for men in families, and a stronger spiritual role for fathers in a society which had a lack of formal churches. In many respects, argues Christie, this *ancien régime* form of patriarchy persisted intact in Canada well into the twentieth century, and its resilience challenges the periodisation of changes in masculinity in much recent modern historical scholarship.

The First World War is the subject of vast scholarship, including, in recent years, some work on masculine identity. There are, however, aspects of life in wartime which have been little studied: the sexual activities of soldiers on duty being a key example. Through a study of letters and diaries, Clare Makepeace's chapter explores the different ways in which men narrated their sexual desires, and their use of sanctioned brothels in wartime France. Advice manuals and army rules give a notional structure to the licit and illicit in this regard; the more personal evidence suggests ways in which men negotiated their sense of masculine identity within this frame. As Makepeace argues, whilst wartime undoubtedly provided a different 'space' for masculine identity, what becomes visible during wartime may also be read back into peacetime identities. This is particularly intriguing with regard to married men and the 'uxorious ideal' of the period; issues of status (class/rank) and nationality also played notable roles in mediating the experience, and subsequent narration, of masculine identity.

Victor Jeleniewski Seidler concludes this collection with reflections upon the place of, and developments in, masculinities as a site of critical analysis in the last 20 years, both within the academy and in politics more broadly. In 'Masculinities, Histories and Memories', Seidler places the Birkbeck 2008 conference and this collection in the historical context of questions 'around the critical study of men and masculinities into relationship with traditions of social theory and research' that aimed for a 'renewal of disciplinary theory and practice', dating from the groundbreaking Bradford University conference in 1988,[6] which in turn had been inspired by 'men-consciousness raising' among radicals since the early 1970s. Seidler discusses the ways in which he and others, including Joseph Pleck and Jack Sawyer, formed a discussion group at Harvard University (among other discussion groups at this time) with the specific aim of exploring their own inherited masculinities and responding to the challenge of feminism, recognising the 'politics of the personal' in men's lives and the ways in which this framed gender relations (and developing eventually into 'Men's Studies' in the United States). Examining this and other movements in the 1980s, such as the inception of the journal *Achilles Heel*, Seidler discusses the instigation of, and the importance of, historical writing and investigation in questioning the present history of masculinities. He emphasises how unusual it was for heterosexual men 'to explore how their experience had been shaped through the expectations and disciplines of contemporary masculinities', and that the term masculinity itself was not a term in wide usage, except in relational contrast to femininity. Tracing questions of masculinities as a history of ideas in the last 30 years, Seidler provides a fascinating account of the changes and challenges of masculinities as scholarly enquiry in recent years, moving as it has far beyond the rapidly redundant concept of the 'politics of the personal' of the 1970s. He highlights the dangers present in historical research 'that seeks a sense of security through "staying within the context" of the narratives that are invoked to make sense of gender relations in a specific historical period'.

It is precisely this practice that this collection seeks to challenge. *What is Masculinity? Historical Dynamics from Antiquity to the Contemporary World* necessarily and deliberately raises more problems than it provides answers to its provocative question. This book is a route in to the serious, collaborative attempt to question what masculinity *was* and *is* over time and space. The concept of the collection is key to the series within which it is published, 'Genders and Sexualities in History' (Palgrave Macmillan, edited by Joanna Bourke, John H. Arnold and Sean

Brady). It is hoped that both this groundbreaking collection, and the series itself, will foster scholarship in time-period disciplines that look beyond the confines of historical periodisation, context, evidence and discipline, to provide new insights and challenges in questions of the relational qualities of gender – synchronically and diachronically.

## Notes

1. Pierre Bourdieu, *Masculine Domination*, trans. R. Nice (first published 1998; Cambridge, 2001), p. 48.
2. For the explicit suggestion that gender was not the determining issue in Scandinavian warrior society, see Carol J. Clover, 'Regardless of sex: men, women, and power in early Northern Europe', *Speculum* 68 (1993), 363–87.
3. Joan W. Scott, 'Gender: a useful category of historical analysis', *The American Historical Review* 91:5 (1986), 1053–75.
4. Joan W. Scott, 'The evidence of experience', *Critical Enquiry* 17:4 (1991), 773–97.
5. For example, the popular reactions to government propaganda revealed in Paul Addison and Jeremy Crang, *Listening to Britain: Home Intelligence Reports on Britain's Finest Hour May-September 1940* (London, 2010).
6. Organised by Jeff Hearn, David Morgan and the British Sociological Association.

# Part I
# Paradigms and Nomenclature

# 2
# The History of Masculinity: An Outdated Concept?

*John Tosh*

It may seem premature to raise the possibility of a redundant specialism when, as recently as the mid-1980s, the history of masculinity did not yet exist in Britain. Indeed, the very idea was absent from academic and popular discourse. Its modest beginnings were associated less with the discipline of history than with sociology; politically and conceptually it was indebted to socialist feminism. Those influences were critical at what turned out to be foundational moment for the history of masculinity. In September 1988 the theory section of the British Sociological Association convened in Bradford. The event was dominated by academics in social theory and social policy. Interest in history on the part of the delegates was minimal.[1] But the conference was attended by a small number of historians, and the outcome for them was an informal study group – the first forum of any kind in Britain in which the history of masculinity was discussed. In due course the group produced the first theorised collection of essays on the history of masculinity in Britain.[2] Even so, progress thereafter was slow. A panel on masculinity at a History Workshop in 1992 was thinly attended. The following year the theme of the Institute of Historical Research's annual Anglo-American Conference was gender, but only a few papers on masculinity were featured. R.W. Connell was not far wrong in stating in 1993 that serious historical work on themes of masculinity was 'extremely rare'.[3] All one could say in mitigation was that this was an improvement on his earlier scathing dismissal of histories of masculinity as 'embarrassing'.[4] Fifteen years on we have no reason to be embarrassed. Whereas in 1989 the founding editors of the journal *Gender and History* struggled to commission any article on masculinity, their successors today have no such difficulty: there are typically two or three such articles in every issue, not to mention those contributions which subsume masculinity in a comprehensive gender approach.[5] The Birkbeck conference at which the papers in this volume were first presented is eloquent testimony to the variety of historiographical points where a perspective of masculinity is now being applied. The sense that we were sniping from the boundaries has entirely disappeared.

So, in one sense, the question in my title can be roundly answered in the negative. But the denial is rather less convincing when we pause on the phrase 'the history of masculinity'. The passage of 20 years has changed the way we conceptualise our subject and our sense of what we as historians are attempting to do. Perhaps the most significant shift is that we seek to address the questions which interest cultural historians, whereas in the 1980s there was still some ambition to meet the expectations of a broader non-academic audience committed to a critical discourse around gender. My purpose here is to urge a partial rehabilitation of the approaches which were current 15 or 20 years ago, on two grounds: first, questions of behaviour and agency have for too long been sidetracked by a historical practice dominated by questions of meaning and representation; and, second, until we re-engage with those earlier questions we are unlikely to reach beyond our captive audience of students and academic peers. Given the current deficit in public history, that is a salient issue.

## Men's history as liberation

Consider first of all the origins of the history of masculinity. Inevitably, they are more complex than the version I have just outlined. Viewed from an Anglo-American perspective, 1988 was not so much the beginning as the end of the beginning. British work was more than ten years behind its American counterpart. Historical scholarship on masculinity can be traced back to the late 1970s in the work of Peter Filene and Peter Stearns.[6] There was a distinctly liberationist tone. Indeed, historicising masculinity can be regarded as one of the last historical manifestations of the 1960s. Filene, for example, prefaced his study of sex roles in modern America with a confession of his commitment to personal authenticity and egalitarian values.[7] This was a 'New Men's History' for the edification of the 'new man'.

Quite suddenly the historical record began to be seen as a largely unexploited resource to critique what was generally regarded as natural and fixed in men's lives. History was expected to offer inspiration and guidance in the reformation of masculinity. The earliest interventions were made, not in academic seminars, but in a milieu which has almost disappeared – 'workshops' and open conferences. The audience for this new history also read magazines like *Changing Men* in the United States and *Achilles Heel* in Britain. Indeed, historians of masculinity contributed to these magazines, and also to more broadly based organs of the Left.[8] The audience for this new history, writers and readers alike, looked to remove the heavy burdens that a patriarchal social order imposed on the male sex. They wanted some demonstration that masculinity was not an unchanging endowment – that its prescriptions were not set in stone. The surest means of dismantling the stereotypes which 1980s men found so constricting was to document past behaviour which contradicted them; to recover men's lives conducted on different lines. For many of us, the kinds of historical difference which came to light from these early enquiries *were* liberating: for example, the overt and expansive sexuality of eighteenth-century London, which seemed innocent of the binary divide between gay and straight;[9] or the emotional display which was commended in early Victorian men (before the stiff upper lip triumphed later in the century).[10] The tension between work and family relationships – the central conundrum in the men's anti-sexist movement – began to make more sense when set against the self-made work-driven breadwinner of the nineteenth century. Histories of this kind demonstrated that the dysfunctional aspects of modern masculinity were historically contingent, and that change might be anticipated in areas of life which hitherto had been assumed to be part of the unchanging order of things. In some of this writing there was an inspirational quality – if not a call to arms, then certainly a call to raised consciousness.

An extended time depth was integral to these early efforts. This not only served to bring into play different (and maybe preferable) masculine models in the past; it also might reveal the historical processes which accounted for the evolution and mutation of masculine roles. Donald Bell was a pioneer in this respect. In a 1981 article titled 'Up From Patriarchy,' he contrasted the rigid allocation of sex roles in the modern industrial age with what he saw as the humane and flexible household order of early modern society. This served to demonstrate that the rigid patriarchy associated with the Victorians was not the natural order of things. Indeed, in the post-industrial age which was dawning in 1981, its time was up; surviving attitudes of male dominance were a 'historical lag', as Bell called them, destined to give way to the ascendancy of a new male sex role.[11] The same concern with time depth produced the two most considerable works of men's history in the 1990s: Anthony Rotundo's *American Manhood* of 1993 (but widely circulating as a thesis from the mid-1980s), and Michael Kimmel's *Manhood in America*.[12] Kimmel's book was structured round the self-made man, and his *alter ego*, the man who was inwardly destroyed by the failure to measure up. These books were histories of masculinity in the sense that they looked at masculinity over an extended period – never less than a hundred years, and in Stearns' case the entire modern era in Europe as well as the United States. They testified to the assumption that masculinity would have its own history – like nation and class.

No synthesis of the kind produced by Stearns or Kimmel has been published in the past ten years. None has ever been attempted for Britain. In 2005 the *Journal of British Studies* devoted the better part of an issue to masculinities in Britain, with five contributors spanning the sixteenth to the twentieth centuries. The guest editors explicitly asked us to consider issues of periodisation – that is, whether a focus on masculinity presupposed accepted chronologies or suggested new ones. In response, no one ventured beyond the limits of a single century.[13] No overarching periodisation of Western masculinities has been proposed since Connell's pioneering article, 'The big picture,' of 1993.[14]

It is a commonplace that ambitious surveys are more easily written when scholarship is in its infancy than when it has become encumbered by a luxuriant growth of primary research and conflicting interpretation. But the explanation for the reluctance to write that kind of history runs deeper still. The history of masculinity has virtually disappeared as a free-standing strand. No one today proposes to write such a history. Historians today are enlisted in a different project. The history of masculinity in its pioneering days was based on the twin assumptions of singularity and linearity: masculinity, it was thought, could be meaningfully treated as a unit of analysis, and its development over the centuries could be reconstructed. Those assumptions are no longer current. The idea of a discrete specialism or paradigm has gone. Instead, masculinity has become part of the conceptual apparatus of historians, and of cultural historians especially. Few historians today see their work as a contribution to a discrete history of masculinity, but rather as an enrichment or a leavening of some other theme – be it the history of the family, post-colonial history, or political history. In these areas masculinity takes its place as one lens, among several, through which the texture of society and culture may be more fully understood.

## Women's history and gender history

This is the point at which to draw out some comparisons with women's history. From the beginning the history of masculinity was closely associated with the women's movement. It arose out of an anti-sexist men's politics, promoted by men who not only supported feminism, but whose masculinity was (in many cases) challenged on a daily basis through living with feminist partners. Not surprisingly, this early men's history dovetailed with the preoccupations of women's history. Already by the 1970s feminist historians such as Natalie Zemon Davis were pointing out that, in order to understand the historical dynamic of women's oppression, it was necessary to understand men's stake in that oppression – to view patriarchy as part of men's history. Hegemonic masculinity was the concept which allowed patriarchy to be treated as something more than a blunt instrument in men's history, and the scholar who elaborated it – R.W. Connell – was profoundly influenced by socialist feminism.[15] Homosocial bonding – a popular theme among historians of masculinity in the 1980s – matched 'the female world of love and ritual';[16] manliness, it turned out, was instilled in family and school, just as codes of femininity were.

Yet these parallels concealed crucial distinctions between the two histories. In the first place, whereas the rhetoric of women's history was based on the proposition that women as a sex needed liberation, only a tiny minority of men saw themselves as being in a comparable predicament. Men as a sex did not aspire to liberation. If the notion of a collective men's consciousness had any validity at all, it corresponded to the outlook of the silent majority who were more persuaded of the benefits of patriarchy than its penalties. Indeed, by the end of the 1980s the tone of men's gender politics was increasingly set by the neo-traditionalism of Robert Bly's mythopoetic movement, which was more concerned to repair the bonds between men than to question their relations with women.[17] There simply did not exist the critical mass of anti-sexist men to sustain the political project of a 'men's history'.

The major exception was the gay movement. Here the liberationist perspective had real purchase, leading to a historiography which, initially at least, centred on a few clear-cut themes of repression, resistance and self-discovery.[18] The potential implications for the history of masculinity were important. Gay history, after all, can destabilise many of the untested assumptions about heterosexuality. It also provides the clearest evidence of the uneven extent to which men have been beneficiaries of the patriarchal dividend. But it remains broadly the case that gay history has been a separate specialism, mirroring the detachment of gay culture and politics from a broader focus on masculinity – and vice versa. Queer theory, by advancing into the terrain of heterosexuality and demonstrating all its fragility and ambivalence, signals a breaching of the gay–straight divide, but its impact on history – as opposed to literary studies – has so far been limited.[19]

The second distinction between women's history and men's history concerns the weight accorded to experience and agency. The aim of women's history in the first instance had been to redress the exclusion of women from history. Simply to document women's lives and to reveal women as historical actors – whether in the mass or as exceptional individuals – met that requirement. That programme was problematic when adapted for the other sex. Men's lives were the stuff of traditional history, so there was no radical frisson in writing 'about men'. Historical figures in Britain who exemplified a masculine counterculture can be counted on the fingers of one hand; in the British context Edward Carpenter – the figure who corresponds most closely with that requirement – has only just received a full-length biography (by Sheila Rowbotham, a longstanding feminist historian).[20]

Lastly, women's history is still the subject of free-standing histories with an appreciative audience. Identification with feminist objectives is distinctly patchy, but the historical rediscovery of those who were once 'hidden from history' retains its appeal. There is still a sense that to write about women in the past is to write about women today, whether in biographies of the eminent, like June Purvis on Emmeline Pankhurst, or in grand surveys, like Olwen Hufton's *The Prospect Before Her*.[21] In short, women's history remains a recognisable genre, with a non-academic readership, because it addresses themes such as prostitution, the single woman, or grass-roots activism, which have a purchase on the present. There is no equivalent body of work on the history of masculinity.

It is against this background that we can understand the impact of gender history during the 1980s. The new terminology and the commitment to the relational nature of all gender identities potentially brought women's history and the history of masculinity into a single project. While there were plenty of women's historians who resisted the trend, historians of masculinity quickly signed up to the new dispensation. Men-only histories of club, sport and regiment became redundant, unless informed by an awareness of the full range of gender relations: women might be physically absent from these institutions, but they still fuelled man's fantasies and furnished the idiom in which deviant masculinities were disparaged. Much early work on the history of masculinity had aimed to reconstruct the homosocial environments of the past, and to trace the process of socialisation from boy to man. Konstantin Dierks has remarked of this work that it had an 'internalist' aspect, in which codes of masculinity simply begot more codes of masculinity.[22] The history of gender signalled a rejection of that inward gaze. Masculinity could not be understood outside a structure of relations with the other sex, of power, nurture and dependence. Seen from this perspective, masculinity became of much greater interest to women historians. Major works by women now made their appearance, notably Davidoff and Hall's *Family Fortunes* and Anna Clark's gendered reworking of E.P. Thompson's *The Making of the English Working Class*.[23]

## The cultural turn

Initially gender history was founded on a theoretical base derived from sociology – evident, for example, in *Family Fortunes*.[24] But by the 1990s it was becoming subsumed in the cultural turn. Now in one sense the history of masculinity already had a cultural bias. Historians of masculinity had soon come to the conclusion that what was most lacking in the traditional historiography was not so much men's behaviour as the gendered logic which explained that behaviour. Hence their emphasis was less on narratives of action and events than on the normative codes which underpinned men's lives in the past – typically in family, school, youth organisations and the armed services. J.A. Mangan and James Walvin accurately conveyed the trend in the title of their 1987 collection, *Manliness and Morality*. George Mosse, who signed up to the project late in a distinguished career as a German cultural historian, based *The Image of Man* entirely on what he took to be *the* enduring stereotype of Western manhood, formed in the late eighteenth century, and still recognisable in the mid-twentieth century.[25] In other words, the project of a history of masculinity had already moved away from the reconstruction of men's lives, and had found a resting place in the study of norms and stereotypes – essentially a cultural project.

However, the cultural turn implied a more rigorous and exclusive notion of culture. Three features are central to my theme: the privileging of representation over experience, the dissolution of the integrated subject, and the abstraction of power relations. Prioritisation of representation is the fundamental feature of the cultural turn. For some, such as Patrick Joyce, it is the only approach which is consistent with history's grave epistemological defects and it entails the 'end of social history'.[26] Most devotees of the cultural turn are less absolutist; for them its appeal lies in the enhanced control of the text which deconstructive techniques offer them. The implication in each case is a downgrading of experience. Graham Dawson's *Soldier Heroes*, which appeared in 1994, is an exemplary text. This was a virtuoso analysis of the heroic persona of two imperial icons, Henry Havelock and T.E. Lawrence, employing the full resources of cultural and Kleinian psychoanalytic theory, and one of the most sophisticated and accomplished works on the representation of masculinity to date. But Dawson does not investigate the social reach of these representations, or the light they shed on men's active engagement with the imperial project.

The second key feature of the cultural turn is the problematic and unstable relationship between gender and other markers of identity. The individual is recognised to be the site of different constructions, to the point where the whole concept of identity becomes blurred. Identity is multiple, porous and contingent. Masculinity cannot be abstracted out of this complex, because it only has meaning in relation to other identities of sexuality, class, age and religion. Contextualisation and interconnectedness are all. Hence historians do not so much attempt a history of masculinity as explore the relationship between men's gender and the other ways in which their identity is structured. To take an influential example, Mrinalini Sinha's *Colonial Masculinity* does not herald a history of masculinity as such, but an analysis of social relations which were structured as much by race and class as by gender.[27] If masculinity is everywhere in the historical record, it no longer makes sense to identify oneself as a historian of masculinity. There is a further consequence. If masculinity is embedded in the cultural texture, it follows that it is best studied in synchronic mode. Writing the history of masculinity in a longer time perspective is then open to the charge of retrospectively imposing concepts of gender derived from the present. Stefan Dudink has called attention to the dangers of naturalising masculinity, of placing it beyond history.[28] The earliest ventures in the genre – by the likes of Stearns and Kimmel – can certainly be criticised on these grounds.

Third, the cultural turn has a very distinctive take on questions of power. Given the pivotal importance of gender inequalities, structures of power are integral to any theorisation of masculinity. Foucault was the main influence in this area, but in most of his writings Foucault showed surprisingly little interest in gender. That defect was made good by Joan Scott. Her 1986 article, 'Gender: a useful category of historical analysis,' was crucial.[29] She placed power relations at the very heart of gender. But, in defining power largely in cultural terms, as symbol and metaphor, she severed the connection between studies of power and actual social relations. She popularised the notion that idioms of gender are signifiers of power in every context, including formal politics. The stimulus this offered to historians of masculinity was most clearly visible in the field of political history, largely ignored up to this point as the province of the old regime in history-writing. Gendered metaphors of power were now unravelled in relation to the Founding Fathers of the United States,[30] the new language of fraternity in revolutionary France, and so on.[31] It should be noted, however, that there wasn't the same level of interest in gendered forms of political practice.[32] Kathleen Canning has remarked that Scott's agenda indicated 'a whole new kind of historical investigation, the history of homosexuality instead of homosexuals; of "blackness" instead of blacks; of the construction of the feminine instead of women'.[33] The cultural turn not only raised the standing of 'culture' as a historical theme, but prescribed a culturally inflected approach for everything else. As Carolyn Steedman observed, culture was now treated as 'the bottom line, the real historical reality'.[34]

If I sound somewhat disenchanted, this is not because I doubt the quality of work done in the new cultural history. It is because the aggrandisement of the cultural turn – as *the* historical paradigm – weighs the scales against other, equally telling approaches. As long ago as 1973, Clifford Geertz warned against the danger that cultural analysis would 'lose touch with the hard surfaces of life', by which he meant political, economic and physical realities.[35] Those hard surfaces are not very evident in today's scholarship. In a recent historiographical review of work on masculinity and war, Robert Nye concludes that the pressing task for historians is to continue to explore the construction of the image of citizen–soldier.[36] Yet this theme has been comparatively well worked. What we most lack is analyses of the experience of combat and its impact on peacetime masculine conduct. Or take a recent article on male domesticity in Britain since 1945. Martin Francis challenges the assumption that British men signed up to domesticity with enthusiasm after the war; but the argument is conducted entirely at the level of popular culture, particularly film, with no attempt to address the family life of the period.[37] It is not the interest in film as such which is at fault, but the assumption that this is the appropriate medium for such an enquiry. More serious still, the study of working-class masculinities has more or less ground to a halt in Britain, in part because working-class sources hold little appeal for the prevalent modes of cultural analysis.[38] The current emphases in historical work on masculinity are a world away from R.W. Connell's definition of gender as 'a configuration of practice', focused on 'what people actually do, not on what is expected or imagined'.[39]

How useful is a scholarship which discounts experience and which regards the interpretation of texts and images as being not only more practicable, but more important, than the reconstruction of events and experiences? Why should questions of identity be treated as more significant than the materiality of power relations or the subjectivity of experience? Recent critical reflections on the history of masculinity have brought these questions to the fore. Looking back on nearly 20 years in the field, Michael Kimmel observes that 'in no way is historical interrogation of American and British masculinities the same thing as a history of actual, corporeal *men*'.[40] In introducing the *Journal of British Studies* symposium, Karen Harvey and Alex Shepard distance themselves from the cultural turn, and call for 'a revived emphasis on men's social relations with each other and with women'.[41] In a closely argued critique, Michael Roper takes issue with one of the central claims of the cultural turn – from Joan Scott onwards – that it holds the key to uncovering historical subjectivities. What it actually uncovers, he argues, is cultural constructions whose purchase on individuals remains obscure.[42]

These criticisms have attracted considerable interest within academia. But they are even more persuasive when viewed from the perspective of public history. A generation ago the new men's history was centrally about masculinity as *lived* in the past, in the belief that that was the soundest basis for reaching better grounded conclusions about what was inherently masculine, what was contingent, and what could be regarded as an agenda for change. Naïve and ideologically driven this history may have been, with its quest for a good past and inspiring role models. But it made the all-important point that masculinity as experienced in the late twentieth century was not the eternal state of men, and that fundamental aspects of men's lives were historically conditioned. Analysing the masculinities of the past as cultural constructs is scarcely adequate as a response to that agenda. It conveys the unfortunate impression that historical scholarship has little or nothing to contribute to today's agenda.

## Imperial masculinity

Thus far the argument has been pursued in somewhat abstract terms. I turn now to demonstrate its application to ground-level historical work in respect of two contrasted themes – the history of colonial emigration and the history of fatherhood. The first touches on a global history of nation-making; the second addresses one of the most intimate aspects of masculine identity.

On 29 July 1872 James Randall wrote his first letter home from Picton, New Zealand. He had arrived from England two weeks earlier, an experienced navvy recruited as a ganger on the new railway being constructed on the South Island. He wanted his wife and 16-year-old son to join him. There were no feather beds, he conceded, but wages were high, food was plentiful, and pig-hunting was open to all. It was better to live 'like a gentleman' in New Zealand than starve back home. 'I am feeling double the man I was when I left England.'[43] By that ringing phrase he meant that he was physically restored by a reliable diet, socially empowered by an enhanced income, and able once again to assume sole responsibility for maintaining wife and child. The appreciative mention of pig-hunting reminds us of an aspect of manly accomplishment which was acutely frustrated by the poaching laws of nineteenth-century England.

Rollo Arnold's study of English settlement in New Zealand, from which this passage is drawn, stands at some distance from the tone of post-colonial studies today. Partly this is because there is much greater awareness of gender now. The gloss I have given to Randall's 'double the man' comment is mine, not Arnold's. We now have highly sophisticated studies of Empire as the site of the heroic *par excellence*, where English manhood was tested, and where its triumphs had a special allure; these images had a formative impact on popular thinking about the imperial periphery throughout the Victorian era, but most of all with the advent of Stevenson and Haggard in the 1880s. The obverse of heroic white masculinity was the demonised colonial other, speaking to white masculinity not only as a projection of disowned negatives, but as a means of realising forbidden sexual impulses. Following in the wake of Edward Said's work, post-colonial literary studies have been a particularly important influence here.[44]

As an interpretation of the life of empire in the imagination, these are revealing insights. Yet this work has a curiously bloodless feel. It gives the impression that imperialism was essentially a mindset – a set of metaphors even – rather than an exercise of authority. It is not that these accounts exclude a power analysis, but it is power detached from its material context. It is one thing to uncover the workings of power-knowledge, and quite another to analyse the operation of power between groups on the ground. This is why Catherine Hall's *Civilizing Subjects* is so significant. Race, slavery and emancipation are her central themes, and the way in which their representation in metropolitan culture was reworked over a period of 40 years is done with great subtlety. And it is traced not through the iconic texts of the time, but through the utterances of the men and women who performed the work of empire – men such as Edward Eyre and the Baptist missionary William Knibb. The subtitle foregrounds 'the English imagination', but in Hall's rendering it is imagination manifested in social action and inflected by it.[45]

The materials for Hall's study are richly abundant, because the theme of slavery touched such a sensitive nerve in British society: it was the dominant strand of imperial discourse throughout the nineteenth century. Compared with slavery, emigration is very much 'the poor relation' of imperial history.[46] And one reason is that the questions which emigration provokes, and the sources that need to be consulted for answers, do not sit well with the priorities of cultural history. The common emigrant lacked the visibility of the soldier or the missionary. In novels for the educated classes he or she featured only as a means of disposing of a redundant character – a kind of *deus ex machina* in reverse (as Australia was for Dickens' Mr Micawber). In working-class culture, emigration was one of the stock themes of ballad and music-hall song – materials which rank rather low in the cultural historian's scale of esteem.[47] Overall, emigration was a discursively impoverished theme in nineteenth-century Britain. Indeed, I suspect that the cultural turn is part of the explanation why emigration has not been given the attention it merits. Yet this was the process – extending over the entire century and beyond – which created a sense of personal attachment between metropole and colonies: arguably a more solid basis for pro-empire sentiment in Britain than the romantic appeal of glory and adventure on the African frontier.

Emigration from England received less attention at the time because it was composed of individuals and small groups, rather than entire communities as in Ireland and Scotland. But it survives in emigrant sources, dispersed between private collections and archives in both Britain and the overseas countries. They include letters to the authorities requesting assisted passages, shipboard diaries, progress reports sent to kin or friends back home, and reminiscences written in affluence and old age. They are no more transparent or authentic than any other personal sources. One has to be alert all the time to the distortions of self-making: the settler who gilded the lily of harsh colonial conditions in order to persuade others to join him; or who, writing for his children years later, preferred to draw a veil over just how wretched his circumstances had been when he boarded ship in England.[48] James Randall's letter home, on the other hand, accurately reflected both living conditions in New Zealand and the gender values through which these conditions might be appreciated. The language in which he crisply summarised his good fortune is not difficult to unpack: 'double the man' expresses an understanding of masculinity which was both commonplace and immediately relevant to Randall's circumstances; it was about bodily strength, earning power and independence. These were at the core of his self-respect, and they translated directly into social standing among his male peers.

In the early and mid-nineteenth century, the largest category of emigrant men were husbands with children: men who had achieved the formal qualifications for full masculine status, but whose circumstances usually made a bitter mockery of it; one might call them casualties of the patriarchal order. Adventure certainly figured in their aspirations, particularly in the case of youngsters, but the principal goal was 'independence', measured in the acquisition of cheap land or – as in James Randall's case – good wages. These aspirations were not culturally innocent. Misleading prospectuses from the Colonial Office cynically played up to the ambition for land; the cult of adventure was derived as much from the pages of Captain Marryat or R.M. Ballantyne as from any hard information about the likely destination. But what makes emigrant writings historically significant is the way in which they addressed aspirations and values which were rooted in emigrants' lives, in a way which does not hold true of novels, or propaganda, or even writing for the popular stage. Focusing on the quotidian reality of men's lives as revealed in personal correspondence does not, of course, mean renouncing cultural analysis. But it does direct our attention to forms of representation which arose directly from social experience.

## Fatherhood

The history of emigration may never loom large in histories designed to enhance a critical perspective on masculinity in a lay readership. But the same cannot be said of my second case study. Fatherhood is one of the most contentious dimensions of masculinity today. It is both a pervasive idiom of authority and protection in our culture and an intensely personal experience, which for most men is divorced from any sense of the historical. Current conceptions of the father turn on two polar opposites. One view, reflecting a particularly pessimistic strand of feminism, sees in the father the root of patriarchy (as the etymology asserts) as manifest in exploitation, physical abuse and abandonment, leading to the assertion that fathers are superfluous. The other view regards the absent authority figure as a cruel distortion of men's potential, and calls for a new fatherhood, based on a convergence of roles between mother and father which may break down the artificial polarity of masculine and feminine in the next generation. Whereas the anti-father lobby regards the absent or oppressive father as the nature of the beast, the pro-father lobby sees him as a challenge to its radical reforming credentials. But both start from a common assumption about the traditional baseline. And the image of the unsmiling and quite possibly abusive patriarch is one which precludes a proper appreciation of the historical record.

Family relationships are an area particularly prone to stereotypic expectations. No one did more than the late Peter Laslett to shake up our settled notions about the pre-modern family; but even he expressed surprise at an eighteenth-century description of a husband spending long winter evenings cobbling shoes, mending family clothes and attending to the children while his wife span.[49] Yet, given the fluidity of gender roles in the household economy and the wife's role in production – both of which are routinely stressed by

Early Modernists – it is hardly a surprising observation. The prevalence of such stereotypes means that research in social practice is all the more necessary. Yet the most influential work on the history of fatherhood has chosen instead to concentrate on prescriptive writing and highly opinionated contemporary critiques. This is particularly true of the nineteenth century. It is not that these accounts perpetuate a monolithic stereotype. In the nineteenth century fatherhood was enough of a discussion point for quite divergent views to be canvassed – as Claudia Nelson has demonstrated in *Invisible Men*, based on a close reading of 13 periodicals between 1850 and 1910.[50] But, because her analysis is confined to this kind of material, it does not provide much insight into how fatherhood was practised or experienced. John Gillis's better-known work, *A World of Their Own Making*, prompts the same reservations: while sensitive to broad historical developments, its main focus is on 'the myth, ritual and family values' spelt out in the book's subtitle, and these themes remain somewhat detached from their social moorings.[51] Neither of these works is doctrinaire in its application of cultural theory. Claudia Nelson's work carries minimal theoretical baggage. What they share is a prioritisation of representation which has the effect of moving the focus away from fatherhood as a lived experience.

Yet the earliest scholarly works to deal with historical fatherhood confronted the issue of paternal behaviour head-on. They appreciated that domesticity was a lived environment, not just a set of precepts. Take Davidoff and Hall's *Family Fortunes*. Of their findings, perhaps none was more surprising than the picture they drew of the hands-on, 'nursing father' in the era of William Cobbett, the very antithesis of the Victorian paterfamilias. They certainly did not take Cobbett's word for it, but drew on a string of local family records in Essex and Birmingham.[52] More striking still was the earlier work of David Roberts, published in a symposium on the Victorian family in 1978. Roberts analysed the paternal practice of the nineteenth-century governing class under three headings: remoteness, sovereignty and benevolence. That may sound like a crude summary of the didactic literature. In fact, Roberts made no reference to those texts. His article was based instead on 168 families, studied through the biographies and autobiographies of fathers and children. In Roberts' account neither sovereignty nor benevolence is attributed to the influence of didactic texts: they stemmed primarily from the great wealth of these men, together with their personal prestige in the wider world. Remoteness, sovereignty and benevolence not only produced a distinctive character formation in children; they also served to reproduce the paternalist style of public authority in the next generation.[53]

I am not suggesting that the prescription and ideology should be ignored. Rather, the challenge here is to set paternal behaviour in the context of the considerable weight of contemporary discourse. In my own work on Victorian middle-class fatherhood, I read a great many homilies on parenting, but in turning to family materials my intention was not to start from the discursive high ground and look for confirmation of its authority, but to reconstruct the domestic experiences of fathers and children, which in some cases did bear out the views of the advice-book writers.[54] One of the central themes of middle-class Victorian fatherhood was the separation of work from home. Personal correspondence repeatedly testifies to the contradictory implications for patriarchal power. On the one hand, it placed the material fortunes of the household entirely in the father's hands; on the other hand, it excluded him from a close network of relationships controlled by his wife, leading in some instances to a pathological display of domestic authority over both wife and children – of the kind which regularly came before the divorce court (as James Hammerton has shown).[55] Detached from these often painful negotiations with material and social circumstance, the history of discourse about fatherhood would be a very unreliable guide. A recent symposium edited by Trev Broughton and Helen Rogers provides further grounds for reflecting on the sensitivity of fathering to a range of economic and ideological circumstances; it also reminds us that a society standing in the line of direct descent to our own struggled with comparable dilemmas.[56]

## Conclusion

In the 25 years which have elapsed since serious work on the history of masculinity began, two developments have changed the landscape: one intellectual, the other political. First, the range and sophistication of work within the cultural turn means that a return to the old social history is not an option, except for diehard defenders of the faith. As Geoff Eley has remarked, social history on the terms which were current in the 1970s 'has ceased to exist'.[57] The creative fault-line in historical practice now is the negotiation between cultural and social approaches, summed up by the title of the journal of the Social History Society, *Cultural and Social History*. There is growing support for 'a cultural materialist approach which sees cultural history as inseparable from, and of necessity questioning, political and economic interests'.[58] Yet the hold of the cultural turn on younger scholars remains strong. The journals are full of articles which focus on representation, even if they are now more wary of heavily theorised language. Conferences tell the same story: the two most recent edited collections deal, respectively, with the representation of the male citizen in the modern world and the relation of masculinity to its varied 'others'.[59]

The other development relates to men's anti-sexist politics. As a collective endeavour it has disappeared. There is no 'movement' to which progressive historians of masculinity might be affiliated, and with whom their research strategies might be hammered out. What we have instead is intense social concern about a number of issues around masculinity, operating in a historical vacuum. The most high-profile of these at present is fatherhood, and I have suggested how historical work can contribute to a clearer perspective on work–life balance and on the abusive father. In the case of imperial history, the link between recent work on masculinity and current cultural debate is less direct; but how the British evaluate their imperial record today depends not only on its multiple legacies overseas, but on the nature of the imperial commitment itself – the mixture of considerations (greed, duty, self-improvement or escape) which prompted a significant percentage of the British people to go overseas.

These developments have clouded over the clarity and ambition which marked the first ventures in the history of masculinity. Those qualities have not entirely disappeared. The last ten years have produced two wide-ranging studies of manhood in early modern England, in which command of the didactic literature is grounded in a sound grasp of social practice.[60] The same period has seen some vividly realised historical work on homosexual men, alert to place, experience and agency.[61] As the following chapters demonstrate, the Birkbeck conference was impressive for foregrounding social, religious and intellectual, as well as cultural, approaches. Nevertheless, it is hard to identify in today's scholarship anything which might be called the history of masculinity. We need to reconnect with that earlier curiosity about experience and subjectivity, while recognising that experience is always mediated through cultural understandings. In a recent conference lecture on the history of fatherhood, Joanne Bailey deplored the gulf which has divided the 'social history of men' from the 'cultural history of masculinity', and urged that it be overcome.[62] I endorse that suggestion. What I am advocating is not in the least original – a culturally inflected social history which keeps its moorings in social experience – with its boots firmly strapped on, to adapt a metaphor of R.H. Tawney.

I realise too that the gulf between practice and meaning can be overstated, and that much social theory is dedicated to reconciling the two, particularly through the notion of culture as performance. But at root my argument is not theoretical but pragmatic. I am disturbed by a mode of doing history which frustrates a legitimate social expectation – one on which the long-term health of our discipline may depend. In order to engage the kind of audience that has some reason to read our work other than professional obligation, we need to restore the focus on agency and experience which was beginning to attract a lay readership to the history of masculinity in the 1980s. That doesn't mean reducing our practice to a functionalist formula. But it does mean making a larger space than we do at present for a history which has some connection with the priorities and interests of the non-specialist and the non-historian: the desire for a perspective on the present, for an awareness of past alternatives, and of the processes which have produced the present gender order. The history of masculinity as formulated in the 1980s is an outdated concept. But the task remains to create a body of historical material, grounded in men's experience in the past, which touches some of the most keenly felt issues in gender politics today.[63]

## Notes

1. David H.J. Morgan and Jeff Hearn (eds), *Men, Masculinities and Social Theory* (London, 1990).
2. Michael Roper and John Tosh (eds), *Manful Assertions: Masculinities in Britain since 1800* (London, 1991). This volume was preceded by J.A. Mangan and James Walvin (eds), *Manliness and Morality* (Manchester, 1987): an important collection of case studies, but lacking a theoretical overview.
3. R.W. Connell, 'The big picture: masculinities in recent world history', *Theory and Society* 22 (1993), 606.
4. Tim Carrigan, Bob Connell and John Lee, 'Hard and heavy: toward a new sociology of masculinity,' in Michael Kaufman (ed.), *Beyond Patriarchy* (Toronto, 1987), p. 176.
5. Editorial, *Gender and History* 20 (2008), 2.
6. Peter Filene, *Him/Her/Self: Sex Roles in Modern America*, 2nd edn (Baltimore, 1986); Peter Stearns, *Be A Man! Males in Modern Society* (New York, 1979).
7. Filene, *Him/Her/Self*, p. xvi.
8. These two magazines were founded by anti-sexist activists in the 1970s: *Changing Men* in the United States, and *Achilles Heel* in Britain. The latter has appeared irregularly since then.
9. Alan Bray, *Homosexuality in Renaissance England* (London, 1982).
10. David Newsome, *Godliness and Good Learning* (London, 1961).
11. Donald Bell, 'Up from patriarchy: men's role in historical perspective', in Robert A. Lewis (ed.), *Men in Difficult Times* (Englewood Cliffs, 1981).
12. E. Anthony Rotundo, *American Manhood* (New York, 1993); Michael Kimmel, *Manhood in America: A Cultural History* (New York, 1997).
13. *Journal of British Studies* 44 (2005). The editors of the special feature were Alexandra Shepard and Karen Harvey; the other contributors were Michèle Cohen, Michael Roper and John Tosh.
14. Connell, 'The big picture'.
15. R.W. Connell, *Gender and Power* (Cambridge, 1987). For an assessment of Connell's theory of hegemonic masculinity, see John Tosh, 'Hegemonic masculinity and the history of gender', in Stefan Dudink, Karen Hagemann and John Tosh (eds), *Masculinities in Politics and War* (Manchester, 2004), pp. 41–58.
16. Carroll Smith-Rosenberg, 'The female world of love and ritual: relations between women in nineteenth-century America', *Signs* 1 (1975), 1–30.
17. Robert Bly, *Iron John: a Book About Men* (Shaftesbury, 1990). It is interesting to note that, despite Bly's high profile, there was very little that could be described as a backlash men's history.
18. Jeffrey Weeks, *Coming Out: Homosexual Politics in Britain from the Nineteenth Century to the Present* (London, 1977); Randolph Trumbach, 'London's sodomites: homosexual behaviour and Western culture in the eighteenth century', *Journal of Social History* 11 (1977), 1–13; Bray, *Homosexuality in Renaissance England*.
19. For a study which engages with Queer theory, see Sean Brady, *Masculinity and Male Homosexuality in Britain, 1861–1913* (Basingstoke, 2005).
20. Sheila Rowbotham, *Edward Carpenter: A Life of Liberty and Love* (London, 2009).

21. June Purvis, *Emmeline Pankhurst* (London, 2002); Olwen Hufton, *The Prospect Before Her: A History of Women in Western Europe* (London, 1995).
22. Konstantin Dierks, 'Men's history, gender history, or cultural history?', *Gender and History* 14 (2002), 150.
23. Leonore Davidoff and Catherine Hall, *Family Fortunes: Men and Women of the English Middle Class, 1780–1850* (London, 1987); Anna Clark, *The Struggle for the Breeches: Gender and the Making of the British Working Class* (Berkeley, 1995).
24. See also Leonore Davidoff, *Worlds Between: Historical Perspectives on Gender and Class* (Cambridge, 1995).
25. George L. Mosse, *The Image of Man: the Creation of Modern Masculinity* (New York, 1996).
26. Patrick Joyce, 'The end of social history?', *Social History* 20 (1995), 73–91.
27. Mrinalini Sinha, *Colonial Masculinity: the 'Manly Englishman' and the 'Effeminate Bengali' in the Late Nineteenth Century* (Manchester, 1995). For her theoretical reflections along these lines, see Sinha, 'Giving masculinity a history: some contributions from the historiography of colonial India', *Gender and History* 11 (1999), 445–60.
28. Stefan Dudink, 'The trouble with men: problems in the history of "masculinity"', *European Journal of Cultural Studies* 1 (1998), 419–31.
29. Joan W. Scott, 'Gender: a useful category of historical analysis', *American Historical Review* 91 (1986), 1053–75.
30. M.E. Kann, *A Republic of Men: The American Founders, Gendered Language, and Patriarchal Politics* (New York, 1998).
31. Lynn Hunt, *The Family Romance of the French Revolution* (Berkeley, 1992); Joan Landes, *Visualizing the Nation: Gender, Representation and Revolution in Eighteenth-Century France* (Ithaca, 2001). For further examples, see Dudink, Hagemann and Tosh (eds), *Masculinities in Politics and War*.
32. An impressive exception is Thomas Welskopp, 'The political man: the construction of masculinity in German Social Democracy, 1848–78', in Dudink, Hagemann and Tosh, *Masculinities in Politics and War*, pp. 257–75.
33. Kathleen Canning, *Gender History in Practice* (Ithaca, 2005), p. 74.
34. Carolyn Steedman, 'Culture, cultural studies and the historians', in Lawrence Grossberg, Cary Nelson and Paula A. Treichler (eds), *Cultural Studies* (New York, 1992), p. 617.
35. Clifford Geertz, *The Interpretation of Cultures* (London, 1975), p. 30.
36. Robert A. Nye, 'Western masculinities in war and peace', *American Historical Review* 112 (2007), 438. Similarly, most of the contributors to Dudink, Hagemann and Tosh, *Masculinities in Politics and War*, write about politics or war at one remove from party meeting or the battlefield, as if experience can take care of itself while they focus on the complexities of representation.
37. Martin Francis, 'A flight from commitment?', *Gender and History* 19 (2007), 163–85.
38. I owe this point to Mike MacDonnell of the University of Sydney.
39. R.W. Connell, *Arena* 6 (1996), quoted in D.Z. Demetriou, 'Connell's concept of hegemonic masculinity: a critique', *Theory and Society* 30 (2001), 340.
40. Kimmel, *Manhood in America*, p. ix.
41. Karen Harvey and Alexandra Shepard, 'What have historians done with masculinity? Reflections on five centuries of British history, circa 1500–1950', *Journal of British Studies* 44 (2005), 276.
42. Michael Roper, 'Slipping out of view: subjectivity and emotion in gender history', *History Workshop Journal* 59 (2005), 57–72.

43. James Randall to wife, 29 July 1872, quoted in Rollo Arnold, *The Farthest Promised Land: English Villagers, New Zealand Immigrants of the 1870s* (Wellington, 1981), p. 11.
44. Dane Kennedy, 'Imperial history and postcolonial theory', *Journal of Imperial and Commonwealth History* 24 (1996), 345–63.
45. Catherine Hall, *Civilising Subjects: Metropole and Colony in the English Imagination, 1830–1867* (Cambridge, 2002).
46. A. James Hammerton, 'Gender and migration', in Philippa Levine (ed.), *Gender and Empire* (Oxford, 2004), pp. 247–81.
47. J.S. Bratton, Richard Allen Cave, Breandan Gregory, Heidi J Holder and Michael Pickering, *Acts of Supremacy: The British Empire and the Stage, 1790–1930* (Manchester, 1991); Andrew Thompson, *The Empire Strikes Back? The Impact of Imperialism on Britain from the Mid-Nineteenth Century* (Harlow, 2005).
48. For a fuller consideration of these issues, see my '"All the masculine virtues": English emigration to the colonies', in John Tosh (ed.), *Manliness and Masculinities in Nineteenth-Century Britain: Essays on Gender, Family and Empire* (Harlow, 2005), pp. 173–91.
49. Peter Laslett, *The World We Have Lost Further Explored* (London, 1983), p. 120. For a corrective, see Bridget Hill, *Women, Work and Sexual Politics in Eighteenth-Century England* (Oxford, 1989), pp. 120–22.
50. Claudia Nelson, *Invisible Men: Fatherhood in Victorian Periodicals, 1850–1910* (Athens, 1995).
51. John Gillis, *A World of their Own Making: Myth, Ritual, and the Quest for Family Values* (New York, 1996).
52. Davidoff and Hall, *Family Fortunes*, pp. 329–35, 345–48.
53. David Roberts, 'The paterfamilias and the Victorian governing classes', in Anthony S. Wohl (ed.), *The Victorian Family* (London, 1978).
54. John Tosh, *A Man's Place: Masculinity and the Middle-Class Home in Victorian England* (London, 1999), ch. 4.
55. A. James Hammerton, *Cruelty and Companionship: Conflict in Nineteenth-Century Married Life* (London, 1992).
56. Trev Lynn Broughton and Helen Rogers (eds), *Gender and Fatherhood in the Nineteenth Century* (Basingstoke, 2007). See also the chapters in this present volume by Joanna Bailey, Rachel Moss and Robert Rutherdale.
57. Geoff Eley, *A Crooked Line: From Cultural History to the History of Society* (Ann Arbor, 2005), p. 189.
58. Hsu-Ming Teo and Richard White (eds), *Cultural History in Australia* (Sidney, 2004), p. 13.
59. Stefan Dudink, Karen Hagemann and Anna Clark (eds), *Representing Masculinity: Male Citizenship in Modern Western Culture* (Basingstoke, 2007); Heather Ellis and Jessica Meyer (eds), *Masculinity and the Other: Historical Perspectives* (Cambridge, 2009).
60. Elizabeth Foyster, *Manhood in Early Modern England* (Harlow, 1999), and Alexandra Shepard, *Meanings of Manhood in Early Modern England* (Oxford, 2003).
61. Matt Cook, *London and the Culture of Homosexuality, c. 1885–1914* (Cambridge, 2003); Matt Houlbrook, *Queer London: Perils and Pleasures in the Sexual Metropolis, 1918–1957* (Chicago, 2005).
62. Joanne Bailey, lecture delivered at conference on 'Masculinities and the Other', Balliol College, Oxford, 29 August 2007. See further Joanne Bailey's chapter in this volume.
63. The argument of this chapter is explored in relation to the practice of historians in general in my *Why History Matters* (Basingstoke, 2008).

# 3
# Can the Hegemon Speak? Reading Masculinity through Anthropology

*Diederik F. Janssen*

> There a lover stamps around and is in love only with his passion. There one is wearing his differentiated feelings like medal-ribbons. There one is enjoying the adventures of his own fascinating effect. There one is gazing enraptured at the spectacle of his own supposed surrender. There one is collecting excitement. There one is displaying his 'power'. There one is preening himself with borrowed vitality. There one is delighting to exist simultaneously as himself and as an idol very unlike himself. There one is warming himself at the blaze of what has fallen to his lot. There one is experimenting. And so on and on – all the manifold monologists with their mirrors, in the apartment of the most intimate dialogue!
>
> Martin Buber, *Between Man and Man* (1947)[1]

Prefacing a recent edited collection on late antique gender, Virginia Burrus observes that 'our own mappings of the mappings of ancient texts extend an iterative process of transformation that conveys both orders of intentionality and degrees of unpredictability that exceed teleological constraint'.[2] Twentieth-century ethnography has similarly delivered gender as a remapping of what is always already mapped. My interest in this chapter is the use of anthropology in relation to 'masculinities', as a late addition to the gender studies portfolio. In part, I wish to reflect upon whether anthropology can fault philologists and others for their 'myths', 'errors' and 'failure [...] to ask the most basic questions' regarding gender/sexuality categories, as Holt Parker put it some years back.[3] More generally, can anthropology act as cultural critique, and, all the while, 'avoid a rhetoric of a clash of paradigms in order to confront more directly the extreme fragmentation of research interests and the theoretical eclecticism of the best work'?[4] Can anthropology *help*, in other words?

These are obviously historicisable questions. Around the advent of masculinity's anthropological hour, in the early 1980s, anthropological thought itself had been branching off into various interdisciplinary directions, including post-colonial theory, feminism, deconstructive approaches to ethnography spearheaded by Clifford and Marcus's edited collection *Writing Culture* (1985),[5] cultural studies, the comparative appraisal of 'homosexualities', and ideas later to coalesce under the moniker of 'queer' theory. The theoretical mobility of gender was pivotal to most of these contenders for academic limelight; and, whilst the editors of *Writing Culture* apologised for not addressing gender, various contributions to *Women Writing Culture* (1995), building on more than two decades of 'feminist anthropology', historicised the anthropological canon, methods and theories in terms of an effective or intentional masculinism, which tended toward a male 'bias' and excluded feminist input.[6] Whereas others had doubted that feminism and anthropology could aspire to more than a 'particularly awkward dissonance', as Marilyn Strathern had assessed matters in 1987, what still held anthropological sensibilities together conceptually was generally understood to be caught up in gender at root level.[7]

Questions of dissonance surfaced largely in regard to the admissibility of feminist and postmodernist ethical and epistemic approaches to representing the Other, and hence concern over the potential erasure of the architectural hybridity of each in the face of the Other's territorial tendencies.[8] This scramble for attention tended to focus on radical ontologies of the Subject, as they appeared to resonate with ethnographies of personhood, gender and embodiment. Gender theory, however, commonly asserted itself as a critical narrative of the *Alltag* (the 'everyday'), variably reckoned as a pre-reflexive, unwittingly complicit, or strategically uncritical and obscurantist scene of representation. Thus gender theory's intentions entail an assault on that symbolic *Alltag*: a 'damaging' of language (Sunderland), a writing 'against culture,' as Lila Abu-Lughod put it – an attempt to mark that which is unmarked.[9] However, this critical project becomes self-limiting when attempted from within, rather than against, the genre of ethnography, where the latter is understood as a commitment to accurate documentation, translation or 'evocation' – expressions of 'concern' (identified by James Clifford as ethnography's *salvage* and *redemptive* modes) unavoidably discordant with an aggressive politics 'against' culture or language. Ethnography was nonetheless considered as staging a continuity between 'gender theory', as academic accomplishment, and the mundane gender practices recognised as its substrate; the recognition of practices as 'gendered' resulted in their being shown to articulate, and thus potentially entrench, much the same range of epistemic and ontological postures as those that defined and divided academic texts. From this continuity, a central problem emerged: to what extent 'genders' can be legible through circumscribed evaluative schemas, containing ('encoding') circumscribed repertoires of identity negotiations. To what extent does the schema of classification predefine the object under study, and hence lead to an analytical circularity which loses any critical force?

The problem is particularly acute for the study of 'masculinities'. I will turn below to a historical appreciation of this particularity, but will first preface this by noting anthropology's familiar double epistemic ambition (that of intellectual care regarding local representational templates and that of theoretical significance beyond local or regional pertinence) as it coincides with a familiar third: a place at the interdisciplinary table of political leverage. In appreciation of Gayatri Chakravorty Spivak's well-known question, 'Can the subaltern (as woman) speak?', I ask that we venture the possibility of asking, 'Can the hegemon (as man) speak?'[10] By this I mean that the political and ontological question of the marginal voice can be extended to the realm of privilege, to question the idiomatic and theoretical contractions which paradoxically surround forms of privilege. This requires 'masculinity' to be queried in terms of historical analytic–literary grounds and burdens, sites of ascription, and ontological closure. Critiques of 'closure' in gender narratives – that is, critiques of the bounded, ascriptive function of gender – may not come from 'within' or 'outside' anthropology, or even 'both'; as I argue below, the discursive and epistemological locality of 'anthropology' must also be analysed as integral to the problem.

## Common ground

The late modern project of gender theory envisioned, apart from equity and other kindnesses, an unsettling of 'gender' as it related to common sense – 'a cultural system; a loosely connected body of belief and judgment, rather than just what anybody properly put together cannot help but think'.[11] This project of recalibration has included forms of dissemination that beg continued anthropological attention. For example, late 1990s popular men's magazines in Japan identified men's studies as a 'trendy activity'.[12] Trendiness is certainly evidenced by ongoing global elevation of women, men, sexuality and gender as epistemologically critical rubrics and orientations, rather than administratively effective categories. This elevation has proven to be an elementary feature of the post-1960s code of 'gender' (*jendâ*, in Japanese). What is critical must be incessantly shown to underlie: gender's melodramatic necessitation of visibility, disclosure and *démasquer* proved paradigmatic for a more generalised, redeeming emplotment of subaltern positions facing everyday life contractions of representation. Studies have recognised regionally specific historical burdens when examining these contractions, thus diversifying the academic stakes of 'masculinity' in Japanese, German, circum-Mediterranean, Chinese and Middle Eastern studies. Euro-American, especially Anglo-American, intellectual mobilisation around 'gender variance' and 'gender regimes' importantly sketched out the late modern drama between minority interest and majority fiat. 'Masculinism' and 'hegemonic masculinity' thus figure in a range of strategic appellations of cultural fiat associated with men, adding to the earlier corpus of terms such as *patriarchy, male chauvinism, sexism, androcentrism* and *phallogocentrism*. 'Masculinity' would identify the world as it was to be re-historicised, as delimiting, invading and plundering 'woman', as a universal subject recuperable through self-assertion.

Anthropologists have provided important elements to this recuperation, by co-legitimising specific forms of cross-cultural legibility. For 'masculinity studies' as well as anthropologists, the focal question was how directly masculinity could identify and distinguish men, if strict, confrontational dichotomies were themselves the working level of gender.[13] Anthropology at this point can be shown to rehearse and restage the myriad analytic standoffs that underlie the social sciences at a more general level. This has been well demonstrated by objections to Bourdieu's *habitus* as it sought to qualify feminism's 'symbolic revolution' and consciousness-raising by reference to a preconscious 'embedding of social structures in bodies'.[14]

The 1990s consolidation of masculinity as a research theme, then, calls for an ongoing reassessment of Strathern's and Bourdieu's early scepticisms. Masculinity, however, has never been at the epicentre of anthropology's attempts to trouble gender. Post-structural approaches to gender in anthropology were preoccupied with 'transgenders', 'homosexualities' and 'women of the world'. The occidental structure of gender politics required these notions to explain themselves vis-à-vis the rubrics of the *human, universal, natural, cultural* and *occidental*. This has often involved a precarious attempt to secure common ethico-ethnographic grounds on the basis of which gender could be properly ascribed and generically represented. In interpretative anthropology, this process of ascription would seem to require elements of *rubrication* – resembling the scribe's humble task of highlighting in red ink the outlines, subsections and critical passages in original manuscripts, and thus, following their contours, enacting both a facilitative role vis-à-vis its proper reading and a caring, calligraphic service. But the metaphor dies if we consider the constitutive role played by the invocation of analytic rubrics; even more so where the academic code of 'gender' wishes still to revise the poetics of everyday life. For instance, Towle and Morgan lamented the 'typological errors', 'inconsistent' and 'illogical' political arguments, 'ethnocentrism' and 'caricaturisation' in popular uses of anthropology that seek to 'romanticise' the 'third gender' native, and imagine that these issues are resolvable by an empirical ethnography of 'lived quotidian realities' and 'appropriate use of cross-cultural examples'.[15] The same problematic posture is encountered, for instance, in Ana Mariella Bacigalupo's analysis of the Mapuche *machi* (shaman), in which she suggests that 'Colonialism rarely sees indigenous people as they really are: crossing boundaries, having overlapping cultures, and juggling multiple cultures, perspectives, and epistemologies,' and, more specifically, that 'Colonial assumptions and modern Chilean misreadings of colonial texts had distorted Reche [colonial Mapuche] gender epistemologies and *machi weye* [male shamans'] subjectivities.'[16] This familiar post-colonial admonition for interpretative recall and restraint, however, appears inadequate as a positive definition of an appropriate analytic approach, and seems to valorise the paradoxical idea of a disinterested empiricism systematically moderating the otherwise ubiquitous manhandling of fragile identity statements, so as to reinstate 'social and political solidarity'.

## Straw men

Towle and Morgan conclude their proposal for de-romanticising gender by positing a growing challenge to it, namely the 'heavy traffic across borders in images, bodies, ideas, technologies, and transgender political activism'.[17] This situation (save the activism) informs masculinity studies' polemic structure. If we look at how 'masculinity' has come to function in anthropological parlance, and anthropology in 'masculinity studies', we see opportune, if still awkward, idiomatic reverberations, the historical assessment of which is vital for developing a productive reading strategy. *Masculinity* often names and encodes negotiations over second-wave feminist cultural diagnostics, most clearly between American pro-feminists and their pet nemesis, the mytho-poet. Their rough-and-tumble over narrative and poetics saw a series of publications and dissertations in the mid-1990s, intended to contain the 'primitivism', 'essentialism' and claims to 'deep truth' by public spokesmen and popular men's organisations.[18]

These 1990s interlocutions ostensibly served to stage 'masculinity studies' as a watchdog task: a fending off of popular, non-feminist parables of maleness through a register of historical and ethnographic realism. Robert Bly's anthropology, particularly the trope of 'male initiation', was considered 'selective', 'distorted' and 'misguided', thus reaffirming the image of a common battleground for social scientific rigour and the species of cultural therapy emerging from popular movements. American pro-feminists' attacks upon domestic poets had the latter act as straw men: politically unviable representations could be rejected without having to insult anthropologists dedicated to ethno-theoretical as well as ethno-political subtleties. Gender theorists' have more generally used anthropological texts to frame or support rejections of projected 'binaries', abusive and neurotic gender schemas ('masculinities') and obsolete formulae ('sex roles', 'honour and shame', 'sex vs. gender'). This has been done by projecting a conclusive mandate onto selected ethnographic texts that could be shown to resonate with politically viable theorems. They found in anthropologists an ally against 'Western' folk ontologies thought to misrepresent and thus oppress 'marginal' gender subjectivities and 'systems'.

Anthropologists thus became stakeholders in a triumphalist occidental gender movement, organised through the discursive form of a juridical dispute over what constitutes 'fair' and 'unfair' representation (in the double connotation of representational leverage and ethnographic viability). Early anthropological responses thus tended to inherit the politicised, argumentative structure of circum-Atlantic, specifically American, gender narratives. Yet 'gender', as for any politically informed concept, shows a diversified polemic structure, upheld by ways of arguing that always strategically exceed projected norms of scientific temperance. The late twentieth-century rejection of alleged excesses of 'masculinism', 'binarism' and 'essentialism', more precisely, entailed the use of anthropology to feed a positivist rhetoric of bias and refutation that served largely polemic functions. Masculinity, in these narratives, served to figure forth an embodied site of grotesque excess, an opposable and refutable position, vital for a proprietary plot of political controversy: 'owned', 'used' or 'claimed' by men, and thus instrumentalising oppression.

These connotations (which invite scrutiny of the epistemic conditions of controversy, rather than involvement in the disputes) demonstrate a pluriform resistance to analysis. Anthropology, in its classic role, describes a clash of epistemic orders in which and through which gender was elevated beyond a strictly oppositional ordering of the sexes. This entailed unearthing pre- and per-colonial elements of such orders, as in Michael Horswell's work, 'to interrogate the performative nature of [the] tropes of sexuality found in early colonial texts; and to recover the subaltern knowledge of the colonized third-gender subjects misrepresented by the rhetorical figures'.[19] For Horswell this included an archaeology of 'symbolic rupture' of the hierarchical binaries at the site of third-gendered *ipa* or *orua* (ritual attendants, witnesses to an Andean model of gender, functionally tied to 'complementarity'). The challenge, equally felt in work by Sylvia Marcos and Rosemary Joyce, is clear: 'How do we read for subjectivities in the profane, frozen word-images of an outsider's mirror when those same subjects were inscribed in their culture's collective memory through ritual, sacred performances in an oral tradition?'[20] The challenge extends to reflection on the continuity of colonial (medieval) and post-colonial textual practices, considering the absence of present-standard ethnographic scrutiny of both the clashing epistemological orders. Whether we can arrive at a subjectivity-based idea of 'misrepresentation', then, has turned out to depend on the 'new reading strategy'[21] that anthropologists brought to the field in order to enable such an arbitration. Since gender was being shown to be a process of *bricolage*, and figured forth through ongoing strategies of (dis)identification, this process – the narrating of its intentions, agents, products and effects – would be able to resist gender's formulaic face; yet any such resistance could only be launched from another 'trendy' layer of (dis)identification strategies. Only such an additional overlay can authorise the historicising of cultural encounters in terms of *mis*representation: a problem that has haunted the post-colonial project ever since Edward Said's *Orientalism*. It is worth noting that post-colonialism clearly provides a parallel with gender (post-feminist) studies and queer (post-sexualities) theory in that important and even founding texts have been both appreciated and criticised as *polemics*, such that discussions of authorial intent became elementary to their argumentative organisation.[22]

## Site of ascription

This problem, the epistemology of the encounter, applies equally to the historical appreciation of masculinity as intercultural 'stereotype', such as Matthews Gutmann's *macho* and Fred Gardaphé's *gangster*.[23] Indeed, from what typological basis can we tell a stereotype from a type? Gutmann observes that 'Determining the systemic character of machismo is predicated on following the historical tracks of the term,' and finds that young Mexican men of the 1990s identified typically as 'Ni macho, ni mandilón' ('neither macho nor henpecked'), suggesting that masculinity, as a labelling procedure, may involve the *rejection* of labels felt to be anachronistic, where they do not distinguish current façade from past entitlement, or are found to be 'pejorative and not worthy of emulation'.[24] The Mexican *macho*, then, may amount to 'a joke that outsiders (foreigners) do not get' or elsewhere 'a playful role [men] can perform on demand', or else may articulate 'a certain element of nostalgia [being] cultivated by those who feel they have been born too late'.[25]

This question leads to another, that of the cultural life of the abstract category, and of its cross-contextual mobility. For example, a recent study which presents a historical typology of 'masculinities' in Papua New Guinea does not contextualise or historicise either the notion of *typology* or its situated application or relevance, and admits that some of the proposed types are never discussed as such, or at all, by interviewees.[26] In fact, most anthropologists can similarly be shown to waver in their deployment of gender as a typological incursion. Gutmann's 1997 review of masculinity as an anthropological trope was limited to, and engaged in, the variable ways in which men could be located 'as men'.[27] Clearly masculinity is the tale of how 'men' can be shown to be 'not men', 'half men' and 'girls'. The question remains as to what element of 'theoretical rigour' should guide an anthropologist's attention to practices of categorisation, if the mere recognition of the category itself historically tied him or her into a project critical of the cultural authority carried by categories and theories. As a consequence, Gutmann's discussion of feminism wavers between an admonition to take more account of feminist contributions, 'incorporate' women's opinions, and study 'woman' as an instance of analytically necessary or *a priori* ethnographically compelling implication. We see here, in fact, the conventional image of a cumulative, triangulatory project in which more and diverse 'opinions and experiences' are thought to effect an increasingly inclusive, hence increasingly productive, *Darstellung* (representation/depiction).

Yet this model would do well to accommodate the question of whether it can see itself mirrored at the sites which it diagnoses: as a model. Whilst anthropology imagines its role as an excavation of 'masculinities' behind the cruel stereotypes, anxious façades, phobic projections and academic biases it seeks to (en)counter, it also needs a view of itself as an archive *of* and *for* representational exercises. This approach led Strathern to ask whether gender can be said to be anchored semantically through attributions, relations or transactions, and to suggest that accounts of pre-capitalist Papuan 'masculinisation' rites should be read as unresponsive to an analytic insistence on a 'totalistic sexed identity'. Melanesian gender would rather pertain to contingent and temporary cross-significations between ritual interlocutors' bodies, body parts, body products and ritual paraphernalia, such that the implied gender of their origins, media and functions proved dependent on situational gift exchanges. Gender was relative to the idiomatic conditions for speaking about origins, media and functions. This compositional, relational, 'transactible', 'partible' or 'dividual' view prompted reflection on the way in which ethnographic data is recruited into the service of a contemporary politics of 'gender identity', 'sexual orientation' and 'power', themselves historically organised by narratives of accountable, entitled and developmental subjectivities. Strathern argued that such narrative elements depend on interpretative or exegetical practices based upon root metaphors whose analytic reach proves limited. Clinical, civil and social scientific notions of gender privilege a proprietary logic which encodes sociality as a clash of competing identities legible through and semantically contained by inalienable attributes, ownership and authorship.

Strathern explains that, while 'indigenous exegetical activity [for example, concerning gender symbols] consists in the creation of further symbols and images', anthropological exegesis, likewise, 'must be taken for what it is: an effort to create a world parallel to the perceived world in an expressive medium (writing) that sets down its own conditions of intelligibility'.[28] This creation of a parallel written world is especially tangible in Fitz John Porter Poole's poetic sketch of Bimin-Kuskusmin (Papua New Guinea) androgyny, as providing 'a more or less constant background presence, appearing in illuminated form now and again, fleetingly, and ambiguously, to alter suddenly one's sense of the forms, hues, and textures of gender', and through which we encounter 'an oscillation not only between singularity and duality of gender, but also among embodied reality, iconic artifact, discursive construction, and cultural fantasy'. Hence,

> the multifaceted character of androgyny is better illuminated in an unfolding representational process loosely interconnecting arrays of images in flux

and without a stable center or, perhaps, even a clear distinction between reality and illusion.[29]

While Strathern's pausing at the sites of individuality and sociality proved negotiable in comparative discussions,[30] her caveats remain salient in appraising cross-cultural and cross-disciplinary work on 'masculinities'.[31] If responsive to key issues in 'gender studies', such work would ideally foreground the ethno-linguistic and wider ethnographic conditions for evaluating and distinguishing between notions approaching those of *manhood, masculinity, masculinities, manliness, maleness, emasculation, femininisation* and *(re-)masculinisation*. The work of Melanesianists suggests that, in profusely gender-inflected cosmologies, analysis of 'masculinity' as a property of the person can quickly become complicit with ontological resolutions of the body as a source for metaphoric extrapolation, rather than a shifting density, the gendering and wider semiotic and metaphoric contours of which depend on ongoing iconographic and exegetical routines. This has been the key conundrum in the study of ritual as well as of personhood. Gender opens up to a range of intersecting discussions, requiring arbitration between domestic, analytic and vernacular idioms. In short, anthropologists will have to reflect on the 'inside and outside' of ethno-theoretical narrative, with the implication that any analytic usage of gender should acknowledge polyvocality's inherent propensity for dissonance. Comparative anthropology, for instance, may not be able to evade propagating formulaic ontologies of gender if considering it an 'inherently integrative subject',[32] as bridging 'the ontological gap between material and symbolic worlds by simultaneously anchoring itself in biological sex and cultural ideology' and thus, in Gregor and Tuzin's conclusion, as showing a 'primordial character'.[33]

It is exactly this element of anchorage and characterisation that provoked dissent across disciplines. Judith Butler's famed proposition of performativity–citationality came to rub against the myriad anthropological shades of 'performance theory', which, as Don Kulick suggests, creates friction between identity-focused and (dis)identification-focused understandings, and, according to Rosalind Morris, entailed 'a movement from representation to formation, from meaning to force'.[34] Butler refers to Strathern's work in several places, but curiously does not include discussion of her work on gender. Unlike later critical commentary on kinship theory, Butler herself has shown little interest in extending ontological reflection on gender to anthropological genres beyond 'criticism of hegemonic Western representation and of the metaphysics of substance that structures the very notion of the subject'.[35] Yet it seems curious that anthropology is endnoted rather than foregrounded in literary analyses: Strathern found that 'the image of the active agent at the creative or created center of relations is missing' in Melanesian manhood, while Butler, two years later, contended that the gendered body had, in general terms, 'no ontological status apart from the various acts which constitute its reality'.[36] In that same year, Laqueur argued that in pre-Enlightenment texts:

> what we call sex and gender were [...] explicitly bound up in a circle of meanings from which escape to a supposed biological substrate – the strategy of Enlightenment – was impossible. [...] Sex before the seventeenth century, in other words, was still a sociological and not an ontological category' [to the effect that] 'the biological is not, even in principle, the foundation of particular social arrangements.[37]

These canonical findings show obvious resonance across disciplines; Laqueur's work was considered critical, for instance, for conceptualising gender across Chinese historical as well as Iranian contexts.[38] Yet it seems necessary at this point to reflect on the direction of theoretical exchange. What rendered Strathern's, Butler's and Laqueur's formulations analytically compelling may have been a general turn against the body as the irreducible bedrock of and canvas for constructivist theory. Laqueur reminds us that his thesis had been anticipated as a generally instrumental formula in 1970s feminism and Foucaultian genealogy, and that he was writing from a well-established 'fraught chasm between representation and reality, seeing-as and seeing'.[39] Likewise, the problems dealt with in Strathern's work can be securely considered, as she did herself, as straddling contemporary social scientific stakes in agency and practice theory, as well as regional ethnographic interests in gender, personhood and commodity/gift-inflected epistemes.

Most theorists will endorse the idea of unbounded bodies in late modern 'masculinities', given testosterone, Viagra, sperm and egg donation, and pregnant trans-men. Only in part cued by these considerations, an idiomatic reverberation of 'fluidity' and radical contingency was to echo down the academic discourse of the 1990s. Yet it could not prevent 'masculinity studies' developing primarily as an extension of an American sociology-of-the-sexes, which in turn had inherited much of its working idioms from social psychology and psychoanalysis. As sketched out above, a common parlance was introduced by pro-feminists, whose authorial role was slanted to the parochial task of *speaking to* an (Anglo-American) context rather than the more salvational challenge of *translating* the conditions that render discussions contextual and thus legible. In work not located within this tradition, masculinity often pertained to a neo-Freudian functional dynamic, theoretically exchangeable with a 'sense of maleness', manhood or male adulthood. For instance, where historian John Tosh arrived at masculinity as importantly driven by 'the need to repress the feminine within – a psychic universal maybe', the Lokutian cross-cultural approach by David Gilmore rather envisioned 'a "Ubiquitous Male" [...] [a] quasi-global personage' characterised by an evaded regression to primordial symbiosis: 'a hard-fought renunciation of the longing for the prelapsarian idyll of childhood'.[40] These conclusions, however, similarly privilege twentieth-century depth psychology over careful exegesis and Geertzian concerns for local knowledge; and thus, expectedly, the reading of Gilmore's *Manhood* by gender-minded anthropologists has been essentially negative.

## 'Masculinities' and burdened white men

Many anthropologists have co-opted canonical sociological formulations of gender. We find a Gramscian notion of *hegemony* applied to gender by R.W. Connell in the 1980s but also, apparently independently and in the context of anthropology, by Sherry Ortner's 1989 reference to Raymond Williams's *Marxism and Literature* (1977).[41] When the concept was popularised in an oft-cited 1985 article co-authored by Connell, the stakes of the phrase *hegemonic masculinity* were identified by its pinpointing of 'a particular variety of masculinity to which others – among them young and effeminate as well as homosexual men – are subordinated'.[42] This seeming slippage of categories indicates that gender was seen as indexically linked to the category of 'man', which is taken to precede and remain ontologically unaffected by the social reckoning of age, demeanour and sexuality. A Marxist sociological conception, it speaks of a male-bodied subject who finds himself interpellated by rivalling male-typed codifications of comportment (*masculinities*), a persona in other words largely irresponsive to ontological doubts but whose existential 'crises', on the other hand, proved exhaustively intelligible through an idiom of privilege, ('patriarchal') dividend and accumulation.

According to Barbara Evans Clements, 'What seems clear at this very early stage [in 2002] in the development of the historiography of masculinity is that the notion of what was appropriately male changed with notions of the nature of sovereignty and governance.'[43] By laying bare the inner working of capitalist power structures, Gramsci's *cultural hegemony* presumes an economically legible referent and projects the scope of class struggle onto the field of gender. By comparison, Ortner, a first hour theorist of sex-based status across cultures, considered hegemony as a shorthand for 'cultural prestige system' (although it was to improve on structuralist notions such as 'system'), bridging 'the pervasiveness of culture and the biased nature of ideology' as well as discursive and institutional embeddedness of sex-based values (although not considered by Ortner, the Foucaultian notion of *dispositif* seems useful). Accordingly, societies were to be classified as either 'egalitarian hegemonies' or 'male dominant hegemonies'. However, at the same time these were complicated in order to account for the 'multiplicity of logics operating, of discourses being spoken, of practices or prestige and power in play [...] a relative dominance of some meanings and practices over others'.[44]

While both Ortner and Connell were interested in rethinking sex-coded prestige differentials, Ortner's guarded renegotiation of structuralism produced an application of hegemony different from Connell's, whose much more mainstreamed phrase, 'hegemonic masculinity', projected genders as bounded 'configuration of practices' or 'positions' in relation to hegemony, articulating 'the currently accepted answer to the problem of legitimacy of patriarchy' – theoretical projections shifting *by definition*. Connell's schema, assuming exclusionary if mobile and contestable 'forms', 'kinds' or 'types' of gender, was proposed in an attempt to 'cure' the 'startling ethnocentrism' of Anglo-American psychoanalysis and sex role literature, and came with clear warnings against reification; in fact, Connell was 'forced to wonder' about the mere applicability of *masculinity* across cultural domains.[45] Connell's predicament was and remains 'the contemporary world order', requiring a challenging of white men as 'agents of global domination', and precluding elaborate attention to ontological plurality beyond that informing Marxist practice theories. However, it also precluded a nuanced view of identification practices beyond what could be exposed as male power play – masculinities was the grammar of male–white–colonial–entrepreneurial authority claims and 'masculinity studies' the burdened white face of a global theoretical thrust to undo sex-based authorisation. Its rooting in an 'evidential' routine of historical self-reflection would 'wipe out [...] any ontological or poetic account of male essences' as a 'credible' account.[46] Connell's 'political sociology of men', in other words, evidences little mercy for ethno-theoretical plurality. Reasoning from this basis, Connell has repeatedly announced the end of masculinity's 'ethnographic moment' and come to consider the ethnographic record an archive of 'rapidly internationalized' mappings of an encroaching 'world gender system' in which further ethnography would be too local and further historical inquiry too historical.[47]

Ortner, following Williams, argued that from an anthropological perspective the benefit of *gendered/sexed hegemony* over *hegemonic gender* lies in differentiating hegemony from ideology by an appeal to holism, a taking into account of 'the whole lived social process as practically organized by specific and dominant meanings and values'. How and when any such practical organisation translates to classificatory men's identitarian status, as variously implied by Connellian 'masculinity', would require both ethnographic scrutiny and, as Kate Crehan reminds us, a perpetual reflection by anthropologists on whether they should hold on to a distinct, traditional, anthropological notion of culture as a 'whole lived process'.[48] Connell's concomitant notion of gender multiplicity was hailed as a corrective to self-serving folk taxonomies, whose monistic and biological conception of maleness would preclude viable socialities (less advantage and privilege) as well as psychological tranquillity (less identity angst). But plurals may only sustain, rather than disrupt, ideas of indivisible personhood. In Connell's recent book on *Southern Theory* (2007), consequently, we find little in the direction of a critical engagement with proprietary ontologies that are not ultimately driven by the prospect of tying in to an all-contextualising world-system theory and of resisting the heat of an alienating, globalist macroeconomic present.

In a critical light this theoretical and political presentism seems unfortunate: a politics uncritical of its implicit ontological messages may turn out to be fundamentally complicit in that which it seeks to address. But then, the area of gender studies has been organised by a necessary tactic of speaking the language people are likely to appreciate. Can a folk ontology of sex/gender be challenged by gender theory if that theory renders the problem knowable only through the idioms that re-inscribe that very same ontological framework? What may be productive for an assessment of this question is a comparative historical cartography that critically locates gender as an epistemic routine, according to which any citation of gender is taken to inform some ontological claim. Such claims may find themselves oscillating between ontological options, even if organised by the now largely revoked grooming of genders as 'local' and 'traditional' treasures. For instance, Kodi (south-east Asia) theories of the nature of the person would create 'a dualism within the individual, represented by male and female "souls" attached to different parts of the head'; individuals are thus 'composed of attributes passed on to them along maternal and paternal lines'. However, the idiom speaks of blooming flowers (female) and fruit (male), while '[m]ale agency is active, mobile and transformative; female agency is stable, unmoving, and substantive'.[49] Hoskin's account of local gender, in sum, can only take the form of a partial cartography of the many sites in which [male/female] turns out to encode a double presence, temporary crossing, oppression, futility or complementarity, without the connotation that we should be entitled to more than a kaleidoscopic spectrum of solicited clarifications. Strathern's solution, similarly, can only count as an identification of one among many remarkable and contrastive dimensions, and can present no hope of a conclusive political commensuration. This is precisely to argue that ethnography should not be contained by the doubly reductive anticipation of global gender justice, and should take theoretical refractions as its ultimate theme.

## Idiomatic fixations

Gender can thus be said to pertain to a range of images, metaphors, idioms and other lexical devices used to facilitate classification, arbitration, demarcation and comparison by appeal to ethical or aesthetic standards. In *Guardians of the Flutes* (1981), one of the first monographic essays on non-Western masculinity, Gilbert Herdt centralised 'instances of verbal idiom, along with their manifest and tacit content, as parts of a wider communicative system'.[50] At this point, however, Herdt's decades-long re-theorising of ritual efficacy was increasingly slanted toward catering to Euro-American needs for post-psychiatric narratives of 'homosexual identity formation', even while he came to reject 'homosexuality' as an analytically viable category. This precarious intertextual predicament informed the translation of anthropological theory for a popular audience receptive to 'coming out' as 'an implicit rite of passage'.[51]

A focus on language use remains productive, then, but specifically now to decipher the citational and reiterative status of 'gender' on a world scale. The word 'gender' itself has become widely adopted across extra-academic genres of publication, but remains a loanword in, for instance, Dutch and Japanese; resists translation in other languages; and predominantly serves to signal a constructivist posture. Thus, the translatability of *gender* can be considered a central obstacle to feminist internationalism and related us/them debates.[52] A three-volume series examining *Gender Across Languages* (2001–03) set out to avoid 'a narrow western perspective on other languages', but its synoptic comparative focus falls short of a linguistic anthropological approach, sensitive to the use and functional contingency of speech in everyday life.[53] Standard paragraphs allow a glimpse of formal and legal aspects of 'language politics' with respect to gender talk, but do so in theoretically limited terms of 'sexism', 'stereotyping' and 'fairness' that prove disjunctive where used together with other terms like 'discourse'.

Suzette Heald suggests that general, explanatory uses of 'power' may be in competition with alternative interpretative strategies structured around notions such as morality or vernacular psychology, the study of which would provide a sense of how such notions 'directly structure the psychological field in which the individual is prepared and made capable of acting'.[54] This suggestion has broad implications for the localisation of privilege and exclusion. In pre-twentieth-century Chinese history, Charlotte Furth suggests:

> Both the place of the family in society and the norms of gender difference were constructed by Confucian moralists around a bifurcation of spheres into inner (*nei*) and outer (*wai*) terms that demarcated separate spaces but also claimed a complementarity between them [...] best imagined as nested and overlapping spheres whose boundaries shifted with circumstance, while the family model of the state gave the conduct of domestic life more than private significance.

*Nei* and *wai* articulated a yin/yang pair encoding 'an interlocking network of signs binding a wide range of phenomena to a common system of signification that was metaphysically grounded [...] not attributes of sexed bodies, but themselves the foundation of gendered meanings diffused in bodies and in the world at large'.[55]

There is nothing to preclude a feminist reading here; however, approaches comparing the medical narratives springing from the Confucian episteme with those of the European Enlightenment will risk elucidating feminism more than Confucianism. It is this risk that will have to occupy centre stage. Likewise, *relationality* and *positionality* have become common operators on gender; however, the distinction, made by Nancy Chodorow, was productively taken up in anthropology as a contingent one. The influential work by Ortner and Whitehead,[56] largely following Chodorow, argued that females', but not males', gender universally translates to the relative salience of relational roles as semantically and ethically informing a wider spectrum of relational dynamics. In the research by Peletz,[57] however, Malay (Negeri Sembilan and Aceh) masculinity is, likewise, 'best understood as dialectically related to constructions of adult men's kinship roles', particularly that of the elder brother; or, rather, an 'increasingly lofty and heavily mythologized set of ideals that comprise the fantasy of the perfect elder brother'. Thus, 'in the practice of everyday life, certain male relational roles – those of elder brother, husband, and father – may not only dominate the category of "male" but may also inform the meanings of all other male relational (and "positional") roles.' Peletz concludes that the *a priori* dichotomy of positional/relational genders does not hold in a comparative view. This is pertinent to a whole range of academic conventions, where a realm of cultural classification is studied through the lexicon of another: for instance, classifying boys in terms of 'young masculinities' and fraternal interests in terms of 'patriarchal' ones.

As with Peletz's approach, Osella and Osella's observations in India criticise the transcultural applicability of psychogenetic idioms, both in terms of the core dynamics thereby referenced (*repression* versus *renunciation*, in their case) and where such idioms identify the individual rather than various layers of imagined socialities that form the semantic conditions and contours for agency.[58] Comparable work by Staples addresses different ways of becoming an Indian *man* and an *adult*, drawing, however, on 'shared Indian idioms of what it is to be a complete person'.[59] In other words, ethnographic research may not deliver a ubiquitous personage, as in Gilmore, but a degree of immersion in overarching semantic orders that facilitate a way of making sense of the very notion of personhood.

Such immersion may well sit uneasily with Anglo-American analytic idioms (often used uncritically) such as 'reaching', 'earning' or 'proving' manhood. While rich monographic studies of *masculinity* have been offered for Persian *jawanmardi*, Greek *andreia* and Latin *virtus*, in much anthropological work we do not have so much a confusion as an under-analysis of gender as an abstraction, that is, an incomplete or absent attestation of its textualities. Allow me to illustrate with a number of examples. According to Kam Louie, the well-known Chinese wen/wu (culture/force) dichotomy defies easy translation and is best approached through the 'many traditional idioms' by which it has been articulated.[60] As Louie observes elsewhere, *The Great Chinese Dictionary* lists 26 definitions of the word *wen* while *wu* has 20.[61] Wu/wen pertains to demarcations, first in terms of its exclusive applicability to Chinese men at the exclusion of women, eunuchs and barbarians, and secondly as being a dual ideal, sorting achievers and losers according to their simultaneous, balanced and/or dual presence. So, whereas Asians have variably been said to be 'emasculated' or 'feminised' in terms of American norms, ideals and stereotypes, Americans, *as barbarians*, would, rather, be excluded from the Chinese idiom that makes men ethically commensurable as men, and would thus be located with women in an extra-idiomatic realm.[62] Ethnographic research by Hillman, however, suggests that 'both Tibetan men and majority Han attribute a wu masculinity to Tibetan men' in the absence of clear-cut relations of domination and subordination, and research by Teng suggests that, at least during the Six Dynasties (220–589) and Tang (618–907) periods, there was a tendency to 'feminize the southern barbarians and masculinize the northerners'.[63] Note that these latter authors elevate 'wu masculinity' to an analytic rubric but do not elucidate how the Tibetan term *phokhyokha* ('real man') coincides with Mandarin *wu*, other than in terms of a sharing of evaluative parameters.

The anthropological question, in other words, is whether 'masculinity' can be considered a universal evaluative category, varying merely in terms of its metaphoric nestling and parametric nuance. An underlying problem is how meaning is to take account of medium and genre. How does a 'marking of the unmarked' privilege representational genres? Studying nineteenth-century Ionian knife fighting as a 'plebeian form of duelling', Gallant found that the recognised ultimate cause for a knife fight was usually an insult. The author notes that 'certain words had extremely evocative power in this society because they tapped into a set of core metaphors through which men made sense of their world.'[64] Even if *the knife*, and in vendetta killings *the gun*, takes over from *words*, words were the most outstanding of exchanges, from insult to bystander testimony and court proceedings. Gallant's article insightfully sketches how and where idioms of ritualised violence articulate both historically and contextually with idioms of slander and insult; but where and how these idioms intersect with idioms of masculinity (as promised in the title of the article) remains largely anecdotal if not conjectural.

A similar problem concerns the cross-idiomatic emergence of local gender, as can be studied in Dorothy Hodgson's ethno-historical study of 'Maasai masculinity'. As elsewhere in East Africa, we encounter 'a range of masculinities cross-cut by generation [or rather: by age-set]'; more precisely, a dialectic between *ilmurran* (warrior) and elder status, a series of contrasts 'predicated on significant differences in [men's] relationships (sexual, dietary, and social) with categories of women'.[65] As with the Chinese wu/wen idiom, the cultural drama of 'masculinity' here is contingent on contrastive discourses greasing homosocial networks, thus animating shifts between traditional and modern (in the Maa words, *ormeek*) attitudes to the system of male age-sets. In Hodgson's analysis we see masculinity only in terms of a dialectic of *historicisable categories of men*, much more than we see a historical dialectic involving *men as a category*. This may even be too much to ask of the data: warriorhood and elderhood are arguably more saliently pseudo-fraternal, generational, familial, ethnic and territorial indices than gendered ones. More importantly, Hodgson argues that 'the Maasai warrior' became a species of *masculinity* mostly through European (both colonial and tourist) idioms of fascination. The twentieth-century study of so-called initiation rituals in general offers a historicisable instance of Occidental narrativisation of what is variably and interchangeably called *the male life course, masculinity* or *manhood*. The notions of *adolescence* and *adulthood* have been equally intrusive as the European, selective and 'exaggerated reification' of *warriorhood* Hodgson identifies. However, the essentially negative term *ormeek* ('modern') may not, as Hodgson suggests, inform *ormeek masculinity*, where it seems rather to ventilate an ethnicised anti-modernism observed in male Maasai, indeed a 'core metaphor through which men made sense of their world'. This problem may result from the analytic jargon of sociological theory on masculinity Hodgson utilises, a political jargon that insists on an asymmetric and confrontational division of 'gender identities' within a positive gender category. As in many current ethno-histories, there is the projection of a cultural centrality and an idiomatic prevalence of 'masculinity' where neither the semantic category nor its internal complications are ethnographically attested beyond, in this case, the historicised administrative equations of males with tribal affairs, through their membership in an age-set system. By consequence, while *ormeek* might have become a less totalising and less negative semantic device during the twentieth century, the statement that it became a less masculinised or less feminising signifier seems unsupported; there is a lack of demonstration that it, beyond a seeming sex-specific application, was in effect a gendered descriptor in Maa idiom.[66] In other words, even if an idiom of culture or cultural change can be said to cater exclusively to males, it is not by implication a cultural–historical idiom of masculinity (we are offered little evidence of this in Hodgson's paper).

## Concluding men

In anthropology, *gender* and *culture* as vectors of analytic commitment have become competitively oriented, betraying their rhetorical stakes and strategic tendencies most clearly if studied through a simultaneously historical, comparative and reflexive approach to past and emergent idiomatic contractions. The interdisciplinary study of gender/sexuality classically resides in an affective *dubio*, oscillating between melancholy (lamenting 'gender systems' and hegemony by commemorating the bleeding margins) and anarchic elation (celebrating mobility through tentative refutations of structural confinement). Organising this bipolar outlook, and profusely mirrored in historical work, one encounters a schism between an explanatory (evolutionary, ecological, psychological and sociological) ambition and an interest in exegetical variance. 'Gender's' internationalist as well as 'ontologically radical' momentum has predominantly fed off counter-ideological mobilisation, and therefore enacts a counter-ideological emplotment. The notion of an anthropological gaze driven by a care for authentic and recalcitrant marginalities, however, all too immediately interpellates the margin into a counter-ideological project. Neither the hegemon nor the margin may be speaking. A reconstructive anthropology 'enabled' by an ethical stance of performativity, plurality, contingency and hegemony cannot but recognise the world worth analysing as constituted by essence, monism, determinism and abject privilege. The degree to which this has entailed a 'straw man' argument – specifically, a refutation of a hostile episteme that appears to mistake the world, but only in the light of a reductive projection – can be linked to ongoing controversy over two questions: whether this metaphor necessarily implies an untenable etic/emic distinction, and whether 'gender' generally translates to falsifiable propositions.

Where Melanesianists have classically proffered historical models of gender antagonism and domination, the male body, *pace* Strathern, may just as well be thinkable, even writable, in terms of a nexus, a transfer node, an amalgam of relations. Regardless, it seems that, if masculinity can but figure in a clash of ethical commitments and thus in a clash of strategic ontologies and idioms, the analytic moment cannot simply consist of the application of well-rehearsed ontological strategies, for whilst these may be intellectually stimulating and politically vital they may not be effective in studying exegetical variability. In a world where gender theory has importantly come to precede gender through a 'constitutive reiteration' and where theory can now be projected back in showing that gender never materialises except through epistemic practices, we encounter the thoroughly anthropological problem of academic exceptionalism. This may consist only in part of a masculinist or anti-feminist grammar of social science (informing the scope and historical direction of feminist studies in and of anthropology). A critical anthropological stance, one that of necessity localises and historicises the cogency of 'gender theory', may (as concluded in feminist encounters with French thought well before masculinity's transdisciplinary moment) enduringly have to focus on discourses of theory, and on disciplinary demarcations of analytic dedication more specifically.

Accordingly, in appreciating ethnographies of gender, we need to appreciate first and foremost the confrontational model of reactionary and dissident varieties of perspective. The double ambition to do theory across time and language may seem to have been more acutely felt at times and in contexts where the need for theory building was informed by a sense of political alarm. Depending on our audacity to identify aftermaths and ability to look back on various such contexts and moments still contemporary, we observe that the ethnographic record lies before the historical anthropologist as it does before the historian of anthropology: as a vital archive of tentative cross-formulations of 'kinds' of sexualities, genders, sexes, sexual anatomies, sexual biologies and sexual maturities. Again, the same goes for the anthropology of 'sexualities/maturities' (which is largely coextensive with that of gender), especially of those recalcitrant to the famed occidental dualities (homo/hetero, male/female) against whose banner comparative conclusions were to experience their *floruit*. In matters gender, anthropology should map varieties of conclusiveness before it can pride itself on conclusions regarding variety.

## Notes

1. Martin Buber, *Between Man and Man*, trans. Ronald Gregor-Smith, 2nd edn (first published 1947; London, 2002), pp. 34–5.
2. Virginia Burrus, 'Mapping as metamorphosis: initial reflections on gender and ancient religious discourse', in T. Penner and C. V. Stichele (eds), *Mapping Gender in Ancient Religious Discourse* (Leiden, 2007), p. 3.
3. Holt N. Parker, 'The myth of the heterosexual: anthropology and sexuality for classicists', *Arethusa* 34 (2001), 313–62.
4. George Marcus and Michael Fischer, *Anthropology as Cultural Critique: An Experimental Moment in the Human Sciences* (Chicago, 1986), p. xi.
5. James Clifford and George Marcus (eds), *Writing Culture: The Poetics and Politics of Ethnography* (Berkeley, 1985).
6. Ruth Behar and Deborah A. Gordon (eds), *Women Writing Culture* (Berkeley, 1996). See further Henrietta Moore, *Feminism and Anthropology* (Minneapolis, 1988), pp. 1–2.
7. Marilyn Strathern, 'An awkward relationship: the case of feminism and anthropology', *Signs*, 12 (1987), 277; Marilyn Strathern, *The Gender of the Gift: Problems with Women and Problems with Society in Melanesia* (Berkeley, 1988), ch. 2.
8. For discussions see *Anthropological Quarterly*'s April and July 1993 special issues; Rosalind C. Morris, 'All made up: performance theory and the new anthropology of sex and gender', *Annual Review of Anthropology* 24 (1995), 567–92; Frances E. Mascia-Lees, Patricia Sharpe and Colleen Ballerino Cohen, 'The postmodernist turn in anthropology: cautions from a feminist perspective', *Signs* 15 (1989), 7, with comments by Vicky Kirby (*Signs*, 16 (1991), 394, reply on 401; Bonnie McElhinny, 'Genealogies of gender theory: practice theory and feminism in sociocultural and linguistic anthropology', *Social Analysis*, 42 (1998); Henrietta Moore, 'Gendered persons: dialogues between anthropology and psychoanalysis', in S. Heald and A. Deluz (eds), *Anthropology and Psychoanalysis* (London, 1994), pp. 131–52; David Chioni Moore, 'Anthropology is dead, long live anthro(a)pology: poststructuralism, literary studies, and anthropology's "nervous present"', *Journal of Anthropological Research* 50 (1994), 350; Tom Boellstorff, 'Queer studies in the house of anthropology', *Annual Review of Anthropology* 36 (2007), 1–19.

54  *Diederik F. Janssen*

9. Jane Sunderland, *Gendered Discourses* (Basingstoke, 2004), p. 191; Lila Abu-Lughod, 'Writing against culture', in R. Fox (ed.), *Recapturing Anthropology: Working in the Present* (Santa Fe, 1991), pp. 137–62. For a critique see Daniel Martin Varisco, 'Reading against culture in Edward Said's *Culture and Imperialism*', *Culture, Theory and Critique*, 45 (2004), 107–9.
10. Gayatri Chakravorty Spivak, 'Can the subaltern speak?', in C. Nelson and L. Grossberger (eds), *Marxism and the Interpretation of Culture* (Illinois, 1988), p. 296.
11. Clifford Geertz, *Local Knowledge: Further Essays in Interpretive Anthropology* (New York, 1983), p. 10.
12. Mark J. McLelland and Romit Dasgupta, 'Introduction', in McLelland and Dasgupta (eds), *Genders, Transgenders, and Sexualities in Japan* (London, 2005), p. 4.
13. This argument was raised in the late 1970s by Baudrillard and Derrida. See Diederik Janssen, 'The obscenity of gender theory: Baudrillard's masculinities', *Culture, Society and Masculinities*, 2 (2010), 75–92.
14. Pierre Bourdieu, *Masculine Domination*, trans. Richard Nice (Stanford, 2001), pp. 40–1, 116–17. The book, originally published in France in 1998, was developed from an article in *Actes de la Recherché en Sciences Sociales* 84 (1990), 2–31.
15. Evan B. Towle and Lynn M. Morgan, 'Romancing the transgender native, rethinking the use of the "third gender" concept', *GLQ* 8 (2002), 469–97. Compare Mark Johnson, 'Transgression and the making of "Western" sexual sciences', in H. Donnan and F. Magowan (eds), *Transgressive Sex, Transforming Bodies* (Oxford, 2009), pp. 167–89.
16. Ana Mariella Bacigalupo, 'Rethinking identity and feminism: contributions of Mapuche women and Machi from Southern Chile', *Hypatia* 18 (2003), 35; id., 'The struggle for Mapuche Shaman's masculinity: colonial politics of gender, sexuality and power in Southern Chile', *Ethnohistory* 51 (2004), 495.
17. Towle and Morgan, 'Romancing the transgender native', p. 492.
18. A species of manifesto was published in 1995 under the editorship of Michael Kimmel: *The Politics of Manhood: Profeminist Men Respond to the Mythopoetic Men's Movement (And the Mythopoetic Leaders Answer)* (Philadelphia, 1995).
19. Michael J. Horswell, *Decolonizing the Sodomite: Queer Tropes of Sexuality in Colonial Andean Culture* (Austin, TX, 2005), pp. 3, 5.
20. Horswell, *Decolonizing*, p. 5; Sylvia Marcos, *Taken from the Lips: Gender and Eros in Mesoamerican Religion* (Leiden, 2006); Rosemary A. Joyce, *Gender and Power in Prehispanic Mesoamerica* (Austin, TX, 2000).
21. Horswell, *Decolonizing*, p. 6.
22. See Daniel Varisco, *Reading Orientalism: Said and the Unsaid* (Seattle, 2007). For a note on 'feminist orientalism' see J. Zonana, 'The sultan and the slave: feminist orientalism and the structure of Jane Eyre', *Signs* 18 (1993).
23. Fred L. Gardaphé, *From Wiseguys to Wise Men: The Gangster and Italian American Masculinities* (London, 2006); Matthew C. Gutmann, *The Meanings of Macho: Being a Man in Mexico City* (Berkeley, 1996).
24. Gutmann, *Meanings of Macho*, ch. 9.
25. Américo Paredes (1967), cited by Gutmann, *Meanings of Macho*, pp. 227, 234.
26. Anastasia Sai, *Tamot: Masculinities in Transition in Papua New Guinea*, unpublished doctoral dissertation, Victoria University, 2007, p. 313.
27. Matthew Gutmann, 'Trafficking in men: the anthropology of masculinity', *Annual Review of Anthropology* 26 (1997), 385–86, 404.
28. Strathern, *Gender of the Gift*, pp. 17, 101, 211–13; M. Strathern, 'Introduction', in M. Strathern (ed.), *Dealing with Inequality: Analysing Gender Relations in Melanesia and Beyond* (Cambridge, 1987), pp. 6–7, 24.

29. Fitz John Porter Poole, 'The procreative and ritual construction of female, male, and other: androgynous beings in the cultural imagination of the Bimin-Kuskusmin of Papua New Guinea', in S.P. Ramet (ed.), *Gender Reversals and Gender Cultures: Anthropological and Historical Perspectives* (London, 1996), pp. 211–12.

30. e.g. Mark S. Mosko, 'Motherless sons: "divine kings" and "partible persons" in Melanesia and Polynesia', *Man*, new series, 27 (1992), 697–717; Cecilia Busby, 'Permeable and partible persons: a comparative analysis of gender and body in South India and Melanesia', *Journal of the Royal Anthropological Institute* 3 (1997), 261–78; Alan Rumsey, 'Agency, personhood and the "I" of discourse in the Pacific and beyond', *Journal of the Royal Anthropological Institute* 6 (2000), 101–15.

31. See, for example, David Lipset, 'What makes a man? Rereading *Naven* and *The Gender of the Gift*, 2004', *Anthropological Theory* 8 (2008), 219–32.

32. Thomas A. Gregor and Donald Tuzin, 'Comparing gender in Amazonia and Melanesia: a theoretical orientation', in Thomas A. Gregor and Donald Tuzin (eds), *Gender in Amazonia and Melanesia: An Exploration of the Comparative Method* (Berkeley, 2001), p. 8.

33. Gregor and Tuzin, *Gender in Amazonia*, pp. 338–39, 342.

34. Don Kulick, 'No', *Language and Communication* 23 (2003), 139–51; Morris, 'All Made Up', pp. 572, 578.

35. Judith Butler, *Gender Trouble: Feminism and the Subversion of Identity* (London, 1990), p. 14.

36. Strathern, *Gender of the Gift*, p. 269; Butler, *Gender Trouble*, p. 136.

37. Thomas Laqueur, *Making Sex: Body and Gender from the Greeks to Freud* (Cambridge, MA, 1990), p. 8.

38. S. Brownell and J.N. Wasserstrom, 'Introduction: theorizing femininities and masculinities', in S. Brownell and J.N. Wasserstrom (eds), *Chinese Femininities/Chinese Masculinities* (Berkeley, 2002), pp. 25–32; Tani E. Barlow, *The Question of Women in Chinese Feminism* (Durham, NC, 2004), ch. 2; Azam Torab, *Performing Islam: Gender and ritual in Iran* (Leiden, 2007), pp. x, 10, 16.

39. Laqueur, *Making Sex*, p. 14; M. Foucault, *The History of Sexuality*, I, trans. R. Hurley (New York, 1990), p. 154.

40. John Tosh, 'What should historians do with masculinity? reflections on nineteenth-century Britain', *History Workshop Journal* 38 (1994), 196; David Gilmore, *Manhood in the Making: Cultural Concepts of Masculinity* (New Haven, CT, 1990), p. 29.

41. Although they cite each other's work, Ortner and Connell nowhere seem to discuss or even cite each other's application of hegemony. Sherry B. Ortner, 'Gender hegemonies', *Cultural Critique*, 14 (1989/90), 44–6; Raymond Williams, *Marxism and Literature* (Oxford, 1977), pp. 108–09.

42. T. Carrigan, R.W. Connell and J. Lee, 'Toward a new sociology of masculinity', *Theory and Society* 14 (1985), 587.

43. Barbara Evans Clements, 'Introduction', in Barbara Evans Clements, Rebecca Friedman and Dan Healey (eds), *Russian Masculinities in History and Culture* (Basingstoke, 2002), p. 7.

44. Ortner, 'Gender hegemonies', pp. 45–6.

45. R.W. Connell, 'The big picture: masculinities in recent world history', *Theory and Society* 22 (1993), 600–01, 605–06.

46. Ibid.

47. Raewyn Connell, *Gender*, 2nd edn (Cambridge, 2009), p. 44; id., 'Globalization, imperialism, and masculinities', in M.S. Kimmel, J. Hearn and R.W. Connell (eds), *Handbook of Studies on Men and Masculinities* (London, 2005), pp. 71–2.

48. Kate A.F. Crehan, *Gramsci, Culture, and Anthropology* (Berkeley, 2002), pp. 50–1, 99–105, 188–99.
49. J. Hoskins, 'Doubling deities, descent, and personhood: an exploration of Kodi gender categories', in J. Atkinson and S. Errington (eds), *Power and Difference: Gender in Island Southeast Asia* (Stanford, 1990), pp. 291, 305.
50. Gilbert Herdt, *Guardians of the Flutes: Idioms of Masculinity* (Chicago, 1981), p. 68.
51. Gilbert Herdt, *Same Sex, Different Cultures: Gays and Lesbians across Cultures* (Boulder, 1997), p. 110.
52. Karin Widerberg, 'Translating gender', *Nora* 6 (1998), 133–38; Samia Mehrez, 'Translating gender', *Journal of Middle East Women's Studies* 3 (2007), 106–27.
53. Marlis Hellinger and Hadumod Bussmann (eds), *Gender across Languages: The Linguistic Representation of Women and Men* (Amsterdam, 2001), I, p. ix.
54. Suzette Heald, *Manhood and Morality: Sex, Violence, and Ritual in Gisu Society* (London, 1999), pp. 2–3, 31.
55. Charlotte Furth, *A Flourishing Yin: Gender in China's Medical History, 960–1665* (Berkeley, 1999), pp. 6, 7, 301–02, 304–12; Martin W. Huang, *Negotiating Masculinities in Late Imperial China* (Honolulu, 2006), pp. 3–4.
56. Sherry Ortner and Harriet Whitehead, 'Introduction', in Ortner and Whitehead (eds), *Sexual Meanings: The Cultural Construction of Gender and Sexuality* (Cambridge, 1981), p. 21.
57. M.G. Peletz, 'Neither reasonable nor responsible: Contrasting representations of masculinity in a Malay society', *Cultural Anthropology* 9 (1994), 155–56; M.G. Peletz, *Reason and Passion: Representations of Gender in a Malay Society* (Berkeley, 1996), pp. 330–33.
58. F. Osella and C. Osella, '"Ayyappan saranam": masculinity and the Sabarimala pilgrimage in Kerala', *Journal of the Royal Anthropological Institute*, 9 (2003), 729–54.
59. J. Staples, 'Becoming a man: personhood and masculinity in a south Indian leprosy colony', *Contributions to Indian Sociology* 39 (2005), 279–308.
60. Kam Louie, *Theorising Chinese Masculinity: Society and Gender in China* (Cambridge, 2002), pp. 11–13; Kam Louie, 'Chinese, Japanese and global masculine identities', in K. Louie and M. Low (eds), *Asian Masculinities: The Meaning and Practice of Manhood in China and Japan* (New York, 2003), p. 4.
61. Louie, *Theorising Chinese Masculinity*, p. 10.
62. Teng, however, notes that 'the feminization of southern peoples and the masculinization of northern peoples served to center the ideal "Han" self of the central plains as a normative identity': E.J. Teng, 'An island of women: the discourse of gender in Qing travel writing about Taiwan', *International History Review* 20 (1998), 353–70, on 362–63.
63. Hillman, citing Teng.
64. T.W. Gallant, 'Honor, masculinity, and ritual knife fighting in nineteenth-century Greece', *American Historical Review* 105 (2000), 370.
65. D.L. Hodgson, '"Once intrepid warriors": modernity and the production of Maasai masculinities', *Ethnology* 38 (1999), 126–28.
66. Hodgson, 'Once intrepid warriors', 135.

# 4
# The Whig Interpretation of Masculinity? Honour and Sexuality in Late Medieval Manhood

*Christopher Fletcher*

I

The history of masculinity has recently encountered a general problem which has often arisen in the study of past societies. A number of commentators have drawn attention to the difficulty of reconciling modern categories of analysis with the cultural concepts of their object of study.[1] Two divergent tendencies have been identified in the study of masculinity. Some writers, it has been suggested, have favoured a sociologically informed approach, taking their agenda from modern social theory, whilst others have followed a primarily cultural historical method, focusing their efforts on the explication of contemporary structures of ideas.[2] A certain dissatisfaction with the 'linguistic turn' in historical studies has arguably contributed to focusing criticism on the second of these two perspectives, in that a primary cultural approach might be accused of reducing lived social realities to just so much discourse.[3] Weighing up these two tendencies, commentators on recent developments in both history and ethnography have expressed similar dissatisfactions, invoking the need for a primarily sociological perspective to enable broad comparisons over time,[4] or noting the limitations of 'symbolic' studies which are 'often remarkable, but partial'.[5]

In truth, this tension between sociological and cultural perspectives is nothing new, especially when it is the work of historians which is at issue. On the one hand, historians have always asked questions about past societies because these questions seem interesting to them. Since the mid-twentieth century, it has seemed natural to draw on modern ideas about similar questions where these are available, whether that involves drawing on philosophy, psychology, anthropology, sociology or cultural studies. Yet, at the same time, historians have always found it difficult to ignore the fact that past actors had their own ideas and priorities. Sometimes their concerns seem tantalisingly close to our own. On other occasions they seem quite different, even disconcertingly alien. Both sociological and cultural historical perspectives bring their own characteristic dangers if pursued exclusively. How do we keep in mind the ideas of contemporaries without losing sight of why we became interested in a certain set of questions in the first place? Or, again: how do we make sure we are studying something we are interested in, without reducing the society under study to a mere illustration of our own pre-existing categories of analysis?

As the history of masculinity begins to negotiate these familiar problems, it seems worth considering how older historical sub-disciplines have dealt with them in the past, with what successes and what failures. For late medieval historians, the classic example of the second trap – what can go wrong with an unreflectively diachronic perspective – is well known under the title of 'the Whig interpretation of history'. As Herbert Butterfield saw it, the Victorians and their Edwardian successors had been guilty of writing history, and especially the history of English political institutions, to present a narrative of political progress whose apogee was themselves.[6] This excessively present-centred approach distorted their account of the past, forming part of an ideological proof that the late-nineteenth or early-twentieth-century Englishman lived in the best of all possible political worlds.[7] In the course of the twentieth century, inspired by Butterfield and others, a radical critique unfolded which gradually undermined almost every received truth about late medieval politics. In some regards, this critique took a materialist form, in that it placed new stress on the material interests which underlay the actions of the nobility or gentry.[8] In other ways, it could be regarded as cultural historical in focus, placing renewed stress on how contemporaries perceived the political institutions in which earlier historians had found the roots of English liberty.[9]

The anti-Whig assault on present-centred accounts of late medieval political culture had a number of virtues, in that it yielded a more accurate picture of past societies. But it also brought with it a number of negative consequences, especially the risk of losing the bigger picture. A purely historicist approach risked losing sight of why historians had become interested in all this in the first place.[10] Only in recent years have historians been able to fight their way out of this historiographical quagmire to give a broader perspective on the development of the late medieval state and the way this interacted both with existing culture and with longer-term social and political changes.[11] They have been able to do so by pursuing an approach which combines an analysis of contemporary language and assumptions with an awareness of the force of the material considerations which arose from the nature of social organisation.

The long-term historiography of English governmental institutions holds lessons for newer disciplines, such as the history of masculinity, which are just embarking on similar journeys. Like English constitutional history, the history of masculinity came into existence because it was found interesting both for reasons within academia and because of broader social developments. It made it possible to pursue the implications of the advances made in the study of women's history beyond that academic sub-discipline. It also sought to address problems still faced by feminism in the West once women had obtained formal rights in the political, economic and reproductive domains. It offered the possibility of exploring the more subtle forms of subjection which persist after formal legal freedoms have been established. One of the central aims of this project was consciousness raising. A historical perspective offered a way to demonstrate that the socially accepted qualities of adult males, just like those of women, had varied over time.[12] Since masculine roles are particular and changing characteristics of particular societies, and not biologically determined universals, they might be reformable in the present day. At the very least, the exposure of the historical particularity of past gendered orders would make it possible to demonstrate the arbitrary nature of current arrangements.

Just as in the early days of English constitutional history, the agenda for the history of masculinity has been set by the interests of its day. Now, this is all very right and proper. It would be a perverse history which only asked questions that were of no interest to those living at the time of writing.[13] It could also, very rightly, be pointed out that Victorian and Edwardian accounts of medieval political institutions were *unreflectively* conditioned by the priorities of those who wrote them, whereas the history of masculinity is far more self-conscious. This field has, if anything, been characterised by an explosion of theoretically elaborated approaches.[14] Nonetheless, I would suggest that this very burgeoning of theoretical perspectives has sometimes allowed unstated assumptions to return by the back door. As the history of masculinity cut its teeth, the multiplicity of approaches pursued was arguably conducive to creative innovation.[15] As this sub-discipline nears maturity, it is the drawbacks of this diversity which have come to the fore. Too often, the modern connotations of 'masculinity' – notably its primary association with sexuality – have served as an unacknowledged organising schema, conveniently linking a wide variety of fields without the reasons for this association always being clear.

Butterfield argued that it was in the composition of a general synthesis that the greatest dangers lay in store for even the most rigorous of scholars, especially as they strove to present detailed empirical work to a wider audience.[16] When Ruth Mazo Karras undertook the first, pioneering general synthesis dedicated to the history of medieval masculinity, she faced a particularly virulent form of this general problem: how to present in a single survey such a variety of approaches, whose common themes, or even broad outlines, had yet to emerge clearly. The imposition of an overarching theoretical framework might fulfil this role, but could it succeed in imposing unity on such diverse material?

In the first work to take on the theme of medieval masculinity with comprehensiveness as a goal, Karras thus began by setting out an approach which draws on the work of the sociologist R.W. Connell.[17] The method initially advanced is consequently a socially constructivist one, intended to demonstrate how society 'shaped roles and defined norms for men' in a variety of social groups, just as it did for women.[18] This approach makes it possible to divide up current research by social group, between the nobility, the university and the towns. Nonetheless, despite this theoretical framework, it proves difficult to maintain this unity as the argument proceeds.

The difficulty of reconciling the diverse conceptions of masculinity inherent in early work on medieval masculinity becomes clear, for example, in a consideration of the masculinity of late medieval university students. In the course of this discussion, the theoretical underpinning of each subsection necessarily bends to accommodate the varied agenda which early historians of masculinity have brought to a consideration of this social group. Initially, the method pursued is close to that of the anthropologist David Gilmore, focusing on how the status of an adult male is something which needs to be won, and is not just something which is conferred by reaching a certain age.[19] Masculinity is thus a matter of rites of passage and 'becoming' male (or at least becoming a 'man'), in an investigation of how the norms of the university 'show how young men were expected to take up their masculine position in the world'.[20] But, as the argument progresses, it proves difficult to maintain this single framework, as the focus moves to a second, distinct understanding of 'masculinity' – arguably the key one in recent discussions of medieval masculinity. Considering the sexual activities of students, Karras maintains that the tolerance by the university authorities of sexual relations with certain 'sexually available' women amounted to the acceptance of activities necessary 'to demonstrate their assimilation into manhood';[21] and that there was an 'implicit charge of emasculation' always ready to fall on those who took up a life of chastity.[22] Yet, in moving from male 'ways of life' and 'rites of passage' to male sexuality, sexual activity has been equated with adult-male status without an overt defence of this position. It is taken for granted, rather than argued, that maleness must be performed through heterosexual sex.

The sheer variety of approaches pursued by historians in considering even this relatively small social group becomes still more apparent as the discussion moves to a third approach of a more cultural historical kind, and it is argued that the symbolic combat of university disputation, with its use of military vocabulary, 'provided a forum for the demonstration of masculinity'.[23] Finally, Karras concludes with a fourth approach, in a discussion of the 'bonding mechanisms' by which students were initiated into the university community.[24] Thus, in bringing unity to the work of historians, diverse themes are necessarily grouped together, ranging from norms of social comportment and the attainment of adult-male status, to sexual activity, symbolic conflict in disputation, and bonding in a particular all-male social group. But it remains unclear how these different theoretical approaches relate to one another, and how they relate to medieval cultural categories.[25] Even though a particular theoretical framework is staked out by way of introduction, it proves difficult to avoid falling back on less fully examined systems of association in the course of the argument.

The creative variety which proved so fruitful for the early development of the history of masculinity risks creating confusion as historians reach the level of synthesis. If we are to avoid presenting a Whig interpretation of masculinity, finding only reflections of ourselves in past culture, then social theory alone is not enough. Contrary to the order of priorities recommended by a number of recent commentators, there is still a need to begin with a cultural historical approach, and then move to our own questions. Only by looking at what past societies associated with being male can we hope to avoid organising the history of masculinity around what we have already decided its characteristics are likely to be. Only in that way can we avoid going round the houses which it has taken English political history nearly a century to negotiate.

## II

With the problem presented in these terms, a central difficulty immediately arises, one associated with writing the history of masculinity before the eighteenth century. Put simply, there was no word for it.[26] In English, for example, 'masculinity' is a rare term before this period, restricted to technical and grammatical contexts. To date, historians of masculinity have not generally regarded this lack of correspondence between medieval and modern categories as a very important difficulty. Instead, writers have tended to treat 'masculinity' and 'manhood' (which *was* a current term) as more or less equivalent. Now, if masculinity were something like population or iron production, something whose modern associations are well established, unitary and not too controversial, then this would not present a problem. But the modern term 'masculinity' is not such a simple concept. It brings with it a nest of commonplace assumptions and a wide range of more self-conscious theoretical approaches whose relationship to one another is not always clear. Medieval manhood, meanwhile, is at least as complex and ramified in its associations as modern masculinity. These associations are not identical to those linked with masculinity in modern culture. Certainly, they often overlap, sometimes enough to make us think that we are dealing with very similar concepts, but this is not always the case.

In particular, the relationship between medieval manhood and sexuality is rather different from that suggested by the close association in the modern mind between masculinity and sexuality. Instead, the associations of 'manhood' are organised around strength, vigour, steadfastness and a certain kind of concern with status and honour, including largesse and conspicuous expenditure.[27] They only secondarily impinge on sexual activity. This should give pause before assuming that the associations between sexuality and male identity were the same in late medieval England, for example, as they are in the present day. In particular, it draws into question the approach taken by a number of commentators on the gender status of the later medieval clergy, who have been regarded as a third sex, or even an 'emasculinity', on account of their exclusion from legitimate sexual activity.[28] On the contrary, I would suggest that, because the logic of manhood was organised not around sexuality but around strength and honour, it was relatively straightforward for the celibate clergy to redirect the values of manhood to a form of spiritual combat in which sin was the ultimate enemy to be fought.[29] Indeed, this tactic was so successful that it was to enjoy a healthy afterlife in later lay forms of spirituality and correct moral life. Medieval laymen, also, were advised to show their manhood, in contrast to youths, women and the pursuit of mere worldly honour, by seeking to win salvation in the next life through the fight against sin.

I would suggest that, contrary to what is often assumed, abstinence from sex need not have impeded the self-identification of medieval men as men. Abstinence from honour, however, was quite another matter. This is not to say that the insistence of the Church on clerical celibacy from the eleventh century onwards did not present difficulties for male clergy,[30] or for devout laymen. It is clear that sexual desire was a quality seen to be inherent in the human body which could be fought by self-imposed bodily suffering, resisted by will, or expunged by mystical deliverance – even by a kind of metaphysical castration.[31] Nonetheless, these problems were related to embodiment (both male and female) in a way which was not as directly linked to 'manhood' in medieval language and commonplace assumptions as modern masculinity is to sexuality. Certainly both men and women were considered to possess lustful bodies, and this was sometimes dealt with by appeal to a military metaphor, perhaps more characteristically for men than for women.[32] Certainly young men especially (and women of all ages) were assumed to be vulnerable to sexual sin, not least because they lacked the strength and constancy of mature men.[33] But we need to acknowledge that there is an important difference between our classification of sexuality, when it involves men, as being 'masculinity' and the rather different associations of contemporary 'manhood', notably with personal honour and status, and with strength and fighting. Although we can observe that it was implicitly accepted in the Middle Ages that it was natural for human bodies to be lustful from the age of puberty onwards, and although we can note the male-gendered nature of the spiritual combat by which this threat might be overcome, it is worth observing that, for medieval people at least, the (military) solution was more explicitly labelled as 'manly' than the (sexual) problem it purported to solve, however odd this might seem to the modern observer.

It is worth considering why it has seemed self-evident to scholars that warfare was the 'quintessential masculine activity' in the Middle Ages, or what it means to say that 'the ideal lay male body was above all the body of the knight'.[34] This has tended to be regarded as the consequence of the dominance of medieval society by the military class,[35] and it would certainly seem wrong to deny that this dominance played its role. That said, medieval manhood was not simply a matter of downward cultural diffusion. The links of manhood with honour, strength and constancy had deeper roots, which pre-dated this dominance, and which would long outlive it. The association between manhood and warfare appears 'quintessential' not only as a result of the importance of the lay nobility as 'those who fight' but also because of the well-established nature in medieval language and culture of the association between men and a form of quasi-military honour. To develop these remarks more fully, the remainder of this article will explore what happens if we come from the opposite direction from that pursued even in studies which integrate sociological and cultural historical approaches to the history of masculinity. What happens if we start with the medieval language of manhood, and then consider how this fits in with modern ideas of masculinity, rather than taking modern social theory as the starting point of our inquiry?

## III

We can begin with what is now becoming quite a famous milestone in the history of masculinity, one which seems to take us to the core territory of this subject area – namely, sexuality – but which on closer inspection is revealed to relate to manhood in quite a different way. This fine example of the interaction of commonplace assumptions about manhood with a rather surprising set of social circumstances was brought to light some years ago by Richard Helmholz.[36] It occurs in the course of a discussion of the procedure for marriage annulment on the grounds of the man's impotence. It appears that the ecclesiastical courts of the archdiocese of York would, if it came to that, recruit seven women to verify that a man really was impotent. Their testimony provides a fascinating account of what certain fifteenth-century 'honest women' believed would stand up in court, as it were, when it came to testing male sexual capacity.[37]

In July 1432, John Skathelok was examined by Joan Semer in the presence of six other 'honest women':

> The same witness exposed her naked breasts, and with her hands warmed at the said fire, she held and rubbed the penis and testicles of the said John. And she embraced and frequently kissed the same John, and stirred him up

in so far as she could to show his virility and potency (*virilitatem et potentiam suam*), admonishing him that for shame he should show then and there and prove and render himself a man (*probaret et redderet se virum*).[38]

I would like to draw out two things which have so far been neglected in commentary on this episode. First, there is the question of heat and the fire. Second, what seems the most surprising part of this procedure: that the women in question (at least for the sake of a church court deposition) seemed to believe that taunting a man to show his manhood would somehow cure his impotence?

The first of these procedures, quite apart from its potential practical efficacy, may bear witness to contemporary medical ideas about manhood, ideas which by the fourteenth century had spread beyond the university to influence popular conceptions of the operation of the human body. Heat was a characteristic of manhood, which bore witness to the more efficient functioning of a mature, male organism by comparison with that of women, children and old men.[39] This heat, the product of the correct coction of humours, produced the vigour of the organism in question.[40] Nonetheless, in the context of an impotence trial, it might be thought (reasonably enough) that the attention to heat and manipulation was simply a sensible way to go about resolving the problem in question. What is rather more surprising is the final method which the 'honest women' deployed, namely taunting: 'admonishing him that for shame he should then and there prove and render himself a man'. In fact, the logic of taunt and response which underlie this procedure, and in particular the demand for John to show himself a man, is tied to the deep involvement of the notion of manhood, not with sexuality, but with a system of honour, shame and vengeance. To explore further how this logic operated, it is necessary to put aside our own categories for a moment, and to pursue the medieval associations of 'manhood', as they are revealed by the use of language.

Perhaps the most closed and specific, but nonetheless characteristic, use of the substantive 'manhood' and the adverb 'manly' in late medieval England was to denote the actions of a man who has to act vigorously and steadfastly, especially to defend himself in a tight spot. These connotations were ancient ones, found also in the Latin 'viriliter', but they were retained and used with frequency in English.[41] So, for example, in an early fourteenth-century Middle English version of the romance *Richard Coer de Lyon*, the hero king shows might and energy in battle when he assaults a Sicilian town, and fights 'so manly' that none of his men perish:

> And at the londe-gate Kynge Rycharde
> Helde his assawte ylyke harde,
> And so manly he toke one,
> He lost of his men neuer one.[42]

Such behaviour averts not only death, but also shame and subjection. Thus, in one version of the romance of *Horn*, the hero's father, faced with the invading Irish, calls all who 'hold their land free' to fight, for it is

> Better manly to be slayn
> Than long to liue in sorwe & pain
> Oghain outlandis thede.[43]

'Manly' behaviour in contexts like these prevents shame and confirms the actor's status, often explicitly his status as a nobleman. In another example, this time in the mid-fourteenth-century alliterative romance *William of Palerne*, we see the king of Spain, overtaken by his enemies, addressing his knights. He tells them to defend themselves doughtily, or else they will die, that no profit lies in flight:

> And more mensk it is manliche to deie
> than for to fle couwardli, for ought that mai falle.[44]

It seems that, as part of this system of associations, 'manhood' or 'manship' could serve as synonyms for honour or renown, what late medieval English speakers called 'worship'. 'Manhood' in this sense appears most often when it had to be defended with the swift taking of vengeance in the face of a slight, lest it be damaged by the presumption of the enemy. So, when William himself addresses the same troops before they ride out to battle, he appeals to their 'manship' and for the need to act 'manly', saying:

> Men, for youre manchipe, namore that suffreth,
> but wendeth ought wightli and with your fon meteth![45]

and:

> Yif ye manli with hem mete, the maistry worth oure
> theigh thei be five so fele as we in fere alle.[46]

These recurrent scenes appeal to the basic physical vigour, and the refusal of shameful inaction, which underlie the use of the language of manhood. The martial associations of this terminology have a tendency to arise even when they are not strictly relevant, for example in a context in which the meaning of 'man' is at first sight simply 'adult'. Thus, in the late romance *Sir Eglamour of Artois*, the hero is separated from his son, Degrebelle, who is raised by the king of Israel. When Eglamour subsequently defeats his unrecognised son, and is then apprised of his identity, he declares to the king of Israel:

> 'Lord,' he said, 'God foryelde thee!       [i.e. God grant you]
> thou hast hym broghte to man.'[47]           [var: 'made hym a manne']

On one level, the king is simply being congratulated for having brought up Degrebelle to the age of adulthood, but the context also suggests that the inculcation of knightly virtues and prowess have played no small part in bringing him to be a man. In this passage, there seems to be more to being made a 'man' than the simple passage of years. More than just adulthood, it also seems to denote a certain status, and certain specific qualities, which a man ought to show to win and maintain his 'manhood'.

Returning to the York bedroom scene with these associations in mind, the taunts of the 'honest women' start to make more sense. It seems that the associations of manhood with strength and honour were so well established in late medieval culture that they could pass from this realm into that of sexuality, without practical experience exposing the absurdity of this transference. Since 'manhood' was the status of an adult male, which was defended above all by vigorous, violent reaction to a potential shame, then it was simple enough to follow a similar logic in the sexual domain. If manly action were above all vigorous action in a tight spot and in response to a taunt, then taunting might seem a rational way to go about inspiring a suitably manly reaction even in the sex of an impotent man.

## IV

The importance of the values of strength, steadfastness and honour in the logic of manhood gives reason to reconsider the prominence which has been given to sexuality in recent discussions of medieval masculinity. This impression hardens when it is considered that it was these associations, more than any link to sexual activity, which served to link the diverse areas which late medieval culture associated with the status of a 'man'. Far from the context of cures for impotence, the pursuit of manhood as honour figured as a struggle with sin, a kind of conquest of the impulses of pride, the body and the world. As with the vocabulary of manhood itself, the roots of the metaphor of manly combat against the assaults of the devil ran back to the early Christian church,[48] and further back into the promptness with military metaphor of Roman culture in general and the Latin language in particular.[49] But, again, as with the associations of the language of manhood itself, these themes were also very much alive in late medieval England, adapted to a very different social and cultural atmosphere. Particularly interesting is the extension of this metaphor, in which it is not just that fighting sin might be characterised as 'manly', but that this spiritual battle leads to the accumulation of renown or 'manhood' of a kind which is analogous with the worldly honour of the battlefield, even as it claims to supersede it.

Take, for example, a didactic poem composed by one William Shoreham, vicar of Chart-Sutton, in the first half of the fourteenth century.[50] The aim of this poem is to prove in common sense terms that Creation was clearly willed and done by God. This leads on to the problem of evil, for Shoreham asserts that the Almighty did not create evil, although He did permit evil to come into existence. In seeking to explain why this should be the case, Shoreham deploys the values of manhood to provide an explanation for the role of evil in the scheme of world salvation. Why did God allow evil to come into existence? Well, the answer runs, the first thing that God created was heaven, which was made in such a fashion that every kind of bliss would be fulfilled in it. Now, if you receive advancement through a gift meant for you, then you are very happy; if you find yourself the heir of a large and fair kingdom, you are even happier. Yet none of this, Shoreham holds, can be superior to the joy of conquest through God:

> Ac nys no blysse ne no feste
> Agheyns the ioye of conqueste
> Thet hys thorgh god;
> Ne mey me more ioye aspye,
> Thane wanne a man thorgh mestrye
> Keth hys manhod.[51]

Evil thus exists so that men can make the joy of heaven complete by winning the manhood – that is renown and honour as well as the status of a man – which comes with victory and conquest. Since no conquest can come about without strife, thus God suffers evil to exist. For, if there were no evil, there would be no strife, nor victory, and so heaven would lack that glory.

A similar logic, in which the associations of manhood are taken up in the steadfastness required for the fight against sin, leading to a kind of spiritual renown, occurs scattered through late medieval preaching. Thomas Brinton, for example, bishop of Rochester from 1373 to 1389, made much use of the metaphor of manly combat against personified sin. In one sermon, he incites his audience to combat the devil, the flesh and the world, saying:

> But in what way were we revived and nourished alike through faith? Certainly in three ways. By overcoming manly three kingdoms, that is of the devil, of the flesh and of the world.[52]

On another occasion, Brinton urged on a clerical audience the example of another manly defender of the church, St Thomas of Canterbury. The words of the theme 'laus eius in ecclesia' ('his praise/renown in the church') might be appropriately applied, Brinton argued, to Thomas. For:

> The fresh memory of the just man comforts us so that we imitate him manly, 'because of his renown'.[53]

Thomas Becket's *laus* – the praise of him, his reputation, or even his chivalric renown – inspire us to imitate him 'manly'. In Brinton's sermon, it is implied that if we keep the praise Thomas has won in our minds, like the deeds of some exemplary knight, we can undertake the hard path before us. As in Shoreham's poem, Becket's manly battle against the forces of the devil leads to the accumulation of a fund of merit, just as in romance texts manly deeds led to the accumulation of manhood, meaning honour and renown. Like earlier hagiography and monastic devotion, these sermons and devotional texts do not attack the cult of manhood head on, nor seek to undermine the worth of knightly honour, but instead take up the values of manhood with enthusiasm in their effort to direct its emotionally stirring potential towards spiritual ends.

To an extent it is tempting to dismiss the trope of spiritual combat and its resulting heavenly renown as a piece of clerical special pleading, a rather contrived attempt to convince men that they can be men by fighting, not their neighbours in a county community or their opponents in war, but those truly more dangerous enemies, the devil, the flesh and the world. We might wonder if everyone was as convinced by this argument as Brinton and Shoreham apparently were. But it should be noted that the fundamental markers of masculine worth which the proponents of a more clerical lifestyle felt the need to accommodate are not organised around the expression of masculinity through sexual activity, but are based on the demonstration of manhood by physical violence in the face of shame.

It is clear, moreover, that rhetorical tactics similar to those used by Shoreham and Brinton enjoyed popularity not just in the writings of late medieval preachers, but in the works of devout laymen also. Similar strategies, although without an overt use of the language of manhood, are found, for example, in a prose treatise known as the *Two Ways*, composed by Sir John Clanvowe probably sometime in the late 1380s and certainly before his death on crusade in about 1391.[54] The 'Two Ways' in question are, respectively, the broad way which leads to hell and the narrow way that leads to salvation. In order to follow the narrow way, we must first pass through the narrow gate which leads to it. This gate is guarded by three strong enemies that we must fight in order to enter.[55] These enemies turn out to be our old friends, the devil, the flesh and the world.[56] This battle is hard, but we are aided in our efforts by the example of the saints of heaven who have passed by the gate in spite of these enemies. 'And therefore, it is a great shame to us, and endless harm, unless we hold the way after those saints.'[57] Then, in perhaps the most famous passage of *The Two Ways*, Clanvowe turns in detail to 'the worships of this wretched world'.[58] If we are well advised we will know that they are not really 'worships'. Before God, such things are neither riches nor 'worships', 'for before God all virtue is worship and all sin is shame'. In this world, Clanvowe claims, the reverse is true, for the world holds them to be 'worshipful' who are great warriors and destroy and win many lands, and waste and give to those who have enough, and spend outrageously in food and drink, in clothing and building and living in ease, sloth and other sins. Vengeance too is rewarded by the world, for 'the world worships them much who are avenged proudly and without pity for every wrong that is said or done to them. And of such men, folk make books and songs and read and sing of them to hold in mind their deeds the longer here on earth. For worldly men desire greatly that their name might last long here on earth. But whatever the world might think about such men, they are judged 'right shameful before God and all the company of heaven', for before them all sin is shame and 'unworship'.[59]

Again, there is nothing very new in what Clanvowe says.[60] But once more this ought to sharpen our awareness of the deep currency and import of such views, not blunt it. The constantly present military metaphor in Clanvowe's text appeals to the deeply held assumption that physical courage, in defence, and in a good cause, is in itself desirable. Even in the moralised world of the *Two Ways*, the good deeds of virtue still lead to a form of honour analogous to chivalric honour. The social approbation or condemnation of the knight's peers is simply replaced by the opinion of 'God and all the company of heaven'. That he chose to support such views with liberal use of a ninth-century model emphasises their continuing currency, just as the affection for 'manly' fighting in a tight spot marks romance writers' awareness of the links of such activity both with an ancient heritage and with what current linguistic usage took to be a 'man'.

## V

If we put aside for a moment the associations suggested by modern concepts of masculinity, and place the focus of inquiry on medieval manhood instead, then, although similar themes do sometimes emerge, it begins to become apparent that a different order of priorities pertains than now operates in modern concepts of masculinity. Although sexuality is undeniably present amongst the associations of manhood, it most often seems to be a secondary phenomenon. It is not central in the same way as sexuality lies at the hub of modern concepts of masculinity. Instead, strength, personal honour and a kind of reactive vigour appear to be the organising concepts of manhood. Consequently, to invoke these values in a sexual context could be just as much a matter of transferral or redeployment as the invocation of manly action in the context of spiritual combat.

This invites a reassessment of how historians have approached late medieval masculinity, and above all the masculinity of the clergy.[61] If what was most important to manhood was less sex than honour, strength and steadfastness, how might this affect accounts of changing ideals of manhood, particularly with the insistence on clerical celibacy which gained pace from the eleventh century? Might the attempt to appropriate the values of manhood and redirect them to the battle against sin represent an attempt not (or not mainly) to reconcile aristocratic males to an abandonment of sexual activity (and hence masculinity) but instead a largely successful attempt to reconcile the same men to a more central aspect of their social status – the defence of honour, if necessary through violent action? It seems that manhood could exist without sex; what is less clear is that manhood could exist without strength and honour. The language of manhood and renown shows itself just as capable of being redirected to spiritual life as it was, in very different circumstances, to sexual life. The continuing success, even amongst devout lay audiences, of the strategy of opposing the fight against sin to the manly impulses of worldly honour, or to the bodily desire for sex, suggests that we should take care before regarding the late medieval clergy as doomed to 'emasculinity'.

Contrary to recent critiques of the undesirable consequences of the cultural or linguistic turn, such an order of priorities need not imply the abandonment of a general perspective or of a broader narrative, although it would alter the way in which such a long view was composed. The logic of the language of manhood explored in this article shows the power of concepts of honour and shame in the definition of the status of a 'man' in medieval England. It suggests that a view of manhood more commonly associated with Mediterranean societies was well established in England in the later Middle Ages, and for some time before and afterwards.[62] This should, I think, destabilise further the picture presented by the earliest theoretical frameworks proposed for the history of masculinity, which portrayed a series of gender eras, each with their characteristic qualities, and each replaced in turn by successive crises of masculinity.[63] Historians have already noted the weakness of such an approach in terms of the illusion of uniformity it can give for a particular epoch. They have underlined how men always had a variety of possibilities at their disposal to pursue socially valued roles in their respective social group.[64] But in doing so scholars have perhaps run the risk of emphasising diversity rather too much, and of overlooking the fact that some masculinities related more closely than others to certain culturally valued forms of behaviour, notably those linked to the status of a 'man'. I would suggest that we still risk underestimating the power of deeply established cultural concepts of manhood, notably a strong substratum of association between being a 'man' and requiring recognition of a certain status, face-to-face, if necessary by violence. This association was alive and well in fifteenth-century York, seventeenth-century Cambridge or nineteenth-century London, despite the long-established tension with the sober values of the patriarch or priest who fights sin instead of his fellow Christians, or the less respectable priorities of the youth, dedicated to fashion, sex and drink. As well as stressing the multiplicity of socially located masculinities, we need to consider each culturally valued masculinity as one configuration amongst competing sets of values which, if not eternal, changed at a far slower rate than early studies suggested. The present article has served only to scrape the surface of how this enterprise might be undertaken, and to raise some as yet unanswered questions, but, if we are to avoid giving a Whig interpretation of masculinity, it is with these questions that we must begin.

## Notes

Earlier versions of this paper were presented at the Leeds IMC, the Cambridge Historical Society, Southampton University and Birkbeck College, London. I am indebted to the audiences on each of these occasions, and to Ewan Johnson, David Pratt, Leonie Hicks, John Arnold and Sean Brady for the opportunity to explore these issues.

1. Karen Harvey and Alexandra Shepard, 'What have historians done with masculinity? Reflections on five centuries of British History, circa 1500 to 1950', *Journal of British Studies* 44 (2005), 274–80.
2. Harvey and Shepard, 'What have historians done?', 276. For similar remarks concerning 'materialist' or 'symbolic' approaches to masculine domination in ethnography, see Pierre Bourdieu, *La domination masculine* (Paris, 2002), p. 13.
3. Joan Hoff, 'Gender as a postmodern category of paralysis', *Women's History Review* 3 (1994), 149–68. For a more moderate view, see Elizabeth A. Clark, 'The lady vanishes: dilemmas of a feminist historian after the "linguistic turn"', *Church History* 67 (1998), 1–31.
4. John Tosh, 'Masculinities in industrializing society: Britain, 1800–1914', *Journal of British Studies* 44 (2005), 330–42, on 330–31, 342.
5. Bourdieu, *La domination masculine*, p. 13.
6. Herbert Butterfield, *The Whig Interpretation of History* (London, 1931).
7. For comment on the origins of this distaste, given Butterfield's own grand historical projects, see Stefan Collini, 'Whigissimo', *London Review of Books* 27 (2005), 14.
8. For a combative summary of early developments, see K.B. McFarlane, 'An early paper on crown and parliament in the later middle ages', in his *The Nobility of Later Medieval England* (Oxford, 1973), pp. 279–97. An example of noble interests: R.A. Griffiths, 'Local rivalries and national politics: the Percies, the Nevilles and the Duke of Exeter, 1452-55', *Speculum* 43 (1968), 589–632. An example of gentry society: Christine Carpenter, *Locality and Polity: A Study of Warwickshire Landed Society, 1401–1499* (Cambridge, 1992).
9. The early attacks of H.G. Richardson and G.O. Sayles on the significance of the Commons in parliament are brought together in Sayles, *The King's Parliament of England* (London, 1975). For a more moderate view, see J.W. McKenna, 'The myth of parliamentary sovereignty in late medieval England', *English Historical Review* 94 (1979), 481–506 and the remarks of McFarlane, 'Early paper', pp. 287–94.
10. See Christine Carpenter, 'Political and constitutional history: before and after McFarlane', in R.H. Britnell and A.J. Pollard (eds), *The McFarlane Legacy: Studies in Late Medieval Politics and Society* (Stroud and New York, 1995); Edward Powell, 'After "After McFarlane": The poverty of patronage and the case for constitutional history', ibid.
11. G.L. Harriss, *Shaping the Nation: England 1360–1461* (Oxford, 2005); Jean-Philippe Genet, *La genèse de l'Etat moderne: Culture et société politique en Angleterre* (Paris, 2003); W.M. Ormrod, *Political Life in Medieval England, 1300–1450* (London, 1995); Simon

Walker, *Political Culture in Later Medieval England*, ed. M. Braddick (Manchester, 2006); and, from the European perspective, John Watts, *The Making of Polities: Europe, 1300–1500* (Cambridge, 2009).
12. Joan Scott, 'Gender: a useful category of historical analysis', *American Historical Review* 91 (1986), 1053–75; Alan J. Frantzen, 'When women aren't enough', *Speculum* 68 (1993), 445–71; Clare A. Lees, 'Introduction' to *Medieval Masculinities: Regarding Men in the Middle Ages* (Minneapolis and London, 1994).
13. Quentin Skinner, 'Sir Geoffrey Elton and *The Practice of History*', *Transactions of the Royal Historical Society*, 6th ser., 7 (1997), 301–16.
14. This is not least because much early work on medieval masculinity has emerged in the form of closely focused case studies, producing many overlapping insights but no clear consensus as to the core object of study. The variety of approaches can be sampled from the contributions to Lees (ed.), *Medieval Masculinities*; D.M. Hadley (ed.), *Masculinity in Medieval Europe* (London, 1999); J.J. Cohen and B. Wheeler (eds), *Becoming Male in the Middle Ages* (New York, 1997); Jacqueline Murray (ed.), *Conflicted Identities and Multiple Masculinities: Men in the Medieval West* (New York, 1999); P.H. Cullum and Katherine Lewis (eds), *Holiness and Masculinity in the Middle Ages* (Cardiff, 2004). For an attempt at a broad categorisation of current approaches to medieval masculinity, see Christopher Fletcher, *Richard II: Manhood, Youth, and Politics, 1377–1399* (Oxford, 2008), pp. 4–5.
15. See, for example, the sanguine remarks of Peter G. Beidler, 'Introduction' to Beidler (ed.) *Masculinities in Chaucer* (Woodbridge, 1998), pp. 1–5.
16. Butterfield, *Whig Interpretation*, for example pp. 5–6, 24, 28–9, 33.
17. R.M. Karras, *From Boys to Men: Formations of Masculinity in Late Medieval Europe* (Philadelphia, 2003), p. 1. Cf. R.W. Connell, *Gender and Power* (Oxford, 1987); Connell, *Masculinities* (Oxford, 1995).
18. Karras, *From Boys to Men*, p. 3.
19. David Gilmore, *Manhood in the Making: Cultural Concepts of Masculinity* (New Haven and London, 1990).
20. Karras, *Boys to Men*, p. 68.
21. Ibid., p. 81.
22. Ibid.
23. Ibid., p. 90.
24. Ibid., pp. 95–100.
25. Christopher Fletcher, 'Manhood and politics in the reign of Richard II', *Past and Present*, 189 (2005), 3–39, on 13–14.
26. This issue, and its attendant implications, is not restricted to pre-industrial England: see Diederik Janssen, above, in this collection.
27. In addition to the material presented below, see Fletcher, *Richard II*, chs 2–3.
28. The coinage is that of R.W. Swanson, 'Angels incarnate: clergy and masculinity from Gregorian reform to reformation', in Hadley (ed.), *Masculinity in Medieval Europe*. A similar assumption is evident throughout recent work which approaches the insistence on clerical celibacy through the danger this is held to pose, in an implicit psychoanalytic framework, to male identity, notably: Jo Ann McNamara, 'The *Herrenfrage*: the restructuring of the gender system, 1050–1150' in Lees (ed.), *Medieval Masculinities*.
29. See Jacqueline Murray, 'Masculinizing religious life: sexual prowess, the battle of chastity and monastic identity', in Cullum and Lewis (eds), *Holiness and Masculinity*. An excellent summary of the tradition of spiritual combat up to the twelfth century is provided by Katherine Allen Smith, 'Saints in shining armour: martial asceticism

and masculine models of sanctity, ca. 1050–1250', *Speculum*, 83 (2008), 572–602, on 576–82.
30. P.H. Cullum, 'Clergy, masculinity and transgression', in Hadley (ed.), *Masculinity in Medieval Europe*; Cullum, 'Learning to be a man, learning to be a priest in late medieval England', in Sarah Rees Jones (ed.), *Learning and Literacy in Medieval England and Abroad* (Turnhout, 2003).
31. John H. Arnold, 'The labour of continence: masculinity and virginity in the twelfth and thirteenth century' in Anke Bernau, Ruth Evans and Sarah Salih (eds), *Medieval Virginities* (Cardiff, 2003); Jacqueline Murray, ' "The law of sin that is in my members": the problem of male embodiment', in Samantha J.E. Riches and Sarah Salih (eds), *Gender and Holiness: Men and Women and Saints in Late Medieval Europe* (London, 2002).
32. Smith, 'Saints in shining armour', p. 595; Murray, 'Masculinizing religious life'.
33. Fletcher, *Richard II*, ch. 4.
34. Megan McLaughlin, 'The woman warrior: gender, warfare and society in medieval Europe', *Women's Studies* 17 (1990), 194; A. Dunlop, 'Masculinity, crusading and devotion: Francesco Casali's Fresco in the Trecento Perugian *Contado*', *Speculum* 76 (2001), 315–36, on 328.
35. See, for example, Karras, *Boys to Men*, p. 108; Smith, 'Saints in shining armour', p. 595; Dunlop, 'Masculinity, crusading', pp. 317, 328.
36. R.M. Helmholz, *Marriage Litigation in Medieval England* (Cambridge, 1974), p. 89. Further discussed by Jacqueline Murray, 'On the origins and role of "wise women" in causes for annulment on the grounds of male impotence', *Journal of Medieval History*, 16 (1990), 235–49, on 240–41.
37. It seems that the women were, in fact, known to the court as prostitutes, although this is not mentioned in the trial record itself. See P.J.P. Goldberg, 'Women in Fifteenth-Century Town Life', in John A.F. Thompson (ed.), *Towns and Townspeople in the Fifteenth Century* (Gloucester, 1988), p. 119, n. 128; R.M. Karras, *Common Women: Prostitution and Sexuality in Medieval England* (New York and Oxford, 1996), p. 97.
38. *Ipsa iurata ostendebat mammillas suas denudates ac manibus suis ad dictam ignem calefacis virgam et testiculos dicti Johannis palpavit et tenuit ac eundem Johannem amplexabatur et sepius osculabatur ac eundem Johannem ad ostendum virilitatem et potentiam suam in quantum potuit excitauit, precipiendo sibi quod pro pudore tunc ibidem probaret et redderet se virum.* Helmholz, *Marriage Litigation*, p. 89. For fuller translated extracts of the proceedings see *Women in England, c. 1275–1525*, trans. and ed. P.J.P. Goldberg (Manchester, 1995), pp. 217–22.
39. Danielle Jacquart and Claude Thomasset, *Sexuality and Medicine in the Middle Ages*, trans. Matthew Adamson (Oxford, 1988), pp. 51, 59–60, 68, 117; Joan Cadden, *Meanings of Sex Difference in the Middle Ages* (Cambridge, 1993), pp. 52–3, 171–72, 181, 184–85.
40. Fletcher, 'Manhood and politics', pp. 22–3; Fletcher, *Richard II*, pp. 62–7.
41. Fletcher, *Richard II*, pp. 31–2. See also Rachel Stone, in the present volume. I would suggest that there is considerable unity in the examples of acting *viriliter* which she furnishes, and a shared frame of reference with the examples given in the present article. In particular, manly action keeps the same reference to vigour and steadfastness, even when this behaviour is invoked, for example, in the pursuit of reform or the defence of the Church. Compare the semantic field of *virtus* and *viriliter* in classical Latin, discussed in the works cited below, n. 50.
42. *Der Mittelenglische Versroman über Richard Löwenherz*, ed. K. Brunner, Wiener Beitrage zur Englischen Philologie 42 (Vienna and Leipzig, 1913), ll. 1908–12: ('And at the

land-gate King Richard held the assault so hard, and acted so manly, that he lost not one of his men.')
43. *Horn Childe and Maiden Rimnild*, ed. M. Mills (Heidelberg, 1988), ll. 166–68. ('Better manly to be slain than long to live in sorrow and pain under a foreigner's yoke.')
44. *William of Palerne*, ed. G.J.V. Bunt (Gröningen, 1985), ll. 3900–01. ('And it is more noble to die manly than to flee cowardly, whatever may happen.')
45. *William*, ll. 3337–38: ('Men, for your manship, suffer this no more, but go out valiantly and meet your foes!')
46. *William*, ll. 3341–42. ('If you meet with them manly, the mastery will be ours.')
47. *Sir Eglamour of Artois*, ed. F.E. Richardson, Early English Texts Society 256 (London, 1965), ll. 1315–17 (Lincoln Cathedral Library 91 of c.1430-1440, the 'Thornton' MS). Variant from BL Cotton Caligula A.II (c.1446–1460).
48. See Smith, 'Saints in shining armour', pp. 576–82; Murray, 'Masculinizing religious life'.
49. Carlin A. Barton, *Roman Honor: The Fire in the Bones* (Berkeley and London, 2001), esp. pp. 36–42; Myles McDonnell, *Roman Manliness: Virtus and the Roman Republic* (Cambridge, 2006).
50. *The Poems of William of Shoreham*, ed. M. Konrath, Early English Texts Society, old series 86 (London, 1902), no. 7.
51. Ibid., ll. 349–54: ('And there is no bliss nor celebration to compare with the joy of conquest that comes through God; nor can I conceive of more joy than when a man proves his manhood through mastery.')
52. *The Sermons of Thomas Brinton, Bishop of Rochester (1373–1389)*, ed. M.A. Devlin, Camden Soc. 3rd ser. 85 (London, 1934), sermon 37, p. 106: *Sed quomodo per fidem sumus recreati pariter et nutriti? Certe tripliciter. Tria regna videlicet diaboli, carnis, et mundi viriliter superando.* Cf. *Fasciculus Morum: A Fourteenth-Century Preacher's Handbook*, ed. and trans. S. Wenzel (London, 1989), pp. 40–3. Compare also the examples from the eleventh and twelfth centuries cited by Smith, 'Saints in shining armour', pp. 591–92.
53. *Sermons of Thomas Brinton*, p. 121: *Viri iusti recens memoracio nos comfortat vt eum viriliter imitemur,* quia laus eius.
54. 'The two ways' in *The Works of Sir John Clanvowe*, ed. V.J. Scattergood (Cambridge, 1975).
55. Clanvowe, 'The two ways', ll. 169–71.
56. Ibid., ll. 174–76. Here and below the modernisation is my own.
57. Ibid., ll. 191–93: 'And, therfore, it is greete shame to vs and eendelees harme also but yef we holden the wey after thoo seyntes'.
58. See especially K.B. McFarlane, *Lancastrian Kings and Lollard Knights* (Oxford, 1972), pp. 201–05.
59. Ibid., ll. 477–503.
60. One might also compare the remarks made by Alfred the Great in his translation of Boethius concerning the misleading nature of worldly riches, although the military metaphor is absent from Alfred's comments. See *Alfred the Great: Asser's Life of Alfred and Other Contemporary Sources,* trans. with intro. and notes by M. Lapidge and S. Keynes (Harmondsworth, 1983), pp. 133–34. Many thanks to David Pratt for bringing this similarity to my attention.
61. See also Smith, 'Saints in shining armour', p. 591, although she limits herself to the suggestion that celibate monks might be 'considered fully masculine within their own sphere'.

62. For such values in twentieth-century Mediterranean societies, see J. Peristiany (ed.), *Honour and Shame: The values of Mediterranean Society* (Chicago, 1974); David Gilmore (ed.), *Honor and Shame and the Unity of the Mediterranean* (Washington DC, 1987); P. Bourdieu, 'Le sens de l'honneur', in *Esquisse d'une théorie de la pratique, précédé par Trois études d'ethnologie kabyle* (Paris, 2000), pp. 19–60; A. Blok, *Honour and violence* (Malden, MA, 2001).
63. An approach launched by M. Kimmel, 'The contemporary "crisis of masculinity" in historical perspective', in Harry Brod (ed.), *The Making of Masculinities* (Boston, 1987) and followed notably by McNamara, 'Herrenfrage'; Anthony Fletcher, 'Men's dilemma: the future of patriarchy in England, 1560–1660', *TRHS*, 6th ser., 4 (1994), pp. 61–81.
64. Karras, *Boys to Men*, pp. 161–62; Alexandra Shepard, *Meanings of Manhood in Early Modern England* (Oxford, 2003), pp. 1–17.

# 5
# Masculinity without Conflict: Noblemen in Eighth- and Ninth-Century Francia

*Rachel Stone*

Around the middle of the eighth century near Langres, in eastern France, a *crime passionelle* allegedly took place. The wife of Gangulf, a Burgundian noble, began an affair with a cleric, but her husband discovered their wrongdoing. The cleric then murdered Gangulf. What is unusual is how we know about this story: Gangulf, a cuckold and a murder victim, became a saint.[1] The church of Melun received relics from him at its foundation in 809 and St-Pierre de Varennes was rededicated to him by 870.[2] Several versions of his life were composed: the first surviving one dates from the end of the ninth or early tenth century, and over 60 copies of this text survive.[3] His cult became widespread in Lorraine and Germany. In the second half of the tenth century Hrotsvit of Gandersheim, author of a number of religious poems and plays, composed one on Gangulf; a collection of Gangulf's posthumous miracles was also written at Liege in the eleventh century.[4] Although Gangulf's fame continued for centuries, however, I want to focus on the first *vita* (the written 'life') and its implications for our understanding of masculinity in the Carolingian empire, the vast area (eventually stretching from the Pyrenees to Croatia) ruled by Charlemagne and his successors between 768 and the end of the ninth century.[5]

Before discussing Carolingian ideas, however, there is a preliminary question, particularly appropriate for this collection of essays. Is it justifiable to talk about masculinity (in the sense of culture-specific ideas of what men *ought* to be like) in an early medieval context? Or is it a concept that is simply inappropriate for such a society?[6] The sources suggest that ideas of gender are applicable to this period. The use in Latin texts of terms such as *viriliter* (manfully), applied to both men and women, or *virago* (a man-like maiden) show an understanding of gendered social behaviour as conceptually distinct from biological sex. The mid-ninth-century monastic writer Haimo of Auxerre, for example, in a homily on the feeding of the five thousand, explains why the text mentions only men eating:

> Since only men are said to have been at this refreshment of the Lord, we are warned mystically, that if we should desire to taste how sweet the Lord is, we should be men, that is strong against the devil's temptations... Nor will a woman remain hungry at this refreshment of the Lord, if with feminine sex, she should manfully restrain the attempts of the devil: just as on the contrary, a man by sex is made feminine in mind, if he is found soft and dissolute in his labour against the attack of temptation.[7]

Given that Carolingian Francia did have concepts of masculinity, what can we say about them? Any discussion of the idea of gender in the Carolingian period must be considered against a background of religious reform.[8] For more than a hundred years, a royally inspired programme is visible which aimed at the moral reform of the whole of society. From mirrors for princes intended to inspire kings to godly rule, to the efforts to ensure pastoral supervision of peasants, the whole of Carolingian society was to be ordered (in both senses) to be good. In this hierarchical vision of perfection, gender borders were standard. A model sermon from around 802 announced:

> Let wives be subject to husbands in goodness and chastity, keeping themselves from fornication, sorcery and avarice... Let them nurture their sons in the fear of God... Let husbands love their wives and not say dishonourable words to them, ruling their houses in goodness... Let sons love and honour their parents; let them not be disobedient.[9]

This sermon was one of many reform texts inculcating a set of moral norms for the lay world. Demands for the obedience of subordinates (including wives to husbands and sons to parents) were linked with the responsibility of those in authority to provide pastoral instruction to these subordinates and also to exercise their 'rule' morally. Such a consistent ideology of gendered moral behaviour was propagated not only in royal assemblies and councils, but also at diocesan and even parochial level.

Reformers' views on morality and gender are culturally dominant in the extant texts: we do not possess sources celebrating 'unreformed' men. This is perhaps inevitable, given that the vast majority of Carolingian texts were both written and preserved in monastic and clerical contexts. The wide variety of genres which inculcate such moral norms, however, including legislative texts, letters and annals, as well as hagiography and sermons, suggest that ideas of religious reform also dominated public discourses in the eighth and ninth centuries.

78  Rachel Stone

Yet gaining such ideological control probably involved more of a struggle than is immediately visible. The limitations of early medieval sources mean that, although we can hear the reformers' message clearly, it is far harder to gauge its impact on a lay audience. Since we have only sources written by the elite, there is almost no evidence about the reaction of the lower orders to such moral instruction. We have a handful of texts written by Carolingian lay nobles, which demonstrate the influence on them of ideas of religious reform and moral education.[10] The reactions of most lay noblemen, however, must be inferred from texts written or promulgated by reform-minded clerics, monks or rulers.

Some aristocratic laypeople embraced the new ideas: Paul Kershaw describes the book collection of Eberhard of Friuli and his wife Gisela as demonstrating 'the moral and corrective drives of Charlemagne's *renovatio* [renewal] shrunk to the scale of a single family.'[11] There is also, however, evidence of resistance to new moral demands. Archbishop Hincmar of Rheims worried about men using Biblical texts to justify marriage by abduction, while the reformer Jonas of Orléans reported some husbands objecting to his attempts to limit the times at which they might have intercourse with their wives.[12] Studies of Carolingian marriage disputes show similar patterns, with occasional direct resistance to new restrictions on marriage and divorce combined with more frequent attempts to find loopholes within the system.[13]

One of the products of this reform programme was views on gender noticeably different from those in other medieval societies. To return to Gangulf: to many historians and literary scholars his cult will seem bizarre. How can a cuckold be represented as a saint? Such husbands have been a stock figure of derision and contempt in much western literature.[14] In many cultures, indeed, the dishonour brought by a wife's adultery has been held to justify a husband's slaying her. This was certainly the case in Carolingian Francia, where secular law allowed the killing of adulterous wives. Count Richwinus, for example, killed his wife because of her 'disgrace' (*stuprum*).[15] Yet such male behaviour was not universally accepted. Reforming clerics spoke out strongly against uxoricide. At the end of the eighth century, for example, Paulinus, Patriarch of Aquileia, imposed a severe lifelong penance on a certain Aistulf, who had killed his innocent wife and afterwards alleged she was an adulteress. He stressed that, even if the allegations had been true, Aistulf could have sent his wife away, but not killed her.[16]

The depiction of Gangulf shows an author transforming a story of cuckoldry into one of heroism. He repeatedly and specifically praises Gangulf as masculine. Gangulf is pious even as a boy, but the *vita* focuses on his life 'when the alarms of adolescence had been passed through, and the strength of virile age had resulted'.[17] (This is associated by the author with his deciding to marry.) Gangulf, he recounts, was a 'holy man', carrying out military service for Pippin, then mayor of the palace.[18] He 'contended manfully against the temptations of the old enemy [the Devil]',[19] and he died 'happily' a few days after being fatally wounded by the cleric, the 'circle of this present life completed manfully'.[20] In his relations with his wife, Gangulf is not shown as deceived by his wife's cunning, but instead betrayed. He chooses a wife wisely, marrying a woman of 'very noble birth', whose morals unfortunately do not live up to this birth. Instead, God 'allowed' her to be unworthy, to test Gangulf's virtue.[21] When Gangulf hears rumours of his wife's adultery, he does not act precipitously, but first gains proof of her guilt, via a miracle in which she is burnt by a cold spring after perjuring herself.[22] Gangulf tells her she deserves to die, but he refrains from exercising his legal right to kill her and her clerical lover. From Christian mercy, he simply disowns his wife, going away and leaving her to repentance and God's judgement.[23] Gangulf thus shows by his magnanimity his superiority to mundane concerns of honour. The guilty couple, however, fear that he will change his mind and therefore decide to attack Gangulf pre-emptively.[24]

The author's tactics show how an ordinary framework for correct male behaviour (in response to cuckoldry) could be altered to show an equal or greater masculine virtue via unconventional behaviour.[25] Similar attempts at re-imagining masculinity are visible in other Carolingian sources. It is particularly revealing to examine the discourse of manly action: who is described as behaving *'viriliter'* (manfully) and in what circumstances?[26] Some uses are conventional enough: battles, both literal and spiritual, are often described as being fought 'manfully'. Pope Leo IV in 853 wrote to the Frankish army: 'Take care to act manfully against the enemies of the holy faith and the adversaries of all the provinces.'[27] Alcuin encouraged the religious community at York: 'If we overcome our enemies, with God's help, and manfully resist devilish suggestions, we are going to receive the crown of perpetual praise and the palm of eternal blessedness.' In 839 the nobleman Ratolt made a donation to the church of Freising 'manfully girded with his sword'.[28]

Similarly, rulers, both secular and religious, were expected to govern manfully. Regino of Prüm reports how, in 888, 'The people of Gaul made Duke Odo, a vigorous man, unequalled in beauty of form and height of body and greatness of strength and wisdom, king over them by both council and will; who ruled the state manfully.'[29] Adversity also had to be endured *viriliter*. Haimo of Auxerre claimed:

> For man is named from strength, and that name is especially apt for he who alone was able to wreck the strength of the devil, rising from the dead... Let us therefore also learn to be men, strengthened by him, so that we may bravely resist the temptations of the devil and endure all misfortunes manfully.[30]

Yet behaviour could also be described as 'manly' even when it lacked such obvious masculine attributes as strength or domination. Louis the Pious, in a diploma reforming the monastery of St Denis in 832, says that, while some of the monks have abandoned the monastic life, 'a certain part of them...chose especially to remain manfully in the purpose and habit of holy religion'.[31] Belief itself could be manly: Hrabanus Maurus said that the names of the apostles Andrew and John 'signify peoples who manfully believe Christ'.[32] Exemplary masculinity could also be shown in obedience. Alcuin urges Charlemagne's treasurer and 'devoted helper' Megenfrid, 'to do his will manfully.'[33] Pope Hadrian II called on the Synod of Douzy in 871 to support Bishop Actard of Nantes: 'moved by fraternal charity, take care manfully to aid him with all your powers, humbly interceding before your most excellent king'.[34] To Carolingian authors, therefore, 'manly' behaviour encompassed an enormous range, from boldness in battle to persistence in faith and humble supplication.[35] Nor was the term applied only to men: Alcuin urged Charlemagne's sister Gisla to 'Manfully build an eternal home for yourself in the heavens'; Katrien Heene has argued for *viriliter* being used in a 'sex-neutral' way by Carolingian authors.[36]

If the clearly positive quality of 'manliness' could be possessed by Carolingian women, were Carolingian men at danger of being undesirably 'female'? Carol Clover has argued for such a 'permeable' barrier in her influential study of gender in Norse society. In her view,

> there was finally just one 'gender', one standard by which persons were judged adequate or inadequate, and it was something like masculine. What finally excites fear and loathing in the Norse mind is not femaleness per se, but the condition of powerlessness, the lack or loss of volition, with which femaleness is typically, but neither inevitably nor exclusively associated...what prompts admiration is not maleness per se, but sovereignty of the sort enjoyed mostly and typically and ideally, but not solely, by men.[37]

Clover sees this opposition, summarised in the adjectives *hvatr/blaupr*, working 'more as a gender continuum than a sexual binary'[38] and thinks it may result in the 'frantic machismo of Norse males, at least as they are portrayed in the literature'.[39] Such a gender continuum has also been suggested as characteristic of the Carolingian world;[40] the textual evidence, however, does not support this. In contrast to Norse sources, the failures of men were not strongly marked as female.[41] Accusations of effeminate behaviour are rare, even for those who are seen as cowardly or sexually lax.[42]

Attitudes towards women in the period are also noteworthy. As Katrien Heene demonstrates, texts of the period express relatively low levels of misogyny. Women were not portrayed as fundamentally other by the authors of most sources.[43] In addition, Frankish historians of the eighth and ninth centuries do not criticise prominent women, such as queens and empresses, with anything like the ferocity seen in several near-contemporary cultures. There are no Carolingian texts as vitriolic as Procopius' portrayal of the Empress Theodora or depictions of Merovingian queens like Fredegund and Brunhild.[44]

## Early medieval masculinity

How do these Carolingian attitudes fit into a history of early medieval masculinity? The current narrative has tended to focus on two periods of change: the Western Roman Empire in the period from around 380 to 420 AD and the Gregorian reforms in the eleventh century. The late antique period is often seen as one in which a hegemonic Christian masculinity developed in the West, which exalted celibate clerics and virgins, and denigrated lay masculinity and married women.[45] A deep emphasis on gender is also visible in the eleventh-century church reforms, particularly associated with Pope Gregory VII. These aimed to ensure the separation of the church from the world via prohibitions on clerical marriage and simony. As part of this reform the medieval gender order was definitively established, with clear divisions made between clerics and secular men and both secular and religious women firmly subordinated.[46] The centuries in between have largely been ignored in discussions of medieval gender history. They figure only in the postscripts of books on late antiquity.[47] For many working on masculinity in the central Middle Ages, meanwhile, the period between the fifth and eleventh centuries is a curious limbo, in which late antique Christian ideas are powerless to affect a secular culture assumed to be unchanging in its gender norms.[48]

There are also evidential problems for the study of early medieval masculinity, particularly secular masculinity. Sixth- and seventh-century sources are difficult to use; a number of literary texts are not securely dated, and the evidence for some early medieval cultures is dominated by the views of one or two possibly idiosyncratic authors.[49] Studies of distinctively early medieval evidence, such as gendered grave goods, cannot easily be put alongside late antique letters and theological polemic.[50] The Carolingian period, in contrast, does have a substantial corpus of material that can be used for comparisons with the gender order in both late antiquity and the eleventh century. (They also show that the imposition of celibacy on clerics was not simply an eleventh-century innovation.[51]) Although Janet Nelson has seen continuity in ninth and tenth-century forms of 'anxious masculinity', I would argue instead that there is a noticeable contrast, especially when looking at attitudes towards laypeople.[52] The Carolingian period, with its holy cuckold, low levels of textual misogyny and an unusually inclusive idea of masculinity, is very different from both the late antique and eleventh-century patterns.

How and why do new concepts of gender develop? Many studies of the changing ideology of classical and medieval masculinities have focused on misogyny and a hatred of sexual activity as the driving factors, with men concerned mainly with repressing and controlling women whenever their superiority might be challenged.[53] Recently, however, some scholars have argued that these intense debates over gender are better seen as driven by struggles for power between different male social groups. Misogyny in texts is often used instrumentally to attack other men, with the adverse effects on women themselves occurring more as collateral damage. Kate Cooper and Conrad Leyser, for example, see the controversies around clerical marriage and virginity in the late western Roman empire as primarily a matter of competing claims to authority by male ascetics and the traditional senatorial class (whether pagan or Christian).[54] In particular, Christian ascetics appropriated and reworked the traditional senatorial ideology that used sexual restraint as a sign of a married man's fitness for political office. From the first century AD, the aristocracy of Imperial Rome had used their conjugal behaviour as a privileged sign of their ability to subordinate private interests to the public good. Ascetics such as St Jerome tried to trump this by demonstrating the superior judgement of the celibate: the very uncertainty of marriage meant that only those who had no family, and thus no private interests, were definitely virtuous enough to rule.[55] Similarly, Maureen Miller argues that, in the eleventh century, 'The real struggle in the reform movement was not men against women, but clerical men against lay men.'[56] Such scholarship draws on the insight that many texts supposedly representing women may actually be using them symbolically, as a way of making coded attacks on the men associated with them.[57] As Miller puts it: 'the reformers' sharpest invective about women was mobilised to censure their supposed emasculation of clerical males through their devouring lust...The audience for this discourse is not women, it is men.'[58]

An approach to Carolingian masculinity that considers the dynamics between different elite male groups is revealing. Two significant changes had already taken place in the late fifth and sixth centuries. First, competitive celibacy as a tactic for claiming authority died out, with the disappearance of pagan senators as political rivals and St Augustine's successful ridiculing of extreme ascetics as akin to freak show acts.[59] By the late fifth century, metaphors of spiritual authority rarely drew on the body and sexuality, but instead on such (male) social relationships as lord and man.[60] At the end of the sixth century, Gregory the Great in his *Pastoral Rule* produced a model for a moral overseer which simply ignored celibacy.[61] Similarly, the negative moral significance of nocturnal emissions and the positive moral significance of spiritual marriage declined sharply, and there are relatively few references to these topics in the eighth and ninth centuries.[62]

Second, there was an important shift within Western monasticism. From the sixth century or earlier, a new symbiotic relationship developed in the West between monasteries and lay elites. Noblemen who remained in the world were increasingly responsible for providing both protection and resources for monasteries. This included the human resource of oblates: young children, particularly boys, given as irrevocable gifts to a monastery to be brought up as monks.[63] In return for the protection and resources provided, monasteries became centres for family commemoration and intercession, as well as providing strategies for protecting family property.

These changes in monastic recruitment and support had several important effects on gender relations. Oblation provided a ready supply of 'pure boys' to carry out priestly duties, both within the monastery (where monks were increasingly priested) and as recruits to the episcopate.[64] Male ascetics now had less need to denounce lay life in order to win adult recruits and their estates.[65] A new emphasis on the monastery as a holy space moved concerns about monastic chastity from an individual to a corporate level. Monks were increasingly imagined as a collective group of asexual beings, rather than as individual rivals in the battle for chastity.[66] It also seems plausible that religious men who had been raised within the cloister, and gained their own gender identity there, were less likely to feel hostility towards women or a need to reject them.[67]

Such changes to clerical and monastic ideology were already affecting Francia before the eighth century. What distinguishes the Carolingian period is the systematic attempt by the new dynasty to create alliances between elite men. To fulfil the Carolingian rulers' vision of an expanded and godly kingdom of the Franks under their divinely ordained leadership, clerics, monks and laymen had to be exhorted to work together. There were repeated calls by Charlemagne for bishops, abbots and counts, men who often had opposing interests in particular regions,[68] to love one another.[69] An emphasis on the consensual production of key capitularies (royal orders) was another symbol of this desired concord.[70] Yet this alliance had to be extended even further, beyond this magnate class. The holy hands and pure prayers of monks were seen as essential to the stability of the kingdom.[71] Since Christianisation of the whole society was required, there was a new emphasis on the pastoral role of bishops and rural priests.[72] Nor was this pastoral responsibility limited to clerics: both fathers and mothers were required to participate in what Janet Nelson has called 'Charlemagne's great enterprise of social correction'.[73] The pastoral role of laypeople was also expanded by a greater emphasis on the role of godparents in providing religious instruction to their godchildren.[74]

In this Carolingian project, competitive claims to masculinity were a divisive distraction. If only the self-controlled and celibate were truly manly, laymen were almost by definition inferior. Unlike the eleventh-century reformers,

Carolingian religious had no wish to denigrate lay rulers and magnates in that way. An overemphasis on sexual purity as a prerequisite for authority also risked exposing erring rural clergy to lay derision, increasing splits within the priestly *ordo* itself.[75] Nor could masculinity be understood simply in terms of rule over others, a society made up of patriarchs. The ordinary monk was metaphorically a son, with the abbot as father, but he was still manly in his role as spiritual warrior: asexuality did not remove gender. As a result, masculinity, apart from its Christian connotations, becomes a curiously unfocused concept in Carolingian moral thought.

The *Vita Gangulfi* hints at both the successes and the tensions of this strategy of inclusion. As several scholars have pointed out, it contains the most sustained attempt in any early medieval *vita* to show the life of lay noblemen (and in particular three characteristic markers of it: warfare, hunting and marriage) as virtuous.[76] Gangulf's hunting is justified by his concern to avoid idleness.[77] His military prowess is celebrated, and it is claimed that his weapons are still displayed at his tomb.[78] Even the miraculous confirmation of his wife's adultery is followed by his regrets for the loss of marital harmony.[79] Yet Gangulf's hesitations over whether or not he should kill his wife to protect his own honour suggest how difficult lay noblemen must have found some clerical demands.[80] It is also noticeable that Gangulf is not shown as living an ascetic life, either before or after separating from his wife. He is a generous giver of alms, avoids obscene stories and spectacles, and as a boy memorises much doctrine, but his religious practices are not stressed.[81] Only when he is dying is his partaking in the Eucharist mentioned, for example.[82]

The author, probably a cleric himself, says little about the adulterous cleric, apart from stressing his wickedness.[83] He is a 'faithless apostate' and 'a vessel of the Devil'.[84] After his murder of Gangulf, he returns to his lover and they rejoice. The cleric then promptly dies hideously, like Judas Iscariot and the heretic Arius.[85] Unlike Gangulf, whose lingering death allows him to ensure his own salvation, the cleric thus goes straight to hell.[86] The cleric is shown implicitly as an abominable aberration, whose behaviour has no wider implications. In contrast, there are moments of universalising misogyny in the treatment of Gangulf's wife. She is tempted by the Devil, who had also led Eve astray.[87] When Gangulf confronts her with allegations, 'as is feminine custom, she began to assert with many oaths that she had been unjustly slandered by all'.[88] Such misogyny, however, could not be allowed full expression. If the evil behaviour of Gangulf's wife was shown as typical, it would imply that Gangulf (and other laymen) were foolish to marry in the first place. (In contrast to Hrotsvit's later rewriting, where Gangulf is pressurised into marrying, the initiative for marriage in the first *vita* is entirely his.)[89]

This concern to appeal to an audience of married men may also explain the repeated showing of Gangulf's wife as a scoffer at both God and Gangulf. She bewails Gangulf's action in buying a spring from a peasant, which he is later miraculously able to relocate to his own land.[90] When Gangulf proposes his 'ordeal' to her, 'thinking the words of the man of God were ignorant... she did not hesitate to put her hand into the water without uncertainty';[91] the touch of the water then removes the skin of her arm and hand. After Gangulf's death, she receives her final punishment when she is informed that miracles are being performed at his tomb:

> But she, raving in furious madness, said thus: 'Gangulf's virtues work as much as my arsehole.' Immediately as this shameful voice came from her mouth, an obscene sound was produced from the thrust-out part of her body.[92]

She is then divinely punished by farting whenever she speaks on Fridays (the day of her offence).[93]

The scoffer, who is punished for doubting God's power and the saint's holiness, is a common figure in hagiography.[94] Yet in this case the fact of marriage to a saint adds the overtone that lack of respect for one's husband is also sinful. Even the adultery could be imagined by a hearer or reader as motivated by the wife's inability to recognise Gangulf's merit. Gangulf's story thus contains a potential warning for all wives. It also, however, shows them ways of godly behaviour (initial wifely obedience or subsequent repentance) that were eminently achievable, just as it was more feasible for laymen to imitate Gangulf than ascetic or monastic saints.

The tensions within Gangulf's story suggest that Carolingian attempts at creating inclusive images of masculinity were not always straightforward. The popularity of Gangulf's cult, however, implies that such models were not simply irrelevant clerical propaganda. Enough laypeople (perhaps simply husbands who felt under-appreciated by their wives) must have felt able to venerate Gangulf for his cult to have prospered.

If Carolingian rulers successfully put together a coalition of social groups that discouraged competitive discourses of masculinity, what happened in the post-Carolingian world? The evidence suggests that competing ideals of masculinity soon reappeared in the tenth century, once the pressures to avoid them were released. Phyllis Jestice, for example, discusses what she calls 'the first firmly self-motivated reforming group in the medieval church: the reformed monks of the early tenth century'.[95] The works of Odo of Cluny, one of the key figures in the movement, show his extreme worries about the sinfulness of all sexual activity.[96] Odo's *Vita* of Gerald of Aurillac, like the *Vita Gangulfi*, is one of the earliest medieval examples of a lay saint. Unlike Carolingian moralists and the author of the *Vita Gangulfi*, however, Odo regards warfare and sexual activity as incompatible with a holy life; Gerald must avoid both.[97] Similarly, in the later tenth century, Hrotsvit rewrote the story of Gangulf to show a man who married only reluctantly at his entourage's request, and who triumphed (like Gerald of Aurillac) in bloodless victories.[98]

Older patterns of gendered discourse also become visible again. In the second half of the tenth century Liutprand of Cremona's works, for example, are notorious for their lurid portrayals of lewd women. Ross Balzaretti argues that their main aim is to justify the political claims of Otto I against the pope and other political rivals in Italy: wicked women once again become symbolic of the moral failures of rival men.[99] Italy in the tenth century was also marked by controversy over clerical celibacy, a conflict that pitted groups of clergy against each other. The reformers fulminated about men who could not control their lust, and thus demonstrated their unfitness to rule others, but married clergy may have had their own counter-attack. Rather of Verona reported some clerics arguing that any man who did not keep a woman must be a sodomite. Balzaretti sees this as an indication of 'the sexual fears of the Veronese clergy' and an early example of compulsory heterosexuality.[100] It may instead indicate a tactic for impugning the morals and the masculinity of the reforming party, just as monastic claims in the twelfth century of widespread sodomy by laymen suggest a defensive response to sexual allegations made about themselves.[101]

## Conclusion

A study of masculinity in the Carolingian period can remind us of the obvious point that masculinity is culturally constructed and has no trans-historical core. It also demonstrates again the role of political conflicts in actively generating gender stereotypes rather than simply deploying existing images. But the study of Carolingian masculinity also raises a more difficult question about masculinity as a historical concept. Researchers have rightly stressed the relational aspects of masculinity: it does not simply exist in isolation. And yet the changes in the ideology of masculinity that are visible between the fifth and eleventh centuries do not seem to be driven primarily either by changing concepts of femininity or by substantial changes in women's social position.

Recent studies of late antique and early medieval women have instead often stressed the continuities in their lives, both over time and between social groups. Women's lives in western Europe changed significantly between the fourth and ninth centuries, but remained framed by an ideology of women's presumed inferiority and the structures of domestic patriarchy.[102] Christianity had brought genuine change, in the new possibility of an ascetic life for women, but such a life was still often imagined in domestic terms, with clear parallels between the expected behaviour of religious and lay women.[103]

The evidence suggests that it was conflicts within the male elite (or the lack of them) that powered significant developments in early medieval images of the ideal male, rather than challenges to the patriarchal system as a whole. Can a gender system with this kind of dynamic be understood in the same terms as a modern masculinity influenced by real changes in women's position? What, if anything, do medieval and modern masculinity share?

## Notes

The following abbreviations are used in this chapter: MGH=*Monumenta Germaniae Historica*; MGH Cap.=*Capitularia regum Francorum*, 2 vols, ed. Alfred Boretius and Viktor Krause (Hanover, 1883–1897); MGH Epp.=*Epistolae Merowingici et Karolini aevi*. MGH Epistolae, III–VIII (Berlin, 1892–1939); MGH SRG=*Scriptores rerum Germanicarum in usum scholarum separatim editi* (Hanover, 1871–); MGH SRM=*Scriptores rerum Merovingicarum*, 7 vols, ed. Bruno Krusch and Willhelm Levison (Hanover, 1885–1951); PL=*Patrologiae Cursus Completus, Series Latina*. 221 vols, ed. J.-P. Migne (Paris, 1841–1864); VG=*Vita Gangulfi martyris Varennensis*, ed. Willhelm Levison (Hanover, 1919) (*MGH SRM 7*), pp. 155–170.

1. VG. A French translation is given in J.-P. Royer and M. Goullet, 'La vie de saint Gengoul (*BHL* 3328)', *Annales de Bourgogne*, 75 (2003), 351–73.
2. J.-P. Poly, 'Gengoul, L'époux martyr. Adultère féminin et norme populaire au Xe siècle', *La femme au Moyen Âge*, Collection des journée de la Faculté de droit Jean-Monnet, 2 (Paris, 1992), pp. 47–63, on p. 53.
3. M. Goullet, 'Les Vies de Saint Gengoul, époux et martyr', in M. Lauwers (ed.), *Guerriers et moines: conversion et sainteté aristocratiques dans l'Occident médiéval (IXe-XIIe siècle)* (Antibes, 2002), pp. 235–63, on p. 237.
4. J.-P. Poly, 'Gengoul', pp. 54–7. On Hrotsvit see K.M. Wilson, *Hrotsvit of Gandesheim:The Ethics of Authorial Stance* (Leiden, 1988).
5. In this chapter 'Francia' is used to refer to this imperial area as a whole, rather than in its narrower sense of the traditional heartlands of Frankish power. For an overview of Frankish political history in the period, see R. Collins, *Early medieval Europe 300–1000*, 2nd edn (Basingstoke, 1999), pp. 262–364.
6. Cf. J.A. Schultz, 'Heterosexuality as a threat to medieval studies', *Journal of the History of Sexuality*, 15 (2006), 14–29, arguing that 'heterosexuality' is not a useful concept for the medieval period.
7. Haimo of Auxerre, *Homiliae de temporae*, 49 (PL 118, col. 291): *Cum ergo in hoc convivio Domini tantummodo viri fuisse dicuntur, mystice monemur ut, si quam suavis sit Dominus gustare desideramus, viri simus, id est fortes contra diaboli tentationes... Nec ab hac refectione Dominica femina jejuna remanebit, si sexu femineo viriliter tentamenta diaboli compresserit: sicut e contra vir sexu femineae mentis efficitur, si contra impetum tentationis mollis et dissolutus in opere suo invenitur.*
8. On the reform movement in general, see R. McKitterick, *The Frankish Church and the Carolingian Reforms, 789–895* (London, 1977). On the specific moral demands made on laymen see R. Stone, 'Masculinity, nobility and the moral instruction of the Carolingian lay elite', unpublished doctoral thesis (University of London, 2005).
9. *Missi cuiusdam admonito* (MGH Cap. I no 121 p. 240): *Mulier sunt subiecti viri sui in omni bonitate et pudicitia, custodiant se a fornicatione et beneficiis et abaritiis... Nutriant filios suos in Dei timore... Viri diligant uxorem suam, et inhonesta verba non dicat ei, guberne domus suas in bonitate... Filii diligant parentes suos et honoret illos; non sint inobedientes.* On the genre, date and authorship of this text, see T.M. Buck, *Admonitio*

*und Praedicatio: zur religiös-pastoralen Dimension von Kapitularien und kapitulariennahen Texten (507–814)* (Frankfurt am Main, 1997), pp. 157–238.
10. For an overview of lay authors, see P. Wormald and J.L. Nelson (eds), *Lay Intellectuals in the Carolingian World* (Cambridge, 2007).
11. P.J.E. Kershaw, 'Eberhard of Friuli, a Carolingian lay intellectual', in Wormald and Nelson (eds), *Lay Intellectuals*, pp. 77–105, on p. 102.
12. R. Stone, 'The invention of a theology of abduction: Hincmar of Rheims on *raptus*', *Journal of Ecclesiastical History* 60 (2009), 433–48, on 445–46.
13. R. Stone, '"Bound from either side": the limits of power in Carolingian marriage disputes, 840–870', *Gender and History* 19 (2007), 467–82.
14. For the Roman tradition of the *leno*, the husband–pimp, see T.A.J. McGinn, *Prostitution, Sexuality, and the Law in Ancient Rome* (Oxford, 1998), pp. 171–94.
15. Regino of Prüm, *Chronicon*, ed. Friedrich Kurze (Hanover, 1890) (*MGH SRG 50*), s.a. 883 p. 121. Compare Hincmar of Rheims, Epistola 135 (MGH Epp. 8, pp. 81–7), discussing the case of Ingiltrude, wife of Count Boso of Italy, who, having run off with a lover, refused to return to Boso, claiming she feared for her life.
16. Paulinus, Epistola 16 n. 1 (MGH Epp. 4 pp. 520–21).
17. VG 2, p. 158: *decursis adolescentiae metis, cum robur virilis evasisset aetatis*.
18. VG 3, p. 159: *Ea tempestate regnum Francorum Pippinus strenue gubernabat; cui hic sanctus vir militari officio coniunctus inserviebat* [At that time Pippin energetically ruled the kingdom of the Franks; this holy man, connected to him, was devoted to military office].
19. VG Preface, p. 155: *contra antiqui hostis temptamenta viriliter decertavit*.
20. VG 10, p. 164: *consummatoque viriliter praesentis aevi circulo, felici et iam dudum exoptato transitu migravit ad Dominum*.
21. VG 2, p. 158: *Quae licet nobilissimis adforet orta natalibus, dissimilis tamen extitit moribus... Quam idcirco occultus arbiter permisit degenerem, ut remur esse, ut in illa beati viri patientiae experiretur praeconium et innocentis probaretur simplicitas* [Who, although she was born from very noble parents, yet was unlike this in morals... The secret judge therefore allowed her to be degenerate, as we think, so that the celebrating of the holy man's patience might be tested by her and the simplicity of innocence tried].
22. VG 7, p. 162; Gerald is associated with springs: he has previously miraculously relocated one after purchasing it (VG 4–5, pp. 159–61). Gangulf's testing of his wife's innocence is a miraculous version of the 'ordeal by cauldron', a method of proof often used in the Carolingian period: see R. Bartlett, *Trial by Fire and Water: The Medieval Judicial Ordeal* (Oxford, 1986), pp. 4–9.
23. VG 8, pp. 162–63.
24. VG 9, p. 193: *Verentes itaque, ne forte, zelo iracundiae succensus, beatus Gangulfus repentino ambos interitu necaret, omni conamine coeperunt comminisci, ut quo modo ei necem inferrent* [Thus fearing, lest perhaps, inflamed by zeal of rage, blessed Gangulf might with sudden destruction kill them both, they began to contrive with every effort, how they might cause death to him].
25. There are intriguing parallels with one of the few other texts I know which show a cuckolded husband in a positive light: Thomas Heywood's 1603 play 'A Woman Killed with Kindness.' John Frankford, the husband in the play, similarly marries a wife of good background, who betrays him with a man whom Frankford could have expected to be trustworthy (his friend and dependent Wendoll). Told about their affair, Frankford seeks proof, but then refrains from killing them, although severely tempted. Instead, he banishes his wife, preserving her life to allow her to repent. Unlike's Gangulf's wife, she does so, dying from grief soon after. Such parallels

come not from any common source, but from a similar desire to show how the hero's honour could be preserved in a potentially shameful situation.
26. As Christopher Fletcher points out in his chapter in this collection, such an approach via contemporary terminology can help us avoid imposing our own preconceptions of masculinity on the sources.
27. Leo IV, Epistola 28 (MGH Epp. 5, p. 601): *contra inimicos sanctae fidei, et adversarios omnium regionum viriliter agere studete*. Alcuin, Epistola 43 (MGH Epp. 4, p. 88): *si nostros, Deo auxiliante, superamus adversarios, et diabolicis viriliter resistimus suggestionibus, coronam perpetuae laudis et palmam aeternae beatitudinis accepturi erimus*.
28. T. Bitterauf (ed.), *Die Traditionen Des Hochstifts Freising*, 1 (Munich, 1905), no. 634, p. 539.
29. Regino of Prüm, s.a. 888, pp. 129–30: *Galliarum populi…Odonem ducem…virum strenuum, cui prae caeteris formae pulchritudo et proceritas corporis et virium sapientiaeque magnitudo inerat, regem super se pari consilio et voluntate creant; qui rempublicam viriliter*. Cf Alcuin, Epistola 116 to Archbishop Eanbald II of York (MGH Epp. 4, p. 171): *et si tempestas undique immineat, guberna viriliter navem Christi* [and if the storm menaces from every side, govern the ship of Christ manfully].
30. Haimo of Auxerre, *Homiliae de temporae*, 72 (PL 118, col. 459): *Vir namque a viribus dictus est, et illi specialiter hoc nomen aptatur, qui solus diaboli vires resurgendo a mortuis potuit confringere…Discamus ergo et nos ab illo confortati viri esse, ut diaboli tentationibus fortiter resistamus, et cuncta adversa viriliter toleremus*. Cf Alcuin, Epistola 198 to Charlemagne, on the death of Eric and Gerold, two important military leaders (MGH Epp. 4, p. 328): *Via est haec vita pergentibus ad patriam. Si aspera est, si arta est, viriliter gradienda est* [This life is the road for proceeding to the fatherland. If it is rough, if it is narrow, it is to be walked manfully]. On the continued significance of such metaphors, see Fletcher, this collection.
31. Louis the Pious, Diploma CLXIX (PL 104, col. 1208): *Pars denique quaedam eorum…in sanctae religionis proposito et habitu…elegerunt viriliter permanere*.
32. Hrabanus Maurus, *Commentariorum in Matthaeum libri octo*, book 2, ch. 4 (PL 107, col. 791): *Andreas vero et Joannes significant gentes viriliter credentes Christum, et gratia Dei salvatas*.
33. Alcuin, Epistola 111 (MGH Epp. 4, p. 161): *Et tu…adiutor devotus, viriliter fac voluntatem illis*. Cf. John VIII, Epistola 77 (MGH Epp. 7, pp. 73–4) [to Neapolitans in 878, praising them for choosing Athanasius as bishop]: *state viriliter obedientes illi in omnibus, velut filii charissimi* [remain manfully obedient to him in all things, like dearest sons].
34. Hadrian II, Epistola 34 (MGH Epp. 6, p. 739): *ut fraterna eum charitate commoti viribus totis adiuvare, apud excellentissimum regem vestrum humiliter intercedendo, viriliter satagaris*.
35. The most common use, and the vaguest, is in the Biblical injunction to 'act manfully' (*age viriliter*); see, for example, MGH Cap. I no. 62, p. 150, c. 15: *Ut missi nostri per Dei misericordiam viriliter in omnibus agant* [that our agents act manfully in all things through God's mercy]. Alcuin was particularly fond of this expression: see, for example, Alcuin, Epistola 66, p. 65 (to 'Dodo'); Epistola 183, p. 308 (to Elipandus of Toledo), Epistola 205, p. 342 (to abbots and monks of Gothia), Epistola 209, p. 347 (to 'Calvinus'), Epistola 232, p. 377 (to Eanbald II of York).
36. Alcuin, Epistola 84, p. 127: *Viriliter domum aedificate vobis sempiternam in caelis*. K. Heene, *The Legacy of Paradise: Marriage, Motherhood and Woman in Carolingian Edifying Literature* (Frankfurt am Main: P. Lang, 1997), pp. 248–53.
37. C.J. Clover, 'Regardless of sex: men, women and power in early northern Europe', *Speculum* 68 (1993), 363–87, on 379.

38. Clover, 'Regardless of sex', 377.
39. Ibid., 380.
40. J.M.H. Smith, 'Gender and ideology in the early Middle Ages', in R.N. Swanson (ed.), *Gender and Christian Religion*, Studies in Church History 34 (Woodbridge, 1998), pp. 51–73, on p. 59, argues for this.
41. Haimo of Auxerre's comments (cited above) are one of the few exceptions.
42. The use of key terms is largely restricted to exegetical texts: five out of ten uses of *muliebriter* in Patrologia Latina sources from the Carolingian period are from Biblical commentaries; 48 out of 60 for *effeminatus* and cognates are from commentaries. On accusations of cowardice see also Stone, 'Masculinity, nobility', pp. 66–7.
43. Heene, *Legacy*, pp. 216–48, 69–70.
44. On Theodora, see L. Brubaker, 'Sex, lies and textuality: the *secret history* of Prokopios and the rhetoric of gender in sixth-century Byzantium', in L. Brubaker and J.M.H. Smith (eds), *Gender in the Early Medieval World: East and West, 300–900* (Cambridge, 2004), pp. 83–101. On Fredegund and Brunhild, see J.L. Nelson, 'Queens as Jezebels: the careers of Brunhild and Balthild in Merovingian history', in D. Baker (ed.), *Medieval Women* (Oxford, 1978), pp. 31–77; I. Wood, *The Merovingian Kingdoms 450–751* (Harlow, 1994), pp. 123–36.
45. See, for example, P. Brown, *The Body and Society: Men, Women, and Sexual Renunciation in Early Christianity* (New York, 1988); M. Kuefler, *The Manly Eunuch: Masculinity, Gender Ambiguity and Christian Ideology in late Antiquity* (Chicago, 2001).
46. Differing interpretations of these reforms are given by, for example, J.A. McNamara, 'The *Herrenfrage*: the restructuring of the gender system, 1050–1150', in C.A. Lees (ed.), *Medieval Masculinities: Regarding Men in the Middle Ages* (Minneapolis, 1994), pp. 3–29; M.C. Miller, 'Masculinity, reform, and clerical culture: narratives of episcopal holiness in the Gregorian era', *Church History*, 72, (2003), 25–52; and R.I. Moore, *The First European Revolution, c. 970–1215* (Oxford, 2000), pp. 65–111, but the overall effects are agreed.
47. See, for example, Brown, *Body and Society*, pp. 428–47.
48. See, for example, Yarrow, in this collection.
49. See, for example, P. Wormald, 'Bede, "Beowulf" and the conversion of the Anglo-Saxon aristocracy', in R.T. Farrell (ed.), *Bede and Anglo-Saxon England* (Oxford, 1978), pp. 32–95.
50. See, for example, D.M. Hadley, '"Death makes the man"? Burial rites and the construction of masculinities in the early Middle Ages', in D.M. Hadley (ed.), *Masculinity in Medieval Europe* (London, 1999), pp. 21–38; G. Halsall, 'Gender and the end of empire', *Journal of Medieval and Early Modern Studies*, 34 (2004), pp. 17–39.
51. See M. de Jong, '*Imitatio morum*: the cloister and clerical purity in the Carolingian world', in M. Frassetto (ed.), *Medieval Purity and Piety: Essays on Medieval Clerical Celibacy and Religious Reform* (New York, 1998), pp. 49–80. On the regulation and instruction of secular clerics see C. van Rhijn, *Shepherds of the Lord: Priests and Episcopal Statutes in the Carolingian Period* (Turnhout, 2007).
52. J.L. Nelson, 'Monks, secular men and masculinity, c. 900', in Hadley (ed.), *Masculinity in Medieval Europe*, pp. 122–42. It is debatable how many of Nelson's undoubtedly anxious young men can be regarded as 'Carolingian': see Stone, 'In what way'. I do not discuss in this paper Lynda Coon's claims of the continuity of late antique and early medieval monastic views on gendered bodies (see, for example, L. Coon, 'Somatic styles of the early Middle Ages', *Gender and History*, 20 (2008), 463–86). The

discourse she identifies seems to me to have had little impact on the more 'public' discussions of gender in which laymen participated.
53. See, for example, Kuefler, *Manly Eunuch*, pp. 293–94; McNamara, *'Herrenfrage'*. S.F. Wemple, *Women in Frankish Society: Marriage and the Cloister, 500–900* (Philadelphia, 1981) makes a rather unconvincing attempt to fit the Carolingian evidence into this consciously oppressive pattern.
54. See K. Cooper, *The Virgin and the Bride: Idealized Womanhood in Late Antiquity* (Cambridge, MA, 1996), p. 17; K. Cooper and C. Leyser, 'The gender of Grace: impotence, servitude and manliness in the fifth-century West', *Gender and History* 12 (2000), 536–51, on 539.
55. K. Cooper, 'Insinuations of womanly influence: an aspect of the christianization of the Roman aristocracy', *Journal of Roman Studies*, 82 (1992), 150–64.
56. Miller, 'Masculinity', p. 49. C. Leyser, 'Custom, truth and gender in eleventh-century reform', in Swanson (ed.), *Gender and Christian Religion*, pp. 75–91, on p. 90, in contrast claims: 'Reform begins when monks accuse bishops of being susceptible to womanly influence.'
57. See, for example, Cooper, *Virgin and the Bride*, pp. 10–12. On the impact of the 'linguistic turn' on women's history and gender history more generally, see E.A. Clark, 'The lady vanishes: dilemmas of a feminist historian after the "linguistic turn"', *Church History*, 67 (1998), 1–31.
58. Miller, 'Masculinity', p. 50.
59. Leyser, 'Custom', p. 85; Cooper and Leyser, 'Gender of Grace', p. 543.
60. Cooper and Leyser, 'Gender of grace', pp. 542–46. On the use of this metaphor in the Carolingian world, see in particular D.H. Green, *The Carolingian Lord: Semantic Studies on Four Old High German Words: balder, frô, truhtin, hêrro* (Cambridge, 1965).
61. Leyser, 'Custom', p. 85.
62. D. Elliott, *Fallen Bodies: Pollution, Sexuality and Demonology in the Middle Ages* (Philadelphia, 1999), pp. 19–21; D. Elliott, *Spiritual Marriage: Sexual Abstinence in Medieval Wedlock* (Princeton, 1993), p. 91.
63. On oblation see M. de Jong, *In Samuel's Image: Child Oblation in the early Medieval West* (Leiden, 1996).
64. de Jong, *'Imitatio morum'*, pp. 54–60.
65. Heene, *Legacy*, pp. 269–70, sees the rather different patterns of female religious recruitment (which included girls being educated in convents and then removed for marriage and widows who might be forced into monasticism) as having a similar effect: Carolingian moralists did not think it suitable to denigrate marriage and exalt virginity excessively.
66. A. Diem, 'Organisierte Keuschheit: Sexualprävention im Mönchtum der Spätantike und des frühen Mittelalters', *Invertito* 3 (2001), 8–37.
67. Heene, *Legacy*, pp. 272–77.
68. For conflicts between bishops, counts and abbots, see J. Nightingale, *Monasteries and Patrons in the Gorze Reforms: Lotharingia c. 850–1000* (Oxford, 2001).
69. See, for example, *Pippini capitulare Italicum* (MGH Cap. I, no. 102, p. 209, c. 5 (bishops and counts); *Admonitio generalis* (MGH Cap. I, no. 22, p. 58, c. 62) (all Christian people, bishops, abbots, counts, iudices, all persons of greater or lesser degree); *Capitulatio de partibus Saxoniae* (MGH Cap I, no. 26, p. 70, c. 29) (all counts).
70. D. Hägermann, 'Zur Enstehung des Kapitularian', in W. Schlögl and P. Herde (eds), *Grundwissenschaften und Geschichte: Festschrift für Peter Acht*, Münchener historische Studien, 15 (Kallmünz, 1976), pp. 12–27, lists the key texts.

71. de Jong, 'Imitatio morum', p. 57.
72. See C. van Rhijn, 'Priests and the Carolingian reforms: the bottlenecks of local *Correctio*', in R. Corradini, R. Meens, C. Possel and P. Shaw (eds), *Texts and Identities in the Early Middle Ages* (Vienna, 2006), pp. 219–37, on p. 223.
73. J.L. Nelson, 'Gender, memory and social power', *Gender and History* 12 (2000), 722–34, on p. 722. On one Carolingian mother's wide-ranging understanding of this pastoral role, see J.L. Nelson, 'Dhuoda', in P. Wormald and J. L. Nelson (eds), *Lay Intellectuals in the Carolingian World* (Cambridge, 2007), pp. 106–20.
74. J.H. Lynch, *Godparents and Kinship in Early Medieval Europe* (Princeton, 1986), pp. 318–32.
75. de Jong, 'Imitatio morum', pp. 58–9.
76. See, for example, S. Airlie, 'The anxiety of sanctity: St Gerald of Aurillac and his maker', *Journal of Ecclesiastical History* 43 (1992), 372–95, on 385–95.
77. VG 2, p. 158.
78. VG 3, p. 159.
79. VG 8, p. 162: '*Optaveram*', inquit... '*omnia tecum saeculi discrimina perferre; quaecumque adversa contigissent, quaecumque prospera, collato tecum robore sustinere*' ['I had hoped', he said... 'to finish the whole interval of life with you, to sustain with you whatever adverse things happened, whatever favourable things, with collected strength'].
80. VG 6, p. 161: *sepius enim cordi inherebat, ne eam diutius vivere sineret, ne, crebro in huius volutabri caeno devoluta, decus nobilitatis eius graviter dehonestaret infamiae turpitudine* [For it was always in his heart, that he should not allow her to live longer, lest, having repeatedly fallen in the filth of this mud pool, she might seriously dishonour the glory of his nobility by the disgrace of infamy].
81. VG 1, p. 157.
82. VG 10, p. 164.
83. On the possible identity of the author see Goullet, 'Vies', pp. 238–39.
84. VG 6, 9, pp. 161, 163.
85. VG 12, p. 166: *ut ventrem purgaret, secessum petiit latrinarum; moxque ut diversorium petiit, naturae debitum persolvere, ad instar Iudae proditoris et Arrii heresiarchis...diffusa sunt viscera eius* [So that he might purge his belly, he sought the solitude of the latrines; and soon, as he sought to pay the debt to nature's lodging place, in the manner of the traitor Judas and the heresiarch Arius...his viscera poured out].
86. VG 12, p. 166.
87. VG 6, p. 161.
88. VG 7, p. 162: *Tunc illa more muliebri coepit sacramentis multimodis adseverare, se a cunctis detrahi iniuste.*
89. Goullet, 'Vies', pp. 248–50.
90. VG 4, p. 160.
91. VG 7, p. 162: *Illa, viri Dei verba inertiae deputans...sine ambiguitate manum inicere in aquam non est cunctata.*
92. VG 13, pp. 166–67: *At illa, furiali amentia debachata, sic ait: 'Sic operatur virtutes Gangulfus, quomodo anus meus'. Statim ut haec vox nefanda ab ore exiit, a parte obstrusa corporis obscenus sonus prodiit.*
93. VG 13, p. 167: *Talique postea subiacuit obprobio, ut...quot eo die protulit verba, ab illa parte corporis quasi tot prodierunt probra* [She afterwards lay under such a disgrace, that...as many words as she said on that day, it was as if that many disgraces were produced by that part of the body].
94. S. Reynolds, 'Social mentalities and the case of medieval scepticism', *Transactions of the Royal Historical Society*, 6th series, 1 (1991), 21–41, on 29–30.

95. P.G. Jestice, 'Why celibacy? Odo of Cluny and the development of a new sexual morality', in Frassetto (ed.), *Medieval Purity and Piety*, pp. 81–115, on p. 81.
96. Jestice, 'Why celibacy?', pp. 91–8. Odo's thought also shows the re-emergence of late antique ideas of monastic continence as a constant individual spiritual battle: see C.A. Jones, 'Monastic identity and Sodomitic danger in the *Occupatio* by Odo of Cluny', *Speculum* 82 (2007), 1–53, on 15–16.
97. A. Barbero, 'Santi laici e guerrieri. Le trasformazioni di un modello nell'agiografia altomedievale', in G. Barone, M. Caffiero and F. Scorza Barcellona (eds), *Modelli di santità e modelli di comportamento: contrasti, intersezioni, complementarità* (Turin, 1994), pp. 125–40, on pp. 128–35; Airlie, 'Anxiety'. It is unfortunately not possible to date either of these *vitae* precisely, but, even if they are contemporaneous, the *Vita Geraldi* clearly shows a new style of discourse.
98. Goullet, 'Vies', p. 250.
99. R. Balzaretti, 'Men and sex in tenth-century Italy', in Hadley (ed.), *Masculinity in Medieval Europe*, pp. 143–59, on pp. 154–57.
100. Balzaretti, 'Men and sex', pp. 150–51.
101. M.S. Kuefler, 'Male friendship and the suspicion of Sodomy in twelfth-century France', in S. Farmer and C.B. Pasternack (eds), *Gender and Difference in the Middle Ages* (Minneapolis, 2003), pp. 146–81, on p. 162.
102. On the (limited) changes in the post-Roman period, see J.M.H. Smith, 'Did women have a transformation of the Roman world?', *Gender and History*, 12 (2000), 552–71.
103. For the late antique period see G. Clark, *Women in Late Antiquity: Pagan and Christian Life-styles* (Oxford, 1993), pp. 94–105. For the Carolingian period see J.M.H. Smith, 'The problem of female sanctity in Carolingian Europe c. 780–920', *Past and Present* 146 (1995), 3–37; V.L. Garver, *Women and Aristocratic Culture in the Carolingian World* (Ithaca, 2009).

# Part II
# Masculinity and Hegemony

# 6
# Masculinities in Early Hellenistic Athens

*Henrik Berg*

## Introduction

This chapter focuses on masculinities in early Hellenistic Athens, approximately 323–275 BC, based on an analysis of literary sources from this time and place. Of special interest here is to see what the literary sources can tell us about ideal masculinity in Athens during this time. This is achieved through using gender theories, including theories from masculinity studies, when analysing the material. When applying such theories to the study of different historical periods, new insights into the past can be gained, which also is the aim of this chapter. But the more distant the period studied is from the present time, the more problematic the study becomes. This is, of course, because the knowledge of cultural and social aspects of distant periods is less certain, and because the materials that can be analysed are far from complete and can be difficult to interpret. In many ways, this is similar to when researchers try to apply Western masculinity theories to non-Western societies, something that scholars of Asian masculinity have pointed out.[1]

The chapter focuses on how to use literary material to acquire greater knowledge of masculinities during a specific period in history and what can be learnt from it. This is also of interest as the Hellenistic period has been little studied through the gendered perspective in general and through the perspective of masculinity in particular. The chapter begins with some background to the historical period in question, and a synthesis of the current research regarding gender, questioning why Athens is focused upon by scholars, what materials we have from the period, and why they are useful and interesting in a study of masculinities. This is followed by the analysis of the texts and the conclusions that can be drawn from them.

## The Hellenistic period

The Hellenistic period in ancient history is defined as the time between the death of Alexander the Great in 323 BC and the Battle of Actium in 31 BC which marked the fall of the last of the Hellenistic kingdoms, Ptolemaic Egypt. The start and end of the period are defined by historical events with political significance; but the period itself is defined through its political phenomena, and also its cultural phenomena.[2] This is of interest when studying gender and especially, as in this case, masculinities, if genders are regarded as social and cultural constructions. With Alexander's conquest Greek culture spread to new areas. Greek cities were established around the conquered territories, and this in turn meant that Greek society became influenced by other cultures, such as Persian and Egyptian. The period is often described as a time of city-cultures, migration, secularisation (the meeting of religions and the coming of new ones as well) and cultural meetings. It was also a time of great cultural developments: for example, the *Museion* in Alexandria, an institution that hosted a great number of scholars and authors who were salaried by the Ptolemaic monarchs, and significant focus upon literature, including the development of new literary styles.[3] The period was also marked by great unrest and several wars, in which mercenary soldiers were of great importance and the old ideal of citizen–soldiers lost some of its significance. New centres of culture and political power arose, taking over the position of the earlier Greek city-states in this respect – a shining example being Alexandria in Ptolemaic Egypt. These centres were also the capitals of the new Hellenistic monarchs, who profoundly changed the political structure of the Greek world. The period also saw the growth of Roman influence and power around the Mediterranean. It is also claimed that the new political situation during the period brought about a change in society, whereby the focus shifted from the city-state, the *polis*, to the home or family, the *oikos*. Such a shift also indicates that the dominating all-male focus on previous periods, such as those of, for instance, *paiderasia* and political *eros*, would diminish. The notion of the shift from *polis* to *oikos* has been established and discussed in several recent studies.[4] The *oikos* did not only consist of family members, but was also a larger structure including several generations, servants and slaves.[5] A focus on the *oikos* also contributes to a focus on genders and their construction, and on the significance of one's place in family and society. The foundation for the *oikos* was marriage and the begetting of legitimate children, which also is of significance when considering questions of gender.[6]

## Gender, masculinity and the Hellenistic period

Gender and masculinity during the Hellenistic period have scarcely been studied. This is partly because the period itself has not captured the same great interest as classical Athens and imperial Rome, which preceded and succeeded the period. However, during the last decades this has changed somewhat and the period has received much more attention from recent classical scholars. This notwithstanding, studies concerning the Hellenistic period and gender are still few and focus upon women and families. These studies are also geographically specific, often limited to Ptolemaic Egypt. Sarah Pomeroy's books *Families in Classical and Hellenistic Greece* (1997) and *Women in Hellenistic Egypt* (1984) are perhaps the best-known examples of studies carried out in this field. There are also several studies regarding women and New Comedy, especially Menander's comedies. Ariana Traill's *Women and the Comic Plot in Menander* (2008) is of specific interest for this chapter.[7] Broader studies on gender and how it was constructed and perceived during the period are still lacking but would be of great value, as this was a time of great political and social changes that had specific implications for conceptions of gender.

When it comes to studies of masculinities in the period, even less work has been done. In the collections *When Men Were Men* (1998) and *Thinking Men* (1998), edited by Linn Foxhall and John Salmon, there are four articles dealing with masculinity during the period; one is about the masculinity of the Hellenistic king and the other three are connected to New Comedy, one of which deals with the issue of rape and young manhood.[8] Another study that deserves mention is Angelos Chaniotis' *War in the Hellenistic World* (2005).[9] In this study Chaniotis addresses several different aspects of war and warfare during the period, and several of them deal directly or indirectly with gender and masculinities: for example, the chapter 'The Gender of War: Masculine Warriors, Defenseless Women, and Beyond'. Even if the study's main aim is to create a social and cultural history of war and warfare, it addresses gender in several interesting ways, though only in connection with war. In the scholarship thus far regarding gender and the Hellenistic period there is an emerging consensus that the beginning of the period saw substantial changes in how gender was perceived, as well as significantly changed relationships in gender structures.

## Why Athens?

So why is Athens of special interest in a study of masculinity during the Hellenistic period? As we have seen, the beginning of the Hellenistic period saw major political changes in Greek society, and these were perhaps especially noticeable in Athens. From having been the leading power during the classical period, Athens declined during the fourth century BC, and, with the rise of Macedonian power and influence, the sovereignty of Athens also changed. The early Hellenistic period was a turbulent time in the history of Athens, as it tried repeatedly to break away from its dependency on Macedonian rulers, and failed in this respect several times. Dependency upon Macedonia led to changes in the governmental system and the ability of the Greek city-states to act independently in international politics, which affected the people of Athens in different ways. This, and the changes in the whole Hellenic world during and after the conquests of Alexander the Great, also affected Athenian society in many ways, not only politically but also socially and culturally. In the period following the rise of Macedonia, Athens had to witness other cities and states surpassing it in power and prestige. It was still an important centre of learning and culture, but cultural development and innovations moved away from Athens during the period, most especially to Alexandria. At the beginning of the period Athens could still be seen as the cultural capital of the Hellenistic world, with the development of New Comedy and its various philosophical schools. These schools would endure and become the features with which Athens was most associated, as a city of learning, far into the Roman era.

Athens during the classical period has been studied from several angles regarding masculinities. Examples are Joseph Roisman's *The Rhetoric of Manhood, Masculinity and the Attic Orators* (2005) and Barry Strauss's *Fathers and Sons in Athens* (1993). So in some ways there is some recent comparative material regarding Athens that can help us discern how masculinities changed or developed during the early Hellenistic period. Another important aspect regarding Athens and the Hellenistic period is the increasing focus on the *oikos*, of which the Menandrian comedies are an example, which can be regarded as highly significant in Athenian society.[10] This was due to the citizenship laws of Pericles (451/450 BC), which decreed that in order to be counted as an Athenian citizen one had to be the child of citizens (*astos* and *aste*).[11] It is also interesting that the new dramatic style that developed in Athens during this period, the New Comedy – which is one of the two main sources used in this study – concentrated upon the *oikos* and marriage in much of its material.

In this chapter, two source materials are examined, namely the comedies of Menander and the *30 Characters* of Theophrastus. The surviving texts of the two authors provide excellent material for studying relationships between people as well as scrutinising constructs of gender and other social phenomena. As mentioned earlier, Menander's New Comedy dealt with the microcosm of society, the household or *oikos*, while Theophrastus' *30 Characters* addressed negative traits or behaviours in human beings, exemplified through differing situations in society. Both sources could be said to have the character of being comical. This is of great value when studying human behaviours and relations, because comical text and comedy, as several scholars have pointed out, have close connections to human weaknesses, human behaviour, the emotions, and everyday life more generally.

As Henri Bergson has pointed out, 'the comic does not exist outside the pale of what is strictly *human*', which shows that for events to be thought of as comic they must be linked to and identified with human behaviour.[12] Comedies are also closely linked to jokes, and, as Stott argues, these emerge

> from within the social framework and necessarily express the nature of their environment, which means that all jokes are necessarily produced in a relative relationship to the dominant structures of understanding and the epistemological order.[13]

This quotation indicates that comedy also can be of great value when looking at the dominant structures in society, which are important factors when studying masculinities in a patriarchal society like Hellenistic Athens. Power is also a focus in most masculinities studies, as in R.W. Connell's influential work regarding hegemonic masculinity. If we accept that in patriarchal societies there existed a hegemonic or ideal masculinity, it must have been the norm everyone was forced to relate to or compare themselves to.[14] Viewed together, these ideas are of use when seeking information or when analysing comedies with regard to how masculinities, and especially the ideal (hegemonic) masculinity, could have been perceived and constructed during a specific period in history.

Even if comedy is not always thought to be closely linked to everyday life and values, the comedies of Menander have historically always been associated with a high degree of realism and with everyday life. The Alexandrine scholar Aristophanes of Byzantium (c. 257 BC – c. 185/180 BC) has been credited with pointing this out by saying, 'O Menander and Life/ Which of you are imitating which?'[15] Another source from antiquity, Plutarch, credited Menander with important knowledge of human life and stressed how important his message was as an influence on good moral behaviour.[16] In our own time, scholars have also stated that Menander is of great value when studying issues of everyday life and social situations. David Konstan, for instance, writes that Menander 'adapts the plots to a subtle and sympathetic examination of contemporary social issues', and many of these issues are factors that can be seen as or used for the construction of gender.[17] All this emphasises why Menander is examined in this kind of study; but what of the *30 Characters* of Theophrastus? First of all, the *Characters* are closely connected to comedy, exemplified by the fact that several now-lost comedies have the same titles as some of the characters. Furthermore, the characters deal with negative human traits, and a frequent way masculinities are constructed in many societies is through demonstration of examples of what masculinity is not; it's vilified antithesis. There is also the fact that history has always linked the two authors to each other by claiming that Theophrastus was Menander's teacher, and that they had several links in common. It is therefore also necessary to have some knowledge of the authors and their works that are left to us.

Theophrastus (372/371–288/287 BC) was not a native Athenian or a citizen of Athens, but came from the island of Lesbos and lived the larger part of his life in Athens. He was active at the Lyceum (the philosophical school established by Aristotle), which he came to lead after the retirement and death of Aristotle.[18] Theophrastus was held as a person of great popularity in Athens and was granted the right to own property in his own name, exceptional for a non-citizen, though during one period he had to leave Athens and the running of the Lyceum due to xenophobic sentiments.[19] He was a very active writer in various fields, and besides the *30 Characters* there are numerous works and fragments left of his vast literary and scientific outpouring. The most famous of these are his botanical and other scientific works, some of which were used until the eighteenth century as important, informative works. When it comes to the *30 Characters*, the exact purpose of these is not known, but they all deal with different negative human traits or behaviours.[20] Many factors indicate that the *Characters* were written in 319 BC; predominantly references to specific historical events, but also the absence of certain key events and changes in society in the period.[21]

Menander, or *Menandros* in Greek (344/343–292/291 BC), on the other hand, came from a wealthy Athenian family and as previously mentioned, was probably educated by Theophrastus, which gives them both a connection to Aristotle and his philosophy. Another important person to whom both seem to have been connected was Demetrius of Phaleron; as a politician he was closely linked to Macedonia, and he also enforced an oligarchic constitution in Athens for a short period of time in the late fourth century.[22] Menander is claimed to have been the creator, or the developer, of, what we today call New Greek Comedy. He is said to have written over a hundred comedies, of which there remains only one complete one, the *Dyskolos* or *The Ill-tempered Man*, but we also have sufficient material from another six plays to discern the plots and main events in them. It is claimed that Menander's first play was performed in 321 BC; this has been established in the same way as Theophrastus' *Characters* have been dated, even if we have some exact dates for some of Menander's comedies as they won theatrical competitions in specific years.[23] The comedies have a standard plot which always ends with two citizens getting married after a number of *imbroglios* that usually involve children of uncertain parentage, and/or other situations that make a marriage between the hero and heroine impossible, either because they are not both citizens, or due to some other social obstacle. It is important to note that the *imbroglios* usually involve issues of ethnicity or belonging to different social groups, a point that will be discussed below. These plots are in many ways gendered, as they deal with the relationship between men and women, but also very much the relationships between men, as marriage in many ways was a homosocial activity.[24] It is worth noting that, of the preserved plays, the lines for females consist of approximately 10 per cent of the material only.[25] In the plays there are also examples of relationships between social groups and between different age groups. Another important factor regarding the works of Menander is that several scholars, such as Susan Lape in her *Reproducing Athens, Menander's Comedy, Democratic Culture and the Hellenistic City* (2004), have been able to use them to interpret different aspects of Athenian social history during the period, such as views on democracy, sexuality and civic education.

## Masculinities in the texts

What, then, can be found in the texts that create masculinities, and which different aspects seem to have been the most important for ideal Athenian masculinity in the period? Let us use Aristotle as the starting point, since he influenced not only both of the authors in question, but also the entire period, having been Alexander the Great's teacher. In one of his works, Aristotle wrote the following in regard to how to look after fellow Greeks: 'as friends and relatives, and to deal with the barbarians as plants and beasts'.[26] It was also common for slaves to be looked upon as 'animated tools', and the way in which women were viewed in society during a certain period depended on their role, as the quotation from Pseudo Demosthenes exemplifies: 'Mistresses we keep for the sake of pleasure, concubines for the daily care of our persons, but wives to bear us legitimate children and to be faithful guardians of our households'.[27] These are some of the thoughts that formed the basis for how the Athenians or even all Greeks viewed themselves and others during this time in history.

Naturally, this influences how and whether one could talk about masculinities or masculinity in Hellenistic Athens; or did one merely speak about citizens, foreigners, women and barbarians? And, if this is the case, was the notion of an ideal masculinity only something that applied to or was sought after by citizens, or perhaps ethnic Greeks? We must consider these issues when approaching material utilising gender theories in general and, in this case, masculinity theories in particular. Thus the question is: in the texts of Menander and Theophrastus, can we find traces of what Aristotle and others have pointed out in regard to male citizen behaviour, and, if so, what does this tell us about which aspects were important to create ideals and masculinity?

Starting with the quotation from Aristotle, it seems that ethnicity or geographical background played a large part in how a person was viewed. As pointed out earlier, this even affected Theophrastus, who was expelled from Athens for a period, even though he was a Greek. Ethnicity and geographical background must have been very important factors if they could result in even a popular and respected person like Theophrastus being expelled. In the Menandrian comedies, the importance of having Athenian or citizen parents is one of the most important aspects to several of the plots. That the hero or heroine does not share the same citizenship or geographical background is often an obstacle to their getting married; for example, in both the plays *Sikyonis* and *Misoumenos* the girls the men want to marry are thought not be of citizen descent, and a marriage is not conceivable. This is supported by Theophrastus' *Character the Slander*, in which the first verse deals with a person's lineage and shows the importance of being first of all Greek and especially a citizen of Athens. This is achieved by the implication that a man's mother was not an Athenian but a Thracian, even though of noble heritage, and therefore the man could not be an Athenian citizen due to his mother's ethnicity.[28] The texts also seem to stress the importance of staying loyal to one's own ethnic group, as Theophrastus points out in *Character Obsequiousness*: 'He tells foreigners that they have a better case than his fellow citizens,' as it was regarded as harmful not to support your fellow Athenians.[29] This also demonstrates the degrees of difference between different Greeks (albeit in Athenian concepts) and not simply between Greeks and non-Greeks.

In any case, the main point seems to be whether or not one was Greek, and being thought of as having another ethnicity was considered a gross insult. We have an example of this in Menander's play *Samia*, where an older man insults the young hero Moschion by saying: 'You brute, you Thracian goat...'[30] This must have been a terrible insult, as the Thracians were claimed to have a reputation for lasciviousness and violence.[31]

In the Menandrian comedies the characters to whom a non-Greek ethnicity is attributed are usually slaves, and different ethnicities are linked to different traits that seem to have been common knowledge during the time. One such example is from the comedy *Aspis*, where there is a conversation between two slaves:

WAITER: ... Where do You come from?

DAOS: Phrygia.

WAITER: That means you're no good,
  A queer. We Thracians, though, we're men, unique –
  The Getic tribe, by Apollo – yes real men.
  That's why we fill the grain-mills.[32]

The remark about the grain mill also indicates further that Thracians were considered problematic and violent, and often punished by being sent to the mills; but it also implies that Phrygians were less than manly. So it seems clear that the geographical background and/or ethnicity of the characters were of utmost importance, not only for their possibilities in life in Athens, but also for how they were perceived and which traits they probably held.

Another important factor for how characters were regarded in the texts and in society was the question of which social group they belonged to, and also their economical possibilities and potential. In the *Characters* Theophrastus gives several examples, as in the *Character Slander* mentioned above. In it there is a man (a citizen) who is claimed to have a father who, from the beginning, was called Sosias, which was a slave name.[33] This meant that the man could not be a citizen, as his father was a slave or a freed slave and not an Athenian; and as such the man did not have the right to be a citizen. At the least, this theme was something people could readily question. In the *Character Boorishness*, we have a behaviour that breaks the barriers between social groups, and even the barrier between the sexes and between master and slave, as 'the boor seduces his cook without anyone's knowing, but then joins her in the grinding up the daily ration of meal and handing it out himself...'[34] Here a citizen performs tasks that the slave is supposed to carry out, and by doing so places himself far below his position in society. This quotation also carries implications regarding sexuality and keeping one's self-control, subjects that will be discussed later in this chapter. Similar behaviour of breaking the social boundaries occurs in the *Character Bad Taste*, when the master chews his baby's food, a task that was supposed to be carried out by the child's wet nurse or, if the family was poor, by one of the females of the household.[35]

When it comes to social groups, the texts also demonstrate that the important thing was not only not to cross borders to other social groups, such as slaves and foreigners, but also to behave correctly towards members of one's own social group (if we define one such group as the free citizens of Athens). This applies even when there are great differences in economic and educational standing between the citizens in question. One example of this is in the *Character Authoritarianism*, where the Authoritarian says: 'I wonder what the men getting involved in politics are after. The common people show no gratitude, they always follow anyone with a handout or a gift.'[36] The common people in this case are other citizens of Athens, less wealthy and educated than the Authoritarian. His negative behaviour is that he is condescending towards members of his own group, men who officially should have the same rights in society as he does, even if in reality the exercise of those rights might be different. This theme recurs in the Menandrian comedies, and some scholars have interpreted this as reflecting a conflict in Athens at this time between wealthier and poorer citizens, which in turn can be seen in connection with Demetrius of Phaleron's attempt at a more oligarchic constitution that would bar poorer citizens from participating in the government of Athens. One of the most frequently used examples from Menander is the *Dyskolos*. In this play, one of the fathers, Kallipides, a very wealthy man, talks about his future daughter-in-law and son-in-law as paupers, saying they are less worthy and not suitable for marriage to his children. He therefore tries to stop the marriages, until the error in his reasoning is pointed out to him. In this case it is also questionable whether the poor were so very poor, as the future son-in-law was able to give his half-sister, Kallipides' future daughter-in-law, quite a large dowry.[37] This also indicates the importance of being self-sufficient, of which Gorgias in the *Dyskolos* is one example. Even in the play's prologue he is described in terms that show him as hard-working and capable of providing for himself and his mother.[38] The theme of being self-sufficient is one that Menander returns to in other plays, such as the *Aspis*, where a young man, Kleostratos, has been serving as a mercenary in order to provide his sister with a proper dowry.

This is also an example of the importance of marriage and of creating an *oikos*, which are central in *Dyskolos* concerning ethnicity and social groups. As the *oikos* was the smallest unit of society and the one on which it rested, that seems natural, and explains the vastly important role getting married and creating a household, *oikos*, had for the duties and creation of the image of Athenian male citizens. But it is not only in the standard plot of the Menandrian comedies that marriage and creation of new *oikos* are stressed. It is also visible in the *Characters*, as Theophrastus lets several characters talk about their wives and family life. In the *Character Boorishness* the importance of the smaller circle of the *oikos* and close friends is demonstrated, as it is pointed out how foolish it is not to take advice from your own family and close friends.[39] The importance of being able to trust the members of your household and having a trustworthy relationship with your spouse is emphasised in the *Character Mistrust*, where the man does not trust his wife or slaves.[40] The *Character Lack of Generosity* mentions both being generous when you are giving your daughter away in marriage, and being generous to your wife, partly in connection with a daughter's dowry.[41] This could also be seen as showing the importance of good relationships between two households; it exemplifies how marriage was also a homosocial activity, as it dealt with the two male heads of *oikos* negotiating the dowry, which was also a security for the prospective bride (as the husband should use it for her needs) and which had to be paid back to her original *oikos* if there was a divorce. But there were also things that a man was emphatically not expected to do with his family. One of these has already been mentioned, namely the chewing of the babies' food, but it seems that an overly active interest in infants was regarded negatively, because Theophrastus returns to how men being or acting overly fond of small children are perceived in a negative way.[42] The family should also be kept to the home, as it was private and not a part of the social life in the polis. An example of this can be found in the *Character Superstition*, which commented on how a man takes his wife and children to the temple too frequently.[43] The Menandrian texts focus mostly on the creation of new *oikos* and how to achieve this, but they also highlight at least one problem with the Athenian marriage laws. There existed laws that gave the closest older relative (uncle or cousin) the right to marry nieces or cousins in order to preserve a family's fortune. This could create marriages with vast differences in spousal age, and such marriages might lead to a situation in which there was no reproduction of new citizens, as the elderly man might want to protect his children from a previous union. Whether Menander with his plays and especially with *Aspis* – in which the foulest character we have in a Menandrian comedy, the old uncle Smikrines, is demanding his right to marry his niece – wanted to make a statement regarding these laws is debated, but the implication resonates with this problematic aspect of Athenian law.[44]

Age and marriage are issues on which the texts give us indirect information, as it is expected of a man to create an *oikos* and by doing so secure the birth of new citizens. It also creates a situation whereby older men who already have heirs and become widowers or divorcés can enter into another relationship with a courtesan, which appears socially acceptable. One example of this is in *Samia*, where Demeas, who has an adopted son Moschion, lives with his courtesan Chrysis, the girl/woman from Samos who has given the play its name. Furthermore, in the Menandrian comedies we can draw some information from the fact that the couples who marry are younger, even if the man is older than the woman, which corresponds to other sources regarding marriage during this time.[45] Marriage, like many other things, including different public duties, seems to have been age-related, and a citizen of a certain age was expected to marry. He was also expected to hold certain public offices such as *choragus* or *phylarch*, that is, provided he was from the right social and economic background, such as Moschion was. In some respects, age determined what one was supposed to do in society, and also in some ways age restricted social action, on account of the differing age limits for varieties of positions and offices.[46] Advancing chronological age gave the citizen an increasing number of different social and political possibilities; but, by the same measure, it seems to have been just as important to remain within one's own age group as within one's own social group. Even so, there seems to be a focus on mental age or maturity as opposed to chronological age in the Menandrian comedies. This has been discussed elsewhere; and, when it comes to ideal masculinities, in the comedies it seems that mental age is at least as important as chronological age, even if the latter was a prerequisite for getting access to different public offices and arenas in which masculinities were created.[47]

Both of the sources also raise the question of another age-related issue, namely how important it was for a man not to try to seem younger than he was, or to behave like those of a younger age group. The most obvious example of this is the *Character Rejuvenation*, in which Theophrastus devotes a whole character to pointing out the importance of behaving and looking your age.[48]

Through this character, Theophrastus points out the foolishness of behaving in a manner that does not suit your age group, as well as trying to look younger or being told that you do look younger. Menander also addresses this issue by making fun of old men who act like youths, or by asking age-related questions that highlight an unsuitable behaviour in relation to the characters' age.[49] An example of the latter is found in Menander's *Aspis*, where two middle-aged/old brothers are talking:

> CHAIRESTRATOS (The younger): Do you intend to marry a young girl at your age?
> SMIKRINES (The older): My age?
> CHAIRESTRATOS: I think you're too old.[50]

This conversation carries on for a while, debating the suitability of the marriage in relation to the age difference, but also that the older brother is behaving in an unacceptable way for his age.

Another age-related issue that both Menander and Theophrastus bring up is when older men are fighting over courtesans or prostitutes, something that makes them look ridiculous. It seems more or less expected that younger men would visit prostitutes to have sex and even lose some control over themselves in connection with this, but this does not seem to be the case for a mature man. In the Menandrian comedies, a young man having sex without being married, or having sex outside his marriage, is a usual starting point for the play. In many cases this also involves some degree of violence, as it is often described as the young man raping a girl, which leads to a child being born or expected. This child is always at the centre of the *imbroglios* in the play, as later on it will be shown to be legitimate and able to be married to a young citizen (if time has elapsed during the play), or that the child's parents will be free to marry, with the same outcome. The question of rape in New Comedy has been studied by several scholars, such as Vincent Rosivach and Alan Sommerstein, and it has also been suggested that the trope could be a question of seduction and not rape.[51] This is one of the circumstances when the sources refer to sexuality, even though it sometimes seems more of a way for Menander to create the plot than to give information on how sexuality was looked upon during this time. Even so, both sources mention sexuality, but it is not thoroughly discussed. There are two things that both the sources used here have in common: namely that they only bring up sexuality between men and women, and that the older one is, the less interest one should have in sexual acts. It seems that a man ought to have a sexual appetite, but it should be controlled.[52]

In nearly all the texts the issue of control as self-control seems to be of great importance. One aspect of this is not to lose face or make a fool of oneself.

In the plays of Menander, most conflicts and problems arise from the fear of losing control, or from already having lost control. Here, the most common reason for losing control is falling in love. One of the most obvious examples of this is the elderly Demeas in *Samia*. He loves the courtesan Chrysis but thinks she has been unfaithful, and he even tells himself that he cannot lose control, but does, which must have helped to create a comical situation in the play.[53] Without characters losing their self-control, most of the Menandrian plots would not work as comedy, so it seems that keeping one's control is a central theme in the plays. In the *Characters* the loss of self-control is one of the most frequently occurring themes, which is telling in itself, as the *Characters* by definition are depicting negative traits in a person. One of these examples has already been discussed: the Character *Rejuvenation*, which implies behaving like someone outside one's own age group. And it is also very clear that the *Characters Shamelessness, Garrulity, Obnoxiousness, Bad Timing, Squalor, Bad Taste, Petty Ambition, Lack of Generosity, Arrogance* and *Patronage of Scoundrels* all deal with different aspects of losing one's self-control.[54] In the *Characters* another issue which could be linked to not being able to control oneself, and which occurs frequently, is the behaviour of talking too much or saying the wrong thing. The most obvious examples of this are the *Characters Idle Chatter, Rumour-Mongering, Flattery* and *Slander*. Several of the other *Characters* also depict in various ways the negative side of talking too much.

## Conclusion

So what are the important aspects of masculinities in the texts, and can they tell us something about masculinities in Athens in the early Hellenistic period? To begin with the last question, if the texts and what they say about masculinities bring new knowledge about ideal masculinity in Athens and other concomitant masculinities, this seems to be the case. This is because the comical texts needed to address issues that their audience could readily recognise, albeit in exaggerated form, and obviously the more we compare the messages in the texts with other sources from the period, the more we learn, as they confirm and enhance our previous knowledge as well as contributing new knowledge on this period in ancient history. When it comes to the analysis of the masculinities of Hellenistic Athens, the texts contribute much information but also force us to consider how we analyse them and which factors create historical masculinities. As seen above, aspects like ethnicity, age and civil status are significant, so the question is whether we need to use intersectionality to be able to grasp the realities of masculinities in the period. The construction of masculinities in the texts was achieved through combining several different aspects of social life, and even letting these develop in the plays. This could be one of the reasons why Menander stressed the significance of men's mental age in his work. The action in the plays is set over the course of one day. This did not allow any change in chronological age of the character, and demonstration of maturity seems to have been of the greatest importance.

The most important aspect of masculinity that a character could possess was the right geographical background and/or ethnicity, where being an Athenian was at the top of the social order. This is also demonstrated in the texts, as they focus upon citizens or becoming a citizen. The other group that is given some amount of space in the texts are the slaves, the opposite of the free citizens. It is interesting that there is little space left in the texts for other free Greeks, and when there is mention of them, as in the *Characters*, it is mostly to demonstrate that you should be supportive of your own Athenian group. Not surprisingly, this indicates that it was necessary to be a citizen to maintain ideal masculinity in Athens during this time, but what else was needed? One thing that the ideal Athenian citizen should do was to fulfil his direct and indirect duties towards the state through the creation of a new *oikos*; in this way the citizen secured the future by creating the base for new citizens. Other duties to the state have been discussed to a lesser extent in this chapter, but they exist in both sources used. However, they are problematic in a sense because Athens, during part of the time in question, had an oligarchic constitution that barred some groups of citizens from taking part in government. This notwithstanding, the sources point out the importance of taking part in different public arenas that were connected to citizenship, either by tradition or by earlier constitutions. Is this a sign that the ideal reflected a bygone time and was partly an ideal of nostalgia, or is it, as Susan Lape has indicated, a political message against the prevailing order, at least in the case of Menander?[55]

Other aspects that have to be included in ideal masculinity, but that also could create alternative masculinities if they were lacking or if only a few of them existed, have been mentioned above. Most of them are connected to the citizen, but what kind of masculinity did they create if you had the aspects but were not a citizen, considering that citizenship seems to have been the focal point in ideal masculinity? Talking in terms of Connell's theory of hegemonic masculinity, this might have created different complicit masculinities.[56] One of these aspects is age, and it seems that there was a preferable age, the age of the family father (from the time you could get married until an unspecified older age). This also indicates that an ideal masculinity should have, at least at some time, a wife and children. It also seems that the ideal should be self-sufficient but not stick out as overly wealthy, as the discussion with Kallipides regarding his future in-laws indicates. Another aspect that the texts emphasise in different ways is that of self-control. This applies to all kinds of situations, such as sexuality, temper, talking, and general behaviour, for instance with smaller children; the ideal could not lose self-control.

The conclusion is that the text portrays an ideal masculinity of a responsible Athenian citizen with a family, who can support himself and his family and who never loses his self-control. The last part is probably what makes this an ideal, as probably no one, even in the texts, can have total self-control all the time, but one can come close by having a great amount of it.

This leaves us with some unresolved issues for future research. Even if the ideal seems to be confirmed by other sources, more work needs to be done, including a deeper study of sexuality. The sources in this chapter mention only sex between men and women, and there remains the question of the gender of the slaves; or did they even have one?

## Notes

1. Kam Louie, 'Chinese, Japanese and the global masculine identities', in *Asian Masculinities, The Meaning and Practice of Manhood in China and Japan* (New York, 2003), p. 1ff.
2. A. Erskine, 'Approaching the Hellenistic world', in A. Erskine (ed.), *A Companion to the Hellenistic World* (Oxford, 2003), p. 3.
3. I.C. Cunningham, 'Introduction to Herodas mimes', in J. Rusten (ed.), *Theophrastus Characters, Herodas Mimes, Cercidas and the Choliambic Poets* (Cambridge, MA, 1993), p. 201.
4. Among others, J.B. Burton, *Theocritus, Urban Mimes: Mobility, Gender and Patronage* (Berkeley, 1995).
5. L. Foxhall, 'Household', in S. Hornblower and A. Spawforth (eds), *The Oxford Classical Dictionary*, 3rd edn (Oxford, 1996), pp. 729–30.
6. S. Pomeroy, 'Families', in *Classical and Hellenistic Greece* (Oxford, 1997), pp. 33ff.
7. Another example is Madeleine Henry, *Menander's Courtesans and the Greek Comic Tradition* (Frankfurt am Main, 1988).
8. The one addressing the Hellenistic king is 'The masculinity of the Hellenistic King' by Jim Roy, and the three connected to New Comedy are 'Rape and young manhood in Attic drama' by Alan H. Sommerstein, 'Understanding the men in Menander' by Angela Heap and 'Ideals of masculinity in New Comedy' by Karen F. Pierce.
9. A. Chaniotis, *War in the Hellenistic World: A Social and Cultural History* (Oxford, 2005).
10. S. Pomeroy, *Families in Classical and Hellenistic Greece: Representations and Realities* (Oxford, 1997), pp. 33 ff.
11. D. Konstan, 'Premarital sex, illegitimacy and male anxiety in Menander and Athens', in A.L. Boeghold and A.C. Scarfuro (eds), *Athenian Identity and Civic Ideology* (Baltimore, 1994), p. 225.
12. H. Bergson, 'Laughter: an essay on the meaning of the comic', in W. Sypher (ed.), *Comedy* (Baltimore, 1980), pp. 59–190, on p. 62.
13. A. Stott, *Comedy* (New York, 2005), p. 10.
14. R.W. Connell, *Gender and Power* (Cambridge, 1987); idem, *Masculinities* (Cambridge, 1995).
15. E. Segal, *The Death of Comedy* (Cambridge, MA, 2001), referring to Syrian, in Hermog. (=K.-A. test. 83), p. 153.
16. L.A. Post, 'Dramatic infants in Greek', *Classical Philology* 34 (1939), 193–208, referring to Plutarch, *Quaest. conv.* vii. 8, p. 195.

17. D. Konstan, *Greek Comedy and Ideology* (New York, 1995), p. 4; V.J . Hunter, *Policing Athens: Social Control in the Attic Lawsuits, 420 – 320 B.C.* (Princeton, 1994); and A.C. Scafuro, *The Forensic Stage: Settling Disputes in Graeco-Roman New Comedy* (Cambridge, 1997) have all argued that Menander is a good source for social history.
18. P. Millett, *Theophrastus and his World* (Cambridge, 2007), p. 20.
19. J. Diggle, 'Introduction', in J. Diggle (ed. and trans.), *Theophrastus Characters* (Cambridge, 2004), p. 3.
20. J. Rusten, 'Introduction', in J. Rusten and I. C. Cunningham (ed. and trans.), *Theophrastus Characters, Herodas Mimes, Cercidas and the Choliambic Poets* (Cambridge, MA, 1993), p. 7.
21. Rusten, 'Introduction' , p. 8 ff.
22. C. Habicht, *Athens from Alexander to Antony* (Cambridge, MA, 1999), p. 54ff.
23. W.G. Arnott, 'Introduction', in W.G. Arnott (ed. and trans.), *Menander: Volume I* (Cambridge, MA, 1979), p. xv.
24. R. Garland, *The Greek Way of Life* (Ithaca, NY, 1990), p. 210 ff.
25. D. Bain, 'Female speech in Menander', *Antichthon: Journal of the Australian Society for Classical Studies* (1967), 31.
26. *Fragmenta Historicum Graecorum*, 658.
27. Demosthenes 59/1/122 in N.W. Dewith and N.V. Dewith (eds) *Demosthenes, with an English Translation* (Cambridge MA, 1949).
28. Theophrastus, *Character 28* (Cambridge, MA, 1993), line (l) 2.
29. Theophrastus, *Character 5*, l. 4.
30. Menander, *Samia*, in W.G. Arnott (ed. and trans.), *Menander: Volume III* (Cambridge, MA, 2000), ll. 518–20.
31. A.W. Gomme and F.H. Sanbach, *Menander, A Commentary* (Oxford, 1973), p. 602.
32. Menander, *Aspis*, in W.G. Arnott (ed. and trans.), *Menander: Volume I* (Cambridge, MA, 1979), ll. 239–44.
33. Theophrastus, *Character 28*, l. 1.
34. Theophrastus, *Character 4*, l. 10.
35. Theophrastus, *Character 20*, l. 5.
36. Theophrastus, *Character 26*, l. 5.
37. Menander, *Dyskolos*, in Arnott, *Menander: Volume I*, l. 845.
38. Menander, *Dyskolos*, ll. 25–7.
39. Theophrastus, *Character 4*, l. 6.
40. Theophrastus, *Character 18*, ll. 1–4.
41. Theophrastus, *Character 22*, ll. 4, 10.
42. Among others, Theophrastus' *Characters* 2 and 5.
43. Theophrastus, *Character 16*, l. 11.
44. Among others, D.M. Macdowell, 'Love versus the law: an essay on Menander's Aspis', *Greece & Rome*, 2nd ser., 29 (1982), 45–52; V.J. Rosivach, 'Class matters in the *Dyskolos* of Menander', *Classical Quarterly*, New Series, 51 (2001), 127–34; C.A. Cox, 'Is Sostratus' family urban in Menander's *Dyskolos?*', *Classical Journal*, 97 (2002), 351–58.
45. Pomeroy, *Families*, p. 23.
46. R. Garland, *The Greek Way of Life* (Ithaca, NY, 1990), p. 280 ff.
47. Regarding mental age or maturity see H. Berg, 'The question of age in the construction of Hellenistic masculinities in Menander', *Thymos* 2 (2008), 125–39.
48. Theophrastus, *Character 27*.

49. K. Pierce, 'Ideals of masculinity in new comedy', in L. Foxhall and J. Salmon (eds), *Thinking Men: Masculinity and Its Self-Representation in the Classical Tradition* (New York, 1998), p. 140.
50. Menander, *Aspis*, ll. 258–60.
51. V.J. Rosivach, *When a Young Man Falls in Love: The Sexual Exploitation of Women in New Comedy* (New York, 1998); A. Sommerstein, 'Rape and young manhood in Athenian comedy', in Foxhall and Salmon, *Thinking Men*; it is also discussed by E. M. Harris, 'Did the Athenians regard seduction as a worse crime than rape?', *Classical Quarterly* 40 (1990), 370–77.
52. D. Konstan, *Sexual Symmetry: Love in the Ancient Novel and Related Genres* (Princeton, 1994), p. 228.
53. Menander, *Samia*, ll. 326, 357–58.
54. Theophrastus, *Characters* 6, 7, 11, 12, 19, 20, 21, 22, 24 and 29.
55. S. Lape, *Reproducing Athens: Menander's Comedy, Democratic Culture and the Hellenistic City* (Princeton, 2004).
56. R.W. Connell, *Masculinities* (Cambridge, 1995), p. 76 ff.

# 7
# Masculinity As a World Historical Category of Analysis

*Simon Yarrow*

I would like to begin this chapter by citing two passages at length. First:

> King Overami came into Benin City with a large following, amounting to 700 or 800 people, all unarmed, headed by messengers with a white flag in front. He was supported in the usual way by chosen men holding him up by each arm. Some twenty of his wives who accompanied him, were of a very different class from those seen previously. They had fine figures, with their hair worn in the European chignon style of some years ago, really wonderfully done in stuffed rows of hair, the head not being shaved on top like those of the lower classes, and they wore coral necklaces and ornaments and hairpins galore…. The next day on the sixth, the king…came down to the palaver house with 400 of his own 'boys'(men), all of whom were stark naked, as was their custom in the presence of the king…The king who is a stout but fine man of considerable intelligence, about forty years of age, was…simply covered with masses of strings of coral, interspersed with larger pieces, supposed to be worth many pounds. His head dress, which was in the shape of a Leghorn straw hat, was composed wholly of coral of excellent quality, meshed closely together, and must have weighed very heavily on his head, for it was constantly being temporarily removed by an attendant. His wrists up to his elbows were closely covered with coral bangles, so were his ankles. He only wore the usual white cloth of a chief, and underneath, a pair of embroidered and brocaded trousers; he had nothing in the way of a coat, but his breast was completely hidden from view by the coral beads encircling his neck…There was a crowd of some 900 to 1000 people standing around when the Resident called upon Overami the king to make his submission. The king was visibly agitated, and after much consultation with the chiefs, the chief Aro asked that the king might do so in private, as he did not like to abase himself before the crowd. The request was naturally refused by the Resident, and then, supported by two chiefs, who assisted him, the

king made obeisance three times in the usual manner, rubbing his forehead on the ground three times....[1]

Second:

Meanwhile though, we learned for certain that the king was approaching. He...offered that he would entirely make satisfaction to God and St Peter and also to ourself, and undertook that he would maintain complete obedience for the amendment of his life, if he could but avail to secure from us the grace of absolution and apostolic blessing. After we had for long delayed this by many deliberations and sharply reproved him for his transgressions through all the messengers who passed between us, at length, showing nothing on his part that was hostile or rash, he came with a few followers to the fortress of Canossa in which we were staying. And there for three days before the gate of the castle, having laid aside all kingly adornment, wretchedly, as being unshod and clad in woollens, he did not cease from imploring with much weeping the aid and consolation of apostolic mercy before he moved all who were there present and to whom a report of this came to such great pity and merciful compassion that, making intercession for him with many pleas and tears, all indeed wondered at the unaccustomed hardness of our mind, while some protested that there was in us not the graveness of canonical strictness but the cruelty of tyrannical brutality. At last, under pressure of his compunction and overcome by such great supplication from those who were there present, we at length released the bond of anathema and received him into the grace of communion and the bosom of holy mother church...[2]

The first of these passages is excerpted from an unattributed contemporary British account of the surrender and trial of Oba Ovonramwen, king of Benin, during what has become known as the British punitive expedition of 1897 to Benin City. The second belongs to a papal letter of late January 1077 that documents the famous encounter between Emperor Henry IV and Pope Gregory VII at Canossa. Whatever actually happened during the encounters recorded in each of these sources, both accounts are narratives of humiliation and reconciliation intended to capture and crystallise an official, public understanding of the primacy of one source of legitimate authority over another. The authors of both polemical accounts took pains to achieve this goal by describing in their work the spectacle of authority encoded on the male body as artefact or icon.

The papal letter is one small fragment of a whole series of legal and theological reform propaganda deployed during Gregory's pontificate in the recruitment of episcopal and archiepiscopal assent to papal authority at the expense of sacral kingship. It is addressed to the German bishops and lay-princes, an audience whose participation during the 1070s was politically and religiously crucial to the relative advancements of rival papal and imperial ideologies.[3] The practical manifestation of this rivalry, which endured well into the twelfth century, was the ritual of investiture and the exclusive claim of the pope to grant the ring and the staff that symbolised apostolic legitimacy among the episcopate.[4] Papal monopoly on the distribution of these symbolic objects demonstrated the unmediated and apostolic continuity of papal authority with that of St Peter and, ultimately, God.

The adornment of the male body with symbolic dress comprised of highly prized decorative materials receives extended treatment in the first account, just as the importance of its absence is emphasised in the second. The divine kings (*obas*) of Benin governed their West African inland territory through their patronage and exclusive control of the craft guilds, hereditary castes of craftsmen who specialised in the production of ivories, bronzes and coral wear, all of which were used to furnish the royal palace and adorn the body of the ruler himself, and which provided the ceremonial resources for rehearsing political and social relationships. The king-artefact was made through a ceremony that included poetry, invocations and adornment with potent substances and materials. He was a symbol of political continuity and cosmic order as complex and subtle as the papal monarch, and, like the papal monarchy, his history was subject to political and economic disruptions and phases of ritual accretion, recession and inflation. A period of political fragmentation in seventeenth-century Benin separated two periods of political centralisation, in tandem with increased connectedness with Portuguese merchants from the fourteenth to the sixteenth century, and from 1800 onwards with the Dutch and increasingly the British.[5] The 1897 punitive expedition of the British to Benin City was also the confrontation of two kinds of iconic masculinity and the forces for which each stood, the European colonial officer and merchant, advancing commerce and trade, and the cosmic king, whose monopoly over the production, circulation and ceremonial deployment of key material resources supported his hegemonic claims among his people.[6]

So both extracts concern the contestation of power; and both narratives focus upon a male figure, whose authority stands at the apex of, but also rests upon, a wider social and political hierarchy. Through reflection upon moments such as these, this chapter explores the potential for masculinities to be studied in world historical perspective. It will offer the insight that a perennial but changing and under-theorised constituent of hegemonic masculinities is the mobilisation of material and male bodily display in social practices designed to rehearse relations of power between elite males and others. The concept of 'iconic masculinity' will be evoked as a means of comparing the way ritual, social practice and the manipulation of material culture is encoded in affective displays of hegemonic authority.

The historical predominance of patriarchy is undisputed. Its origin has been explained in many ways across different disciplines and is best contained in world historian David Christian's formulation of patriarchy as a fundamental sexual division of labour established in historical response to increasing social complexity.[7] In this chapter I want to sketch some potential benefits of placing masculinities in a world historical context. The study of changing configurations of masculinities and the varied gender differences and complementarities that inflected them can and should be made part of the broad synchronic comparative accounts of world history that have been published increasingly since the 1990s. An examination of the material and embodied aspects of these configurations, it is suggested, might offer insight into long-term processes of globalisation and modernisation. We need an integrated and comparative analytical framework applicable to the broadest range of historical evidence in order properly to address questions of patriarchy, the history of men and masculinities, and with it, necessarily, that of women. To this end, I shall offer first a partial summary of some of the relative concerns, approaches and goals of these two fields of history and then rehearse the case for combining them better to cast old stories in new, more inclusive and enriched historical contexts. I shall argue that we stand to gain from a gendered approach to world history that adopts insights from theories of social and material practice, particularly in the context of iconic mobilisations of the male body. When conducted in a world historical perspective, the initial exercise can hardly be more than one in selective comparison, classification and the provisional observation of patterns and possible research directions.

# I

It is difficult to think of the history of masculinities independently of feminist historiography. A place was reserved for men in feminist history by Natalie Zemon Davis as early as 1975, when she drew parallels between the relationships of men and women with those of lords and peasants.[8] Davis's inclusion of men within the parameters of women's history was controversial to some of her contemporaries, for whom women's history was naturally a separatist form of identity politics. Its formulation in structural terms spoke to the intellectual interests of many others engaged in refining historical materialist models of social history in order to enrich and problematise them with women's experiences of the sexual division of labour.[9]

Both the separatist and the inclusive impulses within feminist history mined new intellectual seams in the late 1980s with the invention of gender as a category of historical analysis. Joan Scott made the clearest programmatic statement on behalf of the new gender history. Scott saw gender first as 'a constituent element of social relationships based on perceived differences between the sexes', second as 'a primary way of signifying relationships of power', and finally as emblematic of 'the meaning of the male/female opposition'.[10] For women's history, 'gender' became a tool for interrogating the difference encoded in cultural – by which was predominantly meant literary – constructions of femininity, and a means of highlighting the asymmetries between men and women. For a minority of the 'separatists', gender was a further betrayal of the core cause of women's history.[11] It seemed to substitute writing on behalf of women with writing on behalf of a vague and disparate notion of feminine identities. Yet many adopted gender as a powerful critical tool for deconstructing historical sources. It appealed to the inclusive instincts of feminist historians, who began to trace difference and dissenting, marginalised voices across a range of texts and other media. The ontological emphasis moved gradually from men and women's social experiences to that of cultural discourse.

The historical study of men and masculinities emerged in the 1980s and 1990s, generally in sympathetic response to these continuing achievements and opportunities opened up by historians of women.[12] The male side of the sexual binary generated different questions, concerns and challenges. Questions of motivation and purpose were less clear than they had been in the feminist movement. Historians asked: what value was there in rendering the personal experiences of men historically visible? How might this history relate to ideas of class and other meta-narratives that took male agency for granted? How did the feminist insistence on alternative women's perspectives and experiences problematise the falsely universal grounds on which historians had previously written history? Was there a history of male social bonding analogous to the female solidarities being discovered in women's history and, if so, what was its historical significance?

The cultural turn in the study of men and masculinities took place during the 1990s, John Tosh being among the earliest to develop and articulate a historical approach to the subject. Tosh taught us to see nineteenth-century masculinities as: socially constructed through *practice* absorbed from and fostered in institutional surroundings; opportunities for subjective and psychological *identification*; and encoded, archived, debated and appealed to in discursive *constructions* of 'manliness'.[13] Tosh's approach addressed the social and cultural in that it proposed the autonomous interaction of discourses of 'manliness' with historically contingent social institutions broadly differentiated by class. An equally influential model that emerged at the same time was R.W. Connell's sociological formulation of masculinities in terms of a set of practices and relations 'internal to gender order'. The scheme offered a social matrix of subordinated, complicit and marginalised masculinities, all positioned in relation to a singularly 'culturally exalted' hegemonic masculinity.

'Hegemonic masculinity', according to this scheme, was the 'configuration of gender practice which embodies the currently accepted answer to the problem of the legitimacy of patriarchy'.[14] In any given society, hegemonic masculinity subordinated femininities and other masculinities, and tended to subordinate the latter by associating them with the former. It was also anchored by institutional and material resources and subject to 'crisis tendencies' determined, similarly to Tosh's scheme, by the 'ebb and flow' of historical contingency.

## II

The cultural reframing of gender studies gave historians the critical tools to interrogate their sources in new and powerful ways. But the advance beyond structure came with new challenges and some potential pitfalls. Despite the enduring association of men's with women's history, a habitual division of methodological labour has often restricted historians' attentions to discrete sides of the gender divide.[15] The commitment to exposing difference in discursive constructions of gender can produce an artificially antagonistic view of male/female relations, in what Denise Riley has called 'an invariant and monotonous men/women opposition'.[16] To help relieve the monotony, some critics have pointed out that the grounds on which the antagonism has been played out are inflected by race, by age, by sexuality and by geopolitics in ways that complicate notions of female priorities and solidarities.[17] In short, gendered difference can sometimes unintentionally cramp our understanding of the plurality of female and male identities and agencies.

An associated risk in the practice of gender history is too literal a reading of its normative and discursive claims. This can lead to a rather vague emphasis on the common oppressive properties of all patriarchies rather than on the internal elements that might differentiate them. The historian Kathleen Canning has noted – citing Joan Scott – how the cultural approach to gender falls foul of the 'one-dimensional notion that language or discourses "position subjects and *produce* their experiences" '.[18] This collapsing of discourse into agency again has implications for the way we think of female agency, and also of masculinities. For example, too much emphasis on the discursive claims of particular hegemonic masculinities can obscure our understanding of the social context within which individuals and groups accomplished, maintained and reproduced their gendered claims to hegemonic status and lead to a rather static, monolithic and hierarchical analysis. The fragility of hegemonic masculinities becomes harder to explain as a result of this slippage of discourse into agency. In the case of female agency the editors of *Gender and Change*, a recent collection of reflections on the last 20 years of gender historiography, made the similar observation that 'gender blind scholarship has not been alone in producing partial accounts of female agency, several contributors confront the uncomfortable reality that women's agency did not only occur in progressive domains, but could sustain and benefit from systems of oppression.'[19]

These criticisms of gender and its potential distorting effects expose a subtle range of emphases with which gender historians personalise their *a priori* notions of identity, agency and power. At one end of this range, gender analysis emphasises masculinity as a contest between men for power; at another, it emphasises women's exclusion from or subjection to that power. In pursuit of the maximum sensitivity to multiple identities (such that even sex is no retreat for essentialist assumptions), the separatist splitters risk discounting female solidarity. Conversely, in their desire to understand the full range of female agency by emphasising the complementarities between male and female experience in the past, lumpers risk blunting the critical edge of gender as a tool for exposing the powerful effects of difference.[20]

Written into the concepts of difference and hegemony as they tend currently to be used is a tacit commitment by historians to the static, oppositional quality of gender in the *longue durée*. Feminist historians have been quick to note that, despite the great progress made in recent decades in women's history, its effect on periodisation has been limited. The workshop held in Cambridge in 2007 that resulted in the publication of *Gender and Change* concluded that feminist gender history has disappointed in its attempts to reclassify the past in ways that incorporate the changing experiences of women.[21] Judith Bennett pleaded for a re-engagement with the *longue dureé* in feminist history, and has explained its modernist myopia in terms of the strategic focus and institutional arrangements of history departments in higher education, and with the fact that the very achievement of feminist scholars of remoter periods has removed something of their golden age veneer.[22] Moreover, Bennett suggests that world history in part has contributed to the problem by diverting attention to transnational modernity and away from the concerns of women's historians closer to home. Judith P. Zinserr has made the similar point that, in its historical frameworks and the themes and periods it continues to favour, and because of the male-oriented content resulting from these factors, world history has failed to engage with historians of women. She throws down the gauntlet to world historians, commenting that 'unless world historians, female or male, include full descriptions of women's varied past and of the gendered reality of both sexes' lives, they will have failed in their stated goal to present the global narrative of all human experience'.[23]

## III

A common problem with all these current positions, I would suggest, lies in their implicit understandings of hegemonic power as a series of zero-sum games effecting relational closures. If the critical insights discussed above are valid, then we need a more refined theory of hegemonic power: not all of which involves the power to command; some of which countenances power that is collective in practice if distributive in effect;[24] that sees discourse as separate to and not simply dictating behaviour; and that accepts that hegemony never achieves absolute relational closure. One way of doing this is to problematise the consensus-making side of hegemonic processes, by reflecting on the conundrum that, in its effort to appropriate and close off alternative options, hegemony requires and enables diffuse cultural and interpretive practices.

Hegemony is, of course, a theory of power borrowed and adapted from Gramscian cultural Marxism. It was originally intended as an intellectual device for thinking about processes of cultural negotiation and structural transformation (i.e. revolution). Gramsci was interested in the way in which the Italian media stabilised class relations through their ideological capture of the diffuse range of cultural settings within which social relations were forged. His theory addressed the need for intellectuals to disrupt that hegemony through the raising of class-consciousness in the mass media. That Gramsci had his own political goal does not detract from the value of his abstractions. The basic point is that hegemony is not static or hierarchical, but processual and rhetorical, participatory and open to interpretation.[25] Manuel Castells talks of the desired result of such consensual actions as 'a relational capacity that enables a social actor to influence asymmetrically the decisions of another social actor(s) in ways that favour the empowered actor's will, interests, and values'.[26] Hegemony is not 'relations closed' or 'status achieved' but an indefinitely deferred aspiration to control social encounters by those with sufficient material, practical and ideological resources to rehearse and maintain relational capacities. We might thus envisage hegemonic masculinity as one index of collectively negotiated power implicated in and balanced among other indices such as race, ethnicity, age, wealth, sexuality and caste. Claims on behalf of hegemonic masculinities frequently involved the bracketing and indexing of binaries that illustrated and rehearsed relational capacities between, say, man and God (or gods or angels), man and animals, man and women, man and wife/family, and so forth. Rarely did one exclusive male group get to monopolise the full set of these hegemonic indicators, because these often belonged to mutually exclusive types of relational repertoire; put simply, it is difficult to pose as the head of a warrior dynasty if you have taken a vow of celibacy and renounced violence. Consequently, hegemonic masculine indicators tended to be distributed between different elite male groups, and necessitated trade-offs and accommodations that often multiplied and cut across gender binaries, whether represented as differences or complementarities.

At the same time, however, and for this very reason, different configurations of masculinities might present opportunities for interpretive licence, choice and agency among subordinated and marginalised groups. Only limited numbers of men enjoyed the full material and cultural resources to effect these collective/relational capacities, but many others partially imitated them, played them off one another, or engaged in derivative 'masculine games' of their own that allowed them to draw what Connell has called the 'patriarchal dividend'.

What I have just rather dryly and technically described as male hegemonic bracketing and indexing practices, I would like now to label 'iconic masculinity'. The term is meant to encapsulate the affective efforts of elite males to reproduce the likeness of a hegemonic position, and the role of the viewer in recognising, reading and responding to that likeness. The two textual examples with which I began this chapter were vivid polemical statements of relations between iconic masculinities. The authors of both conspicuously build audience into their narratives, the first noting the 'crowd of some 900 to 1000 people standing around when the Resident called upon Overami to make his submission', the latter noting that Henry IV did not just 'move all who were there present' with his behaviour, but 'all to whom a report of this came, to such pity and merciful compassion'.[27] In each case, also, the iconic dimension of hegemonic masculinity is embodied in elite male social practice, a site for the display of symbols, gestures and qualities, all designed to prompt normative interpretive responses.[28] Through institutional and material displays, aspirant males coaxed and coerced certain forms of interpretive labour from those before whom they enacted their hegemonic aspirations. Since constructions of femininity were the most frequently evoked foils and complements for iconic male practice, the interpretive labour of real women and other men in response to embodied male material display – though almost invariably auxiliary and implicitly inferior (and in modern terms demeaning and exploitative) – was socially important.

A history of masculinities might usefully recast hegemonic masculinities in terms of iconic capacities and the ability of individuals, male or female, to affect, reject, usurp or take secondary advantage of these capacities. For iconic masculinities to overcome historical inertia they must be mapped out socially and their enactment traced in diverse institutionalised forms of social practice.[29] Our assumption of patriarchal closure might then be historically differentiated with social analysis of the complementary work of interpretive labour done by men and women in their daily encounters with elite male carriers of iconic meaning. By suspending our assumptions of closure and opening patriarchy up to questions of social practice, we might recalibrate subordinate male and female agencies with reference to the complementarities as well as the differences found in gendered discourse.[30] There is no denying the distributive power wielded by patriarchal formations, but such power is invariably accompanied by the collective power realised in complementary social roles, themselves dependent on and subject to diffuse historical contingencies, whether incremental, cyclical or catastrophic.

Similarly, gendered roles ascribed to women, however limited, afforded them fields of interpretive expertise that underpinned iconic masculinities. Sherry Ortner has described these as opportunities for 'women's games', or times when some women got to subvert, resist, appropriate, reinterpret, perhaps even occasionally usurp positions of iconic masculinity.[31] Beneath the rhetoric of the iconic male type, whether from a subaltern, world historical perspective or a gendered perspective, lies the chance for subordinated agents to infuse their gender roles with hidden, consolatory meanings. Caroline Walker Bynum's study of medieval female spirituality in relation to food examines such an intimate niche of consolation and meaning, an example of what Tom McCaskie has called the 'history of conscience'.[32] My suggestion is that we adjust our emphasis from the monolithic to the embodied, material and iconic nature of masculinities; a way of reminding ourselves that hegemonic masculinities often display aesthetically desirable values and qualities to draw attention toward and to focus social action through them. It therefore has potential for helping us to connect the cultural meanings generated by gender with the social structural patterns and agencies that are an important concern of world history. I mentioned above that a better understanding of gender in terms of social practice – by providing a link between discourse and agency, between the cultural and the social – might overcome some of the current limitations identified with gender history. This is to say that dominant discourses mediate gender, but so too do oral texts and everyday social practices.[33]

The preceding discussion is ultimately a reassertion of the care with which historians like Tosh and Scott have taught us to separate the analytical strands of gender when attempting to explain its historical significance. Overemphasis on discursive difference can obscure the history of everyday resistance, of conscience and of the hidden transcripts that emerge out of the analysis of gender complementarities in practice.[34] The claims hegemonic masculinities make are not empty verbiage; they put down their roots in social fact. But that social fact depends upon the interpretive labour elicited from men and women through the investment by elites of diverse institutional resources in symbolic, performative and iconic prompts, often crucially directed at women.

## IV

The call for a synthesis of gender and world histories made by Bennett and Zinserr has not gone unanswered.[35] Two general surveys of gender history in a world perspective have been published in the past ten years. Both have focused primarily on the uniformly exploitative effect of patriarchies on women, perhaps helping to confirm Bennett's fears of a creeping disillusionment of feminist historians with the pre-modern past. In her book *Gender in History*, Merry Wiesner-Hanks offers a health warning to her readers on behalf of her general account 'of women's subordination'. Her thematic arrangement of chapters, however, helps to mitigate the worst effects of too conflictual a model of gender systems.[36] In *Gender in World History*, Peter Stearns presents a series of case studies illustrating the development of 'gender-systems' from the fourth millennium BCE to the present.[37] For the period 500–1500 he selects a series of cross-cultural encounters as settings in which to trace changing configurations of male–female relationships: the reception of Buddhism in China (the fourth to the ninth centuries), the impact of Islam in India and Africa (the tenth to the fourteenth centuries), and the influence of China in Japan (the eleventh to the sixteenth centuries).[38]

Stearn's coverage is necessarily selective and general. Three working principles guide his arrangements of the material: first, that gender and world history is the study of relations between men and women in their different civilisations; second, that doctrines of the world religions are the basic reference points for understanding those relationships; and, third, that the historical dimension of gender configurations is best examined in the contacts made between the world's civilisations.[39] He concludes that the world religions have patriarchal gender systems and that new syncretic configurations of gender emerge when they connect that tend increasingly to subordinate women. In short, the more connected civilisations become the greater the oppression of women.[40] Stearn's and Wiesner-Hank's work has done much to open the subject to examination over a broad chronological span. A reservation is that gender still tends to be associated with women, and gender systems tend to be linked primarily and sometimes solely to a view of increasing patriarchal oppression.[41] An approach that challenges conventional periodisation; offers a broader account of female agency, including the kind of interpretive agencies by which women are so often co-opted into patriarchy; and interrogates the different configurations of masculinities, and their vulnerability to and interaction with incremental, cyclical and catastrophic change, is what masculinity as a category of world historical analysis might have to offer.

## V

Histories of gender and of the world have converged in two obvious areas in the last decade and a half. First, both have sought to problematise traditional chronological classifications of the past. Second, each has aimed to enrich existing histories by recovering the voices of neglected communities, groups and identities. The traditional grand narrative of world history has tended to be Eurocentric and focused on explaining modernity. At the risk of caricature, it presumed that, of all the old world civilisations, Europe was the setting for the replacement of traditional agrarian society in the eighteenth and nineteenth centuries with industrial capitalism, democracy and the nation state.

The achievement of a uniquely European modernity, so versions of the story continue, was relayed through a series of golden legacies from Europe's classical, medieval and early modern past. This nineteenth-century romantic metanarrative of history as destiny was present at the birth of academic history and the social sciences; it was built into the language of Cold War geopolitical analysis, with its talk of 'agricultural involution', Rostovian take-offs, 'underdevelopment' and 'blocking factors', and it has been sustained in the last 20 years with increasingly shrill talk of the 'end of history' and the 'clash of civilisations'.[42] But a new literature is gradually beginning to refine the Eurocentric orthodoxy of a monolithic, uniquely Western modernity.[43] Historians are beginning to explore beyond the 'parochial modern',[44] the chronologically foreshortened Eurocentric perspective on the world, for instance in their attempts to explain the 'great divergence' of the eighteenth century by re-imagining the familiar in a more fully integrated, textured and comparative manner. Economic historians, for example, have pointed out a 'world of surprising resemblances'[45] in the economic circumstances among regions dispersed across the Eurasian landmass, and convincingly explained Europe's advance to industrial production as later than customarily thought and as the result, not of systemic causes or some notion of Destiny, but rather of the contingencies of coal being near areas of heavy industry and the benefits of the New World plantation complex.[46]

The teleological and structural certainties of the historical materialist framework upon which this traditional narrative was founded have been most consistently challenged in the last decade by historians influenced by anthropology and post-colonial studies, on cultural grounds that favour discourse, plurality and 'affective histories' over grand narratives of unilinear economic development and industrial production.[47] Just as feminist scholars have challenged the false universals inherent in traditional history, post-colonial scholars have destabilised Eurocentric modernity by highlighting and problematising its dependence on the categories, concepts and labels of the nineteenth-century Western historicist moment. An eloquent example of this more radical subaltern critique of European-led modernisation is that of Dipesh Chakrabarty's collection of essays on post-colonial thought and historical difference, *Provincializing Europe*.[48] Chakrabarty identified historicism, whether in its liberal or Hegelian–Marxist variants, as the narrative means by which Western scholars asserted a political pre-eminence over the non-Western world. Chakrabarty sought not to deny the practical achievements of modernity but to insist that its articulation through Western analytical categories, terms and language reduced the phenomenon to an essentialist, binary rhetoric of non-Western retardation: 'Historicism,' he argued, '– and even the modern, European idea of history – one might say, came to non-European peoples in the nineteenth century as someone's way of saying "not yet" to somebody else.'[49] For non-Europeans, history becomes not destiny, but a waiting room. Chakrabarty sub-alternatively insisted on many points of entry into modernity and multiple perceptions and practices of it,[50] including some misrecognised in and thereby excluded from Western historicist accounts, simply because they didn't conform to classical European sociological or political typologies.[51] *Provincializing Europe* is an invitation to escape the parochiality of modernity and to rethink the categories, concepts, labels and themes of world history in light of the increase in research on Eurasia over the *longue dureé*. It is one that would appeal to historians like Bennett and Zinserr, if it were to respond positively to their desire for gender to be incorporated into new reflections on periodisation.[52]

Gender offers post-colonial and new global historians concepts and insights with which to challenge modernity in ways that extend beyond economic comparison into areas where the very possibility of selecting value-neutral historical labels and categories, not least those dealing with periodisation, becomes moot. The conventional periodisations of classical, medieval and early modern circulate with little obvious explanatory value beyond the Mediterranean, and tend to get allotted arbitrarily and inappropriately to the history of other parts of the world.[53] Periodisation is, of course, only a small part of the wider and thornier problem of difference and cultural translation and the question of what vocabularies and analytical categories we adopt for world comparative purposes. World historians need shared categories in order to facilitate cross-cultural comparison, but in applying them they invite accusations of distortion and damage to their sources and the cultures that produced them.[54] This aspect of the cultural–social dilemma is an irreconcilable but useful conversation, once again, between historical lumpers and splitters, the latter in danger of endlessly deferring the question of who speaks for whom in their focus on translation, difference and subjectivities (whether defined by race, gender, sexuality, ethnicity or any other kind of 'Other'), the former cavalierly or naïvely reinforcing (because discounting) difference through their desire to apply labels that aid comparison and the explanation of change. It was precisely this dilemma that deterred R.W. Connell from attempting a fully comparative approach to the subject of world historical masculinities in an article he published in 1993. His twofold argument was that 'masculinities' may not have any meaning outside Euro/American culture, and that, since 'the agents of global domination were and are, predominantly men, the historical analysis of masculinity must be a leading theme in our understanding of the contemporary world order'.[55] This paradox left him to chart a familiar succession – from the conquistadores to international businessmen – of European masculine types ultimately characterised by individualism, rationality, heterosexuality and extreme violence. There are grounds for at least attempting a bolder approach. As Kenneth Pomeranz has noted, 'nobody would argue that narratives conceived around externally created terms should be used to the exclusion of narratives phrased in terms that participants might have used (and of course different participants in the same event would often have different vocabularies), but it would be at least equally puzzling to insist on only using "indigenous" categories, even if we could agree on what those were.'[56]

As a result of caution about labels, pre-modern area specialists find themselves isolated or speaking at cross purposes for lack of common time frames and language. It may well be that gender and the study of changing configurations of iconic masculinity can help bring together dispersed but related debates. The new subaltern histories and the world history of global connectedness recast the familiar transformations of European history in terms of a two-way dynamic of domination and resistance, showing how major trends in world history are the result, not simply of unilinear top–down movements, but of multi-directional, polycentric and synchronic patterns of change. The history of masculinities on this new scale provides an additional platform for articulating these patterns and dimensions. In summary, an opportunity exists to incorporate gender into the post-Eurocentric reassessment of history currently being undertaken by world historians. The two approaches of world history and the history of masculinities share converging goals and problems,[57] and have complementary contributions to make to those goals. The study of men and masculinities can contribute to the new global historiographical commitment to combining the work of cultural translation with explanations of social and political transformation. It could provide world historians with cultural units of comparison with which to enrich and articulate the new historical landscape of global connectedness. In return, world history might usefully provide historians of masculinities with social and structural contexts for exploring the historical significance of gender. In the words of Catherine Hall, approaching the topic from a slightly different direction, 'The ghost of Marx is still necessarily with us. Marx needs those Others and those Others need him.'[58]

## VI

But what kinds of comparative opportunity might masculinity bring to world history? In response to the methods already prescribed by Tosh, Scott and Connell, we might adopt an approach that looks for family resemblances between iconic types of masculinity (the holy man/saint, warrior/tribesman, cleric/bureaucrat, magistrate/mentor etc.) and that traces their changing hegemonic indicators and multiple configurations in response to tipping points in institutional histories, cycles of political or religious expansion and contraction, conquests, revolutions and environmental challenges. I shall explore a few examples for further investigation before offering some concluding thoughts.

An important proponent of the new global history which adopts polycentric, multi-directional and synchronic perspectives is C.A. Bayly, the imperial and world historian, who echoes Chakrabarty in talking of *The Birth of the Modern World* not as a 'triumph' but as 'a riddle...a collection of substantive trends, and a perception that these amounted to the modern' and that 'many different agencies and ideologies across the world empowered it in different ways and at different times.'[59] In a recent article, Bayly sketched the pre-modern Afro-Eurasian dynamic from the thirteenth to the middle of the eighteenth century in terms of 'archaic globalization'.[60] Archaic globalisation is a refinement of Wallerstein's world systems theory, that offers a heuristic model of global connectedness linking patterns of social interaction and consumption generated by three major cross-cultural ideologies (quite distinct from those associated with modernisation above): cosmic kingship, universal religion and the humoral notion of the body and bodily practices.

One could consider cosmic kingship as an example of an iconic masculinity that allows comparative insights into the rooting of military leadership in transcendent contexts of legitimate authority, for instance, in Christian kingship of Europe, in the Islamic tradition of the Caliph, or through the Chinese imperial Mandate of Heaven. Each of these centres of cosmic kingship established nodes and networks supporting the consumption, distribution and display of exotic objects and goods that fostered social relations over long distances, and helped to knit together states, empires and a global network. Each of these was periodically renewed and reinterpreted afresh during the age of archaic globalisation, whether by phases of imperial expansion and political centralisation undertaken by the winners of dynastic conflict, or by conquering neighbours, or through the migration of confederacies of nomadic warriors, as in the Indo-Islamic and Chinese worlds.[61]

Reconfigurations of iconic masculinity in contexts of conquest, imperial expansion and colonialism have already been illustrated in our two main examples. The account of the surrender and trial of Oba Ovonramwen presents the British desire for Benin's productive assets in a narrative of civilising intervention, the king's ceremonial feasts, which involved barbarous acts of ritual sacrifice that interfered with the peaceable exchange of goods by British merchants, seen as requiring humane military intervention. The king of Benin henceforth was to become the model of a client ruler under British imperial supervision. Canossa was one dramatic episode in papal reformation of the eleventh-century Catholic Church, a turning point in European history that invites the interpretive use of iconic masculinities. One of the Reform's defining features, after all, was a reconfiguration of gender relationships, best encapsulated by the fact that membership of its chief office – whose title was 'Papa' – depended on the personal renunciation of paternity, and thereby lineage.[62] This particular imperial project, chiefly associated with Gregory VII

(1073–1085), was based on a new accommodation between two discrete forms of late antique masculinity: the hereditary warrior aristocrat and the Christian ascetic. The medieval bishop, like the cosmic king, demanded iconic attention and fostered relational capacities. The ideas underpinning episcopal authority have been discussed by Conrad Leyser and Kate Cooper, who have traced in outline the relative intellectual positions of churchmen on the subject of manliness and authority in late antiquity and the early medieval West.[63] Leyser also shows that late antique philosophers assumed that the social practice of masculinity at the highest political levels was agonistic and that a key contestable indicator of fitness to occupy positions of authority was the degree to which a man could demonstrate moderation and balance in the control of his passions, primarily among them his sexual impulses. Control of private lust corresponded to propriety in public office. Scrutiny of domestic life and marital arrangements provided members of the political elite with the means to regulate, distribute and conduct the business of public authority. Leyser examines the adaptation of these values in the conditions of the fourth and fifth centuries, when Roman imperial authority was disintegrating and the Christian church emerged as its only surviving infrastructure. Jerome, Cassian and Augustine took varying positions on asceticism and authority. The ascetic wing, represented by Jerome and Cassian, raised the practice of self-control to a new level, insisting on a strict accounting for the flow of semen for those aspiring to the morally legitimate authority in Christian society.

Augustine punctured the severe strictures of this ascetic Christianity out of concern for its elitist and misguided assumptions. He offered what Leyser memorably calls a 'low brow satire of [their] phallocentric pretensions'.[64] Christian athleticism in the form of mastery over the penis was a futile gimmick: the impotence of man in the face of his desires was laid bare not in his surrender to lustful desires, but in the fundamental unruliness of his sexual organs, proof of which (as no doubt Augustine knew personally) lay in their failure to function even when a man might in all other respects be sexually aroused. Augustine's radical decentring of male sexual self-control as a powerful means of iconic display did not attract universal appeal because it left elite males in an existentially vulnerable place, subject to God's grace alongside the rest of society.

Clericalism and an episcopal infrastructure were important legacies of the late antique world, but they failed to imbue early medieval Europe with a comprehensively celibate and theocratic structure of authority. Although many bishops tended to live by the social habits and political loyalties of their families, ascetic bodily discipline could also be found within episcopal ranks. But, to the extent that it succeeded in mobilising social practice and interpretive labour beyond elite politics, the real ascetic virtuosi, holy men and saints, tended to be recruited from monastic and eremetical institutions.

130  *Simon Yarrow*

This all changed in the eleventh century, when, as a result of elite competition for land and social status, and by stoking and manipulating the religious anxieties of the people, the Church reinvented itself as a literate, celibate, ordained and male profession, an autonomous and self-governing centralised system of authority.[65] The practical results of reform were varied across different regions, but more importantly, as Leyser has argued, reform rhetoric came to dominate subsequent debates about ecclesiastical corruption and lay morality.[66] For example, one of its aspects – misogyny – was not simply the neurotic backlash of a celibate clergy but the ramping up of a language through which churchmen could hold secular masculinity to moral account. By using 'women to think with', for example in its definition of marriage as a sacrament and a school of morality, clerical masculinity could sow pollution fears among secular elites, dependent as they were on the moral propriety as well as the biologically reproductive role of elite women.[67] The implications for female agency were mixed (as so often was the case), a price of the moral and persuasive agency ascribed to the spouse being interpretive compliance to a new form of iconic masculinity, the parish priest. Meanwhile, clerical masculinity defined itself in relation to God and the Church, rather than to family ties. The 'independent manly bishop', free of female pollution and lay interference, is an increasingly popular pious invention of eleventh-century hagiography, and provides a context for understanding what was at stake in the encounter between and reconfiguration of iconic masculinities depicted in the reform version of events at Canossa.[68] Priests were to become angels,[69] representatives of an overarching authority, empowered through their exclusive repertoire of sacraments, and particularly that of the Eucharist, to shape and process the behaviour of secular institutions like the family or the parish community.

The historian who has done most to draw our attention to the socio-political significance of the rise of clerical masculinities in medieval Europe is R. I. Moore. Not least among Reform's consequences for him were its comprehensive documentation of lay society, and its official co-opting of local religious agents (saints, crusaders, pious wives and female mystics) into a 'universal' institution, and the exclusion of others (Jews, homosexuals and heretics) from it.[70] Moore has recently extended his comparative analysis to include the scholar gentry of China and the Islamic scholars of medieval Damascus; both, he argues, undergoing crises of identity between 1000 and 1200 similar to those of the Catholic clergy, and finding their own ways of relating themselves to society and the political institutions around them.[71] In the remarkably similar conditions of intensive exploitation and social complexity attendant on urbanisation, Islamic scholars bid for authority by hiring out their scriptural expertise and rhetorical talents to serve as popular advocates on behalf of elite urban patrons. In this way Muslim religious acted as powerful advocates of a universal religion grounded in loyalty to fragmented and local social forces.

But when external threats, in the form of nomadic warrior interventions, to this urban social equilibrium took over, the position of urban patrons was superseded by a new dynamic, whose political implications have been illuminated most provocatively by Ernest Gellner in his interpretation of the work of David Hume and Ibn Khaldun.[72] Ibn Khaldun lived in the same post-Caliphate, urbanised world addressed by Moore, in which Muslim rulers were local, dependent on the legitimising influence of scholarly clients, and vulnerable to attack by tribal groupings on the fringes of areas under sedentary cultivation. In Gellner's model, post-caliphal Islam was subsumed in and subjected the state to periodic moral renewals of its leadership by warrior tribesmen, the egalitarian collectivism of their mountain and steppe lives harnessed and unleashed by puritan scholars on incumbent, corrupt regimes. In such conditions, when the cyclical threat of tribal pastoralism was not resolved through assimilation into the state in a broadly feudal process, but, rather, legitimacy was located and arranged apart from the state through local accommodations struck between forces of tribalism and scripturalism, metropolitan elites were always subject to the suspicion of having forfeited the moral purity underpinning their authority. Meanwhile, in the West, minority puritan monotheists dislodged the hierarchical collectivism the late medieval Church had fostered since the eleventh century in association with the state, and forged a new state partnership based on the atomistic egalitarianism of civil society. Their decision to confront the state with the challenge of liberty, according to Gellner, was an uncharacteristic resort by monistic, literate puritans to social tolerance for lack of coercive forces like the nomadic pastoralists to co-opt and lionise. Gellner's broadly Weberian argument is that political and social configurations in the West provided the conditions for merchants and an urban bourgeoisie to form a civil and ultimately modern society, while political configurations in Muslim society were more brittle and less conducive to liberty because the society had to reckon with the nomadic pastoralism at its geopolitical and spiritual core. The archetypal icons of masculinity in these schemes were, of course, Jesus and Muhammad, or at least versions of them that came to dominate tradition: the body of the former an image of universal sacrifice that reinforced Platonic notions of legitimate rule as commensurate only with the pursuit by rulers of the common good; the latter, whose likeness was recollected only in abstraction, legitimately embodied only through the social cohesion (*asabiyah*) exemplified by warrior tribalism, and mediated politically through the scripturalism of Muslim scholar–clerics.

Iconic clerical masculinities developed differently in China, where, in the eleventh and twelfth centuries, the Confucian examination system consolidated the means by which the scholar gentry could mobilise the state to serve the local political interests of their families. This endured until the roughly century-long hiatus in native rule occasioned by the Mongol invasion. A recent article by Beverley Bossler on gender and empire in Yuan China has shed light on the proliferation among the thirteenth and fourteenth-century scholar gentry of poetry written in praise of the heroism and fidelity of their female kin.[73] In this case, argues Bossler, praise poetry gave elite men a means to emphasise their social status and political importance during a period of dislocation from imperial patronage caused by the overthrow of the Southern Song imperial court by the Mongols, which replaced recruitment by exam with a more diversely recruited administration.

## Conclusion

The findings of further comparison are eagerly awaited. I anticipate that its value will come not from more literal readings of religious doctrine and ideology but from a deconstruction of the social and material practices invested in iconic masculinities, and the study of how their multiple configurations were negotiated and maintained. Scott identified four analytical threads that constituted gender: symbols, normative concepts, institutions and subjective identities. The task of the historian, she argued, is to study the changing articulations of these four elements. I have argued that a properly calibrated assessment of female agency would benefit from fuller consideration of the complementarities (in addition to the differences) rehearsed in these concepts, institutions and identities. At first this might seem a regressive step to take, but it is hoped that by doing so a more diverse and broadly representative understanding of women's history might be discovered in the small everyday acts of interpretive labour women undertake in spite of the real (discursive and institutional) patriarchal constraints placed upon them. The aim is not to replace one monolithic concept with another, or to assume that iconic masculinity subsumed and governed all forms of association between groups or individuals. An understanding of how patriarchies functioned, I have argued, must benefit from an approach to hegemonic masculinity that grounds male power in a context of diffuse social practice, and one in which huge material resources and displays of discipline and charisma are invested in the production of iconic masculinities. The study of iconic masculinities in a world historical perspective has the potential to enrich our understanding of current trends in the historiography of global connectedness by providing a set of family resemblances between cross-cultural iconic masculinities (the holy man, the warrior, the cleric, the bureaucrat, etc.), the configuration of which might be usefully traced in the *longue durée*. We have seen examples of such reconfigurations of iconic masculinity in the humiliations of Oba Ovonramwen and Henry IV, cosmic kings operating at opposite ends of our date range, and I have explored the proliferation of clerical masculinities during the advent of citied civilisations, c. 1000–1250, as well as the reinvention of imperial networks by the Confucian scholar gentry of the late thirteenth century under the Mongols. A final speculation that might indicate potential for future investigation is how the traditional narrative of modernisation might be modified by a study of the European colonial bureaucrat as an anti-iconic figure, who accumulates objects, not to foster social relations and shared values in contexts of display, but in order to assign to them market (rather than social) value as commodities serving the cause of trade. It may be that, in exploring this possibility, we might be tracing the origins of the erroneously styled 'universal man' of modern social scientific discourse.

## Notes

I wish to thank Anthea Harris, Chris Callow, Christina Pössel, William Purkis, Miri Rubin and Pauline Stafford for reading and advising me on this paper, Karin Barber for her invaluable advice and encouragement, and the editors of this book for their patience and faith in what, despite its flaws (for which I am solely responsible), I have attempted to do here.

1. H.L. Roth, *Great Benin, Its Customs, Art and Horrors* (London, 1903), Appendix III, 'The Surrender and Trial of the King', pp. xii–xiv.
2. *The Register of Pope Gregory VII 1073–1085: An English Translation*, ed. H.E.J. Cowdrey (Oxford, 2002), pp. 221–22.
3. For a synthesis of events see C. Morris, *The Papal Monarchy: The Western Church From 1050 to 1250* (Oxford, 1989), pp. 113–21, and for sources illustrating the polemical exchanges see B. Tierney, *The Middle Ages Volume I: Sources of Medieval History* (Cornell, NY, 1970, 2nd edn 1973), pp. 123–31.
4. Morris, *Papal Monarchy*, pp. 155–64.
5. K.B. Berzock, *Benin: Royal Arts of a West African Kingdom* (New Haven, CT, 2008), pp. 5–14.
6. P.A. Igbafe, 'The fall of Benin: a reassessment', *The Journal of African History* 11 (1970), 385–400.
7. See M.E. Wiesner-Hanks, *Gender and History* (Oxford, 2001), pp. 12–18, J.P. Zinserr, 'Gender', in M. Hughes-Warrington (ed.), *Palgrave Advances in World Histories* (London, 2005), p. 205, and P.N. Stearns, *Gender in World History* (London, 2000), pp. 10–19, for useful discussions, and D. Christian, *Maps of Time: An Introduction to Big History* (Berkeley, CA, 2005), pp. 263–65, for a general statement.
8. N. Zemon Davis, '"Women's history" in transition: the European case', *Feminist Studies* 3 (1976), 83–103.
9. K. Sacks, *Sisters and Wives: The Past and Future of Sexual Equality* (London, 1979); and for recent reflections on early feminist engagements with Marxist approaches see J.W. Scott, *Gender and the Politics of History* (New York, 1999), pp. 68–90; C. Hall, 'Marxism and its others', in C. Wickham (ed.), *Marxist History-Writing for the Twenty-First Century* (Oxford, 2007), pp. 112–39.
10. J.W. Scott, 'Gender: a useful category of historical analysis', *American Historical Review* 91 (1986), 1053–75, on 1067.

11. The often-cited social critique of 'gender' is J. Hoff, 'Gender as a postmodern category of paralysis', *Women's History Review* 3 (1994), 149–68, which regretted the diversion it imposed from agency and intentionality.
12. See Tosh in this book for a personal account.
13. J. Tosh, 'What should historians do with masculinity? reflections on nineteenth-century Britain', *History Workshop Journal* 38 (1994), 179–202.
14. R.W. Connell, *Masculinities* (Cambridge, 1995), p. 77.
15. An important recent exception to this is L. Brubaker and J.M.H. Smith (eds), *Gender in the Early Medieval World East and West, 300–900* (Cambridge, 2004), and particularly J.M.H. Smith, 'Introduction: Gendering the Early Medieval World', pp. 1–19.
16. Cited in Scott, 'Gender', p. 1065.
17. See A. Davies, *Women, Race and Class* (London, 1981); J. Butler, *Gender Trouble: Feminism and the Subversion of Identity* (London, 1999), and B. Holsinger, citing the work of G. Spivak, in 'Medieval studies, postcolonial studies and the genealogies of critique', *Speculum* 77 (2002), 1201.
18. Cited by J. Alberti, *Gender and the Historian* (London, 2002), p. 130.
19. See A. Shepard and G. Walker (eds), *Gender and Change, Agency, Chronology and Periodisation* (Oxford, 2009), p. 10.
20. J. Hexter, *On Historians* (Cambridge, MA, 1979), who characterised all historians in terms of being analytically either 'lumpers' or 'splitters' of phenomena.
21. Shepard and Walker (eds), *Gender and Change*, and see J. Kelly-Gadol, 'Did women have a renaissance?', in *Women, History and Theory: The Essays of Joan Kelly* (Chicago, 1984), pp. 19–50.
22. J.M. Bennett, 'Forgetting the past', in Shepard and Walker (eds), *Gender and Change*, pp. 274–278. See also J.M. Bennett, *History Matters: Patriarchy and the Challenge of Feminism* (Philadelphia, 2006). And, for a feminist historian dismantling golden age thinking, see P. Stafford, 'Women and The Norman Conquest', *Transactions of the Royal Historical Society*, 6th ser., 4 (1994), 221–49.
23. See J.P. Zinserr, 'Gender', in *Palgrave Advances in World Histories*, p. 210.
24. For definitions of 'distributive' and 'collective power', see M. Mann, *The Sources of Social Power 1: A History of Power from the Beginning to A.D. 1760* (Cambridge, 1986), pp. 6–7.
25. As one African historian has put it, 'cultural representations are arguments in the articulation of consent.' T.C. McCaskie, *State and Society in Pre-Colonial Asante* (Cambridge, 1995), pp. 20–1.
26. M. Castells, *Communication Power* (Oxford, 2009), p. 10.
27. For reference to an anti-papal interpretation of Henry IV's behaviour that depicts it as a form of martyrdom at the hands of a tyrannical pope, see P. Buc, *The Dangers of Ritual Between Early Medieval Texts and Social Scientific Theory* (Princeton, NJ, 2001), p. 242.
28. See T. Reuter, 'Nobles and others, the social and cultural expression of power relations in the Middle Ages', in A.J. Duggan (ed.), *Nobles and Nobility* (Woodbridge, 2000), pp. 86–95, and for the symbolic meanings of ecclesiastical clothing in the early middle ages see G. Constable, 'The ceremonies and symbolism of entering religious life and taking the monastic habit, from the fourth to the twelfth century', *Settimane di studio del Centro Italiano de Studi Sull'alto Medioevo* 33.2 (Spoleto, 1987), pp. 771–834. For a late antique example, see M. Harlow, 'Clothes maketh the man: power dressing and elite masculinity in the later Roman World', in Brubaker and Smith (eds), *Gender and the Early Medieval World*, pp. 44–69.
29. Scott argues for this in 'Gender a Useful Category', pp. 1067–68.

30. The inspiration for this approach comes from F. Bray, *Technology and Gender Fabrics of Power in Late Imperial China* (London, 1997), and M. Strathern, *The Gender of the Gift: Problems with Women and Problems with Society in Melanesia* (California, CA, 1988).
31. S.B. Ortner, *Making Gender: The Politics and Erotics of Culture* (Boston, 1996), pp. 16–20.
32. C. Walker Bynum, *Holy Feast and Holy Fast: The Religious Significance of Food to Medieval Women* (Berkeley, CA, 1987); T.C. McCaskie, *State and Society in Pre-Colonial Asante*, p. 20. Similarly L. Abu-Lughod has explored the complexities and subtleties of female cultural agency in a male-honour-dominated society of Bedouin Egypt, in *Veiled Sentiments: Honour and Poetry in Bedouin Society* (Berkeley, CA, 1986, 2nd edn 1999).
33. For a discussion of these processes see K. Barber, *The Anthropology of Texts, Persons and Publics* (Cambridge, 2007).
34. I use here the language of J.C. Scott, *Domination and the Arts of Resistance: Hidden Transcripts* (London, 1990), as a suggestive analogy.
35. M.E. Wiesner-Hanks concurs: 'too much world history does not involve gender, and too much women's and gender history focuses on the United States' in 'World history and the history of women, gender and sexuality', *Journal of World History*, 18 (2007), 53–67, on 56.
36. M.E. Wiesner-Hanks, *Gender in History* (Oxford, 2001), p. 18.
37. P.N. Stearns, *Gender in World History* (London, 2000).
38. Another great encounter of the period that has not been discussed is, of course, that of the Mongols in China, and I am grateful to M.E. Wiesner-Hanks for sending me a copy of her recent unpublished paper on the subject.
39. Though he makes the points that gender systems do more than articulate asymmetrical relationships between men and women and that world religions have their own contradictions and local variations on the ground, nevertheless he sees them as consistent enough to bear use as units representing packages of assumptions about the sexual division of gender roles.
40. The idea owes something to Karen Sacks's feminist Marxist history of the 1970s, which traces the stages by which women were increasingly marginalised from relations of production in feudal societies and isolated in domestic roles that denied them full adult status. K. Sacks, *Sisters and Wives: the Past and Future of Sexual Equality* (London, 1979).
41. For example, the authoritative gender claims of world religions used by Stearns in defining social systems should not be regarded as having simply reflected social realities, as if all that Buddhism had to offer women was the meditative resources to endure foot-binding: P.N. Stearns, *Gender in World History* (London, 2000), p. 41.
42. See F. Fukuyama, *The End of History and the Last Man* (London, 1993); E.L. Jones, *The European Miracle Environments, Economies and Geopolitics in the History of Europe and Asia* (Cambridge, 1981, 3rd edn 2003), J.A. Hall, *Powers and Liberties: The Causes and Consequences of the Rise of the West* (London, 1985), p. 83, for blocking factors in pre-colonial India; and S.P. Huntingdon, *The Clash of Civilizations: And the Remaking of the World Order* (London, 2002). To be fair, parochiality, albeit without the triumphalism, is written into the social science approaches of the liberal left as well, though the left has done more to eradicate it from its interpretive assumptions. See C. Wickham, 'Memories of Underdevelopment: What has Marxism done for medieval history, and what can it still do?', in Wickham (ed.), *Marxist History Writing*, pp. 32–49.
43. The tunnel vision produced by this Eurocentric world historical teleology is a central theme of J. Goody, *The Theft of History* (Cambridge, 2005).

44. To modify a phrase from M. Hughes-Warrington, 'World histories', in *Palgrave Advances in World Histories*, pp. 1–17.
45. The phrase was coined by K. Pomeranz, *The Great Divergence: China, Europe and the Making of the Modern World Economy* (Princeton, NJ, 2000), whose thesis I have grossly simplified here.
46. P. Parsatharathi, 'Review article: the great divergence', *Past & Present* 176 (2002), 275–93, for a useful review of Pomeranz. For related work, see R. Bin Wong, *China Transformed: Historical Change and the Limits of European Experience* (New York, NY, 1997), and A.G. Frank, *ReOrient: Global Economy in the Asian Age* (Berkeley, CA, 1998). I would like to thank Kenneth Pomeranz for sending me his recently unpublished paper comparing frontier masculinities in North America and China.
47. Among its founders might be counted E. Wolf, *Europe and the People Without History* (Berkeley, CA, 1982), R. Guha, *Elementary Aspects of Peasant Insurgency in Colonial India* (Delhi, 1983), and M. Sahlins, *How Natives Think: About Captain Cook for Example* (Chicago, IL, 1995).
48. D. Chakrabarty, *Provincializing Europe: Postcolonial Thought and Historical Difference* (Princeton, NJ, 2000).
49. Ibid., p. 8.
50. Indeed, M. Sahlins points out in 'On the anthropology of modernity, or, some triumphs of culture over despondency theory', in A. Hooper (ed.), *Culture and Sustainable Development in the Pacific* (Canberra, 2000), pp. 44–61, the sense in which Europe could be seen as the odd one out in that its transition to modernity was not a hybridising third-wave response to colonialism, as it was almost everywhere else.
51. An illustration of this is the Marxist concept of 'pre-political peasant consciousness' coined to designate forms of peasant activism such as magic and recourse to supernatural agency that appear to precede a true peasant awareness of 'the political' necessarily required of a fully realised capitalist formation. In these terms, an element of the 'third-wave infectiousness' of the so-called pre-political peasant might be seen in colonial construction of the Indian holy man, the *sadhu*, who at certain moments mutated in British colonial perceptions from an object of rational derision into a terrific icon of political insurrection. My thanks go to Kim Wagner for drawing my attention to the 'paranoid colonial style', on which he is currently preparing a monograph.
52. It also speaks to the appeal made by Bill Jordan (and echoed by Judith Bennett in the same edited collection) on behalf of cooperation and coexistence between historians of medieval Europe and people of colour in US higher education, for which see 'Saving medieval history; or, the new crusade' in J. van Engen (ed.), *The Past and Future of Medieval Studies* (London, 1994), pp. 259–72 and J.M. Bennett, 'Our Colleagues, Ourselves', ibid., pp. 245–58.
53. As Timothy Reuter has concluded in the case of one particular period, 'medieval, both because of its origins and because it is often used as a purely descriptive or conventional term, will not give much help to historians in a globalized world looking for insight through comparison'. T. Reuter, 'Medieval: another tyrannous construct', in J.L. Nelson (ed.), *Medieval Polities and Modern Mentalities* (Cambridge, 2006), p. 37.
54. The celebrated and controversial indictment of historians on this count was, of course, E. Said, *Orientalism* (London, 1978).
55. R.W. Connell, 'The big picture: masculinities in recent world history', *Theory and Society* 22 (1993), 606–10, on 606.

56. K. Pomeranz, 'Social history and world history: from daily life to patterns of change', *Journal of World History* 18 (2007), 85. Chris Fletcher, in the present book, makes a strong case for the methodological priority of cultural ahead of social structural categories in the proper historical comparison of past masculinities. See also R.I. Moore, 'World history', in M. Bentley (ed.), *Companion to Historiography* (London, 1998), p. 954; and, for a thorough discussion, A. Dirlik, 'Reflections on eurocentrism', in E. Fuchs and B. Stuchtey (eds), *Across Cultural Borders: Historiography in Global Perspective* (Oxford, 2002), pp. 247–84. And, for more on 'emic' and 'etic' categories, see Jansen in this volume.
57. In fact, in their reuse of the Gramscian terms 'hegemony' and 'subaltern', they reveal a common intellectual lineage.
58. C. Hall, 'Marxism and its others', in Wickham (ed.), *Marxist History Writing*, p. 139.
59. C.A. Bayly, *The Birth of the Modern* (Oxford, 2004), p. 12. These include 'bodily practices', such as dress, timekeeping, food, naming practices and sport.
60. Idem, '"Archaic" and "modern" globalization in the Eurasian and African arena, c.1750–1850', in A.G. Hopkins (ed.), *Globalization in World History* (London, 2002), pp. 47–73.
61. V. Lieberman, *Strange Parallels: Volume 2, Mainland Mirrors: Europe, Japan, China, South Asia, and the Islands: South East Asia in Global Context, c.800–1830* (Cambridge, 2009), has recently noted parallels between this land-based predation of the settled by the nomadic and European sea-based intervention in south and south-east Asia from the seventeenth century.
62. See J. McNamara, 'The *Herrenfrage*: the restructuring of the gender system, 1050–1150', in *Medieval Masculinities: Regarding Men in the Middle Ages* (Minneapolis, 1994), pp. 3–29; R.N. Swanson, 'Angels incarnate: clergy and masculinity from Gregorian reform to reformation', in *Masculinity in Medieval Europe* (London, 1999), pp. 160–77; and K. Cushing, *Reform and the Papacy in the Eleventh Century: Spirituality and Social Change* (Manchester, 2005).
63. K. Cooper and C. Leyser, 'The gender of grace: impotence, servitude, and manliness in the fifth-century', in P. Stafford and Anneke B. Mulder-Bakker (eds), *Gendering the Middle Ages* (Oxford, 2001), pp. 6–21.
64. Ibid., p. 13.
65. Priests were to be free of local family control, and to mediate between families disputing over land. Their neutrality was to be guaranteed by their celibacy. R.I. Moore, 'Family, community and cult on the eve of the Gregorian reform', *Transactions of the Royal Historical Society*, 5th Ser., 30 (1980), 49–69.
66. The crux of the matter turns on the subject of marriage and the family as represented simultaneously as a path along which male authority progressed and as a site of rhetorical ambush where the failings of 'suboptimal' men lay vulnerable to exposure, for which see C. Leyser, 'Custom, truth and gender in eleventh-century reform', in R.N. Swanson (ed.), *Studies in Church History 34: Gender and Christian Religion* (Woodbridge, 1998), pp. 75–91.
67. See Guy Halsall, 'Gender and the end of empire', *Journal of Medieval and Early Modern Studies* 34 (2004), 17–39, for an important discussion of the implications for female agency of imagined and real women in late antique high politics.
68. See M.C. Miller, 'Masculinity, reform, and clerical culture: narratives of episcopal holiness in the Gregorian era', *Church History* 72 (2003), 25–52.
69. Swanson, 'Angels incarnate'.
70. R.I. Moore, *The Formation of a Persecuting Society* (Oxford, 1987).

71. Idem, 'The eleventh century in Eurasian history: a comparative approach to the convergence and divergence of medieval civilizations', *Journal of Medieval and Early Modern History* 33 (2003), 1–19.
72. See E. Gellner, 'Flux and reflux in the faith of men', in *Muslim Society* (Cambridge, 1981), pp. 1–85, for his full thesis.
73. B. Bossler, 'Gender and empire: a view from Yuan China', *Journal of Medieval and Early Modern History* 34 (2004), 197–223.

# 8
# Hegemonic Masculinities? Assessing Change and Processes of Change in Elite Masculinity, 1700–1900

*Henry French and Mark Rothery*

Over the last 20 years, a consensus has emerged that historical changes in the gender identity of elite men can be conceptualised best as a series of shifts between forms of 'hegemonic masculinities'. These 'hegemonic' forms have included: 'anxious, patriarchal, godly masculinity' (mid-seventeenth century); 'libertine' or 'foppish' masculinity (the late seventeenth century); 'polite' or 'civil' masculinity (c. 1720–1780); 'sincere', 'serious' or 'evangelical' masculinity (emerging from c. 1790); with the final nineteenth-century displacement of landed gentility by 'middle-class' notions of masculinity based around an ideology of domesticity.[1] R.W. Connell, who first advocated this approach, stressed that the cultural dominance of these norms dictated responses to them, generating subgroups who can be categorised as 'complicit', 'subordinate' or 'marginal' to the 'hegemonic' form.[2] Connell also provided a schematic analysis of the evolution of hegemonic masculinities, by highlighting four developments in the last 500 years which have helped create the 'modern gender order'.[3]

The first of these was the effects of Reformation and Renaissance on 'understandings of sexuality and personhood in metropolitan Europe'.[4] Connell asserts that this instituted a 'slow, contested, but decisive decline' in the intellectual and normative power of religion, the victory of 'marital heterosexuality' over 'monastic denial' as the 'most honoured form of sexuality', and the growing association of masculinity with individualised notions of 'reason' – of 'man' (*as* man) as rational animal.[5] The second development was the growth of European empires, as overtly masculine endeavours, conducted by men, spreading 'male' values of reason and action, through violence, and generating new 'masculine exemplars' in the process.[6] Connell's third development is the growth of cities, particularly mercantile centres such as Antwerp, Amsterdam and London, and the transformation of religious individualism into secular, 'calculative rationality' in ways suggested by Weber's 'Protestant ethic'.[7] In addition, these new cities were also sites for the growth of new sexual subcultures, as evinced by London 'Molly' houses.[8] Finally, Connell highlights the sixteenth, seventeenth and eighteenth centuries as a time of internal civil strife and dynastic foreign wars. While such conflicts threw up millenarian and utopian challenges to the existing social and gender order, Connell suggests that their most enduring effect was the creation of the increasingly centralised 'fiscal–military' state, which 'provided a larger-scale institutionalization of men's power than had ever been possible before'.[9] This power was embodied (and wielded in practice) by 'the class of hereditary landowners, the gentry, who dominated the North Atlantic world of the eighteenth century'.[10] It created a gender archetype that was 'emphatic and violent', reliant on the honour code, 'violent discipline' meted out to the 'agricultural workforce', and 'licence in sexual relationships'.[11]

This 'gentry' dispensation was gradually superseded by the norms, ethics and exemplars of 'men of the bourgeoisie', as these values were enmeshed within the 'spread of industrial economies and the growth of bureaucratic states', 'and the political power of the landowning gentry declined'.[12] However, older notions of the violent honour code remained, particularly in Germany, and 'now combined with rationality ... [and] bureaucratic techniques of organisation and constant technological advance', to produce the large-scale exploitation of late imperialism, world wars and ultimately state-organised genocide and fascism, the 'naked reassertion of male supremacy in societies that had been moving towards equality for women'.[13]

Connell's brief historical sketch of long-term change accounts for only a few pages in a book whose primary purpose is to offer a forensic sociological analysis of masculine identities in modern society. Even so, it is significant, first because Connell has stressed the 'historicity' of hegemonic forms of male identity, and second because this broadly developmental 'modernisation' thesis has attained wider currency among gender historians.[14] Indeed, as long ago as 1999 Jeremy Gregory observed that some historians were echoing Connell's template of transitions involving secularisation and urban subcultures.[15] He noted that change over time in masculine norms between the mid-seventeenth and mid-eighteenth centuries was already beginning to be depicted as a series of step-changes, from 'the "godly man" of Stuart England', who was succeeded in turn by 'the "polite man", the "sentimental man" or the "sexual man" of the Hanoverian period'.[16] However, he warned that this periodisation was in danger of forcing 'studies of manliness to ape the increasingly outmoded characterisations of more traditional political and social history'.[17]

Gregory is not alone in his concerns. A number of scholars have begun to question the explanatory effectiveness of these broad hegemonic shifts and have, instead, emphasised the importance of everyday experience within particular social settings, and the possible continuities in male gender norms.[18]

Even in the mid-1990s, John Tosh argued that masculinity should be analysed as 'a set of cultural attributes' in order to 'consider masculinity as a social status, demonstrated in specific social contexts'.[19] This concern with context was echoed by articles on masculinity in the *Journal of British Studies* in 2005, in which a number of leading historians identified several underlying methodological and conceptual problems.[20] Viewing developments in a broader timescale, Shepard and Harvey, in particular, argued that methodological differences in approaches to the medieval, early modern and modern periods probably accounted for much of the identification of different hegemonic masculinities across time, and (in part) for the tendency to depict change as a series of profound normative shifts. They suggested that these issues needed to be addressed by dealing 'not just in free-floating cultural attributes, but in grounded social or psychic contexts of experience that interact with representations'.[21]

Indeed, Alex Shepard and Elizabeth Foyster have done much to illustrate how such variations could occur even *within* a single lifespan. They have shown how different social positions and life-cycle stages affected the ability of men to realise 'appropriate' male values (particularly those associated with 'patriarchal' power) in the sixteenth and seventeenth centuries.[22] Their work has suggested that these norms could be tailored for particular points in the life cycle or social circumstances, indicated, for example, by the fact that youthful (sexual or alcoholic) 'excess' was tolerated, while such behaviour was deemed incompatible with the responsibilities of mature, male 'householders'.[23] Similarly, in relation to eighteenth-century values of 'politeness', there has been relatively little exploration of the implications for male identity of the kinds of variation found in Paul Langford's discussion of the 'social geography' of 'politeness' in eighteenth-century London.[24] Here, the discourses of 'politeness' had several different social and spatial layers. Historians of 'polite' male identity in the eighteenth century have still to come to terms with Langford's observation that 'what was polite in Berkeley Square was not necessarily what was polite in Finsbury or Hammersmith, let alone in Shadwell or Wapping.'[25] The spatial variation implicit in such findings tends not to disrupt the focus of existing studies (particularly of the 'long' eighteenth century), which has been to reconstruct general templates or tropes of masculinity based on conduct literature, or to contrast such unified 'hegemony' with 'subordinate' sexual subcultures.[26]

In addition, the emphasis on historical step-changes and different forms of 'hegemonic masculinities' is increasingly at odds with the chronology of change sketched out in women's history. Here, there has been considerable acceptance of Vickery's critique of the 'separate spheres' interpretation, and its questioning of the growing separation between public men and private, domestic, women between the seventeenth and nineteenth centuries.[27] Women's history has also generated powerful criticisms of linear models of change in gender relations, notably Judith M. Bennett's concept of a long-term 'patriarchal equilibrium'.[28] These interpretative developments have emphasised the degree to which the history of masculinity is still predicated on the assumption that, because men were 'public agents', the chronologies of economic, social and political 'modernisation' somehow guided their formative experiences and values. As Judith Allen has noted, in part this reflects the fact that the 'histories of femininity and masculinity...are at very different stages of development', with women's history emerging much earlier, and developing a wider range of innovative methodologies and research techniques for reconstructing past gender practices as well as gender prescriptions.[29] Even so, this contrast has thrown light on some of the rather 'Whiggish' assumptions that underlie such notions of change, such as the connections between the growth of 'individualism', 'industrial capitalism' and the 'imperial state', particularly in the eighteenth and nineteenth centuries. In the British context, these assumptions have been most notable in the emphasis given to a shift from the hegemony of elite sensibility to that of middle-class 'self-control' in the early nineteenth century, whose timing has been linked to the conventional narratives of industrialisation, urbanisation and the 'rise of the middle classes'.[30]

In the light of these interpretative difficulties, this chapter will provide a critical evaluation of the way in which the theory of shifting hegemonic masculinities has been formulated and interpreted. We argue that Connell and other scholars working with this theory have conflated transient and changeable social *stereotypes* with aspects of deep-seated and enduring forms of *hegemony*, which may be better understood through Bourdieu's idea of *habitus* – that is, 'the dispositions durably inculcated by the possibilities and impossibilities, freedoms and necessities, opportunities and prohibitions inscribed in the objective conditions',[31] or perhaps, less elliptically, 'his brand name for the difficulty of deciding how much of what one does is one's own and how much the culture's'.[32] The effect of this has been to exaggerate the pace and degree of change in fundamental norms of masculine behaviour and attitude. Instead, we suggest that these deep-seated norms were to be found beneath changeable stereotypes such as the 'Fop', the 'Polite Gentleman' or the 'sentimental man', located within the perennial building blocks of male self-valorisation such as 'virtue', 'honour', 'self-control', 'independence', 'character' or 'gentlemanliness', and their interaction with the enduring normative ideals of female conduct.[33] The subsequent section posits this reformulated theory within a body of empirical evidence drawn from the correspondence of several landed gentry families written between the late seventeenth and the early twentieth centuries. The discussion focuses on the way in which stereotypes were interpreted by gentry men and the meaning of stereotypes in the construction of their masculine identities. The resulting picture is one that places more emphasis on continuities in masculinity than on change, bringing the field closer to other areas of gender history and broader approaches to social, economic and political change in British society.

## I. Theory

Our interpretative problem is not with the concept of hegemony *per se* in relation to gender history, but with the scope and importance attributed to it. First, we are concerned about the underlying teleology inherent in Connell's attempt to 'historicise' masculinity, which depicts a series of 'evolutionary' steps for male identity (and, consequently gender relations) broadly in line with a weak 'modernisation' theory of European history over the last 500 years.[34] Second, we feel that the concept of hegemonic masculinities gathers together social processes that are better understood, and may have greater interpretative value, if considered separately.

We agree that it is possible to identify an underlying and enduring patriarchal 'system' between the seventeenth and twentieth centuries. In this system moral and scientific beliefs, institutions, laws, commentaries, customs, education and inheritance practices entrenched male power, and construed women as 'second-class citizens'. This normative, institutionalised pattern of discrimination had all the hallmarks of a hegemonic system in its Gramscian sense, or in the sense of Bourdieu's *habitus*. It provided a value system that acted both consciously and unconsciously to shape gender relations by constraining and skewing the limits of the 'possible' within society. These limits were internalised, and became 'common sense' knowledge, creating a self-sustaining social 'reality' of male 'enfranchisement' and female subordination that was enduring and extremely difficult to shift.

Even so, we would also argue that this fundamental social 'fact' in society between c. 1500 and c. 1950 is not the same thing, and not the same kind of phenomenon, or causal feature, as is implied by Connell's shifting 'hegemonic masculinities'. For Connell, these hegemonic forms are embodied as much in the 'culturally idealised form of masculine character' that predominates in a particular period as in the actual behaviour of any socially or culturally dominant group.[35] However, this seems to equate the underlying hegemonic patriarchal distribution of power and authority in society between men and women, or between different types of men or women, with what might be regarded as the less rigid, less constraining societal *stereotypes* about appropriate male and female behaviour that prevailed in particular eras. As suggested above, these might have changed over time, and might have been more socially specific and geographically variable than is allowed for by Connell's original notion of hegemony.

In a recent article, however, Connell and Messerschmidt have recalibrated hegemony theory to suggest that dominant codes of masculinity *could* vary at the local, national and global levels.[36] Even so, in this theory the dominant mode of hegemonic masculinity still parcels together normative principles, socially sanctioned ways of behaving, and day-to-day value systems into an all-encompassing gender ideal. This requires it to bear a heavy interpretative burden, and implies that the relationship between these elements can be established relatively easily, after the initial ideal has been detected as a cultural product.

When applied to the past, there is the danger that Jeremy Gregory's fears might be realised, with different 'types' of men being distinguished via simple equations between leading cultural tropes and 'hegemonic masculinities'. As a consequence, in our research we have sought to reconsider the concept of hegemony, in order to try to separate out deeper principles, fashionable norms and immediate diagnostic responses, and (therefore) to try to obtain a fuller impression of *how* elite gender identities persisted by reconciling enduring attitudes with short-term cultural shifts.

We can begin to distinguish a number of layers of causal significance in elite male identities in this period by reference to a famous analogy from the work of Fernand Braudel. This equates three layers of causal significance, and historical time frames, with three oceanic levels.[37] At the bottom, in the deep layer, we have *habitus*-type understandings of patriarchal dominance. These ideas exerted considerable force by being embedded within early modern and modern value systems, and acted in truly hegemonic fashion in two respects. First, they marked the genuine limits of the possible in relation to the gender identities of most of the people, most of the time. Second, they were internalised within individuals and suffused throughout social, political and economic institutions, so as to appear simply as common sense knowledge of 'how the world worked'.

In this way, they became exactly like Bourdieu's *habitus*, and were as constraining and slow-moving as he suggests, precisely because their explanatory monopoly was such that it was extremely difficult for men and women to conceive of a different distribution of power from *within* this system. A general example of this might be the different, asymmetrical conceptions of male and female 'honour', particularly the different weight given to sexual reputation for men and women.[38] More specifically, it is also evident that for the social elite – the subject of this chapter – the notion of 'gentlemanliness' was also internalised as a powerful behavioural norm that encoded general masculine ideals of honour, authority and autonomy in particular ways. However, it may not have impinged as a governing ideal for *all* men in the period.[39] Whatever their social reach, though, such norms changed *very* slowly, with little alteration in the fundamentally 'patriarchal' dispensation of gender power between the sixteenth and the mid-nineteenth centuries.

Above this deep zone we have the Braudellian layer of *conjuncture* – that is, the level at which such profound ordering principles interacted with societal norms, political rhetoric, moral knowledge, economic circumstance and discourses of custom, identity and fashion. Here we observe the formation, projection, negotiation and evolution of those gender stereotypes that Connell posits as hegemonic. We might think of these in terms of the well-known historiographical stalwarts 'patriarchal seventeenth-century men', 'polite, civilised eighteenth-century men' and 'sincere, muscular Christian or domestic nineteenth-century men', although in practice each was subject to considerable internal variation. Stereotypes such as these articulated, channelled and applied deeper masculine notions of honour, virtue, courage and autonomy into normative codes that helped individuals to understand and respond to the surface-layer *événements* of daily life. This was a two-way process – life could also shift values, individually and (to some extent) collectively. An example of this might be Colley's stress on the growing emphasis on martial conceptions of honour among the British ruling elite as a result of European wars in the later eighteenth and early nineteenth centuries.[40] Here, events created new trends and fashions, these shaped normative social stereotypes, and these in turn reconfigured the building blocks of the deeper value set – but without necessarily creating a new *hegemonic* form of masculinity. As is emphasised below, these stereotypes appear more often to have been invoked in relation to social or normative *boundaries*, so as to define, comprehend and respond to 'others', than to provide elaborate or well-articulated models of behaviour to be applied in daily life.

## II. Practices

The remainder of this chapter traces the relationships between these different elements or levels of male identity through several detailed examples drawn from a series of landed families in England in the eighteenth and nineteenth centuries. These form part of the research for an Arts and Humanities Research Council-funded research project into elite masculinity in England, 1660–1918, based on a variety of case studies abstracted from the correspondence of 15 gentry families in this period.[41] The current paper is drawn from the most relevant material in a database of just over 2,500 entries about masculine norms found in family letters and diaries. These letters are often very revealing, but are obviously problematic as evidence of values and practices. They contain a number of structural biases in favour of positive, ongoing relationships as opposed to negative, difficult ones. This material is also entirely subjective, because it represents a 'constructed' account between correspondents, reflecting only the material that the writer chose to relay to the recipient, written in ways that may be sufficiently allusive as to appear vague or inconclusive to a modern observer. So, although this evidence provides a different body of source material for the study of masculinity compared with conduct literature or legal records, it does not (in and of itself) offer insights that are any more 'direct' or 'unproblematic' or any less 'subjective' than these other types of sources. In this respect, we remain prisoners of the subjectivities of our correspondents, but these allow us to attempt to understand *why* these selections and constructions were made, and *why* we only ever get to see part of the picture.

The Windham family of Felbrigg Hall, Norfolk provides a good starting point to chart the interaction between these different elements of male identity. The family had been prosperous landowners in the north of the county since the fifteenth century, and by the second quarter of the eighteenth were moving confidently between local and national power bases, following the lead of their more illustrious neighbour Sir Robert Walpole.[42] This concern with power and authority was reflected in the education provided by Ashe Windham (1673–1749) for his only son William (1717–1761).[43] William was educated at Felbrigg by a private tutor, his second cousin Benjamin Stillingfleet. Eventually, in 1737 William set out for Geneva to complete his education, but before he departed Stillingfleet wrote him a long, didactic letter of advice that reviewed the principles of his upbringing, and enjoined lessons for his future conduct.[44] This text eventually found its way into print as an advice book in 1811, and illustrates many of the base-level values that the tutor had attempted to instil into his charge. Most of Stillingfleet's advice was concerned to point out the dangers of following religious 'Freethinkers', Deists who scoffed at the Church of England.[45] However, he also devoted attention to 'our duty as social beings'.[46] Here, his message emphasised duties above freedom, particularly the constant obligation to consider 'the happiness of others'.[47] This responsibility emanated directly from Windham's wealth, which was 'too large to be spent on yourself alone', and which conferred the obligations to rule and set an example: 'it will not be sufficient that you be regular yourself, unless you also take care to keep your family in order.'[48] Stillingfleet echoed Sir Robert Filmer's patriarchalism, stating that 'every man ought to look to himself as a law-giver in his own house,' but with the Lockean qualifier that such a ruler should:

> think himself as much accountable for his government, as a king in his kingdom … he who is willing to keep up … the privilege of an Englishman to inquire into the management of his superiors, ought to be sure he acts up to his duty in the same way.[49]

Indeed, Stillingfleet emphasised male roles and responsibilities in personal and household government as a *patriotic* duty. 'A vicious husband, an imperious master, a cruel father, an undutiful child, an unmerciful landlord, a quarrelsome neighbour, a debaucher of women & c. cannot be a patriot.'[50] While he advised Windham that most of these negative tendencies could be kept in check by the simple desire to preserve 'the ordinary honour of a gentleman', the danger of sexual incontinence was more serious, 'because custom has almost turned it into an occasion of boast rather than of shame'.[51] Stillingfleet's view was that among men 'unwarrantable freedom before marriage' would 'be the source of much unhappiness after'.[52] As a consequence, he then tailored his advice to Windham 'as an individual', and stressed the importance of establishing a moral regimen:

> The best thing, therefore, to be done is to mark out a plan by which to conduct yourself steadily. In all other affairs, we look on the man as mad who hopes to bring about any end without suiting all the means to it.[53]

This self-government was to be managed through appropriate intellectual pursuits and recreations, particularly 'a relish of country life' instead of a penchant for 'gamesters, dancing-masters, fiddlers, French tailors, and Italian singers'.[54] In particular, he warned Windham to avoid 'a mistake too frequently prevailing with young people, that their studies are finished...', whereas in fact 'it is impossible that they should be much more than begun'.[55] Such studies were essential, because 'if we have not acquired the knowledge of ourselves... if we are not able to make ourselves, and others good and happy... if we remain peevish, impertinent, proud, revengeful, inconstant, lustful, covetous', then they amounted only to knowledge without wisdom.[56]

Stillingfleet's injunctions towards an explicitly Christian understanding of virtue, through personal self-control, familial regulation and public behaviour, were largely conventional. To some extent, they reflect the sheer weight of expectation placed on the shoulders of William (II) as a sole heir, and the focus of all the hopes of his father, family and friends. In this sense they were unrealisable, and may have been intended as a valedictory rhetorical exercise by a retiring tutor, rather than a practical advice manual. However, although Stillingfleet emphasises conventional behavioural self-restraint, this is not 'polite' dissimulation, or 'a vicious coolness or indifference for [to] the good of mankind', but merely the self-control necessary to enable the exercise of authority over others.[57] Therefore, virtue had to come from within, and had, constantly, to be cultivated. It was not a veneer that could simply be laid on top of an inherited social status.

How did Windham translate these ideals into practice away from home? His surviving correspondence consists of a series of dutiful letters to his father, about the history and government of Geneva, and his mountaineering near Mont Blanc.[58] Although these reflect the ways in which William attempted to put his tutor's injunctions to an active, intellectual, public-spirited life into practice, they reveal less about William's opinions. However, while in Geneva he made lifelong friends with a small group of English travellers and students, who put on amateur dramatic and musical events, enthused over Italian opera and old books, and who named themselves 'The Bloods'.[59] The group maintained a long, frequently facetious correspondence into the 1740s, which reveals much more about how these fundamental values were applied to produce (often stinging) judgements about male identity.

Perhaps unsurprisingly, this peer group of young men reinforced their own shared values not by articulating them positively, but by satirising their transgression. In particular, they directed much of their scorn towards their fellow English travellers, particularly the young Berkshire squire Richard Aldworth ('Dicky, commonly called The Berkshire Boy') and the wealthy Devon baronet Sir Bourchier Wrey, known to them as 'Sir Butcher Trey'.[60] Aldworth was satirised for his youth and his lack of worldly wisdom.[61] The 'History' emphasised his dependent, infantilising relationship with his grandmother: 'Dicky had always been a dutifull Child; He would sit whole hours together to hear his Grandmother's Stories or read to Her Pilgrim's Progress.' It also mocked the strictures of his religious upbringing. On learning of his plans to travel in Europe, the 'History' alleges that his elderly relative reminded him that he would 'have no Grandmother there, Dicky, to hear thee say every Sunday Thy Catechism, the Lord's Prayer, the Belief & ten Commandments. Thou wilt be ruined Body & Soul; Thou wilt become a Heathen & I shall die for Grief.' The ridicule then shifted to his preparations for travel. His gaudy, old-fashioned clothes were said to have been made out of his grandmother's chairs, with his waistcoat being made out of her petticoat. His sheltered upbringing was mocked by the depiction of his tearful farewell to his childhood sweetheart, 'Peggy Cinders his Grandmother's Scullion-maid', and his fear and seasickness when crossing the Channel. On arrival in France, his learning was questioned, in the account of how his ignorance of French led to an angry tirade, in which he paraded his very thin stock of learning, 'Locke, Sir Is. Newton, Sir Robert Walpole's Speeches in the House of Commons & the History of the Highwaymen which he laid great stress upon'. Finally, after recounting his attempts to assert his dignity over the French by a pompous description of his family lineage, back to Brian Boroun, king of Ireland, and Cadwallader, king of Wales, the 'History' ended with a childlike letter from Dicky to his 'Honoured Grandmamma', complaining about France, where 'the Foolish Dogs here can't yet talk English'.

Aldworth was satirised for his youth, arrogance, ignorance, cowardice and stupidity. He was depicted as an overgrown schoolboy, too immature, inexperienced and guileless to perform the role of cultivated, cosmopolitan young gentleman to which he aspired. These contradictions between ambitions and reality also formed the basis of 'The Bloods'' comedic description of Bourchier Wrey. Wrey was always depicted as a larger-than-life character, who constantly overstepped the bounds of virtuous modesty, self-control, honour and courage. In 1741 Windham's friend Thomas Dampier reported that Wrey was in Leyden, where 'he gave Himself out for a Person of 20,000 pds. a year.' Here, he 'talked continually of the Plantagenet family...of his being the Chief Man...in seven Counties of England; and of an indisputable Right...to the Crown of England'.[62] Sadly, these boasts were undermined by the arrival of his brother, described as looking like 'a Piece of Cheese with a dirty Shirt on', 'a Country-foolish Looby, without Decency or Modesty...never did there spring from Plantagenet Stock a more unpromiseing Lout'.[63] Dampier added that he could write much more of Wrey's private boasts, 'how he vaunted to the Counts, that he...would accept of a Regiment of horse...would willingly have passed off a pair of Stone Buckles for Diamond ones...has the Name only of the Great hog in Leyden...how all the Inn-keepers from Amsterdam to Rotterdam are better acquainted with his History than you are...How every one speaking of Him concludes with the well-known Proverb, That Lyars ought to have good memories'.[64]

Obviously, for 'The Bloods' Wrey was the butt of all their jokes, a preposterous fantasist who subverted all his claims to high honours by his thoroughly disreputable behaviour. Dampier's satirical 'Short History of that wonderfull Knight' found humour both in being an *accurate* record of the doings of a compulsive liar and in pointing out all the ways in which Wrey subverted the gentlemanly imperative of 'truth-telling' by being a man whose word was worth nothing.[65] His behaviour, and that of Aldworth, was represented among the group as a complete deviation from Stillingfleet's advice to his pupil about the importance of honourable dealing, self-command and (above all) self-knowledge. In this respect, Wrey and Aldworth functioned as behavioural 'others' for 'The Bloods'. They represented the antithesis of their (otherwise implicit) social and gender values, and were moulded into negative behavioural templates or stereotypes who served to reinforce their own group ideals. These stereotypes were, to some extent, coercive. They reveal the group's anxieties about being regarded as callow, boastful young men away from home for the first time, and show how ridicule was used to police the boundaries of acceptable behaviour, and translate deeper values into *conjunctural* moral codes. This peer pressure also allowed the group to put their own 'cultural' inflections on conventional masculine values of 'honour', 'imagination' and 'knowledge', and also to perpetuate them. Significantly, perhaps, Dampier went on to become a master at Eton, tutor to William Windham (III), and one of his guardians after the death of William (II) in 1761.

Of course, 'othering' of this kind could occur within families, as well as between them. It could involve perceptions of a generational shift in values and identity, articulated by men in early adulthood as a reaction to 'family traditions' often embodied by their fathers. Once again, the identification of difference could be a means of fashioning the self, and particularly of asserting an independent manly identity. A good example of this is provided by the struggles in the Acland family of Killerton, Devon, at the end of our period in the late nineteenth century. In the case of Arthur Acland, the second son of Sir Thomas Dyke Acland Bt of Killerton, Devon, his growing autonomy as a student at Oxford in the late nineteenth century, and his adoption of 'radical' political and religious opinions, increasingly forced him to define himself in opposition to the values of his family, and particularly those of his father.

The catalyst for Arthur's rebellion was a family rift over his future career. He had been intended for the church from an early age, and as a child he had delivered sermons to his family in his nightgown.[66] Rugby school had been chosen for him due to the guiding moral influence of Sir Frederick Temple, the Headmaster and a friend of the family. True to his family's expectations, Arthur took up minor orders as a Deacon of the Church of England in 1872. However, very soon after this he began to have doubts about his suitability and ambition for the Church. He adopted delaying tactics with his parents throughout the 1870s, during which he served in various teaching posts in Oxford. For Arthur, as for so many other young gentry men, University was a refuge from his family and from 'the family way'. As he noted in his journal in 1872, 'University is a time for giving men a chance of seeing things for themselves and looking to the roots of things', away from the influence of family expectations.[67]

These differences had not been apparent earlier in his training as a clergyman. Like his father and his grandfather, Arthur had relied on religious principles and practices for important aspects of his masculine identity, particularly his sense of self-control and hard work. Under the heading of 'Divine Guidance of Secular Affairs' he mused in his journal over the influence of religion:

> may we never pray for protection in body and soul but mainly for body as guided by the mind – presence of mind – foresight – self control etc. all which will influence the actions of the body enormously... Object of religion is conduct... It extends to at least ¾ of Human life.[68]

Arthur used his journal for 'self-fashioning', in order to analyse and regulate his behaviour and provide a means of knowing himself and shaping his identity. Such self-management was expressed and enacted through religion. For example, he regularly noted the length of time he had spent in prayer, particularly compline prayer.[69] However, as Arthur's doubts over his chosen profession grew, his sense of self began to be defined less by religion, as more secular value systems and beliefs were imprinted onto his masculine identity. In 1875 he posed himself a rhetorical question 'How does Christianity influence men – it keeps them quiet – is that all?'[70]

Arthur explained his decision to leave the Church to his family as theological in nature, insisting he could not in good faith sign the thirty-nine articles.[71] His journal, however, records other reasons for his decision leading up to the final act in 1879, reasons mainly hidden from his family, although suspected by his father. He had come to believe that the Church as an institution was too reactionary socially and too ineffective politically to achieve the progress he desired. The clergy were 'massed together in advanced public opinion as unwise and retrograde' whereas 'in education etc. there is really very much to be done, and in moral teaching and in example – and daily self-denial for and courtesy to others.'[72] Arthur experienced 'a painful consciousness much too sensitive that people were out of harmony with the clergy' and some embarrassment about the equivocal gender status of clergymen, observing that 'the ordinary man half despised the parson and thought him womanish.'[73] This realisation was compounded by a yearning for independence, through an identity of his own distinguished from that of his family by the adoption of an alternative (and in his mind radical) set of values and prerogatives. He rejected the clerical profession in part because it reflected his parents' wishes and the 'Acland tradition'[74], the force of which Arthur later estimated as 'tremendous'.[75]

After his announcement of his intentions to leave the Church, Arthur's father attempted to control the situation by recommending certain role models for alternative advice to counteract the influence of what he perceived to be subversive elements at Oxford.[76] In particular, he referred Arthur to Frederick Temple, his former headmaster at Rugby, as well as his uncle Leopold, the vicar of the family, living at Broadclyst, Devon.[77] He believed Arthur was surrendering himself to his 'feelings' and lacked self-control and a sense of responsibility to the family. He reminded him that 'there is a great deal to be thought about besides ease to your own feelings.'[78] Arthur responded to this pressure by rejecting the advice of Temple and Leopold, and by laying claim to other influences that *he* had selected for himself, ones more in keeping with his increasingly secular masculine identity. He explained this to his father:

> I know no more helpful representation than that, which has been the support and comfort of many men, by Martineau in his *Endeavours of the Christian Life* or in *Hours of Thought*. So too the very practical...representation by [T.H.] Green in his two sermons has been a help out of great difficulties.[79]

He also hinted at the underlying family tension, noting that 'there is and always will be as a mere fact of human nature some difference between the way in which the young and the old look at such matters.'[80]

Independence and autonomy from his family and its values became the driving force for Arthur's rebellion, nurtured in the protective environment of Oxford. He admitted to himself that he had also 'hoped that marriage would be the solution of everything (and certainly make one grander and more independent)'.[81] Arthur's independence was expressed primarily through political difference from the Conservatism and, later, the Gladstonian Liberalism, of his father.[82]

In line with other radicals he connected the Established Church with landed society, privilege and hierarchical social relations, particularly in rural society. This, naturally, led to a significant level of alienation from his family. His was a new, more 'socialistic' form of Liberalism, aimed at educating and empowering the working classes. His first parliamentary seat, in Rotherham, reflected his ambition to help achieve these goals, as did his involvement in the Cooperative Movement. He contrasted this with the politics of his father and his elder brother, Charles, whom he described as 'exceptionally feudal'.[83] For Arthur, they represented 'gigmanity', a term he borrowed from Thomas Carlyle's writings.[84] Carlyle and Cobden were amongst the main influences on his politics, hardly great friends of landed wealth. Both, also, were according to Arthur 'great men' whom he admired and venerated for their masculine qualities, particularly their devotion to hard work and their attacks on privilege. Carlyle 'has embodied for me my former strong feelings about "gigmanity". He was a big man'.[85]

This point of principle resulted in a psychological distancing from his family, their values and interests, which often emerged in his journal whilst he was visiting Killerton House, the family home in Devon. In one particularly revealing entry he reflected on this distance and the foundations of the rift, which he interpreted in political terms:

> As I look out of my dressing room window on a Sunday morning the chapel bell just going to begin this thought is inevitable. The place is full of my former self whom I look at as if a different creature...the huge trees, the big garden, the mass of servants, how grand I once thought all this, how much to be desired, and how much I shrink from it and seem to dislike it now...the general conditions would become better if there was less gigmanity. The more shocks and bangs to his property a gigman gets – the better for him.[86]

Arthur Acland's experiences and the nature of his break with family tradition, or at least in his perception of a break, underline the problems of applying theories of hegemony and hegemonic shifts to the history of masculinity. Certainly, at one level it was a transition with a similar chronological scope to many of the key 'hegemonic shifts'. Here was a generational shift in values and behaviour, from the landowning, Anglican paternalism of Thomas Dyke Acland in the mid-nineteenth century to that of Arthur in the 1870s and 1880s, whose earnest 'Muscular Christian' piety was transformed into secular 'socialist' thinking. It was a change that matched broader socio-economic, cultural and political developments, a pattern broadly in line with the conclusions of scholars such as Connell and Tosh.

Even so, these changes may not have amounted to 'hegemonic shifts'. Certainly, Arthur's more secular and radical politics and identity stood in stark contrast, at the level of his and his father's immediate experience, to the sober dogmatic (as Arthur would have it) beliefs and traditional landed politics of Sir Thomas. Despite this, though, in many respects Arthur and his father drew on the same fundamental *habitus* of masculine values, which emphasised independence, self-control, hard work, virtue and responsibility to others. The real distinction lay in the configurations of these values, configurations that resulted in alternative stereotypes of masculinity, but which were based on the *same* core values. These represented different stereotypical 'types' of men, rather than a simple duality between a dominant, 'hegemonic' ideal and its 'complicit', 'subordinate' or 'marginal' forms. If not, it is difficult to explain how Arthur could *choose* between such dominant codes of behaviour, particularly in view of the family's financial control over him as a younger son seeking to find a profession. The underlying similarity of values is emphasised by the fact that ultimately his family were persuaded that, although his was a different route to manliness, it was a valid and honourable one nevertheless. Indeed, despite his divergent ideals, Arthur actually trod the traditional path for Acland men during the nineteenth century, into politics via a special interest in education. This convergence was completed when he inherited the estate on the death of his childless older brother in 1919.

Whatever his scepticism about the sources of its wealth and power, Arthur was unable to escape the responsibilities of his family position – in private, as well as in public. Further into the life course he began to realise that he possessed some identity of values and interests with his father, and came to view him, and the Acland family traditions, in less oppositional terms. In his later years, as a father himself, he reread their letters while researching an edited collection of his father's correspondence. This enhanced his admiration of Thomas' qualities as a father, and as a man. Beneath his opposition to Arthur's ambitions was a man who 'cared very much about his children and their work and was very proud of them if they did well'.[87] His father's hardworking character also emerged strongly from his letters, and forced Arthur to revise his perception of his 'gigmanity'. He realised the extent of 'his volunteering, his drawing, his interest in agriculture, in chemistry, his interest in middle-class education, his immense reading in religion and in philosophy and constant thinking of all these things, his work in the county and in parliament which he resented after 50 and left when he was 77'.[88] However, it fell to his sister, Mary, to strike the ultimate blow against Arthur's sense of difference, with her discovery of their father's political correspondence. Pointing out Sir Thomas's encouragement of the Agricultural Labourers Union on his estates in the 1870s, she emphasised the irony of this for Arthur's conception of his father, suggesting: 'I should think in view of all Papa's later opinions you find it hard sometimes to realise him in the days of his real Liberal vigour.'[89] This realisation was compounded as Arthur found that his own life echoed that of his father, as he fretted about his son Francis's apparent lack of ambition ('Floating v. independent self reliant action. I cannot tell what he will be or do at all'), in the same way that his father had worried about him.[90]

## III. Conjectures

As has been suggested, these family materials tend to reveal the use of 'stereotypes' (such as those associated with male 'politeness', 'sensibility' or 'sincerity') to demarcate *boundaries* and provide shorthand diagnostics to allow social or normative categorisation and distancing, rather than being a means of somehow capturing the 'reality' of a form of masculine identity, like a photograph. This means that correspondence often contains much more about norms as they were transgressed or contested than it does about the unspoken assumptions of daily life within these boundaries. However, although this feature skews the evidence towards moments of collision, contest, resistance or evasion, it could also be argued that these moments *were* the ones in which implicit or immanent values were made explicit or embodied. Throughout our period, the most notable boundary for members of the landed gentry was that where social and gender definitions collided – in relation to 'gentlemanliness', which could mean very different things to different elements of the social order, and which, arguably, never had much purchase among unskilled wage-earners. This has two consequences. First, it may mean that such social stereotypes are rarely articulated in detail in personal sources, because they were often unconsidered *until* thrown into relief by confrontation with 'others'. Second, if we call these patterns *stereotypes*, instead of according them hegemonic power, the existence of parallel conceptions of male identity becomes at once simpler to explain and perhaps also less 'subversive'. If the edifice against which they are reacting is less powerful, maybe the reaction to them can also be regarded as less intense.

This is not to say that stereotypes were easy to ignore, reject or evade. Here we should adopt Richard Jenkins's phrase. As in the case of 'The Bloods', stereotypes may have been imagined (that is, they were composites made in the mind, rather than observed directly in daily life), but they possessed a social power that was not simply imaginary.[91] When they combined with the more fundamental normative building blocks of patriarchal hegemony (honour, virtue, gentility or authority), they could exert a tremendous pressure and incur a deep psychological toll on those who found it hard to fit in. These stereotypes also acted as a powerful societal restraint upon associations, behaviour, socialising, dress, gesture, speech and ideas deemed incompatible with prevailing 'manners and tastes'.

Such stereotypes were negotiated *socially* rather than being imposed by leading cultural arbiters. That is, they were formed through societal interaction and public and private discourse, they were subject to intellectual, literary and material fashion, and they required a *currency* (an explanatory relevance) in order to be successful as societal archetypes. So, for example, on leaving school at Douai in 1760, the English Catholic Edward Weld was advised by his Jesuit preceptor, Edward Church, about the importance of maintaining a 'genteel carriage'.[92] Church sought to counter the effects of Weld's formative years in France by stressing the importance of values that compounded diagnostic social, gender and national stereotypes. These included the conventional social injunctions against 'any shadow of affectation' and 'effuse laughter in company', which English people regarded as 'a mark of ill-breeding'.[93] A few weeks earlier, Church had mixed gender and national stereotypes, admiring his 'manly behaviour', but at the same time recommending that he adopt 'a certain degree of the Gaiete Francoise, which sits admirably well in an Englishman & renders him both companionable & agreeable in conversation'.[94]

However, this advice on manners also drew on, and articulated, deeper values. Like Stillingfleet, Church stressed the duty to continue cultivating learning, which would assist 'in the practice of virtue by giving you a just notion of perishable things, which is nowhere better gotten than from histories of the rise, fall & vanity of human grandeur'. The practice of these 'civil' arts would allow Edward Weld to qualify himself 'for the station you are kept for where virtue, learning & polite behaviour will all have their proper sphere of action.' This advice illustrates *how* such notions of 'politeness', 'gentility' and 'manliness' were projected as stereotypes into social 'space', and *how*, as a consequence, they varied according to context, and over time. If this is admitted, it makes these changes easier to understand, account for, and integrate into our explanations. However, because we have downgraded the causal primacy of such social phenomena, it also makes these changes less significant when they occur. They no longer have to provide the single, unified and sufficient explanatory template into which all male behaviour has to fit, or against which it has to resist. Instead, they are simply behavioural and normative archetypes, that were constraining, powerful and far-reaching, but which did not amount to a self-sufficient or self-sustaining *habitus* – that is, a sufficient explanation of 'how the world works'.

On the contrary, these diagnostics for understanding and legitimating forms of behaviour seem not to have established such a hegemonic monopoly. There were always a variety of norms from which men could choose. Indeed, it is possible to argue that some alternatives grew out of another part of the deep layer of behavioural or normative constants, the association of adult manhood with behavioural, even normative, autonomy. This helped ensure that there were always opposing stereotypes at work at any time. So, rakish, sensual, hedonistic masculinity existed alongside polite, restrained and self-conscious 'civilised' politeness. A century later, cynical, metropolitan, caddish masculinity could be contrasted with sincere, Christian, domestic norms. In each case, these elements were two sides of the same coin, two opposed implications of adult male self-determination. The former privileged autonomy over constraint, the latter emphasised the manly dimension of 'self-control', as a prerequisite for the patriarchal privilege of governing and protecting others in the household and in wider society.

As has been suggested, these normative variations were often perceived when accustomed behavioural boundaries were transgressed, situations which could be decisive in *activating* such stereotypes, turning implicit or imagined categories into consequential social judgements.[95] As noted, this was often through a reflexive process of identity formation, as self-identity was created out of clashes of values through which groups of 'others' were also defined. These are particularly evident in the encounters of the Money family in the early nineteenth century. William Money of Whetam was a clergyman, the younger son of Wiltshire landowner William Money of Hom House. William Jr and his wife Emma shared an intense piety, focused on the family ('our little circle')[96] that was, in some respects, at odds with the ostentation and worldliness of many of their peers in the social elite – an elite into which William was projected towards the end of his life in 1843 after inheriting the family estate from his brother Gen. Sir James Money-Kyrle.[97] This distancing of values had two causes, financial and spiritual. As the possessor of a relatively modest living, William was always conscious that he could not keep pace with metropolitan tastes and fashions. Whilst commenting in a letter to his wife on a projected trip to London, William referred to the 'grosser men' in the city whom he would encounter. On the basis of previous experiences he dreaded his conspicuous identity in the city:

> My poor clothes and Willow Hat suit Whetam better than the neighbourhood of London: and though I may relinquish every vestige of fashion yet I may not so soon become insensible to ridicule and contempt.[98]

Elsewhere, he commented on the 'clockwork regularity' of his life at Whetam, whose routines 'may be called by the gay, a dull and stupid existence, no better than the vegetation of a Cabbage'.[99] However, he also drew attention to the spiritual differences of these two forms of existence, observing that even 'a Cabbage eagerly imbibes the dew of Heaven', while 'the gay Lounger like the gaudy butterfly, priding himself on a fine plumage flits thro' the sunshine of his little day', heedless of moral responsibilities or religious obligations.

Emma shared his sentiments about a serious and religious masculinity, and made similar comments on the different behavioural standards of fashionable urban men, perhaps as a means of bolstering her husband's ego. During a trip to Cheltenham she wrote:

> The appearance of everyone here with the exception of two or three I disliked beyond description. Their dress, manners, and idle habits, to us sober

people are really disgusting, & I believe what is still of much greater consequence, sinful in the sight of God. I should feel no shame in walking with my beloved William in his old coat with his elbow near through it...but with my present feeling to walk with the Men of this Place, I should feel real shame.[100]

This shared attachment to 'men with sound heads, and sound hearts... Women of pure and domestic education, equally removed from vulgarity and affectation' was expressed repeatedly by reference to stereotypes that contrasted the fashionable urban sophisticates with the simpler, unpretentious purity of country life.[101] Between them, William and Emma both forged a marital relationship of unusual depth, remarked on by their eldest son, and also (in consequence) created a rather sheltered family 'culture' of restrained, spiritually grounded gender values, partly by reference to stereotypical 'others'.[102]

They also passed on these values to their sons, some of whom were forced by necessity to leave the sheltered confines of Whetam and expose themselves to radically divergent forms of masculinity. These collisions threw their parents' serious, domestic and religious masculine identity into sharp relief, and through transgression made values apparent that had previously only been implicit or taken for granted. For example, after William Money's second son, 16-year-old Edward, joined the East India Company in the autumn of 1826, he found himself in unfamiliar and uncomfortable circumstances as a young cadet aboard a ship bound for Calcutta. In his letters home he contrasted his own masculinity with the irreligious and debauched behaviour of the officers that he was face-to-face with for the first time. He complained about the lack of religious services and the conversations focused on 'gambling, dogfighting, billiards and other sports', during which he said he remained 'mute'.[103] By the following spring Edward expressed a distinct feeling of awkwardness, a sense of being an 'outsider'. He had changed his opinion of the Captain, whom he had previously considered a 'gentleman', but who he now noticed had begun to favour certain of the rougher members of the ship's company and associated increasingly with them.[104]

Confronted with such irreligious, ungentlemanly codes of masculinity, Edward had fallen back on familial norms, stating that he paid 'the strictest attention' to his parents' advice, by being 'very moderate in my eating and drinking' and by 'reading the scriptures' every day. Apart from the third officer, an 'upright, straightforward, quiet' man, 'endowed with sound religious principles', Edward had decided that the ship's company did not meet his ideal expectations of religious manly simplicity, or the 'steadiness' which he found in role models such as his elder brother William and his cousin Roddam.[105] Equally, the impolite manners of his fellow passengers deeply offended his ideas of gentility.

Edward Money's subjective experiences of life on board ship illustrate the complex interactions of gender identities and social context. The upbringing he received from his parents had inculcated a behavioural and normative masculine stereotype, enacted through restrained, retired, religious gentility. Aboard ship, however, Edward encountered men whose governing ideals were of a rugged, hedonistic and distinctly less godly variety. This collision of values made Edward acutely aware of the stereotypes on which his own ideals were based. Despite his schooling away from home, at 16 years of age his own masculine values were still defined primarily in 'familial' terms, through ways of behaving learned from his parents. Undoubtedly, too, such feelings were compounded by acute homesickness and nostalgia for the security of his childhood at Whetam.

Edward's journey to India forced him into the formative transition of his life, from boyhood to adulthood, and from a sheltered English rectory to a more fluid, rackety Anglo-Indian world. This transition involved exposure to notions of masculinity and social groups aboard ship and in the East India Company regiments with which he was entirely unfamiliar. He negotiated this alien terrain by falling back on childhood certainties and family-sanctioned proprieties, in the same way that his parents reached for reassuring diagnostic stereotypes when dealing with the perils of the fashionable streets of London or Bath. These melded together foundational definitions of virtue (as religious commitment, moral seriousness, plainness, truthfulness, modesty and restraint) and societal value judgements (adverse reactions to 'butterflies' who favoured fine clothes, billiards and dog-fighting) into stereotypes that were used as moral reference points by which to navigate the daily hazards thrown up by the world.

## IV. Conclusion

None of these correspondents expressed such values as part of a conscious discourse about the nature of their gender identity. William Windham's friends were merely seeking a cheap laugh at the expense of a couple of preposterous poseurs. William and Emma Money were trying to justify their slightly threadbare gentility by highlighting the moral superiority of their rural retirement. Their adolescent son Edward attempted to blot out his homesickness and alienation aboard ship by clinging to the security blanket of his parents' values. Arthur Acland's reflections were largely generated by long-drawn-out discussions with his family over his future career. If gender ideals or identities were mentioned at all, it was usually only implicitly, or as part of the incessant discourse about the dominant and multifaceted template for elite identity, gentility. 'The Bloods' satirised the social pretensions of Aldworth and Trey, the Moneys sought virtue in shabby-gentility, Edward Money tried to bolster his

Christian virtue in the midst of social heathens, while Arthur Acland sought (not wholly successfully) to fight his family's status and values in the name of social reform.

In this respect, then, it can be argued that the template of the gentleman, as amalgam of social, gender, moral and political identities, did exert a *hegemonic* power among the English landed elite between the seventeenth and nineteenth centuries. It translated an imagined normative code into a 'common sense' understanding of the world. This was experienced as much negatively as positively, by delimiting the acceptable behavioural boundaries to be observed within familial, educational and institutional settings, and justifying the sanctions by which these were to be policed. It was inculcated from birth, institutionalised through education, and enacted throughout life as the touchstone for social, cultural, political and moral judgements.[106] However, this hegemonic power seems to have operated more in line with the model of Bourdieu than with that of Gramsci, as a series of deeply engrained dispositions that limited the bounds of what was possible or conceivable, rather than as a more focused polarity to which all other alternatives had to be configured. There was no single definition of gentility, and consequently no single model of gentlemanly masculinity – even if most contemporaries acted as if an agreed definition did exist.[107] This dilemma meant that contemporaries, like 'The Bloods' or the Moneys, were repeatedly forced to choose between *several* competing forms of elite gentility (and masculinity), and to fashion their own definitions of important diagnostic concepts such as honour, virtue, authority and autonomy accordingly.

This chapter has suggested that in understanding and explaining these choices it can be helpful to deconstruct these compacted amalgams of values, to try to separate out the enduring, internalised building blocks from the more explicit diagnostic value judgements and from the immediate, often confrontational situations in which they were applied. Doing so might help us obtain a better sense of both causation and chronology. If these norms were multilayered, and articulated primarily through composite stereotypes, this implies that the process by which the cultural norms enunciated in conduct literature filtered through into social practices was more complex and less linear than simple notions of hegemony suggest. Similarly, it also indicates that the process of change was less well-defined and less teleological than is indicated by the familiar series of step-changes between different 'types' of man.

Clearly, long-term normative change occurred in male identities, even among a group as stable in terms of wealth, status, power, education, opportunities and authority as the English landed elite. Arthur Acland was a far more self-conscious, and troubled, representative of his family's power and status than William Windham (II) had been 150 years earlier. However, if we recognise that these identities were multilayered, then we can understand change as the reconfiguration of slow-moving, base-level values into more mobile diagnostic templates or stereotypes, that existed reflexively with daily experience, shaping and being shaped by responses to immediate exigencies and experiences. Concepts such as gentility or 'gentlemanliness' emphasise that (in many respects) the division between 'deep' values and 'mid-level' is artificial, because such notions joined the two elements seamlessly, translating core values such as 'honour', 'virtue' and 'autonomy' into specific behavioural guides. However, the distinction is valuable as an explanatory device, because it allows us to show how Thomas Dampier and Edward Money could give the *same* set of values, within the *same* cultural frame of 'gentility', two *different* inflections in two different contexts. They did so because they moulded these ideals into two slightly different composite stereotypes to help them diagnose 'true' gentility.

We have suggested here that these stereotypes are the key to accommodating significant spatial and temporal variation within a relatively static 'patriarchal' dispensation in gender relations, in which there were also long-term continuities in masculine norms. They took general concepts and gave them an agreed 'local' definition, whether that was among the denizens of the 'common room' in Geneva or the parlour at Whetam. These localised inflections, established among peer groups, families, and social, administrative, educational and institutional settings, are difficult to detect, because they were the most unspoken element of this 'common knowledge'. However, they may also be the most important, in illustrating *how* cultural archetypes were actually translated into norms, and used to guide behaviour and shape responses.

This is not to suggest, either, that we should not attempt to generalise, or to look for substantive patterns of change over time. The question is whether or not 'hegemony' is the best vehicle for such efforts, and whether or not the variations in experience can best be typified by identifying a leading cultural ideal of masculinity in a particular period and orienting all other forms as responses or reactions towards it. We wish to argue for the existence of a great plurality of forms at any given time, and over time, because we believe that the conditioning constraints that shaped identities operated more strongly upon the value set from which such identities were constructed than on the leading tropes through which they were eventually expressed.

## Notes

1. See A. Shepard and K. Harvey, 'What have historians done with masculinity: reflections on five centuries of British history, circa. 1500–1950', *Journal of British Studies* 44 (1988), 274–80; later periods are summed up in J. Tosh, 'Gentlemanly politeness and manly simplicity in Victorian England', *Transactions of the Royal Historical Society*, 6th ser., 12 (2002), 455–72.
2. R.W. Connell, *Gender and Power* (London, 1987); idem, *Masculinities* (Cambridge, 1995).
3. Connell, *Masculinities*, p. 186.

4. Ibid.
5. Ibid, pp. 186–87.
6. Ibid., p. 187.
7. Ibid., pp. 187–88.
8. Ibid., p. 188.
9. Ibid., p. 189.
10. Ibid., p. 190.
11. Ibid.
12. Ibid., p. 192.
13. Ibid., pp. 192–93.
14. On 'modernisation' ideas and theories see G. Walker, 'Modernization', in Walker (ed.), *Writing Early Modern History* (London, 2005), pp. 25–48.
15. J. Gregory, '*Homo religiosus*: masculinity and religion in the long eighteenth century', in T. Hitchcock and M. Cohen (eds), *English Masculinities, 1660–1800* (Harlow, 1999), p. 86.
16. Ibid.
17. Ibid., pp. 86–7.
18. Shepard and Harvey, 'What have historians done with masculinity', pp. 274–80; M. Francis, 'The domestication of the male? recent research on nineteenth and twentieth century masculinity', *Historical Journal* 45 (2002), 637–52; A. Milne-Smith, 'A flight to domesticity? making a home in the gentlemen's clubs of London 1880–1914', *Journal of British Studies* 45 (2006), 796–818; W. Stafford, 'Gentlemanly masculinities as represented by the Late Georgian *Gentleman's Magazine*', *History* 93 (2008), pp. 47–68; M. Collins, 'The fall of the English gentleman: the national character in decline, c. 1918–1970', *Historical Research* 75 (2002), 90–111; and J. Bourke, *Dismembering the Male: Men's Bodies, Britain and the Great War* (London, 1996), pp. 15–19.
19. J. Tosh, 'What should historians do with masculinity: reflections on nineteenth century Britain', *History Workshop Journal* 38 (1994), 179–202.
20. *Journal of British Studies* 44 (2005), 274–362.
21. Shepard and Harvey, 'What have historians done with masculinity', pp. 274–80.
22. A. Shepard, *Meanings of Manhood in Early Modern England* (Oxford, 2003), pp. 70–92; E. Foyster, *Manhood in Early Modern England. Honour, Sex and Marriage* (Harlow, 1999), pp. 28–54.
23. Shepard, *Meanings of Manhood*, pp. 93–126; Foyster, *Manhood*, pp. 39–48.
24. P. Langford, 'The progress of politeness', in idem *A Polite and Commercial People: England 1727–1783* (Oxford, 1989), pp. 59–122; L.E. Klein, 'Politeness for plebes: consumption and social identity in early eighteenth-century England', in A. Bermingham and J. Brewer (eds), *The Consumption of Culture 1600–1800: Image, Object, Text* (London and New York, 1995), pp. 362–82; L.E. Klein, 'Coffeehouse civility, 1660–1714: an aspect of post-courtly culture in England', *Huntington Library Quarterly*, 59:1 (1996), 30–51; A. Bryson, *From Courtesy to Civility: Changing Codes of Conduct in Early Modern England* (Oxford, 1998); P. Burke, 'A civil tongue: language and politeness in early modern Europe', in P. Burke, B. Harrison and P. Slack (eds), *Civil Histories: Essays in Honour of Sir Keith Thomas* (Oxford, 2000), pp. 31–48; P. Carter, *Men and the Emergence of Polite Society, Britain 1660–1800* (Harlow, 2001); H. Berry, 'Rethinking politeness in eighteenth-century England: Moll King's Coffee House and the significance of "flash talk"', *Transactions of the Royal Historical Society*, 6th ser., 11 (2001), 65–81; J. Gillingham, 'From *civilitas* to civility: codes of manners in medieval and early modern England', *Transactions of the Royal Historical Society*,

6th ser., 12 (2002), 267–91; N. Cooper, 'Rank, manners and display: the gentlemanly house, 1500–1750', ibid., 291–310; P. Langford, 'The uses of eighteenth-century politeness', ibid., 311–32; P. Carter, 'Polite "persons": character, biography and the gentleman', ibid., 333–54; R.H. Sweet, 'Topographies of politeness', ibid., 355–74; H. Berry, 'Polite consumption: shopping in eighteenth-century England', ibid., 375–94; E. Foyster, 'Creating a veil of silence? politeness and marital violence in the eighteenth-century household', ibid., 395–416; A. Fletcher, 'Courses in politeness: the upbringing and experiences of five teenage diarists, 1671–1860', ibid., 417–30; L.E. Klein, 'Politeness and the interpretation of the British eighteenth century', *Historical Journal* 45:4 (2002), 869–98; D.M. Turner, *Fashioning Adultery: Gender, Sex and Civility in England, 1660–1740* (Cambridge, 2002); M. Peltonen, *The Duel in Early Modern England: Civility, Politeness and Honour* (Cambridge, 2003); J. Jordan, 'Herstory untold: the absence of women's agency in constructing concepts of early modern manhood', *Cultural and Social History* 4:4 (2007), 575–83.

25. Ibid., pp. 313–314.
26. See K. Harvey, 'The history of masculinity, circa 1650–1800', *Journal of British Studies* 44 (2005), 296–311. For conduct literature and concerns about effeminacy, see M. Cohen, *Fashioning Masculinity: National Identity and Language in the Eighteenth Century* (London, 1996); P. Carter, 'Men about town: representations of foppery and masculinity in early eighteenth-century urban society', in H. Baker and E. Chalus (eds), *Gender in Eighteenth-Century England. Roles, Representations and Responsibilities* (London, 1997), pp. 31–57; Carter, *Polite Society*, pp. 124–62; E. Brinks, *Gothic Masculinity: Effeminacy and the Supernatural in English and German Romanticism* (London, 2003); T.A. King, *The Gendering of Men, 1600–1750* (Madison, 2004); M.S. Dawson, *Gentility and the Comic Theatre of Late Stuart London* (Cambridge, 2005), pp. 145–204; J.M. Kelly, 'Riots, revelries, and rumor: libertinism and masculine association in enlightenment London', *Journal of British Studies* 45:4 (2006), 796–818. For advice literature on politeness, see V. Nünning, 'From "honour" to "honest": the invention of the (superiority of the) middling ranks in eighteenth-century England', *Journal for the Study of British Cultures* 2 (1995), 19–41; Carter, *Polite Society*, pp. 15–87; essays by Carter, Fletcher, Foyster and Langford in *Transactions of the Royal Historical Society*, 6th ser., 12 (2002); D. Kuchta, *The Three-Piece Suit and Modern Masculinity. England, 1550–1850* (Berkeley, 2002); R.B. Shoemaker, 'Taming the duel: masculinity, honour and ritual violence in London, 1660–1800', *Historical Journal* 45:3 (2002), 525–45; M. Cohen, '"Manners" make the man: politeness, chivalry and the construction of masculinity, 1750–1830', *Journal of British Studies* 44 (2005), 312–30. For masculinity and sexualities, see R. Trumbach, 'Sex, gender, and sexual identity in modern culture: male sodomy and female prostitution in enlightenment London', *Journal of the History of Sexuality* 2 (1991), 186–203; R. Trumbach, *Sex and the Gender Revolution. Volume 1: Heterosexuality and the Third Gender in Enlightenment London* (Chicago, 1998); G.E. Haggerty, *Men in Love. Masculinity and Sexuality in the Eighteenth Century* (New York, 1999); T. Hitchcock and M. Cohen (eds), *English Masculinities, 1660–1800* (Harlow, 1999); Turner, *Fashioning Adultery*; K. Harvey, 'The substance of gender difference: change and persistence in eighteenth-century representations of the body', *Gender and History* 14:2 (2002), 202–23; K. O'Donnell and M. O'Rourke (eds), *Love, Sex, Intimacy and Friendship between Men, 1550–1800* (Basingstoke, 2003).
27. A. Vickery, 'Golden age to separate spheres? A review of the categories and chronology of English women's history', *Historical Journal* 36 (1993), 383–414; see also M. McCormack (ed.), *Public Men: Masculinity and Politics in Modern Britain* (Basingstoke, 2007), pp. 13–32.

28. Judith M. Bennett, 'History that stands still: women's work in the European past', *Feminist Studies* 14 (1988), 269–83.
29. J.A. Allen, 'Men interminably in crisis? Historians on masculinity, sexual boundaries and manhood', *Radical History Review* 82 (2002), 193.
30. J. Tosh, 'Gentlemanly politeness and manly simplicity in Victorian England', *Transactions of the Royal Historical Society* 12, 6th ser. (2002), 455–72.
31. P. Bourdieu, *The Logic of Practice* (Cambridge, 1990), p. 59, quoted in the best brief introduction to Bourdieu's conception of *habitus*, R. Jenkins, *Pierre Bourdieu* (Oxford, 2002), pp. 74–84. Bourdieu's relatively static conception of gender-power has been criticised by recent feminist writers. See L. Adkins and B. Skeggs (eds), *Feminism after Bourdieu* (Oxford, 2005).
32. F. Inglis, *Clifford Geertz: Culture, Custom and Ethics* (Oxford, 2000), p. 119.
33. M. McCormack and M. Roberts, 'Conclusion: chronologies in the history of British political masculinities, c. 1700–2000', in McCormack (ed.), *Public Men*, pp. 187–202.
34. On 'modernisation' ideas and theories in history, see G. Walker, 'Modernization', in idem (ed.), *Writing Early Modern History* (London, 2005), pp. 25–48.
35. R.W. Connell, 'An iron man: the body and some contradictions of hegemonic masculinity', in M. Messner and D. Sabo (eds), *Sport, Men and the Gender Order* (Champaign, IL, 1990), p. 83.
36. R.W. Connell and J.W. Messerschmidt, 'Hegemonic masculinity: rethinking the concept', *Gender and Society* 19:6 (2005), 829–59.
37. F. Braudel, *The Mediterranean and the Mediterranean World in the Age of Philip II* (London, 1972–1973), II, 892, 1239–44.
38. L. Gowing, *Domestic Dangers: Women, Words, and Sex in Early Modern London* (Oxford, 1996), pp. 59–111; Shepard, *Meanings of Manhood*, pp. 152–85. We agree with Shepard that, although greater emphasis was given consistently to sexual purity in evaluations of female reputation, it was also a component of male 'honesty'. See also L.A. Pollock, 'Honor, gender and reconciliation in elite culture, 1570–1700', *Journal of British Studies* 46 (2007), 3–29.
39. Shepard, *Meanings of Manhood*, pp. 186–94.
40. L. Colley, *Britons. Forging the Nation 1707–1837* (New Haven and London, 1992), pp. 147–94.
41. AHRC research project AH/E007791/1 'Man's Estate: Masculinity and Landed Gentility in England, c. 1660-c. 1918'. The families selected include the Windhams (Norfolk), Money-Kyrle (Wilts), Acland (Devon), Lister (Yorks), Parker (Lancs), Buxton (Norfolk), Weld (Dorset and Lancs), Coffin (Devon and Cornwall), Adams (Cornwall), Huddlestone (Cambs), Cotton (Cambs), Tharp (Cambs), Woolcombe (Devon), Wynell, Mayow and Tremayne (Cornwall) and Lucy (Warwickshire).
42. E. Griffiths (ed.), 'William Windham's Green Book 1673–1688', *Norfolk Record Society* LXVI (2002), 4–10; R.W. Ketton-Cremer, *The Early Life and Diaries of William Windham* (London, 1927), pp. 28–55.
43. E. Cruickshanks, S. Handley and D. W. Hayton (eds), *The House of Commons 1690–1715: The History of Parliament V* (Cambridge, 2002), p. 889.
44. *Literary Life and Selected Works of Benjamin Stillingfleet...* (London, 1811), p. 5.
45. Ibid., p. 24.
46. Ibid., p. 34.
47. Ibid.
48. Ibid., p. 41.
49. Ibid., p. 42.

50. Ibid., p. 47.
51. Ibid., p. 50.
52. Ibid., p. 51. This can be contrasted with Stillingfleet's better-known panegyric against women, written after an unsuccessful courtship. 'Dissembling ever was the sex's trade;/ The study of their lives to please... For they can fawn and look demurely down,/If it but suit their present purposes,/While inwardly they glow with lust or pride'. Ibid., p. 69.
53. Ibid., p. 60.
54. Ibid., p. 55.
55. Ibid., p. 56.
56. Ibid.
57. Ibid., pp. 45–6.
58. Norfolk R. O. William Windham, Geneva to Ashe Windham, 9 April 1738 WKC 7/45/5; Ibid., 21 April 1738, WKC 7/45/8; W. Windham, *An Account of the Glacieres or Ice Alps in Savoy...* (London, 1744).
59. Carter, *Polite Society*, p. 136.
60. R. Sedgwick (ed.), *The History of Parliament: The House of Commons 1715–1754* (London, 1970), II, p. 558; Norfolk R. O. WKC 7/46/18 Letter from Thomas Dampier, 19 April 1741.
61. Norfolk R. O. WKC 7/43/1 'A Short History Containing an Acct. of the actions of *Dicky*, commonly called *The Berkshire Boy*, from the first Day of Sept., to the 20th of October in the year 1739'.
62. Ibid.
63. Ibid.
64. Ibid.
65. S. Shapin, *A Social History of Truth: Civility and Science in Seventeenth-Century England* (Chicago and London, 1994), p. 84.
66. Devon Record Office, Acland Family Papers, 1148M Add 14 Series I/169, Arthur Herbert Dyke Acland to his Father, 28 July 1879.
67. Devon Record Office, Acland Family Papers, 1148M Add 23/F31, Journal of Sir Arthur Herbert Dyke Acland 1871–98, 30 June 1872.
68. Ibid., 13 April 1874.
69. Ibid., 25 February 1872.
70. Ibid., 22 April 1875.
71. DRO 1148M Add 14/Series I/180, Arthur Herbert Dyke Acland to Sir Thomas Dyke Acland 11th Bart, 8 December 1879.
72. DRO, 1148M Add 23/F31, Journal of Sir Arthur Herbert Dyke Acland 1871–98, 31 August 1875.
73. Ibid., 15 February 1880.
74. Ibid., 2 October 1877.
75. DRO, 1148M Add 23/F29B, Journal of Sir Arthur Herbert Dyke Acland 1898–1924, 18 September 1898.
76. DRO, 1148M Add 23/F31, Journal of Sir Arthur Herbert Dyke Acland 1871–98, 15 February 1880.
77. DRO, 1148M Add 14/ Series I/174, Rev. Peter Leopold Dyke Acland to his elder brother, Sir Thomas Dyke Acland 11th Bart, 18 August 1879; 1148M Add 14/ Series I/182, Sir Frederick Temple to Sir Thomas Dyke Acland 11th Bart, 10 January 1880.
78. DRO, 1148M Add 14 Series I/168, Sir Thomas Dyke Acland to Arthur Acland, 21 July 1879.
79. DRO 1148M Add 14 Series I/176, Arthur Acland to Sir Thomas Dyke Acland, 28 August 1879.

80. DRO 1148M Add 14 Series I/186, Arthur Acland to Sir Thomas Dyke Acland, 28 January 1880. Acland was referring to two works by the Unitarian James Martineau: J. Martineau, *Endeavours after the Christian Life: Discourses* (London, 1847) and *Hours of Thought on Sacred Things: A Volume of Sermons* (London, 1876). He also refers to T.H. Green's famous lay sermons at Oxford, which were eventually published after Green's death in 1883; A. Toynbee (ed.), *The Witness of God and Faith: Two Lay Sermons* (London, 1883).
81. DRO, 1148M Add 23/F31, Journal of Sir Arthur Herbert Dyke Acland 1871–98, 15 February 1880.
82. Thomas Dyke Acland, 11th Bart, had been a Tory, but joined the new Liberal Party in 1857. He disagreed with Gladstone's policy of Home Rule, but, out of loyalty to Gladstone, had refused to join the Conservative Party with the other Liberal Unionists. The Aclands were, previous to this, famous Tories, having taken the Royalist side during the Civil Wars and serving as Tory MPs in various south-west constituencies practically throughout the period of this paper. See R.G. Thorne (ed.), *The History of Parliament: The House of Commons 1790–1820*, III (London, 1986), pp. 18–20.
83. DRO, 1148M Add 23/F29B, Journal of Sir Arthur Herbert Dyke Acland 1898–1924, 24 January 1899.
84. http://carlyleletters.dukejournals.org, accessed 29 June 2009. T. Carlyle, *The Collected Letters*, 7, pp. 11–13. Thomas Carlyle to Henry Inglis, 8 October 1833, 'Glory to Heaven! you have quitted Gigmanity forever: not "always keeping a Gig" (to be "respectable"), but always standing on your own two legs (to be honest), will you front the world. Adhere *resolutely* to this plan...year after year I shall find you better and wiser; strong, manlike, ready for the duties and destinies of Time.'
85. DRO 1148M Add 23/F31, Journal of Sir Arthur Herbert Dyke Acland 1871–98, 31 December 1882.
86. Ibid., 3 September 1882.
87. DRO 1148M Add 23/F29B, Journal of Sir Arthur Herbert Dyke Acland 1898–1924, 24 July 1898.
88. DRO 1148M Add 23/F31, Journal of Sir Arthur Herbert Dyke Acland 1871–98, 26 February 1898.
89. DRO, Acland Family Correspondence, 51/12/1/103, Mary Hart-Davies to Sir Arthur Acland, 18 September 1898.
90. DRO, 1148M Add 23/F31, Journal of Sir Arthur Herbert Dyke Acland 1871–98, 3 November 1897.
91. R. Jenkins, *Social Identity* (London, 2004), p. 123.
92. Dorset R. O. D/WLC C47 Edward Church to Edward Weld Jr, 8 April 1760.
93. Ibid., 16 May 1760.
94. Idem, 8 April 1760.
95. F. Barth, 'Boundaries and connections', in A.P. Cohen (ed.), *Signifying Identities: Anthropological Perspectives on Boundaries and Contested Values* (London, 2000), pp. 17–36.
96. Wiltshire R. O. WRO 1720/829 William Money to Emma Money, 15 January 1811 (transcript), p. 36.
97. Wiltshire R. O. WRO 1720/ 829 Correspondence of William and Emma Money, p. 1.
98. Wiltshire R. O. WRO 1720/829 William Money to Emma Money, 24 May 1812, p. 66.
99. Ibid., 12 May 1812, p. 56.
100. Ibid., 8 May 1824, pp. 235–36.

101. Ibid., 12 May 1812, p. 55.
102. Ibid., William Money, verses 'on the 16th day of July being the Wedding day of Papa and Mamma': 'Thrice happy those, whom each succeeding year/Finds more enamour'd of their Union here/Whose love deep centr'd grows yet warmer still', p. 246.
103. Wiltshire R. O. WRO 1720/832 Edward Kyrle Money to Rev. William Money, 1 November 1826.
104. Ibid., 22 April 1827.
105. Ibid., 22 April 1827, 7 May 1827.
106. The best recent illustration of the pervasiveness of such values has been M. McCormack, *The Independent Man: Citizenship and Gender Politics in Georgian England* (Manchester, 2005).
107. See J.P. Cooper, 'Ideas of gentility', in G.E. Aylmer and J.S. Morrill (eds), *Land, Men and Beliefs; Studies in Early Modern History* (London, 1983), pp. 43–77; P.J. Corfield, 'The rivals: landed and other gentlemen', in N. Harte and R. Quinault (eds), *Land and Society in Britain, 1700–1914: Essays in Honour of F. M. L. Thompson* (Manchester, 1996), pp. 1–33; Shapin, *Social History of Truth*, pp. 42–125; A. Bryson, 'The rhetoric of status: gesture, demeanour and the image of the gentleman in sixteenth- and seventeenth-century England', in L. Gent and N. Llewellyn (eds), *Renaissance Bodies: The Human Figure in English Culture c. 1540–1660* (London, 1990), p. 136; Bryson, *From Courtesy to Civility*; Gillingham, 'From *civilitas* to civility', pp. 267–90; P.C. Maddern, 'Gentility', in R.L. Radulescu and A. Truelove (eds), *Gentry Culture in Late Medieval England* (Manchester, 2005), pp. 18–34; H.R. French, '"Ingenious and learned gentlemen": social perceptions and self-fashioning among Parish elites in Essex, 1680–1740', *Social History* 25:1 (2000), 44–66; H. Berry, 'Sense and singularity: the social experiences of John Marsh and Thomas Stutterd in Late-Georgian England', in H.R. French and J. Barry (eds), *Identity and Agency in England 1500–1800* (Basingstoke, 2004), pp. 178–99.

# 9
# Masculinity and Fatherhood in England c. 1760–1830

*Joanne Bailey*

This chapter explores the ways in which a research agenda focused upon gender and identity advances the history of men as fathers.[1] It suggests that our understanding of fatherhood is enriched when historians use a conceptual framework informed by four themes that have emerged from the theorising of masculinities: the plurality of masculinities, the concept of a hierarchy of masculinities, the recognition that masculinities are constructed in relation to each other, not simply in opposition to femininities, and that masculinities change over time and place.[2] This chapter also proposes that explicitly addressing the relationship between manhood, fatherhood and fathering offers new directions for research into masculinity more broadly.[3]

English fathers are found in two areas of historical research. In family history published in the 1970s and 1980s fathers are procreators of children, with a focus on biological rather than social fathering. Their role in childbirth and child-rearing is assessed, often as minimal, and they are typically analysed as a generic parent, undifferentiated from mothers, with the objective of uncovering whether relationships between parents and children were more or less emotionally distant at different times.[4] Embracing gender as a category of historical analysis has nuanced social histories of the family, though work on North American fatherhood developed more rapidly in differentiating fathers from mothers.[5] For the most part, closer attention to fathers is only now emerging in publications on the English family.[6] In studies of conflictual or problem family forms, fathers, if they feature at all, appear as irresponsible begetters of illegitimate children, or as men who deserted their children.[7] Expanding interest in the lives of the labouring poor and paupers reveals failing fathers, unable to achieve a full fathering role because they were forced to prioritise paid labour over their involvement in family life or were unable to provide for their offspring.[8]

Fathers are also found in histories of English masculinities. Many of the accounts of medieval, early modern and Victorian masculinities consider fatherhood because it was part of the process of achieving 'full' or 'patriarchal' manhood.[9] A consequence of marriage, an institution which conveyed privileges to men as heads of household and marked male maturity and economic independence, fatherhood is thus one of a constellation of markers of authority.[10] Work on Victorian masculinity moves from domestic patriarchy to the role of 'domesticity' in shaping manhood. Here, fatherhood is 'a telling touchstone of men's commitment to the home'.[11] There are other differences of emphasis. In medieval studies, attention is on fatherhood as marking virility, lineage and status.[12] With sources more conducive to assessing relationships, Victorianists categorise 'types' of fatherly relationships.[13] The first study devoted to English fathers, *Gender and fatherhood in the nineteenth century* (2007), however, indicates the benefits of investigating fathers through multiple lenses (gender, class and empire), thereby breaking down unitary visions of fatherhood.[14]

To date, both research fields focus on the authority of fathers at the expense of the emotional nature of fatherhood and its experience as a subjective identity.[15] Publications on family history examine paternal authority, how it was expressed, contested or ignored.[16] Since histories of masculinity treat fatherhood in the context of mastery of self, subordinates and resources, they expose issues of power and authority.[17] Yet masculinity studies also make it clear that we cannot unproblematically equate manhood with patriarchy. Early modern men, for example, did not or could not achieve all the components of patriarchal manhood.[18] Thus, while there were numerous rhetorical and political connections between fatherhood and patriarchy, they were as likely to be as unstable and contested as those between manhood and patriarchy. Uncovering this is a promising line of enquiry, as Nancy Christie's study reveals, but work is also required on other facets of fatherhood and fathering, particularly provision and the expression of emotion. Neither is a new dimension of fatherhood, but both are subject to change over time and offer a perspective on the relationship between styles of fatherhood and between fatherhood and manhood.

A further area to be more fully developed is the role of fatherhood in constructing male identity. Historians of family and masculinity have only patchily considered it as a personal and public identity. In contrast, art historians have shown how eighteenth-century aristocratic men commissioned portraits of themselves as devoted fathers to advertise their civilised qualities.[19] Studies of English masculinity do provide insights into the ways in which fatherhood conveyed public reputation as a marker of manhood.[20] It is clear, for instance, that, while biologically fathering children demonstrated virility, it was possible for childless men to display manliness through spiritual or social paternity.[21] We also know that the characteristics embodied in responsible paternity were deployed by men. Men of lower rank used them in campaigns for parliamentary reform from the later eighteenth century onwards to demonstrate their dependability and ability to govern.[22] However, being a father in terms of personal identity and personality remains less studied, despite frequent calls for this approach.[23] As an experience with which most men are familiar, either through being fathered or as fathers themselves, fatherhood is a fruitful site for masculine subjectivity.

It is also impossible to construct a chronology of fatherhood and fathering, due to the patchy nature of research on men in the home and family. Family history has avoided long-term surveys of structures and behaviours in the backlash against earlier sweeping narratives of change. Work on masculinity is tackling patterns of continuity and change at both macro and micro-level, though findings are yet to be reconciled. Fundamental continuities in masculinities have been identified.[24] Male household authority is identified as a central 'enduring' masculinity.[25] Indeed, it is proposed that the impression of shifts in masculinities from early modern to modern may be illusory, the result of incompatible social histories of men in the early modern household and Victorian home and cultural histories of eighteenth-century men in society.[26] A recent study of four lower-middling male diarists in Manchester, responding to the need for more research into eighteenth-century men in the home, concludes from the diarists' interest in family life, religion and employment that considerable continuities exist between early modern and Victorian manhood. Additional research is required on manhood, and fatherhood more specifically, before such apparent continuity can be considered conclusive.[27] This is particularly striking given that micro-studies of nineteenth-century men in the home are indicative of short-term temporal and social diversity. For example, there is evidence of the rise of 'serious' Evangelical manliness, which influenced men's domestic roles, and of middle-class men embracing domesticity in the early to mid-Victorian period, but rejecting it by the 1880s.[28] Both theses have received criticism and further nuance, but there is no doubt that periods of 'domestication' of men and reactions against it are visible throughout the nineteenth and twentieth centuries, and, as will be demonstrated below, the eighteenth; though their impact was as much ideological as societal.[29] Focusing on nineteenth-century fatherhood also reveals its different meanings in different social and cultural contexts.[30] Clearly the picture of differentiation and deep continuity needs further research to clarify and conceptualise it where fatherhood is concerned.

This chapter contributes to the process of exploring fatherhood and fathering in more depth by examining the period 1760–1830.[31] It investigates the relationship between masculinity and fatherhood rather than assuming that the latter is a subcategory or symbol of the former. Less interested in the specifics of the father–child relationship, or in identifying categories of fathering styles, it seeks to evaluate how far fatherhood and fathering contributed to the formation of personal (male) identity as both a public category and a more subjective experience (though I realise that the two are closely intertwined).

170  *Joanne Bailey*

It attempts to do so through brief case studies outlining initial findings on patterns of ideals and their adoption by individuals. The time frame will offer some insights into historicising fathers, and perhaps men, over the long term, since it spans the traditional divide between early modern and modern. An early intervention in this area, it addresses three basic questions, with the aim of stimulating further research. How do the ideals of manhood and fatherhood relate to each other? What evidence is there that these ideals shaped experience in terms of self-identity? And does closer attention to masculinity have the potential to shed light on the extent to which fatherhood/fathering underwent continuity and change?

## Sources and methodology

This study is part of a larger project on parenting in England c. 1760–1830, which aims to understand the terms, values and concepts that informed ideas about parenthood and parenting and its practice and experience. A variety of printed and visual sources are used, including autobiographies, correspondence and print culture. Qualitative research software is used to analyse this diverse material. Data are coded with attention to the language, concepts and understandings expressed in them in order to connect the broader cultural framework, ideals and values with personal reflections, memories and behaviours. This offers the 'methodological comprehensiveness' that Karen Harvey and Alexandra Shepard advocate for the history of masculinity and addresses interaction between discourse and subjective experience.[32] The middle section draws on a small number of case studies in the light of Michael Roper's assertion that 'a biographical perspective allows us to see the assimilation of cultural codes as a matter of negotiation involving an active subject.'[33]

Its conceptual framework assumes multiple masculinities.[34] It acknowledges that there are socially dominant forms in a hierarchy of masculinities, though recognising that they can reciprocally influence each other.[35] In relating ideas to experience, it does so in the light of findings that constructions of masculinity may not correspond exactly with men's lived experiences, but 'express ideals, fantasies and desires' that nevertheless interact with them. The scope for tensions and inconsistencies is a key theme, informed by work in the social sciences which points to the 'layering, the potential internal contradiction, within all practices that construct masculinities'.[36] This is emerging in current research on fatherhood, as Robert Rutherdale's chapter in this volume indicates. Finally, it assumes that masculinities differ over time and place. To aim at further precision, sociological analytical categories are used when discussing men as fathers. 'Father' applies to the processes by which this term becomes attached to a particular individual. 'Fatherhood' refers to the cultural representations of men as fathers, and 'fathering' is the set of practices, actions and activities of 'doing' parenting.[37] These terms recognise the plurality of fathering practices rather than a unified normative model of fatherhood.[38] This is no modern phenomenon, but the proposal that we talk about 'fatherhoods' rather than fatherhood has still to be adopted for England, with only one or two exceptions.[39]

## The relationship between ideals of masculinity and fatherhood

Provision and care are two prominent values associated with fatherhood, though their relationship with each other and other qualities of fatherhood differs over time. In the eighteenth and early nineteenth centuries men had responsibility to provide the necessities of life for their families. This is most clearly seen in legal and poor law records. In matrimonial litigation, for instance, men were evaluated on the level of provision they provided for children as well as wives.[40] The vagrancy laws pursued men who did not contribute to the maintenance of their families in order to reinstate their support and punish them if this were not forthcoming.[41] The Old Poor Laws fixed financial responsibility for illegitimate children upon putative fathers.[42] The inability to provide for children through illness or unemployment was also a significant factor in the award of poor relief. More widely, printed advice for men in marriage and the home promoted the paternal obligation and it underlies some fictional depictions of fathers, usually when the ability to meet this obligation was compromised.[43] After several financial setbacks caused by his trusting benevolence, for instance, Goldsmith's Reverend Primrose was reduced to penury when his house burned down. He set out his situation: 'observe this bed of straw and unsheltering roof; those mouldering walls and humid floor; my wretched body, thus disabled by fire; and my children weeping round me for bread.' He tells his children that he would not swap his situation: 'if you could but learn to commune with your own hearts, and know what noble company you can make them, you would little regard the elegance and splendours of the worthless.' Feelings were thus compensation for material goods.[44]

Indeed, in this period, provisioning fatherhood was overshadowed in several discourses by emphasis upon feeling fatherhood as paternal care and affection. My ongoing survey of novels, poetry, periodical fiction, prescription, correspondence and memoirs demonstrates that perhaps the most popular adjective and noun used to praise and describe fathers were 'tender' and 'tenderness'. This application spans the period, and the following examples are chosen to indicate this. It appears, for example, mid-century in Sarah Fielding's *The Countess of Delwyn*. The interpolated story of Mrs Bilson states that she 'lost her Mother when she was about Eleven Years old; but by her Father's Tenderness, and great Care of her Education, she did not suffer as might be expected from so great a misfortune'.[45] It is found in the expanding genre of children's stories, such as Mary Belson Elliott's 1818 *The Orphan Boy or a journey to Bath*. This refers to a father who '(however mistaken in his management) tenderly loved' his daughter.[46] It features frequently in periodicals such as *The Lady's Magazine*. It also defined men who acted as fathers. Thus, when Mary Dudley, the Quaker preacher, recorded the support of Samuel Neale in her spiritual career, she stated that his 'conduct towards me was like a tender father'.[47] It was visually depicted too. The culmination of Francis Wheatley's series of four paintings 'Married Life', for example, was *Happy Fireside* (1791 and exhibited at the Royal Academy in 1792), in which the attractive father and his infants exchange devoted gazes. He engages with his children, who are located next to him, while his wife sews. The adjective 'tender' was not gender-specific, since it was used to describe good parents of both sexes, though the emphasis upon tender mothers is perhaps more familiar from work on a 'cult of maternity'. While historians of literature and art have begun to analyse the English tender father, it is generally historians of North American fathers in this period who engage most productively with this parental attribute, partly because they pay closer attention to the influence of the culture of sensibility upon the family.[48]

It is this cultural base that historicises and inflects the use of the term and therefore the meaning of paternal care. The adjective 'tender' was applied to parents in the early modern period.[49] Yet an examination of context in such usages implies that its meaning was somewhat different. References to tender fathers are found in sermons, scriptural treatises, more broadly as a metaphor for fatherhood as an abstract concept, and, of course, as a title for God. It seems, however, to become more personalised and individualised over the course of the eighteenth century. The OED defines tenderness as related to mildness, delicacy of feeling, and the gentle emotions, characteristics which were used to denote a number of ideal relationships in the second half of the eighteenth century, since the culture of sensibility celebrated human connectedness.[50] Nonetheless, it held particular resonance when used in conjunction with parents, thanks to changing notions of childhood and child-rearing.[51] Where parents were concerned, its meanings encompassed benign and devoted emotional commitment, a depth of love that was deep, not superficial, and a bundle of empathetic traits, including compassion, care and solicitude. Related to the quality of tenderness, the sources describe further paternal characteristics that demonstrate their origin in the culture of sensibility. These denote the outpouring of feeling through tears, kisses, hugs, opening of hearts and sensitivity as represented by tremulousness and stirred nerves. Such fictional fathers literally overflow with emotion. In 1782 the *Lady's Magazine* published the story of a young woman who was deluded into a sexual relationship by the man she hoped to marry. When she discovered she was pregnant and abandoned she confessed her condition to her parents. Her father, the 'best of men', was shaken by 'silent grief'. On preventing his daughter from committing suicide he clasped 'me with an impassioned fondness to his bosom, he exclaimed, while *all the father melted on his cheek*, "She is, she is my child!"'[52] Clearly there was little distinction between paternity and pure emotion.

Though tenderness was at root non-gendered as a desirable trait for both parents, it was gender-related. It is possible to demonstrate this by contextualising tender fatherhood in contemporary manhood. This provides further evidence for one of the key findings of masculinity studies, that manhood is constructed in relation to other forms of manhood, not only in opposition to womanhood. The caring, nurturing, openly affectionate qualities of the tender father were not formulated in opposition to those of mothers and were not assumed to be non-masculine attributes. However, more research is needed, given the paucity of studies, to establish whether the tender father was constructed in opposition to other 'types' of fatherhood, such as the authoritarian father. It is clear that both providing and tender fathers were closely related to dominant manhood, though the first encompasses more long-standing values and the second more novel ones. Provision was linked to the core values of 'patriarchal' manhood, which conjoined male economic independence with responsibilities for maintaining dependents. But, though dominant manhood had some enduring features, in the eighteenth century it absorbed newly fashionable ideals of male behaviour arising out of sensibility.

Sensibility became part of the way in which men defined themselves as refined models of manhood. The 'man of feeling' embodied emotion, sensitivity and gentleness, and was imagined in a domestic setting. Though the ideal was not without its detractors, the fundamental qualities of compassion and benevolence had widespread cultural power. Philip Carter has shown its cultural prominence for men in the second half of the eighteenth century.[53] William Stafford's survey of the *Gentleman's Magazine* 1785–1815 indicates that 'domesticity, connectedness, sensibility and gentleness' were the most important features of 'gentlemanly masculinities'.[54] While qualities of sensibility were undoubtedly closely associated with elite manhood, they were not class-specific. The literature which depicted these ideals circulated among the middle classes, who used its vocabulary. More humble and plebeian men may well have been familiar with the tender father. For example, Hannah Barker observes that the three men who were fathers in her study displayed 'a sentimental attitude toward family life, and in particular, towards fatherhood and being husbands'. She states, however, that their domestic focus was 'far removed' from that of the 'man of feeling'.[55] In fact this is somewhat misleading, given that the 'man of feeling' was profoundly bound up with the family, home, the pastoral and the provincial. By the later eighteenth and early nineteenth centuries it is also possible to see tender, feeling families in popular ballads and songs.[56]

Manliness was meant to combine new values of sensibility and feeling with traditional admirable masculine qualities such as fortitude, stoicism and courage. In her study of Jean-Jacques Rousseau's profound impact upon English elite men, Claire Brock observes that he 'offered a form of masculinity that entranced and inspired. Intertwining the man of feeling with the man of virtuous action, Rousseau presented an image of a new sort of hero, a figure to be admired and emulated'.[57] Thus, the correct kind of sensibility, deeply felt and not hyperbolic in form and expression, enhanced men's roles rather than undermined them.[58] This helps identify the depths of the culture of sensibility, which can too easily be dismissed as superficial sentimentality. Male feeling was about conveying care and sympathy for the helpless. Those deemed vulnerable and in need of protection included the poor, but, of course, it was children who best demonstrated this attribute of manliness for men who were fathers. Thus the contemporary meaning of 'tender father' conveyed esteemed values of compassion, solicitude, conscientiousness and conscience, which helps us understand why men were willing to be praised as such and to adopt this persona themselves. Tender paternity, after all, also demonstrated virility through the fact of reproduction as well as the newer traits of benevolence and mildness.

The cultural function of alterity in constructing discursive definitions of manhood is currently being uncovered. William Stafford, for example, shows that the dominant ideal of 'manly sensibility' in the *Gentleman's Magazine* was defined partly through disapproval of other masculinities, primarily the 'irresponsibility often associated with young men'.[59] If provisioning and tender fatherhood correlate with the approved qualities of socially dominant manhood, then their antithesis, the bad father, a figure through whom ideals of fatherhood was reinforced, also corresponds with varieties of manhood. A 'bad' father was one who failed to provide economically for his children through refusal or abandonment. New features of ideal manhood were also evident in the period in the frequently used term 'unfeeling' father. It was applied to men who would not allow their child to marry for love. In the story of Charlotte Bateman's attempt to secure a marriage to the man she loves, serialised in the *Lady's Magazine*, in 1782, her friend Amelia, a farmer's daughter, denounces Charlotte's 'unfeeling father!' for commanding her to marry a man she does not love.[60] The phrase also encompassed lack of personal affection and emotional connection, being unmoved by the child's feelings, and not taking pleasure in children.[61]

There are bad fathers, however, who would seem to be more broadly in alignment with 'anti-patriarchal' manhood, which entailed codes of behaviour constructed in opposition to patriarchal ones, such as excessive drinking, womanising or violence.[62] When these characteristics were associated with youth they might be overlooked or tolerated. However, they became far more abhorrent when displayed by fathers. Often described as dissipated or profligate fathers, these were men who succumbed to temptation and thus risked wasting resources and fathering unhealthy, immoral offspring. Indifferent fathers were prioritising other aspects of their lives over fathering. Thus, the ambitious father was condemned for putting his commercial or political ambitions first. However, this was a less risky aberration, since it did not threaten livelihood, as did dissipation, and did not infer weakness or lack of self-control. In effect, good fathers were the antithesis of those who were unreceptive to socially dominant manhood or failed to achieve the correct balance between provision and tenderness.

Thinking about fatherhood in the plural, as we do with manhood, makes it possible to explore how far fatherhoods were competing, overlapping or in tension. This is a helpful way to enrich our understandings of fathers in a period when new behavioural ideals were incorporated into the dominant model of manhood and parents faced novel expectations about their function.[63] Signs of tensions are detectable, though more research is required. A fictional letter from Leonidas to the editor of the *Lady's Magazine* in 1781 explained that he was brought up by his father, a country gentleman, following the death of his mother. Though he knew his father loved him, he abhorred his priorities, which centred on enlarging his already substantial landed possessions and gaining his son 'weight and influence in the county'. To this end he would not let his son marry for love. Leonidas claimed he was not a good father because he was 'a man of narrow sentiments... in short, he does not, and I believe never did possess any real tenderness'.[64] This intimates generational disjunction; one is, after all, not a bad parent for wanting to position a child in a secure dynasty supported by money, land, credit and political position. Moreover, though the overflowing of paternal emotion was mostly seen as positive and beneficial to father and child, there were instances where it posed risk. In excess, exercised without other values of fatherhood, it could lead to the adult offspring acquiring bad habits or being taken advantage of. In a slightly humorous version, the Vicar of Wakefield's extreme sensibility left him unable to rescue his daughter when she nearly drowned. He recalled: 'My sensations were even too violent to permit my attempting her rescue,' which was left to their companion. Nonetheless, he later saved his little 'treasures' from a house fire that struck his family.[65] If we can detect clashes between different fatherhoods in public discourses and some working out of an appropriate balance in print culture, it is helpful to ask what negotiation and compromise ensued when individuals took up elements of these discourses as part of the process of constructing their own identities as fathers and men.

## Evidence for a link between ideals and experience

I have argued elsewhere that the 'relationship between the increasing emphasis on a tender paternal role and lived experience is yet to be unravelled'.[66] The same could be said for the provisioning paternal role in this period, and this section takes an initial step in that process. Provision and tenderness were both values by which men were judged in public, by their families and by themselves. Institutional definitions of men as provisioners shaped how men presented themselves when dealing with them. In their letters requesting relief, poor family men defined themselves as thwarted providers for their children, driven to watch them suffer from want.[67] However, it is unwise to assume that in practice provisioning fatherhood was cast as purely economic support.[68] An advertisement for charity in the *Times*, 1795, indicates the range of characteristics conflated with middle-class provision. The wife explained that her 'worthy, though unfortunate husband', previously a respectable merchant, had suffered financial losses and a broken leg, 'which accumulation of misfortunes has so totally absorbed his mind in grief, that he is at present unable to be the advisor or protector of his family'.[69] It would be possible to examine pauper narratives to examine how far labouring fathers and families saw men's provisioning as a purely economic support for children or whether it incorporated additional qualities. On my reading of men's memoirs so far, the role of provider was only one aspect of their paternal personae, and not one that was forefronted. This may be because the memoirs consulted to date are by relatively wealthy men who were not in dire financial need and that provisioning was only evoked when it was absent or threatened.[70]

There is also evidence that feeling and tenderness were qualities against which men were judged or applauded as fathers. The examples selected here are deliberately scattered across the time period, though research is necessary to achieve precision on change over time. The quality was used to praise or idealise men. Thomas Wright described his son-in-law in the same terms as his eldest daughter Betty in relation to their son's death in 1793 aged one and a half.[71] 'He now rests in peace, and will be found again by his feeling, affectionate parents in that day.'[72] Robert Owenson's letter to his daughter Sydney in 1807 adopted the rhetoric of a feeling father. Writing about his younger daughter Olivia's departure from the paternal home to take up a post as a governess, he declared: 'She will leave me in very, very low spirits; and God only knows what I hourly feel for her, and what I am still to feel when she leaves me.'[73] The longevity of these values is indicated by the fact that this was selected by the editor of her memoir in 1862 to demonstrate that Robert was a good father. Individuals used the concept to judge their own fathers. In her old age in the 1820s Catharine Cappe regretted that her father had been 'generally reserved and distant, from principle', effectively positioning him in stark contrast to the emotionally expressive father of sensibility.[74] Men also used the ideal when defending their own behaviour. George Courtauld wrote to his eldest adult children early in 1815, following some tensions, reminding them: 'I have loved you all from the cradle – I have uniformly been a nursing father to all of you – and I might almost say a nursing mother too – for at different times when several of you were quite infants I was left alone with you, and when not alone how often have I hushed you to sleep walking about the room with you for hours in the night – to ease your pains and lull your sorrows.'[75] That George Courtauld did take active care of his infants is confirmed in other family correspondence and in his children's later recollections. Moreover, while inability to provide was the central factor determining fathering in pauper letters, it was linked to emotion. For instance, Frances Soundy wrote to the parish authorities in Pangbourne, Berkshire, on 2 December 1818 explaining that her husband had left her and her children 'in the gratest disstrees' and she would have written sooner except that her 'undutiful child told me her unfeeling farther would sand me 10 shiling on sataday last but he did not'.[76]

Thomas Wright of Birkenshaw, West Yorkshire (1736–1801), who wrote his memoirs in 1795, offers a valuable case study. He detailed his physical care for his children, for example nursing three of them through smallpox and the measles in 1782, and he devoted considerable space to his deep emotional connection with one of them in particular. Positioning himself as the nurturing, tender, good father had a public aspect for him and was clearly the way he represented himself in his neighbourhood. He proudly reported his ill seven-year-old son John's declaration: '"Bless you! Everybody says you are a good daddy to your children, and so you are."' He explained: 'the poor child had heard the family at Brook-houses (Wright's in-laws) abuse me and say I was a bad father to my children, and behaved ill to them; he had heard all the neighbourhood say the contrary, and from the tenderness with which I treated him and all my children, was satisfied of the contrary himself.'[77] But tender fatherhood also formed part of his subjective identity. For instance, he commented that, when he went up and down stairs day and night to his sick children's chambers without intermission for six or seven weeks, it did not just cause him constant fatigue but also 'depressing sorrow of mind' for his 'suffering children'.[78] He claimed he was by nature a feeling father. Responding to people who censured him for suffering too much sorrow over John's death, he mused: 'Different persons have different feelings, and it had pleased my Maker to endow me with very acute ones, especially with respect to my children.'[79]

Despite its significance in several social and cultural domains for approved manhood, not all men felt it necessary to promote a personal identity based upon themselves as the provisioning head of household. This indicates that at the personal level there was some degree of variation in its use and adaptation to newer norms. Perhaps men used the type of fatherhood at which they were successful in order to offset failures in other aspects of manliness. Tommy Wright stated that he was a caring, tender father in order to lay claim to a good reputation as a man, from which his failure to achieve patriarchal manhood might have debarred him. His memoir turned on his inability to achieve a stable marriage, to run a financially successful household in the face of the increasing financial burden of numerous children, or to obtain any independence of means.[80] Yet, by placing tender fathering at the centre of his personal identity, he was able to present himself as a praiseworthy man. Further questions require more research. What balance needed to be achieved between the two fatherhoods when the quality of tenderness was gaining importance? Were there tensions for men in reconciling or negotiating provisioning, authoritarian and tender models of fatherhood? Achieving balance may have been a recurrent dilemma. McLaughlin's study of eleventh-century 'spiritual fathers' maintains that paternity was riven by ambiguities and instabilities: fathers had to be stern and loving, but not too much of either.[81]

One way to think about this is to consider the way in which some men presented themselves as integrating children with their employment. William Cobbett declared it most explicitly: 'My time, when at home, and when babies were going on, was chiefly divided between the pen and the baby.'[82] It is possible that displaying the ability to work alongside children offered them a way to form an identity as a father that addressed the dual requirements of emotional depth of involvement and provision, showing the capacity to labour on their behalf and to combine this with compassion and care. Such hybrid forms have been uncovered in modern sociological studies of fatherhood and masculinity in which the ideals of breadwinner man and caring father create significant tensions in the performance of masculinities.[83] The men interviewed in one study combined the idea of breadwinner and 'involved' father.[84] The concept of 'hybrid' fathering identity needs further research for historical actors. One avenue is to study correspondence from men who had to work away from home in this period, to see whether any tensions between provisioning and tender fathers were visible.

## Historicising fatherhood and fathering

The notion of plural fatherhoods helps us begin to identify differences in fathering styles across social ranks and periods. There is some evidence of nuances according to social rank. While the qualities associated with provisioning and tender fatherhoods might be similar, their delivery to different audiences was differentiated. Two forms of advice, medical and religious, serve as examples. William Buchan's condemnation of fathers who did not give their infants as much attention as their hounds and horses was a warning obviously aimed at a 'gentleman of the first rank'.[85] In contrast, William Braidwood's 1792 sermon reminding fathers 'that no hurry of business, or any concerns in which they may be engaged, can be admitted as an excuse for negligence' in child-rearing was directed at middling and professional men.[86] As previous examples reveal, there was potential for tension between styles of fatherhood and socially approved manhood. Gentry and middling men were cautioned against prioritising what were suitable activities for their social rank over tender fatherhood. For the middling men in particular, this brought the aspects of provision and tenderness into some conflict.[87] Moreover, different institutions may have favoured different qualities of fatherhood. Thus, ecclesiastical courts, quarter sessions, and poor law administrators were geared to viewing fathers as provisioners. Even this distinction may well be too rigid at times, since tenderness was not entirely absent in these venues. For example, matrimonial separation cases did occasionally attend to parental tenderness when assessing spouses' behaviour.[88]

Given that types of manhood are linked to fatherhood, it is also possible to think about change over time. Studies argue that ideals of masculinity evolved in the early decades of the nineteenth century, positively emphasising male independence and taciturnity.[89] This fits with studies that identify a turning away from the voluble culture of sensibility around the turn of the eighteenth century. Did these lead to changes in fatherhood? John Tosh proposed that fatherhood styles had shifted by Queen Victoria's accession. He argues that William Cobbett's advocacy of physically demonstrative and routine caregiving fathering in 1830 was defensive in tone because it was being rejected as effeminate. By the mid-nineteenth century, he observes, men were repressing the 'feminine within', so that upper middle-class fathers were less able to express intense feelings for their offspring in public than their own fathers had been.[90] It is not difficult to link this shift to changing notions of manhood and cultural fashions. Over this period independence came to be equated with maleness, and thus dependence was firmly gendered as feminine. Male dependence thus connoted passivity, inferred political disempowerment and was judged effeminate. Considerations of dependence shaped debates on poverty. Anxieties over increasing poor relief from the turn of the century sharpened criticism of labouring men who failed to maintain families. Thomas Malthus, for example, characterised the state of labouring men who married without the means to support their children and thus became a burden on the parish as 'dependent poverty', which debased men as well as threatening society's capacity to increase without suffering harsh checks.[91] Moreover, as the culture of sensibility was outmoded, so it goes, overt displays of emotion were suspected as artificial and insincere, and male emotional self-control was preferred. It is possible, therefore, that these developments promoted provisioning/breadwinning fatherhood over nurturing fatherhood.

While this is a promising line of enquiry, it needs further research to establish its precise contours. Recent research offers a more complex pattern. For example, literary scholars now demonstrate sensibility's pervasiveness through cultural, social and political life and its longevity into the early nineteenth century. It is not clear when emotional expressiveness was replaced by taciturnity. William

Stafford concludes that representations of masculinity in the *Gentleman's Magazine* 1785–1815 do not reflect a transformation in manhood with 'the disappearance of the man of sensibility, the onset of reserve and taciturnity, [and] a shift from a "social" to an individualistic self'.[92] So in 1815 tensions between masculinities that might have had repercussions for fatherhood, such as disapproval of the expression of love or of nurturing attributes, were not yet evident. Louise Carter's analysis of two opposing visions of masculinity displayed in the debates surrounding the divorce trial of Queen Caroline in 1820 concludes that middle and working-class defenders of the Queen adopted a model of masculinity 'in which character, sincerity, respectability, piety, duty and domestic steadiness' dominated.[93] She also notes that both sides were attuned to the language of manly feeling, suggesting it remained a rhetorical device that was still useful in defining masculine identity in 1820.[94] Prized though the quality was, independence or autonomy cannot be straightforwardly equated with fathering, since it was class and age-related. The extent to which inability to provide for children due to sickness, employment or financial failure led to loss of manhood requires more finely tuned research. Provisioning a plebeian family required joint effort, not sole male labour, and the role of provisioner had yet to acquire the later political connotations of breadwinning. Moreover, independence could be temporary or short-lived. Thus, the aged father was not independent, since he might require support from children.[95] No doubt research on the ideals of fatherhood and modes of expression from 1800 to 1830 will help delineate the patterns of continuity and change.[96]

Using the conceptual framework of masculinities to study fatherhood helps historians recognise diversity, fluidity and potential gaps between aspirations and actualities. This historicises and nuances the picture of ideals and behaviours. Ideals of fatherhood and their antitheses aligned with 'patriarchal' and 'anti-patriarchal' manhood. These ideals could be in tension with each other in discourse and in the construction of masculine identity. In practice, men may have sought to reconcile the tender father and the provisioning father within their own identities. This probably reflects the reality that the two were not dichotomous and that the emotional and material aspects of parenthood were neither separate nor competing. A gendered study of fatherhood also informs our knowledge of change over time. There is no doubt that there was both 'tidal change and deep continuity' in masculinities, with mastery over the household one of the key 'enduring' features, and an 'ongoing negotiation between a soft and a hard masculinity'.[97] Studying fatherhood in this context helps us to identify the ways in which evolving codes of manhood influenced fathering styles across rank and generation, and shaped what was acceptable in the exercise of authority. It has been argued that, while socially dominant manhood in this period drew on traditional values of authority and autonomy, it also took up qualities of care and feeling. This may indicate that, while the constituents of dominant masculinities were resilient, their precise formulation could differ considerably over time.

Other key aspects emerging from masculinity studies indicate further directions for research in the history of fathers. The histories of family and masculinity have yet to explore fathering as an individual or generational experience in any sustained way.[98] Yet scholarship in the social sciences emphasises the diversity of masculinities inflected by age, social, occupational and marital status, race and ethnicity. It also sees masculinity as a process of becoming rather than a culmination or end point.[99] Both insights could be brought to bear on fatherhood. It would be helpful to look at the life-course element of fathering and how this changed as men grew older, as Rachel Moss does in this volume, and how paternal relationships might differ with different children. Masculinity studies also focus on the ways in which men interact with each other, which would help in formulating the study of father–son relationships.

By conceptualising how fatherhoods interact with different domains within masculinity, a dynamic picture of fatherhood and fathering develops. Being attuned to different configurations between these domains allows the historian to historicise fatherhood, because their importance, meaning and significance change according to wider cultural, political, social and economic contexts.

## Notes

Many thanks to Chris Brooks for taking time to read and comment on drafts of this chapter. I am also grateful for funding from the British Academy, the Scouloudi Foundation, Institute of Historical Research, the Leverhulme Trust, and Oxford Brookes University to carry out aspects of this research.

1. On gendering the history of parenting, see J. Bailey, 'Reassessing parenting in eighteenth-century England', Helen Berry and Elizabeth Foyster (eds), *The Family in Early Modern England* (Cambridge, 2007), pp. 210–11.
2. For an overview of masculinity studies in the social sciences, see R.W. Connell and J.W. Messerschmidt, 'Hegemonic masculinity: rethinking the concept', *Gender and Society* 19 (2005), 829–59; M.S. Kimmel, J. Hearn and R.W. Connell, 'Introduction', in idem. (eds), *Handbook of Studies on Men and Masculinities* (London, 2005).
3. For sociological studies making such links, see E. Dermott, *Intimate Fatherhood: A Sociological Analysis* (London, 2008); J. Hearn, 'Men, fathers and the state: national and global relations', in B. Hobson (ed.), *Making Men into Fathers: Men, Masculinities and the Social Politics of Fatherhood* (Cambridge, 2002), p. 254; D. Lupton and L. Barclay, *Constructing Fatherhood: Discourses and Experiences* (London, 1997).
4. R. Houlbrooke, *The English Family 1450–1700* (Harlow, 1984), chapters 6 and 7; L. Stone, *The Family, Sex and Marriage in England 1500–1800* (London, 1977); K. Wrightson, *English Society 1580–1680* (London, 1982), pp. 104–18. Histories of the colonial American family did not follow this trajectory. See differentiation of fathers from mothers in D.B. Smith, *Inside the Great House: Planter Family Life in Eighteenth-Century Chesapeake Society* (Ithaca NY, 1980), chapter 3.

5. R. Griswold, *Fatherhood in America: A History* (New York, 1993); S. Johansen, *Family Men: Middle-Class Fatherhood in Early Industrializing America* (New York, 2001); L. Wilson, '"Ye heart of a Father": Male Parenting in Colonial New England', *Journal of Family History* 24 (1999), pp. 255–74. Fathers were also a focus of historians of eighteenth-century French political culture: L. Hunt, *The Family Romance of the French Revolution* (Berkeley, 1992); J. Merrick, 'The family politics of the Marquis de Bombelles', *Journal of Family History* 21 (1996), 503–18; L. Tuttle, 'Celebrating the pere de famille: pronatalism and fatherhood in eighteenth-century France', *Journal of Family History* 29 (2004), 366–81.
6. For example: Bailey, 'Reassessing parenting'; H. Berry and E. Foyster, 'Childless men in early modern England', in idem, *Family in Early Modern England*; A. Fletcher, *Growing up in England: The Experience of Childhood 1600–1914* (New Haven, 2008), chapters 8–12. An early example, which was not followed up, was J.R. Gillis, 'Bringing up father: British paternal identities, 1700 to present', *Masculinities* 3 (1995), 1–27.
7. For deserting men see J. Bailey, *Unquiet Lives: Marriage and Marriage Breakdown in England, 1660–1800* (Cambridge, 2003), pp. 36–7, chapter 8. For an attempt to break down stereotypical dismissals of the fathers of illegitimate children, see J. Black, 'Who were the putative fathers of illegitimate children in London, 1740–1810?' and T. Nutt, 'The paradox and problems of illegitimate paternity in old poor law Essex', in A. Levene, T. Nutt and S. Williams (eds), *Illegitimacy in Britain, 1700–1920* (Basingstoke, 2005).
8. For poor fathers, see J. Bailey, '"Think wot a mother must feel": parenting in English pauper letters c. 1760–1834', *Family and Community History* 13 (2010); for labouring fathers see J. Humphries, '"Because they are too menny" children, mothers, and fertility decline: the evidence from working-class autobiographies of the eighteenth and nineteenth centuries', Oxford Economic and Social History Working Papers, September 2006, Reference number: 2006-W64.
9. R. Karras, *From Boys to Men: Formations of Masculinity in Late Medieval Europe* (Philadelphia, 2003), p. 165; A. Shepard, *Meanings of Manhood in Early Modern England* (Oxford, 2003), chapter 3; Shepard, *Meanings of Manhood*; J. Tosh, 'Authority and nurture in middle-class fatherhood: the case of early and mid-Victorian England', in idem, *Manliness and Masculinities in Nineteenth-century Britain: Essays on Gender, Family and Empire* (Harlow, 2005).
10. Karras, *From Boys to Men*, p. 15; Shepard, *Meanings of Manhood*, pp. 73–5.
11. Tosh, *A Man's Place*, pp. 4, 79.
12. Karras, *From Boys to Men*, p. 165.
13. For example: absent; tyrannical; distant; and intimate. Tosh, *A Man's Place*, pp. 93–100.
14. L.T. Broughton and H. Rogers (eds), *Gender and Fatherhood in the Nineteenth Century* (Basingstoke, 2007).
15. For example, see L. Davidoff, M. Doolittle, J. Fink and K. Holden, *The Family Story: Blood, Cand Intimacy, 1830–1960* (London, 1999), chapter 5; Tosh, 'Authority and nurture'.
16. Davidoff et al., *Family Story*, chapter 5; Fletcher, *Growing up*, chapter 10.
17. Shepard, *Meanings of Manhood*, p. 70.
18. Shepard, *Meanings of Manhood*, p. 6 and passim. Tosh, 'What should historians do with masculinity? Reflections on nineteenth-century Britain', in idem, *Manliness and Masculinities*, p. 35.
19. K. Retford, *The Art of Domestic Life: Family Portraiture in Eighteenth-Century England* (New Haven, 2006), chapter 4.

20. See R. Griswold, 'Introduction to the special issue on Fatherhood', *Journal of Family History* 24 (1999), 251.
21. Berry and Foyster, 'Childless men'; Karras, *From Boys to Men*, p. 17; M. McLaughlin, 'Secular and spiritual fatherhood in the eleventh century', in J. Murray (ed.), *Conflicted Identities and Multiple Masculinities: Men in the Medieval West* (New York, 1999).
22. M. McCormack, '"Married men and the fathers of families": fatherhood and franchise reform in Britain', in Broughton and Rogers, *Gender and Fatherhood*.
23. K. Harvey and A. Shepard, 'What have historians done with masculinity? Reflections on five centuries of British masculinity, c. 1500–1950', *Journal of British Studies* 44 (2005), 274–80; M. Roper, 'Slipping out of view: subjectivity and emotion in gender history', *History Workshop Journal* 59 (2005), 57; Tosh, 'What should', p. 47; idem, 'The old Adam and the new man: emerging themes in the history of English masculinities', pp. 72–3.
24. See A. Shepard, 'From anxious patriarchs to refined gentlemen? Manhood in Britain c. 1500–1750', *Journal of British Studies* 44 (2005), 281–82; Tosh, 'Old Adam', passim.
25. Tosh, 'Old Adam', pp. 66–7.
26. Harvey and Shepard, 'What have historians done', pp. 275–76; K. Harvey, 'The history of masculinity c. 1650–1800', *Journal of British Studies* 44 (2005), p. 309; Shepard, 'From anxious patriarchs', p. 287.
27. H. Barker, 'Soul, purse and family: middling and lower-class masculinity in eighteenth-century Manchester', *Social History* 33 (2008), 12–35.
28. L. Davidoff and C. Hall, *Family Fortunes: Men and Women of the English Middle Class 1780–1850* (London, 1987); Tosh, *A man's place*, chapter 8.
29. For criticism see E. Gordon and G. Nair, 'Domestic fathers and the Victorian parental role', *Women's History Review* 15 (2006), 551–59; M. Francis, 'A flight from commitment? domesticity, adventure and the masculine imaginary in Britain after the Second World War', *Gender and History* 19 (2007), 163–85; M. Francis, 'The domestication of the male? Recent research on nineteenth- and twentieth-century British masculinity', *Historical Journal* 45 (2002), 637–52.
30. Broughton and Rogers (eds), *Gender and Fatherhood*.
31. For an examination of the representations of fatherhood in the period, see J. Bailey, '"A very sensible man": imagining fatherhood in England c. 1750–1830', *History* 95 (2010).
32. Harvey and Shepard, 'What have historians done', p. 276.
33. Roper, 'Slipping out of view', p. 69.
34. Connell and Messerschmidt, 'Hegemonic masculinity', pp. 835, 846.
35. The term 'hegemonic' masculinity is not used here, largely because this essay is not attempting to explore the issue at the heart of the concept, which is masculinity as a pattern of practice that facilitates men's dominance over women. Ibid, p. 832.
36. Connell and Messerschmidt, 'Hegemonic masculinity', pp. 838, 852.
37. Dermott, *Intimate Fatherhood*, p. 7; Hobson and Morgan, 'Introduction', in Hobson (ed.), *Making Men into Fathers*, pp. 10–11.
38. David Morgan, 'Epilogue', in Hobson (ed.), *Making Men into Fathers*, p. 278.
39. Griswold, 'Introduction', pp. 252–54.
40. Bailey, *Unquiet Lives*, pp. 62–76.
41. Ibid., pp. 36–7, 170–78.
42. Nutt, 'Paradox and problems', pp. 103–04.
43. Bailey, *Unquiet Lives*, pp. 62–4.

44. O. Goldsmith, *The Vicar of Wakefield: A Tale* (London, 1762), p. 191. Hilliard suggests that this is a story of the redemption of a father from worldly ambition and temperamental weakness by his love for his children. R.F. Hilliard, 'The redemption of fatherhood in *The Vicar of Wakefield*', *Studies in English Literature (Rice)* 23 (1983), 474.
45. Sarah Fielding, *The History of the Countess of Dellwyn: In Two Volumes. By the Author of David Simple.…* 1 (London, 1759), p. 157.
46. M. Elliott (nee Belson), *The Orphan Boy; or, A Journey to Bath; to which is Added, The Orphan Girl. Founded on Facts. By Mary Belson … A New Edition* (London, 1818), p. 59.
47. E. Dudley, *The Life of Mary Dudley, Including an Account of Her Religious Engagements and Extracts from Her Letters, with an Appendix Containing some Account of the Illness and Death of Her Daughter Hannah Dudley* (London, 1825), p. 29.
48. J. Lewis, *The Pursuit of Happiness: Family and Values in Jefferson's Virginia* (Cambridge, 1983); S.M. Pearsall, *Atlantic Families: Lives and Letters in the Later Eighteenth Century* (Oxford, 2008); Wilson, 'Ye heart of a Father'.
49. A search of Early English Books Online shows that it was not uncommon. The earliest example listed in a search for 'tender father' is from 1518.
50. For an excellent overview of the relationship between family and the culture of sensibility in the Atlantic world, see Pearsall, *Atlantic Families*, chapter 3.
51. See H. Cunningham, *Children and Childhood in Western Society since 1500*, 2nd edn (London, 2005); C. Heywood, *A History of Childhood: Children and Childhood in the West from Medieval to Modern Times* (Cambridge, 2001).
52. *LM*, 1782, 126. My emphasis.
53. Philip Carter, *Men and the Emergence of Polite Society in Britain 1660–1800* (Harlow, 2001), chapter 3.
54. W. Stafford, 'Gentlemanly masculinities as represented by the late Georgian *Gentleman's Magazine*', *History* 93 (2008), 47.
55. Barker, 'Soul, purse and family', p. 18.
56. See examples in J. Barrell, *The Spirit of Despotism: Invasions of Privacy in the 1790s* (Oxford, 2006), chapter 5; see the ballads 'The Labourer's return home to his family' and 'The Labourer's welcome home' on Bodley ballads website.
57. C. Brock, 'Rousseauvian remains', *History Workshop Journal* 55 (2003), 149.
58. Stafford, 'Gentlemanly masculinities', pp. 57–60.
59. Ibid., p. 60.
60. *LM*, 1782, 693.
61. Accusations of insensibility were aimed at all kinds of individuals: tyrannical fathers in literature, political enemies in war and political conflict, masters of slaves, slaves, and even entire peoples. Pearsall, *Atlantic families*, p. 88.
62. Shepard, 'From anxious patriarchs', p. 291.
63. For twentieth-century tensions see Rutherford.
64. *Lady's Magazine* XVI (Jan 1781), 37.
65. Goldsmith, *Vicar of Wakefield*, pp. 22, 182.
66. Bailey, 'Reassessing parenting', p. 223.
67. Bailey, 'Parenting in English pauper letters'.
68. For provision as an expression of affection, see J.M. Strange, '"Speechless with grief": bereavement and the working-class father c. 1880–1914', in Broughton and Rogers (eds), *Gender and Fatherhood*.
69. The *Times*, 1795.
70. I intend to pursue this further by using correspondence.

71. T. Wright (ed.), *Autobiography of Thomas Wright of Birkenshaw in the County of York, 1736–1797* (London, 1864), pp. 207–08.
72. Wright (ed.), *Autobiography*.
73. Lady Morgan's *Memoirs: Autobiography, Diaries and Correspondence*, 2 vols (London, 1862), p. 317.
74. M. Cappe (ed.), *Memoirs of the Life of the Late Mrs Catharine Cappe: Written by Herself* (London, 1822).
75. Printed in S.L. Courtauld, *The Huguenot Family of Courtauld*, 3 vols (London, 1966), volume II.
76. Bailey, 'Parenting in English pauper letters'.
77. Wright, *Autobiography*, pp. 154–55, 167–184. For men's role in nursing family, see M. James, 'A Georgian gentleman: child care and the case of Harry Tremayne, 1814-23', *Family and Community History* 9 (2006), 79–90; L.W. Smith, 'The relative duties of a man: domestic medicine in England and France, ca. 1685–1740', *Journal of Family History* 31 (2006), 237–56.
78. Wright, *Autobiography*, p. 153.
79. Ibid., p. 183.
80. Ibid., p. 117.
81. McLaughlin, 'Secular and spiritual fatherhood', p. 26.
82. William Cobbett, *Advice to Young Men, and (Incidentally) to Young Women, in the Middle and Higher Rof life* (1st edn 1830; Oxford, 1980).
83. Lupton and Barclay, *Constructing Fatherhood*, p. 146.
84. This term means actively participating in family life and childcare. A. Terokinas, 'Men on paternity leave in Lithuania: between hegemonic and hybrid masculinities', in A. Teredkinas and J. Reingardiene (eds), *Men and Fatherhood: New Forms of Masculinity in Europe* (Vilnius, 2005).
85. William Buchan, *Domestic Medicine*. This was an extremely popular medical book in the home, with numerous editions. W. Buchan, *Domestic Medicine* (London, 1785), digitised text, accessed at: http://www.americanrevolution.org/medicine.html, p. 5.
86. William Braidwood, *Parental Duties Illustrated from the Word of God, and Enforced by a Particular Account of the Salutary Influence Therein Ascribed to the Proper Government of Children; in Three Sermons, Preached to a Church of Christ in Richmond Court, Edinburgh* (Edinburgh, 1792), p. 6.
87. For current research into modern fathers' negotiation of different fatherhoods, see Esther Dermott, 'The "intimate father": defining paternal involvement', *Sociological Research Online*, 8:4 (2003), <http://www.socresonline.org.uk/8/4/dermott.html>
88. Bailey, 'Reassessing parenting', pp. 219–26.
89. M. Cohen, 'Manliness, effeminacy and the French: gender and the construction of national character in eighteenth-century England', in T. Hitchcock and M. Cohen (eds), *English Masculinities 1660–1800* (London, 1999), pp. 44–62; M. McCormack, *The Independent Man: Citizenship and Gender Politics in Georgian England* (Manchester, 2005).
90. Tosh, 'What should historians do with masculinity?' pp. 48–9.
91. T. Malthus, *An Essay on Population* (1798; London, 1985), pp. 76–7, chapter 5.
92. Stafford, 'Gentlemanly masculinities', p. 68.
93. The other was aristocratic libertine masculinity, espoused by supporters of the King. I think the distinction between the two in practice may have been less sharp. L. Carter, 'British masculinities on trial in the Queen Caroline Affair of 1820', *Gender and History* 20 (2008), 265.

94. She mistakenly attributes feeling to 'refined aristocratic sensibilities', ibid., p. 261.
95. Shepard, *Meanings of Manhood*, p. 241.
96. I plan to do this for my forthcoming monograph.
97. Harvey and Shepard, 'What have historians done', pp. 279–80.
98. Research on this is underway by Henry French and Mark Rothery, University of Exeter.
99. Connell and Messerschmidt, 'Hegemonic masculinity', p. 843.

# Part III
# Maturing and Adulthood

# 10
# Athenian Pederasty and the Construction of Masculinity

*Thomas K. Hubbard*

## 1. Mediterranean masculinity

Due to its origins in feminist critiques of patriarchal social structures, the field of Masculinity Studies has been inspired by a presentist agenda to deconstruct the essentialist assumptions justifying male hegemony and reconstruct masculinity in a gentler and kinder version, more friendly to egalitarian ideals.[1] Although on a theoretical level acknowledging the multiplicity, contingency and social constructedness of masculinities, historically oriented scholars have nevertheless focused their gaze upon favoured themes of male sexual domination, violence, militarism, imperialism and oppression of minorities, which are treated as so historically pervasive that they almost re-essentialise the concept of masculinity.[2] Within the field of ancient studies, there has evolved an unfortunate and usually unstated tendency to assimilate Greek, Roman and Near Eastern men of both antiquity and the modern era to a common stereotype of 'Mediterranean masculinity' that obliterates a range of important differences.[3]

Influenced by the pioneering project of Fernand Braudel and the *Annales* school of historiography, the Mediterraneanist approach to social history has particularly privileged the concepts of 'honour' and 'shame', so pregnant with the potential for masculine violence in defence of reputation.[4] In this assumed system, sexual offences against a woman or, even worse, treating a man as a woman represent the most aggressive forms of dishonour and shame, direct attacks on a man's adequacy as master and protector of his family. From this perspective, Mediterranean patriarchy defined itself principally in terms of men's need never to appear passive, but to dominate and subordinate all groups that did not fit the privileged paradigm of the aggressive, mature, ethnically homogeneous citizen male, and to avenge forcefully any affronts to its authority, either collectively on the battlefield or in individual combat of one form or another.

However, this stereotype is almost wholly the social construct of Northern European and American scholars, tinged with no small degree of condescension and even racism: educated Americans are prone to project the same horror-image onto the males of their own Southern 'Other' (whether of the Spanish-speaking, African–American or 'redneck' working-class Southern white variety). Similarly, Northern European scholars have used this model to assert their own attitudinal superiority relative to their darker-skinned, less affluent Southern immigrant populations, formerly the Italians and Greeks, now the Muslims and Africans. Central to the marginalisation and subordination of the Southern 'Other' is its perceived sexual aggressiveness and supposed disrespect for women. While it may describe a system of values held by some Greek males in some cities of a certain era (even as it may be held by some, but not most, Southern European, Muslim or Latin American males today), this generalisation is far too reductive and schematic to provide an adequate global understanding of all or even most Greek men in the totality of their social roles. I would argue that what is most interesting in historical societies is not the fact of male dominance, but precisely its gaps, discontinuities and vulnerabilities: that is, those points where masculine performance diverges the most from our stereotypical expectations are the most useful for helping us imagine alternative formulations of masculinity even within contemporary cultures.

One of these primary critical points for Greek masculinity was the not infrequent practice, particularly among social elites, of man–boy courtship. As Foucault has suggested in the second volume of his *History of Sexuality*, pederasty was already for the Greeks themselves 'problematised', a point of ethical contestation in formulating discourses and regimens of *askêsis* or self-control. According to Foucault, its practice and articulation offered a critical moment of testing for men and youths alike.[5] However, just as the Greeks themselves confessed a certain ambivalence toward the practice, which was by no means universal,[6] modern interpretations have reflected the regnant paradigms and affects of contemporary academic sensibility. It should come as no surprise that this institution has been widely misinterpreted within the terms of the patriarchal dominance model and assumptions about 'Mediterranean' values. For example, let me quote the eminent historian of sexuality David Halperin:

> Not only is sex in classical Athens not intrinsically relational or collaborative in character; it is, further, a deeply polarizing experience: it effectively divides, classifies, and distributes its participants into distinct and radically opposed categories. Sex possesses this valence, apparently, because it is conceived to center essentially on, and to define itself around, an asymmetrical gesture, that of the penetration of the body of one person by the body – and, specifically, by the phallus – of another. Sex is not only polarizing, however; it is also hierarchical. For the insertive partner is construed as a

sexual agent, whose phallic penetration of another person's body expresses sexual 'activity,' whereas the receptive partner is construed as a sexual patient, whose submission to phallic penetration expresses sexual 'passivity'. Sexual 'activity', moreover, is thematized as domination: the relationship between the 'active' and 'passive' sexual partner is thought of as that obtaining between social superior and social inferior. 'Active' and 'passive' sexual roles are therefore necessarily isomorphic with superordinate and subordinate social status; hence, an adult, male citizen of Athens can have legitimate sexual relations only with statutory minors (his inferiors not in age but in social and political status): the proper targets of his sexual desire include, specifically, women, boys, foreigners, and slaves – all of them persons who do not enjoy the same legal and political rights and privileges that he does.[7]

Although acknowledging that sexual values are never monolithic in a society, David Cohen's respected *Law, Sexuality, and Society* nevertheless adopts the same overall view of classical Athens, so strong is his fealty to the Mediterraneanist stereotype.[8] While this approach may well be apt to those pederastic relations that took place with slave boys, or to pederasty as it was practised within ancient Rome (the actual context for Paul Veyne's ruminations on the continuity of 'Mediterranean' sexual values), I shall argue that it is profoundly mistaken as an interpretation of pederastic relations between men and freeborn boys within classical Athens and most other Greek states of the same period. Scholars such as William Percy and Andrew Lear have emphasised the importance of the pedagogical dimension of Greek pederasty, without denying that it was also hedonistic, in some cases entirely so.[9] What I would add to their insight is to highlight that the pedagogy was not merely or even principally intellectual, but was especially significant in acculturating adolescents in their appropriate gender roles. In other words, it was a process of masculinising, not effeminising, teenage males: it was meant to train them in becoming *active* agents, forging their own destinies through responsible choices at a relatively early age. This emphasis upon pederasty as masculinisation puts me at odds not only with Halperin and his predecessor, Sir Kenneth Dover,[10] but also with anthropological theories that rely on the notion that sexual passivity somehow functions to exorcise boys of their femininity by negative associations (i.e. to be feminine=to be raped by another man).[11]

When classical Athenian pederasty is viewed within the broader context of inter-generational relations in all their forms, the picture that emerges is far more nuanced and double-sided. Our best source for understanding Athenian marriage is Xenophon's *Oeconomicus*, which characterises even the marital relationship as both inter-generational and pedagogical; what differentiates it from pederasty is mainly that marital pedagogy centres upon issues of household management, rather than inculcation of the masculine gender role. We must also situate Athenian pederasty within the spectrum of pederastic practices known from other areas and periods of the Greek world: Spartan pederasty, Cretan pederasty, and what little we know of Theban practice, as well as what many Greeks read back into Homeric warrior comradeships, all suggest a practice of elite mentorship, with particular emphasis upon developing skills as a warrior and defender of state interests.[12] One of our richest sources of evidence for pederasty outside Athens is the extensive poetic collection attributed to Theognis of Megara, a Dorian state next door to Athens; it also characterises the poet's relationship to his younger partner Cyrnus as a form of elite pedagogical pederasty, only in this case not oriented to war so much as to active and responsible citizenship in the *polis* and the symposiastic gatherings where traditional songs would be performed and politics discussed.[13]

In his excellent comparative survey of homosexual practices across all cultures, the sociologist Stephen O. Murray sharply distinguishes between 'age-structured' and 'gender-stratified homosexualities' (as well as the 'egalitarian' form, which he regards as uncommon outside the modern world). Although he does recognise a 'gender-stratified' (i.e. feminising) form within the Greek world, namely the unusual orientation of adult sexual passives ('pathics'), he finds none of the traits otherwise common in 'gender-stratified' homosexualities within the practice of Greek pederasty. Indeed, he explicitly recognises Homeric, Cretan, Spartan and Theban pederasty as 'masculinising' forms of warrior reproduction, but he excludes Athenian pederasty from this category, instead grouping it with the relations that are 'neither masculinizing nor feminizing'.[14] In contrast, I will argue that Athenian evidence also points toward a strongly masculinising elite institution, comparable to what we know of other Greek societies of the same era.

## 2. Sex, age and consent

Far from representing a feminisation of boys, as defined by the passive sexual role, pederasty was understood by its practitioners as a process of masculinisation and maturation, by which boys were challenged from pubescence to take cognisance of their sexual development and make responsible choices whether to accept or reject the offers of an older petitioner. Iconographic and literary evidence shows that freeborn boys frequently rejected suitors and did not in any way feel compelled just because their suitor was older or politically empowered. In a pottery fragment attributed to Onesimus (Figure 1), a man grasps someone else's shoulder, probably a boy's, since the man's bent-over posture suggests that the other figure is quite a bit shorter. Most revealing is the dialogue expressed by the inscribed letters: the man cries *eason* ('let me!'),

*Figure 1* Red-figured ceramic fragment attributed to Onesimus (c. 490 BCE). By courtesy of the Museum of Fine Arts, Boston. 65.873 = *Para*. 360

but the boy makes his displeasure known: *ou pausei* ('won't you stop?').[15] Often the suitors depicted on Athenian red-figure vases are waved away with a mere hand gesture and look of disgust, as we see with the figures on the left on a kylix by Douris (Figure 2). Or boys could inflict emotional pain on their suitor by just walking away (see Figure 3). The rejection could be so emphatic as to involve violence, as in the case of a familiar piece by the Aegisthus Painter (Figure 4), where a boy brandishes his lyre overhead as if to strike a man who reaches out to accost him.[16] Similarly, poetry from the mostly sixth-century collection of Theognis to Hellenistic times characterises boys as often contemptuous of their suitors, not necessarily out of devotion to purity so much as due to the abundance of other options.[17]

On the other hand, we can also see boys assenting to men's advances, jumping for joy at being chosen and showing reciprocal interest by stroking the man's beard (Figure 5)[18] or even playing an active part in furthering the intimacy, as we see in the tondo of a famous cup by the Brygos Painter, where the boy draws his excited suitor's head close to himself for a kiss at the same time that the suitor fondles his genitals (Figure 6). The owner of this cup, the Ashmolean Museum in Oxford, rather anachronistically labels the scene

*Figure 2* Red-figured krater attributed to Douris (c. 470 BCE). By courtesy of the Staatliche Antikensammlungen und Glyptothek, München. 2646 = *ARV*² 437.128

'Paedophile and Victim'.[19] More sensitive is the description by the art historian Alan Shapiro, who observes that the boy,

> far from being intimidated by this lavish display of potency, slips one arm affectionately around the man's neck and enjoys the attention... The bag of knucklebones in the boy's other hand suggests the childhood games he is about to leave behind; the sponge and strigil behind the man, the world of the wrestling school he is about to enter; and the walking stick behind these, the world of the Athenian adult male citizen still to come after that. Here, on the cusp of adolescence, he is initiated into the world of sexual pleasure, perhaps not yet his own, but full of excitement and the anticipation of becoming a man himself.[20]

Indeed, the boy appears to puff out his own chest muscles in imitation of the man's prominent pectorals. What the iconography makes clear is that, no matter how insistent or determined the suitor and no matter how small the boy, the boys remained in control of the situation, able to and even expected to make independent decisions for themselves, either smiling and happily cooperating with the man if they liked him or fending him off if not.[21] However attractive the gifts and benefits an affluent suitor might be able to offer, an innate modesty combined with social pressure from their peers, as Pausanias tells us in Plato's *Symposium* 183c–d, was supposed to deter boys from yielding their favours too easily.

*Figure 3* Red-figured psykter attributed to Smikros (c. 510 BCE). Gift of Nicolas Koutoulakis. By courtesy of the J. Paul Getty Museum, Malibu, California. 82.AE.53

Aristotle certainly credited adolescent boys with a capacity for making responsible choices. In the *Eudemian Ethics* (2.1226b17–1227a5), he introduces the concept of *prohaeresis*, usually translated as 'purposive choice', to describe a deliberate and calculated decision to do something one desires, in which the *nous* ('mind') counterbalances the forces of mere *epithumia* ('appetite' or 'desire'). Later in the same work (*EE* 7.1240b31–34), he says that animals and

*Figure 4* Red-figured pelike attributed to the Aegisthus Painter (c. 465 BCE). By courtesy of the Fitzwilliam Museum, University of Cambridge. GR.26-1937 = *ARV*² 506.21

babies cannot have 'friendship for themselves' (what we might call 'self-esteem') because they lack *prohaeresis*, in other words the capacity to restrain themselves from immediate, unreflective fulfilment of appetites; he says that it is only at the stage when individuals have *prohaeresis* that they can have true 'friendship for themselves', that is, an ability to foresee what is best for themselves. It is, I

*Figure 5* Black-figured cup (c. 520 BCE). Gift of E.P. and Fiske Warren, 1908. By courtesy of the Museum of Fine Arts, Boston. 08.292

*Figure 6* Red-figured kylix interior attributed to the Brygos Painter (c. 475 BCE). By courtesy of the Ashmolean Museum, Oxford. 1967.304 = *ARV*² 378.137

think, significant that Aristotle does not use the generic term *pais* in this passage, but chooses the more specific *paidion*, which never refers to a child older than seven.[22] The implication is that, after this stage, a child progressively develops some measure of *prohaeresis*.

Did adolescent boys have enough *prohaeresis* to be able to make sexual decisions for themselves? What can be said is that Athenians of the classical period saw little need to shield children above the age of seven from knowledge or public discussion of sexual matters. A character in Plato, who was no fan of comedy's licentiousness, says comedy is appropriate for *meizous paides* ('bigger children') (*Laws* 2.658c–d). Aristophanes even says that vulgar stage properties like the leather phallus, especially when it is 'red and thick at the end', are a matter of particular enjoyment to the children (*paidiois*) in the audience, implying that even boys under the age of seven were sometimes present (*Clouds* 539).[23] Aristotle says the young ('those not yet of the age to recline at the symposium and drink strong wine') should not be allowed to attend comedies, because they need to be protected from indecent speech and images

*Figure 7* Red-figured kylix attributed to Makron (c. 480 BCE). By courtesy of the Staatliche Antikensammlungen und Glyptothek, München. 2655 = *ARV*² 471.196

(*Politics* 7.1336a39–b35); however, this section of the *Politics* clearly describes an ideal state, not the way it actually was in the Athens of his time. In many respects, this work of Aristotle aims to suggest reform of current Athenian customs. Elsewhere Aristotle, always a keen empirical observer, notes that even pre-adolescent boys enjoy masturbation (*Generation of Animals* 1.728a10–14). The only real anxiety Greek sources express about adolescent male sexual activity is that boys, who are assumed to be hyper-sexual but as yet unacculturated, will enjoy it too much and go overboard (cf. Aristotle, *Problems* 4.26; Xenophon, *Cyropaedia* 1.6.34).

Sexual contact, at least as represented on Attic vases, is mostly non-penetrative, but focuses on gazing at or fondling the boy's developing genitals, which are treated as an object of fascination. As we have noted, the boy of Figure 6 seems altogether to enjoy the manual stimulation he receives and participates actively and enthusiastically in the physical intimacy; for his part, the man bends himself into an awkward position to place himself on a level of equal height to the boy. Figure 7 is a kylix with three courtship pairs; we should take special note of the pair on the left, where the boy opens up his cloak to expose a full frontal view to his suitor, who bends his head down and trains his line of vision not on the boy's face or chest, but directly on his genitals. The contrast the painter draws between the three pairs is based on the three boys' varying degrees of responsiveness to their suitors and gifts. In each case, responsiveness is indicated by the amount of clothing removed and flesh revealed, ranging from the boy on the right, who remains tightly wrapped and reveals nothing to the older, bearded man who merely offers him a flower, to the middle pair, where at least shoulder and chest are shown to a younger man offering a hare, to the pair on the left, where a younger man's gift of a fighting cock earns him a peek at the ultimate prize. Clearly what excites the boys' lovers in these scenes is not any element of feminine passivity, but evidence of the boys' development into phallic potency. In Aristophanes' *Wasps* 578, Philocleon cites as one of the greatest pleasures of being a juror in Athens that he has the opportunity to examine boys' genitals when they go through the ceremony of *dokimasia*, allowing them to become officially enrolled in their tribe as adult citizens. Something of the sort may be going on in Figure 8, a pelike of the Calliope Painter, where we see an athletic trainer or umpire, as identified by the forked staff, bending over to examine a youth's midsection, perhaps to make an official determination of the age category in which this athlete belongs.[24]

Before proceeding further with our iconographic survey, we must address the question of the age at which Athenian boys might become physically intimate with men. This issue had been a matter of little controversy, with the *communis opinio* being that boys could be courted from the age of 12. However, James Davidson's iconoclastic 2007 book *The Greeks and Greek Love* challenged this assumption and argued that physical contact with those under 18 was strictly illegal and could even be punished with death. As I have demonstrated at greater length in my online review (see n. 12 above), Davidson's evidence for these assertions is highly problematic and appears to be motivated by a broader agenda to fashion the Greeks into appropriate role models for the preoccupations of modern gay identity politics. Based on societies that have nothing to do with ancient Greece, he posits that the age of puberty must have averaged 18.5; however, until late antiquity, ancient sources are uniform in asserting that male puberty occurred around 14.[25] Solon (fr. 27 W) and Aristotle (*Pol.* 1336b37–1337a1) both suggest that 18 was not even a particularly important age boundary for the Greeks, compared with 14 (the age of puberty) and 21 (the age of full physical maturity); although 18 was the age at which Athenian males attained full citizenship privileges during the fifth century BCE, Mark Golden has cogently argued that it may have been 16 during the sixth century.[26] Moreover, not all legal rights and responsibilities came at a single age.[27] Davidson misinterprets a passage from Aeschines' speech *Against Timarchus* (1.139) to assert that the Law of Solon forbade erotic associations with boys who were *akuros* (i.e. 'not yet in control of his own affairs legally'); he also conjures up a mistaken fantasy that youths aged 20 and older were not allowed

*Figure 8* Red-figured pelike attributed to the Calliope Painter (c. 430 BCE). By courtesy of the Tampa Museum of Art, Joseph Veach Noble Collection. 86.68 = ARV2 1262.69bis

into the gymnasium at the same time as boys under 18.[28] Of course, iconographic evidence like the Brygos Painter's cup suggests that boys well below the age of 18 were in fact sexually experienced; Davidson must resort to the desperate explanation that these drinking cups are meant as admonitory paradigms of behaviours to be avoided.[29] Plutarch (*Lycurgus* 17.1) relates very clearly and with no intonation of shock or disapproval that pederastic courtship was customary and fully sanctioned at Sparta from the age of 12; he thus gives us no reason to think that age unusual for the rest of the Greek world. Twelve also appears to be the minimum age at which an Athenian girl could be married, although most girls of the upper class married in their mid- to late teens.[30]

Although more careful and tentative than Davidson, David Cohen suggested that the law of *hybris* ('assault') could be applied against any man who had physical contact with a boy under 18, should the boy's father choose to bring a prosecution.[31] However, he presents no real evidence that the law of *hybris* was ever actually applied in this way, beyond his own conviction that sex with under-18s must have been as objectionable a form of 'dishonour' to the Greeks as it is to moderns. This is clearly not a safe assumption.

As we have observed, most of the 'sex' amounted to little more than looking and fondling, perhaps kissing and embracing. Even where penetration of boys does occur on Attic vases, it is of the intercrural variety (see Figure 9), and thus not really penetration at all:[32] as on the Brygos Painter's cup, we see the man bend himself into an awkward and surely uncomfortable position to put himself on the boy's level. Indeed, here in this scene the man's head is actually bent down below the youth's, and the youth has to embrace the man's shoulders to prevent him from collapsing or tipping over. Contrast this solicitude not to inflict discomfort on the youth with the unquestionably phallocratic domination visible in the iconography of male coitus with women, as in Figure 10.

## 3. Masculine pedagogy and gift exchange

If younger men lacked the same political stature as their elders, it was certainly not out of any desire on the part of the older generation to dominate, so much as a recognition that the young had not yet developed the same level of judgement and masculine self-restraint, what Aristotle called *prohaeresis*. The whole purpose of Greek education beyond the elementary level was precisely to make the impressionable young resemble their elders: literate, physically fit, musical and able to practise the responsibilities of elite citizenship.[33] Pederastic liaisons encouraged the older youths/young men who loved adolescent boys to act as good role models, to 'practice excellence' (Xenophon, *Symposium* 8.27, *askein aretên*; cf. Plato, *Symp.* 178d–e). Hence the teacher was a role model to his students, whom he would typically instruct one-on-one or in small groups.[34] Whether in athletics, philosophy, rhetoric or apprenticeship in a trade, all such training had the ultimate goal of forming youths into independent male citizens.

Moreover, such pedagogical mentorship was often, although not always, implicitly eroticised, as the student's nudity in the schoolroom of Figure 11 suggests;[35] if it was indeed historical practice for prepubescent boys to be nude in the classroom or when singing, as well as in more domestic settings (i.e. small children at play or serving boys at a symposium), we can only conclude that child nudity was so widespread and casual as to suggest that male children were conditioned to feel no embarrassment over their bodies. In such a culture, intimate caresses by well-meaning adults were probably not uncommon and

*Figure 9* Black-figured amphora (c. 530 BCE). By courtesy of the Musée Céramique de Sèvres. 6405 = *CVA* France 13, plate 15.7

were for the most part unproblematic for male children, becoming more difficult only once they reached the age at which they would develop new feelings and sensitivities in those parts of the body, would be clothed most of the time, and would thus have more *aidôs* ('shame') with regard to the *aidoia* ('genitals').

*Figure 10* Red-figured kylix interior attributed to the Briseis Painter (c. 475 BCE). By courtesy of the Ashmolean Museum, Oxford. 1967.305 = $ARV^2$ 408.37

At that point, opening up the cloak to give an older friend a peek or a feel would mean something.

Far from being a form of exploitation, as we might consider such relationships today, a mentor's erotic attraction to a student in a sense equalised the relationship by putting the older man in a position of need and suppliance, where he might be either accepted or rejected by the attractive youth who could choose among many potential mentors.[36] It is for precisely this reason that the ugly old Socrates refuses to accept Alcibiades' offer of his own body in return for Socrates' teaching (Plato, *Symp.* 218b–219d). Such an exchange would not only place him into an inferior position relative to his student, but could suggest that Socrates' wisdom, developed and honed over a lifetime, was equal in value to a few brief moments of mere physical pleasure.

*Figure 11* Red-figured kylix interior attributed to the Eretria Painter (c. 430 BCE). By courtesy of the Musée du Louvre, Paris. G457 = *ARV*² 1254.80

Gift-giving was, of course, central to pederastic courtship as represented on Athenian vases.[37] Educational mentorship could certainly constitute a gift just as tangible as a wreath, lyre, fighting cock or hare: indeed, these common gifts usually imply the suitor's offer to train the youth in the associated realm of activity. The lyre represents musical instruction, as in Figure 12.[38] Wreaths and ribbons are, of course, associated with athletic victory, as we see with the pair on the left in Figure 13.[39] The hare and other gifts of wild game (Figure 14) imply hunting, which has always been a key transitional rite of passage for adolescent boys, as in the myth of Cyparissus or the Cretan pederastic abduction ritual described by the fourth-century historian Ephorus (70F149 *FGrH*).[40] As anthropologists have long recognised, hunting is a vehicle for hardening boys' bodies and spirits, teaching both survival skills in the wilderness and the ability to kill, clean, and dismember animals without any childlike squeamishness or sentimentality. It is, of course, ultimately preparation for the manly resolve necessary to becoming an effective warrior.

*Figure 12* Red-figured pelike attributed to Hermonax (c. 465 BCE). © The British Museum. E374 = ARV2 486.40

*Figure 13* Red-figured amphora attributed to the Dikaios Painter (c. 510 BCE). By courtesy of the Musée du Louvre, Paris. G45 = *ARV*² 31.4

Although less often recognised as pedagogical, the fighting cock (Figure 15) is also meant to harden boys' spirits by engaging them in another variety of blood sport in which they would participate in an intensely competitive form of gratuitous cruelty to animals, one preventing even the slightest degree of emotional attachment to the animal they cared for and maintained.[41] On this particular vase, we see five pairs of bearded men and unbearded youths holding cocks in preparation for a fight. We should not read this scene literally as evidence that cockfights always involved age-different partners; rather, it offers us suggestive symbolism for the love relationship, imaged as a contest of will and endurance between man and youth. Far from effeminising boys by rendering them passive, all these practices aimed at masculinising them and making them more competitive: Alan Shapiro aptly notes 'the cock's age-old reputation as the exemplar of virile masculinity among birds'.[42] In this figure's symbolic playscape, if the youth's cock wins out, then he becomes one of the men.

Pederastic courtship was fundamentally a ritual of gift-exchange in which tangible things, as well as the arts, skills and leisure activities they metonymically

*Figure 14* Black-figured kotyle attributed to Amasis (c. 550 BCE). By courtesy of the Musée du Louvre, Paris. A479 = *ABV* 156.80

*Figure 15* Black-figured kylix attributed to the Painter of Louvre F51 (c. 530 BCE). John Wheelock Elliot Fund. By courtesy of the Museum of Fine Arts, Boston. 63.4

represent, are offered by an adult suitor, in the expectation that they will in turn receive a gift of friendship, affection and perhaps even some form of physical consummation. As in all gift-exchange relations, what is most important is not the exchange of material property, but the affective bonds it creates or signifies. This is what differentiates it from mere prostitution, in which intangible property (money) is exchanged for an interval of bodily service without affective bonds. Fundamental to gift-exchange is that it assumes a basic social equality of the parties involved, who by exchanging gifts and forging affective bonds acknowledge their worthiness of each other. Gift-exchange is inconsistent with any notion of one-dimensional dominance.

## 4. Symposium and *Palaestra* as educational settings

The two principal social settings for pederastic *eros* were the symposium and the *palaestra* (wrestling school). Both were in different ways educational and aimed at making the young more manly: the *palaestra* moulded strong bodies and competitive spirits; the symposium taught good manners, intelligent conversation and the socio-political values appropriate for adult citizens. Symposiastic poetry, such as the work of Theognis or the Attic *skolia*, appears to be intended for precisely such values education. The youths who were most desirable erotically would be those most successful in absorbing these lessons in manhood: victorious athletes and those who could be witty and entertaining at a banquet, or at least those who could, like Autolycus in Xenophon's *Symposium*, listen respectfully.

The social and cultural significance of the Greek symposium has been the object of much recent critical discussion, particularly with reference to the social dynamics of the man–boy relationship. Some believe that only youths above the age of 18 could attend the symposium; however, scholars including Jan Bremmer and Claude Calame have argued for an initiatory model of the Greek banquet, in which boys might progress through a series of steps as in a *rite de passage*, initially sitting on the ground or serving wine as their elders ate, mutely listening to the conversation, then at the age of 18 moving up to the couch to recline along with their *erastês*, possibly performing with the lyre when asked, but still adopting a posture of respect toward their elders.[43] The scene of an unbearded youth of about 17 or 18 reclining beside a bearded man is commonplace on Athenian red-figure vases, as we see in Figure 16.[44]

Moreover, Eve Stehle constructs the symposium as an all-male preserve defining itself in terms of a fundamental 'disconnection' with women and the world of marriage.[45] Even when not explicitly homosexual, the symposium was always 'homosocial', a site of male bonding and concelebration of values imparted from one male age class to another. Sometimes those values might include aggressive exploitation of slave women or prostitutes, once the level of inebriation reached the point of shedding all inhibitions. What I find intriguing in Figure 17 is that we see an older and a younger man joining together to penetrate a single woman from both ends, but we should note that the older man's gaze is not directed toward the woman, whom he is striking with the sandal, but toward the face of the younger man, as if his greatest pleasure is in perceiving the younger man's expressions of pleasure in their acts of phallic domination. Perhaps the prostitute's body has been purchased with the older man's money as a kind of love gift to his younger companion, even as Aeschines (1.42, 1.75–76) tells us that Timarchus' lovers purchased him the services of female prostitutes. This may also be the scenario implied on a much

*Figure 16* Red-figured kylix attributed to Douris (c. 485 BCE). By courtesy of the Museo Archeologico, Florence. 3922 = *ARV*² 432.55

discussed hydria by the Harrow Painter, which previous critics have been wont to interpret as a father taking his son to a brothel.[46]

Whether presented as *skolia*, elegy or tales of paradigmatic heroes, song was an integral part of a boy's symposiastic instruction in the political values of his social class, as well as in the proper forms of self-fashioning as an elite adult male. Theognis' pederastic elegies addressed to Cyrnus present themselves explicitly as such moral and political education. Through hearing such songs recited by others and ultimately performing them himself, a boy apprehends, enacts and promulgates the elite values he is supposed to learn; in time, he will implement them in his role as a participating adult citizen.[47]

It should be emphasised that the symposium was no less competitive an arena for masculine self-display than the wrestling ring, although of an intellectual rather than a physical form. Plato's *Symposium* centres upon a contest to determine which speaker could praise the god Love most eloquently. Similarly, Xenophon's *Symposium* (3.3–5.10) challenges each guest to deliver a clever speech on his greatest source of pride; it also features a beauty contest between the young Critobulus and the elder Socrates, which is really a verbal duel in defining beauty. Derek Collins's recent work has shown just how deeply ingrained in Greek culture the tradition of verbal duelling and contestation is.[48] It was certainly a favoured pastime at symposia for guests to display their learning and verbal skill through learned disquisitions and verse

*Figure 17* Red-figured kylix attributed to the Pedieus Painter (c. 510 BCE). By courtesy of the Musée du Louvre, Paris. G13 = $ARV^2$ 86(a)

recitations or songs fitting the situation, as Athenaeus' deipnosophists do.[49] Another favoured game was for one guest to recite a poetic verse and challenge the next guest to cap it with a witty and appropriate next verse, as we see in a scene in Aristophanes' *Wasps* (1219–49). The company could also express its solidarity by singing a familiar *skolion* or paean in unison, or by having each guest recite a stanza in turn.[50] Inability to do so would be a humiliating disgrace that marked a man as unworthy to be a participant in the group. Acquiring the musical ability, verbal skills, erudition and self-confidence to hold one's own in such company was an essential part of a well-bred young person's development into full manhood. Otherwise, he might be taunted, 'you don't even know the three (lines) of Stesichorus,' a familiar insult for the stupid or boorish, not the kind of people who deserved to be let into the elite club of upper-class symposia.[51]

The competitive character of athletics is, of course, obvious. That it was considered such an essential part of adolescent education is a sign of the importance the Greeks attached to instilling a competitive spirit in future citizens.[52] And, as the work of Thomas Scanlon has recently reminded us, Greek athletics was a pre-eminently erotic spectacle, glorying in the beauty of the naked male body achieving its maximum potential.[53] Numerous vases, as well as various literary references, make it clear that the gymnasium and *palaestra* were also favoured cruising grounds for mature men who were interested in meeting talented and attractive boys of good family. Indeed, as I have argued in a previous publication, boys' athletic trainers often were their lovers or provided boys with access to other men who might assume that role:[54] in Figure 18 we clearly see the trainer using his forked staff to direct the boys' posture and movements, but note the bearded figure with the ordinary staff on the right, who has been admitted to the gymnasium and appears to express interest in a boy who waves him away. The implied homoeroticism of athletic group scenes on numerous Athenian vases supports the notion that many forms of athletic exercise and competition were additionally contests of beauty and physical display which engendered a community of homosexual sensibility among the youths themselves as well as their more mature audience. The evolution of Greek athletic nudity must have had something to do with the development of a homoerotic aesthetic based on appreciation and even adoration of the male physique. It is perhaps no coincidence that our first evidence for athletic nudity, a separate

*Figure 18* Red-figured kylix signed by Douris (c. 485 BCE). By courtesy of the Musée du Louvre, Paris. G118 = *ARV*² 430.35

boys' category in the Olympic games and pederasty all date to the same period, namely the third quarter of the seventh century BCE.[55]

Indeed, Nigel Crowther has gathered together a wealth of epigraphical evidence for contests called *euandria* at several local athletic festivals, including the Panathenaea, as well as festivals at Sparta, Rhodes and Sestos; these appear to have been male beauty contests, including some kind of performance that displayed bodily size, strength and agility.[56] The *euandria* at the Athenian Theseia were closely linked with the *euoplia*, and the prizes for the winning tribe at the Panathenaic *euandria* were oxen and shields, also suggesting an association with military training. Even more widely attested are the contests of *euexia*, which appear to have been a kind of body-building competition. Whether men or youths, Greek athletes provided the model for the artistic representation of ideal masculinity, as can be illustrated by an examination of Greek sculpture. The pervasiveness of perfect male forms in the sculpted monuments of Greek cities (see, for instance, Figure 19) provided growing youths with an omnipresent and sexually alluring image of what they were expected to become, even as advertising and popular media present powerful visual role models to young people today.

Previous discussions of athletic nudity have neglected its educational role in training boys to shed any vestige of shyness when presenting themselves to the public gaze. As a responsible citizen who may be called upon to undertake affairs of state, a man should properly have nothing to hide, but should be an open book to public scrutiny of both his past life and his conduct in office. Being conditioned to perform nude in front of an audience of hungry eyes prepared adolescents for the transparency which was the proper bearing of a leader competing in the realm of democratic politics. As Pierre Brulé has recently noted, nudity was the distinctive mark of being both Greek and male, since neither barbarians nor women (except perhaps in Sparta) exercised naked.[57] To be uncomfortable with public exposure of one's body would therefore be a sign of femininity or slavishness.

For an adult competitor, winning a conspicuous athletic victory often becomes the basis for a subsequent career of political leadership, since the Greeks viewed victory not only as a manifestation of personal discipline and excellence of character, but also as a matter of divine dispensation, illuminating the victor as in some sense the god's favourite, who could likely bring the god's favour back to his home city.[58] For the adolescent competitor, victory often marks a crossing of the threshold into adult maturity: numerous myths and legends tell of fathers setting up a footrace or chariot race as a test for suitors seeking the hand of their daughter.[59] Only victory in that athletic trial permits them to enter into the adult reproductive community and become a patriarch in their own family. Most famous among these myths is the story of Pelops' chariot victory against Oenomaus for the hand of Hippodameia:

*Figure 19* Roman copy of the Diadoumenos of Polyclitus (original c. 420 BCE). By courtesy of the National Archeological Museum, Athens

this race to the death results in Pelops removing the father-figure and taking his place as both Hippodameia's male master and king of Elis. As related in Pindar's *First Olympian*, Pelops is able to win this newfound status only by virtue of his adolescent interlude as Poseidon's chosen favourite, manifested in a pederastic liaison and confirmed by receiving a team of divine horses as a belated gift-exchange.[60]

Pindar makes clear the association between athletic victory and sexual maturity in two other poems: the *Ninth Pythian* praises the victor Telesicrates with myths that frame him as eminently eligible for marriage.[61] But more interesting is *Pythian Ten* (vv. 56–60), an epinician ode written for a boy victor:

When Ephyrean choristers pour out
My sweet voice around the Peneius,
I expect by my songs to make the crowned Hippocleas
Still more splendid to look upon both among his age-mates and older men,
And a heart-throb for young maids. For
Different loves tickle the fancies of different folks.

In other words, the athletic victor Hippocleas, once he has also been celebrated by Pindar's song, will appear even more attractive to three different groups: boys his own age, older men and young women. That we are dealing with his erotic allure and the different types of sexual opportunity now open to him is made clear by the summary gnomic formula 'different loves tickle the fancies of different folks' (*heterois heterôn erôtes eknixan phrenas*). As I have argued elsewhere, this ode was commissioned by the boy's lover, the Thessalian noble Thorax, whose abiding companionship Pindar goes on to recommend to the boy in the lines that follow.[62] But what is most important to note for our present purpose is that Hippocleas could, if he wished, move beyond that relationship and successfully pursue other boys his own age or even a young maiden. In other words, he could now switch from being an *erômenos* to become an *erastês*.

## 5. Taking the initiative and becoming a man

We see the same dynamic at work on an interesting kylix by the Eretria Painter, owned by the Blanton Museum at the University of Texas. On one side (Figure 20) we have a scene that is very typical of this artist' kylixes:[63] two pairs of youths stand in conversation. The two clothed figures appear to be courting the two naked athletes holding discuses; note that the clothed figure on the right appears to offer a sprig of laurel as a gift or award to the athlete, and his lips are parted as if to show that he is the one now speaking. The mutual

216   *Thomas K. Hubbard*

*Figure 20* Red-figured kylix attributed to the Eretria Painter (c. 430 BCE). By courtesy of the Jack S. Blanton Museum of Art, The University of Texas at Austin, Archer M. Huntington Museum Fund and the James R. Daugherty, Jr, Foundation, 1980. 1980.38 = *ARV*² 1254.73

eye contact of the figures expresses genuine engagement and interest, but the athlete makes no effort to reach out and receive the sprig. Note that the athlete moves his right foot ever so subtly to the side, placing it on top of the foot of the clothed youth with a tall staff who is conversing with the other athlete, as if to make a claim on his attention or as a secret signal that he should take notice.

But it is the other side of the kylix that breaks all the rules (Figure 21). Note the pair on the left this time. Again, we see a sprig of laurel, but it appears to be the naked athlete who is handing it to his friend, who is modestly wrapped up in his cloak. His posture, which strides forward boldly, and the position of his hand as well as the friend's lack of arm extension, make it clear that in this case the athlete is offering a gift, not receiving it. Or perhaps he is proudly displaying it to impress his friend. But what is even more amazing, and quite unprecedented in such scenes, is that the athlete sports a prominent erection that reaches nearly as far as his navel. It is partly obscured by a scratch mark in this area, probably the work of a prudish former owner, as this vase was once in private hands.[64] The laurel sprig is a token of victory; in his excitement, the athlete employs it as an erotic talisman to attract his favourite. So the athlete is no longer the passive object of a public gaze and courtship by others; he has now become self-confident enough to do the courting himself. Note, however, that we again have a subtle game going on with the feet: in this case, the figure

*Figure 21* Red-figured kylix attributed to the Eretria Painter (c. 430 BCE). By courtesy of the Jack S. Blanton Museum of Art, The University of Texas at Austin, Archer M. Huntington Museum Fund and the James R. Daugherty, Jr., Foundation, 1980. 1980.38 = *ARV*² 1254.73

with a forked staff, who must be a trainer, appears to press his heel upon the metatarsals of the excited athlete's foot. Far from being erotic, this can actually be rather painful, the kind of move an athletics trainer might make to suppress undesirable behaviour on the part of a boy under his charge.

Also notable in the work of the Eretria Painter is that the figures all appear approximately the same in age, stature and even facial appearance, regardless of whether they are a trainer, a lover or an athlete. This is not at all unique, but occurs on a number of illustrations throughout the development of Attic red-figure painting. Even in these age-equal scenes, one member of each pair tends to be strongly marked as the lover and the other as the beloved. One figure is aggressive and self-confident, the other either compliant or reserved. What this suggests is that there was a certain interval of youth, which we might roughly identify with the ephebic stage around the ages of 18–20, when one might legitimately be either an *erastês* or an *erômenos*. Different boys would mature and become sexually experienced at different rates; they would show the initiative and masculine self-confidence characteristic of an *erastês* at different times. Conquering their natural diffidence and awkward 'geekiness' was just as much a problem for some classical Athenian boys as it is for many teenagers today; however, the institutions of mandatory athletic nudity and exposure to legitimated sexual pursuit assisted them in overcoming the kind of discomfort with body image that most modern adolescents feel concerning their changing appearance and urges. The competitiveness among elite Athenian boys in attracting the attention of men surely acted as training for the more challenging competitiveness of pursuing boys in turn. Once they started to pursue boys, they would be competing not only against their own age cohort, but against older men as well. At this stage, they would truly be men, even if they still looked the same as the boys they courted.[65]

A demographic factor that is often overlooked in discussions of Greek education and pederasty is that the late age of marriage for most Greek men, combined with much shorter lifespans, left many Greek adolescents and youths without living fathers: studies have estimated that only about half of Greek boys would still have a living father by the time they reached 18, and only a third by the time they were 25.[66] During or after periods of war, the numbers would be even more grim. This situation meant that fatherless boys and young men would tend to look to mentors, teachers, athletics trainers and/or lovers as surrogate fathers, but it also meant that such youths had considerable freedom to choose such companions for themselves without having their choices vetted by their fathers.[67] Even in cases where the father was still alive, he would usually be quite a bit older than his adolescent son and relatively uninvolved in his son's life; considerable evidence suggests that father–son relations, particularly among the upper classes, were not close and were even prone to conflict as sons attempted to assert independence and autonomy.[68]

Boys could use their freedom with modesty and restraint, choosing one wise and beneficent lover to whom they remained loyal, or they could carouse with a succession of irresponsible wastrels and spendthrifts, as Aeschines tells us that Timarchus did. The consequence of a good choice at this stage of life would be useful learning and future respect; the result of a bad choice would be suspicions of having prostituted oneself and possible political disenfranchisement, as happened to Timarchus. Greek popular morality had no concept of forgiving youthful indiscretions, as we are wont to do nowadays. The relative sexual freedom accorded to adolescent boys aimed at building independence, self-assertiveness, judgement and the other qualities of masculine character. But, as Foucault reminds us, it was also a critical moment of both temptation and potential, predicting one's future quality as a citizen under the panoptic scrutiny of the eternal public gaze.

## Notes

1. This explicitly reformist motivation is at the heart of much of the foundational scholarship in 'Men's studies' from the 1970s and 1980s, when essay collections with names like *The Changing Definition of Masculinity* (C.W. Franklin, New York, 1984), *Changing Men* (M.S. Kimmel, Thousand Oaks, 1987) or *Slow Motion: Changing Masculinities, Changing Men* (L. Segal, New Brunswick, 1990) appeared. See also the

influential essays of Harry Brod, 'The case for men's studies', in H. Brod (ed.), *The Making of Masculinities: The New Men's Studies* (London, 1992), pp. 39–62, and R.W. Connell, *The Men and the Boys* (Cambridge, 2000), pp. 197–226. On the explicitly reformist goals of the early Men's Movement in the 1970s, see V.J. Seidler, *The Achilles Heel Reader: Men, Sexual Politics and Socialism* (London, 1991), and the early collection of J.H. Pleck and J. Sawyer (eds.), *Men and Masculinity* (Englewood Cliffs, 1974).
2. See the range of essays in the more historically oriented collections of the last decade especially, such as L.H. Bowker (ed.), *Masculinity and Violence* (Thousand Oaks, 1998) and S. Dudink, K. Hagemann and J. Tosh (eds), *Masculinities in Politics and War: Gendering Modern History* (Manchester, 2004).
3. With regard to ancient Rome, this concept was popularised initially by the work of Paul Veyne, especially 'Témoignage hétérosexuelle d'un historien sur l'homosexualité', in *Le Regard des autres: Actes du Congrès International 'Arcadie' (Paris, 24–27 Mai 1979)* (Paris, 1979), pp. 17–24, and 'Homosexuality in ancient Rome', in P. Ariès and A. Béjin (eds), *Western Sexuality: Practice and Precept in Past and Present Times* (Oxford, 1985), pp. 26–35. J. Davidson, *The Greeks and Greek Love: A Radical Reappraisal of Homosexuality in Ancient Greece* (London, 2007), pp. 155–60, demonstrates the importance of Veyne's work for Foucault's conception of the ancient world in *The History of Sexuality*. D. Cohen, *Law, Sexuality, and Society: The Enforcement of Morals in Classical Athens* (Cambridge, 1991), pp. 35–69, employs the Mediterraneanist approach as an analytic model for classical Athens; for strong criticism of the model, see G. Herman, 'Ancient Athens and the values of Mediterranean society', *Mediterranean Historical Review* 11 (1996), 5–36. C. Blazina, *The Cultural Myth of Masculinity* (Westport, 2003), even attempts to reconstruct an Indo-European basis to the construction of male sexual roles, but, like most such efforts, his thesis rests upon a bed of speculation and generalisation with too little attention to historical context and nuance.
4. See especially J.G. Peristiany (ed.), *Honour and Shame: The Values of Mediterranean Society* (London, 1965); D.D. Gilmore (ed.), *Honour and Shame and the Unity of the Mediterranean* (Washington, 1965); J.G. Peristiany and J. Pitt-Rivers (eds), *Honour and Grace in Anthropology* (Cambridge, 1992). For a general criticism, see J. de Pina-Cabral, 'The Mediterranean as a category of regional comparison: a critical view', *Current Anthropology* 30 (1989), 399–406.
5. M. Foucault, *The History of Sexuality: Volume 2, The Use of Pleasure*, trans. R. Hurley (New York, 1985), pp. 185–225.
6. For the range of moral judgements one finds among the ancient sources, see my remarks in T.K. Hubbard, *Homosexuality in Greece and Rome: A Sourcebook of Basic Documents* (Berkeley, 2003), pp. 7–10.
7. D.M. Halperin, *One Hundred Years of Homosexuality* (London, 1990), p. 30.
8. Cohen, *Law, Sexuality, and Society*, pp. 171–202. From the same era, see also E.C. Keuls, *The Reign of the Phallus: Sexual Politics in Ancient Athens* (New York, 1985), pp. 276–77, who incorrectly assumes anal sex to be the most frequent form of pederastic consummation; later, however, on pp. 282–85, she admits that pederastic relations were often mutual and affectionate.
9. W.A. Percy, *Pederasty and Pedagogy in Archaic Greece* (Urbana, 1996); A. Lear and E. Cantarella, *Images of Ancient Greek Pederasty: Boys were their Gods* (London, 2008), pp. 72–97; M. Griffith, 'Public and private in early Greek institutions of education', in Y.L. Too and S.N. Faroqhi (eds), *Education in Greek and Roman Antiquity* (Leiden, 2001), pp. 61–6. For the more hedonistic approach of Anacreon, see A. Lear, 'Anacreon's "self": an alternate role model for the archaic elite male?', *American Journal of Philology* 129 (2008), 47–76.

10. K.J. Dover, *Greek Homosexuality* (Cambridge, 1978).
11. S. Moscovici, *Society Against Nature* (Atlantic Highlands, 1976), pp. 302–4, cited with approval by B. Sergent, *Homosexuality in Greek Myth* (London, 1987), pp. 51–4.
12. On the Spartan institution, see P. Cartledge, *Spartan Reflections* (Berkeley, 2001), pp. 91–105. On Crete and Thebes, see my remarks and references in *Homosexuality in Greece and Rome*, pp. 56–8. Davidson, *The Greeks and Greek Love*, pp. 255–360, is far too willing to credit questionable sources on these states; he does usefully collect material on epic relationships between warrior and squire, but is too prone to assign a homosexual quality to these relationships from the earliest stages of archaic epic. See my review at <http://h-net.msu.edu/cgi-bin/logbrowse.pl?trx=vx;list=H-Histsex; month=0902;week=b;msg=Ug%2BYuljwHAbsmjyw%2BhMXhQ>, accessed 28 March 2011. This review is also archived at <http://classicaljournal.org/reviews2009.php>. On warrior relationships more generally, see D. Ogden, 'Homosexuality and warfare in classical Greece', in A.B. Lloyd (ed.), *Battle in Antiquity* (London, 1996), pp. 107–68.
13. See my *Homosexuality in Greece and Rome*, pp. 38–47, for a collection and translation of the relevant poems. For a discussion of the poems' interrelated pedagogical and pederastic character, see J.M. Lewis, 'Eros and the *Polis* in Theognis, Book II', in T.J. Figueira and G. Nagy (eds), *Theognis of Megara* (Baltimore, 1985), pp. 197–222; L. Edmunds, 'Foucault and Theognis', *Classical and Modern Literature* 8 (1987), pp. 79–91.
14. S.O. Murray, *Homosexualities* (Chicago, 2000), pp. 34–43, 99–111.
15. Lear/Cantarella, *Images of Ancient Greek Pederasty*, p. 183, interprets the scene as one of intercrural intercourse, but the figures are not close enough together. Intercourse may well be the man's objective, but the boy appears to resist.
16. Dover, *Greek Homosexuality*, p. 93, interprets the man's gesture as an attempt to touch the boy's armpit ('a more tentative approach'), but more likely he had touched the boy's shoulder and the boy shrugged the hand away in the process of raising his own arm defensively.
17. See especially Theognis 1238a–44, 1249–52, 1257–62, 1267–74, 1311–22, 1373–74, 1377–80. Three centuries later, the lover of Theocritus 29 (*Homosexuality in Greece and Rome*, pp. 283–84) laments the same behaviour on the part of his beloved.
18. This gesture is equivalent to the chin-stroking which is a conventional gesture of supplication by the adult, active partner, especially in black-figure iconography: see J.D. Beazley, *Some Attic Vases in the Cyprus Museum* (Oxford, 1989), pp. 4–13; H.A. Shapiro, 'Courtship Scenes in Attic Vase-Painting', *American Journal of Archaeology* 85 (1981), 134, and Lear/Cantarella, *Images of Ancient Greek Pederasty*, pp. 114–15.
19. See M. Vickers and D.N. Briggs, 'Juvenile crime, aggression and abuse in fifth-century Athens: a case study', in G. Rousseau (ed.), *Children and Sexuality: From the Greeks to the Great War* (Houndmills, 2007), pp. 47–8. Davidson, *The Greeks and Greek Love*, pp. 443–44, who rather prudishly refuses to reproduce a picture of this cup, wrongly characterises the vigorous, masculine-looking 'paedophile' as 'a Senior even, with his pectoral muscles dropped to mid-chest'. Not only are his chest muscles clearly not sagging, but the artist goes out of his way to emphasise his virility by depicting chest hair, something featured on relatively few vases.
20. H.A. Shapiro, 'Leagros and Euphronios: painting pederasty in Athens', in T.K. Hubbard (ed.), *Greek Love Reconsidered* (New York, 2000), pp. 31–2. See also Lear/Cantarella, *Images of Ancient Greek Pederasty*, p. 54.

21. For an excellent survey of the various iconographic gestures by which a boy might signal acceptance of his suitor's advances, see Lear/Cantarella, *Images of Ancient Greek Pederasty*, pp. 38–62.
22. See Hippocrates, cited in Philo, *Opif. Mundi* 36.105, and Aristophanes of Byzantium, frr. 37–66 Slater.
23. For other passages in comedy and satyr drama that take for granted boys' fascination with sex and sex organs from the earliest age, see M. Golden, *Children and Childhood in Classical Athens* (Baltimore, 1990), pp. 56–7, 200–1 nn. 29, 31. See pp. 44–6 for evidence that boys both attended theatrical productions and even acted in them on some occasions.
24. The gaze of the trainer may bear some measure of erotic interest as well; see my remarks in 'Sex in the gym: athletic trainers and pedagogical pederasty', *Intertexts* 7 (2003), 8–10.
25. Davidson, *The Greeks and Greek Love*, pp. 80–1. However, see the survey of E. Eyben, 'Antiquity's view of puberty', *Latomus* 31 (1972), 677–97, of which Davidson is unaware. Aristotle, *History of Animals* 581a13–17, clearly states that male puberty hit at 14; Davidson attempts to discredit this evidence by saying that Aristotle places beard growth at 21 and there cannot be seven years' difference between the two phenomena, but what *HA* 582a16–34 actually says is that beard growth occurs at some point until 21 (i.e. 21 is the latest age at which males, whose individual development varies, show a full beard).
26. Golden, *Children and Childhood*, pp. 26–9.
27. Golden, *Children and Childhood*, pp. 40–1, notes that boys could be charged with homicide or act as witnesses in court at younger ages, based on the case described in Antiphon 2.
28. Davidson, *The Greeks and Greek Love*, pp. 68–71. Careful examination of the Greek of Aeschines 1.139 shows that this is merely Aeschines' opinion of what the law 'ought to say', not what it actually did. His assertion that youths and boys could not fraternise in the gymnasia is largely based on a second-century BCE inscription from the Macedonian town of Beroea, but this is irrelevant to Athenian practice; as Davidson elsewhere notes, Macedonian homosexuality was not primarily pederastic, but age-equal and militaristic. See the more detailed arguments in my online review (n. 12 above).
29. Davidson, *The Greeks and Greek Love*, pp. 426–45.
30. See C. Sourvinou-Inwood, *Studies in Girls' Transitions: Aspects of the Arkteia and Age Representation in Attic Iconography* (Athens, 1988), p. 28, and P. Brulé, *Women of Ancient Greece*, trans. A. Nevill (Edinburgh, 2003), pp. 130–31.
31. Cohen, *Law, Sexuality, and Society*, pp. 176–80; against this view, see Golden, *Children and Childhood*, p. 58. That some of the Attic orators apply the term *hybris* to seduction of a married woman or matron proves nothing about its status with regard to boys, given the greater severity of Greek sanctions against adultery. He misinterprets the vague and tendentious paraphrase of the *hybris* law in Aeschines 1.15 as providing evidence that mere seduction of a boy could be defined as *hybris*. If so, then seduction of a slave could also be so defined, since slaves are mentioned in the same list along with women and boys.
32. Where same-sex anal penetration occurs on Attic vases, it is always between age-equal figures, usually bearded men or satyrs, more rarely between two youths. See the excellent survey of Lear/Cantarella, *Images of Ancient Greek Pederasty*, pp. 106–28.
33. On the pederastic model of aristocratic education, see H.I. Marrou, *A History of Education in Antiquity* (New York, 1964), pp. 57–9.

34. That athletics trainers were usually themselves former athletes of some success I have argued in 'Contemporary Sport Sociology and Ancient Greek Athletics', *Leisure Studies* 27 (2008), 285. As such, they were indeed role models. In 'Sex in the Gym', pp. 1–26, I also argue that trainer–athlete relationships were frequently pederastic and could involve the trainer's financial sponsorship of his young protégé. See also Nick Fisher, 'Gymnasia and the democratic values of leisure', in P. Cartledge, P. Millett and S. von Reden (eds), *Kosmos: Essays in Order, Conflict, and Community in Classical Athens* (Cambridge, 1998), pp. 96–8.
35. Such scenes of schoolhouse nudity were common, as were representations of Erotes crowning a teacher's prized student. See my list and discussion in 'Sex in the gym', pp. 17–18 n. 15.
36. See the provocative discussion of Y.L. Too, *The Pedagogical Contract: The Economics of Teaching and Learning in the Ancient World* (Ann Arbor, 2000), pp. 73–5.
37. The most comprehensive survey and discussion of this phenomenon is that of Gundel Koch-Harnack, *Knabenliebe und Tiergeschenke: Ihre Bedeutung im päderastischen Erziehungssystem Athens* (Berlin, 1983). See also Lear/Cantarella, *Images of Ancient Greek Pederasty*, pp. 38–52, 72–97. Both emphasise the pedagogical character of courtship gifts.
38. See also Copenhagen, Nat. Mus. 3634, by the Tyskiewicz Painter (= Figures 84–5 in Koch-Harnack, *Knabenliebe*, pp. 166–67); the opposite side shows a suitor offering a moneybag as a gift to another boy. For a youth of about the same age offering a lyre as a gift to another, see New York 58.11.1, a kylix by the Lyandros Painter (= Figure 2.21A in Lear/Cantarella, *Images of Ancient Greek Pederasty*, pp. 98–100).
39. For wreaths and ribbons as both rewards and love offerings, see my discussion (citing several other vases) in 'Sex in the Gym', pp. 10–11.
40. On the gifts of game and their relation to the pedagogical dimensions of hunting, see Koch-Harnack, *Knabenliebe*, especially pp. 34–58, and Lear/Cantarella, *Images of Ancient Greek Pederasty*, pp. 38–52. On the myth of Cyparissus as a truncated and unsuccessful pederastic initiation of a boy who grew too sentimentally attached to animals, and on its likely classical date, see my remarks in 'Ephebic liminality and the ambiguities of Apolline sexuality', in L. Athanassaki, R. P. Martin and J. F. Miller (eds), *Apolline Politics and Poetics* (Athens, 2009), p. 609; for a somewhat different interpretation in initiatory terms, see Sergent, *Homosexuality in Greek Myth*, pp. 96–101. For Ephorus' supposed abduction ceremony, involving a liminal period of hunting in the woods, see Sergent, pp. 7–39 (who credits Ephorus' account as entirely historical) and D.B. Dodd, 'Athenian Ideas about Cretan Pederasty', in Hubbard, *Greek Love Reconsidered*, pp. 33–41 (who will have none of it). Even if we incline more to Dodd's contention that Ephorus was writing mainly to entertain Athenians with a supposedly ancient ritual that would somehow ground and justify Athenians' own tastes and practices, Ephorus' identification of the summer interlude hunting in the woods as the crucial period of pederastic involvement would have appealed to Athenians, who automatically associated hunting and elite pederasty.
41. On this vase and the cockfighting symbolism in Attic vase painting generally, see H. Hofmann, 'Hahnenkampf in Athen: Zur Ikonologie einer attischen Bildformel', *Revue Archéologique* 1974 (1974), 195–220; Koch-Harnack, *Knabenliebe*, pp. 97–105; B. Fellmann, 'Hahnenkampf', in K. Vierneisel and B. Kaeser (eds), *Kunst der Schale, Kultur des Trinkens* (Munich, 1990), pp. 108–10; Lear/Cantarella, *Images of Ancient Greek Pederasty*, pp. 72–6. On the social practice of cockfighting as a preparation for military pursuits, see Golden, *Children and Childhood*, p. 55.

42. Shapiro, 'Courtship scenes', p. 134.
43. J.N. Bremmer, 'Adolescents, *symposion*, and pederasty', in O. Murray (ed.), *Sympotica: A Symposium on the Symposion* (Oxford, 1990), pp. 135–48; C. Calame, *The Poetics of Eros in Ancient Greece*, trans. J. Lloyd (Princeton, 1999), pp. 94–8. That the host's son(s) might be serving guests at symposia has been suggested by Bremmer and H.A. Shapiro, 'Fathers and sons, men and boys', in J. Neils and J.H. Oakley (eds), *Coming of Age in Ancient Greece: Images of Childhood from the Classical Past* (New Haven, 2003), p. 107. Also see Golden, *Children and Childhood*, p. 35, for children doing the same chores as slaves, based on Aristotle, *Politics*, 7.1333a7–9.
44. See the surveys of Lear/Cantarella, *Images of Ancient Greek Pederasty*, pp. 57–62; J.-M. Dentzer, *Le motif du banquet couché dans le proche-Orient et le monde grec du VII$^e$ au IV$^e$ siècle avant J.-C.* (Rome, 1982), pp. 111–13.
45. E. Stehle, *Performance and Gender in Ancient Greece* (Princeton, 1997), pp. 227–49.
46. Tampa 1986.070 = *ARV*² 276.70. D. Williams, 'Women on Athenian Vases: Problems of Interpretation', in A. Cameron and A. Kuhrt (eds), *Images of Women in Antiquity* (Detroit, 1983), pp. 97–8; Golden, *Children and Childhood*, p. 57; Shapiro, 'Fathers and sons, men and boys', pp. 98–9. Keuls, *Reign of the Phallus*, pp. 260–62, merely interprets it as a family scene with father and son returning home.
47. On the symposium and sympotic pederasty as a preparation for citizenship and political participation, see D.B. Levine, 'Symposium and the polis', in Figueira and Nagy, *Theognis of Megara*, pp. 176–96; P. Schmitt Pantel, *La Cité au banquet* (Rome, 1992), pp. 59–90; Griffith, 'Public and private', pp. 48–59. Griffith observes that the common male messes (*syssitia*) of Sparta and Crete served much the same pedagogical, masculinising function as the more elite symposia of the Athenians. Both were forms of building group solidarity among men of different ages.
48. D. Collins, *Master of the Game: Competition and Performance in Greek Poetry* (Washington, 2004). See also M. Griffith, 'Contest and contradiction in early Greek poetry', in M. Griffith and D.J. Mastronarde (eds), *Cabinet of the Muses: Essays on Classical and Comparative Literature in Honor of Thomas G. Rosenmeyer* (Atlanta, 1990), pp. 185–207.
49. For a guest's performance of song as a central representational motif on sympotic ware that represents the symposium itself, see F. Lissarrague, *The Aesthetics of the Greek Banquet*, trans. A. Szegedy-Maszak (Princeton, 1990), pp. 128–35.
50. For the *skolion*, see Athenaeus 15.694a–c. For the paean at symposia, see I. Rutherford, *Pindar's Paeans* (Oxford, 2001), pp. 7–8, citing Xenophon, *Hell*. 4.7.4, 7.2.23.
51. On this phrase and its likely reference to Stesichorus' famous *Palinode*, see M. Davies, 'The Paroemiographers on TA TRIA TVN STHSIXOROU', *Journal of Hellenic Studies* 102 (1982), 206–10.
52. For a revaluation and extension of Jacob Burckhardt's now classic contention that Greece was a fundamentally agonistic culture, see the thoughtful essay of M.B. Poliakoff, 'Competition', in D. Papenfuss and V.M. Strocka (eds), *Gab es das griechische Wunder? Griechenland zwischen dem Ende des 6. und der Mitte des 5. Jahrhunderts v. Chr.* (Mainz, 2001), pp. 51–64. On the need to instil competitiveness in boys in every realm of their activity, see Golden, *Children and Childhood*, pp. 65–6.
53. T.F. Scanlon, *Eros and Greek Athletics* (New York, 2001); see my review in *Mouseion* 4 (2004), 71–4. See also D.H.J. Larmour, *Stage and Stadium: Drama and Athletics in Ancient Greece* (Hildesheim, 1999), pp. 139–44; S.G. Miller, *Ancient Greek Athletics* (New Haven, 2004), pp. 189–93; N. Fisher, 'The pleasures of reciprocity: *Charis* and the athletic body in Pindar', in F. Prost and J. Wilgaux (eds), *Penser et représenter le*

*corps dans l' Antiquité* (Rennes, 2006), pp. 227–45. From a more modern standpoint, see B. Pronger, *The Arena of Masculinity: Sports, Homosexuality, and the Meaning of Sex* (New York, 1990) and A. Guttmann, *The Erotic in Sports* (New York, 1996).

54. Hubbard, 'Sex in the gym', pp. 1–26.
55. On the date of the earliest Thera graffiti (our first certain evidence of pederasty), see F. Hiller von Gaertringen, *Die archaische Kultur der Insel Thera* (Berlin, 1897), pp. 21–8. For the advent of nudity and the boys' competition at Olympia, see M. McDonnell, 'The introduction of athletic nudity: Thucydides, Plato, and the Vases', *Journal of Hellenic Studies* 111 (1991), 182–93; M. Golden, *Sport and Society in Ancient Greece* (Cambridge, 1998), 65–6, 104; Scanlon, *Eros and Greek Athletics*, pp. 69, 211–12.
56. N.B. Crowther, 'Male "beauty" contests in Greece: the Euandria and Euexia', *L'Antiquité classique* 54 (1985), 285–91.
57. P. Brulé, 'Le corps sportif', in Prost and Wilgaux, *Penser et représenter le corps*, pp. 263–69.
58. For athletic victory as a common route to political leadership, see J. Göhler, 'Olympioniken als Krieger und Politiker: Zur sozialen Stellung der Olympiasieger im Altertum', *Die Leibeserziehung* 19 (1970), 190–95; H.W. Pleket, 'Zur Soziologie des antiken Sports', *Mededelingen van het Nederlands Instituut te Rome* NS 1 (1974), pp. 65–7; C. Mann, *Athlet und Polis im archaischen und frühklassichen Griechenland* (Göttingen, 2001), pp. 66–8; Golden, *Sport and Society*, pp. 169–75. Pindar very clearly links athletic victory with divine election, particularly by the god in whose honour the games are held: see *Pythian* 5.117, *Nemean* 1.1–9, 6.25–27, and *Isthmian* 4.1–5 for his most direct assertions. The connection is also evident in his wishes for future athletic success: see my discussion and references in T.K. Hubbard, 'On implied wishes for olympic victory in Pindar', *Illinois Classical Studies* 20 (1995), 35–41.
59. In addition to the myth of Pelops and Hippodameia (discussed below), see Hesiod, frr. 72–76 MW for Atalanta, the daughter of Schoineus; Pindar, *Pythian* 9.105–25 for the daughter of Antaeus; and Herodotus, 6.126–28 for the daughter of Cleisthenes. For a detailed discussion of the Atalanta myth, see Scanlon, *Eros in Greek Athletics*, pp. 175–98.
60. On this myth's initiatory structure, in which pederasty plays a central role, see Sergent, *Homosexuality in Greek Myth*, pp. 59–67, and T.K. Hubbard, 'The "cooking" of Pelops: Pindar and the process of mythological revisionism', *Helios* 14 (1987), 3–21.
61. On the connection of this poem's myths with the victor's own marriageability, see A. Carson, 'Wedding at noon in Pindar's *Ninth Pythian*', *Greek, Roman and Byzantine Studies* 23 (1982), 121–28; L. Woodbury, 'Cyrene and the TELEUTA of Marriage in Pindar's Ninth Pythian Ode', *Transactions of the American Philological Association* 112 (1982), 245–58; A. Köhnken, ' "Meilichos Orga": Liebesthematik und aktueller Sieg in der neunten pythischen Ode Pindars', in *Pindare (Fondation Hardt, Entretiens* 31) (Vandoeuvres, 1985), pp. 71–116.
62. Hubbard, 'Implied wishes', pp. 41–5, and 'Sex in the gym', pp. 6–7.
63. See A. Lezzi-Hafter, *Der Eretria-Maler* (Mainz, 1988), pp. 135–41, for the most complete catalogue of this artist's kylixes involving young athletes. On this particular kylix, see my earlier discussion in 'Sex in the gym', pp. 13–15.
64. Various experts who have examined the vase under magnification since I first proposed this interpretation in 2003 reach differing conclusions, some in agreement, some still sceptical.

65. I explored the issue of such apparently age-equal relationships in a paper presented at the 2009 meeting of the American Philological Association in Philadelphia ('The Ubiquity of Peer Sexuality in Classical Greece'), a written version of which will appear as chapter 8 in T.K. Hubbard (ed.), *A Companion to Ancient Sexuality* (Malden, 2012). See Golden, *Children and Childhood*, pp. 60–1; Hubbard, *Homosexuality in Ancient Greece and Rome*, p. 5; Davidson, *The Greeks and Greek Love*, pp. 86–8. For numerous examples of age-equal courtship and sexual interaction among youths on both black-figure and red-figure vases, see C.A.M. Hupperts, *Eros Dikaios* (diss. University of Amsterdam, 2000), volume 1, pp. 129–32 and 181–84.
66. B.S. Strauss, *Fathers and Sons in Athens: Ideology and Society in the Era of the Peloponnesian War* (Princeton, 1993), pp. 67–8, applying to Athens the computer-generated models of Richard Saller, *Patriarchy, Property and Death in the Roman Family* (Cambridge, 1994), pp. 43–69. The proportion of boys with living fathers may have been even lower if we accept the less optimistic midlife mortality assumptions of R. Woods, 'Ancient and early modern mortality: experience and understanding', *Economic History Review* 60 (2007), 373–99. For the most up-to-date review of scholarship on this question, see W. Scheidel, 'The demographic background', in S.R. Hübner and D.M. Ratzan (eds), *Growing Up Fatherless in Antiquity* (Cambridge, 2009), pp. 31–40, who notes that in most cases fatherless boys would have no other patrilineal males or even older brothers to become guardians.
67. That fathers sometimes would take an interest in choosing (or at least approving) their son's lover from among their own acquaintances is implied in texts like Aristophanes, *Birds* 137–42; Xenophon, *Symposium* 1.2–4 (which shows Autolycus' father on close social terms with the boy's lover, Callias); and Aeschines 1.42 (expressing outrage that Timarchus' first lover, Misgolas, was not a friend of Timarchus' father). See also Aeschines 1.13–14 for legal protections against a father or male guardian forcing his son into a relationship for financial gain: the law would not have been needed if it had not sometimes happened as a perverted outgrowth of the more usual practice of choosing good companions for a son. See Golden, *Children and Childhood*, pp. 61–2 for discussion of the texts from Aristophanes and Xenophon.
68. Plato's Laches (*Laches* 180b) observes that prominent men of affairs have little time for their children. See Keuls, *Reign of the Phallus*, p. 285; Golden, *Children and Childhood*, pp. 101–14; Strauss, *Fathers and Sons*, passim; Shapiro, 'Fathers and sons, men and boys', pp. 102–7.

# 11
# An Orchard, a Love Letter and Three Bastards: The Formation of Adult Male Identity in a Fifteenth-Century Family

*Rachel E. Moss*

> Sir, our father and I came together in the new orchard last Friday, and he asked me many questions of you, and I told him all as it was, and he was right sorry for the death of the child, and I told him of the good will that the Whigstons and Daltons have to you, and how I liked the young gentlewoman, and he commanded me to write to you that he would gladly that it were brought about and that you laboured it betimes.[1]

In the summer of 1481 Richard Cely, a young wool merchant, wrote to his brother George. He reported that he had met with the sister of a family friend, and judged that she was an appropriate marital prospect for George. Richard discussed the matter with his father, Richard senior, as they walked together in their new orchard, and Richard senior instructed his son to write to George to encourage him to pursue the opportunity. However, these men were not just talking about respectable marriage prospects, but also the death of a child. The child in question was George's illegitimate baby by a woman who lived in Calais, and not only was Richard senior aware of the relationship, he was sympathetic to his son's loss. Richard Cely junior's letter neatly provides examples of why the Cely correspondence is so interesting: here we have evidence of familial affection and paternal authority, courtship patterns, and attitudes toward extramarital relationships. George and Richard junior, both in their early twenties, in this letter appear to be both in friendly confidence with their father and under his paternal authority. At this point in their lives the Cely sons are in a transitional life phase as they begin to move from adolescence into manhood, their sexual behaviour and obedience to their father reflecting their place in the adolescent life stage, whilst their attempts to find wives indicate a shift toward attaining manhood. The Cely letters thus provide an invaluable resource for studying late medieval adolescence and male sexuality.

Examining male adolescence provides an opportunity to address preconceptions about masculinities and manhood. In studying the Celys, it becomes clear that maleness is not synonymous with manliness, and that hypermasculine, life stage-specific behaviours are features of late medieval adolescence. As part of the flourishing field of medieval women's history, there has been attention paid to the concept of 'life cycle'. This has been used to discuss the movement between different female life stages, particularly in terms of the move from adolescence to adulthood and the role of servanthood in this process.[2] In recent years there has been significant work on youthful experience in the Middle Ages, but less attention has been paid to what medieval people meant by adolescence, what purpose it served in medieval thought, and how the adolescent experience is gendered in a way beyond the obviously biological.[3] Barbara Hanawalt addresses the question of gender distinctions in adolescence, but her interest in these differences is largely focused on whether female experience was dissimilar to the male 'default'.[4] This is part of a wider problem. As Michael Kimmel and Michael Messner note, maleness is often treated as the default within Western society.[5] Because patriarchal culture makes men and masculinities the touchstones for normal behaviours and standards within society, maleness becomes taken for granted, creating the paradox of simultaneously privileging men and making them invisible.[6] 'Gender' often really means 'women'. In medieval studies, the past 15 years have seen a shift in this perspective, as there has been an increasing engagement with gender studies, and now with masculinities, but there is still much work to be done.[7] For instance, whilst social scientists have begun to problematise the term 'patriarchy', in medieval studies, just as 'male' has been assumed to be understood, so has 'patriarchy'.[8] Critics have tended to ignore the 'pater' part of 'patriarchy'; the privileging of the father within patriarchal societies is part of its essential nature, but there has been little engagement within medieval studies of what fatherhood meant in the Middle Ages, despite a growing interest in childhood in the Middle Ages.[9] In examining the lives of the Cely brothers the key role of their father in their adolescent experiences becomes apparent. Interactions youths had with their fathers are as important in understanding adolescence as their involvement with their peer group and with the opposite sex.

Youth was a significant life phase in late medieval England, but its boundaries were fluid and are for the historian difficult to identify. The Islamic scholar Avicenna wrote in a work that was translated into Latin and widely disseminated in the twelfth century and beyond: 'There is the age of growing up, which is called the age of adolescence and commonly lasts until the age of thirty.'[10] Whilst our modern conception of adolescence often equates it with puberty, for medieval people these terms were not necessarily synonymous. For many medieval medical writers, puberty was not a phase but a moment in time, marked by an entrance into sexual maturity demonstrated through the onset of menses or the emission of seed.[11] This was related to, but not the same as, the life phase of youth. As Arnold van Gennep argued in 1909, there is a difference between social and physical terms of adolescence.[12] What I am here concerned with is social adolescence, and that, unlike the biological process of puberty, is determined by culture. I argue that, in late medieval England, adolescence extends well beyond puberty into what we would now call 'young adulthood', or the early to mid-twenties, and what characterises the medieval concept of 'adolescence' has more to do with situational instability and mobility than physical (im)maturity.[13]

Adolescent instability features in medieval writing on the stages that made up men's lives. 'The Ages of Man' was a schematic framework used by many medieval thinkers to explain the stages of man's life; there could be as few as three and as many as nine stages, but the usual number was seven.[14] These writers typically imagined a late end to adolescence; Dante wrote that *adolescenza* ended at 25, whilst earlier Isidore of Seville said that *adolescentia* finished at 28.[15] There is no specific event occurring at the age of 25 or 28 that marks the transition from adolescence to adulthood; it seems instead that these ages mark a natural end to adolescent behaviours. Aristotle described man's life as having three basic stages – growth, stasis and decline – and the end of adolescence was a movement into a more stable frame of life.[16] Adolescents' lack of stability was seen in their pleasure-seeking behaviour.[17] John Dalton wrote to his friend George Cely, saying he wanted him to visit because 'it is for merry-making that I would have you here.'[18] John and George also visited taverns and took part in sports, which were typical youthful activities.[19] The life stage following adolescence, meanwhile, was characterised by temperance and reason, and a 'readiness to found a family'.[20] The move toward stability, then, is also a move toward taking on the adult responsibilities of marriage and children, from being part of a family to being head of one. Part of that process was also learning *how* to be responsible; as Lydgate's *Fall of Princes* says, 'in ther adolescence' boys should be well educated to ensure that when they mature they 'do non outrage'.[21]

Whilst the Ages of Man was a framework used by a number of medieval writers, it was still a literary concept found primarily in elite texts. How did this theoretical imagining of adolescence find translation into practice? In legal terms such a relaxed attitude regarding the onset of adulthood was not possible; fixed ages were required for legal purposes such as the age of marital consent and the age of inheritance. In terms of marital consent, boys were considered rational enough to give consent after the age of 14, but legal majority was usually reached at the age of 21.[22] This demonstrates that medieval people recognised the differing kinds of adult responsibility here. If one could theoretically be adult enough to marry but not adult enough to inherit property, the concept of male adulthood must have had a certain degree of flexibility, and attaining it was not necessarily caused by a discrete event – for instance reaching the age of 21 – but by a series of processes working in tandem. Legal thresholds are established to provide a *minimum* age at which someone is likely to be capable of taking on a particular responsibility, rather than an *ideal* age, which is what the writing on the Ages of Man reflects.

The social reality seems to have fallen somewhere in between these two extremes. Hanawalt points to evidence that lawgivers used their own discretion regarding inheritance; while London law put the age of majority at 21, exceptions might be made based on the character of the heir.[23] Meanwhile, though the age of marriage would have varied by social group, amongst the gentry and mercantile classes males seem to marry in their mid-twenties.[24] George Cely married at about the age of 26 in 1484; Richard junior's date of birth is not known, but he was likely close in age to George, and he married in 1483. Their eldest brother Robert was married by 1474, when he was probably in his late teens, but, as we will see later, Robert's behaviour was neither usually typical nor commendable. When adolescent males of the gentry or mercantile class married, it was usually because they were wards and their guardians had sold their marriages, or married them to their own children.[25] For instance, Thomas Stonor purchased the wardship of John Cottesmore in 1470, and later that year seems to have married him to Stonor's daughter Joan.[26] Even in these circumstances, there is evidence that there was a popular sense that early marriages should not be consummated until the couple were older, and so, even if young adolescents were married off, they often did not live as husband and wife until later. In 1453 Sir Thomas Clifford married his daughter Elizabeth to Sir William Plumpton's son William; 'the said Sir William promised the said Lord Clifford that they should not lie together till she came to the age of 16 years.'[27] Clifford's stipulation was probably largely related to the awareness that if girls fell pregnant at an early age they were at a higher risk of complications in pregnancy and death in labour, but there also seems to have been a sense, amongst those arranging marriages at least, that sexual activity was not appropriate for young teenagers, even if they were married.[28] Meanwhile, at a slightly lower social level, apprentices were not allowed to marry without their masters' consent; given that apprenticeships lasted at least seven years, and in the fifteenth century the age of entry into apprenticeship in some elite guilds had risen to 16 or 18, some young men would not be in a position to marry until they were in their early to mid-twenties.[29]

There might, then, be more than a decade between a youth entering puberty and his marriage. Adolescents were known to have sexual desires and reproductive capabilities, and lust was considered to be a particular problem for youths.[30] In addition, medical opinion of the time was that sexual intercourse was useful in maintaining physical health, whilst abstinence could cause physiological and temperamental imbalances.[31] Whilst medical writers did not go so far as to endorse premarital sex, which was sinful, it might perhaps have been preferable to masturbation, which was not only sinful but also potentially emasculating.[32] A popular fifteenth-century saying, 'an angelic young man becomes a devil in old age', shows a certain expectation that youths needed to get wild behaviour out of their systems before they settled down.[33] Apprenticeship indentures, meanwhile, tried to limit adolescent excess through regulations against whoring and gambling, which suggests that these were common enough vices in young men.[34] Jeremy Goldberg concludes that male servants were given tacit permission to engage in sexual activity as long as it was outside their master's household.[35] For youths who were sexually mature but who were culturally encouraged not to marry until later, it was unsurprising that extramarital relationships were formed. With the Cely brothers we will see that they have reached the age where they are beginning to look for suitable wives, but they are still taking part in the kind of sexual encounters that may well have been typical for youths of their age.

At this point a more in-depth introduction to the Cely family and its correspondence is useful. By the later fifteenth century, letter writing was a key means of communication within mercantile society, and was probably taught at a very elementary level.[36] Although there is some evidence that toward the sixteenth century there was an increasing desire to keep the content of letters between writer and recipient, in the main in this period letters were not 'private' in the modern sense.[37] Letters were often dictated, sometimes to a scribe, sometimes to a member of the household. Some letters were written in several hands over the course of a few days. Information, then, circulated quite freely within the circle of the household as it became incorporated into the letters, which then transmitted that information beyond the household.[38] The Cely letter collection is composed of over 200 letters, as well as accounts, memoranda and miscellaneous other items. The letters cover the period 1472–1488, with most of these being written between 1476 and 1484, providing an excellent opportunity to study the day-to-day minutiae of business and family life. Of the history of the family prior to the 1470s little is known. Richard senior was a citizen of London and a merchant of the Fellowship of the Staple at Calais, meaning that his business was in the wool trade. It also meant that a family presence was required both in England and abroad. From around 1479, perhaps when he turned 21, Richard's youngest son George managed business in Calais and also in Bruges. George's elder brother Richard usually remained in London. Their eldest brother Robert seems to have taken little part in the wool business; frequently in financial and social disgrace, he was practically disinherited, his father's estate treating Richard junior as heir.

A large proportion of correspondence in the collection is from Richard junior to George, and this correspondence gives insight both into familial relations, particularly male relationships, and into the way marriages were negotiated by men of their class. Although Richard junior married in 1483 and George was wed in 1484, they were both looking for wives for some time before this, as can be seen in a letter from Richard junior to George in May 1482.[39] Richard reported extensively on meeting the daughter of Thomas Limerick, a meeting orchestrated by family friend William Midwinter, who consulted Richard to find out if he would be interested in the lady. Richard, on hearing that she had £40 a year from her mother, and that her father was the 'richest man in that country', was keen to meet her. This letter gives an interesting glimpse into the use of public space and gifting gestures in opening courtship negotiations. Midwinter told Richard that he could see the lady if he went to church on May Day, and she and her stepmother duly appeared.

After matins, Richard sent them a pot of wine to refresh them, and, with the ice broken, once mass was over he approached them and they issued a dinner invitation, and after dinner they drank together and 'had right good communication'. This was a carefully orchestrated and appropriately chaperoned encounter that allowed the couple to get an impression of one another whilst maintaining appropriate social decorum. Richard, although he pragmatically noted the lady's monetary value, seemed genuinely pleased that they could talk together, and found it important to tell his brother of her good qualities: 'she is young, little, and very attractive and intelligent, and the country speaks much good by her.'[40] Richard then wrote that the success of the negotiations would depend on whether her father liked him, and what he was prepared to settle on his daughter.[41] Marriage making in this class involved family and friends and the balancing of different interests. Either Thomas Limerick did not take to Richard, or he did not offer a big enough dowry, as the marriage did not happen.

The example of the Oxfordshire gentry family the Stonors here serves as an interesting point of comparison in examining courtship and marital negotiations. In 1472 the 23-year-old William Stonor was wooing a wealthy widow, Margery Blount, and he apparently asked Thomas Mull, his father's retainer, to break news of the potential match to his father Thomas Stonor. Like Richard Cely, Thomas Mull emphasised the lady's fortune and good reputation:

> she is in possession of one hundred marks of land, and after the death of her father she shall have half of the residue of all the land of her father... And certainly she is well reputed, and of a worshipful disposition.

Mull was also very particular about ensuring that Thomas Stonor's sense of authority was satisfied: 'I know verily my cousin will in no wise in this case do but as *your good fatherhood* wills he do' [my emphasis].[42] Mull offered the reassurance that, no matter how much William liked Margery, he would not do anything without his father's approval. Shortly afterwards, William sent his father a letter, including the remark that 'I trust verily to almighty Jesus and to your good fatherhood that I shall speed well in my matter, for I have encouraging behaviour by my mistress.'[43] The juxtaposition of divine and fatherly authority is very telling; it gives the impression that Thomas's word is law, his will something that can be appealed to but certainly not challenged. That this was not simply rhetoric intended to flatter Thomas is shown by another letter from Thomas Mull to William:

> I conceive her words were this: 'Sir, I may have 300 marks in jointure, and if I take less when I may have more, my friends would think me not wise etc: and how be it, your father will not give me'.[44]

Fathers were expected to settle the jointures for their sons' wives, and this could be an area of stiff negotiation, though Margery Blount's demand of 300 marks does seem surprisingly high for a gentry marriage.[45] In any case, the discussions clearly broke down, and William was left feeling dispirited, as another letter from Mull to Thomas Stonor demonstrates:

> For God's sake call him forth with you when he is at home with you, and let him walk with you, and give [him] words of good comfort.[46]

William was perhaps seriously disappointed in courtship for the first time, and Mull seems to have expected his master to comfort his son and guide him through a formative experience. Whether or not Thomas Stonor did so, it did not make him relax his stance on the jointure. William's current feelings may have been of less import to his father than the long-term value of the match; marriage negotiations required fine financial calculations, and, in trying to balance the lady's cash value against the cost of her jointure, the result in Thomas's eyes must have been debit rather than credit. William seemed to have accepted his father's decision, even if he did not like it, for no more was said of Margery Blount.

The Cely sons' relationships with their father read as a little more relaxed than the relationship between Thomas and William Stonor. Nonetheless, it was clearly as important to the Celys as to the Stonors that the sons kept their father informed about potential marital prospects. As we saw at the beginning of this essay, Richard Cely junior told his brother about how he discussed a potential match for George as he and his father took a walk through their orchard in June 1481. Although this was at a very early stage in marriage negotiations, Richard senior seemed to be fully in his sons' confidence regarding the matter: as Richard junior says, he 'told him [Richard senior] all as it was', both in terms of George's possible match and of the death of his illegitimate child.[47] This demonstrates, first, that paternal involvement in marriage making began at the earliest stages of courtship, and, second, that fathers were aware that even as sons were seeking marital prospects they might also be engaged in extramarital sexual relationships.

There has been much written on medieval marriage formation, and in recent years there has been some interest in prostitution. However, though there is a great deal of critical interest in medieval *sexuality*, there has not yet been much work about extramarital *relationships* not involving a professional.[48] With the Cely sons we gain some insight into the spectrum of premarital and extramarital relationships, from the opening of marital negotiations to casual encounters to long-term romances to failed betrothals.

The most formal kind of relationship was George's affair with a French or Flemish woman named Clare. In early 1479, she wrote him a love letter in French saying that she had loved him for a long time, but had not previously dared to tell him so, before closing the letter with 'All Clare's heart is yours, George Cely'.[49] The direction is in Flemish, and so Clare may have been based in Bruges at this point, which was a place George frequently went on business.[50] However, he must have decided he would like her closer to him, because he seems to have installed her in a house in Calais.[51] Their relationship continued for at least another year and a half, because in memoranda of June and September 1480 George made references to wool he had stored with 'my Lady Clare'.[52] This would make it plausible for Clare to have been the mother of the child who died in 1481, although it seems more likely that it was another woman, whom I shall come to shortly. In any case, whether or not she had a child, George and Clare had a relationship that seems to have been on a semi-official footing, from the courteous way George referred to her as 'my Lady Clare' in both memoranda, the fact of his provision of her housing and, one assumes, her board, and his entrusting of his property to her. Moreover, her appearance in family records, and the likelihood that it was well known who owned her house, means that their relationship was reasonably public and, presumably, tolerated by his family. This was a long-term and well-established relationship that seems to have been based on at least some degree of mutual affection and respect.

At the other end of the relationship spectrum is Richard, who in May 1482 wrote to George in a panic after getting a woman named Em pregnant:

> Sir, a chance is fallen that lies upon my honesty, but I can keep no council from you, for by guile you and I may find the means to see all things clear at your coming. It is so that Em is with child... It was got on the eve of Shrove Tuesday.[53]

Richard's ability to date the conception so precisely would suggest that either this was a one-off encounter or his liaisons with Em were, at least, very infrequent. Unfortunately, we have no further idea of who Em was, or what happened to the child she bore – or if the pregnancy was even carried to term.

Alison Hanham surmises, from the use of Em's familiar name, that she may have been a servant, as the only women routinely mentioned by first name alone in the Cely correspondence are household servants.[54] With service forming part of the adolescent stage of the life cycle of many people, and with servants living in close proximity to the family they served, this sort of encounter may not have been uncommon. Certainly, though, Richard did not seem to have particularly wanted or expected the consequences of this sexual relationship; he described it as threatening his 'oneste' – his reputation – and he sought his brother's advice, as he was clearly alarmed by what has happened. It is hard to imagine that if Clare had fallen pregnant George would have been this shocked. Was Richard's shock because he did not expect a one-off encounter to result in pregnancy? Richard senior had died earlier in 1482, so Richard junior's panic was not because he would get in trouble with his father, who as head of the household would have been expected to be responsible for protecting the virtue of his female servants.[55] Even without his father's disapproval, Richard may have been embarrassed to have so obviously breached a standard of good conduct. George's relationship with Clare, outside the family home, may have been more respectable than Richard's relationship with someone in his employ.

Richard junior may also seem more panicked than George because he was less sexually experienced than his brother. As well as his long-term mistress Clare, George was also involved with a woman called Margery, a servant in a Calais pudding house. This relationship is particularly interesting in terms of what it says about social conventions regarding extramarital relations and about bastards specifically. In January 1482 George made Margery pregnant. As his close friend John Dalton informed him:

> Also sir, where we ate the good puddings, the woman of the house that made them, as I understand she is with child with [by] my brother that had the Irish dagger from me.[56]

'Brother' was a term used for fellow members of the Staple, and must surely refer to George. Given the way Dalton described her, it does not seem that Margery was a 'mistress' in the established sense that 'my Lady Clare' was; she was still employed in the pudding house, and so one might assume that, like Richard's encounter with Em, George's relationship with Margery had been short-lived and casual. However, George and Margery had been intimate more than once, and over the course of a couple of years. Eight months after George got the news about Margery's pregnancy, William Cely wrote to George, telling him that Margery needed clothing for her churching, as she had required on a previous occasion:

> Margery commands her unto your mastership, and she tells me she should have raiment – a gown and other things – for her churching, *as she had the other time*.[57] [My emphasis]

The timing of these two letters makes it very likely that 'the woman of the house' and 'Margery' are the same person. Churching, a ritual purification following childbirth, would have been a fairly public event.[58] The request that George provide the clothing for this public ceremony may suggest that his relationship to Margery's new child would be known in the community. The 'other time' referred to may well have been the child Richard junior talked about to his father in 1481. There is no evidence one way or another as to whether George and Margery had an ongoing relationship, but certainly they must have been involved sexually at least occasionally from 1480 or even earlier, depending on the age of the 'schylde' that died. George does not appear to have maintained Margery in the way he did Clare. Clare may have been of a higher social status than Margery; she could apparently afford to hire a scribe to write to George, and the fact that she sent him a love letter at all might indicate that she had a reasonable degree of education.[59] This may have made her a more attractive choice to George in terms of establishing a long-term connection; perhaps the pudding house servant Margery, whatever her charms, was, because of her low status, not really mistress material. Whatever the status of their relationship, evidently the encounters were pleasing enough that after Margery bore their first child George kept the sexual connection between them, despite having a relationship with Clare at the same time.

However, we should not be too hasty in assuming that this relationship offered no social complications for George. Three days after John Dalton wrote to George, George's servant Joyce Parmenter wrote informing him that: 'Also I let you know, where you go and eat puddings the woman is with child, as I understand.'[60] There is something very striking in the similarity of the language used by Joyce and John: 'where we ate the good puddings' and 'where you go and eat puddings'. Of course, partly this is simply descriptive; George and John dined out, and at a pudding house they frequented George met Margery. However, the similarity of phrasing, coupled with the circuitous language John used to identify George as the father (the reference to the Irish dagger), gives the distinct impression that 'puddings' is here being used to both cloak and disclose. This tells us something about the nature of this sexual relationship, and also about social attitudes toward such relationships and toward bastards.

It seems that, from the late seventeenth century, 'pudding', which meant a 'sausage' rather than the definition more widely used today, had come to be a slang term for the penis.[61] As Alison Hanham has noted, 'some of the gaps in [the Oxford English Dictionary]...would have been filled had all the Cely papers been available to the editors',[62] but, even if this is the case, there does not seem to be a direct link here to George's 'eating of the pudding', which would in such a definition become a far more taboo act! More usefully, the Middle English Dictionary defines 'pudding' as both a sausage and a type of cheap ale. The conflation of foodstuff and drink may suggest the context in which such 'puddings' were sold. Margery may well have worked in a tavern or alehouse that served this kind of cheap meal, as well as ale. Women played a large part in the brewing and selling of ale. For example, in Chester over half of those retailers brought before the court for breaking the assize of ale were female.[63] This might, of course, merely show that women were more likely to be prosecuted than men, but it still indicates a high proportion of women in the business. Unsurprisingly, the authorities were worried by businesses dominated by women and considered that antisocial activities flourished in alehouses – principally of a violent or sexual nature.[64] Although part of this was probably the result of a misogynistic dislike of female enterprise – Ruth Mazo Karras notes that laundresses and spinsters were also suspected of prostitution – like these industries, it may well have also been rooted in fact.[65] Thus, just as foodstuffs and drinks become conflated, so too do alehouses and brothels, and customers become purchasers of distinct but associated 'products'.

Of course, this is not to say that the pudding house George frequented was actually a brothel. It was probably not, just as the majority of alehouses were likely simply alehouses. However, these letters do allow a glimpse into the recreational habits of two unmarried men, and it is worth noting that both George Cely and John Dalton were, as far as can be seen, perfectly respectable youths, whose potential appetite for more than one kind of pudding did not affect their reputations. All of which supports the idea that social perceptions of young male sexuality accepted and even expected a certain degree of promiscuity, which might well result in the production of offspring.

However, the matter may have been a little more complex than outright acceptance. The use of euphemistic language, as well as providing a kind of shorthand reference to George and John's habits, may have also been employed in order to maintain a certain level of social delicacy. Both John and Joyce seem very careful to avoid naming George as a father, even though they are at the same time revealing him to be one. Young male extramarital sexual activity was tolerated, and there must then have been an acknowledgement that sexual activity would sometimes result in the conception of illegitimate children. Just because there was a certain toleration of youthful sexual behaviour does not mean that siring bastards was entirely socially acceptable, however. Bastards were incontrovertible proof of illicit sex, which may have been acceptable only when it was discreet. Richard Cely junior, referring to Em's pregnancy, was worried about his 'oneste', a term that splices together both his public reputation and his personal virtue.[66] The circuitous ways John Dalton and Joyce Parmenter referred to Margery's pregnancy appear to be attempts at discretion. Given that George's family knew about his previous child, this seems unlikely to be because the matter was meant to be a secret; rather, it seems to be providing a certain distance between George and the child. In English civil courts, an illegitimate child was *nullius filius*, the son of no one.[67] This legal terminology may have had a social resonance. It is striking that George's bastards are never referred to as his children, and he is not called a father. Richard junior refers to the child who dies in 1481 as 'the child' rather than 'your child', and, when William Cely writes in late 1482 to tell George that the child Margery bore in the summer has died, he expresses it as 'Margery's daughter is passed to God.'[68] Of course, medieval letters are not always fully descriptive, but in the world of correspondence, when so much emphasis is placed on establishing relationships between parties – 'my worshipful master', 'my well-beloved brother', 'my right worshipful father' – it seems notable that George is never once called a father.

Is this a polite fiction purely for the medium of letters? Or is it perhaps an indication that bastards were not really viewed as 'proper' children? Richard, as we have seen, certainly seems to have felt a measure of guilt about the siring of his child by Em. In closing the letter, Richard called George 'my ghostly brother', which, as Hanham notes, is clearly a play on 'ghostly father', as in confessor.[69] There is an element of jest here, as Richard recognised that he had been using his brother as a repository for his secrets, but there is also the sense that Richard was looking for absolution – or at least comfort. However, he makes an interesting remark: 'God knows but that once that it was got I deserved it for mine.'[70] Is the sense he is intending to give that, because of his sin, he deserved the consequence – that is, the child? Or does he mean that, once he realised that he had got Em pregnant, he was content to have the child as his responsibility? Perhaps both. Just because a man was not delighted by the news of a pregnancy does not mean he could not subsequently act as a father to the child. Likewise, George might have preferred it if his illegitimate children were not directly referred to as his, but he still bore at least some financial responsibility for their mother, and his father's regret at the death of one of these babies may be an indication that they were at least partly integrated into the Cely family.

Regardless of the extent to which bastards were welcome within the family, it seems very much that their existence was accepted as a part of life. Richard senior did not seem to see them as a challenge to his authority. Although Richard senior, as head of the household, had moral authority over the sexual behaviour of those in that household, from the surviving evidence he seems tolerant of his sons' behaviour. George's escapades, happening outside the household, might have been something about which a father could be indulgent. The siring of bastards, therefore, may well have been, if not a welcome, at least an accepted consequence of socially allowable sexual behaviour for young unmarried men, as long as it happened away from home and in a situation that would not cast the patriarch's authority in a poor light.[71] There is no evidence that George or Richard continued such relationships after their marriages; this may, of course, simply be due to a failure of such evidence to survive, but it seems likely that a certain amount of 'oat sowing' was expected of men of their age, which would then stop once suitable marriages were obtained. Extramarital sex was thus a part of a particular life-cycle stage, but an activity that was meant to be left behind as males reached adulthood.

What was probably more important to Richard senior than his sons' sexual behaviour was that they consulted him in matters of significance to the family. His reaction to the behaviour of his eldest son Robert is telling in terms of what it says both about parental authority and about what kinds of romantic relationships could be accepted by the family. Richard junior and George may have had illicit relationships, but they also sought suitable wives based on factors such as the woman's reputation and fortune, and seemed to find outlets for their sexual or romantic impulses elsewhere. Robert Cely, however, nearly married a completely unsuitable woman and had to be rescued by his father and brothers, which is just one in a long list of bad situations from which he needed help in extricating himself. Despite having been married, perhaps unusually young for a male of his class, Robert does not seem to have grown up. His wife died in 1479, and Robert apparently fell back into being under his father's authority. Despite being the eldest son, Robert seems to have played the role of the perpetual adolescent in the Cely family – and his family treated him as one. In 1478, an exasperated Richard junior reported that Robert had lost on dice 30s. given to him for his board, and two years later Robert wrote a plaintive letter to George asking him to cover debts of £14 15s.[72] The family were regularly critical of Robert's imprudent spending and lack of judgement, or, as Richard junior sourly put it, his 'childish dealing'.[73]

This poor judgement was reflected in Robert's love life. In the spring of 1480 Richard senior wrote to George to report that:

> I feel Robert Cely is at Bruges for fear of getting at Calais into the Bishop's court for the misguided matter of Joan Hart, about which there is much ado in London. Her family have spoken with me about the matter, but they will not give a groat to help them, therefore I have said to them I will not give them a penny... But privily keep these matters private and let me understand his intent, and after I shall write more to you.[74]

Richard's anxiety here is palpable. Joan Hart was evidently trying to get a marriage contract enforced by the consistory court, a marriage that not even her family would support. A few days later, Richard junior wrote to George, informing him of how the matter has been dealt with:

> It is so by great labour that the woman that our brother Robert was tangled with, she has made him acquittance, and she has...all the good that our brother left with her, save a girdle of gold...and a little gold ring with a little diamond.[75]

With some effort, it seems, Joan had been paid off by being allowed to keep the courtship gifts that Robert had given her; she was probably asked to return the ring as it may have been evidence for a marriage proposal.[76] Courtship was an expensive business in general, if Richard junior's widow Anne's claim is true: that George spent the value of more than half of the brothers' common stock on jewels and rich gifts for one Margery Rygon and her friends.[77] The difference between George and Robert's case is that George successfully married Margery, who as a wealthy widow was a good catch. Robert, meanwhile, got entangled so badly with a woman that his parents sent him off to the family's country home to keep him out of further mischief.[78]

The contrast with Richard senior's attitude toward George's sexual relationships is telling. Both Robert's and George's affairs were illicit in the sense that they fell outside the social norm of marriage; but George's behaviour, even though it involved sexual relations outside marriage and the production of children, was less problematic than his eldest brother's behaviour. George did not disrupt the family by producing bastards, and his sexual relationships did not appear to shame it. Robert, meanwhile, unlike his brothers, did not consult with his family regarding suitable brides, and caused his father great embarrassment over his reckless involvement with a woman who brought with her no assets.

Male adolescence in late medieval England was not a brief phase between childhood and adulthood. Instead it was a significant life-cycle stage, a time when youths were expected to be laying the foundations of their adult lives, but also a time when it was expected that they would indulge in activities particular to their age. Male adolescents were expected to learn their profession or trade, but also to take part in sports and merrymaking and to have extramarital sexual relationships. Their lovers were not necessarily prostitutes, but for youths of the mercantile class, at least, they were usually of a lower rank. These relationships did not seem to impact negatively on their reputations, although the occasional result of these relationships, illegitimate children, may have been more problematic in social terms. Adolescents were given a certain amount of social freedom, but it had limits. A youth should not bring his family into disrepute through imprudent behaviour, such as accumulating gambling debt or getting betrothed without his family's approval. In marriage making in particular, an adolescent was meant to be guided by his family. If he failed to do so, his father would probably choose to exert his influence. Youths may have been growing in confidence and moving toward manhood, and fathers could be affectionate and interested in their adolescent sons, but nonetheless authority ultimately remained with the father.

## Notes

1. 'Syr, howr father and I comende togydyr in the new orchard on Fryday laste, and a [he] askyd me many qwestyonys of gyu, and I towlde hym aull as hyt whos, and he whos ryught sory for the dethe of the sch[y]lde, and I toulde hym of the good whyll that the Whegystons and Dawltons hows to yow, and how I lykyd the ȝenge gentyllwhoman, and he commaunded me to whryte to yow and he whowlde gladly that hyt whor brohut abohut and that ȝe labyrde hyt betymys...' Richard Cely junior to George Cely, 4 June 1481. Alison Hanham (ed.), *The Cely Letters* Early English Text Society, o.s., 273 (London, 1975), no. 117, p. 107. All references from the Cely letters are from this edition, hereafter *CL*. Translations from Middle English are my own; some minor vocabulary and syntax changes have been made to ease understanding.
2. See, for instance, P.J.P. Goldberg, *Women, Work and Life Cycle in a Medieval Economy: Women in York and Yorkshire c. 1300–1520* (Oxford, 1992) and Kim M. Phillips, *Medieval Maidens: Young Women and Gender in England, 1270–1540* (Manchester, 2003).
3. Deborah Young provides a useful survey of current scholarship on medieval adolescence in *The Life-Cycle in Western Europe, c.1300 – c.1500* (Manchester, 2006), but seems to mostly consider adolescence to be a time of transition between childhood and adulthood rather than, as I argue, a key life stage. P.J.P. Goldberg and Felicity Riddy's edited collection *Youth in the Middle Ages* (York, 2004) is useful, but uses 'youth' as an umbrella term that also embraces childhood, and does not try to define adolescence. Likewise the interesting collection edited by Konrad Eisenbilcher, *The Premodern Teenager: Youth in Society, 1150–1650* (Toronto, 2002). Barbara Hanawalt's *Growing Up in Medieval London: The Experience of Childhood in History* (Oxford, 2003) attempts a more comprehensive definition (pp. 9–13, 111–13). Ruth Mazo Karras argues that medieval people considered adolescence as a subset of adulthood in *From Boys to Men: Formations of Masculinity in Late Medieval Europe* (Philadelphia, 2002), pp. 13–14. James Schultz, meanwhile, has argued that there was no medieval adolescence in his provocative article 'Medieval adolescence: the claims of history and the silence of German narrative', *Speculum* 66 (1991), 519–39. Schultz's conclusions, drawn from Middle High German texts, do not match my reading of Middle English sources, particularly regarding identity formation and inter-generational conflict.
4. Hanawalt, *Growing Up*, pp. 11–13, 110–11.
5. Michael S. Kimmel and Michael A. Messner, *Men's Lives* (Boston, 1989), p. x.
6. Allan G. Johnson, *The Gender Knot: Unraveling our Patriarchal Legacy* (Philadelphia, 2005), p. 155.
7. Key publications on medieval masculinities include: Jeffrey Jerome Cohen and Bonnie Wheeler (eds), *Becoming Male in the Middle Ages* (New York, 1997); D.M. Hadley (ed.), *Masculinity in Medieval Europe* (London, 1999); Jacqueline Murray (ed.), *Conflicted Identities and Multiple Masculinities: Men in the Medieval West* (New York, 1999); Ruth Mazo Karras, *From Boys to Men: Formations of Masculinity in Late Medieval Europe* (Philadelphia, 2003).
8. An exception is Joel T. Rosenthal, *Patriarchy and Families of Privilege in Fifteenth-Century England* (Philadelphia, 1991).
9. See Shulamith Shahar, *Childhood in the Middle Ages*, trans. Chaya Galai (London, 1992) and Nicholas Orme, *Medieval Children* (New Haven, 2001).
10. Quoted in J.A. Burrow, *The Ages of Man: A Study in Medieval Writing and Thought* (Oxford, 1996), p. 23.

## Adult Male Identity in a Fifteenth-Century Family  241

11. Joan Cadden, *Meanings of Sex Difference in the Middle Ages: Medicine, Science, and Culture* (Cambridge, 1993), p. 145.
12. Arnold van Gennep, *The Rites of Passage*, trans. Monika B. Vizedon and Gabrielle L. Caffee (London, 1977), p. 68.
13. On social puberty, see Hanawalt, *Growing Up in Medieval London*, p. 10. Sandra Cavallo writes usefully on the mobility of Italian urban youths, albeit in an early modern context. Sandra Cavallo, *Artisans of the Body in Early Modern Italy: Identities, Families and Masculinities* (Manchester, 2007), pp. 142–43.
14. J.A. Burrow, *The Ages of Man: A Study in Medieval Writing and Thought* (Oxford, 1996).
15. Burrow, *Ages of Man*, pp. 28–33. See also Karras, *From Boys to Men*, pp. 12–14.
16. Burrow, *Ages of Man*, pp. 5–9.
17. Burrow, *Ages of Man*, pp. 33, 49, 67–77.
18. 'yt ys of meyrth the cavsse I woold haue you for.' *CL* no. 44, p. 41.
19. Hanawalt, *Growing Up*, p. 114.
20. Censorinus, quoted in Burrow, *Ages of Man*, p. 73.
21. Henry Bergen (ed.), *Lydgate's Fall of Princes* (Washington, 1923), ll. 1765–71.
22. Noel James Menuge, *Medieval English Wardship in Romance and Law* (Cambridge, 2001), p. 2; Hanawalt, *Growing Up*, p. 112.
23. Hanawalt, *Growing Up*, pp. 202–03.
24. See Sylvia Thrupp, *The Merchant Class in Medieval London: 1300 – 1500* (Ann Arbor, 1962), pp. 192–93; David Herlihy, *Medieval Households* (Harvard, 1985), pp. 107–09; Karras, *From Boys to Men*, p. 16. On English gentry marriage patterns, see Keith Dockray, 'Why did fifteenth-century English gentry marry?', in M.C.E. Jones (ed.), *Gentry and Lesser Nobility in Late Medieval England* (Gloucester, 1986), pp. 61–80.
25. Kim M. Phillips discusses female wards' marriages being sold, but the principle was likely to have been the same – the earlier the marriage, the quicker the profit for the guardian. Phillips, *Medieval Maidens*, pp. 37–8.
26. Christine Carpenter (ed.), *Kingsford Stonor Letters 1290 – 1483* (Cambridge, 1996), nos. 109–10, pp. 200–02. Hereafter *SL*.
27. '[T]he said Sir William promised the said Lord Clyfford that they should not lygg togedder till she came to the age of xvj yeres.' Joan Kirby (ed.), *The Plumpton Letters and Papers* (Cambridge, 1996), Appendix 1, no. 2, p. 230.
28. Medieval naturalists noted that, whilst adolescence might mark the actualisation of generative ability, it was *not* the perfect age to reproduce. Joan Cadden, *Meanings of Sex Difference in the Middle Ages: Medicine, Science and Culture* (Cambridge, 1993), p. 145. Barbara Harris notes that contracts for dowries often stipulated that the dowry should be returned if bride or groom died before the age of 16, suggesting that before this the marriage would have gone unconsummated. Barbara J. Harris, *English Aristocratic Women* (Oxford, 2002), p. 45. See also Phillips, *Medieval Maidens*, pp. 38–41, and John Carmi Parsons, 'Mothers, daughters, marriage, power: some plantagenet evidence 1150–1500', in John Carmi Parsons (ed.), *Medieval Queenship* (New York, 1997), pp. 63–8.
29. Hanawalt, *Growing Up*, p. 203.
30. Cadden, *Meanings of sex difference*, pp. 146–48, and Fiona Harris Stoertz, 'Sex and the medieval adolescent', in Eisenbilcher, *The Premodern Teenager*, p. 225.
31. Cadden, *Meanings of Sex Difference*, pp. 273–74.
32. Ibid., p. 220.
33. 'Angelicus iuvenis senibus satanizat in annis.' J.A. Burrow, '"Young saint, old devil": reflections on a medieval proverb', *The Review of English Studies*, New Series, 30 (1979), 385. See also Stoertz, 'Sex and the medieval adolescent', p. 226.

34. Karras, *From Boys to Men*, p. 128.
35. P.J.G. Goldberg, 'Masters and men in later medieval England', in Hadley, *Masculinity in Medieval Europe*, pp. 63–7.
36. Sarah Rhiannon Williams, 'English vernacular letters c. 1400 – 1600: language, literacy and culture' (PhD diss., University of York: York, 2001), pp. 44–5.
37. Williams, 'English vernacular letters', pp. 227–30.
38. For more on letter writing in late medieval England, see: Joel T. Rosenthal, *Telling Tales: Sources and Narration in Late Medieval England* (University Park, 2003); Alexander Bergs, *Social Networks and Historical Sociolinguistics: Studies in Morphosyntactic Variation in the Paston Letters (1421–1503)* (Berlin, 2005); and Karen Cherewatuk and Ulrike Wiethaus (eds), *Dear Sister: Medieval Women and the Epistolary Genre* (Philadelphia, 1993).
39. *CL*, no. 165, pp. 150–53.
40. 'we had right good communication...sche is ȝewnge, lytyll, and whery whellfauyrd [attractive *or* prosperous] and whytty, and the contre spekys myche good bye hyr.'
41. 'Syr, aull this matter abydythe the cowmyng of her father to London, that whe may wndyrstonde what some he wyll departte wyth, and how he lykys me.'
42. '[S]he hath in possession C. marks of lande, and after the deth of her ffader shee shall have over that the half of al the residue of al the lande of her ffader...And for certeine shee is well named, and of worshipfull disposicion....I know verely my Cosen woll in no wise in this cas doo but as your good ffaderhode woll he do.' *SL*, no. 121, p. 212.
43. 'I truste weryly to alle myty Jhesu and to youre good fadyhod that I shalle spede well of my mater, for I have comfortabul demenure of my mastresse.' *SL*, no. 122, p. 213.
44. 'I conceyve the [her] wordes wer þees: "Syr, I may have CCC. marcs in joyntur, and I to take þe lesse when I may have þe more, my ffrendes wold þenke me not wyse andc: and how be yt, your ffader wol not geve me..."'
45. Harris, *English Aristocratic Women*, pp. 49–51.
46. '[For] Godis sake callyth hym forth with you when he is at home with you, and let hym walke with you, and gevyth wordes of good comforte...' *SL*, no. 124, pp. 215–16.
47. *CL*, no. 117, p. 107.
48. For instance, Stoertz assumes that the only options open to apprentices were 'celibacy or consorting with prostitutes or concubines'. Stoertz, 'Sex and the medieval adolescent', p. 237. Ruth Mazo Karras discusses this academic assumption in 'Sex and the singlewoman', in Judith M. Bennett and Amy M. Froide (eds), *Singlewomen in the European Past 1250 – 1800* (Philadelphia, 1999), pp. 127–45.
49. 'Tout le coer de Clare est à vous, Jorge Cely.' *CL*, no. 54, p. 50.
50. *Dorse*: 'deseen brief zy ghegeuen tot Jorge Cely.' *CL*, no. 54, p 50.
51. Allison Hanham, *The Celys and Their World: An English Merchant Family of the Fifteenth Century* (Cambridge, 2002), pp. 49–51.
52. 'They [fells] ly in the neder chambyr houyr my Lady Clar.' *CL*, no. 92, p. 81. See also: 'The kay off my ffell chamber ower my Lady Clare, John Wurme hathe ytt.' *CL*, no. 105, p. 93.
53. 'Syr, hyt ys so that a chawns ys fallyn that lyes ap[on] myne oneste, byt I cannat kepe no cwnsell frome yow, for be polesy ȝe and I may fynd the meyn to sawhe awl thyng cler[e] at yowr comyng. Hyt is so that Em ys wyth schyllde, and as Godde knoweys byt that whons that hyt wh[as] gettyn I desarwyd for [m]yn. Hyt whos

gettyn on Schrofe ȝeuyn...' *CL*, no. 169, p. 156. See also Hanham, *The Celys and Their World*, pp. 268–69.
54. Hanham, *The Celys and Their World*, pp. 268–69.
55. Hanawalt, *Growing Up*, p. 186.
56. 'Alsoy syr, wher as we ette the good podyngys, the womon of the hosse that mayd them, as I onderstond sche ys wyth schylde wyth my broder that hayd the Irysch skeyne [dagger] of me.' *CL*, no. 141, p. 129.
57. 'Margery commavndyþ her vnto yowr masterschypp, and sche tellyth me sche schulde hawe rayment – a gowne and oder thyngys – agaynest her chyrchyng, as sche hadd the toder tyme...' *CL*, no. 181, p. 167.
58. Paula M. Reider, *On the Purification of Women: Churching in Northern France, 1100 – 1500* (New York, 2006).
59. *CL*, no. 54, n. p. 262.
60. 'Also I lat yow wyt, þer ye go and ete puddyngys the woman is with child, as I ondirstond.' *CL.*, no. 142, p. 130.
61. 'pudding, n. 9. a. *coarse slang*. The penis. Now only in *to pull one's pudding* and variants'. *The Oxford English Dictionary* (2nd edn, 1989).
62. *CL*, Introduction, p. xxi.
63. Jane Laughton, 'The Alewives of later medieval Chester', in Rowena E. Archer (ed.), *Crown, Government and People in the Fifteenth Century* (Stroud, 1995), p. 202.
64. Judith M. Bennett, *Ale, Beer, and Brewsters in England: Women's Work in a Changing World, 1300–1600* (New York, 1996), p. 122.
65. Ruth Mazo Karras, *Common Women: Prostitution and Sexuality in Medieval England* (Oxford, 1998), pp. 54–5.
66. 'honest(e), also onest(e). 1. (a) Of persons, their reputation, desires: honorable, respectable, noble; also *fig*.; ~ cure, desire for honor or respectability; maken ~, to honor (sb.), enrich (sb.); (b) of actions, conditions, events, etc.: worthy of respect, honorable, noble; of virtue: excellent; (c) of seasons or times: to be honored.' *The Middle English Dictionary* (Ann Arbor, 2001).
67. Norma Adams, '*Nullius Filius*: a study of the exception of bastardy in the law courts of medieval England', *The University of Toronto Law Journal* (1946), p. 361.
68. 'Margery's daughter is passed to God.' *CL.*, no. 188, p. 173.
69. 'No mor to yow, my gostely brother, byt I pray Jhesu that aull thyngys may be whell conwhayd.' *CL*, no. 169, p. 156. See also Hanham, *The Celys and their World*, p. 268.
70. 'as Godde knoweys byt that whons that hyt wh[as] gettyn I desarwyd for [m]yn.' *CL*, no. 169, p. 156.
71. For the head of household's authority over sexual behaviour within his household, see P.J.P. Goldberg, 'Masters and men in later medieval England', in Hadley, *Masculinity in Medieval Europe*, pp. 56–70, and Barbara Hanawalt, *Growing Up in Medieval London* (Oxford, 1993), pp. 186–96.
72. *CL* nos. 32, p. 29, and 102, p. 89.
73. 'chyldysche dellyng'. *CL*, no. 99, p. 87.
74. 'I fele Robard Cely ys at Bregys for fere of fytyng at Caleys into Beschepys corte for the lvde [more commonly used to mean misguided than lascivious] mater of Jonne [Joan] Harthe, the weche ys meche adoe for at London. The frendes [in this context nearly always means 'family' or 'family friends'] of here hath spoke wyt me for the mater, but all they wyll not grant a grote for [to] ȝeve them, werefor I haue sayd to them I wyll not ȝeve them a peny of my good...' *CL* no. 85, p. 75.
75. 'hyt is so be grehyt labor that the whoman that howr brother Robard whos tangyllyd wyth, sche has made hyme a qwyetans, and sche has...aull the good that howr

brother leudy wyth her, saue a gyrdyll of goulde...and a lyttyll golde ryng wyth a lyttyll dyamond...' *CL* no. 86, p. 76.
76. Shannon McSheffrey, *Sex, Marriage and Civic Culture in Late Medieval London* (Philadelphia, 2006), pp. 65–6.
77. Hanham, *The Celys and their World*, p. 311.
78. *CL*, no. 86, p. 76.

# 12
'To Make a Man Without Reason': Examining Manhood and Manliness in Early Modern England

*Jennifer Jordan*

The conundrum of exactly what made a man, or constituted manhood, during the early modern period is something which historians and literary scholars have been puzzling over for the last 15 to 20 years. Much of the current scholarship has focused on relationships between men and women, pointing towards the necessity of marriage, family formation and economic independence in achieving manhood in early modern England.[1] As a result, the significance of patriarchy in determining the prescripts of men's familial and social roles, responsibilities and behaviour has become a prominent feature in studies of early modern manhood. The extent to which manhood was grounded in patriarchal ideology, or was available through many, varied and often contradictory means, is a question that is becoming increasingly pivotal within this burgeoning debate.[2] In strictly prescriptive terms, manhood was identified as being that married, economically independent householder upon whom patriarchy insisted.[3] Pursuing this line of thinking is not an attempt to posit the idea that manhood and patriarchy were synonymous, or that those men who did not achieve such social standing, for whatever reason, were somehow a breed of lesser or non-men. It is an attempt, however, to suggest that those men who did not achieve normative or full manhood could exert their manliness in other ways.[4]

The chief studies of early modern manhood that have been undertaken to date have gone some way towards investigating the defining prescripts of manhood for men in their youth and adulthood.[5] Boys and men in their old age have been given a lesser prominence in studies explicitly focused on the gendering of early modern men. This is not surprising given the relative infancy of the subject area.[6] In particular, adult men have formed the central focus of analysis and, indeed, this chapter does not propose to exclude them either. It is the contention of this chapter that the term 'manhood' has so far evaded a satisfactory definition and that this is in part due to its contradictory and inconsistent usage during the early modern period. As Alexandra Shepard has noted, early modern commentators understood the term most readily as a specific phase of life, but it also had connotations of social status and rank.[7] It is this double meaning which has prompted historians like Shepard and Susan Amussen to utilise distinct phraseology, such as 'normative' or 'patriarchal' manhood, to identify that which is concerned with the economically independent and married householder, and this chapter will also use these terms, although the phrase 'full' manhood will be employed as an alternative.

Two of the central characteristics which were thought to distinguish adult men from women and boys were physical strength and reason.[8] Such attributes worked to enable men to govern effectively both themselves and their social and familial inferiors. Elizabeth Foyster has argued that 'boys' bodies were physically under-developed' and, moreover, that 'from birth until the age of seven, a boy's reason and judgement were feeble'.[9] Likewise, Alexandra Shepard's reading of health guides, medical tracts and conduct books suggests that boys, like men in their youth and old age, lacked the physiological balance which manhood – or 'man's estate' – required and on which reason and strength were founded.[10] Indeed, in terms of medical and anatomical understanding, manhood was presented as a specific and ephemeral life stage.

Criticisms of the earliest histories of childhood, such as the work of Philippe Ariès, Lloyd de Mause and Lawrence Stone, are now well rehearsed, and, whilst there is an appreciation of the merits of the questions at the heart of each of these studies and what they set out to explore, there is an almost universal acknowledgement of their perceived weaknesses and shortcomings.[11] Subsequent histories of childhood, which were spurred on by the inadequacies of these pioneering studies, focused attention on stamping out the myth that there was no concept of childhood before the sixteenth century, on establishing that there has always been an emotional bond between parent and child and, crucially, on establishing that the history of childhood is more one of continuity than of change, each of which appeared to be denied in the older studies.[12]

That childhood is both culturally constructed and historically specific is axiomatic. The term, therefore, is one of classification that possesses shifting meanings according to place, period, social rank and gender. It is doubtful whether any real understanding of a history of collective childhood experience can ever be achieved, particularly for periods of pre-industrial history. Despite her impressive source base of primary material – 416 diaries and autobiographies, of which 98 were written by children – Linda Pollock, for instance, found it difficult to draw any definite conclusions on past children's experience precisely because individual experience is so diverse and so wide-ranging.[13] Indeed, Ralph Houlbrooke has commented that 'the world of early modern

Manliness in Early Modern England 247

childhood is now largely impenetrable save through personal testimony contained in diaries and autobiographies.'[14]

The focus of this chapter, however, is not primarily concerned with childhood experience. In part, it is an examination of both the conceptualisation of boyhood and the father–son relationship. More specifically, this chapter is concerned with assessing the extent to which the inculcation of attributes necessary to achieve manhood occurred during the years of childhood. Will Fisher has asserted that boys 'were quite literally a different gender from men during the early modern period'.[15] This, however, was simply not the case. Rather than being 'a-gendered', early modern boys copied, practised, learnt and went some way toward acquiring the necessary skills of manhood during their childhood years. Indeed, it was Henry Newcome's contention that 'children will imitate what we do.'[16] This chapter will examine the varied ways in which boys were encouraged to learn and display attributes of manliness from a young age. It will be suggested that both moralists and parents alike sought assurances that boys would reach adult age and acquire full manhood. Whilst debarred from the status of manhood by their age and status as dependents, it will be argued that boys could, and were very much encouraged to, achieve traits of manliness, making them entirely male-gendered despite their sexual immaturity.

Elizabeth Foyster has argued that boys were far more likely to learn the attributes of manhood through personal experience and through observation of the adult world around them than they were by reading conduct literature.[17] Her observations are supported by some seventeenth-century men, such as Edward, first Lord Herbert of Cherbury, who suggested that the personal exploits of fathers and grandfathers provided suitable moral guidance and instruction for their offspring. He claimed that:

> It will be found much better for Men to guide themselves by such observations as their Father, Grand-Father and Great Grand-Father might have deliver'd to them, than by those vulgar Rules and Examples, which cannot at all points so exactly agree unto them.[18]

Such was the justification of Herbert for finally recording to posterity what he describes as 'those Passages of my Life, which I conceive best declare me', a work which he began in 1643 and was published posthumously in 1649.[19] It was Herbert's contention that boys and young men would learn more about honour, conscience and virtue through reading or hearing the accounts of the lives of their fathers and grandfathers than by perusing the abstract instructions of conduct literature. In his sixties when he began his memoirs, Herbert says little about his relationships with his sons and daughters, mentioning them only in passing when recounting the preparations for his first voyage abroad. Aged eight when his grandfather died, and called back from Oxford aged 14 at the death of his father, Herbert opens the account of his life by reciting what he remembers of his father and grandfather, and the knowledge passed down to him of his earlier ancestors, before moving on to describing his mother and siblings and the narration of his own life. It is clear from Herbert's writing that he was an advocate of the honour attainable through soldiery, that he placed courtesy and civility at the heart of a gentleman's conduct and that he believed good fathers sought the best possible marital match for their daughters and provided their sons with a good education and, preferably, time spent abroad.[20]

Nevertheless, there is evidence which suggests that conduct literature found a ready market amongst gentry families, and that some mid-seventeenth-century texts were still applicable even into the eighteenth century. In 1729, John Buxton, for instance, suggested to his son that he should study Francis Osborn's *Advice to a Son*, a text first published in 1655. Buxton advised his son that 'allowance must be made for style', but went on to pledge that it was 'so good that I can give you no better than to read it through [...] good sense can never be out of fashion'.[21] Whilst it was common for conduct literature to take the form of advice to parents during the earlier part of the period covered here, whereby it was assumed that parents would take a role in the direction and government of the social and moral education of their offspring, a growing corpus of prescriptive and instructive texts were directed specifically at children as the seventeenth century unfolded.[22] Such works were usually much shorter in length than adult conduct literature, and they tended to assume a male readership.[23] Advice books for children could include academic lessons, such as spelling and basic Latin, catechisms and daily prayers and also more pointed direction on courtesy, civility, good conduct and gender roles.[24] The moral and religious overtones of children's conduct books remained constant throughout the period. John Gother's *Instructions to Children*, for example, took the form of a catechism of questions and answers for a child to learn, and was divided almost exactly into two halves, the first of which was entirely dedicated to devotional teaching whilst the latter was concerned with familial duties and civil behaviour.[25]

*The School of Grace* was also meant as an instruction manual for children.[26] That this book had gone through 19 editions by 1688 is highly suggestive of its popularity. It would appear that this particular book was meant as an instruction manual for children of a fairly young age, and it included lessons, prayers, catechisms and the Ten Commandments to be learnt and rehearsed by children in the home environment. Above all else, the lessons to be learnt were religious studies and deference and obedience to God, the King and parents, thus asserting and reinforcing the ordered principles of patriarchy and the patriarchal hierarchy. Interestingly, there is a list of 'godly books' priced at only 'three pence per piece' advertised in the back of the text which the author considered appropriate for children to read, each of which promoted godliness, sobriety and charity.[27] The cost of these listed books suggests something of the social status expected of the target readership of the work, affordable to the lesser yeomanry and possibly even those of husbandmen status.[28] Whilst it is likely that those children of a lower sort would hear the same or similar lessons and catechisms in Church, it cannot be assumed that *The School of Grace* was representative of the most basic education common to children of all ranks.

It was not unusual for fathers to be involved in the education of their young children, particularly their sons. In presenting evidence to suggest that close and emotional bonds existed between parents and their offspring, Ralph Houlbrooke provided excerpts from a number of diaries which included descriptive passages of fathers schooling their children in reading, history, counting, arithmetic and Latin.[29] Whilst Anthony Fletcher has argued that Latin increasingly became the secret language of the elite – and more specifically of elite men – during the period, Houlbrooke's work seems to suggest that this was a secret shared by fathers with their sons, at least for those sufficiently well educated to do so.[30] Indeed, Sir Justinian Isham, a gentleman scholar and royalist, suggested to his son Thomas that he should keep a record of daily goings-on with the sole purpose of later translating it into Latin.[31] Thomas Willis, a teacher from Middlesex, saw fit to compile and have printed for sale his *Vestibulum Lingue Latine*, which was in the design of a dictionary and intended to aid children in learning Latin. The work was also advertised as an *aide-memoire* for those adults who had forgotten the Latin they had learnt at school and, moreover, it also claimed to be useful for 'those not brought up to the knowledge of the Latin Tongue', as it contained 'interpreted words often used in English Books and Sermons'.[32] That Willis also included some instruction on how the *Dictionary* could best be used in teaching youngsters both English and Latin suggests that the text would have a place in both the home and the school.

It was expected in conduct literature that parents would read lectures, Scripture, moral advice tracts and great histories to their children, and there is evidence which suggests that at least some parents did so. On warning against the vice of pride and noting that it had become more of a virtue during the opening decades of the seventeenth century, Elizabeth Jocelyn noted that 'many parents reade lectures of it to their children.'[33] The author of *The Office of Christian Parents* went further, suggesting that mothers and fathers were not simply the biological – or natural – parents of children but included any number of relations and kin, including uncles, brothers, grandparents, stepparents, wards, masters, guardians and those without their own children who 'doe adopt some other, either of their kindred, or otherwise, and bring them up, and make them their heires'.[34] According to this author, it was the duty of 'govenours and gardians to children' to educate their young and, whilst in the very first years of life this was primarily the responsibility of the mother, both parents played a role in educating their children.[35] The reason for this was that educated children were an honour to themselves and to their parents and, moreover, they bolstered both the church and the commonwealth.[36] So, the instruction given to young boys promoted manly qualities, such as honour, deference and education, which comprised a curriculum of manliness that would continue to be learned and practised into the years of adolescence and youth.

\* \* \*

Leaving the instruction of manliness to one side, the significance of the breeching ceremony needs to be given some consideration. Although the process of becoming a man was one that began during the earliest stages of infancy, the breeching ceremony stands out as one of the most significant milestones in a boy's journey to acquiring manhood.[37] Losing their infancy skirts in favour of breeches provided boys with the outward appearance of manliness. Some historians have assumed that because boys from the age of five or six were dressed in the garb of adulthood this was somehow indicative that they were nothing more than 'miniature adults'.[38] However, the donning of ceremonial breeches did not mark the end of childhood for boys; instead it signified the commencement of a boy's transition into adulthood. Indeed, as Elizabeth Foyster has noted, a boy's first pair of breeches marked out just one of the stages in the rite of passage which a boy went through in the process of becoming a man.[39]

The breeching ceremony was in all probability an important moment in any boy's life, regardless of his social status. As Margaret Spufford's research has shown, clothing constituted the second largest expenditure in the maintenance of orphaned children after food and board.[40] The cost of boys' breeches, for example, before 1660 was on average 3s. 11d., whilst during the years 1660–1700 this cost rose to 5s. 11d., comprising a massive 51 per cent increase in price. However, in 1703 competitively priced breeches could still be found. In Canterbury, for instance, large boys' breeches could be bought from a salesman for 3s. 6d., whilst those for small boys were cheaper at 2s. 6d.[41] Spufford's work has further revealed that, despite the inflation in textile prices, which 'had been nearly continuous from the 1570s until the 1670s', even children of the lower sorts, including those of craftsmen and labourers, would have had the benefit of new clothes.[42] Moreover, for those poorer still, there was the flourishing second-hand clothes trade, which would have provided access to cheaper clothing for the 'millions of lesser folk, making do with secondhand as long as the cost of new materials kept those items out of their reach'.[43] So, at around the age of six years old a boy would be given his first pair of breeches, whether newly made, newly bought or second hand, and this marked the beginning of his journey into the adult world.

The first pair of breeches provided just cause for celebration and remark. Just as Lady Anne Clifford saw fit to record of her daughter Margaret 'the first time the Child put on a pair of Whalebone Bodice' and her 'first coat that was laced with Lace' as well as 'her crimson velvet Coat laced with silver, which was the 1st velvet Coat she ever had', so similar mention was made of boys' first breeches.[44] Sir Henry Slingsby noted in 1641 that he had sent from London 'a suit of clothes for my son Thomas, being the first breeches and doublet that he ever had'. His tailor had made the suit but, as Slingsby further recorded, 'it was too soon for him to wear them, being but five years old.' The reason for such a premature purchase was that 'his mother had a desire to see him in them, how a proper man would be.'[45] In the mindset of Thomas's parents at least, wearing breeches would give the small boy the semblance of a man. Thomas Isham's younger brother had to wait longer for his first pair of breeches. In November 1671, Isham noted in his journal that their servant Katherine 'went to Northampton and bought cloth for Brother Ferdinando's first breeches'.[46] Given that Ferdinando was born in April 1663, he would have been aged eight at the time this diary entry was penned. However, whether or not these were his first pair of breeches or simply the first pair made specifically for him is unclear.

Recording the occasion of giving a son his first pair of breeches was not only significant in terms of his taking the first step in the rite of passage to becoming a man, but it also marked the successful rearing of a child past the age of infancy. The demographers Wrigley and Schofield have estimated that 34.4 per cent of all deaths were those of children under the age of ten years old in pre-industrial England. In addition, their study of the records of eight parishes for the years 1550–1649 establishes that around one-quarter of all children would not live to see their tenth birthday and that, not surprisingly, death was most likely to occur during the first year of life.[47] Conversely, Peter Laslett's research suggests that during the years 1550–1749 roughly 20 per cent of live-born boys died within their first year of life, and this figure dropped to around 15 per cent of those aged between one and nine.[48] Nevertheless, the birth rate rarely fell beneath the death rate during the early modern period and, as Wrigley and Schofield's work suggests, roughly 31 per cent of the population were aged 14 or under in 1686.[49] It might be safe to imagine, as Laslett has, that right up until the Victorian era families were 'in the perpetual presence of their young offspring' and, moreover, that 'in the pre-industrial world there were children everywhere.'[50]

Despite this, rearing boys beyond the years of infancy could be a very difficult and somewhat emotional task that was not guaranteed to be successful. The rather ambiguous conformist minister Isaac Archer, for instance, fathered nine children, of whom only his second daughter, Anne, survived into adulthood.[51] Of his three sons, William, the eldest, did not live beyond the age of three. His second son fared worse and did not live more than a few hours. Unfortunately, his first two sons died within two months of each other, reminiscent of his own childhood when his mother, sister and brother had died within quick succession. Archer blamed the death of his eldest son on his own nonchalant attitude towards the death of the second baby boy and regarded the double loss as God's punishment for his lack of remorse, writing 'the Lord knew how to strike to the heart, by taking away my joy, strength, builder of my house, and by casting my crown to the ground!' Archer later noted in his diary that 'since God tooke away my two boyes I ceased not privately to pray for another to make up my losse.' His prayers were answered and on 14 February 1678 his third son, Isaac, was born. However, his joy was to be dashed just five months later, and Archer's distress at the death of his third son Isaac is evident: 'my son of prayer, desire, and hopes is taken away!'[52]

The death of John Evelyn's first son prompted him to write a rather lengthy tribute honouring the boy in his *Diary*.[53] Either in truth or in mournful hyperbole, it can be seen that at five years old Richard Evelyn was quite a well-accomplished child. Evelyn described the boy as 'a prodigie for Witt & understanding; for beauty of body a very Angel, & for endowments of mind, of incredible & rare hopes'. He claimed of the child that God had 'dressed up a Saint fit for himselfe' and upon the boy's funeral he noted 'here ends the joy of my life, & for which I go ever mourning to the grave.'[54] Evelyn claimed that at just two and a half years old his son could 'perfectly reade any of the English, Latine, French or Gothic letters; pronouncing the three first languages exactly'. By five years of age, Richard could read most writing, had mastered grammar, learnt nearly all French and Latin primitive words, and could translate Latin into English and vice versa. Moreover, he could write legibly, remember and recite verse and plays, had skill in arithmetic, had learnt all of his catechism and demonstrated 'his apt & ingenious application of Fables & Morals', all of which 'far exceeding his age & experience'.[55] The death of such a prodigy was clearly a great loss to Evelyn, and a similarly emotional tribute was penned on the death of his daughter Mary, but one of his sons, John, lived well into maturity.[56]

William Coe, a farmer of gentlemanly status from Suffolk, enjoyed better success in rearing his sons into adulthood than Isaac Archer and John Evelyn, although he too suffered losses. Of his 14 children from two marriages, two sons and one daughter died in their infancy. Four of his sons, William, Henry, Thomas and James, survived at least into their mid-twenties. Coe's diary, however, is not nearly as rich in detail or as family-orientated as Archer's, and so many of the more intimate emotions which have been identified in Archer's accounts are lacking in Coe's.[57] No comment is made of any of his sons' first pair of breeches, although frequent observation is made of their falls, accidents and mishaps, offering some insight into the stoicism expected of boys from a young age.[58] Ralph Josselin, who was the vicar of Earls Colne, Essex, for over 40 years, saw two of his sons, Thomas and John, reach full maturity. Of the two brothers, only John's first pair of breeches is noted in Josselin's *Diary*. The boy was breeched exactly two weeks after his sixth birthday, and it was evidently a moment of pride for Josselin, who wrote: 'John put in breeches, I never saw two sons so clad before.'[59] So it was indeed a cause for celebration when sons reached the age at which they were to be breeched, as the trials of infancy had been overcome and the first step in the rite of passage was complete.

\* \* \*

As we have seen, learning the attributes of manliness in preparation for manhood was a curricular activity for boys of all ages. The lessons of manliness learnt in the earliest years of childhood were to be practised in the years of adolescence, during which time fathers were to be the teachers – at least at the level of prescription. Much of the prescriptive literature, which took the form of a father's advice to his children, was directed at boys, adolescents and male youths who were approaching the age when they would be leaving home for school, university or perhaps travel abroad. Even though such advice books were ostensibly directed towards the author's own children, the very fact they were printed to be sold suggests the intended readership was always beyond that of the immediate family.[60] The author of the 1678 advice manual *The Father's Legacy: Or Counsels to his Children in Three Parts*, which was licensed by Roger L'Estrange, openly stated that, although the book was addressed to his sons, he was writing for a far wider readership. The author explained his intentions for the work in the preface, writing: 'it shall be in this place then, Reader, where I make no difference betwixt thy Son and mine.'[61] It is possible that such advice manuals were not actually intended for the children of the authors, but that addressing them as such was a technique for encouraging more sales, much like the 'true story' performances of ballads identified by Natascha Würzbach.[62] On the other hand, such texts could be examples of those private works of advice, admonition and counsel that entered the public domain through printing, which Martyn Bennett has described as 'crossing the boundary of manuscript and published text'.[63] Nevertheless, the directions given in this type of prescriptive literature always served the same purpose: to instruct boys and young men in the ways and means to properly conduct themselves throughout their lifetime.

There were also those texts which were primarily concerned with piety – mostly written by clergymen – that insisted upon religious devotion, particularly during the years of adolescence. Since many of these types of text were printed during the 1680s, they are perhaps evidence more of political commentary than one specifically concerning the lack of morality amongst the youth of the later seventeenth century.[64] However, even if this is the case, because such works were directed primarily toward a youthful audience, it is highly suggestive that this particular stage of life was open to influence – both good and bad – and needed to be directed by more senior and authoritative persons. So, common to the conduct books directed at youth was the expectation that young men would marry and form their own 'little commonwealth'. As a result, the advice that was given was focused on all aspects of life, both public and private. Sons were counselled on speech, dress, conduct, choosing a spouse, raising their own children, proper treatment of servants, making friends and avoiding bad company, work, reading, piety, eating and drinking and a whole range of other behaviour besides.[65] The chief factor underlying such advice was the importance of acquiring and maintaining a good reputation, which was central to both prescriptions of manhood and manliness.

If Alexandra Shepard's reading of father–son advice books of the earlier half of the seventeenth century is correct, wherein she claimed that the key to achieving manhood was balance, then this is one aspect of conduct literature which remained constant throughout the entire seventeenth century.[66] The words of Henry Massingberd, 'a middle condition renders man most happy,' seem to be particularly pertinent here.[67] In 1649, the advice of Edward Burton to his only son counselled that a balanced life was a godly life, and he further asserted that 'thou must bridle and break thy will in many things, if thou wilt live a quiet life.'[68] Archibald Argyle's instruction to his son, printed posthumously in 1661, also promoted balance when he cautioned: 'be not offended at every injury, wink sometimes at your wrong, but beware of unnecessary revenges.'[69] Argyle's instructions are interesting, too, because those directed to his eldest son and those 'to the rest of his children' were made separately, the indication being that the eldest son was in need of a more pointed tutoring concerning all aspects of life than that of his younger siblings. Indeed, 'the rest of his children' were told 'to your Eldest Brother, who is the Prince of your Family, shew your selves obedient and loving; he is my substitute, your honour is bound up in his.'[70]

Henry Hales's *New-Years-Gift to His Son*, printed in 1685, also proclaimed balance to be necessary during the years of adolescence. It was his contention 'that you ought to be very moderate in your Eating, Drinking, Sleeping and Recreations', because moderation was a lesson in self-government.[71] Self-government, above all else, was what enabled men in full manhood not only to maintain their jurisdiction over all their social and familial inferiors, but to justify such authority too. Strength of reason, which was the cornerstone of self-governance and the governing of others, provided the foundation on which patriarchal authority was built. It was essential to the continuance of the social order that male youths, particularly those of noble birth or wealth, learnt how to control themselves, their tempers and their lusts. Moreover, it was crucial that these lessons were taught whilst in youth to be mastered later upon reaching manhood. And, furthermore, it can be seen that the dictates of the early seventeenth century still carried weight almost a century later. In the year 1697, the anonymous tract *A Word in Season, Or An Essay to Promote Good-Husbandry in Hard and Difficult Times*, which was only 16 pages in length, dedicated seven of these to recounting and synopsising some of the guidance from William Cecil's father–son advice book of 1611.[72] That such advice was repeated and reprinted at the very end of the seventeenth century is highly suggestive of the permanence of moderation and self-government to the prescripts of manhood and manliness.

\* \* \*

The purpose of father – son advice books was to instruct boys and young men on how to master qualities of manliness in a deportment befitting manhood. But books of fatherly advice could also be manuals of instruction for men on how to act as fathers. The information did not only counsel male youths on how to become men; they also offered a useful guide to the kind of advice fathers should be able to give their sons and, as in the case of John Buxton, could be used to substitute fatherly council on matters of some delicacy. That this guidance was presented as father–son advice is suggestive that it was to their fathers (or father figures) that boys looked for instruction and example of how to become a man.

It is also clear that fathers formed strong emotional bonds with their children. We have seen the particularly moving diary entries of men, like Isaac Archer and John Evelyn, mourning the death of their sons. Sir John Reresby was equally afflicted by the death of his fourth son George:

> I received the unfortunate news of the death of my son George by the smallpox, a very beautiful, apt, understanding child. It was a great affliction to me; but God gives, and God takes, and blessed be the name of the Lord.[73]

This is the diary entry which Sir John wrote concerning George's death on 5 April 1689, having heard only seven days prior of his son's illness. It is not a long passage, but it is one which clearly and concisely lays bare the emotional bond between a father and his son. The Puritan Minister Henry Newcome also demonstrated affection for his children, particularly his son Daniel, in his diary entries, describing Daniel as his 'finest boy' and Harry as his 'best child'. Newcome further describes occasions when he sat with the children all evening, helped his sons with their Latin, tended to his son Peter when he was sick, and felt saddened when he had to discipline the children.[74] These are not the musings of men who did not care for their offspring. Rather, these diary entries suggest that fathers formed emotional bonds with their children and, moreover, played an active role in rearing them.[75]

Caleb Trenchfield's advice manual to his son, *A Cap of Grey Hairs for a Greenhead*, printed in 1671, provides tantalising evidence which is suggestive that fathers had hands-on experience in rearing their children from as young as babes. The advice given from father to son, to which I am referring, is concerned with bringing up children. Trenchfield questions the medical advice trumpeted by physicians of how best to feed babies and infants, using his own experience of raising ten children, in advising his son how best to look after very young children. He writes:

> And though the Physicians generally decry the use of Milk, as too Phlegmatick, and not convenient; yet doth not my own experience as much assert it; there being ten of you, who I believe vye with such a number of any one mans in the world beside, for health, strength and straitness, who have been all true Trojans at a milk-bowl.[76]

Whether or not he actually had any dealings with feeding the children, or directed what they were fed, or sought female advice on the matter to pass on to his son, is questionable. But this particular passage is telling that men could and did make it their business to know, and have opinions about, what made the best nourishment for small children. Moreover, it was considered appropriate that a father should impart this kind of knowledge to his male offspring. The passage is also suggestive that Trenchfield read medical treatises concerning the health and welfare of all family members, thus taking responsibility for his family's well-being as well as for his son's education on becoming a man. This responsibility, as Ilanna Ben-Amos has suggested, did not diminish as children grew older.[77]

\* \* \*

As this chapter has suggested, whilst boys were necessarily debarred from achieving the status of full manhood, they were perfectly able and indeed encouraged to demonstrate attributes of their manliness. Boys, even in their infancy, were identified in explicitly male terms despite their sexual immaturity.[78] Not only was children's education purposely gendered during the early modern period, which was meant to prepare boys and girls for their future roles as husbands and wives in adulthood, it was also status-specific, with sons of noble and wealthy birth receiving the most comprehensive instruction with lessons in grammar, Latin, arithmetic, history, scripture and the classics.[79] Conduct books, which were directly targeted at young boys, taught the patriarchal principles of full manhood in an expectation that those sons of the middling sorts and above would begin to learn such attributes whilst in their years of childhood. Moralists and parents alike sought assurances that male children would grow to maturity and acquire full manhood, and this can be witnessed in diarists' accounts of their sons' accomplishments. Whilst the experiences of those boys from the lower sorts cannot be judged in this regard, the expectation that male children of a higher rank could both display their manliness and learn the skills which full manhood necessitated can be identified, and it is evident that the lessons of manhood continued into the years of youth.

The distinction between manhood and manliness, it has been argued here, is an important one: it is one that delineates the dictates of patriarchal ideology surrounding normative manhood from the diverse ways in which men could prove to others, as well as to themselves, that they were indeed men. Put another way, manliness was the method through which men reassured themselves of their masculine identity. So, manhood and manliness – like manhood and patriarchy – were not synonymous. The differing strands of manliness allowed men to reject, ignore, compete with or select only some aspects of the dominant ideology of patriarchal manhood in order to assert their own masculine identity. It is this subtle difference between manhood and manliness which allows for competing and contradictory male identities to exist concurrently. It may be possible to list these as 'subordinate', 'marginalised' and 'alternative', as Alexandra Shepard has, but this suggests that there existed some level of choice by which men could openly choose what sort of man they wanted to be.[80] Instead, it would seem more appropriate if such distinctions were not drawn so markedly. Competing male identities are evident across the early modern period, mutable according to context and drawing selectively on characteristics and traits from the defining principles of patriarchal or full manhood. There existed, then, a complex web of male identities which could concur with, compete against or select only parts of the dominant ideology of full manhood and its patriarchal principles. Finally, and most importantly, not insisting on adulthood as a prerequisite for examining manhood opens the door to more useful explorations of masculine identities across the whole lifespan, including childhood, allowing historians to consider the processes through which boys and male adolescents learned how to become men in early modern England.

## Notes

1. An important exception to this is the work undertaken by Alexandra Shepard; see Shepard, *Meanings of Manhood in Early Modern England* (Oxford, 2003).

2. For the terms 'normative' and 'patriarchal' see Susan Amussen, '"The part of a Christian man": the cultural politics of manhood in early modern England', in Susan Amussen and Mark Kishlansky (eds), *Political Culture and Cultural Politics in Early Modern Europe* (Manchester, 1995), pp. 213–33, especially pp. 216–17; Shepard, *Meanings of Manhood*, pp. 11–12.
3. Shepard, *Meanings of Manhood*, especially pp. 6, 11, 16, 248–53; Shepard, 'From anxious patriarchs to refined gentlemen? Manhood in Britain, circa 1500–1700', *Journal of British Studies* 44:2 (2005), 281–95, especially 290–92. The analytical framework in which Shepard's work is situated builds on the model outlined by the sociologist Robert Connell; see Connell, *Masculinities* (Cambridge: Polity Press, 1995), especially chapter 3.
4. Shepard, *Meanings of Manhood*, especially chapters 4, 5, 6 and 7; see also Shepard, 'Manhood, credit and patriarchy in early modern England', *Past and Present* 167 (2000), 75–106.
5. Anthony Fletcher, *Gender, Sex and Subordination 1500–1800* (New Haven, 1995); Amussen, 'The part of a christian man', pp. 213–33; Elizabeth Foyster, *Manhood in Early Modern England: Honour, Sex and Marriage* (Harlow: Longman, 1999); Bernard Capp, 'The double standard revisited: Plebeian women and male sexual reputation in early modern England', *Past and Present* 162 (1999), 70–100; Shepard, *Meanings of Manhood*; Mark Breitenburg, *Anxious Masculinity in Early Modern England* (Cambridge, 1996); Lyndal Roper, *Oedipus and the Devil: Witchcraft, Sexuality and Religion in Early Modern Europe* (London, 1994).
6. See, for example, Fletcher, 'Manhood, the male body, courtship and the household in early modern England', *History* 84 (1999), 419–36; Foyster, 'Boys will be boys? manhood and aggression, 1660–1800', in Hitchcock and Cohen (eds), *English Masculinities 1660–1800*, pp. 151–66; Shepard, *Meanings of Manhood*, especially chapters 2, 8.
7. Shepard, *Meanings of Manhood*, chapter 2.
8. Foyster, *Manhood in Early Modern England*, pp. 28–32; Shepard, *Meanings of Manhood*, pp. 29–30, 47.
9. Foyster, 'Boys will be boys?', p. 154.
10. Shepard, *Meanings of Manhood*, chapters 1, 2.
11. Philippe Ariès, *Centuries of Childhood* (London, 1962); Lloyd de Mause, 'The evolution of childhood', in Lloyd de Mause (ed.), *The History of Childhood* (New York, 1974), pp. 1–73; Lawrence Stone, *The Family, Sex and Marriage in England, 1500–1800* (London: Weidenfeld and Nicolson, 1977).
12. Linda Pollock, *Forgotten Children: Parent-Child Relationships from 1500 to 1900* (Cambridge: Cambridge University Press, 1983); Ralph Houlbrooke, *The English Family 1450–1700* (London, 1984); Ralph Houlbrooke (ed.), *English Family Life, 1576–1716: An Anthology From Diaries* (New York, 1988); Keith Wrightson, *English Society 1580–1680* (London, 2002 edn). See also Alan Macfarlane, 'The family, sex and marriage in England, 1500–1800 – Lawrence Stone – review', *History and Theory* 18:1 (1979), 103–26. For a discussion on the history of childhood in Germany, see Carmen Luke, *Pedagogy, Printing and Protestantism: the Discourse on Childhood* (Albany, 1989). One text that could also be added here is John Sommerville, *The Rise and Fall of Childhood* (London, 1983). For a historiographical overview of the history of childhood, see Hugh Cunningham, 'Histories of childhood', *American Historical Review* 103:4 (1998), 1195–1208.
13. Pollock, *Forgotten Children*, especially chapters 4, 6 and 7; Cox, *Shaping Childhood*, pp. 3–4.

14. Houlbrooke, *English Family Life*, p. 133.
15. Will Fisher, 'The renaissance beard: masculinity in early modern England', *Renaissance Quarterly* 54:1 (2001), 175–79; see also Steve Brown, 'The boyhood of Shakespeare's heroines: notes on gender ambiguity in the sixteenth century', *Studies in English Literature, 1500–1900* 30:2 (1990), 243–63.
16. Henry Newcome, 'Diary', 9 February 1662, in Houlbrooke, *English Family Life*, p. 159.
17. Foyster, *Manhood in Early Modern England*, p. 39; Foyster, 'Silent witnesses? Children and the breakdown of domestic and social order in early modern England', in Anthony Fletcher and Stephen Hussey (eds), *Childhood in Question: Children, Parents and the State* (Manchester, 1999), pp. 57–73.
18. Edward Herbert, *The Life of Edward, First Lord Herbert of Cherbury, Written by Himself*, ed. J.M. Shuttleworth (London, 1976), p. 1.
19. Herbert, *The Life of Edward*, p. 1.
20. Herbert, *The Life of Edward*, pp. 1–20.
21. A. Mackley (ed.), *John Buxton Norfolk Gentleman and Architect: Letters to His Son 1719–20*, Norfolk Record Society, LXIX (2005), J. Buxton to R. Buxton, 18 March 1728, cited in Henry French and Mark Rothery, '"Upon your entry into the world": Masculine Values and the Threshold of adulthood among landed elite in England 1680–1800', *Social History* 33:4 (2008), 414.
22. For conduct literature directed at parents, see, for example, Bartholomew Batty, *The Christian Mans Closet: Wherein is Contained a Large Discourse of the Godly Training Up of Children* (London, 1581, trans. William Lowth); Richard Greenham, *A Godly Exhortation, and Fruitfull Admonition to Vertuous Parents and Modest Masters* (London, 1584); Anon, *The Office of Christian Parents*. Examples of conduct literature directed at children include Henry Jessy, *A Catechisme for Babes, Or, Little Ones* (London, 1652); George Fox, *A Catechisme for Children* (2nd edn, London, 1657); Anon, *School of Learning: Or, a Guide for Children* (London, 1668); S.T., *The Child's Book and the Youth's Book*; Hart, *School of Grace*; James Kirkwood, *Advice to Children* (2nd edn, London, 1693).
23. Martyn Bennett, 'Gender and education in the early modern period', *Defining Gender, 1450–1910* (London, 2003).
24. As Anna Bryson has noted, courtesy texts, which took a pedagogic form and which were specifically directed at schoolboys, were not the invention of the seventeenth century. Those penned by Erasmus and Seagar in the sixteenth century remained influential into the seventeenth century. Anna Bryson, *From Courtesy to Civility: Changing Codes of Conduct in Early Modern England* (Oxford, 1998), especially chapters 1, 2.
25. John Gother, *Instructions for Children* (London, 1698).
26. John Hart, *The School of Grace; or, A Book of Good Nurture for the Admonition and Instruction of Youth and Age in the Fear of the Lord* (19th edn, London, 1688).
27. Hart, *The School of Grace*, sig. $C_7$.
28. Tessa Watt, *Cheap Print and Popular Piety, 1550–1640* (Cambridge, 1991), pp. 260–62; Wrightson, *English Society*, pp. 32–4.
29. For example, see extracts by John Dee, Henry Newcome, Oliver Heywood, Thomas Isham and Sir Richard Newdigate in Houlbrooke, *English Family Life*, pp. 137, 158, 159–60, 161, 162, 163–64, 166.
30. Fletcher, *Gender, Sex and Subordination*, pp. 302–03; Houlbrooke, *English Family Life*. On education as a civilising process, see Bryson, *From Courtesy to Civility*, pp. 29–31, 67–8.

31. See Houlbrooke, *English Family Life*, p. 249. By 1671 Thomas Isham had taken up his father's suggestion and began to keep a daily journal; for extracts from his journal see Houlbrooke, *English Family Life*, pp. 163–66.
32. Thomas Willis, *Vestibulum Lingue Latine: A Dictionarie for Children* (London, 1651), quotation from frontispiece.
33. Elizabeth Jocelyn, *The Mother's Legacie to Her Unborne Childe* (London, 1625), sig. B$_5$.
34. Anon, *The Office of Christian Parents*, pp. 1–5, quotation p. 3.
35. Anon, *The Office of Christian Parents*, pp. 42–56.
36. Anon, *The Office of Christian Parents*, sig. A$_1$-A$_3$, quotation p. 5.
37. Jennifer Jordan, 'Becoming a Man: Prescriptions of Manhood and Manliness in Early Modern England' (Unpublished doctoral thesis, Nottingham Trent University, 2007); Jordan, 'Boyhood and manliness in early modern England', *Parergon* (under consideration).
38. See, for example, Laura Gowing, *Common Bodies: Women, Touch and Power in Seventeenth-Century England* (New Haven, 2003), p. 193.
39. Foyster, *Manhood in Early Modern England*, pp. 39–40.
40. Margaret Spufford, 'The cost of apparel in seventeenth-century England, and the accuracy of Gregory King', *Economic History Review* 53:4 (2000), 677–705, especially 681.
41. Margaret Spufford, *The Great Reclothing of Rural England: Petty Chapmen and their Wares in the Seventeenth Century* (London, 1984), p. 123.
42. Spufford, 'The cost of apparel', pp. 687–91, quotation p. 687, figures p. 688.
43. Beverly Lemire, 'Consumerism in preindustrial and early industrial England: the trade in secondhand clothes', *Journal of British Studies* 27:1 (1988), 1–24, quotation on 3. For those of a lesser moral fibre – or those with no other choice – the trade in stolen clothes may also have provided opportunity to purchase cheaper, or else barter an exchange for clothing; see Beverly Lemire, 'The theft of clothes and popular consumerism in early modern England', *Journal of Social History* 24:2 (1990), 255–76.
44. Clifford, *Diaries*, 28 April 1617, 2 May 1617, 1 January 1619, pp. 58, 67.
45. Henry Slingsby, 'Diary', 1641, in Houlbrooke, *English Family Life*, p. 147.
46. Thomas Isham, 'Journal', November 1671, in Houlbrooke, *English Family Life*, p. 164.
47. R. Schofield and E.A. Wrigley, 'Infant and child mortality in England in the late Tudor and early Stuart period', in C. Webster (ed.), *Health, Medicine and Mortality in the Sixteenth Century* (Cambridge, 1979), cited in Wrightson, *English Society*, p. 105.
48. Peter Laslett, *The World We Have Lost: Explored Further* (London, 2001 edn), p. 112.
49. Laslett's work suggests that the birth rate fell during the mid to late seventeenth century, and attributes this to higher levels of out-migration, mainly to North America; see Laslett, *The World We Have Lost*, chapter 5, especially p. 108; E.A. Wrigley and R. Schofield, *The Population History of England, 1541–1871: a Reconstruction* (London, 1981), pp. 217–18.
50. Laslett, *The World We Have Lost*, pp. 118, 119.
51. Archer, *Diary*, p. 4. It is not known when Anne died, but she was still alive exactly one day after her 30th birthday (4 April 1700), when she gave birth to her daughter Frances; see p. 184. For Archer's ambiguity regarding religious conformity and his relationship to nonconformity see *Diary*, pp. 21–7.
52. See Archer, *Diary*, September 1649, 25 August 1675, 30 October 1675, 14 February 1679, 16 July 1679, pp. 47, 150–51, 157, 159, quotations pp. 151, 157, 159.

53. See Evelyn, *Diary*, 27 January 1658, 30 January 1658, pp. 350–54.
54. Evelyn, *Diary*, quotations pp. 351, 352, 353–54.
55. Evelyn, *Diary*, quotations pp. 351, 352.
56. Evelyn, *Diary*, 7–14 March 1685, pp. 714–15, 719–20.
57. See Matthew Storey's introduction to the diary in Coe, *Diary*, pp. 27–37.
58. For examples see Coe, *Diary*, 10 December 1711, 13 July 1712, 15 December 1712, 27 January 1714, 18 June 1716, 24 March 1719, 6 April 1720, 29 July 1724, pp. 230, 231, 235, 237, 239, 242–43, 244, 254.
59. Josselin, *Diary*, 3 October 1657, p. 407.
60. See, for example, Henry Massingberd, *The Counsell and Admonition of Henry Massingberd Esq.; to His Children* (London, 1656); Archibald Argyle, *Instructions to a Son by Archibald, Late Marquis of Argyle* (London, 1661); Matthew Hales, *The Father's New-Years-Gift to His Son: Containing Divers Useful and Necessary Directions How to Order Himself Both in Respect to this Life and that Which is to Come* (London, 1685).
61. Anon, *The Father's Legacy: Or Counsels to his Children in Three Parts* (London, 1678), sig. B$_3$.
62. Natascha Würzbach, *The Rise of the English Street Ballad, 1550–1650* (Cambridge, 1990).
63. Bennett, 'Gender and education in the early modern period'; further examples of such include Dorothy Leigh, *The Mother's Blessing: or, the Godly Counsaile of a Gentlewoman, Not Long Deceased, Left Behind For Her Children* (London, 1629); Elizabeth Jocelyn, *The Mother's Legacy to Her Unborne Childe* (3rd edn, London, 1625).
64. Thomas Vincent, *The Good Work Begun in the Day of Grace, with the Addition of a Cautionary Letter, Sent Unto Some Youths by an Unknown Author* (London, 1673); Samuel Peck, *The Best Way to Mend the World, and to Prevent the Growth of Popery: by Perswading the Rising Generation to an Elderly and Serious Practice of Piety* (London, 1680); Henry Hesketh, *The Importance of Religion to Young Persons Represented in a Sermon* (London, 1683); Christopher Ness, *A Spiritual Legacy: Being a Pattern of Piety for all Young Persons Practice* (London, 1684); A. Tompkins, *A Few Words of Counsel and Advice to all the Sons and Daughters of Men; More Especially to the Children of Believers* (London, 1687); Samuel Pomfret, *A Sermon Preach'd to Young People* (London, 1698); Anon, *Serious Advice and Directions to all, Especially to Young People, How They May Hear and Read the Word of God* (Edinburgh, 1700).
65. See, for example, Francis Hawkins, *Youths Behaviour, Or Decency in Conversation Amongst Men* (London, 1646), which discusses such issues as good conversation, how to properly address others, table manners and walking; John Dunton, *The Knowledge of the World: Or the Art of Well Educating Youth, Through the Various Conditions of Life* (London, 1694), which is primarily concerned with the importance of education and on choosing a tutor.
66. Shepard, *Meanings of Manhood*, pp. 30–8.
67. Massingberd, *The Counsell and Admonition of Henry Massingberd*, p. 131.
68. Edward Burton, *The Father's Legacy: Or Burton's Collections* (London, 1649), p. 32.
69. Argyle, *Instructions to a Son*, p. 16.
70. For the instructions 'To His Other Children' see Argyle, *Instructions to a Son*, pp. 20–8, quotation p. 22.
71. Hales, *The Father's New-Years-Gift to His Son*, p. 40.
72. Anon, *A Word in Season, Or An Essay to Promote Good-Husbandry in Hard and Difficult Times: Being, in Part, Advice From a Gentleman to His Son a Tradesmen in London* (London, 1697); cf. William Cecil, *The Counsell of a Father to His Sonne, in Ten Severall Precepts* (London, 1611), cited in Shepard, *Meanings of Manhood*, p. 35.

262  *Jennifer Jordan*

73. Reresby, *Memoirs*, 5 April 1689, p. 570. It is thought that George was born in April 1678, making him circa 11 years old; p. 138.
74. Houlbrooke, *English Family Life*, pp. 156–60. (Henry Newcome (1627–1695) 1657–1665; passages referred to 8 August 1658, 23 October 1661, 4 February 1662, 7 February 1662, 19 February 1662, 8 July 1662, 6 October 1664).
75. Pollock, *Forgotten Children*; Houlbrooke, *English Family Life*.
76. Caleb Trenchfield, *A Cap of Grey Hairs for a Greenhead, Or, The Fathers Counsel to his Son, An Apprentice in London* (London, 1671), pp. 153–4.
77. Ilanna Krausman Ben-Amos, 'Reciprocal bonding: parents and their offspring in early modern England', *Journal of Family History* 25:3 (2000), 291–312.
78. Fisher, 'The renaissance beard', pp. 175–79.
79. Bennett, 'Gender and education in the early modern period'.
80. Shepard, *Meanings of Manhood*; the categories are based on the model put forward by the sociologist Robert Connell; see Connell, *Masculinities*.

# 13
# 'Boys, Semi-Men and Bearded Scholars': Maturity and Manliness in Early Nineteenth-Century Oxford

*Heather Ellis*

In order to show the very different ways in which the categories of 'manliness' and 'masculinity' have been constructed historically, this chapter will focus on the various contexts in which the language of 'manliness' was employed by students and senior members at the university of Oxford in the early nineteenth century. Contrary to the argument of many modern historians, it will suggest that differences of age, generation and maturity were far more important in the construction of manliness in the early nineteenth-century university than distinctions of gender *per se*. By focusing on the construction of manliness in a largely all-male setting, distinctions between men, rather than between men and women, assume prime importance. Nor is the significance of maturity in the construction of manliness limited to Oxford alone; as the *alma mater* of almost half of Britain's political elite in this period, the ideal of manliness cultivated there enjoyed a much wider influence within British society. It helps, in particular, to explain key features of another much-discussed and highly influential contemporary model of manliness, namely that promoted by Thomas Arnold at Rugby School in the 1830s.

One of the most prominent trends in recent work on the history of masculinity has been to investigate how gender identity intersects with, and is affected by, a wide range of other cultural markers including class, 'race', sexuality and age.[1] This move may be understood in large part as a response to an important strand of criticism directed at the discipline in recent years, which maintains that historians of masculinity have over-privileged the gender binary in their analysis at the expense of other axes of difference.[2] Critics suggest that the influence of feminist scholars in the early development of the history of masculinity, and the politically engaged nature of much work still carried out in the field, has led to an overestimation of the differences between men and women at the expense of differences between men.[3]

One unfortunate consequence of this has been a persistent preoccupation with an under-theorised model of power relations, most commonly treated in the form of a straightforward dynamic of dominance and subordination. Ironically, such a model has had the tendency to reify and re-essentialise gender difference, rather than to reveal its constructed and fragmented nature.[4] Even when differences between men are considered, for example, distinctions of 'race' or sexuality, they are frequently described in gendered terms, using the language of effeminacy or femininity.[5]

One of the most interesting attempts to complicate our understanding of male identity in the past has been the increasingly popular study of how distinctions of age and maturity have interacted with gender to alter its significance and meaning in different social contexts. Potentially, an examination of age and generational difference may be one of the most fruitful ways of challenging the still prevalent assumption that gender identity is something essential and unchanging. By its very nature, age, as a social distinction, is shifting and uncertain, and an analysis of how it interacts with, and affects, the impact made by other cultural markers like gender may do much to reveal the fragmented and transitional nature of all facets of identity.

A focus on distinctions of age and maturity also challenges long-standing assumptions about what it has meant to be a man in the past. It forces us to think of men, not simply as gendered beings, but also as adults, defined against boys, children and the immature, in addition to women and effeminate men.[6] This approach has been most prominently employed by historians working in the medieval and early modern periods, such as Ruth Mazo Karras, Alexandra Shepard and Anne S. Lombard.[7] They have argued persuasively for a history not so much of masculinity as of men, which takes account not merely of gendered ideals and practices, but of the whole array of meanings with which the word 'man' has been invested historically, most importantly, 'adult' and 'human'. The focus of attention, they suggest, should be on contemporary institutions, ideals and categories such as manhood, patriarchy and manliness, which, although heavily implicated by gender difference, were much more complicated constructions, in which gender competed and interacted with a whole host of other distinctions including age, marital status and social class.[8]

By contrast, historians who study male identity in the nineteenth and twentieth centuries have often been much less sensitive in terms of the categories they employ. 'Man' is primarily (and sometimes exclusively) understood in its gendered sense, with 'masculinity', 'manhood' and 'manliness' employed as virtual synonyms for each other. In doing this, scholars ignore the significantly different ways in which these ideals and categories have been constructed historically. This contrast between historians of men in a pre-modern context and those examining men in the modern era has not gone unnoticed in recent scholarship. Although the exact point at which the change occurs is contested, many scholars describe and endorse a shift from a focus on 'manhood' to one on 'masculinity'.[9] R.W. Connell is typical of many focusing on the modern period when she dismisses the calls of scholars like Kenneth Clatterbaugh for 'men' in all their complexity to be made the focus of study, rather than one isolated domain of behaviour and identity, however important.[10]

This greater flexibility has allowed historians of the pre-modern era to make important theoretical advances in the understanding of gender as a social distinction. In particular, they have grasped the vital significance, not only of learning how gender functions in society, but also how important, relative to other axes of difference, it has been. They have acknowledged that one of the most important tasks in gender history is to discover under what conditions gender emerges as an important, even the most important, distinction. As Alexandra Shepard has written, 'it is important to ask whether gender was ever eclipsed by other determinants of status and identity in ways which rendered it temporarily irrelevant.'[11]

Precisely why distinctions of gender have been focused on to a much greater degree by modern historians is difficult to say and has rarely been discussed in any depth. Some argue that it simply reflects a genuine historical shift from a society in which age and generational difference gradually ceded place to distinctions of class and gender. This shift is usually linked in some way with the emergence of the modern capitalist economy, which Marxist historians, in particular, see as having simplified the complex, hierarchical system of early-modern social relations into a binary opposition comprising the bourgeoisie and the proletariat. Such a change, they argue, served to strengthen the import of other distinctions traditionally conceived of as binary pairings like gender, rather than more complexly graduated markers like age. A few scholars, such as Øystein Gullvåg Holter, have gone so far as to claim that 'masculinity' and 'femininity' as ideals and identities have been the peculiar products of modern capitalist society.[12] Historically, there has certainly been a close relationship between Marxist scholarship and the development of feminist analysis, whose shared concerns with the suppression of one half of society by the other have left an enduring mark on current masculinity studies.[13] It has also been suggested that certain key features of modern society, in particular the primacy accorded to the individual and the notion of individual subjectivity, have strengthened belief in the existence of a 'deep' masculine and feminine essence which somehow fundamentally defines men and women.[14] More broadly, scholars like Ruth Mazo Karras have argued that the rise of mass society, characterised by mass media, centralised authority, a broad-based educational system and, above all, an ideology of equality, has allowed individuals to identify themselves, for the first time, as forming part of much larger groups of people, be it social classes or genders.[15] Under such conditions, more subtle and graduated distinctions such as age may have come to play a less important and obvious role in men's and women's self-perceptions.

Despite this notable difference in the way historians have viewed men in the pre-modern and modern eras, there have been scholars keen to make those working on the more recent past more sensitive to the role played by cultural markers other than gender. John Tosh and Stefan Collini, for example, have called for a much more sophisticated theorisation of 'masculinity'; in particular, they have stressed the need to distinguish more sharply between discourses of 'masculinity', referring specifically to distinctions of gender, and those of 'manliness', which, in Victorian Britain, were shaped, according to Collini, by contrast 'less with the "feminine" and more with the "bestial", non-human, childlike and immature'.[16] Tosh has commented similarly that ideals of 'manliness' were 'only secondarily about men's relations with women' in this period. 'The distinction which exercised' men in nineteenth-century Britain, he wrote, 'was that between men and boys; worries about immaturity counted for much more than the fear of effeminacy, at least until the 1880s'.[17] Such calls are very much in line with recent work on the theory of identity by scholars such as Stuart Hall, who argues that, 'in late modern times', 'identities' which 'are never unified' have become 'increasingly fragmented and fractured; never singular but multiply constructed across different, often intersecting and antagonistic, discourses, practices and positions'.[18]

Tosh's claim about the relative importance of distinctions of age and maturity in the construction of male identity in modern British history has been investigated only patchily;[19] one of the most potentially enlightening contexts in which to explore the role played by age is the all-male association, highlighted by Tosh as one of the three areas most significant in the formation of male identity.[20] In predominantly single-sex environments, it should be possible to observe the functioning of distinctions *between* men and to explore whether gender, as historians like Alexandra Shepard have envisaged, was rendered less important or even 'temporarily irrelevant' in such contexts. This chapter will therefore focus on the language of manliness as it was constructed and employed by both students and tutors at Oxford, one of England's two ancient universities, in the first half of the nineteenth century. Although it is not absolutely correct to describe Oxford in this period as a single-sex environment, all students and tutors were male, the vast majority of tutors and fellows were celibate, and all lived together in the intimate, sealed-off world of the college or hall. The only women likely to be encountered were visiting female relatives and girlfriends, female servants occasionally employed by colleges, and certain townswomen, most frequently those working in public houses as barmaids and prostitutes.[21] Moreover, an examination of 'manliness' at Oxford is in no sense a parochial investigation. In no other European country were a higher proportion of the nation's political elite educated at just two institutions, so that a study focusing on Oxford men may tell us much about the lives and identities of elite British men beyond the walls of the university. Indeed, in the course of the nineteenth century, the social and political importance of Oxford and Cambridge expanded significantly as they came to serve as training grounds, not merely for Britain's political leaders, but also for those civil servants and other officers responsible for the administration and government of the empire.[22]

From the work carried out by medieval and early modern historians on Oxford and Cambridge, England's ancient universities are potentially one of the most fruitful sites for exploring the possibility that 'manliness' may be constructed primarily according to distinctions of age and maturity, rather than gender.[23] By their very nature, universities are structured according to these distinctions and are often defined as places where males on the threshold of adulthood complete the crucial transition from boyhood to manhood. There has, however, been little attempt by modern historians to study Oxford and Cambridge in this way. The tendency in works such as Paul Deslandes' *Oxbridge Men: Masculinity and the Undergraduate Experience, 1850–1920* has been to neglect the importance of age, maturity and generational difference in favour of a more traditional focus on the gender binary.[24] Following other historians of Victorian masculinity like James Eli Adams,[25] Deslandes identifies a set of masculine types which, he claims, dominated the university between 1850 and 1920: the aesthete, the athlete, the reading man and the aristocratic 'blood' or sporting man.[26] Each of these types is described as having been constructed against overtly gendered 'others', including various incarnations of the effeminate male and, later in the century, the female undergraduate.

Here, by contrast, it will be suggested that, in the first half of the nineteenth century, the University of Oxford placed little emphasis on overtly gendered paradigms of masculinity, perceiving its role rather to be that of turning boys into men. Thus 'manliness', as an ideal, was defined by the possession of maturity, both moral and intellectual, and constructed primarily in opposition to notions of boyishness, rather than overtly gendered ideas of femininity or effeminacy. Although traditional, Oxford's role in negotiating the transition from boyhood to manhood was complicated in this period by a rising student age. From the beginning of the eighteenth century, the average age of matriculants rose from just 17.4 years of age to 18.5 by 1835.[27] What makes this rise of just over a year significant is the fact that the majority of undergraduates now reached 21, the legal age of majority, for the first time while still at university. This new situation placed unprecedented strain on the traditional relationship between tutor and pupil. With students officially emancipated from parental authority, it became increasingly difficult for tutors and other senior members to act *in loco parentis*.

Arguably, this changing relationship is most clearly seen in the contemporary debate about university reform, which witnessed unprecedented public discussion of important questions, including the purpose for which the university existed, which subjects should be studied there, and how authority should be distributed among its various classes of members. The prominence and connotations of the language of manliness in this important discourse will, therefore, be considered first, and it will be suggested that both junior and senior members[28] adhered to an ideal of manliness, defined primarily by intellectual and moral maturity. The significance of this discovery for the wider history of manliness in early nineteenth-century England will then be explored. In particular, it will be suggested that the prevalence of such an ideal at Oxford provides a more useful background against which to assess the concept of manliness developed by Thomas Arnold while headmaster of Rugby School, the example usually focused on by scholars whenever the idea of manliness as maturity has been considered.[29] Rather than being the peculiar product of Arnold's personality, as has often been suggested, the ideal he developed at Rugby will here be interpreted as a logical development of the concept of manliness which dominated the university reform debate when Arnold himself was resident at Oxford, a debate in which he took a prominent part long before his appointment to Rugby in 1828. It will be suggested that an ideal of 'manliness', understood, first and foremost, as maturity, was far more prevalent among elite British men in the early nineteenth century than has often been thought. By examining precisely how and in what contexts the language of manliness was used, it is hoped that the relationship between discourses of manliness and masculinity will be better clarified and that historians may come somewhat closer to answering the question to which this volume is dedicated.

The issue of university reform first became a major feature of life at Oxford in the last quarter of the eighteenth century in the years leading up to the crucial New Examination Statute of 1800. The age and maturity of students was absolutely central to this debate; indeed, it is fair to say that the principle of competitive examination and a uniform course of reading which the Statute introduced were in large part a response to the fact that the average student age was rising.[30] Certainly one of the most common complaints from the parents of undergraduates in the late eighteenth century had been that the work their sons received was too easy and bore too close a resemblance to the kinds of tasks they had been given at school. This fact was rendered particularly troublesome for the university authorities against the background of the French Revolution; among Oxford's senior members, the opinion became increasingly common that the older students became, the more likely they would be to imbibe radical principles and rebel against established authority.[31] Thus, it is possible to see the 1800 Examination Statute as a measure designed primarily to give senior members greater control over student reading while appearing to provide a more challenging system of examination for older students.

The language of manliness is certainly a prominent feature of discussions about the Statute both before and after its introduction; in this context, moreover, it is clear that 'manliness' refers to the moral and intellectual maturity of students. In 1781, Vicesimus Knox justified the need for root and branch change at Oxford with reference to what he saw as the lamentable consequences of young men entering the universities at a later age, referring, in particular, to the increased likelihood that they would crave the independence of manhood and indulge in its vices prematurely. These days, he wrote,

> every one, on putting on the academical gown commences a man in his own opinion, and will often endeavour to support the character by the practice of manly vices. I consider the sending a son thither at present a most dangerous measure; a measure which may probably make shipwreck of his learning, his morals, his health, his character, and his fortune.[32]

These concerns were shared by many supporters of the New Statute. 'J.M.', the writer of an 1800 article in the *British Magazine*, wrote of his satisfaction with the proposed changes. 'In such an exigency', he declared, referring to the French Revolution, the English nation 'calls with a far more earnest and authoritative voice upon her public seminaries of learning... It is high time to think of laying some restraint upon the profligacy which will always be found among young men who are too much their own masters'; and 'no method,' he concluded of the Examination Statute, '[could] be more effectual for the accomplishment of this end'.[33]

Publicly, the changes were most often justified in terms of their ability to promote greater 'manliness' among undergraduates; in other words, to hasten the onset of intellectual and moral maturity. In a set of three *Replies*, designed to answer persistent accusations in the *Edinburgh Review* that Oxford's curriculum and examinations were childish and out of date, Edward Copleston, the greatest defender of the 1800 Statute, emphasised the 'manly and generous discipline' he felt the new system inspired in undergraduates. Although it might be tempting to interpret this phrase in an overtly gendered sense, Copleston's comments make clear that he meant a discipline which did not treat its undergraduates as schoolboys, but rather as young men completing the transition to manhood. 'In the first stages of infancy and boyhood,' he wrote,

> restraint must be continually practiced, and liberty of action abridged. But, in proportion as reason is strengthened, freedom should be extended... On this principle I rejoice to see a manly and generous discipline established among us – a discipline which enjoins nothing, which prohibits nothing... but what reason and common sense declare deserving of the treatment.[34]

When rebutting the charge of the Edinburgh Reviewers 'that in Oxford, in particular, every manly exercise of the reason is discouraged', Copleston once more made clear that he understood the accusation not in a gendered sense, to imply that an Oxford education produced effeminate or emasculated men, but rather that it prevented young men from reaching moral and intellectual maturity. Thus, he asserted plainly that the composition of 'verses, especially Latin verses' (a practice which the reviewers had, in particular, attacked as 'unmanly') was 'looked upon as a boyish exercise' at Oxford and, as such, was hardly ever required from students.[35] In contrast, he took pains to portray an Oxford education as a slow, yet certain, progress towards maturity: 'That finished offspring of genius,' as he described the successful student at the end of his degree,

> starts not like Minerva from the head of Jupiter, perfect at once in stature, and clad in complete armour: but is the produce of slow birth, and often of a hard delivery; the tender nursling of many an infant year – the pupil of a severe school, formed and chastened by a persevering discipline.[36]

The argument that change was needed in order to promote a 'manliness' defined by intellectual and moral maturity remained popular with university reformers throughout the first half of the nineteenth century. Although Samuel Taylor Coleridge had attended Cambridge rather than Oxford, his *Aids to Reflection in the Formation of a Manly Character* quickly became one of the key texts in the reform debate at Oxford when it was published in 1824. He directed the work specifically towards undergraduates at both English universities and linked his ideal of the 'manly character' firmly with the transition from boyhood to manhood. As a work, he wrote, *Aids to Reflection* had been

> *especially* designed for the studious Young at the close of their education or on their first entrance into the duties of manhood and the rights of self-government. And of these, again, in thought and wish I destined the work... yet more particularly to Students intended for the Ministry... to the members of our two Universities [original emphasis].[37]

It is, however, in the debate surrounding the visit of the Royal University Commission to Oxford in 1850 that we see the idea of manliness as maturity most keenly displayed. Appointed by the British government, and supported only by a minority of senior members at Oxford, the Commission, chaired by Samuel Hinds, bishop of Norwich, was charged with inquiring into 'the state, discipline, studies, and revenues of the University and colleges of Oxford'.[38] The system of 1800 came in for unprecedented criticism at the hands of the Commissioners, who elicited an emotional response from Oxford's senior members and former graduates, many of whom defended it on the grounds that it had promoted greater 'manliness' in undergraduates. Thus, in 1848, one writer in *Fraser's Magazine* praised the principle of competitive examination, introduced in 1800, as having brought a new and 'manly element' to university life. Specifically, he referred to the unrivalled 'inducement to self-discipline' it provided and its ability to appeal 'to the more mature part of the student'.[39] Walter Bagehot likewise praised the greater maturity which came to be required of candidates after 1800. In the 1852 article from which the quotation in the title of this chapter is taken, he praised the new examination system as one finally designed for 'grown-up gentlemen and bearded scholars', rather than 'youth[s] and semi-men'.[40] In a pamphlet criticising the recommendations of the Commission, Henry Arthur Woodgate, a former fellow and tutor of St John's College, Oxford, contrasted what he termed the 'infantine simplicity' and 'childishness' of their plans to introduce a system of professorial lectures at Oxford with the 'fine and manly qualities' cultivated in students under the current system.[41]

Crucially, this understanding of manliness as maturity was not restricted to Oxford's senior members and to the university's critics, but was accepted by a significant proportion of the undergraduate population too. The early decades of the nineteenth century saw a significant rise not only in the average age of students at Oxford, but also in their willingness to take an active part in the university reform debate. This new eagerness to participate was yet another sign of the shift in the traditional balance of power between senior and junior members. One of the earliest critiques came from the pen of a 20-year-old undergraduate at Christ Church, James Shergold Boone. In 1818, he published a set of five satirical dialogues under the title *The Oxford Spy*. One of their most remarkable features is the degree to which they mirror the language and ideas of senior members like Copleston. This is certainly the case with Boone's use of the term 'manly', which, as in the *Replies*, is contrasted not with effeminate, but with boyish, behaviour. Thus, instead of a 'puerile and minute accuracy', Boone wishes to see a spirit of 'wide and manly inquiry' encouraged at Oxford;[42] such phrasing is strongly reminiscent of Copleston's contrast just over a decade earlier between the 'manly and generous discipline' which he believed to characterise the system of 1800 and the schoolboy studies which the *Edinburgh Review* accused the university of promoting. Similar attacks upon the childish nature of Oxford studies are to be found in another student publication, *The Undergraduate*, which appeared in six weekly numbers in the spring of 1819 and was clearly influenced by *The Oxford Spy*. Created by John Henry Newman and James Bowden, then undergraduates at Trinity College, the magazine endeavoured to expose what its editors considered the true aims behind the campaign for university reform. In contrast to the 'manly' system which Copleston and others claimed to be promoting, the magazine accused senior members of wanting to introduce a system of humiliating, schoolboy discipline. In a fictional letter of one reforming tutor to his friend in the country, they described the project thus:

> [I]n fact we have lately had much occupation,
> Attempting at college a grand reformation.

> ... We are not without hope that the next generation
> May be made to submit to severe flagellation.
> I'm aware you will say misdemeanours and crimes
> Were not punished thus in the earlier times,
> And that those who at present are bachelors, then
> Were wont to be treated like rational men.
> I confess it is likely they will be amazed
> To see a grown gentleman solemnly raised
> On the back of a scout in the presence of all
> To be whipped by the Dean or the Bursar in hall:
> But such is our plan, and if this should succeed,
> We prohibit all wine, and shall substitute mead.[43]

Bachelors too, who were also classed as junior members, began to play an ever greater role in the university reform debate, articulating a similar concept of manliness defined by intellectual and moral maturity. Charles Stocker, later White's Professor of Moral Philosophy at Oxford, was one such. Shortly before he took his MA in 1820, he published a scurrilous critique of the current classical curriculum at Oxford. What angered him most was the failure of the university to provide 'manly' authors for undergraduates to read. 'When ancient history is to be read', he declared, we would have 'the excellent sense of Polybius and the profound maxims of Tacitus' replace 'writings' which are 'frequently offensive by their puerility'.[44] Another bachelor, Daniel Sandford, who was unsuccessful in his bid for an Oriel fellowship despite his first class honours, penned a similar attack on the hypocrisy of the university's claim to provide a 'manly' education. In particular, he condemned the design of the fellowship examination at Oriel (conducted, notably, in this case by Copleston) for insisting on 'barbarous logic and childish physics'[45] and the writing of 'a school-boy *theme* of four pages, perhaps on a subject that would require a volume [original emphasis]'.[46] Such examinations, he fumed, 'must counteract, in the youthful bosom, all the beneficial influence of ... previous liberal and manly discipline, and reduce the character and intellect ... to the standard of that cast, with which they aim, at the expense of original bent and native excellence, to be for the future identified'.[47]

Having established that maturity was an important element in the construction of manliness at Oxford in the first half of the nineteenth century, can this knowledge provide us with greater insight into other aspects of the history of manliness in England in this period? I would like to suggest that it may allow us to understand better the origins of what is perhaps the most famous example of an ideal of manliness defined by maturity, namely that developed by Thomas Arnold while headmaster of Rugby School in the 1830s. While scholars have repeatedly noted the emphasis which Arnoldian manliness placed on moral and intellectual maturity, it has been generally treated as the peculiar creation of Arnold's personality; the only attempts at contextualisation being somewhat narrow comparisons with the language of manliness in the works of other prominent men of letters. This tendency seems to have begun with David Newsome's 1961 study, *Godliness and Good Learning*. Instead of locating the peculiar features of Arnold's ideal within a wider cultural context, his stress on maturity was merely likened to a similar emphasis in the writings of Samuel Taylor Coleridge and contrasted with the gendered conception of manliness favoured by the most famous protagonists of 'muscular Christianity', Charles Kingsley and Thomas Hughes.[48]

This approach has been continued in more recent treatments of the subject. Thus, in *Sinews of the Spirit* (1985), the only analytical framework presented by Norman Vance for discussing Arnoldian manliness was a comparison with the respective ideals of Coleridge, F.D. Maurice and Thomas Carlyle; and when discussing his emphasis on maturity the only context provided, once again, was a notice of similarity to Coleridge and of contrast with 'muscular Christianity'.[49] Ten years later, in *Dandies and Desert Saints* (1995), James Eli Adams confined his analysis to a similar comparative format, merely contrasting Arnold's concept of manliness with that developed by John Henry Newman and associated with the Oxford Movement.[50]

What I would like to suggest here, by contrast, is that the specific features of Arnoldian manliness can only be assessed accurately in terms of their origins and influence when they are considered against the wider educational and institutional background of the period in which Arnold himself was educated. Key to this is the way in which the language of manliness was used at Oxford when Arnold was resident there between 1811 and 1819. It will be suggested, in particular, that the ideal he later developed at Rugby was deeply influenced by the concept of manliness as maturity which formed such an important feature of the university reform debate in these years.

Apart from the superficial similarity between the two ideals in terms of the emphasis they both placed on intellectual and moral maturity, there was also a shared sense of urgency when it came to cultivating these qualities in the young. One of the key features of Arnold's construction of boyhood, the notion against which his idea of manliness was primarily defined, was his belief that boys were far more susceptible to the temptations of vice than grown men. Boyhood, he wrote, is 'an age when it is almost impossible to find a true, manly sense of the degradation of guilt or faults'.[51] We remember that it was, above all, a fear of similar moral weakness in undergraduates (particularly regarding their vulnerability to the temptations of revolutionary ideology) which drove many senior members at Oxford to support the conservative aims of the 1800 Statute. In particular, reformers like Copleston claimed that the principle of competitive examination would hasten the onset of moral and intellectual manhood in undergraduates; this assumption, of course, has much in common with Arnold's later and better-known attempts to 'anticipate' what he termed the onset of 'Christian Manhood' in his pupils.[52] This he attempted to do through a variety of measures, not least among which was his own adaptation of the competitive principle by ensuring that promotion through the school's forms was not determined by seniority but by the academic and moral progress of pupils when measured against their peers. In addition, as is well known, he entrusted the sixth form with much greater responsibility for disciplining younger pupils. In sermons before the school, Arnold actively inquired 'whether the change from childhood to manhood can be hastened'. 'That it ought to be hastened,' he remarked, 'appears to me to be clear...When I look around, I cannot but wish generally that the change from childhood to manhood in the three great points of wisdom, of unselfishness, and of thoughtfulness, might be hastened from its actual rate of progress in most instances.'[53] Such comments are once again strongly reminiscent of those used by advocates of the changes introduced by the Statute of 1800.

This is, I would suggest, no coincidence. There is strong evidence that the time Arnold spent as an undergraduate and college fellow at Oxford in the early years of the century and his participation in the university reform debate profoundly influenced the ideal of manliness he later developed at Rugby. In his account of Arnold's undergraduate years, his friend John Taylor Coleridge remarked upon how 'essentially' his period of Oxford residence had 'contributed...to the formation of his character in afterlife'.[54] As part of a close group of friends, Arnold flourished under the stricter discipline and more challenging examination system introduced only a decade before his arrival. Above all, Coleridge reminisced, it promoted a sense of 'manly' emulation among Arnold and his peers. 'We might be, indeed we were, somewhat boyish in manner, and in the liberties we took with each other,' admitted Coleridge, 'but our interest in literature, ancient and modern...was not boyish; we debated the classic and romantic question; we discussed poetry and history, logic and philosophy.'[55]

Arnold's biographer, A.P. Stanley, likewise credited his years at Oxford with hastening his transition to moral and intellectual manliness. 'There had taken place,' he wrote, 'the great change from boyhood to manhood, and with it a corresponding...growth of character, more marked and more important than at any subsequent period of his life.'[56] In 1815, at the age of only 19, Arnold was elected Fellow of Oriel College, at that time the bastion of support for the reforms introduced in 1800. Until a few months before Arnold's election, the college head had been none other than John Eveleigh, one of the chief framers of the 1800 Statute; its foremost defender, Edward Copleston, was also a fellow there. This was, moreover, the time when junior members, undergraduates and bachelors like Arnold, were beginning, for the first time, to take an active role in the university reform debate. And Arnold was clearly interested in the discussion, writing later of his 'excessive admiration' for Copleston in this period.[57]

His first public contributions to the debate came as a young MA in the early 1820s. In his 1824 *Address to the Members of Convocation*, Arnold showed his familiarity with the very latest arguments. Clearly influenced by Coleridge's opinion in *Aids to Reflection* that the study of Logic was crucial for maturing the mind and forming the 'manly character', he criticised the recent proposal of the Hebdomadal Board to replace the treatise on Logic, then compulsory reading for all students, with the mathematical 'Elements of Euclid'.[58] The following year, in 1825, he urged the need for further reform of the university's syllabus; in particular, he hoped to see a greater focus on ancient history, a detailed study of which, he felt, was indispensable for the proper development of moral and intellectual maturity. In recent years, he argued, Oxford had begun to decline from the 'manly' standard set by the Examination Statute of 1800. There had appeared, he wrote, a 'general deficiency in the field of classic literature and criticism', with college tutors spending most of their time teaching their pupils how to construe classical texts of a not particularly challenging nature. 'The consequence,' he concluded, 'has been the converting of our universities' into little more than 'great schools'.[59]

This view became even more entrenched following the rise of the Anglo-Catholic Tractarian Movement at the university in the years following 1833. As the place in which he had spent some of the happiest years of his life and the destination to which he sent many of his pupils, Oxford remained of central importance to Arnold as headmaster of Rugby.[60] Indeed, he became the most prominent critic of Newman and the Tractarians, not only (as is well known) from a theological standpoint, but also from an educational perspective. Above all, he lamented what he described as the childishness and immaturity which the dominance of Tractarianism with its ultra-conservative fear of change had brought to university studies. On several occasions, he employed his favourite passage from St Paul to denounce Newman and the other leaders of the Oxford Movement as 'children in their understanding, and men only in the vehemence of their passions'.[61] Interestingly, this passage was also used by Arnold to chastise his pupils at Rugby in the course of many a Sunday sermon.[62]

Significantly, the link between the ideal of manliness promoted by Arnold at Rugby and that which had dominated Oxford in the years following the Statute of 1800 was recognised by many of his contemporaries, particularly in the years after his premature death in 1842. It was not seen as something new and revolutionary, but was welcomed by most commentators as a timely restatement of a valued and temporarily forgotten traditional position. In the course of the 1830s, Oxford came under renewed attack for the childishness and conservatism of its syllabus. Such charges were most often connected with the dominance which the Tractarians under John Henry Newman and

E.B. Pusey were seen to exercise over university studies at this time.[63] Shortly after Arnold's death in 1842, George Moberley recalled how, within a few years of Arnold's appointment at Rugby, 'it soon began to be a matter of observation... that his pupils brought quite a different character with them to Oxford' than that which had recently predominated, 'thoughtful, manly-minded, conscious of duty and obligation'.[64]

Indeed, by the time of the Royal University Commission in 1850, Arnold and his ideal of manliness had become the leading model put forward by university men for the reform of Oxford. This was more than a little due to the fact that many of those involved were former pupils of his, who saw the link between the system they had known at Rugby and that which had been introduced at Oxford in 1800 and which the Commissioners were determined to replace. One such was John Conington, who argued in a *North British Review* article of November 1852 that, following two decades of Tractarian dominance, Oxford should be returned to its former glory by being reformed along the same lines as Rugby had been under Arnold and the other public schools on the same model. 'The fact is,' he wrote, 'that our public schools have taken the place and do the work of what our Universities were in former times.'[65] The remedy proposed by the Commissioners which most struck Conington as likely to succeed was the 'summary removal of idle and extravagant students', which he attributed to the example of Arnold and his determination that while 'it was not necessary that Rugby should be a school of 300, or 100, or 50 boys; it was necessary that it should be a school of Christian gentlemen'.[66] Another article, from *Fraser's Magazine*, which appeared in November 1848, declared that, under the Tractarians, university studies had become so narrow through a paranoid fear of student dissent that though a man is kept 'upwards of three years they often send him on his vocation unable to write his own language, knowing little of any thing, and less... in many respects, than a charity-school boy'.[67] What was needed, he argued, was a return to the sensible compromise of 1800 in which closer control of student reading by senior members had been combined with the manlier system of competitive examination; and the model which struck him as most helpful for achieving this was Arnold's Rugby.[68]

F.W. Newman, writing in *The Prospective Review* in 1849, looked similarly to the example of Arnold's reforms at Rugby for improvement in the university syllabus. He remarked upon the similarity between the way in which the classics had been cultivated at Rugby under his leadership and how they had been studied at Oxford in the years after the 1800 Statute but before the rise of Tractarianism. In preparation for university study, he wrote, Arnold had encouraged the sixth form to read Thucydides and thereby 'to penetrate into the substance of an author with a manly intellect'. Under the influence of

Tractarianism, by contrast, authors of comparable weight such as 'Demosthenes and Cicero are almost entirely neglected', he declared.

> Greek and Latin history is studied with a painful and useless accuracy within certain limits, but is utterly ignored beyond those limits. Three or four treatises of Aristotle are elaborated with slavish anxiety, while the rest are never opened.[69]

'For more than a dozen years,' he continued, 'the appropriate studies of the place ha[ve] languished, all heart being eaten out of them by the new zeal for the Fathers, and by theological speculations, which...were sanctioned neither by Church nor by State.'[70] So central indeed was Arnold to the debate at mid-century that no less a figure than Benjamin Jowett, one of the principal defenders of the system introduced in 1800, identified himself in 1849 as a 'humble imitator of [Thomas] Arnold'.[71]

From the views of contemporaries, then, and, more importantly, from Arnold's own contributions to the university reform debate before his appointment at Rugby, there would seem to be a strong case for arguing that the ideal of manliness he advocated there, characterised by intellectual and moral maturity, was not constructed in isolation, but was rather a logical development of the concept of manliness to which he was exposed during his extended residence at Oxford between 1811 and 1819.

At the beginning of this chapter, I stated that historians of masculinity, particularly those working on the nineteenth and twentieth centuries, continue to equate 'masculinity' with 'manliness' despite repeated assertions from scholars like John Tosh that as concepts they have often been constructed differently. With reference to nineteenth-century Britain, Tosh has suggested that, in most cases, manliness had more to do with distinctions of maturity than of gender *per se*. Despite the considerable potential of this claim to help clarify our understanding of the different ways in which ideals of manliness and masculinity have been constructed, it has not received the attention it deserves. In particular, I wanted to test its applicability in the context of the nineteenth-century university, where the majority of well-to-do parents considered the final transition from boyhood to manhood to take place. By paying attention to the specific contexts in which the language of manliness occurred and the connotations it appeared to have, for both junior and senior members, we saw that it was most often taken to denote the possession of intellectual and moral maturity, rather than any overtly gendered quality.

The language of manliness was particularly prominent in the university reform debate, an important discourse at Oxford in this period and a useful index of the changing relationship between junior and senior members at a time when the average student age was rising. Although traditional, the idea of manliness as maturity acquired a greater importance at Oxford in the final decade of the eighteenth century against the background of the French Revolution and the fear that older students were more likely to imbibe radical principles spread from the continent. Indeed, the need to promote moral and intellectual maturity in undergraduates so as to prevent their descent into rebellion and vice remained the chief justification for further changes to the university's syllabus and examinations throughout the first half of the nineteenth century.

It was further suggested that the prominence at Oxford of an ideal of manliness chiefly characterised by maturity has significance beyond the confines of the university; indeed, that it may help to contextualise better another concept of manliness which scholars have tended to focus on when the importance of maturity has been considered, namely that developed by Thomas Arnold at Rugby School in the 1830s. Usually seen as the peculiar product of Arnold's personality, it is better understood as a logical development of the ideal to which Arnold was himself exposed during his time at Oxford and which he endorsed in his various contributions to the university reform debate in the 1820s. By exploring one important social context in nineteenth-century Britain where ideals of manliness were constructed primarily according to differences of age and maturity, rather than gender, I hope to have shown the need for a more subtle theorisation of masculinity in the modern period. As Tosh has suggested, discourses of manliness can be misleading targets for historians of masculinity. Nevertheless, investigating the conditions under which gender difference has played a secondary, or even negligible, role in the construction of male identity remains a crucial task for historians seeking to answer the question 'What is masculinity?'

## Notes

1. See, for example, Karen Harvey and Alexandra Shepard, 'What have historians done with masculinity? Reflections on five centuries of British History, circa 1500–1950', *Journal of British Studies* 44 (2005), 275. Referring to the September 2003 colloquium on the history of masculinity, they write that participants were asked to consider 'what is the relationship of masculinity to other determinants of status such as age, sexuality, ethnicity, and class?' See also Heather Ellis and Jessica Meyer, 'Introduction', in *Masculinity and the Other: Historical Perspectives* (Newcastle upon Tyne, 2009), pp. 6–7.
2. See, for example, Donald E. Hall, 'The end(s) of masculinity studies', *Victorian Literature and Culture* 28 (2000), 228–29; John Pettegrew, 'Deepening the history of masculinity and the sexes', *Reviews in American History* 31 (2003), 136; Susan Stanford Friedman, 'Beyond white and other: relationality and narratives of race in feminist discourse', *Signs: Journal of Women in Culture and Society* 21 (1995), 9.
3. Ellis and Meyer, 'Introduction', in *Masculinity and the Other*, pp. 1–4.
4. Donald Morton, 'The cultural politics of (sexual) knowledge: on the margins with goodman', *Social Text* 25/26 (1990), 227.

5. Consider, for example, the tendency of some ancient historians to consider the participation of male adolescents in homosexual relations with older men in classical Athens as 'effeminising'. As Thomas Hubbard has suggested in his chapter in this book, such participation was considered by many within ancient Athens to be a normal part of the male maturation process, of the transition from boyhood to manhood.
6. This advantage is not peculiar to distinctions of age alone; the term 'man' may also, of course, refer to that which is human or 'civilised' as opposed to that which is bestial and 'uncivilised'.
7. See Ruth Mazo Karras, *From Boys to Men: Formations of Masculinity in Late Medieval Europe* (Philadelphia, 2003); Alexandra Shepard, *Meanings of Manhood in Early Modern England* (Oxford, 2003); Anne S. Lombard, *Making Manhood: Growing Up Male in Colonial New England* (London, 2003).
8. The growing significance of the history of fatherhood as an area of research within medieval and early-modern history is further evidence of this desire to examine how gender intersects with other social distinctions, in particular, age and generational difference. See, for example, Cyndia Susan Clegg, 'Checking the father: anxious paternity and Jacobean press censorship', in Douglas A. Brookes (ed.), *Printing and Parenting in Early Modern England* (Aldershot, 2005); Joanne Bailey, 'Reassessing parenting in eighteenth-century England', in H. Berry and E. Foyster (eds), *The Family in Early Modern England* (Cambridge, 2007), pp. 209–31. See also Rachel Moss's chapter in this book, which argues for the importance of father–son relationships in the construction of male identity in one elite family in fifteenth-century England. For a study of the relationship between fatherhood and masculine identity formation in the modern period, see Robert Rutherdale's chapter in this book.
9. 'Historians,' writes Karen Harvey ('The history of masculinity, circa 1650–1800', *Journal of British Studies* 44 (2005), 303) 'swap the study of manhood for the study of masculinity around the time of the Glorious Revolution.' For a similar view, see Anthony Fletcher, *Gender, Sex, and Subordination in England, 1500–1800* (London, 1995), pp. 83, 322.
10. See R.W. Connell, *The Men and the Boys* (Cambridge, 2000), p. 16. She is referring to Kenneth Clatterbaugh's article, 'What is problematic about masculinities?', *Men and Masculinities* 1 (1998), in which (p. 41) he suggests that 'talking about men seems to be what [historians of masculinity] want to do'.
11. Shepard, *Meanings of Manhood in Early Modern England*, p. 4.
12. Ø.G. Holter, 'Family theory reconsidered', in T. Borchgrevink and Ø.G. Holter (eds), *Labour of Love: Beyond the Self-Evidence of Everyday Life* (Avebury, 1995), p. 102. In the words of R.W. Connell (*The Men and the Boys*, p. 22), 'Holter's "social forms analysis" gives an account of gender, masculinity and femininity, as historically specific features of social life in modernity.'
13. For a longer discussion of the methodological consequences of the influence of feminist analysis on the history of masculinity, see Heather Ellis and Jessica Meyer, 'Introduction', in *Masculinity and the Other*, pp. 1–4. See also the fairly recent call of Karen Harvey ('History of Masculinity, circa 1650–1800', 298) for more work which 'meets the challenges of feminist women's historians' and 'look[s] to more traditional questions first raised by...historians of women'.
14. On the 'deep masculine', see Connell, *The Men and the Boys*, p. 5; T. Beneke, 'Deep masculinity as social control: Foucault, Bly, and masculinity', in M. Kimmel (ed.), *The Politics of Manhood* (Philadelphia, 1995), pp. 151–63.

15. See, for example, Karras, *From Boys to Men*, pp. 9–10.
16. Stefan Collini, *Public Moralists: Political Thought and Intellectual Life in Britain 1850–1930* (Oxford, 1991), p. 186.
17. John Tosh, 'What should historians do with masculinity? Reflections on nineteenth-century Britain', *History Workshop Journal* 38 (1994), 183.
18. S. Hall, 'Who needs "identity"?', in P. du Gay, J. Evans and P. Redman (eds), *Identity: A Reader* (London, 2000), p. 17.
19. See, for example, Michael Roper, 'Between manliness and masculinity: the "war generation" and the psychology of fear in Britain, 1914–1950', *Journal of British Studies* 44 (2005), 343–62; Jessica Meyer, 'Separating the men from the boys: masculinity and maturity in understandings of shell shock in Britain', *Twentieth Century British History* 20 (2008), 1–22; Heather Ellis, '"The nakedness of boy nature": Thomas Arnold and the anticipation of manhood at Rugby', *Sextant. Revue du Groupe Interdisciplinaire d'Etudes sur les Femmes* 27 (2009), 177–91.
20. Tosh, 'What should historians do with masculinity?', p. 184.
21. Paul Deslandes, *Oxbridge Men: British Masculinity and the Undergraduate Experience, 1850–1914* (Bloomington, IN, 2005), p. 192, details 'three standard categories of women' encountered by male students: 'relatives and girlfriends, servants, and prostitutes'.
22. For the relationship of the ancient universities to the empire, see Richard Symonds, *Oxford and Empire: The Last Lost Cause?* (Oxford, 1991).
23. See Karras, *From Boys to Men*, pp. 67–108; Shepard, *The Meanings of Manhood*, pp. 12–16.
24. In particular, Deslandes continues to use the terms manliness, manhood and masculinity as virtual synonyms without any systematic attempt to distinguish between them. Despite devoting a chapter to 'The transition from boyhood to manhood' (pp. 48–82), Deslandes assumes that the language of 'manliness' was always overtly gendered and does not distinguish the different connotations it may have carried in different contexts. Indeed, on p. 5, he restricts the semantic range of 'manliness' to 'a specific type of gender ideology'.
25. James Eli Adams, *Dandies and Desert Saints: Styles of Victorian Masculinity* (Ithaca, NY, 1995).
26. Deslandes, *Oxbridge Men*, p. 72.
27. Laurence Stone (ed.), *The University in Society Volume I: Oxford and Cambridge from the 14th to the early 19th Century* (Princeton, NJ, 1974), p. 98.
28. Junior members consisted of undergraduates and bachelors, while senior members comprised all MAs, senior fellows of colleges, tutors and heads of houses.
29. See, for example, Tosh, 'What should historians do with masculinity?', p. 183; David Newsome, *Godliness and Good Learning: Four Studies on a Victorian Ideal* (London, 1961), p. 197.
30. On the New Examination Statute, see V.H.H. Green, 'Reformers and reform in the university', in L.S. Sutherland and L.G. Mitchell (eds), *The History of the University of Oxford Vol V. The Eighteenth Century* (Oxford, 1986), pp. 607–38.
31. For the anxiety of the university authorities about the susceptibility of undergraduates to radical principles in the wake of the French Revolution, see Sheldon Rothblatt, 'The student sub-culture and the examination system in early 19th century Oxbridge', in Lawrence Stone (ed.), *The University in Society Volume I*, pp. 285–87.
32. Vicesimus Knox, *Liberal Education* (London, 1781), 2nd edn, p. 350.

33. 'J.M.', 'On the proposed regulations in the University of Oxford', *British Magazine* i (1800), 425–27.
34. [Edward Copleston], A *Reply to the Calumnies of the Edinburgh Review Against Oxford Containing an Account of Studies Pursued in that University* (Oxford, 1810), pp. 158–59.
35. Ibid., p. 131.
36. Ibid., p. 129.
37. Samuel Taylor Coleridge, *Aids to Reflection in the Formation of a Manly Character...* (Burlington, 1829), p. lviii.
38. *Report of Her Majesty's Commissioners Appointed to Inquire into the State, Discipline, Studies, and Revenues of the University and Colleges of Oxford: Together with the Evidence, and an Appendix* (London, 1852), p. 1.
39. 'The Universities [Oxford and Cambridge]', *Fraser's Magazine* 38 (November 1848), 585.
40. [Walter Bagehot], 'Oxford', *The Prospective Review* (July 1852), 360.
41. [Henry Arthur Woodgate], *University Reform: National Faith Considered in Reference to Endowments* (Oxford, 1854), p. 35.
42. [James Shergold Boone], *An Appendix to the Oxford Spy* (Oxford, 1818), 15.
43. [John Henry Newman and James Bowden], *The Undergraduate* (Oxford, 1819), 50–1.
44. [Charles William Stocker], *Reflections Occasioned by the Flirtations of Alma Mater and the Stagyrite* (Oxford, 1820), p. 13. For attribution of this piece to Stocker, see R. Simms, *Bibliotheca Staffordiensis* (1894), p. 436.
45. Daniel Keyte Sandford, *A Letter to Peter Elmsley* (Oxford, 1822), p. 28.
46. Ibid., p. 31.
47. Ibid., p. 20.
48. Newsome, *Godliness and Good Learning*, p. 197. 'Arnold,' wrote Newsome, 'had regarded manliness as something essentially adult', whilst 'Kingsley and Hughes stressed the masculine and muscular connotations of the word and found its converse in effeminacy.'
49. Norman Vance, *Sinews of the Spirit: The Ideal of Christian Manliness in Victorian Literature and Religious Thought* (Cambridge, 1985), p. 71. 'Arnold proposed a rather austere form of Christian manliness,' wrote Vance, 'not the physically vigorous manliness of Tom Brown and Tom Hughes but a self-reliant moral maturity which recalls the Coleridgean ideal of self-superintendent virtue.'
50. Adams, *Dandies and Desert Saints*, pp. 61–106.
51. Thomas Arnold, 'On the discipline of public schools', in Thomas Arnold (ed.), *Miscellaneous Works* (London, 1845), p. 368.
52. Arthur Penrhyn Stanley, *Life and Correspondence of Thomas Arnold, D.D.* (New York, 1846), p. 91. On Arnold's strategies for 'anticipating' the onset of manhood at Rugby, see Heather Ellis, '"The Nakedness of Boy Nature": Anticipating Manhood at the English Public School in the Early Nineteenth Century', pp. 177–91.
53. Thomas Arnold, *The Christian Life: Its Course, Its Hindrances and its Helps* (London, 1844), p. 18.
54. Stanley, *Life and Correspondence*, p. 29.
55. Ibid., p. 30.
56. Ibid., p. 40.
57. Ibid., p. 372.
58. [Thomas Arnold], *Address to the Members of Convocation on the Expediency of the Proposed Statute* (Oxford, 1824), pp. 2–3.

59. [Thomas Arnold], 'Early Roman History', *Quarterly Review* 32:63 (June 1825), 91–2.
60. Stanley, *Life and Correspondence*, p. 260.
61. Ibid., p. 552.
62. See, for example, Arnold, *The Christian Life*, pp. 11–12.
63. See, for example, [F.W. Newman], 'University Reform', *The Prospective Review* 5:17 (January 1849), 3.
64. Stanley, *Life and Correspondence*, pp. 144–5.
65. [John Conington], 'Oxford and the Royal Commission', *North British Review* 18:35 (November 1852), 14.
66. Ibid., 9–10.
67. 'The Universities [Oxford and Cambridge]', p. 590.
68. Ibid., p. 589.
69. [Newman], 'University Reform', p. 6.
70. Ibid., p. 3.
71. Evelyn Abbott and Lewis Campbell (eds), *Life and Letters of Benjamin Jowett III* (London, 1897), p. 53.

# Part IV
# Domesticities

# 14
# St Francis of Assisi and the Making of Settlement Masculinity, 1883–1914

*Lucinda Matthews-Jones*

In 1895 a debate emerged in the pages of the periodical *The Nineteenth Century* over the religiosity of Oxford and Cambridge students. It began with the publication of Anthony C. Deane's article 'The Religion of the Undergraduate', which argued that an 'easy-going agnosticism is the average undergraduate's creed'.[1] Agnosticism, Deane argued, was regarded as the 'symbol of intellectual manhood', an identity encouraged by younger dons and overlooked by older ones. Responses disputing Deane's article were quickly published. Although many sought to refute the accusations, Hugh Legge, for one, conceded that Oxford students' attitude to religion was indeed one of indifference and scepticism.[2] Legge agreed with Deane that in Oxford a 'boy becomes a man', but he also argued that, once men, graduates discovered their spiritual selves by moving from Oxford to one of London's university settlements.[3] Dons might have been indifferent to the spiritual welfare of their students, but, having just spent a year at the university settlement Oxford House in Bethnal Green in London's East End, he declared: 'Let Mr. Deane go to the Head of Oxford House who knows more of and is better known by undergraduates than any one else in Oxford or out of it, and ask him what he thinks about agnosticism. Mr Winnington-Ingram's work is proof positive of what can be done to abolish indifferentism.'[4] Whilst Oxford made boys into men, settlement houses such as Oxford House made them *homines religiosi*, according to Legge.

Oxford House opened its doors to graduate settlers in October 1884.[5] It was followed a few months later by the opening of Toynbee Hall in nearby Whitechapel. Described as 'centres of brightness' by one-time Head of Oxford House, and later Bishop of London, Arthur Winnington-Ingram, settlement houses allowed Oxford and Cambridge graduates to live in 'slum' areas and work alongside their poorer 'brothers'.[6] In their direct action approach to poverty, these houses marked a new phase of urban philanthropy.[7] Once there, settlers were encouraged to draw upon the example of the thirteenth-century Italian saint, Francis of Assisi, who became the unofficial patron saint of settling in late nineteenth-century London. Clare Simmons and Alice Chandler have shown that the medieval period became an ideal in Victorian literature, for example in the novels of Walter Scott.[8] Although separated from this period by some 700 years, settlement leaders such as Winnington-Ingram were certainly thinking about the cultural similarities between the nineteenth and thirteenth centuries.

Masculinity was undergoing a process of transformation in Victorian Britain. According to John Tosh, the period 1880–1914 witnessed a reappraisal of masculine identity through a 'flight from domesticity'.[9] He suggests that settlement houses, together with men's clubs and bachelor flats, provided young men with an alternative space to the familial home. Yet, as Matt Cook acknowledges in this collection, Tosh's discussion of masculinity and the home has been both 'pivotal and extremely troublesome'. Tosh has revised the traditional assumptions of separate sphere ideology to show how men engaged within the private sphere. This reading of domesticity nevertheless perpetuates an image that links men primarily to a domestic sphere centred on the family and women. Domesticity is not such a concrete category. How it was experienced depended on life stage, gender and class. This is true not only of the settlement house. Amy Milne-Smith and Paul Deslandes have considered how late-Victorian men replicated ideas of home in their clubs and university digs.[10] Settlers, too, were not involved in a straightforward rejection of the domestic sphere. At different times in their life they would have experienced and understood domesticity in different ways. Settlers were overwhelmingly young, middle-class and single. They increasingly did not have the material means to establish households of their own. The settlement house, therefore, provided them with the emotional, material and spiritual comforts of the domestic sphere while they were establishing careers. It also provided a space in which to develop a religious self.

The settlement house provided settlers with a sacred sphere. Religious meaning was not created by material goods alone, but also through the settler's imagination.[11] Toynbee Hall's and Oxford House's appropriation of a medieval Catholic saint was, indeed, more than casual admiration. For male settlers, his image facilitated the construction of a new masculine identity. This was all the more important at a time when Victorian spiritual masculinity was undergoing transformation.[12] According to traditional historiography of religion, such as the work of E.R. Wickham and K.S. Inglis, this was typified by men's indifference and hostility towards religion.[13] Such a reading has been confirmed by Callum Brown, who has contended that Christianity underwent a process of feminisation during the period in question.[14] Yet settlers' appropriation of St Francis was not part of the secularising or feminising processes affecting religious belief in Victorian Britain. St Francis typified a masculine identity that was active and adhered to the ideals of practical Christianity demonstrated by Jesus Christ.[15] Eileen Janes Yeo and Richard A. Kaye have demonstrated how

Victorians were able to appropriate Catholic saints for the construction of gendered and sexual identities. Yeo, for instance, has argued that first-wave feminists such as Josephine Butler and Frances Knight 'borrowed' from a number of Christian traditions in order 'to create their identities and empower themselves for public activity'.[16]

This chapter will argue that St Francis served the same purpose for men.[17] His example reassured settlers at a time when they were moving from young manhood to full adult masculinity. Life at Oxford House and Toynbee Hall allowed for a new masculine agency which transcended the *fin de siècle*'s stereotypical paradigm of the homosexual Victorian man.[18] Seth Koven has recently pointed out that settlement houses were 'remaking' and 'redefining' settlers by providing them with the spaces needed for testing 'distinctly heterodox concepts of masculinity and male sexuality'.[19] Koven argues that 'slumming' was not only the desire amongst bourgeois do-gooders to experience the conditions of the poor, but also provided a fantasy space where gender, class and sexual identities could be played out and transgressed. Yet Koven does not figure Christian spirituality fully into this equation. He points out the formal expressions of faith at Oxford House and the controversial religious pluralism of Toynbee Hall, but overlooks the informal spiritual imaginings which played such a crucial part in the refashioning of elite masculinity in settlements.[20] Personal testimonies of settlers will be used here to demonstrate the importance of spirituality in the social imagination of settlers. So too will the hagiographies written of St Francis by the Oxford House Head James Adderley.[21] What these sources reveal is that settlers did not simply think of themselves as reincarnations of St Francis. They modernised his image in order to construct a new masculine identity for themselves. St Francis's example helped a number of settlers who might traditionally have gone into the Church but now wanted to follow the principles of practical Christianity. Even those who had formerly had little interest in religion were captivated by the idea of doing God's work in the poorest parts of London. St Francis was crucial to how these men understood their masculinity and their role within a modern urban and industrial society.[22]

## St Francis and Oxbridge graduates

St Francis was the founder of the Franciscan order. Originally christened John, but called Francesco, he was born around 1182 to Pica and Peter Bernardone, the latter a wealthy cloth merchant. Similarities between St Francis's life and settlers' lives were noted by the Oxford House Head James Adderley.[23] He deliberately drew a parallel between the youthful decadence of Francis and the university graduates of the late nineteenth century. Francis had a tendency during his youth to be 'lordly in manners', 'greedy' and 'fastidious', enjoying nothing but 'jokes and pranks'. He had a tendency for luxurious clothing as well as a love of poetry and music. His banquets were reported to be the best in Assisi. Cambridge and Oxford students during this period were also criticised for the easy-going and indulgent nature of university life, which appeared to encourage drunkenness, laziness and decadence. This behaviour was often criticised by those in the settlement movement. Winnington-Ingram, for example, objected to the level of drunkenness and the practice of gambling that went on in Oxbridge Colleges in his St Mary's Sermon to Oxford students on 29 October 1905. His criticism was all the more damming because, as the Oxford student magazine *The Isis* noted, the 'Bishop has a hold over Oxford which no one else shares with him'. *The Isis* often acknowledged the significance of Oxford in national culture, but was equally self-aware of students' decadent failings.[24] As one *Isis* article entitled 'Oxford and England' had declared eight years before Winnington-Ingram's sermon, 'the public has displayed a desire to know about Oxford.' Yet it argued that Oxford's contribution to the nation amounted to the creation of the slang phrases 'Footer', 'Rugger' and 'Soccer'. This led them to the conclusion that the 'importance of our mission, we confess, weighs upon us somewhat heavily'.[25]

Settler autobiographies, however, were particularly keen to demonstrate that the kind of decadent manliness promoted in Cambridge and Oxford colleges was temporary and confined to undergraduate life. This fitted with Francesco's own conversion. At the age of 21 he began to have callings to the religious life, which at first he tried to dismiss. After his conversion, he made a resolution to restore ruined churches and to work with lepers. His father, apparently disgusted with his son's newfound religiosity, disinherited him.[26] St Francis's example highlighted the possibilities of change in young men in Adderley's hagiography. Settler autobiographies also maintained that a transformation took place in young men upon entering Toynbee Hall or Oxford House. An example can be found in the writings of the Oxford House settler Andrew Bulstrode. He was noted at Oxford for his smart appearance, forcing many to argue that he was a 'dandy', whilst tea in his rooms was always considered to be a charming occasion, with tasty fare on offer.[27] This contrasted with the 'dingy old blue cassock, heavy boots and shapeless hat' he adorned when he became a travelling Franciscan monk after a stint at Oxford House.[28] His new monkish habits, much like St Francis, upset his evangelical father, who considered it 'merely an offensive eccentricity', and to begin with refused to let his son come home unless he came in ordinary dress.[29]

The settlement house thus provided Oxbridge graduates with a space in which to redeem themselves and find their religious selves. '[A] way is open for Christian devotion which young men may enter without painful hesitation and perplexities,' wrote Professor Seeley. 'It is a plain road which you can't easily mistake, and which you will not regret having entered, believe me, twenty hence.'[30] This was, according to leaders and supporters of the settlement movement, all the more true because the Oxbridge graduate played a central role in national life. Oxbridge students were clergyman, barristers and Members of Parliament. As Koven has argued, the settlements 'were also sites to invent a new type of man who was manly but capable of deep empathy, public-spirited because he was attuned to the private grief of his neighbours'.[31] The settlement house needed to provide men entering these careers with something more than secular ideals. This led Hugh Laurie to argue that the settlement house was not only a working-class college in East London, but also a postgraduate college for young Oxford graduates hoping to become MPs, civil servants, lawyers, members of the clergy and so on.[32] For the months or years that settlers were in the movement, they could stand still and consider their future roles. The settlement movement gave these men the means by which to look for their '"Christed" self...[a] self moved with the Spirit of Christ'.[33]

The image of St Francis was essential to this process. As Walter Besant, novelist and founder of the People's Palace, proclaimed in his essay 'On University Settlement',

> What St. Francis command his followers was, that they should be obedient; that they should remain in poverty; and that they should be celibate. They were to be obedient because work of all kinds among men must be organised; very well that law is in full force in the University Settlement. They were to remain in poverty- that law is also in force wherever work is done without reward or money. They were to be celibate- a custom, if not a law, which also prevails in the modern settlement.[34]

This quote challenges Gertrude Himmelfarb's proclamation that Toynbee Hall and Oxford House settlers 'were not to be latter-day St. Francises'.[35] Besant argued that the settlement movement was organised along distinctly Franciscan lines and that it was the first large philanthropic organisation for 600 years to fully adhere to the act of personal service associated with St Francis's work with the medieval poor.[36] This was also the argument of those in the settlement movement. They perceived themselves as Franciscans without having to make the formal declarations of poverty, chastity and obedience. Toynbee Hall and Oxford House were certainly single-sex residences, but vows were not a central part of the movement. Settlers were never asked to formally undertake them, despite Besant's suggestion that they were effectively in play. This meant that when in 1923 Henry W. Nevinson, journalist and Toynbee Hall associate, came to reflect upon his time at the settlement house he was able to describe it as 'a monastic establishment where there are no vows'.[37] He suggested, therefore, that the identity of Toynbee Hall was established through both conventional and unconventional forms of monasticism.

Nevinson's decision to inform his reader that settlers were not tied to the vows of poverty, obedience and chastity also reflected wider concerns with the monastic system in late Victorian Britain. For example, the Reverend John Hartley, curate of Harts Hill in Birmingham, had complained that 'the three vows of celibacy, poverty, and obedience are binding for life. How ruinous and detrimental to the human frame must such a slavish system be! It can only lead to those persons who are confined to physical sufferings and a premature death.'[38] Yet there was simultaneously a growth of missionary zeal in both Anglican and Catholic monasticism in mid to late-nineteenth-century Britain.[39] Adderley, along with other social observers, noted this transformation. For example, the popular author of several devotional writings, the Reverend Fredrick C. Woodhouse, recognised the importance of a nineteenth-century revival of monasticism both for the Church of England and for society as a whole. Whilst many of his contemporaries argued that monasticism was not compatible with modern Protestantism, Woodhouse offered examples of monastic traditions present in Anglicanism. Recognising that the Church Army, founded in 1882 by the Reverend Wilson Carlile, was not in a strict sense 'a monastic institution', Woodhouse nonetheless argued that 'its principles and motives of the founder and its active members are the same as those that, as we have seen, are the root and the moving impulse of Monasticism, love of God and of man, a desire to imitate Christ, and to follow Him literally in the precepts and practices.'[40]

Adderley believed, furthermore, that St Francis's age was 'like our own'. He argued that the thirteenth and nineteenth centuries both experienced mass loss of faith. The object of modern-day monasticism was, therefore, 'to bring religion more to the minds of the people'.[41] Religious revival could occur in two ways, according to Adderley. It could either proceed through the organisation of the Church, or by a deeper holiness and more application of religion in everyday life. Adderley preferred the latter, because it was a 'genuine attempt to realize Christianity in social conduct'.[42] He assumed that a purely Catholic monasticism would be unable to reconcile modern society with Christianity because it was contemplative and other-worldly. Benedictine monasticism, according to Adderley, was contemplative in this sense. In his autobiography he recounted the case of the Benedictine order under Father Aelred Carlyle which chose to leave the Church of England for Roman Catholicism because of its preference for contemplation over action.[43] Franciscan monasticism, on the other hand, was part of the world and was centred on social action. He cited St Francis's work with the poor and with lepers as evidence of the importance of humanistic work within the monastic tradition.

Moreover, Besant believed that the many problems of the present day could be overcome by turning to the late medieval period. He believed that the era between the thirteenth and the nineteenth centuries had been an age of misdirected philanthropy. During this period the rich had established schools, churches and almshouses, whilst social commentators had written great essays on philanthropy. Yet, he argued, nothing had been achieved to offset the terrible effects of poverty in the industrial age, despite these material acts of kindness.[44] In the thirteenth century, the followers of St Francis had demonstrated the importance of settling in 'the poorest and most miserable parts of the towns, and worked among the poorest and most miserable of the people'.[45] Not until the establishment of Oxford House and Toynbee Hall in 1884 had this example been followed, according to Besant.

## St Francis of the East End slum

According to settlement thought, Oxford graduates had two choices when they moved to London to establish their careers. Either they could live in West London and become morally corrupt, or they could undertake God's work by settling in the East End. Canon Scott Holland, speaking on behalf of Oxford House, argued that the settlement promised to solve 'one of the most serious problems of the age', namely 'the problem of the surplus of educated gentlemen'.[46] 'What was to be done with them?' he asked.

> They had a way of accumulating in contested districts, and swarming together in shoals like herrings. One of the districts where they accumulated, and which was terribly congested, was the West End, round about Piccadilly... They sat idling in their clubs, or mooned and caged up and down Piccadilly, and many of them were wholly unemployed [so that]... they got-submerged [laughter]... So it was partly with a view to deal with this problem that labour refuges or shelters for contested gentlemen had been established at the East End. One was Toynbee Hall, another Oxford House. They would bring these poor unfortunate gentlemen under the healthy influence of contact with working men and the poor... they would be surprised to see how it would improve their moral tone, so that they might hope to make them fit to be safely transferred to labour farms, which were sometimes called country seats or country livings.[47]

Holland's comical narrative borrowed imagery from William Booth's recently published *In Darkest England, and the Way Out* (1890).[48] In particular, describing settlement houses as 'labour refuges' for the West End's 'submerged' and 'unemployed' gentlemen who were idly waiting for their country livings struck the same tone as Booth's book. The Army Officer and Toynbee Hall settler Fletcher Vain confirmed this when he suggested that visiting the East End was more 'instructive than always loafing in well-known clubs' whilst waiting for active army business.[49]

The settlement house was, therefore, as much a space for the improvement of the upper and middle classes as of instruction for the working classes. By living in East London, settlers were able to sanctify the settlement house through their adherence to practical Christianity. It did not matter whether settlers were intending to go into the Church or not. Their settlement work allowed them to adhere to a notion of personal service that brought practical Christianity, or what Winnington-Ingram termed the 'gospel in action', to the forefront of a new religious philanthropy.[50] The example of St Francis fitted with this idea. A theological shift had occurred in nineteenth-century Protestantism which emphasised practical theology through the teachings and examples of Christ. Practical theology recognised, first, that faith was not simply a set of ideas but an ongoing experience and, second, that self-transcendence was not egotistical and private but altruistic. Settlers were moving from a faith that had once been dependent on prayer and the Bible to a faith that was practical and for the greater good. Beatrice Webb's famous quote that the Victorian period witnessed the 'transference of the emotion of self-sacrificing service of God to man' suggested not only that religious belief had been superseded by socialism but that, at a theological level, religious belief was no longer confined to a God in heaven but now included God's presence in man.[51]

The religious undercurrent of Oxford House and Toynbee Hall was, at this level, free from denominational constraints. Incarnation theology was central to both houses, despite Oxford House's High Anglicanism and Toynbee Hall's non-sectarian impulse or, as the settlement motto declared 'not money, but yourselves'.[52] Following the teaching of T.H. Green and the exemplars of Arnold Toynbee and Edward Denison, they understood Christianity not only as a personal relationship between God and Man, but an active faith which sought to unite mankind. 'Charity' was perceived, as Fredrick Maurice argued in his *Theological Essays* (1857), as 'the key to unlocking the secrets of Divinity as well as Humanity'.[53] For settlers, this meant that religion was no longer issued to them by a distant authority, but was personal and to be found within themselves.

St Francis became a key example to men like Adderley because he taught Christians to apply religion directly to their everyday lives.[54] He instilled in Victorians 'the need to realize Christianity in social conduct', which in turn led them to follow his work with the poor in urban centres.[55] This was noted by many others, including Besant, and the Reverend J.B. Gilman, who pointed out that

> history repeats itself, and the generous self-abnegation of the early Franciscans is repeated again and again in these days; the motive of power is the same, though the methods differ, as the world maintains its steady course upward in spiritual descent. As the noble Franciscans, in the thirteenth century,

gave up the comforts and luxuries which were theirs by birth and heritage, and took up their abode with the poor and the afflicted, so, in this nineteenth century, in the Toynbee Hall movement, East London, men are devoting themselves to the same noble work.[56]

The interest in St Francis, therefore, fitted the growing interest in social action in late Victorian Britain. A debate in the *Pall Mall Gazette* about accommodation in London for medical students highlights the significance of the settlement house and its monasticism as part of this trend. Dr Stephen Mackenzie wrote to the *Pall Mall Gazette* on 18 December 1885, responding to Major-Surgeon Hamilton Evatt's letter sent eight days earlier. The latter argued that no suitable accommodation was available to those receiving medical training in the metropolis.[57] Agreeing with Evatt, Mackenzie argued that a possible solution was Toynbee Hall's communal living, which would allow the medical student 'to find the companionship from young men of his own age from the universities currently engaged in different professions; and the association of men of culture'. The residence of medical students at Toynbee Hall would also, according to Mackenzie, facilitate the growth of social consciousness in these students at a time 'when character is forming'.[58]

Although Mackenzie understood Toynbee Hall to be a collegiate residence, his argument that medical students' sympathies and interests could be expanded by their involvement in the house indicates the significance that was placed on social action by a growing number of men in the late Victorian era. Mackenzie argued that parents would be comforted by the knowledge that the leader of Toynbee Hall, the Reverend Samuel Barnett, like other settlement heads, would provide counsel and guidance to their young sons. Winnington-Ingram recalled that he asked a young man to 'come and pray with us, and not talk about your doubts'. The young man came to Oxford House and 'for five years he worked among the poor, and he never talked about his faith at all. What was the result? Why, in working for the others his faith came back to him: He saw the Gospel in action'.[59] Barnett also hoped to 'spiritualise life', according to the settler Alfred Spender.[60] The idea that man could be without God was the greatest human calamity for Barnett. During his own time at Toynbee Hall, Spender was experiencing his own religious difficulties.[61] He noted that 'What Barnett was to young men setting out in their life can never be told.' Barnett was, according to him, a 'wise, subtle, and original mind' who helped settlers when they needed help.[62] The divide between the secular and the spiritual was never apparent for Barnett in undertaking this work. He hoped to spiritualise all aspects of settlers' lives, and helped Spender into a career in journalism rather than in the Church.

The pages of the *Pall Mall Gazette* also reveal the criticisms directed at the settlement movement's Franciscan monasticism. In 1886 its front page ran an article under the title 'Communism at Home', which argued that '[W]e are ceasing to live in homes. We are beginning to live in hotels.' Critical of Toynbee Hall's 'modified monasticism', they argued that such communal living should not be made permanent because it undermined the domestic sphere and destroyed men's relations with the opposite sex. Toynbee Hall, according to the author of this article, represented 'the home of the future' for a body of men who found the expense of 'material civilisation' too much. It prevented them from making their own homes with wives and families:

> There can be no home in which there is no marriage and the test by which the new social arrangements will be judged will be the extent to which they facilitate and multiply opportunities for the free and open association and friendship of men and women. It is easy to re-establish the monastery, the common refectory, reading room, and kitchen, so long as the inmates are all of one sex; but although easy it is not profitable. What we want is not barracks but homes.[63]

The *Pall Mall Gazette*'s objection confirms this chapter's argument that monasticism was a popular concern and point of reference in late Victorian Britain. It leads to interesting questions about the settlement movement's role in the cultivation of young men's gendered and sexual identity. Koven has already explored male homosexuality in the movement. Yet it did not necessarily disrupt the traditional domestic arrangements of society as much as he suggests. Many settlers indeed left upon marriage, including Spender, who both met and married his wife Mary at Toynbee Hall. Although Winnington-Ingram never married, he was briefly engaged to Lady Ulrica Duncombe, the youngest daughter of the Earl of Faversham, during his bishopric of Stepney.[64] Samuel and Henrietta Barnett lived together at Toynbee Hall. They initially lived in St Jude's vicarage, but in 1892 moved into the Warden's Lodge with a door from Toynbee's drawing room joining their house directly to the settlement.[65] Toynbee Hall was furnished by Henrietta Barnett with the comforts of the home in mind, despite all its residents being male. As Samuel Barnett proclaimed, 'There must be no affection of asceticism.'[66] The Barnetts were eager for settlers to make the house their home. They modified the traditional vow of poverty, which was to live without worldly goods. They did this by decorating settlers' bedrooms with luxurious wallpapers and carpets.[67] In addition, the drawing room at Toynbee Hall challenged the conventional alignment of monasticism with asceticism. Henrietta Barnett, who was in charge of decorating the house, wanted the drawing room to be decorated in a similar manner to a West End drawing room. She believed that Whitechapel needed lovely colours, which led her to decorate the drawing room with green Japanese wallpaper.[68]

Oxford House's approach to materialism contrasted sharply with that of Toynbee Hall. Their decision not to reproduce the aestheticism of Toynbee Hall demonstrates diverging understandings of taste. The Oxford House Head Herbert Hensley Henson, for instance, noted upon visiting the Barnetts that their 'drawing room impressed me not a little. It was exceedingly pretty and tasteful: but far too luxurious for my taste (fancy S. Paul on that Sofa, contemplating that statuette: & drinking afternoon tea out of those cups!!).'[69] Henson's disdain for the Barnetts' tea cups might, though, have arisen out of bitterness about his own living conditions at the time rather than an absolute commitment to asceticism. The first Oxford House building was a disused schoolhouse that had been basically converted for settlement work. Adderley reminisced about shivering over the sitting-room stove during cold winter evenings, and Aubrey Mynors fondly recalled writing begging appeals with a rug wrapped around his knees because there was no fire.[70] Such were the times that Winfred Burrows, the future Bishop of Truro, could be seen carrying a bath from the house to where settlers were billeted.[71]

Henson's diary also recognised the difficulties of living in Oxford House. The 13 October 1886, he noted, had been a 'very cold day, and with no fire, the House seemed wretched. I am unable or unwilling to be even a *little too cold*: with what face can I talk about asceticism'.[72] In a sense, then, Oxford House's ascetic monasticism was born out of necessity rather than conviction. Indeed, Henson had been living in All Souls College, Oxford, prior to his headship at Oxford House. It was at All Souls that his thoughts had turned towards establishing a religious community with Adderley.[73] Henson's mentor, William Anson, thought that the former's conversion to Apostolic Poverty was hypocritical given that he had got used to living in All Souls, one of the wealthiest and grandest Oxford colleges, and showed no desire to give up his luxurious college life before moving to Oxford House.[74] Henson wrote in his diary following this slight that 'It is not my *will* to remain in luxury. I long to throw all aside, and to be an ascetic as was [St] Francis; but I am not *free* to do what I would. I am not *rich* enough to be poor.'[75] Henson raised an important question when aligning the vow of poverty to the settler: could a life in poverty really be fulfilled if one did not have a secure background to fall back on? Faced with the hardships of Oxford Hous, even he realised that this type of living was difficult. It was generally recognised that a 'larger and more convenient House' was needed if Oxford House were to succeed by the time of Winnington-Ingram's arrival in 1889.[76]

It should not, therefore, be assumed that Oxford House settlers adopted a strictly ascetic lifestyle. Dick Sheppard, another Oxford House Head and later Canon of Canterbury, continued to keep a tailor and barber in the West End. The disjuncture between Sheppard's Oxford House asceticism and his simultaneous use of West End facilities is revealed by his recollection of visiting the barber. After one glance the barber said, 'I'm sorry, sir, but I can't cut your hair.' 'Why on earth not?' demanded the perplexed and affronted Dick. 'I'm sorry, sir: I really can not. Your head, sir, is...ahem!...alive!'[77] This did not prevent Howard Marshall from describing Sheppard as a *'papier mâché'* reproduction of St Francis. Walter Matthews, Dean of St Paul's, objected to this assessment, but acknowledged that 'one must suppose that there is some truth in an analogy which seems to occur spontaneously to different people; to me, however, there appears to be little resemblance, except that both men were devoted to the service of Christ.'[78] He argued instead that Sheppard could not be aligned with Francis because he did not live like a tramp, noting: 'he could do much good with a telephone, a type writer, a secretary, working from the base of a well-ordered house completely "in the world".'[79] Matthews privileged a version of Franciscan monasticism that eschewed the material world and disassociated it from the modern period. He understood this Franciscan monasticism primarily as a process of giving up material objects. This was not surprising, given that Francis's poverty was continually emphasised by Adderley's hagiographies. Barrie Williams has, however, pointed out that 'Francis's poverty appealed to people in the 1890s.'[80] Yet only a handful of settlers embraced an absolutely ascetic life. Those who did, including the Oxford House settlers Adderley, Ernest Hardy (later Father Andrew) and Henry Chappell (later Father Henry), established the Franciscan order the Society of the Divine Compassion (in existence between 1895 and 1952), along with Gordon Bulstrode (later Brother Edward), who became a village evangelist. It was at Oxford House that Hardy read Adderley's semi-autobiographical novel *Stephen Remarx*.[81] Adderley argued in this book that men should join forces with one another and establish monastic institutions in London.

There was, though, a further understanding of Franciscan poverty in the 1890s, namely that Francis's conception of a simple life was not confined to a strictly ascetic existence. Although he asked that his friars live by their begging bowls and sleep in ruined churches, he did not want them to exclude the beauties of music, poetry, romance, gentle manners and the beauties of nature. This meant that settlers' appreciation of art, drama and music would not have been incompatible with Franciscan monasticism. It also meant that Sheppard's use of material objects did not compromise his Franciscan image as Matthews suggested. St Francis himself did not emphasise absolute asceticism. He encouraged a love of the arts. In the Franciscan sense the vow of poverty meant not the total rejection of worldly goods and aesthetic pleasure, but simplicity of life in which personal service to the needy was the ideal. This was not incompatible with Toynbee Hall's aestheticism. Both Toynbee Hall and Oxford House relied for their sanctity on the spiritual actions of settlers. As Adderley pointed out, poverty was the 'primary principle of Christianity' because it emphasises the idea of 'being' rather than 'getting'.[82] The settlement movement allowed settlers to follow in St Francis's footsteps and adhere to acts of personal service. When Douglas Eyre, the longest-serving Oxford House settler, died in 1935, two of his previous Heads, Sheppard and Winnington-Ingram, acknowledged the great debt that the House and Bethnal Green owed to him.[83] His work was informed by 'Christian faith and its practical application', according to Sheppard.[84] Settlers like Eyre were able to bring a 'plain, straight-forward business [and] robust and commonsense Christianity' to the East End by entering the house.[85]

However, there was also realisation among settlement heads that such acts of Franciscan personal service were not always easy to attain. It was dependent on good, hard-working settlers who were prepared to commit to the cause. As Henson noted,

> In social work such continuity is essential, but when work is organised and directed by volunteers, continuity is almost unattainable. The demand on the volunteer's self sacrifice and fixity of purpose is too great for men. Nor can many afford the spiritual luxury of self-dedication to altruistic service. The notion that undergraduates might usefully supplement their normal academic experience by some personal contact with the lives of the poor was not sufficiently correlated with the condition under which alone any permanent influence can be gained. A few weeks spent in Bethnal Green during the vacation might benefit the undergraduate but could hardly have any effect on the East End.[86]

Henson, therefore, decided that the Franciscan premises of the settlement movement were flawed. He was especially critical of the concept of personal service. This led him to declare in his diary that 'the O.H. is, as a fact, an impossible scheme, and must in the long run fail.'[87] Henson's criticism highlighted two problems with the alignment of the settlement movement with monasticism: that settlers were only ever temporarily in service and that the financial burden of the movement on settlers was great. Ironically, the settlement movement was just as dependent on the generosity of older philanthropy in donating money as former movements had been.

Alternatively, others argued that the personal service inherent in settlement monasticism was less about the poor than it was about improving the morality of the middle-class university graduate. Edward Cummings, critic of the settlement movement and Professor of Sociology at Harvard University, argued that 'the discipline of the monastic life' needed to be offered by institutions such as Toynbee Hall in order to prevent 'many of the juvenile eccentricities of college life'.[88] Concerned that the Oxbridge graduate was 'degenerating' as a result of college frivolities, he argued that the student needed to move away from this 'most artificial and ephemeral phrase of civilised life' once he had graduated and undertake a period of personal service. However, like Henson, Cummings was pessimistic about the settlement movement's ability to deliver such monasticism. He thought that the settlement house perpetuated the 'artificial and ephemeral phase' in the graduate's life by 'leaving him with an ideal in which eternal youth, free from the ties of family life, entertains its [working-class] friends with dinners, pipes, lectures, songs and magic lanterns, in ample halls adorned with mysterious things aesthetic, and in the end discusses the evils of society over black coffee and unlimited cigarettes'.[89] Cummings thought that it was no good leaving charity to 'young and inexperienced heads'. It needed to be learnt through monastic discipline and organisation, which, he thought, 'involves a division of work and workers along definite lines'.[90]

## Conclusion

Settlers were able to reconcile their spiritual and masculine identities by making Francis the unofficial patron saint of the settlement movement. The settlement house provided a space for the reformation and the re-figuring of masculinity during this period. Both Oxford House and Toynbee Hall settlers imagined a masculine identity within a monastic framework. This imaginary allowed settlers to be active, social and public men who lived in a space that was neither straightforwardly domestic nor ascetic. The settlement house was a new kind of masculine space which drew upon the monastic model as part of a broader aim to spiritualise the Oxbridge graduate. Such religious symbolism was fundamental to the settlement movement. Settlers' appropriation of St Francis represented more than a simple desire to find a lost feudal past. Incarnation theology had placed greater emphasis on practical theology and the example of Christ. During the Victorian period exemplars from history were drawn upon, and St Francis was one Catholic saint whom British Protestantism took to its heart. This did not imply a return to the past, or a wholesale embrace of Catholicism, but a modernisation of personal service and religious masculinity for an age in which religious belief was changing. Although Toynbee Hall settlers were drawn to St Francis, it was Oxford House settlers who went on to establish fully fledged Franciscan religious orders after leaving settlement work. Brother Edwards and Father Andrew played an active role in restoring an active Franciscan life to the Church of England. Yet the image of St Francis and the broader monastic imaginary was far more important than the revival of monastic orders. It gave a large body of settlement men, many of whom went on to hold important secular positions, a masculine identity that marked a break from the ideals of the previous generation.

## Notes

1. Anthony C. Deane, 'The religion of the undergraduate', *The Nineteenth Century* (1895), pp. 673–80, quote on p. 676.
2. Hugh Legge, 'The religion of the undergraduate: a reply from Oxford', *The Nineteenth Century* (1895), p. 861. For a further response, see in particular Reginald B. Fellows, 'The religion of the undergraduate: a reply from Cambridge', *The Nineteenth Century* (1895), pp. 856–60.
3. Legge, 'Religion', p. 863.
4. Ibid., p. 868.
5. For histories of Oxford House see Mandy Ashworth, *The Oxford House of Bethnal Green: 100 Years of Work in the Community* (London, 1984); Ian Bradley, *Oxford House in Bethnal Green, 1884–1984: 100 Years of Work in the Community, A Short History* (London, 1984). For Toynbee Hall see Emily Abel, *Canon Barnett and the First Thirty Five Years of Toynbee Hall* (University of London PhD Thesis, 1969); Standish Meacham, *Toynbee Hall and Social Reform, 1880–1914: The Search for Community* (New Haven, 1987); J.A.R. Pimlott, *Toynbee Hall: Fifty Years of Social Progress, 1884–1934* (London, 1935). Seth Koven considers both Houses in his *Slumming: Sexual and Social Politics in Victorian London* (Oxford, 2004).
6. Arthur Winnington-Ingram, quoted in 'Meeting at Londonderry House', *Oxford House Chronicle* 6 (1891), 6.
7. Up until this point, college students and graduates had fulfilled their duties towards the urban poor by sending young clergymen, usually former members of their college, to some well-known working-class district to support the local clergy. There was already a growing awareness that sending one or two Mission Curates, as they were known, into the East End was not enough to help the plight of the poor. Histories of such college missions are sparse. See, however, J.W. Dickie, *College Missions and Settlements in South London, 1870–1920* (University of Oxford B.Lit. thesis, 1976). Nigel Scotland considers them in relation to the settlement movement, particularly Barnett's criticism of them, in his *Squires in the Slum: Settlements and Missions in Late Victorian Britain* (London, 2007), pp. 13–19.
8. Clare A. Simmons, *Reversing the Conquest: History and Myth in Nineteenth-Century British Literature* (New Brunswick, 1990); Alice Chandler, *A Dream of Order: The Medieval Ideal in Nineteenth-Century English Literature* (Lincoln, 1970).
9. John Tosh, *A Man's Place: Masculinity and the Middle-Class Home in Victorian England* (New Haven, 1999), p. 170.
10. Amy Milne-Smith, 'A flight from domesticity? making a home in the gentlemen's clubs of London, 1880–1914', *Journal of British Studies* 45 (2006), 798–818; Paul Deslandes, *Oxbridge Men: British Masculinity and the Undergraduate Experience, 1880–1920* (Bloomington, 2005). For a discussion of materialism in female settlement houses see Shannon Jackson's excellent *Lines of Activity: Performance, Historiography, Hull-House Domesticity* (Ann Arbor, 2000) and Kathryn Kish, 'Hull house as a community of women reformers in the 1890s', *Signs: Journal of Women in Culture and Society* 10 (1985), 658–77.
11. See Jane Hamlett, *Gender and the Domestic Interior, 1850–1910* (unpublished PhD, Royal Holloway College, University of London, 2006), p. 199.
12. See John Tosh, *A Man's Place: Masculinity and the Middle-Class Home in Victorian England* (New Haven, 1999).
13. E.R. Wickham, *Church and People in an Industrial City* (London, 1964); K.S. Inglis, *Churches and the Working Classes in Victorian England* (London, 1964).

14. Callum Brown, *The Death of Christian Britain: Understanding Secularisation, 1800–2000* (London, 2001), p. 88.
15. For studies that have also explored Christian manliness, see essays in Donald E. Hall (ed.), *Muscular Christianity: Embodying the Victorian Age* (Cambridge, 1994). See also Norman Vince, *The Sinews of the Spirit: The Ideal of Christian Manliness in Victorian Literature and Religious Thought* (Cambridge, 1985).
16. Eileen Janes Yeo, 'Protestant feminists and catholic saints', in her *Radical Femininity: Women's Self-Representation in the Public Sphere* (Manchester, 1998), p. 133; Richard A. Kaye, '"Determined raptures": St. Sebastian and the Victorian discourse of decadence', *Victorian Literature and Culture* 27 (1999), 269–303.
17. Rene Kollar, *A Universal Appeal: Aspects of the Revival of Monasticism in the West in the 19$^{th}$ and 20$^{th}$ Centuries* (London, 1996).
18. The dominance of sexuality as a historical paradigm stems from the legacy of men's history which emerged from the gay liberation movement and Michel Foucault's *History of Sexuality: Volume One: The Will to Knowledge*, trans. Robert Hurley (Harmondsworth, 1990 [Paris, 1977]). This has meant that the study of monasticism has largely considered the monastery to be a queer space and the monk expressive of a psychosexual practice. See, for example, Hebert Saussman, *Victorian Masculinities: Manhood and Masculine Poetics in Early Victorian Literature and Art* (Cambridge, 1995); Frederick Roden, 'Medieval religion, Victorian homosexualities', *Prose Studies* 23 (2000), 115–30; and David Hilliard, '"UnEnglish" and "unmanly": anglo-catholicism and homosexuality', *Victorian Studies* 25 (1982), 181–210.
19. Koven, *Slumming*, p. 229.
20. See Sarah Williams, *Religious Belief and Popular Culture in Southwark, c.1880–1939* (Oxford, 1999).
21. James Adderley, *Francis the Little Poor Man of Assisi: A Short Story* (London, 1906); James Adderley, *St. Francis of Assisi and His Friars* (London, 1926).
22. This has been particularly important in the field of women's history. See Sue Morgan (ed.), *Women, Religion, and Feminism in Britain, 1750–1900* (Basingstoke, 2002). For two good literature reviews of religion and gender historiography, see Frederick S. Roden, 'Gender and religion in recent Victorian studies', *Victorian Literature and Culture* 31 (2003), 393–403 and Jacqueline de Vries, 'Rediscovering christianity after the postmodern Turn', *History Compass* 4 (2006), 698–714.
23. 'Heard on "the high"', *The Isis* 28 October 1905, p. 31.
24. For example, see 'The art of being idle', *The Isis*, 26 May 1894 and 'Oxford decadence and democracy', *The Isis*, 16 November 1895, p. 85.
25. 'Oxford and England', *The Isis*, 15 May 1897, p. 123.
26. Adderley, *Francis*, pp. 33–6.
27. Packard, *Brother Edward: Priest and Evangelist*, p. 23. A discussion of Oxbridge masculinity can be found in Paul R. Deslandes, *Oxbridge Men: British Masculinity and the Undergraduate Experience, 1850–1920* (Bloomington, 2005).
28. Packard, *Brother Edward*, p. 20.
29. Kathleen E. Burne, *The Life and Letters of Father Andrew S.D.C.* (London, 1951), p. 28.
30. Universities Settlement Association, *Work for University Men in East London* (Cambridge, 1884). p. 3.
31. Koven, *Slumming*, p. 240.
32. Arthur P. Laurie, *Pictures and Politics: A Book of Reminiscences* (London, 1934), p. 72.
33. Henrietta Barnett, *Canon Barnett: His Life, Work, and Friends by his Wife in Two Volumes* (London, 1918), 2, p. 40.

34. Walter Besant, 'On university settlements', in W. Reason (ed.), *University and Social Settlements* (London, 1898), pp. 2–3.
35. Gertrude Himmelfarb, *Poverty and Compassion: The Moral Imagination of the Late Victorians* (New York, 1991), p. 240.
36. Besant, 'University settlements', p. 3.
37. Henry Wood Nevinson, *Changes and Chances* (London, 1923), p. 91.
38. John Hartley, *Monasticism: Its Origin, Influence, and Results with Observations on Sisterhoods, the Lay Deaconate, and the Pastoral Order* (London, 1885), p. 91.
39. Susan O'Brien, 'Terra incognita: the nun in nineteenth-century England', *Past and Present* 121 (1988), 110–44.
40. The Church Army was essentially a working-class Anglican mission that sought to proselytise the working classes. It set up homes, refuges, unemployment workshops, laundries, food depots, dispensaries and shops for second-hand clothing as well as sending out mission vans with preachers and books. Woodhouse, *Monasticism*, p. 297.
41. Adderley, *St. Francis of Assisi and His Friars*, p. 3.
42. Ibid., p. 4.
43. James Adderley, *In Slums and Society: Reminiscences of Old Friends* (London, 1918), p. 78.
44. Besant, 'University settlements', p. 4.
45. Ibid., p. 3.
46. Anon., *The Oxford House in Bethnal Green: Report of Meeting held at the Mansion House in Support of an Appeal for the Building Fund on Wednesday, 21st Jan., 1891* n.p., n.d., p. 9.
47. Ibid., pp. 9–10.
48. William Booth, *In Darkest England, and the Way Out* (London, 1890).
49. Francis Fletcher Vane, *Agin the Governments: Memories and Adventures of Sir Francis Fletcher Vane, Br.* (London, 1929), p. 57.
50. See 'The New Philanthropy', *Pall Mall Gazette (PMG)*, 17 December 1886, 4, which argued that Toynbee Hall was the centre of this new type of philanthropy.
51. Beatrice Webb, *My Apprenticeship* (Cambridge, 1980), p. 130.
52. Besant, 'University settlements', p. 6.
53. Fredrick Maurice, *Theological Essays* (Cambridge, 1853), p. 7.
54. Adderley, *St. Francis of Assisi and His Friars*, p. 26.
55. Ibid., p. 4.
56. J.B. Gilman, 'Toynbee hall, Whitechapel', *Lend a Hand* 2 (1887), 255.
57. 'Hostels for medical students in London', *PMG*, 10 December 1885, 1.
58. Ibid., 1.
59. Winnington-Ingram, quoted in S.C. Carpenter, *Winnington-Ingram: The Biography of Arthur Foley Winnington-Ingram, Bishop of London, 1901–1939* (London, 1949), p. 39.
60. Barnett, *Canon Barnett*, 1, p. 316.
61. J.A. Spender, *Life, Journalism and Politics*, 2 vols (New York, 1927), 2, p. 199.
62. Ibid., 2, p. 199.
63. 'Communism in the Home', *PMG*, 9 September 1886, 1.
64. 'A Bishop who toils in Society', *New York Times*, 1 September 1907, 5.
65. Barnett, *Canon Barnett*, 2, p. 58.
66. Ibid., 1, p. 312.
67. Ibid., 2, p. 58.
68. Ibid., 2, p. 58.
69. Herbert Hensley Henson, 'Monday January 23rd 1888', Herbert Hensley Henson diaries, Durham Cathedral Archives, Journal 4, p. 18.

70. Adderley, *In Slums and Society*, p. 18; 'Gathering of Past and Present Workers', *The Oxford House Chronicle* 9 (1894), 3.
71. Adderley, *In Slums and Society*, p. 17.
72. Herbert Hensley Henson, 'Monday January 23rd 1888', Herbert Hensley Henson diaries, Durham Cathedral Archives, Henson 4, p. 157.
73. Herbert Hensley Henson, 'May 3rd 1886', Herbert Hensley Henson diaries, Durham Cathedral, Henson 3, p. 72. This organisation would have been called 'League of the True Vine', but it was never founded.
74. Herbert Hensley Henson, 'May 25th 1886', Herbert Hensley Henson diaries, Durham Cathedral Archives, Henson 4, p. 55.
75. Ibid., p. 55.
76. *Oxford House Annual Report, Balance Sheets, List of Subscriptions, 1889* (Oxford, 1890), p. 12.
77. R. Ellis Robert, *H. R. L. Sheppard: Life and Letters* (London, 1942), p. 53.
78. Walter Matthews, 'The Impatient Parson', in *Dick Sheppard by His Friends* (London, 1938), p. 33.
79. Ibid., p. 33.
80. Barrie Williams, *The Franciscan Revival in the Anglican Communion* (London, 1982), p. vii.
81. James Adderley, *Stephen Remarx: The Story of a Venture in Ethics* (London, 1906).
82. Adderley, *St. Francis of Assisi and His Friars*, p. 12.
83. H.R.L. Sheppard, 'Mr Douglas Eyre: An Appreciation', *The Times*, 1 November 1935, p. 18; 'Mr Douglas Eyre', *The Times*, 2 November 1935, p. 14.
84. Sheppard, 'Mr Douglas Eyre', p. 18.
85. 'Meeting at Londonderry House', p. 4.
86. Herbert Hensley Henson, *Retrospect of an Important Life*, 3 vols (London, 1942), 1, p. 28.
87. Ibid., 1, p. 31.
88. Edward Cummings, 'University settlements', *The Quarter Journal of Economics*, 6 (1892), p. 273.
89. Ibid., p. 273.
90. Ibid., p. 273.

# 15
# Homes Fit for Homos: Joe Orton, Masculinity and the Domesticated Queer

*Matt Cook*

> Orton would have relished the solemn fakery of sodomite domesticity embodied in the spectacle of Jenny cuddling brain-soaked teddy between Ken and Joe's own prick-proud, severed body.[1]

In his 1986 review of the diaries of Joe Orton (1933–1967), fellow British playwright John Osborne used Orton's murder at the hands of his lover, Kenneth Halliwell, to underscore the patent absurdity of gay parenting and 'sodomite domesticity'. 'Jenny' was the protagonist of the children's book *Jenny Lives with Eric and Martin* (1983), which represented a happy but also queer domestic unit. The book caused a storm and was used by Margaret Thatcher's conservatives to indicate the dangers posed by a permissive society and to attack the 'political correctness' of 'loony left' local councils which stocked this and similar books in their libraries. By imagining Jenny cuddling teddy alongside the bloodied and brain-splattered bodies of 'Ken and Joe', Osborne was keying into a familiar story of the anti-domestic and anti-familial homosexual whilst also conjuring for Orton an embodied and 'prick-proud' masculinity.[2] He stumbled in this way on the under-examined intersection of cultures of homosexuality, of domesticity and of masculinity, and unwittingly presented Orton as an apt case study.

## Preliminaries

For historians and sociologists working on modern masculinities, home and homosexuality are key. Attitudes towards, behaviours within, and rejections of 'home' (as an idea and material locale) become telling indicators of the extent to which middle-class men especially measured up in their expected roles – as, for example, protector and provider; respectable and responsible social actor;

and prudent (literal and figurative) investor in the social and familial future. This relationship between home and masculinity, as John Tosh so brilliantly demonstrates, is both pivotal and extremely troublesome, especially as the domestic sphere became increasingly feminised in the late nineteenth and twentieth centuries.[3] Eve Kosofsky Sedgwick, meanwhile, argues for the central significance to hegemonic masculinities and to heterosexuality of the homosexual – that despicable figure who yet served to give definition to 'real' men. Sedgwick indicates the fine line that separated (and separates) the two, and so the anxious boundary policing necessary to sustain a sense of difference.[4] This understanding of the cultural centrality of homosexuality and more and less associated notions of effeminacy, 'softness', camp and the closet has been important to subsequent analyses of shifting modes of masculinity and sexual normalcy in the west.

Tosh and Sedgwick formulate their arguments chiefly in relation to the later nineteenth and early twentieth centuries, widely seen as periods of particular instability in gender and sexual identification in England, and also, Deborah Cohen would add, of transition in the meaning and function of the home.[5] The immediate post-World War II period that is the focus of this chapter was marked by further social and cultural anxiety in these regards, sharpening and giving further momentum to the ideological imperatives which underpinned Osborne's later comments and the wider 1980s backlash against gay men and lesbians. The binary heterosexual/homosexual understanding of sexuality became more entrenched and widely accepted in the 1950s and 1960s,[6] and there was a new paranoia about 'the homosexual problem' on the one hand and, on the other, new hopes for what (the heterosexual) home and a particular configuration of family might offer the project of national renewal. The threat of the one and the promise of the other were enunciated almost simultaneously, and (adding further support to Tosh and Sedgwick's respective arguments) normative masculinity was configured between and in close relation to both. And yet in our explorations of masculinity we tend to utilise home and homosexuality separately, inadvertently reproducing presumptions about a disjunction between the two. We tend to forget that (to use Sharon Marcus) 'even the most scandalous gay lives had a domestic component', and that, though heterosexuality was a defining feature of home, home was a space and idea that was also utilised by queer men and women.[7]

In this chapter, and through an analysis of Orton's writing and domestic relationship with Halliwell, I consider what difference a direct examination of the conjunction of home and homosexuality might make to our understanding of masculinity, and especially queer masculinities. Orton's pose and plays have tended – like 'homosexuality' and 'masculinity' – to be examined in oppositional terms: he was and is seen to be an iconoclast and his work iconoclastic; Randal S. Nakayama describes him 'continually and self consciously formulating his identity in terms of opposition'.[8] Such oppositional analyses, however, potentially obscured complexities in Orton's identifications and notoriously contradictory accounts of himself. Whilst there is no doubt that he deliberately pitched himself against respectable and bourgeois conventions, it is also true that he did not sit comfortably on one side or the other of the binaries we tend to deploy to understand gender and sexuality. However strident the circulating ideologies and narratives of masculinity, homosexuality or home, Orton (and other men) negotiated them in unpredictable and often contradictory ways, highlighting once more the tensions between cultural histories of discourse and histories of everyday lives.[9]

This chapter, then, looks briefly at some of the discursive productions of homosexuality and home life in the post-war period – in which masculinity and also class were centrally at stake – before embarking on a more detailed analysis of the ways these played out in Orton's more and less self-conscious articulations of himself. Taking the intersection of home and homosexuality seriously, I argue via the Orton case study, brings the fragility of masculine identifications and identities – as well as the care needed to sustain them – into especially sharp focus.

## Homes and homosexuals

British society in the 1950s was 'unprecedentedly home-centred'[10] – rhetorically, symbolically and practically. This has been read as a reaction to the disruption wrought by wartime evacuation, mobilisation and rehousing;[11] as a rearguard attempt to counter 'wartime morality' and to shore up the faltering institution of the family in the face of a rising divorce rate;[12] as a product of the 'biggest improvement in the material standard of living in Britain since the Middle Ages', allowing many more to buy for – and indeed to buy – their own homes;[13] and as part of a retreat from the streets as places of socialisation, courtship and sex.[14] Not for the first time,[15] but more pervasively and intensely than before, the home became emblematic of – and instrumental in – the project of national renewal and the cultivation of a putatively shared set of values.[16] By extension, it was also pivotal in creating and judging cultural outsiders. Deviating from the trumpeted models of home and family was, argues Simon Shepherd, 'not merely a matter of personal failing but a very public symptom of bad citizenship and lax patriotism'.[17]

No wonder, then, that queer public sex and socialisation were more comprehensively attacked and aggressively policed than ever before;[18] or that the 1957 Wolfenden Committee recommendations for the partial decriminalisation of homosexual acts – and the legislation that at last followed in 1967 – could only conceive of tolerating homosexuality in terms of coupledom and the private sphere. The homosexual was to be rendered acceptable to the degree to which he might mimic imagined 'normal', 'respectable' and implicitly middle-class domestic lives. On the passing of the Sexual Offences Act of 1967, Lord Arran famously called on 'homosexuals' 'to show their thanks by comporting themselves quietly and with dignity'.[19] The homosexual was allowed to signify – to use Jonathan Dollimore – 'only to the extent that [he] confirm[ed], or c[ould] be aligned with, the values of the dominant'.[20]

This imagined intersection of the (respectable) homosexual with (idealised) straight lives was predictably problematic. Apart from anything else, the realities of straight lives were very variable indeed, and, as Carolyn Steedman makes vividly apparent, many 'normal' men and women in the 1950s felt alienated and crushed by the sense that they didn't measure up either (it was indeed these 'other' lives that gave many queer men some conceptual and everyday sense of cultural belonging).[21] The vaunted standards of domestic and familial life, moreover, seemed more narrowly defined than before, and there was little evidence that queer partnerships would gain acceptance alongside them. With this and legal prohibition in mind, couples were understandably reticent about living openly – a virtual requirement of respectable domesticity. They also remained absent from the official record (unless they were caught out and arrested – hardly a recipe for respectability either). As Janet E. Gardner observes, whilst under census definitions a married couple without children constituted a 'family' and the place where they lived a 'family home', there was (unsurprisingly) no such designation for a homosexual couple.[22] 'Male persons living together do not constitute domestic life', proclaimed a law society memo of the 1950s.[23] As I have argued elsewhere, queer men were figuratively rendered as either sissy homeboys or as homeless – caught up in a misogynist discursive bind which belittled attention to domestic detail and housework and yet also constructed home as culturally and socially central and so off limits to sexual outsiders.[24] In related ways, homosexuals were seen to be products of family in the sexological and especially psychoanalytic theorisations which gained more cultural sway in the 1950s, yet were, in adulthood, commonly conceptualised as 'exiles from kin', such that, in Kath Weston's words, 'straight to gay' came to be as 'family is to non family'.[25] The homosexual was depicted functioning outside the home and family or else in homes which betrayed the troubling domestic practices that went on within. 'Normal' men had a fine line to tread in asserting their masculinity and heterosexuality: they had to be invested in the home, family and what they both represented, yet display a disdain or charming incapacity for day-to-day childcare, housework, and the details of domestic furnishings and décor.

This notion of judging 'normality' or 'perversity' via attitudes towards, and productions of, domestic space was not new.[26] As homes became ever more tightly bound to ideas of subjectivity and identity, however, and as the 'cult of the domestic' became less elite and more generalised post-war, so growing numbers of people became attuned to signs of conformity and deviance therein. Hornsey's examination of reactions to domestic exhibitions of 1946 and 1953 shows just how sensitive observers could be. A contemporary-styled living room was judged by one to be 'out to impress'. It was 'not sincere' and must belong to 'a rather immoral type of person'. Another felt the same room was 'flippant' and didn't provide 'the right background for children'. A brightly decorated bedsit, meanwhile, was unmasculine: 'the colour scheme is completely wrong for a man to wake up and see.'[27] Hornsey shows morality and gender inscribed on the walls and in the furnishings of these spaces, and underlying both were presumptions and judgements about sexuality – communicated via the telling conjunction of immorality and a lack of masculinity.

Given this sensitivity to domestic styling, it is not surprising that films and novels of the period marshalled the home in the characterisation of contemporary queer 'types'. In Mary Renault's *The Charioteer* (1953), the feminised, flamboyant and self-consciously modern interiors of the discreditable queer (Bunny) are contrasted with the restraint of the model homo (Ralph). In Rodney Garland's *The Heart in Exile* (1953), psychologist Dr Anthony Page's dead lover, Julian, is characterised through his domestic interior, which 'gave a masculine impression in negative good taste, extremely English and genteel'.[28] Barrister Melville Farr in the landmark Basil Dearden film *Victim* (1961) displays a similarly 'traditional' and uncontroversial taste in the home he shares with his wife on the Chelsea Embankment – near to where Oscar and Constance Wilde had lived just over half a century earlier. Two sympathetic film portrayals of Wilde were released in 1960,[29] and *Victim* can be read as a resonant retelling of how the Wilde saga might have turned out differently if only the playwright could, like Farr, have kept his house in order and his desires in check.

The professional, discreet and domestically conventional protagonists in these various works of the 1950s and early 1960s are rewarded ultimately with stable companionship (in Farr's case in the promised reunion with his wife). Feverish, uncertain and dangerous passions are left outside and the home secures a more or less compromised but safer future. There is an echo of these respectable and acceptable homos in Michael Schofield's contemporaneous sociological case study of a middle-class homosexual couple in their 30s:

> Case XVIII. D is a successful business man who lives with H, the editor of a trade paper. Both are in their early thirties and except in working hours, they are seldom apart. They both earn good salaries and they live in an expensive flat. It is furnished in excellent taste and they are extremely proud of their home and lavish attention on it like young newlyweds. There is a certain amount of physical love between them but the most striking thing about them is their complete emotional harmony and the way they rejoice in each others company. The editor described the sexual side of their

love affair as "unimportant". Both of them have masculine physiques and neither of them take, or want to take, the part of the passive partner. They occasionally visit one of the London clubs together, but most evenings they are content to stay at home or entertain friends. Although they are careful to keep their relationship secret from their business associates, they have a number of heterosexual friends.[30]

Despite the attention H and D 'lavish' on their home (rather as you might on a child), Schofield uses the couple's home-centredness to mark out their equivalence to 'young newlyweds'. Their openness to visitors at home, their good taste, their domestic compatibility, their restrained passions and refusal of the 'passive role', and their professional and class status are all also part of Schofield's attempt to squeeze them into the mould of middle-class and masculine normalcy. The couple neatly capture the mode of homosexuality which those beginning to press for reform felt might gain some cultural approval. Not so the 'effeminate', 'isolationist' homosexuals charted in 1948 by the Mass Observation Survey;[31] the criminal, sexually 'twisted' 'aimless young men' described by Gillian Freeman in her novelistic exploration of London's 'youth culture' (*The Leather Boys*, 1961); or, to return to Schofield, those homosexuals who entered queer culture at 'the queer bar level', and who 'will [...] have to be able to hold his own in a vicious, jealous, back biting society where no affair is sacred and every effort will be made to hinder his search for happiness.'[32]

If the homosexual in one current of writing and rhetoric was imagined partially redeeming himself and his flawed masculinity through a putatively conventional middle-class home and pseudo-heterosexual partnership, in another he was inimical to the domestic sphere or else flippant, trivial and insincere in relation to it (and so also to what it represented). The cultural centrality of home in terms of individual and national identity was reaffirmed on both counts, leaving queer men to negotiate for themselves (and probably more self-consciously than most) quite how they were to relate to the domestic sphere and to the associated codes of masculine behaviour.

## At home with Joe and Ken

Joe Orton's diaries and plays apparently underscore his position as sexual, familial and domestic outlaw, and in this he was seen (by Osborne amongst others) as indicative of other queer lives. Orton in some ways cultivated this image. Aside from the diaries, his plays are populated by confident young men who have no family and sometimes no home: Wilson in *The Ruffian on the Stair* (1964) and Sloane in *Entertaining Mr Sloane* (1964) are both parentless and ostensibly seeking lodgings. Their arrival disrupts and forces a reconfiguration of the established domestic set-ups in each play (though importantly each set-up is a little skewed from convention in the first place). John Lahr's biography of Orton also suggests the playwright's distance from domestic and family life – a distance which, Simon Shepherd suggests, Lahr uses to account for the couple's demise.[33] Though Shepherd angrily rebuts what he sees as Lahr's subtext, however, he does not really qualify the core features of this depiction as far as home and family goes: Orton's estrangement from these institutions was part of what made him distinctively queer. What both biographers do, implicitly or explicitly, is to underscore the heterosexual/homosexual, familial/anti-familial, domestic/anti-domestic binaries, fixing these formulations and our historical gaze in ways which, I want to suggest, don't quite work. Orton's negotiation of familial and domestic ideologies complicates presumptions about the relationship between queer lives and home and family and the masculinities attendant to each, suggesting a closer intersection than Osborne, Lahr, Shepherd and commentators on the 'homosexual problem' in the 1950s and 1960s were wont to acknowledge.[34]

George Kaleb has argued that to 'reject being at home mentally or spiritually – to praise alienation – is to accept a burden, but it is the same thing as trying to live honestly rather than living a story'.[35] However desirable, such a 'rejection' is more than a 'burden' – it is well nigh impossible. Quite apart from the fact that this rejection would require yet another story, our narratives of home and family are deeply entrenched;[36] Orton could not easily sidestep them. What he could do was to play with them so that they could, in *ad hoc* fashion, assert an ironic distance – from straights, from 'queens', and from the kind of house-proud homosexual described by Schofield.

If Ralph in *The Charioteer*, Anthony in the *Heart in Exile*, Melville in *Victim* and Schofield's H and D were being touted as the acceptable face of homosexuality partly through their domestic styling, Bunny, with his self-conscious domestic modernism, and Orton and Halliwell in their bedsit were more disturbing queers, more clearly distant from the 'normal' and 'decent' constructions of home, family and masculine comportment. Orton and Halliwell's bedsit served posthumously as a symbol of the couple's dysfunctional lives (as if the bedsit hadn't been a fairly standard home base for many Londoners – including friends sharing – during this period).[37] The bedsit seemed to indicate 'the sterility and self destruction of homosexual love' (as Giovani's room in James Baldwin's 1956 novel did for author Colin MacInnes, writing in 1963).[38] This was not (as Osborne was to suggest) the sort of home to sustain family and acceptable coupledom.

There is precious little to go on in reconstructing Orton's domestic life with Halliwell.[39] Whilst his candour about his public sex is infamous, Orton is evasive about his time at home. One of his unpublished diaries – written at RADA in 1951 – tails off tantalisingly four days after he moves in with Halliwell in West Hampstead. 'The rest,' he says, 'is silence.'[40] As I have suggested elsewhere,

Orton was playing here with the ideas of secrecy and revelation that attended queer life, and he enacts a mock prudery at what might go on behind the couple's closed doors.[41] However ironic Orton was being, however, 'the rest' was indeed 'silence' – at least until Orton resumed his diary in December 1966 at the suggestion of his agent Peggy Ramsay. Of the intervening 15 years we know very little about the couple's home life together. There are the insights of occasional visitors interviewed after the couple's deaths by Lahr, and there are also some letters from Peggy Ramsay recounting Orton's comments on these years (of which more later).[42] From this and other material it would be difficult to persuasively domesticate Orton in 1950s and 1960s terms. What is also true, though, is that Orton and Halliwell lived an intensely insular and domestic life together: like Schofield's couple, they were 'seldom apart', took no part in the London's changing queer scene,[43] and were 'content' to stay at home. Orton's 'silence' on his domestic life is certainly not easy to analyse, but this silence, in itself and in what lay behind it, remains highly significant to our understanding of the playwright, and also the wider queer dynamics surrounding home and home life in this period. Sharon Marcus's observation on Victorian home-making remains apposite for Orton and the 1950s: 'domesticity,' she writes, 'celebrated a privacy that could be put on display'; the emergent homosexual type, meanwhile, 'coalesced around secrecy and evasion'.[44] Excessive privacy for Orton and Halliwell was, as for Wilde and his co-defendant Alfred Taylor in the 1890s, a marker of deviance.[45]

Orton's 'silence' in this respect was, then, not unusual for queer men. Home was not necessarily the safest place for queer men to have sex or to conduct their relationships. In interview men recall the evasive action that was sometimes necessary to dupe landladies, landlords, fellow tenants or room-mates. Rex and John couldn't contemplate installing a double bed in their rented room in Camden, for example,[46] and Michael remembers piggy-backing down hallways so that only one set of footsteps could be heard by others in the house.[47] Such oral history evidence indicates the anxieties that could surround the home space, and which led many queer men to particularly assiduous attempts to judge the safety (or otherwise) of a particular area or domestic set-up, and to try to discern what kind of queer was in residence. Such judgements took in class position, gender identifications and the minutiae of queer categorisation. In this light Orton's wry and highly detailed domestic observations in the diaries and in his anecdotes take on a new significance. He described, for example:

> A room on the ground floor of a large house. The place was damp, not lived in. A smell of dust. He didn't live there. He rented it for sex. There was a table covered in grime. Bits of furniture. A huge mantelpiece with broken glass ornaments on it. All dusty. There was a double bed with grayish sheets. A torn eiderdown. He pulled the curtain which seemed unnecessary because

the windows were so dirty. He had a white body. Not in good condition. Going to fat. Very good sex though, surprisingly. [...] As I lay on the bed looking upwards, I noticed what an amazing ceiling it was. Heavy moulding, a centerpiece of acorns and birds painted blue. All cracked now.[48]

The domestic and sexual detail segue in Orton's depiction; he characteristically described the room like a theatrical set, ready for the action that ensues. The room positions the sexual subject in this account (as in others) and we see Orton reading not only the queer body but also the space and context in which it was exposed. Indeed, the two are conflated: the dirty rented room framing the man's body, which is 'out of condition' and 'going to fat'. The room and the man together suggest a double life; a particular attitude to sex; a distance, perhaps, from a queer scene, subculture and identification; and also a careless masculinity – one that was (unlike Orton) inattentive to body or context.

Orton describes another type of queer man via an anecdote about a pick-up he related to his actor friend Kenneth Williams. The pick-up claimed that rich men could be found in a particular area. 'They're not all effeminate either,' said the man, 'some of them are really manly and you'd never dream that they were queer, not from the look of 'em. But I can tell because they've all got LPs of Judy Garland.'[49] The 'rich' men were definitively queer not so much because of the sex they had but because of the Judy Garland LPs which attached an identity and subcultural identification to their desires. As Margot Finn, Deborah Cohen and (in specific relation to Orton) Richard Hornsey suggest, domestic ephemera took on particular meanings which could then be read back to the inhabitant and/or used as a means of self-creation, affirmation or revelation to others who were 'in the know'.[50]

Orton's domestic observation in relation to these particular queer types was in part about distinguishing himself from them. He and Halliwell were not slovenly in their bedsit like the man in the first example, and if he had Judy Garland LPs he didn't advertise the fact. Despite his general posture of indifference, Orton was acutely conscious of how the domestic spoke of others, of himself and of his relationship with Halliwell. He positioned himself in direct opposition to the aspirational middle-class domestic. He and Halliwell were among the first wave of owner–occupiers who shifted the demographic of Islington in the 1960s, but they (or technically Halliwell since he had the money at this point) bought the bedsit when the area was only just seeing the first seeds of this gentrification.[51] Theirs was, moreover, a set-up not unlike that of many working-class individuals, couples and families nearby (and indeed in the same building). If the bedsit spoke of the couple's queerness after they died, it also figured 'as a symbol of [Orton's] authentic working class roots'.[52] By 1966 Orton was parodying the new influx to Islington. In an interview with the *Daily Sketch* he observed that 'late at night you can hear car doors banging and people singing out "good night darling".'[53] In his diary, meanwhile, he sneered at the suburban Brighton home and family of *Loot* producer Oscar Lewenstein. He also related his attempt to shock the straight American couple at an adjoining table in Morocco by parodying queer and middle-class domestic acquisitiveness and fussiness (in an anecdote underpinned too by a casual racism in relation to the excitability and uncontrollability of Moroccan 'boys'):

> 'We've got a leopard skin rug in the flat and he wanted me to fuck him on that', I said in an undertone which was perfectly audible to the next table, 'only I'm afraid of the spunk, you see, it might adversely affect the spots on the leopard', adding loudly 'he might bite a hole in the rug, and I can't ask him to control his excitement'.[54]

Orton and Halliwell meanwhile pared down the excesses of the apartment they rented in Morocco (the one where Tennessee Williams wrote *Suddenly Last Summer* in 1959).[55] 'We've locked the main salon of the flat,' wrote Orton, 'which is enormous and gives an impression of millionaire elegance. We'll just pretend that the flat consists of the kitchen, bathroom, and two bedrooms.'[56] Amidst the generally middle and upper-middle-class queer ex-patriate milieu, Orton and Halliwell tried to preserve some domestic austerity and so signal a difference from the compatriots they bitchily derided.

Back at home they adopted this approach too. Their bedsit was functional: it had a desk, two chairs, two stools and two single beds. After their deaths a lawyer's letter to Orton's brother detailed the rest:

> Of the articles remaining in the flat it would appear that the most valuable are your brothers typewriter, two student-type table lamps which appear to be new, and a considerable number of gramophone records and books. There is also what appears to be a valuable hi-fi set. Copies of your brothers plays of course will eventually form part of his Estate, and all the paintings in the flat appear to have been collages done by Halliwell. There is a quantity of clothing in the flat including a great coat which Miss Ramsay has suggested you may care to keep. Apparently it was one which she gave to your brother.[57]

The pair did not attempt to create a stylish 'home beautiful' *à la* Wilde and, despite the broader fashion for domestic consumption, they didn't accumulate mod cons either. As consumers, Obelvekich observes, 'men's domain' in this period was 'limited to the car and audio equipment'.[58] Notably, the one expensive item in the flat was the hi-fi, and in this, their otherwise minimal possessions, and their choice of area, we see a reflection and production of Orton's working-class masculine 'swagger'.[59] The single beds preserved them (to an extent) from the conjectures of others, of course, but they also fostered this sense of equal and parallel masculinity and 'matiness'.

'Americans see homosexuality in terms of fag and drag,' Orton wrote in a US production note for *Loot*. 'This isn't my vision of the universal brotherhood. They must be perfectly ordinary boys who happen to be fucking each other. Nothing could be more natural. I won't have the great Great American Queen brought into it.'[60] This idea of brotherhood was more personally usable for Orton than other circulating models of homosexuality during this period. In this Orton was aligning himself with the new homosexual type Matt Houlbrook identifies: he was 'neither a queen nor normal, unequivocally masculine yet exclusively queer'.[61] In framing this form of masculinity the home front was key, though, because of the way home had been ideologically freighted, Orton also had a fine line to tread.

He struggled with what he saw as the feminised roles which could structure queer encounters and relationships. In July 1967, for example, he recounted an argument with Halliwell in his diary: 'I said "are you going to stand in front of the mirror all day?" He said "I've been washing your fucking underpants! That's why I've been at the sink!" He shouted it loudly and I said "Please don't let the whole neighborhood know you're a queen".'[62] Though in his resentment of Halliwell's behaviour he signalled a desire for an alternative domestic model (one they perhaps shared before Orton's success), his discontent sinks back into a familiar misogyny.[63] He was concerned about what Halliwell's 'hysterical' outbursts, vanity and housework might say about him and them both. This had less to do with a fear of exposure, arrest and prosecution (Orton was, after all, cavalier in the face of the law). It was much more about protecting and constructing a particular masculinity, which was also part, for him, of a reconstruction of homosexual style.[64] If, with Orton's rise to fame, Halliwell was more home alone and focused on domestic work, and if (as Orton attests) the couple had largely ceased to have sex, then they were for the playwright no longer 'perfectly normal boys who happen to be fucking each other'.

Orton was similarly defensive about his association with the arts and theatre. 'I mean,' he remarked in an Evening Standard interview, 'there's absolutely no reason why a writer shouldn't be as tough as a brick layer.'[65] Orton certainly had the artistic and cultural references to be part of a (queer) literary and artistic *avant garde* and lineage.[66] His debt to Ronald Furbank, Oscar Wilde and Noel Coward is well documented; John Alderton describes them all figuring in the 'melting pot' of Orton's writing.[67] Orton refused, however, to wear these cultural and implicitly queer pretensions on his sleeve – as Richard Dyer talks about doing as a means of coming out in this period (in an avowed love of opera, for example), and as satirically modelled in Michael Nelson's 1958 novel *A Room in Chelsea Square*.[68] For Orton, behaving in this way would have made him a different sort of queer – one, in fact, he rather despised. In the bedsit there was thus no specially commissioned furniture, none of the latest styles or domestic fashions (aside from the Venetian blinds), no swags of plush velvet, elegant armchairs or carefully embroidered cushions, which, in an unpublished section of the diary, he derisively describes a group of 'queens' working on.[69]

What we do get, though, is a mural collage of cut-outs which Lahr describes as a 'wall of culture' between the couple and 'the mediocre world outside'.[70] It combined those putative markers of queer sensibility – Greek statuary and Renaissance art – but it crucially presented them prosaically. The men did not have a miniature replica statue of a Greek athlete or a carefully positioned and framed reproduction of a Michelangelo. Instead these featured in a mural composed of images torn from library books.[71] It was a promiscuous mingling of 'high' and 'low' art and culture which spread across the walls and dominated the simply furnished room. The mural was excessive and unbounded in a sphere which, wider rhetoric suggested, should be organised and tightly controlled.

Between the bedsit's ordered furnishing and this wild mural, between the artistic references of that mural and the everyday materials used to compile it, Orton and Halliwell marked out their association with but also distance from domestic, artistic and queer cultures. Drawing together these materials in a new formation spoke uniquely of Halliwell (probably the primary mural artist), of Orton, and of their relationship. It was, to use Hornsey, 'an ongoing project [...] a firm and lasting component of [Orton and Halliwell's] domestic life together'.[72] As such, Orton saw the room and the mural as an appropriate frame within which to be viewed. He repeatedly had himself photographed in front of it, including for publicity shots. His nonchalant poses spoke of his working-class masculinity; the mural of his queer difference and also (much more obliquely) of his togetherness with Halliwell.

Peggy Ramsay gave a potted account of the couple's domestic life in a letter to Lahr in 1970. She wrote:

> Kenneth's family left him a little bit of money, which subsidised the two of them in a small room and all day they read the classics aloud to one another, and it was during that time that they studied Firbank and Wilde in such detail. Also, during that time, they wrote very bad novels together [...]. When they began running out of money, they used to work in the daytime and earn their living at night in an ice cream factory in order to save electric light. When Joe sent me *Sloane*, he always spoke of the play as 'we', and after he'd visited me the first time, he always bought Kenneth with him afterwards, and Kenneth always attended rehearsals.[73]

Ramsay (presumably via Orton's own notoriously shifting accounts of his life) described a financially, emotionally and intellectually interdependent couple playing out their relationship in this 'small room'. Orton himself obliquely and romantically described it in *The Ruffian on the Stair* (1963) just after he and Halliwell had been separated for six months during their imprisonment for defacing Islington library books. In the play Wilson and his (now dead) brother 'had a little room'; they were 'happy', 'bosom friends': 'we had separate beds,' he says, 'he was a stickler for convention, but that's as far as it went. We spent every night in each others company. It's the reason we never got any work done.' 'I'm going round the twist with heartbreak,' Wilson adds poignantly on his brother's death.[74] Such intensity, though, was perhaps unsustainable; Orton wrote of his relationship with Halliwell in 1967: 'I think it's bad that we live in each other's pockets 24 hours a day and 365 days a year.'[75]

The bedsit was the near-exclusive setting for Orton and Halliwell's relationship, and ironically in this home-based companionate coupledom they keyed into wider post-war expectations of what intimate relationships should be like.[76] Such a formation went to the heart of modern subjectivity.[77] As I've observed, though, Orton and Halliwell's version of home and coupledom was too undiluted. Their privacy and protection of the home space exceeded that of Schofield's middle-class homosexual couple, whose domestic privacy was normalised through visits from friends and so a (carefully regulated) intersection with the world. Orton and Halliwell's domestic closure, meanwhile, became part of their queer oddity. The gap between the pair's particular set-up on the one hand, and expectations of what a (conventional) home and couple might be on the other, made the relationship difficult to judge, or perhaps easier to dismiss as neurotic, or unloving, or as only those things. After they died Ramsay was highly sensitive to what she saw as the misrepresentation of the partnership. In a letter about Lahr's dramatisation of the diary (A *Diary of Somebody*, 1987), she observed: 'they loved each other. There is no love in the play. I mean the kindliness of affection, the comradery of all their years together, and the fun they had.'[78] The manner of their deaths, and their being *just* too distant from convention at home and in their conduct, made their relationship difficult to read.

### Families of choice

Having read the diaries, Orton's sister, Leonie, poignantly observed the different kind of home and family her brother had constructed in London. She wrote to Ramsay: 'I realise we were nothing to Joe. You and Kenneth were all the family he acknowledged. His natural family were just an embarrassment to him. I think I've always been aware of this but never admitted it before.'[79]

Embedded in Leonie's account is the familiar story I alluded to earlier, of the queer son and brother who leaves his family and reinvents himself through new affective bonds in a new city. Perhaps, though, it was not so clear-cut. Orton sought to sustain a connection with his birth family, and clearly saw these connections as significant, if certainly at one remove from his London life and lifestyle. Leonie Orton observed later to Orton's biographer John Lahr that her brother used to write to his mother, but she never wrote back; 'he kept writing and nobody answered.'[80] Joe also returned home (his use of the word) for two weeks every summer, and Ramsay described to Leonie how 'warmly' he talked of her.[81] What emerges – as for many of the interviewees in Jeffrey Weeks, Brian Heaphy and Catherine Donovan's 'families of choice' project in the late 1990s – is not a simple 'either'/'or', but more of a 'this' *and* 'this'.[82] Orton's new attachments in London did not function to the complete exclusion of his relations in Leicester.

This emerges in the plays too. Orton stays close to home and family in terms of theme and setting, but toys with different structures of loyalty and emotional and sexual connection. Thus in *The Ruffian on the Stair* (1963) we get the cohabiting brothers/lovers; more farcically in *Entertaining Mr Sloane* (1964) we have the eponymous hero entering a time-sharing arrangement with Kath and Ed, and the baby to come. Sloane veers between the roles of lover, son and, beyond the end of the play, father. In *The Good and Faithful Servant* (1965), Ray – another parentless young man – is told by his grandmother that things would have been easier 'if [his] fathers were alive'. Seeking an explanation for the plural, she explains: 'Your mother was a generous woman and your fathers – though one of them must surely have been your uncle – loved her dearly. You were the result.'[83]

As Gardner and Nakayama suggest, in these configurations Orton refused to respect the sanctity of the 1950s family.[84] He infused the domestic matrix with sex and desire (in line with the growing influence of Freudian theory),[85] whilst also casting doubt on the efficacy of the family as social building block (resonating in this respect with R.D. Laing and the 1960s' anti-psychiatry movement).[86] Through what Edmund White calls 'a knack of dialogue collage', Orton drew together 'the elegant, the crude and the ridiculous'[87] to de-sentimentalise family life in his plays. But, rather than creating 'alternative communities' (as Gardner terms them),[88] he played with an existing language, structure and set of relationships to create scenarios that were contingent and pragmatic. He did not articulate a clearly differentiated set of domestic and familial values. The subversiveness of Orton's work lay not in the end result and the formation of a coherent alternative, but rather in the suggestion that home and family were entities which were not fixed but which could shift shape. It was a lesson learned from the necessarily improvised intimacies of queer life in this period and the contexts in which they were acted out.

## Bricolage

In *The Wilde Century* (1994), Alan Sinfield's landmark exploration of effeminacy, Lévi Strauss's notion of *bricolage* is marshalled as a way of analysing the 'new situations' in which men having sex with other men in the nineteenth century found themselves. Sinfield and also Neil Bartlett show how Wilde and other late nineteenth-century queer men forged cultural space for themselves by piecing together in new resonant formations existing places and styles, unevenly drawing together (in Stuart Hall's words) 'the fragments of more ordered or stable meaning systems'.[89] Existing ideas and ideologies were not so much opposed as reworked and repositioned so that they could make sense of themselves and their sexual and emotional relations in a culture which had become newly preoccupied with – and censorious of – male–male sex.[90] Christopher Reed shows how Duncan Grant and Vanessa Bell did something similar through the domestic murals they executed for themselves and their Bloomsbury associates in the 1910s and 1920s.[91] Later in the 1980s Derek Jarman delighted in anachronistically pulling together domineering cultural fragments in his writing, film, art and garden to forge something which might support, sustain and provide a critical and radical language in an especially hostile decade.[92] In all this work we see skewed investments in domineering and hegemonic ideologies, and, touching the growing interest in the contingent amongst historians of sexuality and masculinity,[93] also some of the pragmatic ways in which these men negotiated them in their everyday lives and in their artistry.

Keeping Lévi Strauss, Sinfield, Bartlett, Hall, Grant and Jarman in mind as we explore Orton and the 1950s and 1960s allows us to look beyond the simplistic homo/hetero binary and the accompanying dyads of domestic to non-domestic and family to non-family. They allow us to imagine the relationship of queer men to home and family in rather messier ways than being 'in' or 'out' of them; queer men were differently and contingently invested in these things. We see more clearly, too, that sexual practice and identity were not necessarily the prime determinants of gender identity (as Philip Carter has argued in relation to the early modern period),[94] and that intersecting domestic, class, urban and youth cultures might (amongst much else) have shaped ways of 'being a man'. Approaching the period in this way does not, of course, make Orton's lifestyle any more compatible with a putative domestic norm or with Wolfenden's vision – or, for that matter, any more legal under the 1967 Sexual Offences Act had he and Halliwell lived. But it does allow us to complicate our accounts of queer lives and to draw domestic spaces and affective and familial bonds more fully into the analysis. We also gain more of an insight into some of the strategies queer men used to work round (and through) prevailing rhetorics and restrictions.

With Orton, the preoccupation with home and family in the plays; the elaborate mural; the orderly bedsit; the working-class but gentrifying area; and the intense domestic brotherly relationship bring us up against the youth, class, homosexual, artistic, domestic and familial ideas, ideals and cultures within which he was shaped and through which he shaped himself. Threading through this complex fabric were varying overlapping and conflicting masculinities which reconnect us repeatedly to home as a space and idea. Home, we find, was pivotal in articulations, experiences and understandings of the gendered and sexual self, and was also crucial to the ways in which ideas about masculinity circulated culturally and were modulated by individuals.

\* \* \*

When Osborne described Orton's 'prick-proud severed body' he conjured an aspect of the playwright's masculinity and then promptly and figuratively negated – it's tempting to say castrated – it. Other reviews of the diaries gratuitously suggested that, had Orton not been murdered by Halliwell, he would surely have become an early 'victim' of the AIDS pandemic.[95] There is almost an excitement at the devastation Orton supposedly wreaked – or would have wreaked – on himself and his body as a result of his sexual lifestyle and identity. This kind of man was a threat at both historical moments. In the 1950s and early 1960s he hardly fitted into the prevailing gendered (homo)sexual typology of the restrained middle-class homosexual or the camp effeminate; by the 1980s, had he lived, he would have gained pariah status for (the reviewers assume) spreading and succumbing to the HIV virus whilst maintaining a mode of masculine comportment which did not immediately signal his queerness. On both counts, Orton is envisioned as an outsider, one who would, in Osborne's account, have been amused and bemused by the 'loony left' attempt to enfold gay men into the culturally central realms of home and family. What I have argued in this chapter, however, is that Orton's outsider and oppositional status was and is not so clear-cut. The way he negotiated the intersecting ideologies of home, homosexuality and masculinity indicate investments, refusals and reconfigurations of domineering cultural stories. Such stories and discourses, in this analysis, retain their power, but their localised effects are – crucially – uneven and contingent.

## Notes

1. John Osborne, 'The diary of a somebody', in *The Spectator* (29 November 1986), p. 3. For further discussion of Osborne's comments in relation to John Lahr's editing of Orton's diaries, see Matt Cook, 'Orton in the archives', *History Workshop Journal* 66 (2008), 163–80.

2. Osborne, p. 3.
3. John Tosh, *A Man's Place: Masculinity and the Middle-class Home in Victorian England* (New Haven, 1999).
4. Eve Kosofsky Sedgwick, *The Epistemology of the Closet* (Berkeley, 1990).
5. Deborah Cohen, *Household Gods: The British and their Possessions* (New Haven, 2006).
6. For more on this shift in queer identity, see especially Matt Houlbrook, *Queer London: Pleasures and Perils in the Sexual Metropolis 1918 – 1957* (Chicago, 2005).
7. Sharon Marcus, 'At home with the other Victorians', in *South Atlantic Quarterly*, 108 (2009), 120–45, 139; Matt Cook, 'Queer domesticities', in Chiara Briganti and Kathy Mezei (eds), *The Domestic Space Reader* (Toronto, 2010).
8. Randall S. Nakayama, 'Domesticating Mr Orton', *Theatre Journal* 45 (1993), 185–196, 194.
9. For a brief account of the debate on this tension amongst historians of masculinity, see Karen Harvey, 'The history of masculinity, c. 1650 – 1800', *Journal of British Studies* 44 (2005), 296–311; Karen Harvey and Alexandra Shepard, 'What have historians done with masculinity? reflections on five centuries of British history, c. 1500 – 1950', *Journal of British History* 44 (2005), 274–80.
10. James Obelkevich, 'Consumption', in James Obelkevich and Peter Caterall (eds), *Understanding Postwar British Society* (London, 1994), p. 144.
11. Chris Harris, 'The family in post-war Britain', in Obelkevich, *Understanding*, p. 48.
12. Jonathan Dollimore, 'The challenge of sexuality', in Alan Sinfield (ed.), *Society and Literature 1945 – 1970* (London, 1983), pp. 60–1. See also Lesley A. Hall, *Sex, Gender and Social Life in Britain Since 1880* (London, 2000), ch. 9.
13. Obelkevich, 'Consumerism', p. 141. See also Alistair Davies and Peter Saunders, 'Literature, Politics and Society', in Sinfield, *Society*, p. 21.
14. Houlbrook, *Queer*, p. 192.
15. For the significance of 'home' in the formation of the Victorian middle class, see especially George K. Behlmer, *Friends of the Family: the English Home and its Guardians, 1850 – 1940* (Stanford, 1998); Catherine Hall and Leonora Davidoff, *Family Fortunes: Men and Women of the English Middle Class, 1780 – 1850* (London, 1988); and Tosh, *A Man's Place*.
16. On this point see Peter J. Kalliney, *Cities of Affluence and Anger: A Literary Geography of Modern Englishness* (Charlottesville, 2006), p. 122.
17. Simon Shepherd, *Because We're Queers: The Life and Crimes of Kenneth Halliwell and Joe Orton* (London, 1989), p. 137.
18. On this point see Matt Cook, *A Gay History of Britain: Love and Sex between Men since the Middle Ages* (Oxford, 2007), pp. 167–71. See also Patrick Higgins, *Heterosexual Dictatorship: Male Homosexuality in Postwar Britain* (London, 1996).
19. *The Times*, 28 July 1967.
20. Dollimore, 'Challenge', p. 76.
21. Carolyn Steedman, *Landscape for a Good Woman: A Story of Two Lives* (London, 1986). See also Penny Summerfield, 'Women in Britain since 1945: companionate marriage and the double burden', in Obelkevich, *Understanding*; Houlbrook, *Queer*, ch. 7; Cook, *Gay*, pp. 159–60.
22. On this point see Janet E. Gardner, 'A normal family: alternative communities in the plays of Joe Orton and Caryl Churchill', in Francesca Coppa (ed.), *Joe Orton: A Casebook* (New York, 2003), p. 79.
23. Cited in Houlbrook, *Queer*, p. 110.

24. Cook, 'Queer Domesticities'.
25. Kath Weston, *Families We Choose: Lesbians, Gays, Kinship* (New York, 1991), p. 22; see also Matt Cook, ' "Families of choice"? George Ives, queer lives and the family', *Gender and History* 22 (2010), 1–20.
26. On the interiors of Wilde and his circle see, for example, Ed Cohen, *Talk on the Wilde Side: Towards a Genealogy of a Discourse on Male Sexualities* (London, 1993), p. 180; Matt Cook, *London and the Culture of Homosexuality, 1885 – 1914* (Cambridge, 2003), ch. 4; Neil Bartlett, *Who Was That Man?: A Present for Mr Oscar Wilde* (London, 1988). On the Bloomsbury group see Christopher Reed, *Bloomsbury Rooms: Modernism, Subculture and Domesticity* (New Haven, 2004).
27. Richard Hornsey, *The Spiv and the Architect: Unruly Life in Postwar London* (Minneapolis, 2010), pp. 208–10.
28. Rodney Garland, *The Heart in Exile* (1953; Brighton, 1995), p. 47. For more detailed analysis of these domestic interiors and the 'type' of homosexual they portend, see Hornsey, *The Spiv*, p. 206; and also Matt Houlbrook and Chris Waters, '*The Heart in Exile*: Detachment and Desire in 1950s London', *History Workshop Journal* 62 (2006), 142–66.
29. *Oscar Wilde*, starring Robert Morley, and *The Trials of Oscar Wilde*, starring Peter Finch.
30. Gordon Westwood (pseud. Michael Schofield), *Society and the Homosexual* (London, 1952), p. 132.
31. Liz Stanley, *Sex Surveyed, 1949 – 1994: from Mass Observation's Little Kinsey to the National Surveys and the Hite Report* (London, 1995), pp. 199–203.
32. Schofield, *Society*, pp. 139–40.
33. John Lahr, *Prick Up Your Ears: The Biography of Joe Orton* (Harmondsworth, 1978); Shepherd, *Because*.
34. For 1950s analysis of the 'homosexual problem' in Britain see, for example, J.T. Rees and H.V. Usill (eds), *They Stand Apart: A Critical Survey of the Problem of Homosexuality* (London, 1955); Gordon Westwood, *A Minority: A Report on the Life of the Male Homosexual in Great Britain* (London, 1960).
35. George Kateb, 'Exile, alienation and estrangement', *Social Research* 58 (1991), 138.
36. On this point see Alan Trachtenberg, 'Home as place and center for private and family life', *Social Research* 58 (1991), 211.
37. Though Nakayama claims that 'in a room that was 16 × 12' there could be 'no subterfuge' that they were 'just room mates', in the strained and expensive post-war housing market such 'room mate' arrangements were in fact relatively common. Nakayama, 'Domesticating'. See also Hornsey, *The Spiv*, pp. 244–45.
38. Colin MacInnes was writing in *Encounter*, 21 (August 1963). Cited by Dollimore, 'Challenge', p. 78.
39. On this point see also David Van Leer, 'Saint Joe: Orton as Homosexual Rebel', in Coppa, *Joe Orton*, p. 112.
40. Joe Orton, 'Diary' (19 June 1951), Leicester University Library (hereafter LU), Joe Orton papers, ms 237/21/1. I am grateful to the Orton estate for permission to quote from the archive.
41. Cook, 'Orton', p. 166.
42. Van Leer rightly criticises Lahr for failing to position the interviewees in this way: Orton and Halliwell's deaths necessarily coloured their memories. See Van Leer, 'Saint Joe'.
43. See Cook, *Gay*, pp. 150–58; for an autobiographical account of the Soho scene in the 60s see Peter Burton, *Parallel Lives* (London, 1985), esp. p. 45.
44. Marcus, 'At Home'.

45. On this point see Cook, *London*, ch. 2; and Robert A. Nye, 'Kinship, male bonds and masculinity in comparative perspective', *American Historical Review* (2000), 1656–66.
46. Interview with Rex, 23 March 2009; see also Rex Batten, *Rid England of this Plague* (London, 2007).
47. Interview with Michael, 1 July 2007.
48. John Lahr (ed.), *The Orton Diaries* (London, 1986), 30 December 1967, p. 45.
49. Kenneth Williams, *The Kenneth Williams Diaries*, cited in Alan Sinfield, 'Is there a queer tradition and is Orton in it?', in Coppa, *Joe Orton*, p. 91.
50. See Margot Finn, 'Men's things: masculine possession in the consumer revolution', *Social History* 25 (2000), 133–55; Cohen, *Domestic Gods*; Hornsey, *The Spiv*.
51. See Jerry White, *London in the Twentieth Century* (London, 2002), pp. 63–4. On the national rise in home ownership in the 1950s see Obelkevich, 'Consumption', p. 144.
52. Hornsey, *The Spiv*, p. 244.
53. Cited in Shepherd, *Because*, p. 85.
54. Lahr, *Orton Diaries*, 25 May 1967, p. 187.
55. *Suddenly Last Summer* features desirable but ultimately uncontrollable and cannibalistic Sicilian 'natives', signalling, alongside Orton, particular racialised structures of homoerotic desire which also relate to levels of investment or disinvestment in northern European conceptions of home and the domestic.
56. Lahr, *Orton Diaries*, 8 May 1967, p. 159.
57. Laurence Harbottle to Douglas Orton, 16 August 1967, British Library (hereafter BL), Deposit 9635: Peggy Ramsay papers, b.37, f.13. I am grateful to the trustees of Peggy Ramsay Foundation for permission to quote from this archive.
58. Obelkevich, 'Consumption', p. 149.
59. Coppa, 'Introduction', in Coppa (ed.), *Joe Orton*, p. 4.
60. Lahr, *Prick*, p. 248.
61. Houlbrook, *Queer*, p. 193. See also Houlbrook and Waters, *The Heart in Exile*.
62. Lahr, *Orton Diaries*, 17 July 1967, p. 243.
63. Shepherd, *Because*, p. 130.
64. On this point see Van Leer, 'Saint Joe', p. 116.
65. Lahr, *Prick*, p. 152.
66. For an incisive discussion of Orton's relationship to the queer theatrical tradition, see Sinfield, 'Is There a Queer Tradition'.
67. See Simon Shepherd, 'A colored girl reading proust', in Coppa, *Joe Orton*; and 'A Conversation with John Alderton and Leonie Orton', in Coppa, *Joe Orton*, p. 157.
68. Richard Dyer, *The Culture of Queers* (London, 2002), p. 16.
69. Orton, 'Diary', 30 April 1967, Howard Gotlieb Archival Center at Boston University (hereafter BU), John Lahr Collection. For discussion of the status of the diary held at BU, and for citation and discussion of this particular section, see Cook, 'Orton', p. 174.
70. Lahr, *Prick*, p. 138.
71. Around 1,653 of them, according to Islington library. Maurice Charney, *Joe Orton* (London, 1984), p. 7.
72. Hornsey, *The Spiv*, p. 242.
73. Peggy Ramsay to John Lahr, 29 May 1970, Peggy Ramsay collection, deposit 9635, b.37, f.17.
74. Joe Orton, 'The ruffian on the stair', in John Lahr (ed.), *Orton: The Complete Plays* (London, 1976), pp. 49–50.
75. Lahr, *Orton Diaries*, 30 April 1967, p. 146.

76. Summerfield, 'Women in Britain'.
77. Tamara Hareven, 'The home and the family in historical perspective', *Social Research* 58 (1991), p. 258.
78. Ramsay to Dan Crawford, 12 May 1987, BL Deposit 9635, b.37, f.17.
79. Leonie Orton to Peggy Ramsay, 19 October 1986, BL Deposit 9635, box 37, f.13.
80. Lahr, *Prick*, p. 88.
81. Ramsay to Leonie Orton, 22 October 1986, BL Deposit 9635, b.37, f.13.
82. Jeffrey Weeks, Brian Heaphy and Catherine Donovan, *Same-Sex Intimacies: Families of Choice and Other Life Experiments* (London, 2001). On the need for flexible understandings of kinship in our approach to the past, see Nye, 'Kinship', p. 1658.
83. Joe Orton, 'The good and faithful servant', *Complete Plays*, pp. 166–67.
84. Gardner, 'A normal family'.
85. Dollimore, 'The challenge of sexuality', p. 64. See also Chris Waters, 'Havelock Ellis, Sigmund Freud and the state: discourses of homosexuality in interwar Britain', in Lucy Bland and Laura Doan (eds), *Sexology in Culture: Labelling Bodies and Desires* (Cambridge, 1998).
86. Dollimore, 'The challenge of sexuality', p. 61; and Dollimore, 'Orton's black camp', in Coppa, *Joe Orton*, p. 97.
87. Edmund White, 'The importance of being Joe', *Sunday Times*, 23 November 1986.
88. Gardner, 'Normal', p. 76. See also Randall Nakayama, 'Sensation and sensibility: Joe Orton's diaries', in Coppa; and Nakayama, 'Domesticating'.
89. Alan Sinfield, *The Wilde Century: Effeminacy, Oscar Wilde, and the Queer Movement* (London, 1994), p. 11. Sinfield cites Stuart Hall from 'Deviance, politics and the media', in Paul Rock and Mary McIntosh (eds), *Deviance and Social Control* (London, 1974), p. 293.
90. Bartlett, *Who Was That Man*.
91. Reed, *Bloomsbury*.
92. See Matt Cook, 'Wilde Lives'.
93. See especially: on the early modern period, Anthony Fletcher, 'Men's Dilemma: the Future of Patriarchy in England, 1560 – 1660', *Transactions of the Royal Historical Society* 4 (1994), 61–81, and Helen Berry, 'Scrutinising men: current trends in the history of British masculinity, 1600 – 1800', *History Workshop Journal* 52 (2001), 283–86; on the late Victorians: Seth Koven, *Slumming: Sexual and Social Politics in Victorian London* (Princeton, 2004); on the post-war period in France: Julian Jackson, 'Sex, politics and morality in France', *History Workshop Journal* 61 (2006), 77–102.
94. Philip Carter, *Men and the Emergence of Polite Society, Britain 1660 – 1800* (London, 2000).
95. See, for example, Jonathan Meades, 'The fully formed artist', in *The Tatler*, November 1986, 15.

# 16
## Three Faces of Fatherhood As a Masculine Category: Tyrants, Teachers, and Workaholics As 'Responsible Family Men' during Canada's Baby Boom

*Robert Rutherdale*

How useful 'masculinity' is as a category of experience and identity is a question that has been pursued by growing numbers of historians for over a generation. Initially, scholars raised it as part of the debate that took place during transitions from women's to gender history. More recently, historians of masculin*ities* – approaching the category consciously and explicitly in the plural – have applied it in their studies of boys and men *as* history rather than simply *in* history: as children and youths, as bachelors or married subjects, as heterosexual, gay or, more recently in some work, transsexual subjects, as studies of particular masculinities in past evidence drawn from public and private lives on varied historical sites. Since gendered categories are created by history, rather than as reified objects detached from the past, any making of masculinities – fatherhood included – can refer to how becoming and being masculine appeared in diverse forms only in intersection with others across time. And, as several contributions to this volume reveal in compelling detail, varied fatherhoods as an expression of changing masculinities in given places and periods produced highly revealing and still largely unexplored social histories, located on the shifting boundaries that divided public and private domains.

Joanne Bailey's perceptive examination of the emergent ideal of the 'sentimental' English father in the second half of the seventeenth century considers a category of masculine parenting in which the traditional domains for fathers as procreators, providers, protectors and educators were tempered by a more refined masculine sensibility. New signs appeared in art and literature of intimate relations marked more by a 'tender, loving engagement with children' than older models of the patriarchal father allowed. The rising importance of the domestic realm expanded the scope of fatherhood, but did not diminish the investment in public duties, roles and legally sanctioned privileges fathers pursued or enjoyed. Nancy Christie's evocative work on fatherhood and religious practice in Protestant Upper Canada in the Victorian era challenges assumptions that fathers played only minor roles compared with their spouses – at home in the domestic sphere – fostering societal prescriptions of faith rooted in their denominations, congregations and churches. Indeed, it was also and to a hitherto overlooked extent, Christie argues, through their private rituals in family faith observances that fathers found considerable scope for leading their families in their respective faith traditions that connected home life to wider communities.

The varieties of traditional and new forms of fatherly practices expressed on both sides of the Atlantic from the colonial to the modern periods continued to give rise to evidence that historians of masculinities are actively investigating at present – using new models or expressions of this category – to better understand what it meant to be a family man, a father whose masculinity was invested in the shifting regimes of gender and family life in which private and public relationships overlapped. The father figure, fatherly signs and practices, and fatherhood itself as a category of historical experience are undergoing fresh reconsiderations. In addition, as Heather Ellis argues through her critical examination in this volume of maturing men at Oxford University in the early nineteenth century, historians need to address the relationship between age and masculinity: manhood and maturity as historical constructs are rooted in shifting histories of masculinity as a category of experience and practice.

Fatherhood is a key, indeed ideal, site to consider this. In his review of recent work, John Tosh affirms with inspiring insight that fatherhood continues to offer a remarkably fruitful and yet comparatively untapped field of inquiry. The evidence of experience in particular, Tosh recommends, needs to be more actively pursued in ongoing and future work; and this is the approach which I have taken to oral history and life writing in my own efforts to assess postwar Canada in the baby boom period. As a masculine category, fatherhood has been experienced as intrinsically relational to other kinship ties and historical forces inside and beyond the home. Its complex and multiple roles are located, and thus help historians locate, a considerable array of gendered histories in relational contexts. What responses to sexual differences among family members, one might, for instance, ask, have shaped histories of fatherhood history in periods of economic changes such as the conversion after 1945 from wartime to consumer-based production? The search for combined elements in the making of masculinities is central to a keener understanding of how masculine positions – including those of fathers – have originated and functioned.

My work on family manhood in English-speaking Canada in the 1945 to 1975 period – a specific masculinity – sees fathers as gendered beings as a consequence of how their own life stories took shape through formative influences that mark their classed, ethnic and generational life paths. How their biographies intersect with the periods and places they were rooted in as they grew up, matured and became fathers concerns me more than simply drawing isolated examples of fatherhood practices from diverse source material. Oral history and autobiographical life writing can serve as particularly revealing sources for this. From intimate family relations to their public roles in work and local community-based leisure, fathers' varied masculinities emerge in identifiable categories – as 'faces of fatherhoods' – but only as outcomes of their parenthood that were relationally constructed over the life course. Fathers exercised their responsibilities through a variety of potential behaviours connected to their basic functions of provider and parent. Fatherhood's many potential *faces*, as John Demos suggested shortly before work on the subject began its fruitful escalation, are a useful way to conceptualise and categorise their masculinity as family men.[1] Below, I consider fathers in this period as tyrants, as teachers and as workaholics: again, faces of fatherhood that appear as intersecting outcomes evident in the life stories of fathers, in the cases below, as part of a generation of fatherhood in English Canada.

That the many gendered faces of fatherhood, as providers, nurturers, guides and models of manhood for their children, negative and positive, cannot be seen as outcomes entirely of their own making may seem obvious. But I raise this, in part, because this was something surprisingly absent from the teller's perspectives in many of the life stories I collected in my oral historical fieldwork.[2] Conceptually, my approach explicitly attempts to focus on connections evident between the autobiographical elements of a life story and the broader social forces, situations and relationships within which interview subjects invariably attempt to place themselves: 'At the heart of what is social in oral history,' as Samuel Schrager has expressed it, 'is the symbolic quality at the boundaries of actions and characters, of the "I" that stands for the one doing the speaking and the "we" that designates the speaker's membership in groups.'[3] Family men look back to their life and times as fathers both as individuals *and* as part of a generation, as providers and parents *and* as agents in history. 'Experience,' Schrager continues, 'is pulled toward the universal and grounded by the particular: it is mythic and historical at once.'[4]

To cite a recurring masculinity in the gendered texts of memory, I refer here to the myth of the 'self-made' man. This narrative figment emerged repeatedly in my interviews when the fathers who raised children in the post-war decades (all grandfathers and some great-grandfathers today) also spoke of their individual roads to self-sufficiency – how they 'made it' after the Second World War. In many ways, of course, many did 'succeed' as consistent providers, as reliable parents and as active citizens in the wider society. As John Tosh points out in his influential earlier work, it is in the home, at work and in relations to other men that fathers have made their appearances in history.[5] Their masculinities as fathers, again, are relational. But, using life stories, what *types* of fatherhood, what categories of specific masculinities, emerged during the baby boom years? My concern is with how anglophone Canadian men, either Canadian-born or newcomers, who grew up in the late 1920s and 1930s and matured during the war years, constructed their fatherhoods in the era that followed – of the baby boom, of the Cold War ethos, of increased consumerism, of contexts rarely rehearsed with any broad force in the preceding interwar and wartime periods. My focus here is on fathers' relationships with their children during this period, an era of the so-called 'generation gap' of the 1960s. What connections can be drawn between masculinity, fatherhood and responsible manhood? Within their family relations, how did fathers express their masculinity as their children grew up in the 1950s and matured themselves in the 1960s and early 1970s?

We should begin by noting that masculinity and fatherhood both were often seen in the 1950s, as the baby boom intensified, as entering a period of crisis.[6] As James Gilbert points out in reference to this salient masculinity panic that spilled back and forth across the Canada–US border in the 1950s, economic, bureaucratic and institutional forces were blamed for eroding the 'traditionally' assertive, 'self-directed' masculinities of men in 'former times'. These, too, were little more than mythical figments. Within this new mid-century discourse, personnel departments in large corporations, along with mass culture, suburbanisation and consumerism, were often blamed for the crises men were to have faced as authentic beings. So were the popular middle-class prescriptions for family 'togetherness', along with the tranquillising 'good citizenship' and 'group dynamics' men were said to be encouraged to foster in their own behaviours. In the course of developing such narratives, women became a primary target. The 'increasing feminization of culture', Gilbert notes, as a part of post-war normalisation was said to be threatening modern men *as men*, as essentialised masculine beings.[7] As part of a broader masculinity crisis, family men – with fathers in the middle at mid-century – were said to be losing their paternal authority, undergoing extreme instabilities despite the obvious signs of material progress. They were no longer 'heads' of their own households.

## Masculinity crisis?

The 'masculinity crisis' at mid-century that became prominent in a series of popular texts during the 1950s can, in fact, be seen as part of a recurring mythology of the 'lost man' in modern times, a prominent figure in literature since the late Victorian period, in the First World War's lost generation, and in both fiction and memoirs drawn from the Great Depression. The end of the Second World War and the beginning of the Cold War, by the early 1950s, soon ushered in the new archetype: the endangered 'modern man'. This figure faced the crisis of traditional masculine virtue giving way to the emasculating, even effeminising forces of 'other-directed' imperatives in work and home life.

This caricature is, of course, hardly unique to Canada. Fathers as masculine beings across the industrial democracies, often conceived as 'mass society', were seen as losing their autonomy and manful agency. At stake was the question of how masculinity could be preserved in the face of post-war modernity. The authenticity of the existential 'man', popular commentators opined, inspired by a new sociological discourse, was entering a crisis caused, not alleviated, by modern life.[8] Were men, including fathers, trapped in the rat race – were they, collectively, in crisis?

The repeated framing and reframing of the new instability in masculine culture in glossy magazine articles, in radio commentaries, and even in certain aspects of the new sitcom television shows broadcast in both Canada and the United States by the early 1950s, reflected primarily White, middle-class orientations, perceptions and moral panics. Many commentators, and a new army of professional experts, feared that such men, family men among them, had lost their completeness as assertive, masculine beings. Apart from the much more varied historical realities mature men were actually experiencing across class and ethnic lines, such diagnoses for 'modern men' as a whole echoed across a considerable array of representations, from psychological journals to magazine articles, from novels to Hollywood films.[9] Sociological works like William H. Whyte's *Organizational Man* (1956) or relevant portions of David Reisman and his collaborator's compelling treatise of 1950, *The Lonely Crowd*, became best-sellers. They reflected anxieties in the popular media over manhood and modernity.[10] Fathers, it seemed, increasingly faced uncertain futures as breadwinners, as parents and as husbands. This new discourse tended to reify fatherhood as an alienated, subjugated category within complex social systems. Moreover, the much-debated Canadian-based study, *Crestwood Heights*, addressed similar themes when it considered the place of family men, somehow lost between home, work and their everyday selves – emasculated fathers, grown estranged from their inner resources as they confronted the constraints of post-war 'opportunity'. Life, so the archetypes of men in crisis appeared, had become routinised and empty: work, home, ambivalent family contact, and back to work again.

At one point, *Crestwood*'s authors go as far as to bemoan a diminished patriarchy in the post-war family of the 1950s. Fathers stripped of traditional powers remained responsible for more than they could handle: 'Even though the patriarchal powers once associated with his role have dissipated, the father still stands as the symbolic head of the family.' The upshot, as the authors saw it in historical perspective, was that the 'father now seems to have more responsibility within the home, but without commensurate authority.' In 'previous decades', they generalise, without reference to historical evidence, fathers enjoyed a greater degree of separation between 'occupation and home'.[11] A Toronto *Star Weekly* article of 1951 declared in this vein that 'father is no longer the head of the family.' He could not fit in because he no longer had a 'proper place', as post-war life and patriarchal ideals seemed suddenly at odds. Its author, R.S. Hosking, blamed wives, and offered simplified, distracted images of wrong-headed companionate marital relationships he sensed emerging. 'What's the Matter With Father?' Hosking asked, in pointing his finger at wives who no longer knew 'their place': 'Already we have a good idea of what we're up against – the changing role of woman in society. This has naturally done more than anything else to affect the status of man – which was never lower than present.'[12] Variants on this theme might locate the lost man within prescriptive advice to wives to 'help' their husbands be better parents, especially better infant caregivers. 'What comes naturally to you as a mother does not come naturally to him as a father,' as Lila Chapman put in the *Christian Home*, published by the United Church of Canada.[13]

Fathers seemed trapped by this conundrum. They did not fit in at home, so what about work? Would they not be, again, lost to their families within their expanding roles as providers as the economy grew? What if they ignored their family's emotional needs in search of the almighty dollar? By the end of the 1950s, increased discretionary incomes and domestic consumption patterns underpinned a revival of the discourse of the Lost Man – the father without a purpose beyond breadwinning: 'At fifty-five,' as this same Christian family journal put it, 'Sam is a bitter, unhappy man. His good job does little for him because it is only a job to earn money. His friends are limited because he has used friends for his own advancement and suspects them of like motives. His employees are acutely aware of his disdain for them because they were halted on the ladder of success. But most tragic of all, his family seems cruelly ungrateful for all the unsolicited wealth he has given them. One by one they have become aware of the emptiness of their life with him. Now at fifty-five he has found a partial solution, tragic as it is. He has found the oblivion of alcohol if not inner peace.'[14]

My research points in different directions. Some lost family men can indeed be found, but not within a crisis of masculinity. Family men appeared in my oral histories and life writing to be raising children as they themselves matured, though they seldom admitted or perceived changes in their fundamental self-concepts. What they did try to exercise, successfully or not, was masculine power and control as male parents attempting to achieve 'responsible family manhood', a social category of masculinity that recognises a father's formal powers defined by both the state and social sanction. Informally, and in the flow of daily life, it can often leave open the question of how responsible fatherhood is exercised. Wielding power and control over one's offspring or child dependents can mean many things.

## Father as tyrant

Tyrannical fatherhood is approached here as a parenting practice that reflects a boldly assertive, sometimes cruel, masculinity. While sons and daughters may resist this model as they grow up, negotiation is displaced by the imperative that children follow a tightly controlled, overtly patriarchal 'father-rule' script in the stories of fatherhood that emerge. Sons and daughters and other children under their care must conform to the father's demands.

The first two examples here come from contexts that may appear unusual at first for discovering the tyrannical fatherhood masculinity. Across Canada during the baby boom period, from the late 1940s to the mid-1960s, fathers increasingly were called upon to serve their local communities as parents who helped guide the recreation of their own children and their peers, particularly in growing towns and cities where rapid family formation rates produced a high demand for male volunteers. While few fathers in such settings emerged as full-blown tyrants, this could be a site of such encounters, especially when the strain of parenting one's own children and those of others came into potential conflict. Coaching and scouting leadership roles could introduce this in terms of fathering sons and their teammates and fellow scouts. Fathers *in loco parentis* often found themselves transmitting principles observed at home to groups of boys drawn from local communities, and a pattern of fatherhood in the home might spill over to the type of father that appeared in the public hockey rink, scout hall, or other venue of children and youth recreation. Such sites could even heighten the tyrannical face of fatherhood.

In Prince George, Roy Gibson remembered his community service most distinctly this way as a Scoutmaster. His leadership philosophy seemed influenced by a Depression-scarred childhood. Both as a father and a Scoutmaster, Gibson felt that self-reliance, more than anything, had to be instilled in boys. He remembered hoping that his hard lessons might serve as their best example. 'You were in a corral,' he said of his childhood, 'and within that corral certain things had to be done and that was all there was to it. Whether you liked it or not, you did it. Now that's – my years with the Scouting movement – this is what I put across to the boys.'

His three sons all joined Scouts. He claimed to show no favouritism, but more significantly he suggested close parallels between the values he espoused as a parent and those upheld as a Scoutmaster. When asked in a general way what good fatherhood was all about, Gibson replied: 'teaching the kids to paddle their own canoe...If you can't take care of yourself nobody else is going to. And yet, they're teaching in the schools, and this I found very difficult to counter in Scouting – I was teaching one set of values and they would see another set. And they couldn't make up their minds as to who was right. And it was the older group of boys, basically after they left my group – where they went in Venturers – where you'd see it finally, where the boy made up his mind. And he fell off the fence one way or another. And, if they fell off on my side of the fence, OK, they're still around the community. They're members of the community – some of the others are in jail!'[15]

Sam Taylor's life story unfolded partly though a difficult relationship with his own father he recalled from growing up in the Depression in Prince George, British Columbia. He recalled an alcoholic father, an abusive father, and a father who ultimately deserted Sam and his family in the middle of Canada's depression years. One telling instance of his father's tyranny was recalled as follows:

> I can remember running all the way home from that school up here all the way downtown to tell my father that I stood second in the class of forty kids. I never stood second, up that high. And this one girl beat me because she was the school inspector's daughter and got teaching at home and so on. But I stood second. And that big idiot stood there and said 'What the hell good is that, standing second? If can't stand first, don't stand anything.' I expected a dime, or a reward, or a kind word. And then he walks away. I never worked in school after that. He took it out of me – in grade five! At eleven years of age, or ten I think it was at the time. He knocked it right out of me, right there.

Taylor, who fathered six sons, struggled with his upbringing when his turn came to parent boys at that age in the 1950s and early 1960s. He remembered, through a narrative he considered pivotal in influencing his parenting thereafter, a moment of tyrannical community-based fatherhood when coaching one of his boys in bantam hockey in the early 1960s. He had been acting, as he admitted, as an autocrat behind the bench that stretched any reasonable limit. Finally, the pleading face and beseeching words of one of the boys playing alongside his son reminded him of a fathering face he was ashamed had become, to some degree, his own: 'I'm trying to do what you say, coach,' the lad looked up to say, 'but I'm just an eleven-year-old boy.' And yet, in summing up his notion of what a father should be in essence, Taylor stated: 'A father first of all has to be a leader. Somebody has to be a leader. If the woman is a leader, the other men laugh at the father, don't they?...."Oh hell, you know who wears the pants in the family," y'know.'[16] Noting the potential censure of other men, other fathers perhaps, the face of father as tyrant appeared in Sam Taylor's invocation of what a family man had to become in his masculine conduct. He confessed to seeing, at his worst, his father's face in his own behaviour. Taylor also claimed he had fought against it, and even won over it in the end.

Tyrannical fathers, of course, have appeared in many guises in history. Their manifestation in the 1960s, however, could sometimes appear as a period-specific feature, but was always more than that when the life story of the father as a whole is considered. Rock and roller Carole Pope recalled a father, Jack Pope, she did not love, who languished in a marriage that did not last. In telling her own story, she often incorporated a series of brief vignettes to describe her father, delivering often startling portraits of both him and herself: Jack Pope, the tyrant either responding, or unable to in the end, to the changes his daughter was going through as an adolescent in the 1960s of suburban Canada: 'I have to bear the flower-bedecked cross of the baby boomer,' she wrote:

> For me the sixties consisted of taking every drug possible, hallucinating Shiva and Vishnu cartoons on hardwood floors, and having really bad sex with everybody... I moved away from home when I was eighteen. My family was living in Don Mills, a suburb of Toronto. The landscape was flat and monochromatic, relentless in its conformity. I knew I'd lost whatever semblance of sanity I had if I stayed in that house. I was the oldest of four kids. My childhood had been heaven until my father decided we had to move from England to Canada.

Pope casts a dark portrait of her father, Jack, describing him, in several narratives, as a failure as a husband, a father, a provider:

> My parents Jack and Celia, were an odd match. Dad was a Canadian who'd moved to England in the forties. He dressed like a gangster, favouring black shirts and white ties. He had wavy hair and a pencil thin mustache. He was, quite frankly, wacko – a certified manic depressive. He was sexually Victorian and politically left-wing. He was always running some sort of scam. During the war he had done duty as a fireman and he openly admitted to me that he'd ripped off people's belongings while putting out fires in their houses. He'd won my mother in a three-month courtship. They were both into ballroom dancing and that was how they met.

Pope's depictions of being a daughter of father Jack are subjective, but very usefully: as evidence of her experiences they point toward an authentic sense of her childhood relations with her father, grounded in negative sentiments. Her father was, as she put it, hung up on controlling the sexualities and freedoms of all his daughters in the Don Mills of the early 1960s. 'When Diane [Pope's sister] and I came home after hanging out with our friends, he'd call us sluts.' Carole Pope describes herself as very much the precocious adolescent of a sexual revolution meeting suburbia in the Sixties: 'Sex was becoming an obsession with me. I used it as a shock tactic to get attention. I loved the way people would react to my sense of humour, which was riddled with sexual innuendo. For the first time in my life I felt connected with a group of people.

I felt an affinity for the kids in my class. We were all dispossessed art students who shared the same warped outlook on life.'

At that point, he turned to chase some unspecified scheme, among his many get-rich schemes, and the whole family faced a hiatus in Vancouver: 'we were soon ripped out of school again by Daddy Dearest,' as Pope put it, for a period in which Jack seems to all but disappear. Then, '[o]ur somewhat idyllic life was shattered by my father's announcement that we were moving back to Toronto. It was always the same broken record – he had some scam going on that was going to make us rich. We wanted to kill him.' It is difficult to tell what sort of life Jack wanted for Carole, or for any of his four children. Earlier, Pope suggested that '[m]y parents' quick-fix solution for the problems with their marriage was to have more kids.' Jack's role as a father, throughout their growing-up years, was described as profoundly negative: 'When I asked my father to help me with my math homework, he'd get abusive, calling me stupid if I didn't get the right answers.'

But as she and her younger sister returned to adolescent life in Don Mills, Jack seemed increasingly lost, petulant, unattached to all that was going on in Carole's life. Her dream of going to the Ontario College of Art meant nothing to a father who just wanted his daughters out working at anything to make money. This last long sketch set the stage for father about to lose nearly all meaningful contact with his eldest daughter – depicted in the tempo of suburban teenage life in the Sixties:

> We went back to school, and Jack was on our backs about everything we did. We lived in the middle of a cul-de-sac, where all the neighbours could watch us turn the street into a drag street when our parents went out. We were supposed to be baby-sitting Howard [Pope's much younger brother], and would threaten to beat up Elaine [her kid sister] if she ratted on us. Boys would tear into our driveways in Corvettes or on Harleys. They'd make a shitload of testosterone-induced noise. It was all show. We weren't bad girls. It makes me cringe to even use that term. Diane met a boy named Danny in the midway at the Canadian National Exhibition. Both my parents disapproved of him, so she started sneaking out with him.
>
> I desperately wanted to go to the Ontario College of Art, but Jack wouldn't let me. He didn't consider art a money-making career. He told me to get a job. I dropped out of high school and went to work with Diane at Philco, a factory that manufactured televisions...Diane and I were traumatized; we quit after eight months. Diane left home and moved to a room downtown to be close to Danny. I got a job as a junior artist in a business forms printing plant. That job was the beginning of the end of my button-down life. I was living every angst-ridden teenager's nightmare. I was rebellious and self-righteous. I didn't want to spend the rest of my life carpooling to some

loser job. The insipid vacuum of suburbia would not claim another victim. Right on!!
I started hanging out in Yorkville...

Jack and Pope's mother, Celia, soon slipped almost entirely into the background. Her father may have long lost his daughter's love, but was rendered, in our last narrative from Pope, all but silent at seeing her in the ambience of her 'cool pad' on Huron street in downtown Toronto:

> I had a room on the top floor. The colour scheme was puce. I surrounded myself with music and books. My first real artistic influence was the poetry of Sylvia Plath. I related to her dark and bitter sensibilities, but I was not crazy about the oven thing. I remember my parents' first and only visit to my cool pad. I'd drawn a picture of Queen Elizabeth on the wall brandishing a huge cock. Jack and Celia dropped by unannounced with a bag of groceries to see if I was still alive. Both my parents eyed the offending piece of artwork and said nothing about it.[17]

Pope portrays a father who struggled not only with his ability to communicate with his daughters, but with capacity to mature as a parent while they grew up. For some fathers, the potential conflict of the sexual revolution, parenting, and a sense of fundamental values as a family man could inspire a tyrannical face.

David Benson of Prince George showed this in expressing the 'right way' to bring children up – the search for responsible family manhood in the face of perceived changes that were seen as threatening to a father's sense of basic 'family values'. Here, we see a an authoritarian face of fatherhood in the 1960s that perhaps fell short of the tyranny that Pope and her sister lived under but one that moved, more commonly in many fathers, toward an 'either/or' system of discipline, a black-and-white moral code. The 'right way' to grow up during the sexual revolution seemed clear to Benson as a father of boys in this period. As he put it,

> We always had a problem, y'know, after the flower children days, and so forth – the 'freedom of sex.' Sex freedom and, y'know, sleep with anything you want and whenever you can and whatever. This wasn't in our generation and it wasn't in our bringing up, eh? And trying to instil that in our sons, y'know, when they're in their prime, y'know. My influence on them was that: 'hey mister – be careful who take out,' y'know. 'If she's good enough to take her to bed you'd better be thinking about marrying her – because that's the way it is done and that's the right way.' So that, that's the thing that raised my family, and how I was raised.'[18]

Benson, as the last example here, sat somewhere on the edge of tyrant and teacher, whereas Jack Pope was clearly an example of the former in his daughter's memoir. Attitudes toward sexuality and maturation during Canada's sexual revolution pushed many fathers to be more authoritarian in their control of their daughters' sexuality than that of their sons, reflecting the double standard in sexual relations of the 1950s that was challenged on so many fronts from the early 1960s onwards. What, for Canada's baby boomers, Doug Owram approached as the disappearance by the late 1960s and early 1970s, particularly on college campuses, of the 'cult of virginity' that unmarried daughters in the 1950s endured may have challenged a paternal authority that was, in fact, seldom exercised by fathers teaching sons about sex.[19] Clear examples of fathers teaching their sons about sex are relatively rare in the primary evidence. The following case thus provides a somewhat unique and useful illustration of the 'responsible' father as teacher rather than tyrant. The role is gendered. The masculinity of a moderate paternal figure displaces the fiercely controlling patriarch.

## Father as teacher

Everett Barclay and his son, Linwood, were part of a nuclear family of four that included Linwood's mother and an older brother. Linwood recounts many influences in his life, but none more than his father. His sensitive portrait of father as teacher, delivered here as a tender story set squarely in the sexual revolution, serves as a reminder that fatherhood's relational aspect often takes shape through the eyes of an adolescent dependent: 'Dad and I were alone in our new improved, sixty-foot-long house trailer,' Linwood recalled, speaking of his life as a teenager when his parents ran a trailer park campsite in Ontario cottage country in the late 1960s. He recalls his father

> asking me how I liked this girl from high school I was seeing at the time, and I said I liked her quite a bit. He said he didn't want to intrude on my privacy or anything like that by demanding that I tell him what exactly this girl and I might be up to, but he said there were some things I should know, even though I was only fifteen, and just because he was going to tell me these things didn't mean he was promoting anything, if I got his drift. It was just that I should be informed, he said.
> 
> He got a pencil and paper and proceeded to sketch out the basics of condom use. Given that he was a trained artist, his drawing, while not exactly *Gray's Anatomy*, was clear enough for the purposes of this lesson. 'You have to wear one of those,' he said, 'and it has to be on right. All the way on. You get what I'm saying?'
> 
> I nodded. I didn't know what to say, so I said nothing. I couldn't recall Dad being this direct before, or quite this honest about what went on between the

sexes. I felt uncomfortable, but at the time very close to him. That was due to the fact that this was not the kind of talk Mom would ever have with me.

As though he'd been reading my mind, when he finished the lesson he looked worriedly at his drawing. 'I guess we'd better get rid of this before your mother sees it,' he said. 'She'll say, "Everett, what's *this*?"' And we both laughed as he tore the paper into small bits, crumpled them up, and stuffed them deep into the garbage. He was wise to destroy the evidence.[20]

To the memories of a boy who later wrote poignantly about a father he missed so much after he passed away (Linwood's father died of cancer two years later) many such accounts could be added. Fathers, hardly in crisis about who they were as men, often simply went about their daily lives as fathers who taught through example, as role models, or, occasionally, in direct interaction with their children.

This often came about if fathers as providers were observed by their children. David Zieroth grew up on a family farm in Manitoba in the 1950s. His close contact with a providing father, which his agricultural upbringing necessitated, was in this case fondly remembered. Perhaps to emphasise this fact, Zieroth chose a present-tense narration: 'I love my father, and he loves me,' began one passage describing a father who

shows me how to handle a machine, or we bend our heads over a tool, and, and he talks to me, and sometimes we laugh about something I don't understand. He tells me what to do, and I do it. I'm eager to help because I believe it will gain entry to my father... I can tell my father is looking at me from the distance of the forty-five years he's already put under his belt when I'm born, the last of his four kids... After lunch, before he goes back to his work, he lies on the couch in the living room to snooze for fifteen minutes, not really sleeping, eyes closed, doing some private calculation that restores him.[21]

Zieroth recalled trying to get as deeply as possible into the mindset of his father, especially when he worked. Most telling was Zieroth's yearning to know everything that his father appeared to know about the world around them: 'I would like to follow him into his dreams, to see him the way he sees himself. Since I can't, I stay close to him, go where he goes.'[22] Zieroth suggested how his father became a young boy's guide to the world of work partly because they lived on a farm, but fundamentally because his role as a manful provider and teacher melded with masculine role modelling that held a special appeal for young Zieroth.

Wayne Johnson's intimate portrait of his father often points toward his family's Newfoundland heritage as well as that of father as teacher. His father,

Art, completed his formal training as an agricultural technician in 1948, graduating from the agricultural college in Truro, Nova Scotia, just before the Province of Newfoundland and Labrador entered Confederation a year later. Art Johnston claimed to have left the Avalon Peninsula to study agriculture in order to help save modern Newfoundlanders from their traditional reliance on the sea. He then worked at an experimental farm near St Johns, set up under Premier Joey Smallwood, which ultimately closed. From there, he moved on to a fisheries research station in the city's downtown core. His job in a modern, lab-coat environment, working on projects to improve the marketing and exploitation of cod and other species, seemed to negate his anachronistic sense of island pride. 'He lived in denial of these contradictions,' his son maintained. 'By my time, he was well used to it. He had become what my mother called a "fishionary," part missionary, part visionary when it came to fish. Though he still regarded the sea with a mixture of awe, dread and revulsion, he preached the gospel of the fishery, predicted the imminent invention, by scientists and technologists like him, of new and more efficient ways of catching and preserving fish. Where the farm had failed, "the Station" would succeed.'[23]

His father also taught him all that he thought he should know about fish, from the Latin nomenclatures of cod, herring, turbot and mackerel to his clowning imitations of a flatfish's prey-roving eyes, which 'always sent me into hysterics'.[24] In his son's eyes, Art Johnson's provider's face, like much about this misplaced man, could never be separated from a romantic sense of island nationalism that, fundamentally, defined his father for him. As it might for many gainfully employed men and fathers in raising their sons, Art Johnston's work spilled over into his particular domain of father as teacher.

The last illustration here introduces a case in which play rather than work shaped the masculinity of father as teacher. It also serves, again through the role of ice hockey coach, as a contrast to Sam Taylor's illustration above. Mike Zuke grew up in Sault Ste Marie, a steel mill city located in northern Ontario, during the Second World War. His father had worked in the mill, and he became a postal worker. He married after the war and parented two daughters and three sons, all baby boomers. He also acquired considerable local notoriety as a community-based parent through sports, namely ice hockey, a favourite pastime among male youth throughout the city's history. He coached, established a huge and well-provisioned backyard hockey rink that became a local landmark, and was a teacher of hockey to boys all his life. Locals are proud of their hockey hero 'sons' of the Soo, including several professional players of national and international renown, from the Esposito brothers, Tony and Phil, to Ron Francis. Mike Zuke raised one boy, Mike Jr, who played eight seasons with the National Hockey League, the premier professional league in Canada and the United States.

Zuke Sr grew up playing and loving hockey, stealing away free time to watch senior hockey games, a community entertainment mainstay. 'As a youngster,' sportswriter Chris Cuthbert relates, 'he'd hide in the basement "dungeon" of the old Gouin Street rink to avoid paying admission to senior games. He lined up in three- or four-block queues for the ferry to witness the Can-Am battles at Pullar Stadium in Sault, Michigan. His most cherished memory is opening night of the Sault Memorial Gardens in 1949 when the Sault Indians, featuring brothers Walter and Bill, entertained the Port Arthur Bearcats.'[25] He never gave up his enthusiasm for the game, especially as a father and teacher of both his own sons and of many others. Zuke's backyard rink began even before he and his wife, June, had children: 'The year after we were married, we went to a city skating rink,' he recalled. 'There were about four hockey games going on and pucks whizzing all over the place. We skated for about twenty minutes and left. As I'm walking back, I looked at all the land I had and said, why can't we have our own rink? I started one the next day.'

For Zuke, preparing the surface and first flooding became a 44- year ritual that grew to embrace the local neighbourhoods at a time of expanding family formation in the Sault, as elsewhere, with plenty of local children filling the streets, schools, parks and arenas. Zuke's enthusiasm for the game and for teaching it as a hockey coach gradually became a popular part of the city's social history. 'There has only been one complaint issued from a tranquil neighbourhood regarding Zuke's winter amusement park,' Zuke mentioned in a story that came back to his role as teacher of the sport and community-based father: 'We had an old couple across the street,' he said, pointing to the house as he recalled a chance event that he claimed had made him an even better teacher of the game. 'The guy used to get up for work at five in the morning. Late at night in twenty below weather, you could hear the puck hitting the boards for miles. His wife called over and asked us to keep the noise down. So I decided to use a ball. It was the best thing that ever happened. I read a book by the Russian coach Tarasov twenty-five years later. He said the best way to develop shooting accuracy is with a ball. I thought, Holy geez, we've been doing it all along.'[26]

As a father, Mike Zuke's enthusiasm for his rink clearly revived the boy within the man, a strong sentimental attachment to the joy of movement, play, and identity with team sporting excellence: 'When kids would come over to play I'd join in,' Zuke was to have declared as he laughed with a 'hooked nose', as Cuthbert describes, 'rearranged by at least one high stick': 'I'd call my son Michael and say, "Come on, let's play." He'd say, "I can't until I finish my homework." Usually, it's the parent telling the kid to do his homework.'[27] When Zuke's backyard rink responsibilities increased as his children grew up, his sense of himself as a teacher of hockey came into focus throughout the city. He coached Bantam (11–12 years) and Junior (14–18 years) hockey, always as an amateur who loved the game and all that it could teach. And no doubt backyard rink fathers elsewhere in Canada, holding with freezing hands a garden hose in night-time darkness when the temperatures are often best for flooding, shared Zuke's sense in that era that winter recreation was going to be good for their sons and their son's friends.

As a father and son encounter at a time, in the 1960s and early 1970s, when girls' recreational hockey had yet to find its fair place in Canada, Zuke provided scope for the masculine face of father as recreational coach and teacher of the sport. As he neared the normal retirement age of 65, he was able to quit his paid job as a postal employee to devote time to coaching and spend time with his wife, June, after their children had long since left home. 'I could have worked for more years for a full pension,' he recalled in reference to his ongoing volunteer responsibilities. 'I had three jobs and only one paid. I decided to retire from the job that paid. I gave the post office one month's notice and that was it.'[28] As much as his backyard rink and local civic arenas for children's and youth hockey could be considered a potent site for father as teacher in Canada, his decision as paid provider was unusual for his generation of fathers. Of course, father-as-teacher in many cases had little to do with formal education. In each case, no doubt, fathers acted to assist children to grow up, mature and prepare for their lives ahead. Preparing their children, sons especially, for their lives ahead as paid workers was something they often did in the post-war economy as role models rather than active parents.

## Father as workaholic

In many interviews, fathers often underscored as their biggest single regret the time spent working when, in retrospect, they feel today they should have been at home with their families. It seems too common, has nothing to do with the crisis of masculinity feared to have swept the modern world after the Second World War, and stands now, arguably, as a significant lament of a generation of family men. Their efforts to be good providers and 'responsible fathers' could lead down the wrong path, even if they did not realise where they were heading at the time. Moreover, for some fathers, even volunteer public service, at nights and weekends too, could become a regret.

As one father, Roy Phillips, put it: 'As a father I was not too good with the kids. Because I was too involved [in community service work]. Sometimes when I'd come home from work, they'd say "Daddy, are you going to play with us tonight?" I'd say "Nope, sorry kids – teaching St John's Ambulance tonight." Or "Sorry kids, no, I'm going to armouries tonight." Or "Sorry kids there's a church meeting tonight." I've eaten my *heart* out over that. Because I missed so much time with those kids when I *should* have been – sitting with them, y'know. Bigshot. Gotta be, gotta be part of the community. That's a *painful* thing when you realize "What the *hell* did you do it for?" Yeah, you spent time, you made friends. You had fun. Matter of fact, in the army you gotta a bit of money. You got two bills, payday twice a year, sorta thing. And there was a good social life there too.'[29] But that came with costs recognised only in hindsight.

With respect to paid work, the responsibility of earning became a time constraint without limits in the gendered family regime, especially in cases where the father was the sole breadwinner. His provider's role eclipsed his parenting and spousal roles. But at the time he may, in fact, have felt that his work schedule reflected his willingness to assume *more* responsibility for his family, not less. He was doing the right thing. He was exercising his masculine privileges as a father with a keen eye to financial security and his family's well-being over the long run.

But, for many fathers, the long run never ran out. 'Do I have regrets?' former national evangelist, provincial politician, one-time actor, novelist, inventor, advertiser and journalist Charles Templeton asked himself in the early 1980s. Templeton had worked most of his life in Toronto in a career in public life that began at age 17 with an illustration for a political cartoon page in the depths of Canada's Great Depression. Templeton parented five children, two from his second wife's first marriage, but later admitted after they had left home: 'I have often been so immersed in what I am doing that I have neglected friendships, even my family,' as he admitted.[30] His son, Brad, born toward the end of Canada's baby boom in 1960, nonetheless recalled his father with considerable fondness. Brad Templeton remembered a time when his father actually worked out of the home. But not, at least so it appears, to spend more time with his family. As Brad Templeton related, when his father 'took on the role of morning newscaster he arranged to be able to do the news from a room built at the back of our garage. This gave him time to try more independent pursuits, namely writing and inventing.'[31] It might be said that Templeton Sr was an ideal role model for the post-war 'Renaissance man' of his generation in English Canada who travelled across the country to pursue his many avocations and paid professions. But he was also, by his own admission, an erstwhile workaholic. His business hours and waking hours, as he described them in terms that modelled assertive masculinity in the workforce, he saw as one and the same. On his success he wrote: 'If I have been successful in what I have done it has usually been because all my energies have gone into the work at hand. I knew nothing about "hours of business" - for me they have been all my waking hours.'[32]

Of course, countless fathers may regret, and with cause, time spent at work. The pervasiveness of this lament should prompt historians of this particular masculine trait in fathers at work to contextualise it within both the career course and the life course of any individual father's history as a father. This particular face of fatherhood, in other words, appears in fathers who may have overworked at one point in their career but learned to adapt to parenting demands within their respective family as a gendered and classed regime. Family lives had long life courses, and, while some fathers may have grown accustomed to, even comfortable with, the masculine face of father as workaholic, it was not always worn by family men as a sign of their drive for success.

The following illustration introduces this potential ambiguity between the judgements made by a father in the post-war period facing considerable stress and conflict between his home life, challenged by a daughter with cystic fibrosis, and his demanding career in the lumber business, a family business in his case, that thrived in southern Ontario during the 1960s as suburbs grew.

This portrait of a lumber firm owner and father from Brantford, Ontario, Doug Summerhayes, comes through the memoir of his daughter, Heather. She recalled a father distracted by the dual demands of parenting a chronically ill child. Her sister would have died during her childhood without intensive, ongoing treatment at home and in hospital. Doug Summerhayes dealt with this and with his daily demands at the office, at the lumberyard and on the road. His daughter writes of a father who loved her, yet forgot she was even there from time to time: 'my father was indeed sad, profoundly sad,' she recalled of him during a period in their family's past when the local paper, the *Brantford Expositor*, ran stories like 'Saddened Father Tells Cystic Fibrosis Story.'

Perhaps as compensatory behaviour, Doug Summerhayes seemed to bury himself in his work: 'He distanced himself from sorrow with activity,' his daughter remembered. 'He was always on the telephone or on the fly. Out the door, in the car, off to the lumberyard. Late for a meeting, gone to make a speech, rushing to the airport. Even when he was home he was distracted.' In the process, Heather describes the family waiting for their husband and father to come home: 'Night after night, my mother waited dinner until long after he told her to expect him, buying our patience with raw carrots and celery. Gregg pressed his nose to the window, watching the daylight hours fade, waiting for his dad to come home and play with him. Finally, my mother simply had to feed us and, of course, that's just when Dad would walk into the door... His mind was always somewhere else. He constantly forgot things.'

Two incidents, from this period, remained marked in his daughter's memories. The first was when he took her to the lumberyard at Tillsonburg and told her to wait in the car: '"I'll be just few minutes," he promised. As she described: 'Two hours later, when I wandered into the showroom complaining that I had to pee, he looked at me stunned, and asked me where the hell I'd come from.' The next was more dramatic: 'A few months later, on a cold January afternoon, he forgot to pick me up from my ballet lessons at the YWCA. I waited and waited, watching the shadows lengthen outside the lobby window.' After calling home and his office and with 'no dimes left to take the bus' she decided to walk: 'I slipped and stumbled down the glistening sidewalk in the freezing twilight, hatless, bootless, without mittens, wearing only my coat, ballet slippers, and leotard.' Then, she saw her father race past in the car: 'Frantic, I yelled and waved. He made a U-turn in the middle of the hill and sped back where I stood. I clambered into his car, all snotty and frosted red. We did not know whether to laugh or cry. He handed me his big linen hankie so I could blow my nose. "You forgot me," I exploded in tears. "Aw, come here," he said chuckling, folding me up in his long arms and pulling me to his chest. "Why, Daddy?" I wept into his overcoat. "What made you forget?" "I don't know." His arms fell away from me. He removed his glasses and pinched his nose between his eyes. He sighed deeply. "I guess I've just got a lot on my mind lately."'[33]

Family men like Summerhayes, Templeton and Thompson can be found across the social classes. Thompson had begun his road to self-sufficiency during the war, working as a labourer in a pulp mill in Espanola, Ontario when Summerhayes was still in college and Templeton was drawing huge audiences as an evangelist leading Billy Graham's crusade north of the Canada–US border. Our final instance here focuses on a public figure, whose sense of family responsibility and masculine assertiveness combined *on* rather than off the job. It is drawn from the memoirs of J. Angus MacLean, former Premier of Prince Edward Island and federal cabinet minister in the Conservative government of John Diefenbaker, in power in Ottawa from 1957 to 1963. MacLean and his wife, Gwen, had four children during the baby boom years. The following segment from his life story begins with a moment when his daughter, Jeannie, may have looked up to him as a powerful public man, but only as an absent-presence, that is, as a father whose work outside the home and presence within it began to meld together in the figure of public father. His life story, published under the title *Making it Home*, develops as a broader narrative in which 'home' – Prince Edward Island, his family, his rural community roots – blends nostalgically into the imagined place any man would wish to be at the end of his journey, both daily and lifelong. As MacLean records:

> In my first year in cabinet, Gwen and I rented a fully furnished house from a physician who was taking a postgraduate course in university. When we returned to Ottawa, we rented a house owned by a CCF MP who had been defeated in the 1958 election. Our next door neighbour was a retired civil servant. One day our daughter, Jeannie, who was then about six, was with him in the yard, playing with seed pods from a maple tree, tossing them in the air and watching them spin to the ground. Our neighbour was fascinated by this phenomenon. 'Where did you learn that?' he asked. 'My daddy showed me,' our neighbour said, 'well, I guess he is fairly smart,' said Jeannie. 'He would hardly be minister of Fisheries if he wasn't.'

Jeannie may have been impressed by my exalted estate, but it did not leave me much time to spend with her or the other children. By the late 1959s we had four pre-school age children...I recall when Robert arrived, I took a box of cigars to the next cabinet meeting, as was the custom of the day. As cabinet minister, I had to travel to various parts of Canada and sometimes overseas. Once when I was packing to catch a plane for a conference in Newfoundland, I explained to the children where I was going. I arrived back in Ottawa a couple of days later, but as usual my workdays began early and ended late. Three weeks after I came back, one of the children asked Gwen, 'When is Daddy coming home from Newfoundland?'[34]

Father as workaholic does not imply an addiction to work, but rather a chosen work life that has an impact on absences at home – a masculine drive for power in the public sphere through work. Self-employed fathers, professionals and politicians were among those in this period, like MacLean and Templeton, who took pride in their hard work, often measuring this by the sacrifice they had to make at home. But working-class fathers too, working shifts, at distant work sites from their homes, or moving from job to job to make ends meet also often had little choice but to place work demands before those of family. These illustrations do not suggest a crisis in masculinity. They do not recount the experiences of men and perceptions of children who felt their masculinity as fathers was under attack. Some fathers may, in retrospect, have come to wish they could have spent more time home as involved parents, but perhaps only through a kind of life myth provided by memory. Lévi-Strauss argued that myths can 'provide a logical model capable of overcoming an apparent contradiction'.[35] In this case, a 'time away' myth, when expressed by the fathers themselves, can reflect the dual sense of power and achievement as masculine agent some fathers feel when looking back at their accomplishments as men, but not when looking back at their accomplishments as fathers. Their 'greatest single regrets' become a mythical lamentation, a life myth rehearsed in memories of family life, used to overcome the logical contradiction of not being home to parent. Masculine power in the public sphere was, and is in memory, the *preferred* category of manhood for fathers who moan and groan in old age that they wish they could turn back the clock and return to spend more time with children who have long since grown up. Fathers did not face a crisis over their masculinity as providers. For fathers, wearing the workaholic face either periodically or constantly in their working lives could be a chosen, if not preferred, avenue of time expenditure. In labour markets that discriminated against women and in gendered family regimes that privileged male breadwinning, masculine power and privilege were often exercised by fathers through this face, father as workaholic. Ironically, it was often worn at the time – when Canada's post-war generation of children were growing up – as a face of responsible family manhood.

## Conclusion

At one extreme, being 'responsible' could translate into authoritarian fatherhoods that verged on the tyrannical. Indeed some 'lost men' did not succeed in their masculine search for effective male parenting in some of the examples above, but not because their masculinity had eroded. They did not know how best to apply male assertiveness as fathers either with their children or acting *in loco parentis*. In many cases of tyrannical fatherhood, if anything served to influence how this dysfunctional category of masculinity was expressed it was how these men had grown up themselves, how particular models of fatherhood and parenting had taken shape for them when they were boys and youths in the interwar period.

For many fathers, too, work demands were satisfied to pursue what was considered to be *responsible* fatherhood. During part of these fathers' careers, employment gains led to workaholic patterns that some may have been able to correct, but others failed to address throughout their working lives. But this was not a disruption of masculine assertiveness in shaping the provider's role. Rather, it was a question of balance, or lack thereof. Fulfilling the drive for security was a sign of a father's masculinity, not its erosion. Laments for this were often expressed in hindsight, and were undoubtedly, for some, their biggest single regret when looking back on their own lives. To the extent that other choices *could* have been made, this 'time away' lament may also have served, in memory, as a life story myth deployed to overcome the logical contradiction of actually having had some freedom to be off the job yet choosing not to return home to family lives.

Between the tyrants and the workaholics fell many fathers, who nurtured, who taught their children whatever they thought was important in a non-authoritarian manner, or who became in their children's eyes good role models as teachers of how to live and how to grow up. These family and fatherhood histories, again, did not signify a masculinity crisis; quite the reverse. In such cases, masculine role modelling as seen in the face of father as teacher demonstrated a category of masculinity that suited the activity or problem at hand in guiding children toward some recreational pursuit or new level of understanding. For purposes of historical interpretation, fatherhood histories emerged in this period through types of male parenting connected to their efforts to be responsible parents, good or bad, successful or not. Carole Pope's life story, more than most, indicates an impact of a Sixties 'generation gap' dislocation between herself and her father, but as a relational outcome Jack Pope's own reactions seemed to contribute.

As a category of masculinity, responsible family manhood can offer a useful analytical spectrum. At one extreme, some fathers emerged in the post-war decades as tyrants through their relationships with their children. In a more positive light and within their intimate relations at home, others emerged as male parents who were, in fact, not in crisis at all, either as fathers or as role models. Still others did seem, as the prescriptive literature warned, unable to rectify very real, even destructive, tensions between their provider and parenting functions. Work could become a hazardous yet empowering form of escape in workaholic patterns some fathers later came to regret. But even this face of fatherhood was not a failed category of masculinity so much as a misapplied one that foiled efforts to be an effective, involved parent. Being on the job too much took its place among the less successful aspects of male parenting in the flow of daily experiences for many fathers.

These categories – tyrant, teacher and workaholic – were constructed over the family's life course through relationships with spouses and children. For the tyrants, who were consistently authoritarian, this was tragic. They wished to be 'responsible' but did not know how to express it. For the teachers it was not. They faced little contradiction; again, no real masculinity crisis in becoming and being fathers. For workaholics, again, no crisis of diminished masculinity and fatherhood appeared. They did not try to control too much in their children's lives. They simply were not there. Of course, not all fathers fell into these categories as their children grew up in the 1950s and became adolescents and youths in the tumultuous decade that followed. Nonetheless, from the 30 oral interviews and approximately 120 memoirs and autobiographies, as well as popular media representations of fatherhood, that constitute the evidence of the larger study from which this chapter is drawn, these three categories of masculinity and fatherhood reflect a significant range of manful relationships engendered by the role of father in post-war Canada.

## Notes

1. See John Demos, 'The changing faces of fatherhood', in idem, *Past, Present, and Personal: The Family and Life Course in American History* (Oxford, 1986), pp. 41–67.
2. As noted in the conclusion of the paper, approximately 120 life stories, as memoirs, autobiographies and biographies, and 30 oral history interviews (fathers and other family members) have been assessed in the larger project from which this is drawn. In a variety of Canadian locales (located in Nova Scotia, Ontario, Saskatchewan and British Columbia), life story interviews were conducted in English and followed the ethics guidelines of the Social Sciences and Humanities Research Council of Canada. I have also incorporated life writing rooted in the memories of family experience in the period from Newfoundland to British Columbia: approximately 120 memoirs and autobiographies from the perspectives of daughters, sons, wives and mothers, and husbands and fathers.
3. Samuel Schrager, 'What is social in oral history?', in Robert Perks and Alistair Thomson (eds), *The Oral History Reader* (London, 1998), p. 297.
4. Ibid., p. 298.
5. See John Tosh, 'What should historians do with masculinity: reflections on nineteenth-century Britain,' in *Manliness and Masculinities in Nineteenth-Century Britain: Essays on Gender, Empire, and Family* (Harlow, 2005), pp. 29–56.

6. Canada's baby boom was concentrated in the 1949 to 1961 period. See Doug Owram, *Born at the Right Time: A History of the Baby Boom Generation* (Toronto, 1996), especially chapter 1.
7. James Gilbert, *Men in the Middle: Searching For Masculinity in the 1950s* (Chicago, 2005), p. 217.
8. Apart from the large extent to which American and Canadian families confronted and responded to post-war conditions in a period marked by both the Cold War and the baby boom, often with dissimilar results, recent literature on modernism, family life and social changes in the 1950s in Australia indicates intriguing points of comparison. See Tony Dingle and Seamus O'Hanlan, 'Modernism versus domesticity: the contest to shape Melbourne's homes, 1945–1960' and 'A new kind of manhood: remembering the 1950s', in John Murphy and Judith Smart (eds), *The Forgotten Fifties: Special Issue of Australian Historical Studies* 28 (1997), 33–48, 147–57.
9. See, for example, Brian Moore, *The Luck of Ginger Coffee* (Boston, 1960) and Hugh McClennan, *The Watch That Ends the Night* (Toronto, 1959). *The Man in the Grey Flannel Suit* (produced and released by 20th Century Fox, February 1956), starring Gregory Peck, typified a popular American film version of the modern man's angst in the post-war period.
10. William H. Whyte, *The Organization Man* (New York, 1956); David Reisman in collaboration with Reuel Denny and Nathan Glazer, *The Lonely Crowd: A Study of the Changing American Character* (New Haven, 1950).
11. John R. Seeley, R. Alexander Sim, and Elizabeth Loosley, *Crestwood Heights: A Study of the Culture of Suburban Life* (Toronto, 1956), p. 176.
12. R.S. Hosking, 'What's the matter with father?', *Star Weekly*, 21 November 1951.
13. Lila Chapman, 'Help your husband be a good dad', *The Christian Home* (February 1960), 38.
14. Esther L. Middlewood, 'I find it good', *The Christian Home* (February 1960), 34.
15. Roy Gibson interview, Prince George, British Columbia, 22 March 1995 (pseudonyms are used in all references to interview subjects).
16. Sam Taylor interview, Prince George, British Columbia, 15 March 1995.
17. Carole Pope, *Anti Diva: An Autobiography* (Toronto, 2000), pp. 1–8.
18. David Benson interview, Prince George, British Columbia, 4 April 1995.
19. See Doug Owram, *Born at the Right Time,* especially chapter 10. See also Christabelle Sethna, ' "Chastity Outmoded!" The *Ubyssey*, Sex, and the Single Girl, 1960–70', in Magda Fahni and Robert Rutherdale, *Creating Postwar Canada: Community, Diversity, and Dissent, 1945–1975* (Vancouver, 2008), pp. 289–314.
20. Linwood Barclay, *Last Resort: Coming of Age in Cottage Country* (Toronto, 2000), pp. 101–02.
21. David Zieroth, *The Education of Mr. Whippoorwill: A Country Boyhood* (Toronto, 2002), pp. 7–8.
22. Ibid., p. 10.
23. Wayne Johnston, *Baltimore's Mansion: A Memoir* (Toronto, 2000), p. 124.
24. Ibid., p. 128.
25. Chris Cuthbert and Scott Russell, *The Rink: Stories from Hockey's Home Towns* (Toronto, 1997), p. 259.
26. Ibid., p. 258. Anatoly Tarasov has been called the father of Soviet hockey. For over two decades Tarasov was the head coach of the Moscow Red Army Team. He also coached Olympic and world championship teams representing the USSR. Tarasov wrote over 20 books about hockey.

27. Cuthbert and Russell, *The Rink*, p. 259.
28. Ibid., p. 258.
29. Bill Thompson interview, Sault Ste Marie, Ontario, 11 May 2004.
30. Charles Templeton, *Charles Templeton: An Anecdotal Memoir* (Toronto, 1983), p. 348.
31. Brad Templeton's memories of his father are found on his webpage. See 'Charles Templeton (1915–2001),' http://www.templetons.com/brad/cbt.html, accessed 1 September 2010.
32. Templeton, *Charles Templeton*, pp. 348–49.
33. Ibid., pp. 97–9.
34. J. Angus MacLean, *Making it Home: Memoirs of J. Angus MacLean* (Charlottetown, 1998), pp. 174–75.
35. Claude Lévi Strauss, *Structural Anthopology* (London, 1958), p. 229.

# Part V
# Modern Frontiers

# 17
# Cow Boys, Cattle Men and Competing Masculinities on the Texas Frontier

*Jacqueline M. Moore*

The cowboy has become an icon of masculinity to generations of Americans and, indeed, around the world. From the Virginian to John Wayne, Teddy Roosevelt to George W. Bush, men have 'cowboyed up' to tame both literal and figurative frontiers and to prove their manhood and that of their country. The masculine cowboy hero of film and literature usually straddles the frontier between civilisation and the wilderness; sometimes siding with the townspeople against the wilderness, and sometimes, as in the case of the anti-hero or friend of the Indian, against 'civilisation'. But, whether he accepts or rejects white society, his manhood is never in question; indeed, it is usually superior to those around him. In most depictions it is the cowboy's scorn for society and simplicity that makes him the most manly, in contrast to a similarly mythified and feminised city 'dude' in fancy clothes. But in truth, historically, cattlemen and the surrounding townspeople did not think the cowboy was manly for his 'uncivilised' ways. In fact, from the late 1870s on, as the Texas frontier became more settled, the real cowboys faced increasing demands from the people around them to rein in the very traits that Americans considered the most masculine.

The focus of this study is the Texas cattle frontier from 1865 to 1900. Texas was the birthplace of the modern cattle industry as well as the birthplace of the cowboy. While large-scale cattle ranching spread across the Great Plains in the 35 years following the Civil War, it was Texans who first adopted Mexican techniques of caring for cattle from horseback, and who were some of the most prominent cattle barons. Texas cowboys took cattle – and cowboy culture – up the trail through Oklahoma, Kansas and Nebraska and into the Northern ranges. The end of the Civil War and the opening of the railheads in Kansas and the meat packing plants in Chicago made cattle raising a profitable investment, leading to the rise of long cattle drives north. Although there were always a few absentee owners, many of the early cattlemen worked the ranches themselves, often operating on a small scale. As the industry attracted more investors in the early 1880s, however, many of the smaller ranches sold out to neighbouring larger landholders or corporate syndicates. The cattle industry, like other industries in this period, turned to mass production and systematic approaches to earning profit. These changes significantly affected the men who worked on the ranches.

But, at the same time as these changes were taking place, dime novelists and Wild West show promoters in the late nineteenth and early twentieth centuries created romanticised images of the cowboys and cattlemen. Anxious about their own masculinity in the face of new immigration and women's encroachment into the workplace and voting booth, white middle and upper-class men on the East Coast, like Teddy Roosevelt, exalted these images. As sociologist Michael Kimmel describes it, 'the vast prairie [was] the domain of male liberation from workplace humiliation, cultural feminization, and domestic emasculation.'[1] The historical truth is less romantic. Most historians now recognise that, at base, cowboys were essentially working-class men, who, far from being free, were subject to the same restraints that late-nineteenth-century workers faced across the country.[2] They defined masculinity as their ability to perform their work, to control their own lives, and to respect other men who did the same. Like workers elsewhere in the country, they usually expressed their masculinity through public rituals of drinking, gambling and fighting.[3] Although some chose the job specifically to escape the responsibilities of everyday life, cowboys lived outside 'civilised' society mainly because of the nature of their work. They relished their freedom, but they also read the Montgomery Ward and Sears & Roebuck 'Wish Books' in their free time while dreaming of settling down.[4] Theirs was an all-male fraternity and they prized male camaraderie and friendships above most else, but it is also true that their economic and social circumstances often prevented them from pursuing other paths.

In many ways the distinction between early cattlemen and the later corporate investors has also been mythologised. The pioneers in the cattle industry were just as likely to come from middle-class backgrounds as their corporate counterparts. And, if some of the iconic cattle barons, such as Richard King, came from rough and tumble backgrounds, their successors, like King's son-in-law, attorney Robert J. Kleberg Jr, who took over the King Ranch in 1886, were decidedly middle-class in outlook.[5] Cattlemen always saw themselves first and foremost as businessmen, tamers of the frontier. Moreover, as the business world as a whole became more corporate in the late nineteenth century, many cattlemen adjusted to the new style of business themselves and adopted the methods of the corporations. The cattlemen's goal was to bring civilisation to the West and to profit from it, and civilisation, to them, meant steady economic growth and the foundation of stable community institutions. They enjoyed their interaction with civilised society, and their middle-class brand of masculinity emphasised responsibility and restrained behaviour.[6] Their concept of civilisation was also predicated in part on a female presence and stable family life. The usual prerequisite for the presence of respectable women was law and order, something which the cowboys often resisted.

Thus, there was a clear class distinction between cowboy and cattleman. A cowboy was a hired hand who worked cattle on horseback on the ranch and/ or up the trail, but who occasionally did other work on foot for the ranch, such as repairing fences. Conversely, a cattleman was simply a ranch owner or manager who employed cowboys. In truth, while there were certain conditions unique to the frontier, social and economic relations differed little from those elsewhere in the country. Settlers imported class and social hierarchies wholesale into the region along with gender and racial biases.[7] Attitudes about masculinity on the frontier did not differ substantially from the rest of the United States either. As middle-class men elsewhere reclaimed their sense of manhood by bringing immigrants and factory workers under their control, cattlemen made efforts to control cowboys as a way of asserting their own values of masculine behaviour.

In the early years of cattle ranching in the 1860s and 1870s, the boss often rode with his hands and did his share of the work. Many spoke of the cowboys as being part of their ranch family. But even then, as their ranches grew in size, cattlemen did less of the work and used paternalistic language to separate themselves from their 'boys'. Most cowboys were between the ages of 18 and 40, and the relative youth of the men made it easier for the ranchers to think of them as 'boys'. Since many had started work on ranches in their early teens, in some cases the ranchers were father figures to them. But, while ranchers usually had great affection for their cowboys, like stern fathers, they also expected to exercise strict authority over them. Zeke Newman, co-founder of the Niobrara Cattle Company, was known as 'Uncle Zeke' to his men, who respected him as 'one of the greatest men that ever was in the cattle business'. In return, however, Newman expected absolute loyalty, 'and he sure as hell got it.'[8] Charles Goodnight, who was responsible for founding large-scale ranching in the Panhandle, took good care of all of his employees but forced them to sign contracts promising to abide by his rules before going up the trail, even enforcing his standards against any outside men who bothered his 'boys'.[9] Taking their cues from the early ranchers, even some corporate ranch managers adopted similar paternalistic styles with their men. Both Spottswood Lomax and Fred Horsbrugh of the Espuela Ranch tried to find jobs elsewhere for the hands they had to lay off, and would often lend them horses to ride to their new jobs or money to tide them over for the winter.[10] But the use of paternalistic language and concern by the cattlemen and ranch managers was not all altruistic. The ranch was primarily a workplace, and disloyal hands were an economic drain on the ranch, as they could mistreat the cattle, do poor work in general, and perhaps even steal some of the owner's stock for themselves. But, whatever the motive for the control, the fact that it was done in paternal terms asserted a gendered hierarchy in which cowhands were always cow*boys* no matter their age, while those who owned the ranches were always cattle*men*.

Both cowboys and cattlemen measured manhood in part as the ability to do one's job. For cowboys to treat a newcomer as a man, he first needed to prove he had both the skills and the self-reliance to handle the work.[11] When Rollie Burns got his first job on a ranch he had to prove himself by breaking 50 horses for the owner in a period of three months, a feat which proved his skill, but convinced him never to willingly ride a bronco again.[12] Charlie Siringo underwent a similar hazing process even after being hired as a trail boss for the LX Ranch. The local foreman told him that, since he looked too young to most of the other hands, it would be best if he just roped with them on an even basis for a while. Charlie earned the older men's respect only by showing his roping skills and breaking a horse that the others had considered too wild to ride.[13]

In addition to basic skills, what made cowboys men in their own judgement was often steadfastness as much as skill. Account after account notes the loyalty of the men who worked on the ranches, even on the large, corporate ranches. As XIT Ranch foreman's wife noted, 'its men were vigilant and devoted, if not always impregnable.'[14] The *San Antonio Light* described the cowboy as 'faithful day and night, to the sacrifice of his life, if necessary'.[15] Such loyalty, however, was not necessarily a reflection of admiration for the owners. As Teddy Abbott recalled, 'To tell the truth, it wasn't thinking about the owners' money that made them so anxious to turn out their herd in good shape. What they cared about was the criticism of the other cowpunchers.'[16] Men who could not follow through with the job or who complained about it were objects of scorn among cowboys and ranchers alike.[17] Respect from their fellow cowboys was a clear measure of their manhood.

As the work was often dangerous, cowboys also had to be willing to take risks. Risk-taking, in fact, was possibly one way in which cowboys were able to gain self-respect, as their choice of risks they took emphasised their special expertise and allowed them to have some level of self-control. To perform their duties, cowboys had to push cattle to the limits of endurance. The logistics of range grazing meant that cattle had to travel large distances to reach the market under tight control and sometimes without water. The practice of herding cattle on horseback necessitated the use of the rope, snagging calves by their hind feet to subdue them for branding and castrating.[18] But the key factor was the large size of the herds, numbering in the thousands, which the cowboys had to deal with on a regular basis. It was not possible to take time with each animal at branding, nor was it possible to spend much time taming horses. Thus the cowboys 'threw' cattle and 'busted' broncs in an abrupt way. Moreover, they saw the ability to handle the danger involved in these activities as part of what made them true men.[19]

With the rise of corporate methods of ranching in the mid-1880s came increasing regulation of workers, and risk-taking became a primary target for restraint. Cattlemen admired the bravery and skill that their men showed, and early cattlemen in particular recognised something of the same spirit in their own entrepreneurship. But the sort of heroic manliness the cowboys embodied was rapidly becoming a thing of the past to many middle-class businessmen, including ranchers. For the most efficient business, the new businessman had to practise self-control and restraint as he entered the workplace, and his workers had to do the same.[20] With this attitude it was not surprising that the cattlemen began to question the skill of their hired hands. Ranchers regularly complained about cowboys' rough handling of the cattle. The Young County Cattleraisers Association met in 1885 for the sole purpose of addressing the matter. Concluding that the cowboys cared more about display of skills than the actual cattle, they resolved to give them instructions to be more careful and to require their wagon bosses to enforce these instructions.[21] The *Texas Livestock Journal* printed regular complaints of rough handling. One experienced trail boss reported seeing a herd in which 75 per cent of the trail cattle were lame because the cowboys, trying to complete their work early, had driven them too fast. His proposed solution was closer control over the cowboys on the job. He concluded: 'There is as much in a boss knowing how to handle men as there is in knowing how to handle cattle.'[22]

The rise of corporately owned ranches furthered the antagonism between cowboys and cattlemen. Absentee foreign investment corporations hired professional ranch managers primarily for their business abilities or their knowledge of cattle breeding, not for their cowboy skills, and in fact most of them had not done cowboy work before. The lack of personal relationships between cowboys and cattlemen contributed to the growing antagonism. B.B. Groom, the manager of the Diamond F Ranch, 'was a pompous Kentucky colonel who treated the cowboys as if they were stableboys'.[23] In fact, ranch owners and managers increasingly became an annoyance to the hands rather than people they looked up to. In 1889, John McNab, one of the English directors of the Espuela Ranch, wanted to go out with the hands on a round-up. He insisted on walking rather than riding, and wore his business suit and bowler hat and carried an umbrella to shade him from the sun. When the cattle became skittish as a result, one of the hands took on the responsibility of shepherding him around. The cowboys eventually became fond of McNab, and, in a great role reversal, on subsequent visits it was they who took on the paternal role and looked out for him when he wandered off. Such interactions could only reinforce any anxieties the foreign cattlemen might have had about their masculinity in comparison to that of the cowboys. Most other visitors to the ranch avoided any interaction with the working men.[24]

On the corporate and larger ranches, cowboys became objects of condescension at best and suspicion at worst. South Texas sheep rancher Walter W. Meek described the cowboys on a neighbouring ranch in condescending terms as he watched them scramble to be first to get to the coffee can at the ranch house. 'Poor wretches,' he told his fiancée, 'as I stood looking at them I thought of thy query about the heathens: "why should we try to give them more light", and I applied the words not to their religion, but to their way of living – civilizing these people would take away much of their happiness.'[25] Despite his paternal attitude and easygoing reputation, Fred Horsbrugh reported to his Espuela employers that 'I have found that as a rule one cannot depend on the ordinary cow-hand...He will work faithfully and look after his employer's interests...and he will frequently ride a long way round to prevent seeing what might be inconvenient'.[26] The XIT owners in particular felt the need to closely supervise their men. Colonel Abner Taylor proposed placing 'some good men on the Ranch who were not identified with the Cow Boys,...and [who] would take our side in any controversy'.[27]

Like the paternalistic ranchers, large ranches instated rules limiting the men's drinking, gambling and gunplay. The XIT had the most infamous set of 23 rules, with the usual provisions against gambling and drinking, but also forbidding them to carry six-shooters and bowie knives, keep private horses in camp, or feed their own horses with company grain. Any violation, including tearing down a copy of the rules, was grounds for dismissal.[28] The new impression of the cowboy was that he was not a man, but an unruly child who, left uncontrolled, would either steal the livestock or destroy it through his carelessness.

Efforts to resist, from sabotage to strikes, proved futile as the cattle industry entered a slump in the 1890s and there was a labour surplus. Cowboys who had scorned work that was not on horseback were reduced to seeking work of any kind. In 1888, W. Jones sought work on the Matador, writing: 'I am now a Cow Boy but claim that I can do as much as any one such as farm work making fence...'[29] If the cowboy could not achieve middle-class respectability through marriage to a good woman, property ownership or independent wealth, he had at least hoped to control his working conditions. But the corporatisation of ranching, the resulting increased regulation and the employment situation meant he had fewer opportunities to have any control of his work life. Cowboys thus more frequently looked to their leisure time to prove their manhood. Unfortunately, 'respectable' society had different ideas in that regard as well.

It is clear that cattlemen and other prominent local citizens did not just want to control the cowboys on the range and trails; they wanted to regulate their leisure time in town as well. Texas frontier newspapers in the 1860s and 1870s were full of accounts of cowboys coming in to town on a spree, and, indeed, such stories were part of the masculine image of the cowboy. 'Fighting rustlers and attending a herd was a he-man's job, so when the cow hand played, he played as a he man,' recalled former cowboy Earnest Cook.[30] Much of the cowboys' town spree was a public performance, for each other as much as for the townspeople. The spree involved a number of rituals associated with male bonding and masculinity, such as gambling, drinking and fighting. These rituals allowed the cowboy to show his friends and the locals that, whatever else, he was a man.[31]

Gambling, for working-class men, allowed them to strengthen bonds of reciprocity, since each shared the risks and often ended up both winning against and losing to the same people. It was also a way to escape the workplace and its regulation.[32] Assuming the game was an honest one, the risks men took were dependent on luck and shared equally by all, and at the gambling table, unlike the workplace, they had a chance at financial success. But gambling took courage, as a man could just as easily lose.[33] Gambling thus became a public show of manhood for cowboys, even if it seemed profoundly irrational to the people around them. A broke former cowboy, Jim Gober, tried to rebuild his fortune by gambling despite having a job offer in hand. He lost his last dollar in a rigged poker game but, instead of quitting, he asked a friend to loan him $50, and went right back to another poker table. He ended up winning $590, justifying his risk, and also likely earning the admiration of the men around him.[34]

If gambling allowed men to choose their own risks, public drinking rituals defied efforts to control them further. Drinking in public was associated with manhood, since taverns and saloons were off limits to respectable women, and generally men went there to be with each other and relax.[35] As a result, drinking was big business, and saloons proliferated in the frontier towns (as did brothels). Although many townspeople objected to saloons and the numerous violent incidents that resulted from drunken sprees, they could do little to stop them in the early years. Shopkeeper Andre Anderson stated that, in the early days of the city, the citizens of Fort Worth had to choose either rough entertainment or no trade at all, and so they chose to provide what the cowboys wanted.[36]

Numerous violent incidents resulted from drunken sprees. In the early 1870s, many Texas cowboys resented the lawmen in the northern states because most of them were ex-union soldiers and the cowboys were ex-confederates. As a result the cowboys often picked fights with them when they were arrested and ended up getting killed.[37] A group of Texas cowboys in town in Wyoming got drunk and rowdy, and when one cowboy tried to get his buddy to go sleep it off the buddy shot him, and in the uproar another drunk shot the sheriff. The sheriff arrested both men and the buddy was seriously hurt.[38] When a group of cowboys tried to 'take' the town of Marionfield, a battle ensued between the cowboys and the sheriff and his posse, ending with one cowboy dead and another mortally wounded.[39] Drunken violence usually backfired on the cowboy when it came to confrontations with the law, but it was part of the ritual of public drinking and could also enhance a cowboy's manly reputation. In a fight, the winner proved his manhood and dominance, but as long as the loser stood up and fought as well he maintained his own honour, so there was no reason to continue the argument. Unfortunately, the results of gunfights were often lethal for the losers.[40]

In the 1870s and 1880s, most violent incidents went unpunished, especially against non-whites. Will Hale shot a Mexican gambler who had cheated him at cards, and when his victim's brother showed up to avenge him Hale shot him as well. However, although Hale was arrested, he was released, and the case never came to trial.[41] In this case, is likely that no Anglo jury would have convicted him, since there was great prejudice against Mexicans. Teddy Roosevelt wondered at the fact that cowboys came from every different national background and yet blended in so well that they all resembled each other, with one exception: 'Some of the cowboys are Mexicans, who generally do the actual work well enough, but are not trustworthy; moreover they are always regarded with extreme disfavor by the Texans in an outfit, among whom the intolerant caste spirit is strong.'[42]

But even murder of Anglos was not necessarily grounds for punishment. When C.B. Burnett killed a man who had stolen some of his cattle and who, upon discovery, 'approached B[u]rnett in a threatening manner', the jury ruled the death a justifiable homicide.[43] Similarly, few cases in the early years of Donely County, in the Panhandle, ever made it to trial, despite the many charges of murder.[44] Crimes against property, however, such as cattle rustling, often faced very steep fines. This fact conforms to Southern honour-based culture, in which it was more honourable to kill than to steal in some circumstances, particularly if it involved theft of livestock. Moreover, few people took disputes over personal insults into courts, preferring to settle the matter between themselves, perhaps believing *real* men fought it out rather than complaining to a judge.[45] In 1876, W.E. Race and Henry Gadberry were indicted for challenging each other to a duel in Uvalde County, but charges were dropped as there had been no clear legal violation.[46]

Cattlemen did not always oppose violence if done for a 'just cause'. Will Hale, as the son of a rancher and eventually a ranch owner himself, seemed to identify with a Southern ideal of honour that many of the older cattlemen embraced. While not all cattlemen came from Southern backgrounds, and in fact after 1880 most ranch owners came from outside the South, a number of them adhered to the older form of masculinity that centred on honour. As such, these men were not above violence themselves. Moreover, some of the early cattlemen came from less than genteel backgrounds. Historian Tom Lea reports that Richard King was fond of a little fisticuffs on occasion.[47] Still, King was not a typical cattleman in any way, and his actions reflected as much his working-class New York Irish background as any Southern sense of honour. As historian Lewis Atherton reports, violence and shows of force were rare among cattlemen. But, in the absence of other authorities on the frontier, cattlemen were also used to enforcing the law – at least their law – with the threat of lynchings and violent retaliation. Charles Goodnight claimed that south of Mobeetie, before 1882 when Donely County was officially organised, the cattlemen enforced the law, including a ban on whiskey, and there were no murders as a result.[48]

But these concepts of honourably justified violence were not universally held. In 1878, even the *National Police Gazette*, a sensationalist true crime magazine popular in the bunkhouse, carried out a campaign against violence in the state, charging that 'the murderer is a hero with the people, press and clergy of Texas'.[49] In the mid-1880s, when Walter W. Meek, a Pennsylvania native, served on the grand jury in Duval County in South Texas, he was astonished at the prevailing values among his fellow citizens. He reported that horse stealing received the harshest punishment, with some even advocating the death penalty for rustling, whereas murderers received far more lenient treatment. Meek personally believed the death penalty should be reserved for murder and that murder was by far the worst crime.[50] But Meek was somewhat in the minority at the time.

Nonetheless, in later years, as the frontier became more settled, violence came to seem counterproductive to most cattlemen and townspeople. Moreover, it was increasingly clear that not all violence was as honourable as either cowboys or cattlemen would have liked to claim. By the 1890s, most violence did get a hearing in the courts. W.D. Browning was arrested and brought to trial for assault with intent to kill after attacking J.B. Atkinson, who had called him a lying son of a bitch in the course of a debt dispute, an affair of honour that perhaps would not have reached the court in earlier years.[51] Convictions were most likely if the death involved an employee of one of the large ranches and the killer was from elsewhere. In these cases the ranch owners would marshal the whole outfit to go to court to testify against the killer. An example of such a case was the trial of George Jowell for assault with intent to murder John Lindley, who died of his wounds in late September 1902. The Spur's lawyer reported to the ranch manager that, although the grand jury had indicted Jowell, the 'best men' had all excused themselves from the petit jury, leaving a less than law-abiding panel to decide the case. The result was a hung jury, so the lawyer got the venue changed to Armstrong County and told Fred Horsbrugh to make sure all the Spur 'boys' who had witnessed the attack would show up to the new trial. The tactic seems to have been effective, as the new jury convicted Jowell, who was sentenced to two years in the state penitentiary.[52] The increasing involvement of the courts and ranch managers in these disputes reinforced a changing attitude between ranchers and cowboys. For cowboys, violence was necessary to restore order and honour; for the modern cattlemen, violence destroyed order and was itself generally dishonourable.[53]

One of the reasons for the changing view of violence was the decline in the traditional basis for patriarchy. In an industrial world, property loss was impersonal and far more common, and thus the concept of male honour was less relevant. Since it was easier to lose property, it was no longer feasible or rational for gentlemen to resort to violence against an impersonal market force. Thus violence among the middle and upper classes no longer had a purpose, at least when aimed at each other.[54] Middle-class men in the late nineteenth century expected to be aggressive in the marketplace, but tried to control and channel their aggression into activities such as sport, or bodybuilding, in their leisure time. Physical strength was part of the new ideal of manhood, but not brute force.[55] Untamed aggression was limited to boyhood. Novels like *Huckleberry Finn* celebrated boys as harmless savages with only a crude sense of morality, such as respecting women and being loyal to a buddy. Novelist Charles Dudley Warner, in his 1877 book *Being a Boy*, argued that a good boy was a natural savage who inhabited an ideal world that was a refuge from sentimental women and too much civilisation.[56]

To middle-class men, the distinction between a boy and a man increasingly became the ability to restrain aggression and impulses, as well as a sense of responsibility to family and the larger society.[57] George Littlefield advised his nephew, who was nearly cut to death in a fight, to trust the courts to punish the man rather than to try to retaliate himself.[58] Matador Ranch manager Murdo Mackenzie credited the fact that he did not carry a gun as the reason he avoided further violence.[59] Manhood became equated with self-discipline, and those who did not practise it were stigmatised as less manly.[60] Not surprisingly, judged by these standards, the cowboys looked more like boys than men, and accordingly were in need of restraint.

Denied the middle-class masculine privileges of property and family, however, cowboys clung to their working-class male privileges of drink, cards and fighting, thus reinforcing their status as morally suspect.[61] One by one, the towns began to restrain these particular forms of unbridled masculinity. They tried to impress upon the cowboys that truly masculine behaviour was non-violent. Newspapers praised peaceful resolutions of disputes. In 1877, the *Lampasas Dispatch* printed letters of apology ending a feud between two ranches, which had resulted in several shootings. The editor commented: 'This is manly, and exhibits more true courage than to shoot down an enemy.'[62] The cowboys' weapons were a major target. Even the notorious town of Fort Griffin, in Shackelford County, started to regulate use of guns within town limits. Beginning in the late 1870s, the townspeople began efforts to stop cowboys from openly carrying rifles and six-shooters. They repeatedly petitioned the governor to declare that Shackelford County was no longer a frontier county so that they could enforce the state laws against side arms. The governor finally did so in 1881.[63] In that year the *Fort Griffin Echo* admonished the boys for a disturbance at one of the local brothels. 'This shooting does no good but may unintentionally cost a life; it is not an indication of bravery or manly spirit, but evidence of a depraved nature.'[64] Similar movements occurred in cowtowns across Texas in the 1880s, though prosecutions for unlawfully carrying a pistol continued well into the early 1900s in some areas.

Having got the guns under control (at least partially), the towns next turned to what they considered the cowboy's immoral behaviour. Townspeople recognised that much of the violence stemmed from the cowboys' presence at dancehalls, saloons and gambling houses, and so had additional reasons to want to pass morals legislation. Cattlemen already enforced sobriety on their ranches, and many avoided excessive drinking themselves, whether under the influence of wives, trying to set an example for the men, or by choice.[65] Indeed, self-discipline and middle-class manhood depended on being able to control behaviour like drinking. The added fact that excess alcohol could lead to a loss of restraint in other areas made it an easy target. Nonetheless, prohibition on the frontier was primarily an attack on the saloons, the site of masculine bonding and cowboy revels.[66]

Most towns passed laws licensing sellers and prohibiting the sale of alcohol on Sundays, and by 1895 53 counties were completely dry.[67] Beginning in the 1880s, the townspeople had additional help in their fight against drunken cowboys in unlicensed drinking establishments. Once they had driven all the Indians out of the region, the Texas Rangers were reassigned to maintain order in the frontier towns. 'Respectable' citizens increasingly relied on the Rangers and the courts to deal with rowdy cowboy behaviour, but very few convictions of the sellers ever resulted, only fines for individual cowboys, which had little long-term impact.[68]

The attempts to restrict gambling also focused on passing local ordinances limiting the practice on Sundays and arrests of people for violation of these laws. While there were a few exceptions, most cattlemen did not gamble, once again marking a distance between themselves and their men. J.S. Wynne reported that, while range bosses or trail bosses would often gamble in a nearby town, he only rarely saw any ranch owners gamble.[69] Cattleman George W. Littlefield despised gambling parlours and advised one of his nephews that 'business men do not like for their employees to go to such places – They do not improve the business relations or knowledge of young men.'[70] For middle-class men, gambling was irrational and the sure road to disreputability. Businessmen might gamble on the stock market or an investment, but their risk was always calculated and rational. Moreover, the ties between gambling and the saloon gave more incentive to advocate prohibition, and, by banning both gambling and drink, reformers hoped to eliminate 'tavern fellowship' of working men in exchange for more 'enlightened' and respectable leisure.[71]

Cowboys perceived these new restrictions as part of a general effort to control them, but the towns' leading men tried to couch them in terms of paternalistic advice, further asserting their greater claim to masculinity. Many newspapers regularly lectured the cowboys on what was proper 'manly' behaviour. *Jacksboro/Fort Griffin Echo* editor G.W. Robson directly addressed the cowboys when there had been incidents of violence. 'Go slow on the racket, our citizens do not want to see you punished but you are almost certain to be [cala]boosed or fined-maybe both – if you do not chop on the noise.'[72] The *Texas Livestock Journal* advised cowboys on how to spend their leisure time between seasons. A good cowboy should beware of liquor, go straight home to his family, visit his sweetheart, and save money for the next year so he did not have to borrow more from the boss.[73] Such advice continually emphasised restraint as the proper manly model for leisure.

When cowboys did not respond well to paternal lectures on manly restraint, the townspeople denigrated their manhood in racial terms. In late nineteenth-century Texas, as elsewhere in the United States, racism was an accepted social practice and white Americans frequently based their own concept of manhood on being white. Being white was intimately tied into middle-class ideals of masculinity in the late nineteenth century, as manifested in the many calls to build up white manhood. Only by building up the manly white American race could the United States reach its full potential, and miscegenation would only weaken it. Victorian-era white Americans also believed that the 'primitive' non-white races had not evolved sufficiently to achieve true manhood. By their understanding of evolutionary standards, the most advanced races had to have the most perfect manliness, and thus white supremacy and masculinity were linked.[74]

Anglo prejudices generally prevailed in the cattle industry. While there are no clear figures, some historians have estimated that one-quarter to one-third of all cowboys were black or Hispanic.[75] Whatever the total, a typical outfit was from eight to ten men and usually had at least one Hispanic or black worker as a cook, a horse wrangler or, occasionally, a regular hand. These figures varied within different regions of Texas. On the upper Coastal Prairie, where there was a strong slave plantation tradition, there were more black cowboys and even a few all-black outfits. Similarly, near the Mexican border and on the King and Kenedy ranches, Hispanic cowboys predominated. Typically, on Panhandle ranches such as the IOA Ranch or the T-Anchor there might be two or three African–Americans in each outfit, often in the position of horse wrangler or cook.[76]

If a black cowboy had exceptional skills, moreover, he could earn respect at a time when African–Americans faced increased hostility in other fields. Matthew 'Bones' Hooks earned a reputation as one of the best bronco busters around and made a living going from ranch to ranch in West Texas and the

Panhandle breaking horses. When his name came up another old cowboy praised him, remarking, 'Yes, Bones is a Negro, but those who know him say he is one of the best riders the United States has ever known.'[77] Ironically, Bones had learned his skill so well because the white cowboys had tried to embarrass him by making him ride tough horses all the time. As Bones put it: 'They made me the best rider in the country, but they weren't trying to make me a rider.'[78]

While Anglo cowboys occasionally gave credit to talented black cowboys, they almost never name the vaqueros in their accounts and give little or no praise of any individual Hispanic cowboy's skill, despite several generic assertions that Mexicans were good ropers and riders.[79] Ironically, the term vaquero implied a certain knowledge of cattle work, so that even Anglo cowboys co-opted it at times. The South Texas hero of J. Frank Dobie's 1929 *A Vaquero of the Brush Country* is in fact John Young, an Anglo cowboy, who in his description of his outfit names every Anglo cowboy individually and then says (as was typical of almost all cowboy narratives) 'there were two Mexican vaqueros in the crowd, and two negroes.' Whilst in subsequent stories Young provides the names of the black cowboys, he never gives the individual names of the Mexicans.[80]

However varied the degree of racism they faced, non-whites ultimately found themselves on the wrong side of the colour line. Anglos often used the supposed superiority of whites not only as justification for taking land and economic exploitation of workers, but also to reinforce their own social status. Such practices were particularly important for Anglos who were at the bottom of the economic scale and had little chance of rising beyond manual labour. This category included cowboys, and, while there were many individual cases of reaching across the colour line in friendship, the reality was that it was in their interest to have a group of men lower on the social scale than they were, as it gave them some self-esteem in comparison. Thus, given the view of non-whites as childlike, to impugn a man's 'whiteness' was to impugn his manhood as well.

Joseph McCoy, who helped establish the system of shipping cattle from Kansas railheads, described the cowboys in Abilene, Kansas as having lives that bordered 'nearly upon that of an Indian', and humour 'wherein abounds much vulgarity and an animal propensity'. He did excuse their behaviour, however, as in part a result of drinking alkali water on the trail. 'No wonder the cowboy gets sallow and unhealthy and deteriorates in manhood until often he becomes capable of any contemptible thing; no wonder he should become half-civilized only, and take to whisky with a love excelled scarcely by the barbarous Indian.'[81] In 1873, the Ellsworth, Kansas newspaper compared Texas cowboys to Indians. 'The Lipan and Comanche are not more unlike civilized white man than is the nomadic herdsman to the Texan who dwells in the city or cultivates the plains.'[82] In 1883, the *San Antonio Light* compared a group of rowdy cowboys who had stolen apples from some local Mexicans to Indians on the warpath, calling them bullies and praising the 'brave' police who 'taught' them to obey the law.[83]

When cowboys did not respond well to paternal lectures or racial characterisations, the papers used another, more insulting, method of restraining 'the boys': public ridicule. In one such report, a wild cowboy came into San Antonio on a spree, only to face charges for being drunk and disorderly. At his court appearance he 'hung his head in a vain endeavour to choke down his sobs' and 'left amid the audible smiles of the spectators'.[84] A unique genre of humorous anecdotes at the cowboys' expense appeared in the mid-1880s which downplayed the cowboys' masculinity in the face of better and wiser 'dudes'. In one story, three cowboys attempt to intimidate a well-dressed salesman on a train platform, but the salesman turns out to be a rapid shot medal winner and sends them away 'completely cowed'.[85] In another story, 'the doodest dood', who dresses in ridiculous clothes and only drinks lemonade, beats up one of the toughest men in the local bar who had tried to get him to drink gin. The dude's fighting skills are so impressive that when he asks the other men to drink lemonade with him they quickly agree to do so.[86] This tale has the added benefit of proving the value of temperance. While we can only guess the response of the cowboys to these stories, they were clearly intended to make them feel less manly. The Dude, long the object of derision among cowboys, now owned the ranch where the cowboys worked, and therefore by middle-class standards had a greater claim to manhood.

While cowboys resisted complying with many of the regulations in town, when the ranchers made good behaviour a prerequisite to keeping their jobs, they had little choice. XIT men knew that if they got a bad reputation in town for drinking, fighting, or gambling the ranch would not rehire them the following year.[87] Teddy Abbott experienced similar supervision on the FUF Ranch in Montana, when the New Englander owner banned the *National Police Gazette* from the ranch and followed the men in town to make sure they did not drink. Unfortunately for the cowboys, 'We couldn't do nothing but to give in to him, more or less. We were strangers up north and winter was coming on. We were getting big wages. We had to take a tumble.'[88]

Faced with arrests in town and punishment on the job, cowboys had little choice but to comply with the regulation of their public leisure. While the saloons and brothels never completely disappeared, and cowboys did not stop gambling or drinking, they did so out of the public eye in the more settled towns. As in urban areas in the south and east, by the end of the century, working-class male recreation had become restricted and sanitised in public.[89] By the 1890s, stories of cowboy sprees had all but disappeared from the newspapers.

Two competing images of the cowboy emerged in the late nineteenth century. He was either a miscreant – if sentimental – boy who could not adapt to modern times, or a manly hero, fulfilling America's destiny of taming the continent. By local standards cowboys were a throwback to a more primitive time. However, for middle-class men outside the West, who worried that they had become over-civilised, the cowboy became a symbol of masculinity at this time precisely *because* of his 'primitive' masculinity. To Teddy Roosevelt, for example, the cowboy possessed 'few of the emasculated milk-and-water moralities admired by the pseudo-philanthropists; but he does possess, to a very high degree, the stern, manly qualities that are invaluable to a nation'.[90] By the 1920s, his image had gained heroic proportions even among Westerners themselves. Editor J. Marvin Hunter dedicated the *Trail Drivers of Texas* (1925) to 'the old trail drivers...to the young and the brave who fought manfully for proud, imperial Texas' and who made possible 'the development of an empire so vast in its possibilities as to excite the envy of the world'.[91]

In many ways this image accurately reflected a process that had taken place in the late nineteenth century. In the course of taming the frontier, the cattleman tried to tame the cowboy and impose his own standards of behaviour on him, including ideals about masculine behaviour. Not surprisingly, the new heroic image of the cowboy reflected a restrained and virtuous ideal of masculinity that still celebrated the 'boys' for being somewhat wild. This image was perpetuated in both literature and early Western films. Tom Mix set the tone for the tamer cowboy persona in the 1920s. His serials were aimed at children, and so he did not drink, kill or smoke in any of them. A number of imitators followed, culminating in the 1930s with Gene Autry, the singing cowboy, who codified the cowboy's alleged restraint in his Ten Cowboy Commandments. Autry's cowboys are always gentle to old people, children and animals; never smoke or drink; are never racially or religiously intolerant; are always clean in thought, deed and personal grooming; respect women and the law; and above all are patriots.[92] Ironically, many of his commandments would have been equally at home as a list of rules on the bunkhouse wall of a corporate ranch in the 1890s.

In truth, the historical cowboy was far from restrained in his behaviour, and, indeed, much of his masculine self-image lay in that freedom from restraint. However, the cattlemen ultimately maintained social hierarchies in part by asserting their own version of masculine behaviour as being superior to that of the cowboys. Masculinity was not dependent on physical strength but on manly restraint, which by definition the cowboys, however strong or skilled, could never hope to achieve. In this way, the cowboys remained permanent adolescents, and were no threat to the class structure. By the twentieth century, many of the former cowboys embraced a heroic mythical image of themselves, perhaps in part to counter the attacks on their ideals of masculinity. But the myth of the masculine cowboy who answers to no man was largely a fiction. Cattle raising was an industry as much as any factory out East, and the cowboys were employees who required close supervision. To the cattlemen and townspeople around them, they were simply out-of-control, overgrown boys, not real men.

## Notes

1. Michael Kimmel, *Manhood in America: A Cultural History* (New York, 1996), p. 150. For discussions of masculine anxiety at the turn of the century the major sources are ibid., pp. 43–78; E. Anthony Rotundo, *American Manhood: Transformations in Masculinity from the Revolution to the Modern Era* (New York, 1993), pp. 178–93; Gail Bederman, *Manliness and Civilization: A Cultural History of Gender and Race in the United States, 1880–1917* (Chicago, 1995), pp. 10–15, 77–120; Peter N. Stearns, *Be A Man!: Males in Modern Society*, 2nd edn (New York, 1990), pp. 48–79; and Peter G. Filene, *Him/Her/Self: Sex Roles in Modern America*, 2nd edn (Baltimore, 1986), pp. 72–93.
2. See such sources as Ernest Staples Osgood, *The Day of the Cattleman* (1929, reprinted Chicago, 1966), pp. 131–32n, 149–50, 228–29; Edward Everett Dale, *The Range Cattle Industry: Ranching on the Great Plains from 1865 to 1925* (1930, reprinted Norman, OK, 1960); William W. Savage, Jr (ed.), *Cowboy Life: Reconstructing an American Myth*, rev. ed. (Niwot, CO, 1993), pp. 101–02; William W. Savage, Jr, *The Cowboy Hero: His Image in American History and Culture* (Norman, OK, 1979); David Dary, *Cowboy Culture: A Saga of Five Centuries* (Lawrence, KS, 1981, 1989), pp. 308–38; Joe B. Frantz and J.E. Choate, *The American Cowboy: The Myth and the Reality* (Norman, OK, 1955); Don D. Walker, *Clio's Cowboys: Studies in the Historiography of the Cattle Trade* (Lincoln, 1981); Douglas Branch, *The Cowboy and His Interpreters* (New York, 1961); Laurence I. Seidman, *Once In the Saddle: The Cowboy's Frontier, 1866–1896* (1973, reprinted New York, 1991), pp. 122–24; David Hamilton Murdoch, *The American West: The Invention of a Myth* (Reno and Las Vegas, NV, 2001), pp. 4–5; Paul H. Carlson, 'The myth and the modern cowboy', and Robert E. Zeigler, 'The cowboy strike of 1883', in Carlson (ed.), *The Cowboy Way: An Exploration of History and Culture* (Lubbock, TX, 2000). This is just a sampling of the many sources that have discussed this issue.
3. This article is partly excerpted (with permission) from my larger work, entitled *Cow Boys and Cattle Men: Class and Masculinities on the Texas Frontier, 1865–1900* (New York, 2009), in which I address the questions of the nature of cowboy and cattleman masculinity in much greater detail.
4. For examples of sentimental cowboys, see the narratives of George L. Flanders and John J. Baker, from Texas, WPA Federal Writers' Project Collection, Manuscript Division, Library of Congress, pages 16 and 19 respectively. Found at <http://memory.loc.gov/ammem/wpaintro/txcat.html> (accessed 10 October 2005; hereafter cited as 'WPA Life Histories'). Note on sources: The Library of Congress has digitalised most of the WPA Life Histories and posted them online as part of their American Memory Project. The web address is the introductory page for the Texas narratives, of which there are 445 in total. Since the narratives do not have stable URLs, anyone wishing to access these accounts should go to the Texas page and then link to the list of all Texas narratives. They are listed in alphabetical order, not by last name but by first letter of the entry (Jim Smith is therefore alphabetised under 'J', not 'S').
5. Vaqueros on the King Ranch referred to Kleberg as 'El Abagao' (The Lawyer), and King and Kleberg sent their sons to elite academies for their education; Tom Lea, *The King Ranch*, 2 vols (Boston, 1957), pp. 325, 482–83, 510, 523, 560–64. Even cowboy and rancher Will Hale, despite his seeming wildness, was educated in New York

and St Louis at several gentlemen's boarding schools; Will Hale, *Twenty-Four Years a Cowboy and Ranchman in Southern Texas and Old Mexico: Or, Desperate Fights with the Indians and the Mexicans* (Santa Barbara, CA, 2001), pp. 16, 36, 41–2.

6. Karen R. Merrill, 'Domesticated bliss: ranchers and their animals', in Matthew Basso, Laura McCall and Dee Garceau (eds), *Across the Great Divide: Cultures of Manhood in the American West* (New York, 2001), p. 171; J. Marvin Hunter (ed.), *The Trail Drivers of Texas*, 2nd edn (1925, reprinted Austin, 1985), p. 25. For a discussion of middle-class emphasis on restraint, see Stearns, *Be A Man!*, pp. 81–2, 129, 139; Theodore Roosevelt, *The Strenuous Life: Essays and Addresses* (New York, 1911), p. 257; Thomas Winter, *Making Men, Making Class: The YMCA and Workingmen, 1877–1920* (Chicago, 2002), pp. 6–7; Judy Hilkey, *Character is Capital: Success Manuals and Manhood in Gilded Age America* (Chapel Hill, NC, 1997), pp. 142–44.

7. Richard Slotkin, *The Fatal Environment: The Myth of the Frontier in the Age of Industrialization* (Norman, OK, 1985, 1994), pp. 45–7; Richard Slatta, *Comparing Cowboys and Frontiers* (Norman, OK, 1997), p. 33. Some historians, such as Susan Johnson, Linda Gordon and Mack Faragher, have argued that before the arrival of middle-class settlers there was a period of relative equality. I would argue, however, that such a situation did not exist in the cattle industry, where there were middle-class employers and working-class employees from the very beginning.

8. E.C. 'Teddy Blue' Abbott and Helena Huntington Smith, *We Pointed Them North: Recollections of a Cowpuncher* (1939, reprinted Norman, OK, 1955), p. 85.

9. Philip Durham and Everett L. Jones, *The Negro Cowboys* (1965, reprinted Lincoln, NE, 1983), p. 99.

10. William C. Holden, *The Espuela Land and Cattle Company: A Study of a Foreign-Owned Ranch in Texas* (Austin, TX, 1970), p. 123.

11. James R. Wagner, '*Cowboy*: origin and early use of the term', in Carlson (ed.), *The Cowboy Way*, pp. 17–18.

12. William C. Holden, *Rollie Burns: Or An Account of the Ranching Industry on the South Plains* (College Station, TX, 1932, 1986), pp. 14–20, 24, 38–9.

13. Charles A. Siringo, *A Texas Cowboy: Or Fifteen Years on the Hurricane Deck of a Spanish Pony* (1886, reprinted New York, 2000), pp. 103–04.

14. Cordia Sloan Duke and Joe B. Frantz, *6,000 Miles of Fence: Life on the XIT Ranch of Texas* (Austin, TX, 1961), p. 116.

15. *San Antonio Light*, 17 March 1884, found in bound typescript, 'History of grazing in Texas: excerpts from newspapers, 1880–1884, II,' Box 2R333 Grazing Industry Papers, 1537–1940, 1973, Center for American History, University of Texas, Austin, Texas (hereafter CAH-UTA).

16. Abbott, *We Pointed them North*, pp. 212–13.

17. See, for example, the poem by Woodson Coffee, 'Reminiscences of the open range': 'Eating your breakfast while the stars are still shining/ Complaint from a man was considered just whining/ He did not last long – too soft for the job/ As he could not keep up with the rest of the mob', in 'Memories, Incidents and Tales', p. 18, bound typescript Papers of Woodson Coffee (1862–1953), Woodson Coffee Collection, Panhandle Plains Historical Museum, Canyon, Texas (hereafter PPHM).

18. Robert V. Hine and John Mack Faragher, *The American West: A New Interpretive History* (New Haven, 2000), p. 310.

19. There are many accounts and first-hand narratives that stress such heroics. 'Brave and fearless' almost inevitably appear in any description of the cowboy. For a few good examples of this connection with manhood, however, see G.F. Boone Narrative, p. 14,

WPA Life Histories; Earnest Cook Narrative, p. 8, ibid.; Pat Bullis, 'Ranging the East Panhandle', pp. 6, 8; Bullis (Pat), Box 2H 468, Vandale (Earl) Collection, CAH-UTA.
20. Cecilia Morgan, '"Better than diamonds": sentimental strategies and middle class culture in Canada West', *Journal of Canadian Studies* 32 (1998), 135.
21. *Texas Livestock Journal*, 25 July 1885, p. 4.
22. *Texas Livestock Journal*, 8 August 1885, p. 1.
23. Willie Newbury Lewis, *Tapadero: The Making of a Cowboy* (Austin, TX, 1972), p. 118.
24. Holden, *The Espuela*, pp. 50–1.
25. Walter W. Meek to Eliza Duis, 1 May 1887, 'Meek Letters', 35, bound typescript, Box 516A, A 1989-021.002, Walter Meek Family Papers, 1845–1981, South Texas Archives, Texas A and M University, Kingsville, TX.
26. Fred Horsbrugh to [J. Earle Hodges], 4 January 1901, quoted in Holden, *The Espuela*, p. 215.
27. Abner Taylor to B.H. Campbell, 4 February 1886, Letters to B.H. Campbell from Abner Taylor, 1886, E.2, D.3, XIT Ranch Records, PPHM.
28. 'General Rules of the XIT Ranch, January, 1888', in J. Evetts Haley, *The XIT Ranch of Texas and the Early Days of the Llano Estacado* (1929, reprinted Norman, OK, 1967), pp. 241–45.
29. W. Jones to H.H. Campbell, 22 February 1888, Folder 2, Box 13, Matador Land and Cattle Company Records – Headquarters Division, Southwest Collection, Texas Tech University, Lubbock, Texas (hereafter SC-TTU).
30. Earnest Cook Narrative, 8, WPA Life Histories.
31. For a discussion of the performative aspects of working-class masculinity, see Craig Heron, 'The boys and their booze: masculinities and public drinking in working-class Hamilton, 1890–1946', *Canadian Historical Review* 86 (2005), 451.
32. Ann Fabian, *Card Sharps, Dream Books and Bucket Shops: Gambling in 19th-Century America* (Ithaca, NY, 1990), p. 41.
33. Gunther Peck, 'Manly gambles: politics of risk on the Comstock Lode, 1860–1880', in Basso, McCall and Garceau (eds), *Across the Great Divide*, pp. 77–9.
34. Jim Gober, *Cowboy Justice: Tale of a Texas Lawman*, James R. Gober and B. Byron Price (eds) (Lubbock, TX, 1997), pp. 164–76.
35. Heron, 'Boys and their booze', p. 412.
36. Andre Jorgenson Anderson Narrative, p. 6, WPA Life Histories.
37. Abbott, *We Pointed Them North*, pp. 23–4.
38. *Texas Livestock Journal*, 13 September 1884.
39. *El Paso Lone Star*, 28 February 1885.
40. Elliott J. Gorn, '"Gouge and bite, pull hair and scratch": the social significance of fighting in the southern backcountry', *American Historical Review* 90 (1985), 36, 43.
41. Hale, *Twenty-Four Years*, pp. 82, 85.
42. Theodore Roosevelt, *Ranch Life and the Hunting-Trail* (New York, 1899), pp. 8, 11.
43. *Fort Griffin Echo*, 14 June 1879.
44. See, for example, the charges for the 1887 session and *State of Texas vs. G. W. Arrington*, 8 July 1887, Minutes of the District County Court, 286-87, Civil Record No 1 District Court of Donely County, County Clerk's office, Donely County Courthouse, Clarendon Texas.
45. Grady McWhiney, *Cracker Culture: Celtic Ways In the Old South* (Tuscaloosa, AL, 1988), pp. 166–67, 169.
46. District Court Minutes 2 Uvalde County, 187, District Clerk's Office, Uvalde County Courthouse, Uvalde, TX. This is the only duel I found explicitly mentioned in the

court records, which suggests either that such charges were rare or that duels were disappearing in a formal sense in Texas after Reconstruction.
47. Lea, *King Ranch*, 327–28. Interestingly, historian Lewis Atherton describes one such fight as restoring 'a sense of harmony and good will, as well as increased respect on both sides'. By Atherton's measure violence again restored order. Lewis Atherton, *The Cattle Kings* (Bloomington, IN, 1961), p. 121.
48. Charles Goodnight, 'A Sketch of the First Settlement of the Panhandle', 3, undated typescript, Literary Productions: Miscellaneous written by Charles Goodnight, undated, Box 2Q74, Charles Goodnight Papers, CAH-UTA.
49. Murdoch, *The American West*, pp. 52–4.
50. Walter W. Meek to Eliza Duis, 1 August 1887, Meek Letters, 81–82, bound typescript, Box 516A, A1989-021.002, Walter Meek Family Papers, South Texas Archives, Texas A and M University at Kingsville, Kingsville, TX.
51. *State of Texas vs. W.D. Browning*, 15 May 1891, #23, District Criminal Court, County Clerk's Office, Armstrong County Courthouse, Claude, Texas.
52. J.N. Browning to Fred Horsbrugh, 14 August 1902 and 30 July 1902, Folder 15, Box 2, J. Earle Hodges to Fred Horsbrugh, 17 September 1902, Folder 16, Box 2, J.N. Browning to Fred Horsbrugh, 30 August 1902 and 19 September 1902, Folder 3, Box 3, Espuela Land and Cattle Company Records, SC-TTU. Characteristically, the Spur disputed paying the doctor's and hotel bills for the 67 days Lindley lingered before his death. Eventually the doctor, noting that the expenses were very high and had been largely 'borne by the friends of the poor boy who have manifested such noble traits of character', reduced his bill by $50, but three months after Lindley's death the bill was still in dispute. Quote comes from J.D. Stocking to Fred Horsbrugh, undated, Folder 4, Box 3, ibid. See also J.H. Pirtle to Horsbrugh, 17 September 1902, W.H. Patrick to Horsbrugh, 3 October 1902, Folder 3, Box 3 and T.W. Carroll to Horsbrugh, 30 December 1902, Folder 15, Box 2, ibid.
53. Dickson D. Bruce, Jr makes this distinction in *Violence and Culture in the Antebellum South* (Austin, TX, 1979), p. 99.
54. Stearns, *Be A Man!*, p. 50; Shawn Johansen, *Family Men: Middle-Class Fatherhood in Early Industrializing America* (New York, 2001), p. 85. Bertram Wyatt-Brown argues that, while duels declined and were viewed as oddities after the Civil War, Southern violence to defend 'honour' did not entirely disappear; instead, it was channelled into lynchings of blacks. While I agree that violence did not completely lose legitimacy, it was not the elite who were involved in lynchings, as he himself acknowledges. Therefore I cannot see a correlation between the decline of duelling and the rise of lynchings, or a direct evolution of the idea of honour; only a working-class co-optation of the concept of honour as a justification for racist violence. Bertram Wyatt Brown, *The Shaping of Southern Culture: Honor, Grace, and War, 1760s-1890s* (Chapel Hill, NC, 2001), pp. 270–71, 283–88.
55. For a discussion of the rise of the concept of physical manhood and the importance of organised sports as a way to build up manhood, see Joe L. Dubbert, *A Man's Place: Masculinity in Transition* (Englewood Cliffs, NJ, 1979), pp. 163–75.
56. David I. Macleod, *Building Character in the American Boy: The Boy Scouts, YMCA, and Their Forerunners, 1870–1920* (Madison, WI, 1983), pp. 53–4.
57. E. Anthony Rotundo, 'Boy culture: middle-class boyhood in nineteenth century America', in Mark C. Carnes and Clyde Griffen (eds), *Meanings for Manhood: Constructions of Masculinity in Victorian America* (Chicago, 1990), pp. 31–2.
58. Quoted in J. Evetts Haley, *George W. Littlefield, Texan* (Norman, OK, 1943), pp. 77–8.

59. Murdo Mackenzie to J. Evetts Haley, 22 August 1932, 1-2, JEH II J-I, J. Evetts Haley Memorial Library and Historical Center, Midland, Texas (hereafter JEH-MLHC); W.M. Pearce, *The Matador Land and Cattle Company* (Norman, OK, 1964), pp. 39–41.
60. Hilkey, *Character is Capital*, p. 9.
61. Dee Garceau, 'Nomads, bunkies, cross-dressers and family men', in Basso, McCall and Garceau (eds), *Across the Great Divide*, pp. 153–54.
62. *Lampasas Dispatch*, 9 August 1877. This was the infamous Horrells–Higgins feud. See C.L. Sonnichsen, *I'll Die Before I'll Run – The Story of the Great Feuds of Texas*, 2nd edn (New York, 1962).
63. *Fort Griffin Echo*, 26 July 1879, 2 April 1881, 18 May 1881.
64. *Fort Griffin Echo*, 12 March 1881.
65. Charles Goodnight and D.H. Snyder banned alcohol on the ranches and William Lewis confessed to never really drinking very much, even when in town with fellow cowboys. See Lewis, *Tapadero*, 98–9, 104–05; Abner Taylor to B.H. Campbell, 1 November 1885, Letters Received by B.H. Campbell 1885–1887, E.1, D.3, XIT Ranch Records, PPHM; J.G.K. McClure, 'Among the Cowboys of Texas April 23-May 7, 1896', Manuscript Interview, PPHM; Holden, *The Espuela*, p. 48; Mose Hayes to J. Evetts Haley, 8 November 1931, p. 2, JEH II J-I, JEH-MLHC.
66. Ted Ownby, *Subduing Satan: Religion, Recreation, and Manhood in the Rural South, 1865–1920* (Chapel Hill, NC, 1990), pp. 167–170, 172.
67. *Handbook of Texas Online*, s.v. 'Prohibition', <<http://www.tshaonline.org/handbook/online/articles/PP/vap1.html>> (accessed 7 July 2008).
68. See, for example, the many cases dismissed against stores illegally selling intoxicating liquors on Sunday in Armstrong County in 1890: *State of Texas vs. George B. Berry*, 21 August 1890, *State of Texas vs. George Ireland*, 23 May 1890, *State of Texas vs. Jess Gumm*, 23 May 1890, *State of Texas vs. C. M. Johnson*, 12 August 1890, Folders 12–17, Records of the District Court, County Clerk's Office, Armstrong County Courthouse, Claude, TX. The profusion of cases in that year seems to suggest an attempt to crack down on such establishments, however.
69. J.S. Wynne to J. Evetts Haley, 15 July 1926, 9, Manuscript Interview, PPHM.
70. George W. Littlefield to J. 'Will' White, in typescript of letters 'September 15, 1860-Dec 12, 1868', 49–51, Reel 1, George W. Littlefield Papers, SC-TTU.
71. Fabian, *Card Sharps*, pp. 6, 40.
72. *Fort Griffin Echo*, 9 August 1879. See also ibid., 14 February 1880, for a similar warning.
73. 'The Cowboy's Vacation', *Texas Livestock Journal*, 25 October 1884.
74. Bederman, *Manliness and Civilization*, pp. 23–31. There is a growing literature on the racialisation of manhood and the attempt to use whiteness as a way of improving one's own masculine image. See, for example, David Roediger, *The Wages of Whiteness: Race and the Making of the American Working Class*, rev. edn (London, 2007); and Timothy Tyson, *Radio Free Dixie: Robert F. Williams and the Roots of Black Power* (Chapel Hill, NC, 2001).
75. These numbers are extremely difficult to arrive at, given the lack of clear data. For a discussion of the number of black cowboys see Sara R. Massey (ed.), *Black Cowboys of Texas* (College Station, TX, 2000), pp. xiii–xiv and Savage, *The Cowboy Hero*, pp. 6–9. Savage argues that most estimates are not based in fact, as we cannot know the total number of cowboys with any certainty.
76. Kenneth W. Porter, 'Negro Labor in the Western Cattle Industry, 1866–1900', *Labor History* 10 (1969), 347–48; Holden, *Rollie Burns*, p. 218.

77. Bruce G. Todd, *Bones Hooks: Pioneer Negro Cowboy* (Gretna, LA, 2005), p. 13.
78. Ibid., pp. 37, 65–6, 76–7.
79. Mark Withers, for example, took a herd up the trail to Chicago of Joseph McCoy with two Mexican cowboys and commented that 'The Mexicans were fine ropers, as fine as I ever saw.' However, he did not name them, although he named his Anglo buddy who went with them. Mark Withers to J. Evetts Haley, 8 October 1932, 14 JEH II J-I, JEH-MLHC.
80. J. Frank Dobie, *A Vaquero of the Brush Country* (New York, 1929), p. 13.
81. Joseph G. McCoy, *Historic Sketches of the Cattle Trade of the West and Southwest* (Kansas City, MO, 1874), pp. 10, 137–38.
82. Quoted in Jack Weston, *The Real American Cowboy* (New York, 1985), p. 24.
83. *San Antonio Light*, 1 October 1883, found in 'History of Grazing in Texas: Excerpts from Newspapers, 1880–1884 II', Historical Records Survey, Works Progress Administration, 1935, Box 2R 333, Grazing Industry Papers, 1537–1940, 1973, CAH-UTA.
84. *San Antonio Light*, 28 May 1884, 'History of Grazing in Texas: Excerpts from Newspapers, 1880–1884 II', Historical Records Survey, Works Progress Administration, 1935, Box 2R 333, Grazing Industry Papers, 1537–1940, 1973, CAH-UTA.
85. *Texas Livestock Journal*, 12 September 1885.
86. *San Antonio Light*, 26 March 1884, ibid.
87. J.G.K. McClure, 'Among the Cowboys of Texas April 23 – May 7, 1896', 19–21, Manuscript Interview, PPHM. McClure, an English visitor to the ranch, could not praise the rules highly enough, as he said otherwise the cowboys would all gamble and drink, and now they were all really well behaved.
88. Abbott, *We Pointed Them North*, p. 74.
89. See Ownby, *Subduing Satan*, pp. 176–77.
90. Roosevelt, *Ranch Life*, p. 56.
91. Hunter (ed.), *Trail Drivers of Texas*, pp. xix–xx.
92. Edward Buscombe (ed.), *The BFI Companion to the Western* (London, 1988), pp. 24–5, 28–31, 35–6.

# 18
# Valorising Samurai Masculinity through Biblical Language: Christianity, Oscar Wilde and Natsume Soseki's Novel *Kokoro*

*Kasumi Miyazaki*

*Kokoro* (1914), meaning the heart, is a novel written by Natsume Soseki; it is, in fact, about blood rather than a heart. While this novel eloquently describes blood in its pages, it talks less about the heart itself. The Japanese word 'kokoro', the simplest word meaning a heart, does not completely correspond to the English word 'heart'. The English equivalent signifies 'heart' as both an organ of the body and a locus of passion, whereas the Japanese word, *kokoro*, carries the passionate connotation only. The Japanese language has a different word signifying the organ, that is, *shinzo*. Although in Japanese a distinction is made between the two usages, Soseki, in *Kokoro*, seems deliberately to try and confuse the two meanings. The novel's title, *Kokoro*, evidently signifies a heart as organ, unlike an ordinary Japanese usage. One can say that this novel is obsessed with blood, through its corporeal connection with the heart, circulating from the heart and returning to the heart itself.

For those not familiar with this work, I will briefly introduce here the plot of *Kokoro*. It consists of the memoirs of a young man/narrator ('I') and the testament letter of Sensei – also a Japanese word for a respected teacher or elder figure. They accidentally meet each other and soon start a friendship, initiated mainly by the innocent young man, who is attracted to Sensei. Sensei is an introverted man, and closed in regard to his past. 'I' is eager to know Sensei's past and for Sensei to share his past with him; but 'I' is rejected in his overtures. Sensei's inner pain and secretiveness concern his betrayal of his friend, known simply as K, which supposedly led K to commit suicide. Sensei has had to live with this sense of guilt, revealing his secret to no one, not even to his wife, who, as a young woman, was the cause of the breakdown of the friendship between Sensei and K. At the last, he finally breaks free from the burden of guilt in that Sensei kills himself, just like K, and leaves his written 'testament' to the young man/narrator, revealing the truth of his inner suffering.

Toward the end of the novel, a key element of the plot describes how, when the Emperor Meiji died on 30 July 1912 after a reign of 44 years, a veteran member of Japan's military elite, General Nogi, decided to take his life in a feudal act known as *junshi* – meaning 'following one's lord in death' – as atonement for losing the emperor's flag in battle 35 years earlier. This real event shocked contemporary Japanese society so much that Soseki, as a response, turned his meditation upon Nogi's death into literary expression in the form of a novel. In his final 'testament', Sensei confessed that he came to the decision to commit suicide inspired by the news of General Nogi's suicide. On hearing this long-forgotten word *junshi*, that is, self-immolation, Sensei, too, sees that the time has come for him to atone in his reverence for 'the spirit of Meiji', resolving to commit suicide.[1]

## A brief history of the literary criticism of *Kokoro*

*Kokoro* is a canonical work in modern Japanese literature. This novel has been the subject of a wide range of theoretical and literary studies since its first publication. This novel is special, in that many critics have suggested a possible link between the novel, as a canon representing modern Japan, and modern nation state formation in Japan. James Fujii, among others, has proclaimed the novel's capability as a canon, contending that it was seen to exemplify an important move toward 'true' literary modernity.[2] It successfully imitated the 'authentic' European model of the novel in its depiction of a modern individual subject, in contrast to the incomplete characterisation found in traditional Japanese literature. In response to Fujii's contention, this essay will demonstrate that the novel describes how the inner life of modern Japanese men was constructed through internalisation of Christian biblical language.

While Soseki was still alive and writing, criticism of his work was considerable, and published criticism on *Kokoro* has been incessant ever since. But the burgeoning body of criticism on Soseki's work occurred in the years after 1985, when the so-called 'debates on *Kokoro*' were launched.[3] This tranche of criticism was sparked by the publication of Yoichi Komori's essay, 'The "heart" that generates *Kokoro*', in 1985. The highly controversial nature of this essay aroused new critical interest in *Kokoro*, and provoked a flurry of impassioned reactions in Japan. In the essay and his reading of the text, Komori sees the possibility that the narrator has married Sensei's widow. The narrator has fathered a child with her, which Sensei was unable to do. Komori detects this in the textual rupture between the present time of the narrator and the novel's end as the end of Sensei's testament. Many scholars who gave weight to the ethical importance of *Kokoro* in modern Japan found Komori's reading unacceptable and scandalous. Among these, the mightiest opponent was Yukio Miyoshi, professor emeritus at the University of Tokyo and an authority in Soseki studies. Although this debate apparently seemed to be a generational confrontation, it in fact emanated from their different approaches to the text. The debates on *Kokoro* stimulated a critical field in Japanese literary studies, and fostered a variety of approaches to the text in *Kokoro*.

Komori's further contribution to these debates has been the presentation of new approaches to the historical problematisation of homosexuality, newly introduced to Japanese society in the Meiji period. As for the new reconfiguration of modern bodies and the construction of sexual subjects in the Meiji era, about which I will explain in more detail later, Komori pays attention to the pressure exerted not only by the West but from within modern Japanese culture itself. He suggests that 'homosexual energy', centred upon the young Meiji emperor at the time of the Restoration, was an important motivation among the young soldiers who were gathered around the emperor, and channelled toward 'revolutionary' change. Komori's analysis has helped Stephen Dodd conceptualise 'the new libidinal economy' of the Meiji period, which came to reflect the powerful influence of Western codes of sexuality.[4] Though he was preceded in his argument by the psychiatrist Takeo Doi in 1969, Dodd's extensive study should be counted as pioneer in its emphasis upon homosexuality and its distinguished scholarly contextualisation of history and literature. What is remarkable in Dodd's analysis is that, in approaching the triangular relationship in *Kokoro* between Sensei, K and a 'daughter of the lodge', he does not regard the 'daughter of the lodge' as the romantic catalyst in attracting the two young men, but dismisses the daughter character as marginal in this triangular relationship. Instead, Dodd focuses on the rivalry between the two men, and reads into it a certain degree of mutual attraction and even homoerotic desire. Dodd adopted Eve Sedgwick's analysis of homosocial desire in his approach to this aspect of the text.

Although *Kokoro* is unanimously considered canonical, it has singularly defied easy analysis concerning Sensei's resolution to 'die for the spirit of Meiji'; this crucial aspect of the novel remains one of its mysteries. As Jay Rubin frankly admitted, 'critics have had difficulty explaining exactly how the suicide of General Nogi is related to the suicide of Soseki's protagonist.'[5] Doris Bargen bravely challenged this apparent paradox through her thoroughgoing analysis of the phenomenon of *junshi*, suicidal honour.[6] Her analysis, synthesising and applying the most resonant of the exciting interpretations proposed by many scholars in regard to *Kokoro*, approaches the crux of the piece: why does Sensei decide to commit the act of suicide for the 'spirit of Meiji', being urged on by Nogi's *junshi*? She regards Sensei's suicide as a sacrifice offered to the young narrator, and 'Soseki establishes intergenerational sacrifice in *Kokoro* in order to create and maintain kinship between men and men'.[7] Bargen's analysis comes closest to the arguments in this chapter. Despite the fact that she notices that the language of *Kokoro* refers to 'ritual sacrifice' and casts Sensei as 'an Aztec priest sacrificing to the gods', she has not discerned the crucial external associations in the work, namely Christianity or the Bible. Her analysis gets very close to the centre of the work's enigma. Its limit lies in the assumption that Sensei's suicide is unproblematically identifiable with General Nogi's *junshi*. Instead, my interpretation is that Nogi's *junshi* is rather a guise or a cover for something quite new at the time when Soseki wrote: 'the antiquated word (=*junshi*) had a new meaning for me'.[8] What is this 'new meaning' of the word *junshi* he refers to? The purpose of this chapter is the quest to discern the meaning of this 'new meaning'.

## The construction of modern sexuality in Meiji Japan

In order to contextualise Soseki's life and work, it is necessary to outline the rapid changes in body politics and sexual mores in his lifetime.[9] After the so-called restoration of imperial rule in 1868, Japan began its rapid transformation into a centralised nation state along the lines of the Western imperialist powers. These political changes involved not only new governmental and civic institutions, but also a reconfigured regime of sexual regulation to help sustain a new national order. The Meiji government in the new Japan had to fashion the modern subject who managed to modernise his or her own body; that is, a sexual subject who was 'Japanese' for the first time, in contrast to the situation prior to 1868, in which no such nationally authoritative standards for sexual behaviour existed.

The cultural era brought about after the Meiji restoration has generally been termed that of 'civilisation and enlightenment'.[10] For the Japanese, the concept 'civilisation' represented the final destination on an evolutionary path, upwards from 'barbarism', a goal understood as having been achieved most fully by the Western societies. Along this evolutionary axis, Japan's current stage of development lay half-enlightened. The imitation of Western practices thus seemed indispensable in order for Japan to join the comity of civilised nation states. This conviction, together with the aim of persuading the treaty powers to relinquish extraterritorial privileges, was embraced by Meiji leaders, helping to initiate reform through launching policies ranging from the adoption of Western-style governmental and civic structures to the prohibition of social practices that might offend Western sensibilities and diminish Japan's cultural status in Western eyes. The latter was especially intended to fashion 'civilised' subjects from the 'half-barbarian' people of the Edo period. In codifying 'civilised' standards of sexual behaviour, the Meiji government had to establish new penal codes concerning sexuality, which included prohibitions against mixed bathhouses, public nudity and semi-nudity, the sale of erotic images (*shunga*) and phallic objects, and public urination.

At the centre of 'civilised morality' lay male–female sexuality within the framework of state-sanctioned marriage, and the family based upon the monogamous system.[11] As Japanese men and women had never formed this kind of heterosexual relationship, supposed to be motivated by romantic love, it brought about much embarrassment among men. The introduction of 'civilised morality', however, had a heavier impact upon homosexual love between men.[12] The new legal regime put an end to the non-criminal status of sexual acts between men. Such acts now came to exemplify sexuality beyond the bounds of 'civilised morality'. The first legislation to punish sexual acts between men was the 1873 *Kaitei ritsuryo* (reformed penal codes), which focused on regulating the practice of anal intercourse – a central element of *shudo* (a former name for homosexual love) that now came to exemplify sexuality outside the bounds of 'civilised' order.

The medical authorities established a new attitude towards male–male sexuality through the rapid influx of medical knowledge from the West during the Meiji period. It coincided with a vigorous wave of theorising the construct of 'homosexuality' by Western sexologists. As Meiji doctors were quick to domesticate the new medical knowledge and to embrace its premises, they readily advocated a pathological view of 'homosexuality'.[13] They coined Japanese equivalents for this term as early as the 1890s, which by the 1920s would become established as *doseiai* or 'same-sex love'.[14] The earliest work that introduced medical knowledge on 'same-sex love' into Meiji Japan was an 1894 translation of *Psychopathia Sexualis* by Richard von Krafft-Ebing, which was published under the auspices of the Japanese Forensic Medicine Association only eight years after its initial appearance in Europe. Through the influence of this work and others, male–male sexuality would increasingly be viewed not as an erotic discipline like *shudo*, or even a moral failing as in the 'civilised' paradigm, but as a sexual pathology or as a symptom of 'degeneration', which, Krafft-Ebing maintained, considered an individual homosexual as a 'hereditary taint' running in a particular family or a race doomed to decline.[15]

Soseki, born in 1867, just one year before the restoration, spent his youth in times of revolutionary changes, though he was brought up with the remnants of the masculine culture of the past, which valorised homoeroticism and tolerated sexual acts between men. He had been familiar with a culture that would readily express exchange of erotic feelings between men. With the advent of the Meiji era, however, the situation changed profoundly, as described above. Certainly, he was a member of a Japanese society that came to regard itself as entering the civilised stage, where homosexual relationships were now considered as not only barbarian, but even pathological. He himself not only possessed some of the better-known sexological works, including *Studies in the Psychology of Sex* (1905–08) by Havelock Ellis, *Degeneration* (1898) by Max

Nordau and *Marriage and Heredity* (1890) by J.F. Nisbet, but also read them, leaving some notes and marks in them.

Furthermore, he was witness to the ostracisation of a genius such as Wilde in the intensely homophobic society of Britain at this time. This experience might temporarily have driven him also into the so-called 'homosexual panic', creating in him fear of expressing love between men. But the experience did not make him homophobic. As a student of English literature, more particularly in his reading of Oscar Wilde, he was able to overcome his fears by learning that literary language potentially could express everything, even the unspeakable, in hidden terms, or closeted language, which he in turn mastered later in his literary career.

## Reading *Kokoro* (1914) by way of the Bible and the Christian symbolism of blood

Having outlined the plot in the introductory paragraphs, I will analyse *Kokoro* by focusing on the topic of *junshi*; the crucial theme at the end of the novel. Sensei's motive to commit suicide was inspired by the word *junshi*. He wrote, on hearing the long-forgotten word, that he saw that the time had come for him to atone for his reverence for 'the spirit of Meiji'.

Although the custom and practice of *junshi* in its fully developed form are unique to Japanese culture, we can find similar customs in other cultures in antiquity.[16] In its prototypical form, *junshi* is voluntary human sacrifice upon the death of a secular lord who was venerated like a deity, and was performed by *seppuku*. *Junshi* expresses so strong a bond between lord and retainer that the bond cannot be severed by the lord's death. It demonstrates the retainer's gratitude for the benefits and favours of the feudalistic and patriarchal lord–retainer relationship. What should be noted here is that this heroic act of following one's lord into death is supposed to be suffused with homoeroticism, if not always fully sexual, between the lord and the retainer. In the first half of the seventeenth century, at the end of the period of civil wars between daimyos, and in the early days of the Edo period (1603–1867), the practice of *junshi* reached epidemic proportions, to such an extent it concerned the Tokugawa shogunate and was banned officially in 1663. Although the ban was followed by frequent prohibitions, the practice was not completely uprooted, because it remained culturally the most heroic act for samurai to commit. The Tokugawa era's prohibition continued in effect after the Meiji restoration. The barbaric custom of *junshi* had been forbidden and more or less forgotten for centuries until Nogi enacted it in 1912. Nogi was 'an anachronistic lawbreaker and a heroic upholder of Japanese tradition'.[17]

From this point of view, *Kokoro* seems to be symbolic of the last respects to and nostalgic praise of noble samurai masculinity, much more identifiable with the early feudal Edo period than the capitalist and westernised nation born after the Meiji restoration. Certainly, Soseki sometimes expressed his hatred toward capitalism and the modernisation of Meiji Japan. This plot, however, was not only motivated by nostalgic eulogy for feudal masculinity but also by his sympathy with Christian masculinity. I use the word 'testament' when describing Sensei's last letter and the word 'atonement', signifying Sensei's death. They both are terms drawn from the Bible, and are culturally specific to Christianity. I use them intentionally, because Soseki *intentionally* created a plot that would correspond with some elements in the New Testament. The work *Kokoro* describes the formation of the heart, the interiority, of intellectual men of the Meiji era, and, through creating this piece of work, it can be said that Soseki proposed, for the new era, a new masculine presentation, drawing inspiration from the Bible.

It will be useful at this juncture to cite some examples that demonstrate the influence of the New Testament in *Kokoro*. The character K is a student who is pursuing a means of salvation through the academic study of the religious thought of Buddhism. Besides this, K also has a copy of the Bible on the desk in his room. Among a not inconsiderable number of references, the most suggestive Biblically influenced expressions in the text are as follows:

> I returned to the house. As usual, I went into K's room in order to get to mine. It was then that my conscience to K *resurrected*... Suddenly, I wanted to kneel before him and beg his forgiveness. It was a violent emotion that I felt then. I think that had K and I been alone in some *wilderness*, I would have listened to the cry of my conscience. But there were others in the house. I soon overcame the impulse of my natural self to be true to K, which, unhappily, was never to *resurrect*.[18]

In the above quotation, the italicised words are expressions that I have altered deliberately from Edwin McClellan's extensively used English translation of *Kokoro*. For example, McClellan's translated sentence 'It was then that I felt guilty for the first time' should read instead 'It was then that my conscience to K resurrected.' The major alteration is that I adopt the English word 'resurrected'. I do this deliberately to highlight the biblical connotation contained in the original Japanese word *fukkatsu*, as used by Soseki in the novel. As the meaning of the word *fukkatsu* has not been limited to the biblical context in Japanese language usage of recent years, placing the word 'resurrect' as an equivalent expression to the Japanese word *fukkatsu* here might seem, at first glance, a peculiar intervention to make. But, significantly, the Japanese word *fukkatsu* was a new word, a neologism, in use only since the 1890s, and it was Christian authors in Japanese who used it enthusiastically (and predominantly) in the early days of its existence, when describing Christ's resurrection. Though my deliberate emphases may still seem too overt in stressing the biblical at this point in the analysis, the biblical emphasis in *fukkatsu* is truer to Soseki's linguistic intentions. *Fukkatsu* would have conveyed its biblical connotations and cultural meaning much more clearly at the time, given the usage of this new word by Christian writers in Japanese.[19] Moreover, 'wilderness' is a word cited from the New Testament. Its usage in the above passage would seem culturally alien to the Japanese reader in 1903 – and stylistically abrupt. We can detect the author's special intention in his deployment of new words and imported expressions, which aim to evoke the biblical context.

In another passage, Sensei, who visits K's grave, is described as penitent, and performs penance for his guilt before K's grave. He does this by kneeling down. This expression appears very strange. First, the word 'penitent' is peculiar to Christianity; and, second, one does not kneel down to a grave in Japanese culture. Kneeling down is acceptable in Japan if it is a Christian grave, situated as it is nearer to the ground; but most emphatically not at a traditional Japanese grave. This close reading reveals that Sensei's betrayal of a male friend, his suffering and profound guilt, and his performance of penitence, are described in the language of Christianity. To put it another way, the formation of Sensei's heart, his secret inner part, was constructed through biblical metaphors.

One more example from *Kokoro* is illustrative, as it evokes a celebrated scene in the Gospel according to St John, where Mary Magdalene meets the resurrected Christ in the garden of the sepulchre, and the weeping Mary Magdalene supposes the apparition to be the gardener.

> Not far from us in the cemetery, a man was levelling off a piece of rough ground to make a new grave. He stopped, and, resting on his hoe, he watched us.[20]

The narrator of the above passage is Sensei's young friend, and the gardener watched Sensei and him. Sensei regularly visits K's tomb, and the young friend came to catch him in the cemetery. This passage urges us to interpret some meaning, for it apparently has no logical connection with the context. In the above citation, the man who was levelling off ground by use of a hoe is evocative of Christ, whom Mary Magdalene supposed to be the gardener (John 20:15). According to Christian symbolism, Christ traditionally is represented holding a hoe when he is figured as the gardener. The cemetery also is evocative of the New Testament references to the sepulchre where Christ was buried; the tomb was new and one where a man had never yet lain. The cemetery in the novel is given a name as *Zoshigaya-bochi*, which exists near the centre of Tokyo, and was in reality new when *Kokoro* was written. It was constructed in 1874, and extended in 1900.

This close reading leads us to conclude that *Kokoro* includes elements of the narrative structure of the New Testament in its plot, and that the story of Sensei's betrayal is modelled on the most infamous betrayer in the New Testament, Judas. *Kokoro* has been canonical in modern Japanese literature since its publication, not only because no other work has been more widely read in Japan but also because it served as a national narrative of the self-making of Japanese people in the new era of modernity. Furthermore, *Kokoro* describes the construction of the heart of Japanese men explicitly in the language of the Bible, introducing such linguistic concepts as 'conscience', 'repentance', 'penance', 'guilt', 'betrayal of one's friend', and so on, ahead of any other novel. These words were brought into the fictional world of *Kokoro*, and served to make one's soul like a Christian's, fostering the development of a critical gaze inward to the soul.

## The reconstruction of masculinity through Christianity and General Nogi

If we accept that *Kokoro* is suffused with biblical concepts, what role, then, does Oscar Wilde play in this intertextual relationship between *Kokoro* and the Bible? The influence of Wilde as the catalyst for Soseki's adoption of biblical metaphors, and the Christian symbolism of blood in the novel, is compelling. Specifically, it was Wilde's letter to Lord Alfred Douglas, known as *De Profundis*, which included his extraordinarily beautiful essay about Jesus and art, which was of direct influence. Soseki possessed a copy of *De Profundis* and certainly read it, for he left several check marks and underlines on his copy of it, particularly concerning passages about art and the symbol. For example, he underlined Wilde's words 'Art is a symbol, because man is a symbol.'[21] This theme is precisely what Soseki attempted to express through his literary works. Besides this, he quoted Wilde's writing in his novel, *The Three Cornered World* (*Kusamakura*, 1906): 'I see a far more intimate and immediate connection between the true life of Christ and the true life of the artist.'[22] It can be inferred from these empirical traces how deeply Soseki was impressed by Wilde's *De Profundis*. We can understand the reason, when we see the marks Soseki left in the margin along the following of Wilde's sentences:

> On November 13th 1895 I was brought down here from London. From two o'clock till half-past two on the day I had to stand on the centre platform on Clapham Junction in convict dress and handcuffed, for the world to look at. I had been taken out of the Hospital Ward without a moment's notice being given to me. Of all possible objects I was the most grotesque. When people saw me they laughed. Each train as it came up swelled the audience. Nothing could exceed their amusement. That was of course before

they knew who I was. As soon as they had been informed, they laughed still more. For half an hour I stood there in the grey November rain surrounded by a jeering mob. For a year after that was done to me I wept everyday at the same hour and for the same space of time.[23]

This overt hostility toward the homosexual male was precisely what Meiji Japan was trying to imitate and to appropriate to itself. Soseki must have been frightened when he read this passage, as the miserable, abject figure Wilde could easily be his double in different circumstances. Soseki could be labelled as a sodomite, in the new Japanese morality, though he succeeded in avoiding naming anything 'unspeakable', or to be named thus. Most certainly, the masculine culture of Edo he admired was considered sodomitical in the new social order, and vilified. Significantly, the three main characters in *Kokoro* have no names. It is arguable that Soseki decided to take Wilde's tragic fate upon himself by creating his own piece of work that would absorb his innermost fears. In order for Soseki to achieve this, the spiritual atonement evident in *De Profundis* and its overtly religious overtones provided the inspiration for him to use the Christian symbolism of blood for vicarious atonement in *Kokoro*.

What Soseki learned from Wilde, through Wilde's treatment of Christ in *De Profundis* and his dedication of the essay to Christ, was the possibility of seeing Christ as literary symbolism. As evident from passages of Wilde cited by Soseki in *Kusamakura*, Wilde points to Christ's outstanding temperament as a poet. Christ saw the 'One Life' at the cores of all human existence, realised only through man's poetic temperament, according to Wilde. Wilde wrote that:

> He (=Christ) was the first to conceive the divided races as a unity. Before his time there had been gods and men. He alone saw that on the hills of life there were but God and Man, and, feeling through the mysticism of sympathy that in himself each had been made incarnate.[24]

As Wilde conceived Christ to be the ultimate symbol, 'What God was to the Pantheist, man was to him.' Because of the typological relationship between the Old Testament and the New, the life of Christ symbolises the race's history of the Kingdom of Israel in the history of humanity. Christ's power as a symbol made it possible that 'the supreme office of the Church should be the playing of the tragedy *without the shedding of blood*, the mystical presentation by means of dialogue and costume and gesture even of the Passion of her Lord...'[25] As 'art is a symbol',[26] art can encapsulate human tragedy as a vicarious play, '*without the shedding of blood* [my italics]'. Soseki adopted the symbolic power of the New Testament by internalising, or interweaving, its narrative structure into the text, and thereby made his own art, *Kokoro*, a vicarious narrative.

*Kokoro* is, however, haunted by another ghost arising from Japan's long-forgotten past, more explicitly stated in the work. The ghost of General Nogi, in *Kokoro*, embodies the heroic, and even homoerotic, passion of samurai comradeship, which is expressively consummated by Nogi's carrying out of *junshi*. When the Meiji Emperor died, Sensei felt that the spirit of the Meiji era had begun with the Emperor and had ended with him, and that Sensei and the others, who had been brought up in that era, were left behind to live as the leftovers. When he told his wife so, she suggested *junshi* to solve his problem, as a joke. This almost forgotten word, *junshi*, impressed Sensei:

> I had almost forgotten that there was such a word as '*junshi*.' It is not a word that one uses normally, and I suppose it had been banished to some remote corner of my memory. I turned to my wife, who had reminded me of its existence, and said: 'I will commit *junshi* if you like; but in my case, it will be through loyalty to the spirit of the Meiji era.' My remark was meant as a joke; but I did feel that the antiquated word had come to hold a new meaning for me.[27]

What is the new meaning the antiquated word, *junshi*, had come to hold? At this point, however, we are not given any clue to this enigma, and his wife's remark is suspended like a prophecy. About a month later, *junshi* is actually carried out by General Nogi. The antiquated and long-forgotten word was suddenly embodied by the corpses of Nogi and Nogi's wife:

> A month passed. On the night of the Imperial Funeral I sat in my study and listened to the booming of the cannon. To me, it sounded like the last lament for the passing of an age. Later, I realised that it might also have been a salute to General Nogi. Holding the extra edition in my hand, I blurted out to my wife: '*Junshi! Junshi!*'
>
> I read in the paper the words General Nogi had written before killing himself. I learned that ever since the *Seinan* War, when he lost his banner to the enemy, he had been wanting to redeem his honour through death. I found myself automatically counting the years that the general had lived, always *with death at the back of his mind*...'When did he suffer greater agony – during those thirty-five years, or the moment when the sword entered his bowels?'
>
> It was two or three days later that I decided at last to commit suicide. Perhaps you will not understand clearly why I am about to die, no more than I can fully understand why General Nogi killed himself.[28]

While the new meaning in the word *junshi* is not yet made explicit, the above quotation shows that Sensei's decision to commit suicide is superimposed upon General Nogi's *junshi*. Moreover, Nogi's wife, who was also found dead beside him, has the same name as Sensei's wife, Shizuko. What makes these two people, General Nogi and Sensei, seem particularly identical is their way of living *'with death at the back of his mind* [my italics]'. Sensei also lived 'with death at his back'. In the case of Sensei, his 'death-in-life' came from his profound sense of guilt:

> I felt very strongly the sinfulness of man. It was this feeling that sent me to K's grave every month, that made take care of my mother-in-law in her illness and behave gently towards my wife. It was this sense of sin that led me to feel sometimes that I would welcome a flogging even at the hands of strangers. When this desire for punishment became particularly strong, I would begin to feel that it should come from myself, and not others. Then I would think of death. Killing myself seemed a just punishment for my sins. Finally, I decided to go on *living as if I were dead*.[29]

The reference to 'death-in-life', as well as 'life-in-death', can also be regarded as derived from Christianity, to which paradoxical inversion between life and death is intrinsic. The ideas of living and dying being one and indivisible are strong themes in the narratives both of the New Testament and of *Kokoro*. To cite the New Testament: 'Always bearing about in the body the dying of the Lord Jesus, that the life also of Jesus might be made manifest in our body. For we which live are always delivered unto death for Jesus' sake, that the life also of Jesus might be made manifest in our mortal flesh' (*2 Corinthians*, 4: 10–11). As both the above citations from *Kokoro* show, the causes of Nogi's and Sensei's senses of guilt are quite different: Nogi's is the loss of the battle; Sensei's the universal sinfulness of man, originally arising from his own sin committed against K. In this context, however, his own sin, committed personally, needs to be interpreted as not only his own, but the universal sin of the whole of humanity. This displacement could be achieved through the narrative structure adopted in this novel: that of the New Testament. As a novel, this work casts three main characters and describes what happened to them, and at the same time it aims to relate the abstracted and generalised sense of the fate of mankind, simultaneously throughout the text.

The two quite different motives for suicide, originating from the distinct personal and cultural circumstances of Nogi and Sensei, are conflated into one single expression of *junshi*. The vicarious atonement of Christ is slipped covertly into another form of atonement, *junshi*, of which samurai masculinity was once proud. The latter context is revived so vividly that it has veiled the meaning and significance of the former, rendered latent in the work through the passage of time and anachronism in the specific meanings of words used by Soseki. Arguably, this heroic act peculiar to Japanese culture was connected, through Sensei's motives to commit *junshi*, with the vicarious atonement of

Christ, mediated through the vicarious sacrifice of Oscar Wilde. The practice of *junshi* originated in the milieu of samurai comradely love in the feudal period, but the devotional passion initially contained within the word was, by Sensei's time, all but forgotten. At Sensei's wife's remark, the word suddenly came back from oblivion, *resurrected*. Nogi's body, on the other hand, dedicated entirely to the Emperor of Japan, recalled explicitly and vividly a form of culturally specific eroticism that had long been forgotten and forbidden. Nogi killed himself by thrusting a sword into his bowels. But the traditional act of *junshi*, with shedding of blood by thrusting a sword through the bowels, gains a new meaning and dimension through Sensei's mysteriously idiosyncratic act of *junshi*, from the Christian symbolism of Christ's blood-sacrifice as atonement for the sins of the world. In Sensei's fashioning of *junshi*, the masculine ethos of samurai comradeship represented by the word *junshi* becomes connected intimately to Christ's passion and blood, which in turn is eroticised through Oscar Wilde's suffering and the beauty of his language in his lament to his male lover, in Wilde's essay dedicated to Christ.[30]

## Heritage of the masculine ethos and the subverted language of blood symbolism

If this is the case, then what did Soseki intend to express by borrowing the Christian symbolism of blood for Sensei's *junshi*? It is certain that he aimed deliberately to suffuse *Kokoro* with the blood metaphor. At the beginning of Sensei's 'testament', he explains why he decided to confess his past.

> In the end, you asked me to spread out my past like a picture scroll before your eyes. Then, for the first time, I respected you. I was moved by your decision, albeit discourteous in expression, to grasp something that was alive within my heart. You wished to *cut open my heart and see the blood flow*. I was then still alive. I did not want to die. That is why I refused you and postponed the granting of your wish to another day. Now, I myself am about to *cut open my own heart, and drench your face with my blood. And I shall be satisfied if, when my heart stops beating, a new life lodges itself in your breast.*[31]

This is the most crucial and the most often quoted passage in the work. Its impressiveness results from the culturally alien metaphor of the heart and blood, which suggests a hint of Christ's atonement, not through the traditional form of *junshi*, for he does not mention anywhere the cutting of Sensei's bowels, but his heart. Close attention to the last expression, 'a new life lodges itself in your breast', is important; this peculiar interpretation of blood in the novel begins to reveal a new meaning; the reproduction of a new life between males. Does this passage, then, intend to express the succession of a life from male to male? In this metaphor of life-succession between males, the heart seems to be allegorised as a male womb, in which 'a new life lodges itself.' It is as though a womb has been replaced through the male homoerotic relationship by a heart.

Also, what precisely is it that is figured as a 'new life' here? If were a heterosexual relationship being described, the metaphor of the circulation of blood would evoke notions of spermatic economy, prevalent in sexological thought at the time, which originally denoted circulation of sperm between man and woman. In this context, sperm, or blood, figuratively served as a conduit of heredity, or physical inheritance. Indeed, Soseki fictionalised heterosexual relationships in the light of European notions of spermatic economy in his novel *And Then* (*Sorekara*, 1909). Its male protagonist is described as a degenerate aesthete somewhat resembling Oscar Wilde, being endowed with a degenerate body; the assumption is made that the character's degeneration is rooted in his ancestor's sin. It is represented as a metaphor of aberrant erotic customs, chiefly varieties of male–male sexual intercourse, from the Edo period. This label of degeneration also cast a shadow over the future of Japanese society as a whole, in the concepts of the time.

In *Kokoro*, however, he drew the blood metaphor, not from spermatic economy, but from Christian symbolism. This shift in influences accompanied the shift in erotic relationships implied in the blood metaphors in *Kokoro*, away from the heterosexual, toward relationships between males. In short, the metaphor of Christian blood symbolism introduced the suggestion of homoerotic desire in the text. Through this semantic and metaphorical shift, Soseki set free the love between Japanese men in his novel from the doom-laden prison of 'degeneracy'. For, in concepts of 'degeneracy', a man–woman union would deliver not only offspring but also the degenerate 'germ' to the future generation.

The nostrums of degeneration introduced into Meiji Japan, suffusing everything from medical discourses to literary tropes, unanimously condemned the Japanese people of the Meiji era to a future destiny of racial decline. Men of letters in Meiji Japan, such as Soseki or Mori Ougai, were superb masters of foreign languages and effective introducers of information and the culture of the West. Ironically, they were at the forefront of adopting the discourses of degeneration. It is worth noting that Mori Ougai was an army surgeon. These thinkers inevitably had to confront a dilemma: informing the Japanese of new Western discourses on degeneracy, which at the same time condemned the Japanese for their degeneracy. To illustrate the extent to which concerns about degeneracy were shared also by the leaders in the Meiji government, the words of Okuma Shigenobu, the then Prime Minister, uttered in 1915, are illuminating:

> Must we Japanese accept such a state of affairs as our inevitable destiny because we are an inferior race? No! It is my idea, without being unduly

partial to the Japanese, that we cannot be *a priori* inferior to the Europeans. Most certainly it is the power of long habit and tradition that caused such a physical degeneration of this people. This degeneration is, so to speak, *a posteriori*, being of a temporary kind. Our awakening and consequent endeavour to develop will restore to us our original place in the course of time. The correctness of the view that Japanese have great potentiality of development is more than sufficiently proved by the amount of work they have completed in the last 50 years. We Japanese must become more self-confident in our intrinsic value. We must take firm resolution to fight our way with our own energy and ability, boldly confronting the pressure of the white races.

In fact, for my part, I am of the firm belief that we Japanese were not originally and essentially inferior to the white peoples, but only that the combinations of various unfortunate circumstances checked the natural progress of evolution. Therefore if we should in future pay close attention to this point and do all in our power to eliminate causes that may act harmfully on our physical constitution, then it would be quite possible for us to recover the well-balanced physical proportion of our ancestors to have a corresponding increase of bodily capacity and present a bold front against the aggressive expansion of the white races.[32]

This originally was published in the form of a newspaper article, printed in *The New York Sun*, 4 December 1915. Okuma made this impassioned appeal in the United States, fearful that American public opinion, surely anxious about degeneration, might be prone to racial prejudice against the Japanese, and therefore create higher obstructive barriers to Japanese immigrants into the USA.

Soseki, of course, in his role as a national narrator, was also concerned with notions of Japanese destiny. In his late masterpiece, *Grass on The Wayside* (*Michikusa*, 1915), the serial publication of which in *The Asahi Shimbun* commenced nine months after the first issue of *Kokoro*, he expressed his anxiety as follows:

> He had to think also of his sister and brother – and of course of Shimada [=his ex-stepfather]. They all carried with them the stink of decay and degeneration. And his life was tied to theirs by blood and flesh governed by their history.[33]

This piece, *Grass on the Wayside,* is an exceptional novel in that it deals with Soseki's own private life. This style of novel, with the assumption that the protagonist is also author, is a tradition in Japanese modern literature. But Soseki did not follow this genre, except in this particular work. Shimada, the character in the citation, is modelled on his real ex-stepfather. Soseki had been returned to his original family at the age of nine from the care of his ex-stepfather. But even after the separation on the official family register when he was 21, the ex-stepfather stalked him, hoping to extract money from Soseki. By this time, Soseki was a respected lecturer of English Literature at the University of Tokyo.

The line from the above citation, 'the blood and flesh governed by their history', is yet another expression meaning hereditary traits; and the future of the protagonist's family prophesied by new hereditary principles would be nothing but 'decay and degeneration'. The protagonist, modelled upon Soseki himself, cannot be freed from the dark legacy of the family's history. At the end of the novel, his wife gives birth at home before a midwife comes. The protagonist himself is forced to face the childbirth and to assist with it, picking up a newborn baby from the bloodbath. He is not only in panic in this unexpected situation, which was thought not fitting to be witnessed by a man, but also is terrified by the baby itself, because it seems to be too visceral, all jelly-like protein, as if it were an elemental form of life in physical material. At the moment he doubts whether it is breathing or not, the baby begins to make its first cry with vigour. This experience makes the protagonist realise the succession of lives as a physical, palpable reality. The new life is originated in blood, and delivered in blood. Blood, thus, runs from older generations to new ones, transmitting in it life as a body, replete with the sins of his ancestors casting a shadow over the future.

Conversely, the blood image of *Kokoro* is completely subverted by the covert introduction of Christian symbolism. In opposition to the image of blood described in the heterosexual union, love between males, as in *Kokoro*, had nothing physical or material to deliver to the future, except a spiritual legacy of the historic masculine culture. The ominous shadow of degeneration, though regarded as resulting from Japan's eroticised past, gave another new meaning to homoerotic relationships between men. This kind of erotic relationship stood free from the prison of heredity. In order to overcome the allotted place and the condemned fate of the Japanese people in the evolutionary axis of degeneracy, Soseki attempted through his literary works to subvert the concept of degeneration through the introduction of Christian symbolism of blood.

In *Kokoro*, there is a structural conflict between blood signifying kinship and the blood suggesting atonement, drawn from Christianity. The narrator, 'I', oscillates between his biological father and 'Sensei', his spiritual father. Indeed, he is attracted more to Sensei, assuming him to be his 'more real' father, and grows to despise his biological father because of his 'provincialism':

> I compared my father with Sensei. Both were self-effacing men. Indeed, they were both so self-effacing that as far as the rest of the world was concerned, they might as well have been dead... But while my chess-loving father failed

even to entertain me, Sensei, whose acquaintance I had never sought for amusement's sake, gave me far greater intellectual satisfaction as a companion... Indeed, it would not have seemed to me then an exaggeration to say that Sensei's strength had entered my body, and that his very life was flowing in my veins. And when I discovered that such were my true feelings towards these two men, I was shocked. For was I not of my father's flesh?[34]

At the end, 'I' is with his dying biological father. But, when 'I' receives the last letter from Sensei in which he confesses his past and his resolution to commit suicide, 'I' chooses Sensei and jumps onto a train for Tokyo, leaving his dying father. In other words, it is a choice between a father of flesh and the father of the Covenant in the Christian sense. Again, we need to affirm that this text, *Kokoro*, contains the narrative structure of the Bible. Christianity has an intrinsic motivation which tends to disintegrate a blood or familial relationship, and to construct a new one directly between God and an individual, as perceived by Max Weber in his *Protestantism and the Ethics of Capitalism*. Blood, in the context of Christianity, signifies specifically that which was shed by Christ in atonement, rather than the concept of blood coursing through the veins of kinship.

The Bible, furthermore, is a work of literature that records ambivalent traces of eroticised feelings existing in bonds among all males on earth. Soseki learned this from Wilde. This erotic feeling had not been allowed to exist in society, not even in language, so that it had been rendered nameless. Had it not been embedded in literary language, it would have vanished into the air, and remains unrecognised. Similar to the subtext of homoeroticism in parts of the Bible, *Kokoro* built a subtext of *Eros* between males for the modern period, in an era of new abhorrence of such sensibilities. This is *Kokoro*'s key contribution to posterity. Through close reading and thorough contextualisation of his texts, it is possible to discern this literary device in Soseki's works. The device was only made possible by Soseki's extraordinarily sympathetic appreciation of Wilde's writings, and Wilde's own sorrow and sufferings. *Kokoro* is another New Testament, written by a Japanese novelist, honouring the memory of the lost bonds between males. These masculine bonds were swept away and vanished like mist, or ghosts, in the profound changes that transformed a modernising Japan after the Meiji restoration.

## Notes

1. This summary is based on Damian Flanagan, 'Introduction', in Natsume Soseki, *Kokoro*, trans. Edwin McClellan (London, 2007 [1968]).
2. James Fujii, 'Writing out Asia: modernity, Canon, and Natsume Soseki's *Kokoro*', *Positions* 1 (1993), 194–223.
3. Atsuko Sakaki, *Recontextualizing Texts: Narrative Performance in Modern Japanese Fiction* (Cambridge MA, 1999), p. 31.

4. Stephen Dodd, 'The significance of bodies in Soseki's *Kokoro*', *Monumenta Nipponica* 53 (1998), 473-98.
5. Jay Rubin, 'Soseki on individualism', *Monumenta Nipponica* 34 (1979), 22-3.
6. Doris G. Bargen, *Suicidal Honor: General Nogi and the Writings of Mori Ogai and Natsume Soseki* (Honolulu, 2006).
7. Ibid., p. 177.
8. Soseki (2007), p. 245.
9. This paragraph is based upon Gregory M. Pflugfelder, *Cartographies of Desire: Male-Male Sexuality in Japanese Discourse, 1600–1950* (Berkeley, 1999), p. 11.
10. This paragraph is based upon ibid., pp. 146–49.
11. Ibid., p. 149.
12. Ibid., p. 153.
13. Ibid., pp. 244–45.
14. Ibid., p. 248.
15. The latter half of this paragraph is based upon ibid., p. 249. About degeneration theory in Japan, see also Stephen Dodd, 'The significance of bodies in Soseki's *Kokoro*' , p. 475.
16. Bargen, *Suicidal Honor*, pp. 20–9.
17. Ibid., p. 29. As for the custom of self-immolation, *junshi*, see also Ogai Mori's *The Abe Family* (1913), which deals most intensively with this theme.
18. Soseki, *Kokoro*, pp. 224–25. Alterations and italics are mine.
19. The project to translate the Bible was launched by the Committee for the Translation of the Bible into the Japanese Language in 1872. The members included James C. Hepburn (Presbyterian Church, USA), Samuel R. Brown (Dutch Reformed Church, USA), Daniel C. Greene (the American Board of Commissioners for Foreign Missions) and Robert S. Maclay (Methodist Church, USA), in cooperation with other Japanese, English, Scots and Canadian missionaries. As a result, the Meiji version of the Bible was published in 1880, in which they did not adopt the word '*fukkatsu*'. By the time the transformed version was published in 1912, after frequent unfavourable criticism of the style of Japanese in the Meiji version, the Meiji version adopted '*fukkatsu*' in new editions, which, in the meantime, had been in regular use and had been popular with Christian writers. For more on projects of translating the Bible into Japanese as a whole, see Norihisa Suzuki, *Seisho no Nihongo* [*The Japanese Language in the Bible*] (Tokyo, 2006).
20. Soseki (2007), p. 11.
21. Oscar Wilde, *The Complete Letters of Oscar Wilde*, Merlin Holland and Rupert Hart-Davis (eds) (New York, 2000), p. 740.
22. Natsume Soseki, *Kusamakura*, in 3 of *Soseki-Zenshu* (Tokyo, 1994) p. 143.
23. Wilde, *Complete Letters of Oscar Wilde*, p. 757.
24. Ibid., p. 741.
25. Ibid., p. 743. Italics are mine.
26. Ibid., p. 740.
27. Soseki (2007), p. 245.
28. Ibid., p. 245. Italics are mine.
29. Ibid., p. 243. Italics are mine.
30. As for analysis of Christ's body as the site of erotic desire, see Stephen Arata, 'Oscar Wilde and Jesus Christ', in Joseph Bristow (ed.), *Wilde Writings: Contextual Conditions* (Toronto, 2003). Although Arata suggests the possibility that Wilde elaborately tried to avoid mentioning Christ as eroticised, he points out that, from the Renaissance onward, the physicality of Christ has been a key tenet of Christian theology as well

as Christian art. See also Leo Steinberg, *The Sexuality of Christ in Renaissance Art and in Modern Oblivion*, 2nd edn (Chicago, 1983).
31. Soseki (2007), p. 129. Italics are mine.
32. The Record of the Senate of the United States, 10 January 1916. The original article in the newspaper attracted the attention of a senator, who asked for it to be printed in the Record of the Senate.
33. Natsume Soseki, *Grass on the Wayside* [*Michikusa*], trans. Edwin McClellan (Chicago, [1971] 2000), p. 39. Insertion and alteration are mine.
34. Soseki (2007), pp. 49–50.

# 19
## 'Proper Government and Discipline': Family Religion and Masculine Authority in Nineteenth-Century Canada

*Nancy Christie*

> [W]hat is it that lightens labour, what is it that makes a man act a manly part under his own roof tree, what is it that makes the Father of a Family surrounded by his filial flock teach them good examples and moral precepts, what but the certainty of a better world beyond this vain chimera, yes, Walter, God is the end of everything.[1]
>
> There is, in some households, no family government, no order, no subordination.[2]

The above quotation from John Grubb, a yeoman farmer in Upper Canada (Ontario), to his brother in Scotland underscores the extent to which he believed spiritual growth was best nourished within the family. More importantly, he stressed the degree to which manliness, meaning masculine authority, was affirmed first and foremost within the home and that the central pillar of that authority was constituted by the cultural power of religion. While historians have now begun to focus upon the degree to which masculinity was constructed within the household, thus drawing historiographical attention to the importance of fatherhood in the nineteenth century, the power which men wielded over their familial dependents – including their wives, children and servants – has often been considered in terms of their mastery over the labour and sexuality of those subordinate to them in the home.[3] While historians have accentuated the importance of the conjugal unit and marital status to men's sense of identity and power in the nineteenth century, they have for the most part seen the moral authority of men within the family as merely episodic and occluded by what has been interpreted as the dominant discourse relating to moral motherhood. Thus, whilst men may have had a large presence within the family, historians have continued to see the moral sphere of the family and the building of character as a predominantly female preserve. John Tosh was one of the first historians to identify the cultural dominance of 'domesticated manhood' in Victorian England; nevertheless, he has also concluded that in industrialising Britain the concept of manliness was by and large a secular one, for, as he observed, 'manliness had much more to do with one's own standing in the sight of men than with one's standing with the Almighty.'[4]

If in the United States and Britain the cultural status of fatherhood – and in particular the spiritual role of fathers within the family – began to decline somewhere between 1790 and 1830,[5] a reverse process occurred in the British North American colonies that became Canada. There, the ability of men to discipline and govern their families was directly linked to their role as religious heads of the household. Both symbolically and in daily social relations, the power of men descended directly from God, to the monarch, to fatherly magistrates in the homes, and it was the father and husband's spiritual authority which determined all other sources of masculine mastery in colonial society. From the perspective of this older patriarchalism, man's right to govern in the civil realm flowed directly from the efficacy with which he spiritually disciplined and governed his familial dependents. Historians of the United States and France have argued that the age of revolutions overthrew this intertwining of the political and the personal, and that much of republican discourse focused upon eviscerating the power of family patriarchs, which was then transferred to moral mothers, whose authority derived from educating their sons to become virtuous citizens.[6] If republicanism encouraged the construction of the ideal of a moralising and domestic role for women, what of societies like Canada, which did not experience a revolution? Despite recent attempts to posit a vibrant culture of moral motherhood among Canadian evangelicals,[7] this paper will argue that such discourses and practices remained relatively weak because, first, the religious pluralism of a 'frontier' society created a stronger patriarchal role for men in the family; second, the paucity of formal church institutions in early colonial society reinforced this trend towards Christian patriarchy; and, lastly, throughout the nineteenth century and into the early twentieth century, clerical leaders in the mainline Protestant denominations saw the link between the family and denominational identity and expanding church membership. Thus, the institutional church continued to reinforce the key spiritual role of fathers in religious acculturation. Indeed, Canada's formative religio-political moment reflected in a more acute form the counter-revolutionary discourse and institutional arrangements which occurred in Britain between 1790 and 1830 and, because of the peculiar nature of this society,[8] patriarchal and hierarchical social and cultural relations were sustained in Canada much longer than they were in Britain. The cultural status of fatherhood remained virtually intact in Canada until the early twentieth century and the analogy between the family and the state persisted, thus preserving the family, the church and the state as explicit masculinist institutions. In this cultural milieu moral mothers occupied a significantly reduced cultural space. Spiritual patriarchy, that great trope of early modern societies, retained its cultural currency until the 1930s, when it was replaced with an economic definition of fatherhood and political citizenship anchored upon the breadwinner ideal.[9]

In colonial Canada clergymen were particularly concerned with the need to erect churches in order to promote the public authority of religious culture in a new society, which many perceived as disorderly because of the plethora of religious opinions and practices. However, the financial constraints placed upon the process of church building meant that, in practical terms, household religion occupied a much greater role than it otherwise would have. Immigrants from all classes, including pauper emigrants from southern England, sought spiritual comfort in the parish church,[10] but many, like James Gibson, a tenant farmer from Scotland, were forced to feed their spirits by 'keeping the Sabbath in reading and to deal with a fearing God', even though Gibson recognised the social advantages of the visible church, instructing his son, a storekeeper, to become a regular churchgoer so that he might be 'respected above all things'.[11] In a society where the power of the laity was particularly robust prior to the 1880s, many people preferred household prayer, where the head of the household could exert control over the type of religious experience on offer, and there is much evidence from family correspondence of strong views on religion pitting parishioner against clergyman.

In a larger sense, clergymen wished to encourage greater participation in the public and communal aspects of church rituals because they desired to make visible the cultural authority of religion in a society perceived to be 'irreligious' because of the paucity of churches. However, a large proportion of the clerical elite took a positive view of household religion because they considered it a 'public benefit' for several reasons: it made faith more accessible to the individual, it anchored the religious experience in the affections of the family, and, perhaps most importantly, it disciplined family members, especially women, children and female servants.[12] In so doing, it upheld those notions of social hierarchy which were fundamental to counter-revolutionary notions of governance. Rev. John Strachan, the Anglican Bishop of Toronto, recognised how the intense religious pluralism in the British North American colonies put a great strain on overseas missionary societies, which could not keep up with the great demand for clergy, and the ever-present difficulty that the majority of clergy sent out from Britain were considered to be below par in terms of both social status and intellectual training.[13] As late as 1846, even after an intense period of church building, Strachan continued to urge fathers to become surrogate priests in their families: 'In this and in all countries far removed from places of public worship and the sound of the Church Bell, the

Father of a family if possessed of a Prayer Book can call his household together with holy confidence and read devoutly the morning and evening service.'[14] In so strongly proclaiming that the edifice of both the institutional church and the civic polity rested upon the spiritual obligations of fathers, colonial leaders were bestowing a vast amount of power upon men in a society which had already amplified the mastery of men over their families by virtue of the weakness of civic and state institutional life, by the availability of land, which allowed a high proportion of men access to holding property, and by the complete absence of state parish relief, which meant that care of the poor occurred almost exclusively within the household.[15]

Placing fathers at the head of the spiritual household, however, did much greater cultural work than just supplanting absent clergymen. The conventional notion that fathers were dethroned, both literally and figuratively, from their position of moral mastery in the home either as a result of the age of revolutions or irrevocably by the industrial transformation of the mid-nineteenth century[16] has now been convincingly refuted by the work of J.C.D. Clark. As he argues, in the wake of both the American and French Revolutions, in England the 'aristocratic ideal' was in the ascendancy, and with it was revivified the family–state analogy, which argued that both elites and fathers in general were the natural rulers of society and that this was sanctioned, as was the monarchy itself, by divine right. This ideal validated a model of society characterised by deference and hierarchies of gender, class and age, which was reinforced at their foundation, within the family circle.[17] Although, as Rachel Weil has suggested, even after the impact of the Lockean challenge to the older Filmerian patriarchalism, the only real alteration in the dominant political ideology was that monarchs, and by analogy fathers, were no longer deemed tyrannical or absolute.[18] Fatherhood and the civil government continued to be sanctioned by God and the family was still considered the origin of the state.

If, as Clark argues, patriarchalism remained hegemonic until at least 1832 in Britain and staved off secular and contractarian notions of governance, it received further reinforcement when it was translated to the colonial setting. As in Britain, 'bourgeois domesticity' was restrained by anti-modern notions of patriarchal authority; but in British North America, by contrast, those aspiring to uphold the aristocratic ideal tended towards the more conservative axis of a more general Whig political temperament, in which even the now outmoded European *ancien régime* idea of divine right monarchy was refurbished. Rev. John Strachan, the leading Anglican apologist on the colonial scene for what he himself termed conservative Whiggism, wrote a discourse on the character of King George III in 1810, at the height of the counter-revolution. Describing the monarch, he proclaimed:

> he regards the Supreme Being as the common Father of all, and mankind the children, the members of one family. He is not therefore puffed up with

vain glory as if he were an independent being and his subjects beneath his regard; he looks upon them as his children who turn to him for protection, and to promote whose happiness becomes the first of his duties; and it is his conviction that determines him always to prefer the public to private good.

Accepting the principle of the tripartite balanced constitution as good Whigs would have done, Strachan clearly assigned to the monarchy, and fatherhood itself, the central importance in sustaining the social and political order, for, as he stated, the King was a 'watchful guardian' of people's liberties and 'holding the balance between the nobility and commons, become[s] their common father.'[19] Clark has argued that the aristocratic and patriarchal socio-political system of thought was propped up principally by the continued authority of the Anglican Church. While this might have been so in England, in British America the patriarchal ideal had much greater cultural currency, and was not simply a function of Anglicanism but was diffused among dissenting religions. It spread, for example, to the Methodists, the largest religious group amongst American and British settlers, who, in the wake of both the American Revolution and the failed rebellions of 1837–1838 in Upper and Lower Canada, embraced a conservative mindset in order to cleanse themselves of the radical taint and preserve their legitimacy in the colonial order.[20] Just as did the Anglicans, Methodist writers saw the family as the natural terrain of political debate and just as forcefully saw society as a hierarchical structure in which authority descended from God, to the King, to the Father as head of the temporal household. Rev. Samuel Bingham from Beamsville, Upper Canada drew the analogy between Christ's headship of the church and male supremacy over women. Like Strachan, he saw a direct link between the authority of men on earth, civil society and divine laws. As he wrote in 1834 to *The Christian Guardian*, the leading Methodist periodical:

> In order for the existence of society, whether civil or religious, there must be governments, laws, officers, as well as subjects. The father of a family, the constituted authorities of a nation, and the ministers of the Church of God, must all have a sufficiency of power invested in them to enjoin and enforce obedience to laws and regulations as are necessary to the peace, good government and prosperity of the community over which they are placed.[21]

The patriarchal analogy between the father-centred domestic governance and the civil polity was even more explicitly stated in the wake of the republican-inspired rebellions that shook colonial society in 1837. In that year, the Methodist newspaper, *The Christian Guardian*, once again reiterated that all government rested upon the shoulders of a Christian father and drew an organic connection between the father's moral and material duties. He who 'governs and controls' his dependents, stated *The Christian Guardian*, must act as a prophylactic against the reign of sin, which was identified with the 'authority of self'.[22] From this perspective fathers were seen to be the pre-eminent 'guardian[s] of public morals', and this public function of family life was emphatically intended as a counterweight to the privatised domesticity and individual liberty which were believed to characterise republican societies. In short, the father was both spiritual leader and civil magistrate within the domestic circle. Here, religion did not uphold visions of sentimental fatherhood, and this concept of pious fatherhood conferred a great deal of power upon men in the society, for it was upon them that the entire edifice of the state was believed to rest, because both derived their power from God himself.[23]

Where Clark's synthesis of ideology and political practice falls short is that it cannot demonstrate how these values were internalised and deployed in the daily practice of family social relations. Historians like Suzanne Desan, who have studied the identification between family and the political order in revolutionary France, have, in the absence of private family correspondence, analysed court records in order to uncover popular social mores which, as she suggests, challenged patriarchal power during the revolution. In order to trace the way in which patriarchalism was embedded in personal relations I have utilised family letters and diaries, which are available in abundance in Canada for the nineteenth century. These sources conclusively demonstrate that household prayers and rituals were undertaken by the male heads of households and were a near-ubiquitous practice among all socio-economic, ethnic and religious groups, including even the most radical of dissenters, the Primitive Methodists. Not only did the Seceder Presbyterian clergyman William Proudfoot make family prayer a prerequisite for baptism, but he equated true piety with the practice of household worship. He observed in 1833 that 'most families in the district are decidedly pious. All of them keep up their worship of God in their families.'[24]

What these colonial families had in common was the view that the family was a 'Society', which functioned by rules of duty and obligation that informed the civil polity. Gentry women, like the widow Anne Powell, referred to 'family society', in a similar manner to Rev. William Proudfoot, from an artisanal background, who stressed the 'socialities of common life'.[25] In a similar vein, the 1839 obituary of the Methodist James Willson defined the 'domestic circle' as that realm in which the 'relations of private and social life'[26] were united. Within this cultural world view the realms of the domestic and the political were never far removed from one another, because public conduct was merely an expression of private character.[27] This explains how both clerical leaders and the laity could affirm that family religious discipline formed the cornerstone of political governance, all of which shows that across all social classes very little interest was evinced in Lockean concepts of individualism prior to the mid-nineteenth century.

Significantly, almost all references to family worship are expressed in the letters and journals of men. William Gibson, a Scottish farmer of modest means, regularly held family prayers largely because he was unable to choose a new religious identity for himself in the pluralist religious environment of Upper Canada: 'I felt last winter that it was my duty to change my line of conduct and set before my family a better example by keeping family worship and have continued it to the present time.'[28] For Gibson the decision to adopt family worship was an expression both of religious liberty and of his status as head of the family. Indeed, those men of more precarious livelihoods, like Gibson and the engraver Frederick Brigden, whose work was not steady, accentuated their spiritual rule in the family as their uncertain breadwinner status called into question their status as head of the household. Interestingly, the accounts of family worship by women studiously stressed the primary role played by their fathers and husbands. Jessie Robb Henderson, a Presbyterian, recounted that 'we had family worship, morning and evening, following breakfast and the evening meal. In the early days or until my father's throat gave out we sang a psalm or a hymn... We knelt at our chairs while our father led us in prayer... After worship the younger children gathered at their father's knee and said their prayers.'[29] Gentlewomen like Mary O'Brien were well acquainted with Anglican doctrine and the rituals of the Book of Common Prayer and read privately on a range of religious topics, but she never initiated family prayer, viewing this as the sole prerogative of her husband. It is clear that family worship was not a site for the empowerment of women, and, whilst both men and women could read the printed word of the Bible, sermons and devotional books, men dictated the timing and form of household prayers.[30] Most men did not explicitly speak of how their sense of mastery of their household depended upon their religious authority, largely because their spiritual patriarchy was not in question. It is significant, therefore, that the two most explicit references to male spiritual power related to younger men just on the threshold of manhood. Thus John Grubb, a struggling farmer in Upper Canada, expressed success in terms of his control of the religious discipline of his children. Writing to his brother in Scotland in 1837, during the rebellions when this young radical's manhood was being challenged by the dominant patriarchal discourse which linked paternal authority with conservative political values: 'A Father so commands the respect of his own children must worship & address God daily by prayer or by reading a portion of the scriptures.'[31] The conduct of household prayers was one of the most important occasions for the exercise of male power and the daily reinforcement of gender roles, and such household discipline in turn inscribed public notions of the social order. 'Your nephew,' wrote George Murray to Miss Eliza Powell in 1846, 'is quite a patriarch to his family... Morning and evening prayers selected by their Father from the prayer book and their attention to Sunday School of which John is a teacher, and their deportment in Church, will impress feelings of trust that will never be lost sight of during life.'[32] To be a man was to be first and foremost a Christian ruler within the household, which would in turn prepare one to be a responsible governor in the public realm.

If, according to the patriarchal political principle, the central purpose of the divine family, in which authority flowed from the father as the spiritual and civil magistrate to his dependents, was to reinforce gender and class subordination and thereby uphold the politics of deference, there was no clearer articulation of this than the way in which servants were treated in nineteenth-century British North America. Although in terms of everyday social relations religion conferred models of both paternal discipline and paternal affections, especially with the rise of evangelicalism, the persistence of masculinist family authority was made more explicit in terms of master–servant relations, and it is here that one can best perceive the broader public uses of family life. Far from being an anachronism, domestic service and apprenticeship were in fact rejuvenated in Britain's overseas societies, and the notion that servants should be considered family members remained one of the most persistent pillars of the aristocratic ideal. As I have argued elsewhere, well into the latter half of the nineteenth century domestic service was not generally conceived as a contractarian relationship, but this form of work, largely undertaken by women, was perceived as part of the moral economy of service in which servants,[33] apprentices and ordinary labourers were included as part of the household and, as such, fell under the fatherly care of their employer. It is in the treatment of servants that the role of the father as master was most apparent, and it is in the context of the master–servant relationship that the link between household religion and masculine power was most explicitly articulated. If, within the changed tenor of family life, it became increasingly difficult to blatantly articulate the vast authority fathers had over their wives and children, family rulers had no compunction about doing so when speaking of the right relation between masters and their servants.

If the service relationship was thought to replicate that of parent and child, it followed that servants must be morally disciplined during morning and evening household prayers. What is particularly revealing about the cultural penetration of the patriarchal family ideal was the belief that servants must demonstrate obedience by participating in household devotions. This non-contractarian notion of work was adhered to by a wide cross section of families, but the importance of the moral conduct of servants was discussed at greatest length within gentry families, and it was they who put the greatest store by family prayers as a means to inculcate proper attitudes to obedience to one's 'natural' superiors. Mary O'Brien, a gentry woman, described at length her and her husband's preoccupation with regulating the religious views of their servants and farm labourers, and it is clear that her husband's sense of class position was best articulated in his role as spiritual master of the household, for, as she wrote in her diary:

> E[dward] reads a psalm and prayers from the liturgy, he is sufficiently aristocratic in politics & essentially so in habits but he makes a point of this occasion of bringing the servants as much as possible into the same circle with ourselves. In the morning, the employments of the family scatter them too much to admit of any regular assembling but the female servant generally joins in our prayers.[34]

So fundamental was the master–servant relationship to the maintenance of patriarchy that, even when absent from the home, the arch Tory lawyer and politician, John Hillyard Cameron, demanded that his wife Lizzie remain at their home rather than decamp to her parental home so that she could continue to conduct household prayers with the servants. Although their marriage was a love match and their relationship was intensely sexual and affectionate, it was also one characterised by subordination and obedience to the husband's rule. Cameron was obsessed with asserting his authority in the home by means of his relationship with his servants. It was through their subordination that he articulated the seamlessness of his role as master and husband. In a tart missive to his wife, he ordered her to remain at his home because her absence might 'occasion irregularities in our household which would be avoided otherwise, not the least among which is the absence of family prayers, which once commended should never be dropped unless from the most urgent necessity'.[35]

If the authoritarian nature of fatherhood was laid bare through men's attitudes to their servants, the central role religion played in undergirding the sense of masculine power was exposed through the ways in which patriarchy was resisted. Certainly, servants had greater power to resist their masters in colonial Canada because of the dearth of this type of labour, and there is evidence that adolescent males chafed under the authority of their fathers, but for the most part wives seem to have internalised societal norms and for the most part, at least at the beginning of the marriage, they deemed obedience to be part and parcel of the marriage contract. Where in revolutionary France disgruntled wives deployed the rhetoric of republicanism to refute the perceived arbitrary power of their husbands,[36] in Canada women had few cultural touchstones, other than religion, with which to contest the rule of men in the family. The unique diary of Anna Ardagh, the daughter of an Irish evangelical divine who was forced to leave County Wexford after forcing Catholics to convert to Protestantism, demonstrates how pivotal men's spiritual mastery of the household was to their sense of masculine authority.[37] As dominant as Anna's husband Gowan believed himself to be, there were two aspects of his life that undermined the unassailable character of masculine authority to which he subscribed: he was childless, and he was not a convert to evangelicalism and so did not hold household devotions. It is significant that, while the issue of their childlessness distinctly rankled with Gowan, Anna never challenged him on this score, but rather chose to assault his masculinity by challenging his right to spiritual fatherhood of the domestic realm. Anna's own devotion to her evangelical faith grew in direct proportion to her unhappiness in the marriage.[38] By 1855, as Anna recounted, while discussing his failure to convert – and his failure as a spiritual patriarch – 'tears came to both our eyes he cried bitterly lamenting his sins & weakness in the most humble & Christian manner & prayed that we might be led to walk aright casting all our care upon Him.'[39] As time went by Anna employed the higher power of God to break apart the natural elision between divine and mortal fatherhood and sought to undermine Gowan's power over her, first by converting children in the neighbourhood, then by directing the religious conversion of Gowan's own father. By thus winning the elder patriarch to Christ, Anna was overtly disrupting conventional gender and age hierarchies. Lastly, but most importantly, Anna further challenged Gowan's masculinity by converting their servants, an act that allowed her to become the symbolic master of the household when she began to hold household prayers. If cultural convention had constructed a hierarchy of gendered power both within the household and within society, Anna Ardagh derived greater moral authority as a result of her relationship with God in order to create her own conception of the well-ordered home. It was her appeal to her 'One Comforter', God, which at the end of her life bestowed sufficient spiritual authority upon Anna that she openly disobeyed her husband. As she wrote to Gowan: *'Truly I am thankful indeed that it seems as if God would restore my voice – to speak even as I do is much to be grateful for – it all comes from Him, no matter how it comes & thank God He has given.'*[40]

By the mid-nineteenth century, the old patriarchal ideal was in decline with the incremental burgeoning of companionate marriage. However, this transition did not shoulder aside the importance of religion to inform conjugal affection, nor did it eviscerate the importance of fatherhood and masculine control within the family. This can best be illustrated in the marriage of Frederick Brigden, a London engraver who later emigrated to Canada, and his wife Fanny Higgins, a domestic servant and daughter of a bricklayer. In many ways Brigden, although a skilled worker, fits Tosh's paradigm of 'bourgeois masculinity' in so far as he reflected the values of industrial London by seeing work and home as the chief pillars of his identity. As he confided in his diary in 1861, just prior to coming of age at 21: 'I am essentially a family man and my *greatest* pleasures are found in the affections of the family circle to have them and come back to drudge on among strangers and casual acquaintances is always a disagreeable occurrence.'[41] On his birthday he announced that he had entered the stage in the 'character of man' in which one must 'fight the battle of life, with a determination to gain the victory under the will of Providence to gain for myself a comfortable independence, skill in my art, a well educated mind, and a character unimpeachable for truth, honesty, and industry, and for the right carrying out and engagement of all, a healthy and disciplined body'.[42] But, as Brigden himself made clear, his vision of masculinity was not individualistic or 'selfish', for it depended upon making God (and later his family) his chief goal in life.

Between 1861 and 1863, Brigden, who was deaf, underwent a painful and protracted conversion experience, which he identified as significant in placing him at the 'threshold of manhood',[43] as was the successful completion of his apprenticeship and his pursuit of a marital partner. Prior to his conversion experience, Brigden was a devotee of the mechanics' institutes, trained at the Working Men's College, read Ruskin and Charles Kingsley, and was a representative of respectable working-class culture. From Ruskin he derived the notion that industry and work were the route to self-mastery and that the 'power of manhood' derived from having a sense of duty and a determination to strive in one's profession.[44] During his conversion, he began to reject this notion of economic individualism and the prospect of 'ceaseless toil' which so characterised Victorian men. Throughout this process, Brigden self-consciously began to turn away from competing practices of working-class masculinity characterised by drinking, sexual conquest and gambling.[45] After reading Kingsley's *Alton Locke*, Brigden began to interpret progress and working-class uplift in terms of religion.[46] Once he became a dedicated Methodist man, Brigden no longer saw self-mastery in terms of economic independence; rather, he characterised masculine self-control as 'regulated by the Spirit', with labour and upward mobility as entirely due to 'a sense of the presence of God, always and the constraining influence of it in every employment',[47] for, as he later argued, there is 'harmony between religion and labour'[48] because both were embodiments of God in the home.

Thus, to Tosh's interplay between home and work in informing Victorian masculinity needs to be added the important integrating force of evangelical religion. Moreover, it was religion that shifted masculinity away from excessive individualism. For Brigden, individual self-control was but a preliminary stage in masculine formation, which only saw its completion in marriage, for only the family, a divine institution, served as the basis for social relations and a corrective against living too much for oneself. Brigden, once he became a businessman who owned the Toronto Engraving Company, admonished his son in 1894 that work was as much for God as for the male self and that 'true manliness'[49] was not achieved through work, which creates too much 'self pleasure', but through familial relationships and 'losing oneself' in one's divine duty to others.[50]

It is significant that Brigden believed that he had achieved full manhood once he converted to Methodism. Even more significantly, he was able to secure the status as head of his birth family and surrogate father-figure to his brothers and sisters and a surrogate husband to his mother, by using the moral authority of his conversion to chastise his own father, a saddler whose business had failed. In Brigden's view, his father had been transformed from being 'one of the kindest of Parents' and 'a prosperous tradesman'[51] to a failure as a man, not because of his drunkenness or improvidence, but because he no longer believed in a redemptive God and had taught his sons to be enemies of Christ. Once Brigden viewed himself as the spiritual father of the family, he wrote a scathing letter to his father, chastising him as one would a wayward child: 'surely my dear father you cannot so deceive yourself as to think that you have the least shadow of a hope of anything but the sad expectation of eternal misery should you die as you now are.' Not only did he accuse his father of dragging his children's souls 'down to Hell', but he added that his father's rejection of God had the effect of 'despising and rejecting, degrading your manhood, ruining your soul'. It is significant that, after assuming his father's role as spiritual head of the family, Brigden then became the economic master of the household when his mother, a shopkeeper whose creditworthiness was affected by her husband's unemployment, signed her business over to her son,[52] thus making him the surrogate 'breadwinner' of the family.

It was after acquiring this status as the spiritual governor of his extended family, which he understood to comprise all those he converted, including his Aunt Henty and, perhaps, more significantly, his best friend, Henry Beale, that Brigden began to consider marriage. Brigden and Beale had studied art together at the Working Men's College in London, and he, along with several other male friends, offered Christian companionship to Brigden as he was undergoing his conversion experience. However, although he had intense feelings for Beale, he was chary of the strong affections of men and used his religion as a means to distance himself from Beale's desire for emotional intimacy. This allowed Brigden to consider men merely as objects of his spiritual ministerings, thus casting a close friend like Beale as a representative 'holy earnest strong-minded man'.[53] It is clear that Brigden perceived the turning away from the society of men as instrumental to his achievement of mature manhood, for, as he informed his fiancée Fanny Higgins when his friend Beale was departing for Canada, heterosexual marriage was the only relationship in which he could fully express the same kind of emotional intensity which he had communicated only to Christ.[54] For Brigden, companionate marriage was not simply a meeting place of affections between husband and wife; rather, all conjugal sympathy was brought about through the religious compatibility between husband and wife. When Brigden observed that 'a good wife is from the Lord' he saw it both in metaphorical and literal terms: the only reason he opened a courtship with Fanny Higgins is that, while working as a servant for his Aunt, she had helped convert her. Her chief attraction was her piety. In turn, Fanny informed Fred that she was agreeable to opening a correspondence with him only because she saw him as a fellow Christian 'one whose sympathies on religious subjects correspond with my own'.[55] Indeed, they agreed to be married only because Brigden's conduct was ruled by the 'teachings of God'.[56]

For both Fred and Fanny religion was at the heart of their concept of marriage, and marital happiness was directly linked to their mutual feelings of intimacy with Christ and God. As Fanny later told him, even while apart, knowing that they both prayed to Christ at certain hours of the day would bring them closer together, for 'it is comforting to feel we can look up to him as to a Father in everything.'[57] Similarly, Brigden pictured his marriage always in terms of his praying with Fanny on the Sabbath, and he conceived their mutual advance in Grace as always occurring within the domestic relationships of the home.[58] If family and marriage were both crucial to Brigden's sense of manly development, they were no less essential for the affirmation of his religious authority, for the concept of spiritual and temporal fatherhood permeated all his correspondence to Fanny.[59] Indeed, Fanny herself made little gesture towards current notions of moral motherhood or pious domesticity for women, for she too alluded frequently to the masculinist content of evangelical religion.[60] If, as Brigden frequently stated, marriage was a divine idea and its relationships were analogous to those in heaven, what he was alluding to was that his power as spiritual head of the family flowed directly from God. This idea was particularly important to articulate to his new bride, for Fanny was extremely well versed in contemporary theological argument and church doctrine, much to Brigden's chagrin, given his preference for a wife to be a passive helpmeet rather than an intellectual or moral equal.[61] On the threshold of marriage, Brigden was particularly alarmed that his mother and aunt were joking about how Fanny might not be obedient or listen to his advice.[62] But rather than asserting his masculine dominance by referencing his breadwinner status and by alluding to prevailing notions of separate spheres – Brigden actually desired his wife to work after marriage – he used religious metaphors to express his ownership of Fanny and bombarded her with religious tracts which instructed her on her subordinate status as a Christian wife. As he told her, 'we have as it were a kind of property in each other, this is my own exclusive property in the heart of the other.'[63] As an evangelical, Brigden would have been thoroughly aware of the religious discourse of moral motherhood, whose precepts were being passed from his female relatives to Fanny, and his courtship can be read as a deliberate attempt to deflect female religious empowerment by elevating his own powerful sense of religious patriarchy. Not surprisingly, Brigden only ever wanted sons, and throughout his diary the parenting role of Fanny is completely obliterated.[64] By 1872, when Brigden was living in Toronto and running his own engraving company, he stated that all his family depended upon him, an allusion to both his economic role as the principal breadwinner and his ability to better the moral culture of his children: 'I need more thought going out from self to them. The Eternal Father. I a Father here represent Him to the little ones.' He envisioned himself as giving 'Christlike care of my family' and saw his position in monarchical terms as 'anointed of God' for the 'teaching and salvation of these dear ones'.[65] Thus, although his evangelical religion and its companionate ideal of marriage had softened the edges of divine right patriarchy, even among more radical workers like Brigden who evinced youthful sympathy with Chartism, it had not been entirely supplanted by more liberal and egalitarian notions of social relations.

By contrast with Brigden, who saw marriage in wholly religious terms, Isaac Buchanan, a Scottish merchant who emigrated to Canada in the 1840s to expand his family's wholesale grain business, viewed religion in rather more instrumental terms. For him, Christ was not a personal friend, and he defined his relationship with God in contractual terms. Like Brigden, Buchanan was an evangelical, but he was a Free Church Presbyterian, and thus his predilections were towards a more Calvinist and providential view of God. At the time of his marriage, Buchanan, like his working-class counterpart Frederick Brigden, addressed Agnes Jarvie, his prospective bride, on the religious reasons as to why she should become a wife obedient to her husband. As he informed her, her duties to her husband would become 'the necessary breads on which her spirit will live.'[66] Buchanan tutored his wife on the view that happiness must not be grounded upon outward circumstances but upon 'God's blessing alone'. However, as his business fortunes began to precipitously decline in the late 1860s in Hamilton, Ontario, he and Agnes subscribed to the theology of the atonement, in which God was seen as a heavenly banker with whom one banked credit through one's faith.[67] According to this rubric, faith was a 'treasure for time as well as eternity'.[68] As a result, Isaac and Agnes both turned to their faith as he headed towards bankruptcy in 1867, for, according to the precepts of the religion of the atonement, bankruptcy was a moral judgement on businessmen and was a stimulus to faith. But the Calvinistic survivals within their religious world view meant that they did not see sin as personally related to their own actions, for in their view God worked with 'infinite Wisdom which cannot err in its superintendence of affairs', and happiness lay entirely in God's gift,[69] thus leaving little room for human agency. The Buchanans clearly saw religion largely in terms of their ability to succeed in the business world. On the verge of bankruptcy, Agnes assured her husband that they would always have worldly success, for they believed not in a retributive God but in a hopeful providence. As Agnes made clear, their years of faith and regular church attendance had left them with such an enormous amount of spiritual credit that God would give them all they asked for: 'we have a never failing Treasury to apply for and God's own letter of credit.'[70] The spectre of bankruptcy held no fears for Isaac Buchanan, for he could turn to his ancestral Scottish Calvinism for the consolation that the elect would never be punished. As Isaac confided to Agnes, God 'gives everything to richly enjoy'.[71]

Neither Isaac nor Agnes adhered to the conventional evangelical elision between religion and the home; rather, they saw religion as the adjunct of the marketplace. Because of his business and political concerns, Buchanan was largely an absent father, and he did not subscribe to the patriarchal views of Christian authority within the home. Rather, he and Agnes equally shared in the affectionate enjoyment of their children,[72] and what moral tutoring the children received was not undertaken during household prayers, which Isaac eschewed as 'wearisome' and overly 'formal', as he preferred solitary reading of the Bible, but by hired clergymen–tutors.[73] Theirs was a religion of external conformity: Isaac was a heavy contributor to Knox Presbyterian Church in Hamilton as well as to Presbyterian churches throughout Upper Canada, and both he and Agnes were faithful church members, seeing regular Sabbath attendance as a means to uphold their social status within Hamilton. We have little sense from the extensive correspondence between Agnes and Isaac that they directly shaped the moral awareness of their children, and it is apparent that they did not see this as the principal task of the parent, preferring instead to have the institutional church undertake this educational role. While the Buchanans remained fervent evangelicals throughout their lives, they did not see the home as the bosom of spiritual growth; rather, they extolled the ideal of 'the visible church'. And, as they informed their son James, becoming a man was coextensive with church membership, even though they recognised that this must be preceded by a distinct inner decision to follow the Saviour. And, while they encouraged him to take such a step, neither Agnes nor Isaac saw it as their purview to discipline their children in terms of their religious choices.

More significantly, they saw religion in very functional terms. First, Isaac believed that teaching religious precepts was important for children, if only to develop that mental culture which would make a man a worldly success.[74] From the perspective of Isaac and Agnes Buchanan, religion served individualistic ends, for, as Agnes informed her son, his decision to become a church member would allow him to serve God rather than man, but in reality its purpose was to advance James's business prospects: 'Even from a selfish point of view you will find this to smooth your path in your walk in the world while not being of the world for being avowedly and openly a follower of the Saviour.'[75] In the final analysis, Buchanan's sense of masculine authority did not hark back to the old culture of divine right patriarchy but looked forward to a more truncated view of masculinity as founded upon men's position as economic breadwinners. As a leading pillar of the Liberal–Tory coalition, a staunch advocate of protective tariffs and an exponent of the producer ideology, which promoted a partnership between industrial capitalists and workers, Buchanan preached what he called his 'social economy', which maintained 'the only thing of comparative importance is the employment of our own people.'[76] Though seemingly anchored in the outmoded religion of Calvinism and having been raised in the milieu of an older commercial society, Buchanan espoused a very modern view of masculine power.

By 1880 economic definitions of masculinity and fatherhood appeared to be challenging the efficacy of the older spiritual patriarchy that had sustained the early modern social order. It was the spectre of such views gaining wider currency in the new industrial centres like Hamilton and Toronto against which a plethora of religious tracts on the benefits of household religion were directed. Although writers such as the Rev. John Lanceley, who wrote *The Domestic Sanctuary* (1878), and Donald C. Hossack, a Methodist layman, who wrote *The Gospel of the Home* (1903), gave token recognition to the view that the mother had influence, but not leadership, in the home and that the home should be the primary field of her service, their real concern was the decline in male exercise of authority within the household. They directly linked masculine power to male spiritual headship of the family as a concerted attack on the economically driven bourgeois masculinity. It is significant that Lanceley's volume was directed mainly at the business and working classes of the industrial city of Hamilton, which had been dubbed Canada's Birmingham[77] and where men such as Buchanan were the local leaders. These authors were also responding to the vast institutional growth which characterised late-nineteenth-century urban Canada: they tolerated Sunday schools, but they preferred that children learn the foundational elements of religion from their fathers (with the mother playing a supportive role), and, more significantly, in a clear reference to the older vision of patriarchal control of household dependents, Lanceley and Hossack both eschewed the kinds of institutional charitable endeavours such as the industrial schools patronised by Agnes Buchanan, believing that these innovations promoted contractual views of labour and service. For these religious writers, social paternalism, which literally flowed from domestic patriarchy outwards to the wider society, would harmonise the growing antagonism between worker and capitalist. This was a distinctly different remedy from that proffered by Buchanan, who recommended protective tariffs which would sustain higher wages for working-class breadwinners.

In a manner directly echoing the divine right analogy between God, the monarchy and domestic fatherhood, Hossack claimed that the man 'is the head of the family. In order to succeed, every organisation must have a head: there must be a final authority',[78] and, as he made clear, the ultimate template for modern masculinity must be the Divine order. Thus the husband was the head of the wife as Christ was head of the church, a direct reaffirmation of early modern arguments for women's subordination. Although Lanceley accepted aspects of the new liberal order in so far as he gives a nod to the concept of political freedom and individual choice, his real message wholly recapitulated the old language of Robert Filmer, the seventeenth-century architect of the patriarchal divine right discourse. As Lanceley wrote, 'no one can overestimate the value of a proper family training in regard to the nation's life and prosperity. The throne can be secure in freedom only when the family life is sacred, - when the relations of the family are recognised and socially observed and guarded.'[79] And, as he went on to argue, the government of the family depended wholly on the 'father as the priest', for 'the husband, being the head of the house, as king and priest of the whole, and to him only, is deputed the authority of law and order. It is his right to rule. The outer world cares to know no one but him.'[80] There could be no clearer statement of the absolute authority of fathers and husbands within the family, even though by the late nineteenth century Protestant discourse allowed a much greater role for affection, both conjugal and fraternal, within the home, which slightly mitigated the hierarchical nature of the social polity which they were upholding. Where the eighteenth-century patriarchal discourse saw the family as the precursor of the church and state, these later commentators continued to delineate a connection between the 'private' family and the 'public' social order, with the connection seen in entirely masculinist terms, since it lay with the husband and father. As Lanceley so well put the case, 'man is everywhere a man.'[81] Although Hossack and Lanceley still termed the family a form of 'government', they also saw it as the cornerstone of patriotism, economic prosperity and the wellspring of 'social relationships',[82] which indicated the penetration of liberal values into the wider culture. Despite some slight integration of liberal principles, however, the overall tendency of their thought was to reaffirm hierarchical social relations. This can be best illustrated through their discussion of parenting. Lanceley, for example, could well have been writing a century earlier, as he did not uphold the ideal of the loving and sentimental father. By contrast, while Hossack clearly saw the father as the supreme authority within the family, he also recommended that the father be patient with his children, be affectionate, and avoid homosocial companionship offered by associational life. In short, fathers were instructed to take on female attributes with regard to the care of children and to make the home their primary sphere.[83] This obvious feminising of the father's role may have been a reaction against the increased militarisation of masculinity in the midst of the Boer War, but, whatever its purpose, it did not entail a diminution of the reach of the father's influence, as he was in practice to be both 'mother' and 'father' to his children. Lanceley set less store by affectionate models of masculinity and liberal principles of voluntary citizenship, for he declared firmly that children 'must be punished to be governed',[84] despite making a weak allusion to Locke's idea that the relationship between parent and child was that of a voluntary covenant. More significantly, Lanceley wholly embraced the traditional notion of the moral economy of service, declaring that the family must still be defined by the regulation of servants, whose work must not be defined in contractual terms; they must be treated like children and thus be morally tutored and physically corrected! Only religion 'creates in the master an affectionate interest in the welfare of his servants' and it 'renders the rich man the guardian and benefactor of the poor' and it 'makes the poor cheerful, contented and honest'.[85] Given Lanceley's anti-modern response to concepts of individualism and liberty and the growing anomie of social relations in the industrial city, it is not surprising that his vision of the properly regulated household was that of order and subordination by gender and age. This was principally affirmed in the 'good government' of household prayers guided by the earthly priestly father. As Lanceley concluded:

> All government originated in parental authority, and families contain the rudiments of empires; and as the happiness of a nation may be promoted by the wisdom and justice of the legislature, so the welfare of a family depends most essentially on its government. He who is at the head of the family is bound to govern it... The government of a householder over his domestics should be exercised for moral and religious purposes.[86]

According to Lanceley, 'true manliness'[87] was almost entirely defined by a man's spiritual authority in the home, for only religion, not work, could confer the degree of 'self-mastery'[88] which would allow men to govern without being arbitrary or tyrannical in both the private and public realms of modern citizenship.

By the late nineteenth century the views of Lanceley and Hossack regarding spiritual patriarchy may not have been in the ascendancy, but they continued to represent a dominant discourse within Protestantism, and in particular Methodism, a denomination usually identified by evangelical individualism. Their arguments about the father-centred family and its importance in defining broader social norms were in part a reaction against the growth of women's campaigns for the vote and against the growing influence of Christian women's organisations, such as temperance, missionary work and charitable institutions, all of which deployed arguments of maternal feminism to undergird their campaigns. Lanceley and Hossack both focused upon the elision between the male-centred family and the masculinist politics of church governance. Literally, late-nineteenth-century Canadian churches demanded the presence of men and upheld an ideal of male social citizenship.[89] More significantly, their vociferous defence of spiritual patriarchy and their eschewing of

Lockean liberalism must also be viewed in the context of all forms of masculinity – namely the military characterisation of Canadian culture at the height of imperialist fervour and the breadwinner ideal, both of which were on the rise. In fact, the breadwinner ideal, with its emphasis on the concept of the male living wage, was becoming increasingly central to working-class politics, and, more particularly after the 1930s, it became firmly embedded in government welfare policymaking.[90] However, spiritual patriarchy remained sufficiently robust culturally that the religion of the father legally determined the religion of the child until the twenty-first century, although it had probably been a dead letter after the enactment of the Charter of Rights and Freedoms in 1982.

Outside this legal definition, the *ancien régime* culture of domestic patriarchy remained largely intact, and its cultural influence had not just penetrated Anglicanism, the conventional prop of the aristocratic order, but had spread across all Protestant denominations and social classes. As a result, it remained an important facet of masculinity, and, while it had shed over time its direct associations with the aristocratic temper of the eighteenth century, it did forestall the ascendancy of bourgeois domesticity, represented by the life of the Hamilton merchant Isaac Buchanan. More significantly, it ensured that the concept of moral motherhood remained a subordinate discourse, which, while gaining a purchase within Canadian society at the end of the nineteenth century, was quickly shouldered aside by the persistent masculinist institutional demands of church and state. Divine right patriarchy was, in the words of John Tosh, *the* 'resilient masculinity'[91] which remained the dominant value system in Canadian society between 1780 and the 1930s.

## Notes

I would very much like to thank the editors of this volume, Sean Brady and John Arnold, for their helpful suggestions for revision, as well as those of Michael Gauvreau, Carmen Mangion and John Tosh. Above all, I would like to extend my deepest appreciation to Douglas McCalla for directing me to the Isaac Buchanan Papers. The research for this article was supported by the Social Sciences and Humanities Research Council of Canada.

1. Archives of Ontario (AO), John Grubb Letterbook, MS 207, Grubb to his brother, ca. 1850.
2. Rev. John Angel Jones, quoted in Rev. John Lanceley, *The Domestic Sanctuary or the Importance of Family Religion* (Hamilton, 1878).
3. See, for example, Toby Ditz, 'The new men's history and the peculiar absence of gendered power: some remedies from early-American gender history', *Gender and History* 16 (2004), 1–35; Thomas A. Foster, *Sex and the Eighteenth-Century Man: Massachusetts and the History of Sexuality in America* (Boston, 2006).
4. John Tosh, 'Masculinities in an industrializing society: Britain, 1800–1914', *Journal of British Studies* 44 (2005), 332, 335. On the dominance of moral motherhood in the

nineteenth-century transatlantic world, see John Tosh, *A Man's Place: Masculinity and the Middle-Class Home in Victorian England* (New Haven, 1999), pp. 90–1; Mary Ryan, *The Empire of Mother: American Writing about Domesticity, 1830–60* (New York, 1982); Mary Ryan, *The Cradle of the Middle Class: The Family in Oneida County, New York, 1790–1865* (Cambridge, 1981); Barbara Epstein, *The Politics of Domesticity: Women, Evangelicalism and Temperance in Nineteenth-Century America* (Middletown, CT, 1981); William Westfall, *Two Worlds: The Protestant Culture of Nineteenth-Century Ontario* (Montreal and Kingston, 1989); Marguerite Van Die, 'Revisiting "separate spheres": women, religion and the family in mid-Victorian Brantford, Ontario', in Nancy Christie (ed.), *Households of Faith: Religion, Family and Community in Canada, 1760–1969* (Montreal and Kingston, 2002), pp. 234–63; Cecilia Morgan, *Public Men and Virtuous Women: The Gendered Languages of Religion and Politics in Upper Canada, 1791–1850* (Toronto, 1996).

5. For this interpretation, see John Tosh, *A Man's Place*. For a more recent reassertion of this argument, see Trev Lynn Broughton and Helen Rogers, 'Introduction', in Trev Lynn Broughton and Helen Rogers (eds), *Gender and Fatherhood in the Nineteenth Century* (London, 2007), p. 1.
6. For this line of argument, see J. Fliegelman, *Prodigals and Pilgrims: The American Revolution against Patriarchal Authority, 1750–1800* (Cambridge, 1983); Lawrence Stone, *The Family, Sex and Marriage in England, 1500–1800* (Harmondsworth, 1979); Lynn Hunt, *The Family Romance of the French Revolution* (Berkeley, 2003); Joan Landes, *Women and the Public Sphere in the Age of the French Revolution* (Ithaca, 1988). For an important critique of this chronology which argued for the rehabilitation of patriarchy under Napoleon, see Suzanne Desan, *The Family on Trial in Revolutionary France* (Berkeley, 2004).
7. On this theme, see Marguerite Van Die, *Religion, Family and Community in Victorian Canada: The Colbys of Carrollcroft* (Montreal and Kingston, 2005), pp. 5, 54, 108. For other interpretations which emphasise the prominent role of fathers in the religious socialisation of children, see Ollivier Hubert, 'Ritual performance and Parish sociability: French-Canadian families at mass from the seventeenth to the nineteenth centuries', in Christie (ed.), *Households of Faith*, pp. 37–76; J.I. Little, 'The fireside kingdom: a mid-nineteenth-century Anglican perspective on marriage and parenthood', in Christie (ed.), *Households of Faith*, pp. 77–102.
8. See Nancy Christie, 'Introduction: theorizing a colonial past', in Nancy Christie (ed.), *Transatlantic Subjects: Ideas, Institutions and Social Experience in Post-Revolutionary British North America* (Montreal and Kingston, 2008), pp. 3–44.
9. For a more extensive discussion of this transition, see Nancy Christie, *Engendering the State: Family, Work and Welfare in Canada* (Toronto, 2000).
10. Thomas Adsett to Rev. Robert Ridsdale, 21 December 1832, quoted in Wendy Cameron, Sheila Haines and Mary McDougall Maude (eds), *English Immigrant Voices: Labourers' Letters from Upper Canada in the 1830s* (Montreal and Kingston, 2000), p. 87.
11. AO, David Gibson Papers, MS 95, James Gibson to David, 8 July 1819.
12. 'Queen Margaret', *The Christian Recorder* 1:1 (March 1819); AO, Mary O'Brien Diary, February 1837.
13. Michael Gauvreau, 'The dividends of empire: church establishments and contested british identities in the Canadas and the maritimes, 1780–1850', in Nancy Christie (ed.), *Transatlantic Subjects*, pp. 199–250.
14. AO, John Strachan sermons, MS 767, 'Consecration Sermon', Psalm 127:1, Psalm 87:2, no. 190, preached at Markham 11 July 1846.

15. See Nancy Christie, '"A painful dependence": female begging letters and the familial economy of obligation', in Nancy Christie and Michael Gauvreau (eds), *Mapping the Margins: The Family and Social Discipline in Canada, 1700–1975* (Montreal and Kingston, 2004), pp. 69–102; Nancy Christie, 'Strangers in the family: work, gender, and the origins of old age homes', *Journal of Family History* 32 (2007), 371–91. On the expansion of patriarchal rule in colonial America, see Carole Shammas, *A History of Household Government in America* (Charlottesville, 2002); Mary Beth Norton, *Founding Mothers and Fathers: Gendered Power and the Forming of American Society* (New York, 1988).
16. John R. Gillis, *A World of Their Own Making: Myth, Ritual and the Quest for Family Values* (New Haven, 1997), pp. 187–88; Robert Griswold, *Fatherhood in America: A History* (New York, 1993).
17. J.C.D. Clark, *English Society, 1688–1832: Ideology, Social Structure and Political Practice During the Ancien Regime* (Cambridge, 1985), pp. 197–216. Where Clark stressed social continuity, Boyd Hilton has recently argued that patriarchalism was refurbished, although he concurs with Clark's periodisation. See Boyd Hilton, *A Mad, Bad, and Dangerous People?: England 1783–1846* (Oxford, 2006).
18. Rachel Weil, *Political Passions: Gender, the Family and Political Argument in England, 1680–1714* (Manchester, 1999), pp. 7, 72–3. She states that Whigs believed not simply in a symbolic analogy between kings and fathers, but in a literal elision between these roles.
19. Rev. John Strachan, *A Discourse on the Character of King George the Third, Addressed to the Inhabitants of British America* (Montreal, 1810), 13, 22. On the link between religious masculinity and public virtue in the eighteenth century, see Jeremy Gregory, 'Homo religiosus: masculinity and religion in the long eighteenth century', in Tim Hitchcock and Michele Cohen (eds), *English Masculinities, 1660–1800* (London, 1999), pp. 85–110.
20. See Todd Webb, 'How the Canadian methodists became British: unity, schism, and transatlantic identity, 1827–54', in Nancy Christie (ed.), *Transatlantic Subjects*, pp. 159–98.
21. Quoted in Morgan, *Public Men and Virtuous Women*, p. 127. Significantly, the constitution that established the Dominion of Canada in 1867 conferred upon the central government the awesome residual power of making laws for the 'peace, order, and good government', a phrase which harks back to the masculinist patriarchal ideal.
22. Quoted in Morgan, *Public Men and Virtuous Women*, pp. 152–3. Morgan argues that Methodists did not articulate a link between religious fatherhood and the state. Given that Methodists so clearly framed their political ideology in *ancien régime* terms, her argument can only be considered fallacious.
23. 'The Pious Father's Prayer', *The Christian Guardian*, 1 September 1845, quoted in Morgan, *Public Men and Virtuous Women*, p. 152.
24. Proudfoot Diary, 2 June 1833. See also William Bell Reminiscences for the Presbyterian discourse on family religion. Library and Archives of Canada (LAC), Robert Bell Papers.
25. Toronto Central Library (TCL), Baldwin Room, William Dummer Powell Papers, L16, Anne Powell to brother, n.d. AO, William Proudfoot Diary, 13 December 1837. Since personal diaries were considered public property, it can be inferred that, because Proudfoot wrote this in the midst of the Rebellions, he was attempting to make himself appear less of a radical by alluding to conservative notions of family organisation.
26. James Wilson, obituary, quoted in Morgan, *Public Men and Virtuous Women*, p. 131.

27. On the family as both an individual and a communal entity, see Powell Papers, Samuel Jarvis to Mary Powell, 30 August 1818; Anne Powell to brother, 9 May 1839.
28. LAC, William Gibson Papers, David Gibson to Uncle William, 6 March 1843.
29. AO, Proudfoot Papers, MS 54, Jessie Robb Henderson, 'Sketches of Pastors of the English Settlement', typescript, n.d.
30. AO, Mary O'Brien Diary, 8 March 1830, 25 February 1832.
31. AO, John Grubb Letterbook, MS 207, John Grubb to brother, n.d. 1837.
32. Powell Papers, George Murray to Eliza Powell, 26 November 1846.
33. See Christie, 'Strangers in the family: work, gender, and the origins of old age homes; Nancy Christie, '"The plague of servants": female household labor and the making of classes in upper Canada', in Christie (ed.), *Transatlantic Subjects*, pp. 83–132. For the moral economy of service, see Tim Meldrum, *Domestic Service and Gender, 1660–1750: Life and Work in the London Household* (London, 2000). For the importance of domestic service as a benchmark of patriarchalism, see Clark, *English Society*, pp. 85–6.
34. Mary O'Brien Diary, 28 October 1830.
35. TCL, Baldwin Room, John Hillyard Cameron Papers, S8, John to Lizzie, 4 October 1843.
36. Suzanne Desan, *The Family on Trial in Revolutionary France*.
37. AO, Anna Ardagh Diary, passim. For a more complete discussion of Anna Ardagh and the place of 'private' religion as a space for female resistance to patriarchal authority, see Nancy Christie, 'Time, space, modernity and the transatlantic family', in Brigitte Caulier and Yvan Rousseau (dirs), *Temps, espaces, modernité: Mélanges offerts à Serge Courville et Normand Séguin* (Ste-Foy, 2009), pp. 69–82. On religion as contested terrain in Victorian marriages, see Tosh, *A Man's Place*, pp. 69–73, 96. On different views of marriage as a variable of class, see Desan, *The Family on Trial in Revolutionary France*, p. 89. For an interpretation that sees gender as the key to varying views of marriage, see A.J. Hammerton, *Cruelty and Companionship: Conflict in Nineteenth-Century Married Life* (London, 1995).
38. AO, Anna Ardagh Diary, 30 October 1854.
39. AO, Anna Ardagh Diary, 13 March 1855.
40. LAC, James Gowan Papers, Anna Gowan to dearest love, Friday 5 p.m., n.d. The underlining emphatically belonged to Anna Ardagh.
41. TCL, Baldwin Room, Frederick Brigden Papers, S138, Diary 22 April 1861. For Tosh's paradigm, see 'Masculinities in an Industrializing Society', p. 331.
42. Brigden Papers, Diary, 20 April 1861.
43. For a larger discussion of Brigden's life, see Nancy Christie, '"On the threshold of manhood": Working-Class Religion and Domesticity in Victorian Britain and Canada', *Histoire Sociale/Social History*, 36:71 (2003), 145–74.
44. Brigden Papers, Diary, 20 April 1861; February n.d. 1861.
45. For an exploration of these aspects of working-class masculinity, see Jacqueline M. Moore, 'Cow Boys, Cattle Men and Competing Masculinities on the Texas Frontier,' in this volume.
46. Brigden Papers, Diary, 19 February 1861.
47. Brigden Papers, Diary, 7 April 1866, 11 April 1866.
48. Brigden Papers, Notebook, n.d.
49. Brigden Papers, Fred to brother, 15 March 1867. Fred states that the advance towards God and the love and care for others is true manliness.

50. Brigden Papers, Frederick Brigden to Son, Frederick, n.d. August 1894.
51. Brigden Papers, Fred to Fanny, 23 May 1867.
52. Brigden Papers, Fred to mother, n.d. October 1863.
53. On Brigden's wariness of living in a homosocial world, see Brigden Papers, Diary, March 1863; 24 June 1863; 28 February 1865. It was Beale who brought Brigden to Toronto to be an engraver and later bequeathed the Toronto Engraving Company to him. On the male-centredness of his conversion experience, see John Anderson to my dear young friend, 15 August 1862; William Sleight to Fred, 2 October 1862.
54. Brigden Papers, Fred to Fanny, 13 May 1868; Fred to Fanny, 9 July 1868.
55. Brigden Papers, 4 March 1867; Francis Higgins to Mr Brigden, 3 May 1867. They were married 13 October 1868.
56. Brigden Papers, Francis to Frederick, 6 May 1867.
57. Brigden Papers, Francis to Frederick, 21 May 1867.
58. Brigden Papers, Aunt Henty to Brigden, 29 February 1867; Diary, 22 February 1867.
59. Brigden Papers, Fred to Fanny, 7 November 1867.
60. On the fatherhood of God, see Brigden Papers, Fanny to Frederick, 4 June 1867.
61. Brigden Papers, Diary, 18 September 1865.
62. Brigden Papers, Frederick to Fanny, 1 September 1868.
63. Brigden Papers, Frederick to Fanny, 29 November, p.m., 1867.
64. On Brigden's desire for male heirs, see Brigden Papers, Mother to Fred, n.d. 1870.
65. Brigden Papers, Diary, 22 December 1872.
66. LAC, Isaac Buchanan Papers, MG 24 D 16, 6, Isaac to Agnes, 11 January 1843, 15 January 1843.
67. On the theology of the atonement, see Boyd Hilton, *The Age of Atonement: The Influence of Evangelicalism on Social and Economic Thought, 1785–1865* (Oxford, 1988). Buchanan does not entirely fit Hilton's paradigm, as Hilton is most interested in the link between evangelicalism and free trade theories of political economy, and Buchanan emphatically rejected free trade.
68. Buchanan Papers, 6, Agnes to Isaac, 26 January 1851, in which she quotes extensively from a sermon by Mr Lundie in Glasgow.
69. Buchanan Papers, 6, Agnes to Isaac, 4 September 1854; Isaac to Agnes, 5 March 1843.
70. Buchanan Papers, 6, Agnes to Isaac, 28 February 1867.
71. Buchanan Papers, 6, Isaac to Agnes, 20 February 1868.
72. On the new fatherhood which stressed playing with one's children, see Stephen M. Frank, *Life with Father: Parenthood and Masculinity in the Nineteenth-Century American North* (Baltimore, 1998).
73. Buchanan Papers, 6, Isaac to Agnes, 5 March 1843.
74. Buchanan Papers 22, Isaac to Rev. Dr Craig, Glasgow, 5 June 1860.
75. Buchanan Papers, 12, Agnes to James, 24 August 1870; James to Agnes, 26 August 1870.
76. Hamilton Public Library, Buchanan Papers, Box 2, file 1, 'Isaac Buchanan and the mechanics', 7 September 1867.
77. This was a reference to Birmingham, England, 'The Workshop of the World'.
78. Donald C. Hossack, *The Gospel of the Home* (Toronto, 1903), p. 25. Interestingly, the preface written by Rev. Nathanael Burwash, Chancellor of Victoria University, the leading Methodist College, stressed the importance of mothers in sustaining a family's religious lineage, even though this was not the principal goal of Hossack's tract.

79. Rev. John Lanceley, *The Domestic Sanctuary or the Importance of Family Religion* (Hamilton, 1878), p. vi.
80. Ibid., pp. 10, 13.
81. Ibid., p. 39.
82. Hossack, *The Gospel of the Home*, pp. 5, 29; Lanceley, *The Domestic Sanctuary*, pp. 12, 50. For the continued association between family and the state and society with the emergence of liberalism, see Jennifer Huer, *The Family and the Nation: Gender and Citizenship in Revolutionary France, 1789–1830* (Ithaca, 2005); Judith Surkis, *Sexing the Citizen: Morality and Masculinity in France, 1870–1920* (Ithaca, 2006).
83. Hossack, pp. 27–31, 63–6.
84. Lanceley, *The Domestic Sanctuary*, pp. 51, 67–70.
85. Ibid., p. 70.
86. Ibid., p. 13.
87. Ibid., p. 106.
88. Ibid., p. 118.
89. On this theme, see Nancy Christie, 'Young men and the creation of civic christianity in urban methodist churches, 1880–1914', *Journal of the Canadian Historical Association*, new series, 17 (2006), 79–105; Patricia Dirks, 'Reinventing christian masculinity and fatherhood: the Canadian protestant experience, 1900–1920', in Christie (ed.), *Households of Faith*, pp. 290–316.
90. Nancy Christie, *Engendering the State*.
91. John Tosh, 'The old Adam and the new man: emerging themes in the history of English masculinities, 1750–1850', in Hitchcock and Cohen (eds), *English Masculinities, 1660–1800*, p. 225.

# 20
# Punters and Their Prostitutes: British Soldiers, Masculinity and *Maisons Tolérées* in the First World War

*Clare Makepeace*

No chapter in the history of masculinity has undergone such a proliferation in recent years as that concerning the Tommy and his officer. In little more than a decade, the subject has been transformed from a blank field to one of the most burgeoning cultural historiographies on the First World War, with historians focusing their attention on whether or not modern warfare triggered a crisis in masculinity[1] and how masculinity was reconstructed upon homecoming and in the context of commemoration.[2] One area of investigation has remained notably unexplored, despite its centrality to conceptions of masculinity: soldiers' heterosexual lives and, more specifically, their commercial indulgences.[3] This omission is surprising considering how many soldiers were preoccupied with discussing the subject of sex,[4] if not physically indulging in their desires,[5] and that the unfortunate minority inflicted with its infectious repercussions vastly outnumber their more renowned shell-shocked comrades and disabled veterans.[6] My research has delved into this less celebrated side of soldiers' lives by focusing on three aspects of their forays into commercial sex when stationed in France: their motives for visiting brothels, their reactions to the brothels and women themselves, and their contention with the less salubrious consequences – venereal disease.

The main objective for this research was to understand self-conceptions of masculinity and, more particularly, heterosexuality during the Great War. The conditions of warfare also make this research feasible and provide it with resonance beyond the combat sphere. Warfare can offer the historian a unique insight into behaviour and self-conceptions that we simply cannot 'get at' during peacetime. In the alien circumstance of war, individuals were prepared, even obliged, to record their experiences in a manner that was either unnecessary or intolerable during other peacetime periods. Geographical separation required relationships to be sustained through regular letters; the horror of combat demanded greater introspection in the form of diaries; and the dislocation of war legitimatised the recitation of certain 'inappropriate' behaviours. These three points, along with licensed brothels in France being officially accessible to the British soldier for most of the war, make a study of the prostitute's British punter, whose ubiquity has been largely ignored by historians of all periods due to his inaccessibility in the sources, a viable topic during the Great War.[7]

This research was able to draw upon 15 men's diaries, letters or memoirs, which were written either during the war or in the following decade, as well as a further 18 personal testimonies written or recorded much later in the century, in which each soldier either discusses his own visits to brothels or observes the visits of others. A similarly rich set of autobiographical sources relating to brothel visits in peacetime simply does not exist. Of course, the historian must still exercise caution: these men, in describing their commercial sexual experiences, were far from typical and such openness may render them unrepresentative.[8] We should be wary of the temptation to attribute the sexual behaviours of these few, vocal individuals to all men, as previous historians have done.[9] Yet, however skewed and fleeting, there is no doubt that the testimony of these men provides us with an insight into sexual behaviour that was only documented because of the conditions of war.

Through these autobiographies, we are able to approach masculinity as it was experienced: a relatively recent 'turn' in gender studies and a particularly enlightening approach for examining heterosexuality. Many histories of masculinity in the First World War have taken a cultural constructionist approach to masculinity, whether focusing on social ideals of key public figures, such as military officials or medical experts,[10] or literary representations.[11] Whilst such representations are crucial for conceptions of masculinity, since, in Frank Mort's words, 'the whole paraphernalia of government reports and professional knowledge does set the broad conditions for the way we experience our sexual identities,'[12] historians have tended to leave unanswered the way in which these public codes of masculinity related to men's actual behaviour.[13] Focusing solely on cultural representation is particularly problematic for exploring sexuality: unlike some subjects for which ideologies of masculinity or manliness also provide a description of actual life, public codes of purity reveal little about sexual behaviour.[14] For example, historians' frequent citation of Kitchener's personal warning to every soldier to avoid the dangers of French wine and women[15] tells us little about masculine self-conceptions if we fail to consider the recipients' views that 'they may as well have not been issued for all the notice we took of them.'[16]

However, this does not mean that sexual experience was acquired within some sort of male licentious vacuum. Although cultural representations, such as advice manuals or newspapers, are not enlightening here, we can examine the institutional rules and regulations of the British Expeditionary Force (BEF), which not only prescribed the ideal patterns of male sexual conduct during the war but also formally enforced them and so directly altered men's experiences. This forms one half of the system of power relations examined in this research. The other half is composed through the informal strictures instigated by the men themselves, which are particularly insightful in the circumstances of war given the amassing of men of different classes, ages, nationalities and races. Together, these constitute the 'homosocial dynamic' or 'the considerations which govern men's relations with each other *as men*',[17] which has so far received little attention from either sociologists or historians.[18]

In this chapter, I will demonstrate the effectiveness of these two approaches in tackling conceptions of masculinity. First, my work on experience has revealed an as yet undocumented code of masculine behaviour in which premarital and extramarital sex were an acceptable, but not essential, component of masculinity, which was not to be flaunted. Second, the importance of homosociability for the examination of heterosexuality will be demonstrated through the context of Empire. By applying this approach, I will set out the limits of even the *maison tolérée* as a patriarchal institution. Finally, I shall reflect on the resonance of these findings for conceptions of masculinity outside times of war.

In 1916, the Cairo Purification Committee (a civil–military body appointed to recommend ways of reducing venereal disease among troops)[19] noted that a considerable proportion of young men in civil life, as well as in the Army, considered sexual intercourse before marriage a legitimate compliance with natural human instincts, not involving any moral stigma for the male, provided its indulgence was not openly flaunted in the face of society and of his relations.[20] The observation in this report that 'indulgence is not openly flaunted' is crucial to this research and challenges some of historians' most orthodox ordering of male behaviour. One model of masculinity that has received a disproportionate amount of attention from historians is that of R.W. Connell's hegemonic masculinity. In her wake, historians have endeavoured to identify which masculine attributes were essential to masculine status, how such features were achieved or upheld, and how their absence resulted in vilification. Yet the Cairo Purification Committee, in discussing one of masculinity's key components – heterosexuality – introduces the need for a very different social organisation of masculinity. Its report, along with the findings I set out below, describes an aspect of masculinity – sex before marriage – that was not essential but acceptable, and which was condoned, as long as it was hidden.

In the first instance, through analysing men's reasons for visiting brothels, we can ascertain that premarital and extramarital sex were not vital to conceptions of masculinity. In Britain, during this period, historians have tended to agree that demand for the services of prostitutes existed among all classes of men; John Tosh argues that 'commercial sex was a masculine rite of passage' for the majority of men in the nineteenth century. Nevertheless, the subject was shrouded in a 'massive silence' since it conflicted with the 'pieties of manly discourse' as well as the law.[21] In war-torn France such legal impediments were removed. The *maisons tolérées* (licensed brothels) – of which there were some 137 in 35 towns – were only placed out of bounds for the British soldier, and other Crown troops, from 18 March 1918.[22] One might also suspect that, in this all-male environment, the discursive deterrents were loosened. Despite this, whilst some evidence exists from observers of how men, officers and captains urged their fellow soldiers to 'show himself a man',[23] many were equally prepared to resist such provocation and leave their mates 'to their joys'.[24] A further analysis of men's reasons for either entering or abstaining from brothels supports such equivocation. The reasons men offered for consorting with prostitutes conform to one of four tropes: meeting their physiological need;[25] desiring feminine company;[26] living life to the full in the face of imminent death[27] or celebrating their survival of battle.[28] However, the men who abstained appear to have been drawing from a much more diverse range of explanations – from more urgently needing food and sleep to staying faithful to one's wife to fearing that they might contract venereal disease.[29] Given that the level of autonomy observable in explanations of behaviour is often proportional to the acceptability of that conduct, we can conclude that pre-marital and extramarital sex were not essential components of masculinity. Indeed, abstainers from such carnal indulgences do not seem to have faced or felt any tarnishing of their masculinity: Lieutenant A.E. Macgregor felt 'happy and strong and manly' upon declining his Captain's invitation to consort with prostitutes. Likewise, Private Ted Rimmer, despite going months without seeing a woman and not being 'really mad about sex', concluded that the war had 'made a man of me'.[30]

Similarly, during the brothel visit itself, the acceptability but not essentiality of performing with a prostitute becomes evident. In many cases, joining a brothel queue was the preliminary requirement for visiting a *maison tolérée*, to which men do not seem to have had any hesitation in conforming.[31] Indeed, rather than being a pragmatic measure, moving up this rather different line also became a ritual of the brothel visit and a site of homosocial bonding.[32] For some it was a sign of gentlemanly conduct, for others it was a means of demonstrating one's sexual prowess, whilst one man equated it to a 'cup tie at a football final in Blighty'.[33] Yet, despite this public demonstration of intent, there was still no shame in a hasty retreat. Private Eddie Bigwood, Private Hawtin Leonard Mundy and Private Leo McCormack all took fright and flight when they stepped inside the brothel and saw barely clad whores. Since McCormack had already paid his fee, he was given a chocolate bar in compensation and, more revealingly for the acceptability of his continence, did not hesitate to relate this tale back to his fellow soldiers when he returned to the camp.[34]

This conclusion is also evident during the final stage of the brothel visit: preventing venereal disease. The acceptability of extramarital intercourse can be seen in the authorities' reluctance to punish those who contracted VD in the British Army on the grounds that this would only lead men to conceal their infections.[35] The only 'direct' penalty for contracting the disease was for concealment, which resulted in up to two years' imprisonment with hard labour.[36] However, men were still unwilling to flaunt the potential consequences of their promiscuity.[37] In early 1916, compartments were provided for each British Unit containing potassium permanganate solution and calomel ointment, but this was, on the whole, deemed to be unsuccessful. It was thought that men were reluctant to be seen going to use this equipment, which had been openly placed in the urinals.[38] The Army Council sympathised with such coyness, arguing for disinfectants to be accessible to men returning to the barracks 'under proper means of privacy',[39] and, when the British Government finally instituted early treatment in the army in 1918, it ensured that the treatment could be procured on their return 'without the knowledge of anybody'.[40]

One might argue that such reticence was less about conceptions of masculinity and more about a reluctance to acknowledge such undignified diseases. The context of war allows us to compare how other nations responded to similar predicaments, and we can see that the classification of premarital and extramarital sex as an accepted, but not essential, component of masculinity was peculiar to Britain. Just before the war, Abraham Flexner asserted that in Europe 'certain forms of venereal experience have been popularly treated as marks of maturity.'[41] France, during the subsequent four years, appears to be no exception. French soldiers were entitled to sexual interactions with women: not only did they have a duty to produce children for the nation but the army's morale was also dependent on it – *Courage*, written by Drs Huot and Voivenel in 1917 and dedicated to Marshal Joffre, contended that courage and sexual prowess were linked.[42] Consequently, it took until autumn 1918 for the French authorities to agree to a system of prophylaxis for their soldiers, since they were concerned that such measures would limit their sexuality; even then, they failed to impose disciplinary measures on those contracting venereal disease.[43] For the American soldiers, quite the reverse was the case. Disinfection was made easy and compulsory within three hours of contact with a prostitute.[44] If a man disregarded this procedure and subsequently developed venereal disease, he could be tried for neglect of duty.[45] Any commander with a disease rate above a minimum within his unit was liable to lose his command, and, for those Americans at embarkation ports and training areas, brothels were completely out of bounds for soldiers.[46] These steps could be taken because non-sexual physical prowess among American men was prized, and they were advised that chastity did not contradict their masculinity; rather, the overuse of sex organs might exhaust them.[47]

418  Clare Makepeace

This classification of premarital and extramarital sex as acceptable but not essential amongst British men demonstrates the diversity of acceptable masculine behaviours, even for a subject as fundamental to masculinity as sexual desire.[48] Here we find abstainers and indulgers alike not experiencing any slight on their sense of masculinity. More paradoxically, it appears that flaunting this promiscuity was unacceptable, even though it was condoned by both men and the authorities within this libidinous army culture.[49] This questions whether demonstrations were, in fact, 'absolutely central to masculine status'.[50] Indeed, for certain groups of men, although their sexual indulgences received greater endorsement than did others, their brothel visits were accorded more privacy, as in the case of officers and married men.

As is commonly known, brothels during the Great War were divided into red lamps for men and blue lamps for officers.[51] Less acknowledged is that the latter were granted exceptional permission for visiting them. According to one witness, 'the needs of men if they were officers were officially recognised.'[52] Officers were given leave to go to Amiens, Paris and other neighbouring towns[53] and were able to issue road passes so that they could take women from Amiens – 'the recruiting ground for prostitutes for the Fourth and Fifth Armies' – into the war zone (although the authorities subsequently put a stop to this practice).[54] Unsurprisingly, therefore, the Cairo Purification Committee of 1916 'heard that the habit of fornication is more prevalent amongst officers than amongst the rank and file'.[55] However, in spite of having greater access to brothels, officers were admonished if seen in public with prostitutes, a striking contrast to the queues formed by the other ranks. The Army Provost Marshal (APM) at Rouen took the names of officers seen talking to prostitutes in a local hotel in March 1915, and in October 1916 the base commandant at Le Havre ordered APMs to record the names of any officers 'disgracing His Majesty's uniform' by being 'seen in the streets in the company of prostitutes'.[56] Similarly, amongst those unlucky enough to develop venereal disease, the officer class was accorded greater privacy. At Le Havre, the two classes were treated in different locations[57] along with a special camp being allocated to padres who were suffering from VD.[58] Such exceptional treatment for officers met the objection of the Surgeon General of the BEF, who asked: 'why shouldn't they be treated like everyone else – After all what's a little clap?'[59]

Married men also received greater authorisation for their brothel visits: in the absence of their regular marital indulgence, a prostitute was now regarded as an acceptable alternative.[60] An 18-year-old, Bert Chaney, noticing a long queue of soldiers standing outside a red lamp brothel, was told that those places 'were not for young lads like me, but for married men who were missing their wives'.[61] Private Percy Clare remembered being addressed by the Brigade Chaplain, who excused unfaithfulness to wives in the present circumstances but advised the men to restrict themselves to the *maisons tolérées*; otherwise they might contract disease.[62] Such beliefs were also resonant overseas: Hirschfeld noted that in almost all countries 'a great proportion' of those with venereal disease were 'older married men' and described how, in Germany, Dr Albert Neisser put this down to their being 'accustomed to a certain routine in erotic fulfilment and that, torn away as they were from their normal family life, they were particularly oppressed by long continued abstinence'.[63]

Again, echoing the exceptional treatment received by officers, precautions were also taken to ensure these sanctioned visits remained hidden. For the first two years of the war one of the reprisals for contracting venereal disease was informing relatives at home of the true nature of the soldier's affliction: something which, according to Colonel Gibbard (Royal Army Medical Corps), men feared 'more than anything else'.[64] Despite this, the army appears to have suspended notification when a major committed suicide on hearing that his wife had been informed: instead, the next of kin was told that their relative had been admitted to hospital but using vague wording, such as 'not yet diagnosed'.[65] Yet this change of policy also took place within weeks of married men being conscripted, at which point the likely profile of the next of kin changed from a parent to the wife, which meant a different set of repercussions if the soldier's fate was revealed at home.[66] One could speculate that the conscription of married men triggered the decision to withhold information on venereal infections. At the very least, this decision was taken in spite of the fact that it was now even more imperative for the next of kin to be informed of the nature of her relative's illness, since, as a wife, she and her future children were at risk. This was the conclusion of the majority of the Cairo Purification Committee, who agreed that 'in the case of all married men the wife should be warned that her husband has been infected.' Yet a minority disagreed with such exceptional treatment, and the Commander-in-Chief went on to reject the majority Committee's recommendation.[67]

The behaviour of these two groups of men, and the codes of conduct that surrounded them, questions whether the most visible masculine codes were the most acceptable. It shows that, although the acceptability of premarital and extramarital sex dramatically altered according to a man's class and marital status, this did not necessarily entail any change in actual behaviour; provisions were simply put in place to disguise it.[68] This leads to some fascinating questions regarding historians' previous conclusions that promiscuity was much more innate to the working class,[69] as well as to what extent men believed in the uxorious ideal. It also raises a more fundamental challenge to historians' methodological approach towards masculinity: what do codes of masculine behaviour that were acceptable but hidden tell us about masculine ideals and the power hierarchies that controlled them?

In addition to comparing conceptions of masculinity across country borders, as historians have traditionally done,[70] an alternative, less-explored path, open to us in circumstances of warfare, looks at how interactions among different nationalities and races may have affected and changed conceptions of masculinity during the war itself. A focus on men fighting under the Imperial banner during the First World War offers us the opportunity to see how the formal rules and regulations on sexual conduct, drawn up by the BEF, were different for British and colonial forces. It also affords us the chance to see how informal strictures, formed among both Dominion and British men who served and were billeted in closer proximity than their colonial counterparts, altered masculine self-conceptions.

The interaction between the Dominion and British soldiers offers particular insight into men's preferences for the amateur or professional prostitute.[71] Historians have agreed that a shift in the male client's preference for the amateur took place during the first half of the twentieth century.[72] What triggered this shift would be worthy of more thorough investigation – Lesley Hall suggests there was a growing public intolerance of men visiting prostitutes and it was considered an affront to male pride to pay for female company. She also quotes the social purity organisations, which argued that the squalid *maisons tolérées* repulsed men from this particular vice whilst still encouraging them to satisfy habits of sexual indulgence elsewhere.[73]

Some men in this sample were undoubtedly put off by the mechanisation of brothels. Ashurst did not fancy 'them things', being 'so common' and 'all sorts of ages'. Private H.G.R. Williams had 'never seen such an unattractive collection of females in my life. I would have thought it enough to put anyone off completely even if he had gone in with the usual intention'. Similarly, Lieutenant H.E.L. Mellersh found his first brothel 'so revolting, the girls dressed so garishly, the female but moustached owner so monstrous, that we came out hurriedly'.[74] Other men drew a moral distinction between amateurs and professionals. Private Frank Richards remembered how he and two 'old birds' went into a red lamp in Béthune. They 'had a drink and left at once,'

> the Old Soldier remarking that if we three old birds couldn't find something better than this it was about time we packed our traps and went West; and sure enough, forty-eight hours later in a village not far from Bethune each one of us had picked up with a respectable bit of goods.

When the Old Soldier later intervened in a brothel queue, considering these men to be 'showing up the British Army', Richards retorted that they were 'no different to us, as we were going on the same errand'. The Old Soldier looked at Richards 'in disgust'. Clare also noticed a difference between the peasants and professional prostitutes. Although both involved a financial transaction, the peasant girl had 'a certain strange sympathy with, and response to, the need of our men away from their wives for years at a time and "women-starved" for months'. She did not like 'to be handled roughly or disrespectfully and have it rubbed in that she was paid'. These girls were 'just natural, simple minded affectionate or good natured creatures generally, they were most emphatically *not* prostitutes'.[75]

Stepping away from men's reactions to the brothels and prostitutes and turning instead towards the other clients may offer us more insights. British men may have been attracted to amateurs during and after the war because they simply could not afford the *maisons tolérées*. Financial transaction was a prominent aspect of the brothel visit,[76] and even those who were full of intent were turned away if they did not have enough money.[77] Particularly offensive for the British may have been the sight of their better-paid Australian, New Zealand and Canadian counterparts having their pick of the prostitutes. British men got ten francs a fortnight but Canadians got this amount in less than two days, a matter that made the English private 'rather bitter'.[78] Consequently, when Sidney Albert Amatt (NCO) ventured into a place of 'evil intent' in Le Havre following payday, he saw mostly Canadian, South African and French troops. The cost of paying to get into the bar, paying for a drink, paying the madam one franc and then paying the actual prostitute could not be afforded by the British soldier, whose 'money was so small in those days that all we could buy was a drink and a look round before we came out again'.[79] Bert Fearns remembered how disparate rates of pay meant that at one brothel the Australian soldiers queued outside one door and got the younger women whilst the British formed a separate queue for the older ones.[80] Indeed, it was recognised within the army and government that the larger pay packet of the Australians was one cause of their higher venereal disease rate,[81] and the prostitutes in London targeted Dominion troops because of their wealth.[82] To think of the financial transaction as solely between the prostitute and her British client precludes the possibility that the British soldiers turned to amateurs simply because they had been priced out of the professional prostitutes' market. The homosocial dynamic, here influenced by the Dominion soldiers fighting under the Imperial banner, demonstrates how changes in male sexual morality were not solely the product of encounters with the female prostitute.

It is worth briefly reflecting upon whether this interaction between British and Dominion soldiers has wider significance beyond the brothel setting. Historians have readily noted the role that the Empire played, prior to the First World War, in forming British men's conceptions of masculinity, from distinguishing the 'more manly' colonisers from their 'less manly' subjects[83] to offering imagined possibilities for white masculine mastery.[84] But how did such perceptions accommodate this apparent face-to-face marginalisation of British men by their Dominion counterparts? Did British men's masculine superiority falter in spheres of combat other than the brothel? If so, what was the contingent effect on the significance of the Empire to these men and their loyalty to it? Such questions are beyond the remit of this chapter but would be deserving of further research in the context of both masculinity and Imperial demise.

Whilst Dominion soldiers seem to have squeezed some of the British out of visits to the professional prostitutes, non-white troops are invisible to the brothel scene, despite some 135,000 armed Indian soldiers,[85] 21,000 black South African[86] and 90,000 Chinese labourers[87] serving in France. By looking at the presence, or rather absence, of different male clients we see the limited dominance of patriarchal forces even within the *maisons tolérées*. The imperial mentality included notions of the colonial soldier, whether black or Asian, possessing uninhibited sexual desires:[88] in India, the British authorities would not contemplate the possibility that the lower rates of venereal admission among the indigenous troops could be attributed to greater sexual restraint.[89] Nevertheless, the British had been unconcerned with the Indian units' sexual activity when they disembarked in Egypt on their way to France. They were warned that catching a preventable disease was a punishable offence, but beyond that no effort was made to obstruct their sexual activity.[90] Yet, once in France, the troops faced severe restrictions on their off-base activity and could be given a dozen lashes if they stayed out beyond 11 p.m.: measures designed to prevent sexual interactions between Indian troops and white women, which appear to have been successful if VD rates are any indication.[91] Men in the South African National Labour Corps, like black soldiers in the American Expeditionary Force, were housed in camps surrounded by a wire stockade and given limited leave.[92] The lines of communication promptly repealed an order issued by the APM at Dieppe that allowed the Chinese to enter brothels.[93] Even Alice Neilans, secretary to the Association of Social and Moral Hygiene, instinctively qualified notions of sexual purity when, on hearing that Calais, Dieppe, Rouen, Le Havre and Boulogne had given the Chinese Labour Corps stationed there access to certain French brothels, she proclaimed that it was 'a very terrible degradation for white women', which, if true, demanded protestation. It was only after being reminded by her French counterpart that accepting 'the principle that it is more demoralising to sell a woman to a man of colour than to a white one' was tantamount to complicity with the system of *maisons tolérées* that Neilans reordered her racial prejudices and moral priorities.[94]

Sexual desire between non-white troops and white women was considered 'a threat to the moral order of Western civilisation'.[95] The British authorities feared that white women servicing Indian men would undermine their Imperial power,[96] and would not lower the whore, if she were white, to satisfying the non-white man. This could have been due to the fact that white troops were unwilling to share their prostitutes with non-white men. Such an attitude would not have been against tradition: in India, before the war, brothels were 'reserved for the use of white troops'.[97] Yet, it was not a matter of assigning these men different brothels. When one incorporates the experience of the colonial troops, we see the limits of male–female power hierarchies even within the *maison tolérée*, the most patriarchal of institutions.

The profitability of focusing on the homosocial dynamic echoes other historians' recent enquiries into masculine alterity.[98] It also takes the significance of such an approach one step further: even when the female appears to be absolutely central to analysis, we may benefit from an occasional glance away from her and an exclusive focus on the surrounding men. In so doing, we can ascertain that perhaps the British man's preference for the amateur prostitute, rather than being a deliberate choice, was an uncontrollable consequence of the presence of his Dominion counterparts. For those feminist historians who believe such an approach is methodological heresy, surely the validity of these findings for their ultimate quest – uncovering the subordination of women in history – makes such an investigation worthwhile. By momentarily discarding our preoccupation with the male/female focus we are able to free the female prostitute from the role of passive subjugation. Instead, we can demonstrate not only how British men were subordinated by her other clients, but also that the prostitute made a choice to pursue the more lucrative Dominion soldiers. By looking outside the brothel, we can also identify the clients who were not even permitted entry and demonstrate the limitations of patriarchy, even in the *maison tolérée*. Further research into whether non-white clients and prostitutes defied such regulations would be fascinating. For example, did the white, European prostitute choose or reject non-white clients fighting for the British army when the opportunity arose?[99] In this way, paradoxically, by removing the focus from the female prostitute we may actually re-emphasise her agency in history.

Warfare provides gender historians with a unique insight into conceptions of masculinity: the documentation of experiences that may have gone unrecorded in peacetime, the delimitation of the formal army regulations on male conduct and the intersection of different nationalities, races and classes. Some historians will undoubtedly argue that these experiences and their contingent codes of masculine behaviour are as unique as the war itself, that they are simply the product of a libidinous army culture and have little relevance for peacetime historians. In some cases, this is undoubtedly correct. For some of the male clients 'the Red Lamps faded away completely,'[100] for they belonged to the 'topsy-turvy world of the battle-fronts'.[101] Yet, I am advocating for a move away from historians' preoccupation with the war's effect on masculinity as one of change or continuity and instead encouraging historians to question their assumptions about peacetime masculine behaviour using the conditions of war. One enlightening example here relates to the prevalence of the uxorious ideal. We can start to question how much purchase this ideal actually had amongst married men who, when denied their regular physiological indulgence, found in the brothel an acceptable alternative. Indeed, the brothel was not just an opportunistic outlet for such men: these extramarital visits appear to have demanded a change in army codes so that they could accommodate the needs of these civilian, married men.

As well as questioning the components of masculinity through the conditions of war, this chapter has also demonstrated the value of applying two relatively unexplored approaches to masculinity. By focusing on masculinity as experience, the diversity of acceptable masculine behaviours has been demonstrated and, in doing so, a new code of conduct has been unveiled: hidden but accepted masculine behaviour. By applying the homosocial dynamic to these codes of sexual behaviour, and taking the focus away from the prostitute, we can see how conceptions of masculinity were informed by a man's marital status, rank, nationality and race, which, at times, superseded patriarchal forces.

Adopting these approaches may, for some, entail an unthinkable abandonment of the relational analysis of gender. For others, they may involve an unforgivable underestimation of the power of representation. Neither is my intention. It is simply to demonstrate the malleability of masculinity: how certain forms of masculine behaviour were at once both adhered to and abstained from, that sometimes their acceptability actually depended on their invisibility, and that we can only fully understand masculinity in the context of other self-identities. Only by adopting methodological approaches that are as fluid as masculinity itself, and by traversing the wartime and peacetime divide, will historians start to unravel the varieties, paradoxes and hierarchies that are all contingent to masculinity's content and construction.

## Notes

With thanks to the Trustees of the Imperial War Museum for allowing access to the collections and to each of the copyright holders. Whilst every effort has been made to trace all copyright holders, the author and the Imperial War Museum would be grateful for any information which might help to trace the families of Lieutenant R.G. Dixon, Lieutenant A.E. Macgregor, Lieutenant H.E.L. Mellersh and Private J.W. Roworth. The following abbreviations are used: IWM – Imperial War Museum, London; TNA FO – Foreign Office Papers, The National Archives, Kew, London; TNA HO – Home Office Papers, The National Archives, Kew, London; TNA WO – War Office Papers, The National Archives, Kew, London.

1. E.J. Leed, *No Man's Land: Combat and Identity in World War I* (Cambridge, 1978); G. Mosse, *The Image of Man* (Oxford, 1996).
2. J. Meyer, *Men of War: Masculinity and the First World War in Britain* (Basingstoke, 2009); J. Bourke, *Dismembering the Male: Men's Bodies, Britain and the Great War* (London, 1999); G. Dawson, *Soldier Heroes: British Adventure, Empire and the Imagining of Masculinities* (London, 1994).

3. Far more attention has been paid to homoeroticism on the Western Front: see P. Fussell, *The Great War and Modern Memory* (Oxford, 1975), p. 272; E. Showalter, *The Female Malady: Women, Madness and English Culture 1830–1980* (London, 1987), p. 171; M. Taylor, *Lads: Love Poetry of the Trenches* (London, 1989), pp. 27, 53. For historians who have looked at soldiers' heterosexual lives, see Bourke, *Dismembering the Male*, pp. 155–61; K. Craig Gibson, 'Sex and soldiering in France and Flanders: the British expeditionary force along the western front, 1914–1919', *International History Review* 23 (2001), 535–79.
4. IWM Sound Archive, 22739/2, interview with Leo McCormack, 1996; IWM Department of Documents, p. 271, The Papers of H.E.L. Mellersh, 'Schoolboy into War', pp. 100–01, 233–34.
5. It was reported that 171,000 men visited the brothels in one street in Le Havre over 57 weeks: L.W. Harrison (1923), 'Venereal diseases', in W.G. Macpherson (ed.), *History of the Great War Based on Official Documents, Medical Services Diseases of the War, Volume II* (London: HMSO), pp. 124–25.
6. Four hundred thousand cases of venereal disease resulted in men being out of action, compared with 80,000 cases of shell shock and 41,000 men who underwent amputations. Harrison, 'Venereal diseases', p. 118; Showalter, *The Female Malady*, p. 168; Bourke, *Dismembering the Male*, p. 33.
7. The handful of studies which have analysed prostitution and masculinity outside Britain have taken advantage of the regulation setting, such as T. Gilfoyle, *City of Eros: New York City, Prostitution and the Commercialisation of Sex 1790–1920* (New York, 1992).
8. L. Hall, 'Impotent ghosts from no-man's land, flappers' boyfriends, or crypto-patriarchs? Men, sex and social change in 1920s Britain', *Social History* 21 (1996), 57.
9. For example, Devonport-Hines, Bourke and Hall have all drawn upon the forthright Brigadier-General Frank Percy Crozier, a professional soldier whose lasciviousness is not necessarily representative of those who enlisted after 1914. R. Davenport-Hines, *Sex, Death and Punishment: Attitudes to Sex and Sexuality in Britain since the Renaissance* (London, 1990), pp. 180, 226; J. Bourke, *Working-Class Cultures in Britain 1860–1960: Gender, Class and Ethnicity* (London, 1994), p. 37; L.A. Hall, '"War always brings it on": war, STDs and the military and the civilian population in Britain 1850–1950', in R. Cooter, M. Harrison and S. Sturdy (eds), *Medicine and Modern Warfare* (Amsterdam, 1999), pp. 212–13. For Crozier's background, see P. Orr (1989), 'Introduction', in Frank Percy Crozier, *A Brass Hat in No Man's Land* (Norwich, c.1930), pp. 11–26.
10. See Roper for relevant discussion in M. Roper, 'Between manliness and masculinity: the "war generation" and the psychology of fear in Britain, 1914–1950', *Journal of British Studies* 44 (2005), 345.
11. See, for example, Fussell, *The Great War and Modern Memory*; S. Hynes, *A War Imagined* (London, 1990); S.M. Gilbert and S. Gubar, *No Man's Land, The Place of the Woman Writer in the Twentieth Century*, 2 (New Haven, 1989), pp. 258–323.
12. F. Mort, *Dangerous Sexualities: Medico-Moral Politics in England since 1830* (London, 1987), p. 4.
13. Roper makes this observation in Roper, 'Between Manliness and Masculinity', p. 345.
14. J. Tosh, 'What should historians do with masculinity?', *History Workshop Journal* 38 (1996), pp. 181–2.
15. See, for example, L. Hall, *Hidden Anxieties, Male Sexuality 1900–1950* (Cambridge, 1991), p. 38; Hall, '"War always brings it on"', p. 212.

16. F. Richards, *Old Soldiers Never Die* (London, 1933), p. 11.
17. J. Tosh, 'Hegemonic masculinity and the history of gender', in Stefan Dudink, Karen Hagemann and John Tosh (eds), *Masculinities in Politics and War: Gendering Modern History* (Manchester, 2004), p. 54.
18. See M. Flood, 'Men, sex and homosociality: how bonds between men shape their sexual relations with women', *Men and Masculinities*, 10 (2008), p. 342. My own doctoral research, which looks at the subjectivities of British prisoners of war in the Second World War, will address this omission.
19. M. Harrison, 'The British army and the problem of venereal disease in France and Egypt during the First World War', *Medical History* XXXIX (1995), 52.
20. TNA FO 141/466/2 – Part I, Report of the Cairo Purification Committee, Cairo, 1916, p. 14.
21. Tosh, 'What should historians do with masculinity?', p. 182. See also Hall, *Hidden Anxieties*, p. 47; E.M. Sigsworth and T.J. Wyke, 'A study of Victorian prostitution and venereal disease', in Martha Vicinus (ed.), *Suffer and Be Still: Women in the Victorian Age* (Bloomington, 1972), p. 87. Following the 1885 and 1912 Criminal Law Amendment Acts, men engaging in the services of prostitutes in Britain avoided legal liability; however, the owner or occupier of any premises used for prostitution could be prosecuted: TNA HO 45/10557/166505, Suppression of disorderly Houses: Special Purposes Committee Report, 17 January 1917; *Criminal Law Amendment Act 1885: Victoria. Chapter 69*, London; *Criminal Law Amendment Act 1912: George V. Chapter 20*, London: The Stationary Office.
22. Harrison, 'The British army and the problem of venereal disease', p. 142; E.H. Beardsley, 'Allied against sin: American and British responses to Venereal Disease in World War I', *Medical History* 20 (1976), 198.
23. IWM Department of Documents, 05/53/1, The Papers of R.H. Wilson, 'Liverpool Medical Institution: Some Dangers a Soldier May Avoid', by Captain R.W. McKenna, RAMC. See also S. Graham, *A Private in the Guards* (London, 1919), p. 256.
24. IWM Department of Documents, 80/40/1, The Papers of J.W. Roworth, 'The Misfit Soldier', p. 38.
25. Graham, *A Private in the Guards*, p. 256.
26. Wilfred Saint-Mandé, *War, Wine and Women*, 10th edn (London, 1936), p. 325.
27. IWM Department of Documents, 92/36/1, The Papers of R.G. Dixon, 'The Wheels of Darkness', p. 58.
28. F.P. Crozier, *A Brass Hat in No Man's Land* (London, 1930), p. 118.
29. The variety of these explanations has been documented by Bourke in *Dismembering the Male*, pp. 160–61.
30. IWM Department of Documents, Con Shelf, The Papers of Lieutenant A.E. Macgregor, MC, 27 April 1917, 2, 387; IWM Sound Archive, 22745/2, interview with Ted Rimmer, 1996.
31. For reference to brothel queues see IWM Sound Archive, 10604/13, interview with Edmund G. Williams, 1986; IWM Sound Archive, 9875/8, interview with George Ashurst, 1987; IWM Department of Documents, 02/40/1, Papers of Sapper A.R. Camidge, MM., 26 November 1917, Notes from first diary; Richards, *Old Soldiers Never Die*, p. 119; R. Aldington, *Death of a Hero* (London, 1929), p. 340; R. Graves, *Goodbye to all That* (London, 1920), p. 163; IWM Department of Documents, 78/27/1, Papers of Major B.A. Pond, 'Old Soldiers Never Die', p. 22; Saint-Mandé, *War, Wine and Women*, p. 533; W. Holt, *I Haven't Unpacked: an Autobiography* (London, 1939), p. 72; Graham, *A Private in the Guards*, p. 256.

32. Levine makes a similar point in relation to brothel scenes in nineteenth-century Calcutta and Cairo: P. Levine, *Prostitution, Race, and Politics: Policing Venereal Disease in the British Empire* (London, 2003), p. 265.
33. IWM 9875/8, Ashurst, 1987; IWM 10604/13, Williams, 1986; IWM Department of Documents, 04/19/1, The Papers of J.W. Wood (NCO), p. 22.
34. IWM Sound Archive, 22733/1, interview with Eddie Bigwood, 1996; IWM Sound Archive, 5868/7, interview with Hawtin Leonard Mundy, 1980; IWM 22739/2, McCormack, 1996.
35. G.D. Howe, 'Military-civilian intercourse, prostitution and venereal disease among black West Indian soldiers during World War I', *Journal of Caribbean History* 31 (1997), 95.
36. TNA WO 32/11404, Mr Macpherson MP (Deputy Chairman of the Army Council), Imperial War Conference, Temptations of Overseas troops, 19 July 1918, p. 7.
37. Crozier contradicts this conclusion, but he is alone in stating that men were not coy in seeking treatment. Crozier, *A Brass Hat in No Man's Land*, p. 144.
38. Harrison, 'Venereal diseases', p. 125.
39. TNA WO 32/5597, B.B. Cubitt (Army Council) to the General Officer Commanding-in-Chief, Commands at Home and the General Officer Commanding, Districts at Home, 18 March 1916.
40. TNA WO 32/11404, Mr Macpherson MP (Deputy Chairman of the Army Council), Imperial War Conference, Temptations of Overseas troops, 19 July 1918, p. 8.
41. A. Flexner, *Prostitution in Europe* (New York, 1914), p. 45.
42. M.K. Rhoades, 'Renegotiating French masculinity: medicine and venereal disease during the great war', *French Historical Studies* 29 (2006), 295; Beardsley, 'Allied against sin', p. 190; J. McMillan, 'The great war and gender relations, the case of French women and the First World War revisited', in Gail Braybon (ed.), *Evidence, History and the Great War: Historians and the Impact of 1914-18* (Oxford, 2003), pp. 142–3.
43. Rhoades, 'Renegotiating French masculinity', pp. 319, 324.
44. IWM Department of Documents, 99/54/1, Papers of Canon F.H. Drinkwater, 16 July 1918; The Women's Library, AMS/07/03 Box 059, Major-General G.T. Bartlett (American Expeditionary Force) to Alison Neilans (Secretary to the Association for Moral and Social Hygiene), 4 March 1918, p. 2.
45. TNA WO 32/11404, Colonel Ireland (American Army), Minutes of Proceedings at a Conference Regarding Venereal Disease and its treatment in the armed forces, 10 May 1918, pp. 23–4.
46. Beardsley, 'Allied against sin', p. 197.
47. Rhoades, 'Renegotiating French masculinity', pp. 313–17.
48. Tosh, 'What should historians do with masculinity?', p. 183.
49. The army discouraged marriage and considered casual sex an acceptable alternative. J. Baynes, *Morale: A Study of Men and Courage, the Second Scottish Rifles at the Battle of Neuve Chapelle, 1915* (London, 1967), p. 211; R. Hyam, 'Empire and sexual opportunity', *Journal of Imperial and Commonwealth History* xiv (1986), pp. 63–5.
50. Tosh, 'What should historians do with masculinity?', p. 184.
51. Harrison, 'The British army and the problem of venereal disease', p. 143.
52. IWM Department of Documents 06/48/1, Papers of Private Percy Clare, 'Reminiscences 1916–1918, volume III', unpaginated.
53. IWM 06/48/1, Clare, 'Reminiscences 1916–1918, volume III', unpaginated; Harrison, 'The British army and the problem of venereal disease', p. 143. Also see Graves, *Goodbye To All That*, p. 231.

428  Clare Makepeace

54. The Women's Library, AMS/07/03 Box 059, John Gower (Church Army and the Church of England Men's Society Recreation Hut), 'Report on Conditions in France', November 1916 to May 1917, p. 11.
55. TNA FO 141/466/2 – Part I, Report of the Cairo Purification Committee, Cairo, 1916, p. 15.
56. Cited in Gibson, 'Sex and soldiering in France and Flanders', pp. 562–63. Levine also notes the difficulty of uncovering officers' liaisons with prostitutes in British India: P. Levine, 'Venereal disease, prostitution and the politics of empire: the case of British India', *Journal of the History of Sexuality* 4 (1994), 594.
57. Levine, *Prostitution, Race, and Politics*, p. 166.
58. Dennis Wheatley, *The Time Has Come… The Memoirs of Dennis Wheatley: Officer and Temporary Gentleman, 1914–1919* (London, 1978), p. 152.
59. The Women's Library, AMS/07/03 Box 059, Rev. H. Basil Cole, Chaplain to the Forces (Army Post Office, BEF) to Alice Neilans (Secretary to the Association for Social and Moral Hygiene), 14 January 1918.
60. According to Tosh, before the war unmarried men made up the largest proportion of the prostitutes' clients. J. Tosh, *A Man's Place. Masculinity and Middle-Class Home in Victorian England* (New Haven, 1999), pp. 130–31.
61. Cited in Modris Eksteins, *The Rites of Spring: The Great War and the Birth of the Modern Age* (London, 1989), pp. 224–25.
62. IWM 06/48/1, Clare, commentary to letter to his mother dated 29 October 1916 in 'Letters written to my mother, 1916–1918.'
63. M. Hirschfeld, *The Sexual History of the Great War* (New York, 1934), p. 104.
64. TNA FO 141/466/2 – Part I, Colonel T.W. Gibbard (RAMC, ADMS, Camps and Effective Troops, Alexandria), 'Suggested methods for the reduction of venereal disease amongst troops in Egypt', 18 April 1916.
65. Harrison, 'The British army and the problem of venereal disease', pp. 139–40.
66. Married men were conscripted in May 1916 and this change took place between 18 April and 11 July 1916; see TNA FO 141/466/2 – Part I, Colonel T.W. Gibbard (RAMC, ADMS, Camps and Effective Troops, Alexandria), 'Suggested methods for the reduction of venereal disease amongst troops in Egypt', 18 April 1916; TNA FO 141/466/2 – Part I, Report of the Cairo Purification Committee, Cairo, 1916, p. 13.
67. TNA FO 141/466/2 – Part I, Report of the Cairo Purification Committee, Cairo, 1916, pp. 13, 18.
68. Harrison notes that the Cairo Purification Committee's report was not published because it revealed the high rates of VD amongst officers. Harrison, 'The British army and the problem of venereal disease', p. 155.
69. See, for example, Baynes, *Morale*, p. 212.
70. See, for example, Leed, *No Man's Land*.
71. A visit to amateur prostitutes may have involved a transaction of goods rather than money. Hall, *Hidden Anxieties*, p. 50.
72. Hall, *Hidden Anxieties*, pp. 50–2; Bourke, *Dismembering the Male*, p. 156.
73. Hall, *Hidden Anxieties*, pp. 49–50, 51, 53.
74. IWM 9875/8, Ashurst, 1987; H.G.R. Williams, cited in P.H. Liddle, *The Soldier's War 1914-18* (London: Blandford, 1988), p. 77; IWM P.271, Mellersh, 'Schoolboy into War', 184a.
75. Richards, *Old Soldiers Never Die*, pp. 118–19; IWM 06/48/1, Clare, 'Reminiscences 1916–1918, volume III', unpaginated.
76. IWM 22739/2, McCormack, 1996; IWM 9875/8, Ashurst, 1987; IWM Sound Archive, 11047/4, interview with James Dixon, 1989; IWM 80/40/1, Roworth, 'The Misfit

Soldier', p. 29; IWM 04/19/1, J.W. Wood, p. 23; Graves, *Goodbye to all That*, p. 163; The Women's Library, 3AMS/B/07/01 Box 059, Dr Helen Wilson (Hon. Sec., Association for Moral and Social Hygiene), Memorandum, On Some Aspects of the Problem of Prostitution in Relation to the Army, August 1916, p. 2.

77. IWM Sound Archive, 10168/4, interview with Donald Price, 1988.
78. Saint-Mandé, *War, Wine and Women*, p. 278; New Zealand troops received six shillings a day whilst the British received just sixpence: see J. Costello, *Love, Sex and War: Changing Values 1939–1945* (London, 1985), p. 288.
79. IWM Sound Archive, 9168/28/5, interview with Sidney Albert Amatt, 1985.
80. Peter Barton (the interviewer) refers to this reminiscence of Bert Fearns during his interview with Leo McCormack: see IWM 22739/2, McCormack, 1996; original material held in the private collection of Peter Barton, First World War historian.
81. TNA FO 141/466/2 – Part I, Report of the Cairo Purification Committee, Cairo, 1916, p. 5; TNA WO 32/11401, Letter from Walter H. Long (Colonial Office) to the Officer Administering the Government of Canada, Commonwealth of Australia, New Zealand, Union of South Africa, Newfoundland, 19 October 1917. Also see Harrison, 'Venereal Diseases', p. 121.
82. Beardsley, 'Allied against sin', p. 192.
83. R.W. Connell, *The Men and the Boys* (Cambridge, 2000) p. 48. See, for example, M. Sinha, *Colonial Masculinity: The Manly Englishman and the Effeminate Bengali in the Late Nineteenth Century* (Manchester, 1995).
84. J. Tosh, 'Masculinities in an industrialising society: Britain, 1800–1914', *Journal of British Studies* 44 (2004), 339–42; Tosh, 'What should historians do with masculinity?', pp. 196–98.
85. Levine, *Prostitution, Race, and Politics*, pp. 146–47.
86. A. Grundlingh, 'The impact of the First World War on South African blacks', in M. E. Page (ed.), *Africa and the First World War* (Basingstoke, 1987), p. 55.
87. Recruited through the British settlement of Weiheiwei. P.J. Marshall, '1870–1918: the empire under threat', in P.J. Marshall (ed.), *The Cambridge Illustrated History of the British Empire* (Cambridge, 1996), p. 78.
88. P. Levine, 'Battle colours: race, sex and colonial soldiery in World War I', *Journal of Women's History* 9 (1998), p. 114; Howe, 'Military-civilian intercourse', p. 90.
89. Levine, 'Venereal disease, prostitution and the politics of empire', pp. 592–93.
90. J. Greenhut, 'Race, sex and war: the impact of race and sex on morale and health services for the Indian corps on the Western front, 1914', *Military Affairs* 45 (1981), 72. However, Levine notes that the Arab Quarter in Port Said was placed out of bounds to Indian troops to limit their access to prostitutes. Levine, *Prostitution, Race, and Politics*, p. 155.
91. Greenhut, 'Race, sex and war', pp. 72, 74.
92. Levine, *Prostitution, Race and Politics*, p. 154; Levine, 'Battle colours', p. 118.
93. TNA WO 32/5597, Letter from G.H. Fowkes (Adjutant General to Field-Marshal Haig), 20 January 1918.
94. The Women's Library, 3AMS/B/07/04 Box 059, Alice Neilans to Madame Avril (Conseil National des Femmes Francaises), 23 July 1918; Avril to Neilans, 12 August 1918; Neilans to Avril, 15 August 1918.
95. K. Mercer and I. Julien, 'Race, sexual politics and black masculinity: a dossier', in R. Chapman and J. Rutherford (eds), *Male Order: Unwrapping Masculinity* (London, 1988), pp. 107–08, also cited in Howe, 'Military-civilian intercourse', p. 90.
96. Levine, 'Venereal disease, prostitution, and the politics of the empire', p. 593; Greenhut, 'Race, sex and war', p. 72.

97. F. Richards, *Old Soldier Sahib* (London, 1936), p. 197.
98. See S. Brady, *Masculinity and Male Homosexuality* (Basingstoke, 2005); H. Ellis and J. Meyer (eds), *Masculinity and the Other: Historical Perspectives* (Newcastle, 2009).
99. Fogarty suggests there were relations between French prostitutes and non-white French colonial soldiers: R. Fogarty, 'Race and sex, fear and loathing in France during the Great War', in D. Herzog (ed.), *Brutality and Desire: War and Sexuality in Europe's Twentieth Century* (Basingstoke, 2009), pp. 59–90.
100. Holt, *I Haven't Unpacked*, p. 73.
101. IWM 92/36/1, R.G. Dixon, 'The wheels of darkness', p. 58.

# Conclusion

# 21
# Masculinities, Histories and Memories
*Victor Jeleniewski Seidler*

A number of people who had gathered for the conference entitled 'What is Masculinity?', with the subtitle 'How useful it is as a Historical Category?', remarked that it had been 20 years since the conference at the University of Bradford organised by Jeff Hearn and David Morgan and the British Sociological Association. In disciplinary terms this had been a public event that sought to place issues around men and masculinities as a central concern within social theory and practice. Issues around men and masculinities had largely been framed within the counterculture as a response to the challenges of feminism. That conference was an attempt to bring questions around the critical study of men and masculinities into relationship with traditions of social theory and research to reveal some of their tacit masculinist assumptions and so set the terms for a renewal of disciplinary theory and practice.[1]

In the early 1970s men began to gather together in men's consciousness-raising groups in order to reconsider ways in which their everyday lives, feelings, bodies and experiences were shaped by their cultural experiences as men. It was in Boston in 1970 that I first joined a group, during a year's visit with Joseph Pleck and Jack Sawyer, who were later to edit one of the first collections on Men and Masculinities.[2] We met in the Psychology department in the William James building in Harvard where Jack Sawyer was visiting. We met weekly to explore diverse aspects of our inherited masculinities and to respond to the challenges of feminism about the ways we had been brought up to be as men. We shared our personal experiences and histories and began to appreciate what it meant for men to recognise that 'the personal is political.' We also began to question the terms of 'role theory' and the ways in which it framed gender relations. Remembering back over 40 years, it is striking to realise how 'consciousness raising' worked in one of the initial men's groups and so marked a beginning of a men's movement in the United States that was to frame itself academically as 'Men's Studies'. This has become part of the history of the present, as men learnt how significant it could be for us to engage in practices of consciousness raising and so question the privatisation of individual experience that had been so integral to our growing up as men within liberal moral cultures. The practice of consciousness raising for men was an *invention* within a larger social experiment in which we were exploring possibilities of more equal relationships between men and women through engaging with our inherited masculinities and the ways we had learnt to think, feel and behave.

As we experimented in these early groups, we explored ways in which we could be together as men and voiced some of the fears and anxieties that emerged in just being a group of men who did not have a specific goal to achieve but were somehow creating a space of reflection in which we could begin to share our histories and experiences as men. An awareness of the significance of history was there from the beginning, though it did not shape the movement in the ways Sheila Rowbotham's pioneering work in women's history, *Hidden from History* (1975) and *Women's Consciousness, Man's World* (1973), helped shape the early women's movement in Britain.[3] Rather, we tended to be aware of a historical void that needed to be filled. There was an awareness of the importance of Edward Carpenter and other men who had supported women's movements, and there was an awareness of the significance of historical exploration into the complex silences around men's relationships to dominant masculinities.[4] This was something that we had learnt from an exploration of our own experiences as men as we traced the connections between the ways we might have felt, say at school, and the structures of institutional power that were organised around individual competition and success.

As a men's consciousness-raising group we had to find our own ways, because we recognised in ourselves a tendency to rationalise and intellectualise our own experience. It was easier for us to perform our identities as men and theoretically explore connections between the 'personal' and the 'political' than it was *to share* our experience with others. This could feel too threatening, because we were so used to a culture in which men would put each other down and in which a showing of vulnerability would be interpreted as a sign of weakness and so as a threat to our male identities. Often we found ourselves on guard with each other, even when we did not want to be. We might have wanted to will ourselves to be different, but we discovered that we could not simply change through an act of will and determination. This was already to implicitly question a rationalist masculinity that had shaped contemporary modernities.[5] Sometimes it could feel as if we were trapped in our own language, which seemed to work as a form of defensiveness that kept us isolated and lonely in ways we often resisted feeling.

As we were later, in the early 1980s, after five years of meeting as a consciousness-raising group, to gather around the setting up of *Achilles Heel* as a journal of men's sexual politics, we encouraged historical writing and investigation. This has been a particular interest of Paul Atkinson, and it was reflected in some of the writing he did for *Achilles Heel*.[6] Also, through the influence of Marx, we were aware of the historical shaping of consciousness and the necessity to engage with histories of the present, but in ways that went beyond the discursive framing that Foucault was to give to this task. We sought a different history of the present that recognised a tension between language and experience and the particular ways in which dominant masculinities did not have to give an account of themselves, for they inherited a power to silence the questionings of others. But often men found it in a way still difficult to articulate that they were somehow 'locked out' of their own experience, unable or fearful to share what was 'going on for them'. At some level we knew that we had to explore our own histories and the institutions that had helped shape the ways we were feeling.

## Men and masculinities

There was an awareness of the dialectical tension between men and masculinities and the complex ways in which masculinities were framed through relationships of power and subordination. There was an awareness that men had inherited a right to legislate for others before we had really learnt how to speak for ourselves. There was an impersonalisation and abstractness that too often marked a dominant heterosexual male voice that marked a kind of disconnection from experience. It was as if masculinities were somehow working to position men as observers of their own experience, removed and displaced within a language of 'impartiality' and 'objectivity' that were themselves the markers of middle-class heterosexual superiority.[7] There were relationships of superiority, particularly in regard to women but also in relation to gay men, that needed to be explored if these patterns of superiority and inferiority were not to be reproduced. Movements around gay liberation were emerging at the same time in different countries, and in Britain there was some dialogue between these different men's movements. In *Achilles Heel* there was ongoing discussion in a collective that moved across straight and gay masculinities.

On reflection, there was an acknowledgement that masculinity was an issue for both straight and gay men but in radically different ways. We appreciated that we needed a sense of the histories of masculinities and the complex interrelations between 'gay' and 'straight' as marking fluid boundaries rather than fixed or given identities. There was an awareness of the importance of experimentation and the need to transgress boundaries so that we could learn from our own experience.[8] There was a language of 'liberation' that was framed through a sense of the repressions and silences of the bourgeois family lives that many people on the left had known when growing up in the 1950s. There was an awareness that appearances had mattered, and an idea of 'keeping up with the Joneses' that had shaped its own hypocrisies. This was part of the widespread critiques of the family that had been shaped by Laing and Cooper and the anti-psychiatry movements whose ideas circulated widely within the countercultures of the times.[9] Questions around gender were being partly framed against wider critiques of the family as an institution that could work to undermine children and destroy their sense of self-worth. Feminism framed these questions around the family in radically new ways, though it tended to share the critiques of marriage.

There was an ongoing relationship between the psyche and the structural, between the personal and the political, that was somehow already in place and helping to shape the explorations within sexual politics. There was also a widespread sense that we had to understand histories of the present, if we really wanted to break with some of these inheritances. But at the same time there were other tendencies suggesting that we could make a radical break with the past and resonating with liberal modernities, a sense that people could put the past behind them as they shaped their identities in the present. There was a concern with inventing and creating new identities in the present that were somehow more 'authentic' and 'honest' than the relationships that people had experienced while growing up in families in the 1950s. There was a recognition of the importance of talking truth to power and an awareness that this would only be possible if people learnt *how* to be more honest with themselves. There was a dialectic between the personal and the political that also offered theoretical insights to men.

Within a history of the present it can be helpful to recognise that 'masculinity' was not a term that was widely used other than as a relational contrast with 'femininity', and it was unusual for heterosexual men to explore how their experience had been shaped through the expectations and disciplines of contemporary masculinities. This can be important for historians to recall when they consider that in the periods they are working in there is more talk about 'manliness' or 'manhood' than there is any reference to masculinity. This explains a reluctance to introduce a term 'externally' that does not seem to have any currency at the time and that might distract from the complex narratives and experiences that you are seeking to illuminate. Tracing these movements within sexual politics of the 1970s, and the ways in which the relationships between men and masculinities were gradually being framed both theoretically and politically, leaves you with a sense of the complexities involved in invoking 'masculinities' as a theoretical category that can be applied to different historical periods.

This wariness is understandable, especially if it is a matter of importing masculinity as if it were a 'universal' that could somehow be brought into any historical moment. But it is also important to recognise not only that the narratives and discourses that are made available through historical archives are limited in relation to class, 'race' and gender, and so who has the means to write and the authority to document, but also that there are other kinds of tensions between discourse and experience that tend to be foreclosed within cultural theories that assume the discursive character of experience and insist that there is nothing beyond it. An awareness of the tensions between language and experience was something that resonated for me through Wittgenstein's later philosophy and the insights made available through feminism and sexual politics. Though considerable theoretical advances were made through post-structuralism, there were also losses, as tensions between language and experience came to be foreclosed.[10]

## Histories/masculinities

If there are issues of importing concerns from the present into our historical reflections on the past, there is also an awareness that complexities we might experience in the present can echo different complexities in the past. As there are competing narratives around masculinities in the present, so there are tensions within the past. It was noteworthy in the framing of the Birkbeck conference that historians were reluctant to pluralise masculinity into masculinities, which has become a familiar move within social and cultural fields. This was not, as Harry Brod noted in his comments to the conference, because people were unaware of the complexity of masculinities in different historical periods. The reluctance seems to be coming from somewhere else, and it is possibly revealing about how issues around masculinity have emerged so strongly within history across different periods in the last decade. It was almost taken for granted that masculinity would be constituted quite differently in different cultures, times and spaces.

There are issues around whether and how masculinity became an 'object' of historical concern and whether it was a 'topic' or 'area' that could be studied within traditional historical methodologies or whether it somehow helped to identify certain masculinist assumptions within these historical methodologies: for example, notions of 'objectivity' that might favour certain written accounts over others and which treat certain narratives as 'subjective' because they refer to a person's feelings or emotions. But it also raises issues about the relative value of written or verbal sources and the ways in which historians are often dependent upon whatever archives and written sources have survived. But this can make it difficult to explore what becomes *silenced* or *unspoken* and the ways in which, for instance, a father's power can show itself in refusal to respond to his son because to question a father's authority is already a sign of disobedience that is deserving of punishment.

Now, feminist historians might insist that it is women who have been silenced through the workings of patriarchal relationships of power. Their imposed silences have often been wrongly interpreted as signs of approval and agreement, and, at different times, it is the wife who has been expected to defer to their husband, who as 'head of the household' was given authority to speak and so to legislate what was good for others in *his* family. It was the possessive nature of relationships that was a focus of concern, and it was the women's movement that illuminated how women were being *undermined* in their sense of self-worth and esteem within liberal marriage relationships that might regard themselves as 'equal', with men and women traditionally having different 'roles' or responsibilities within the family: men traditionally defined as breadwinners and women having responsibility for the household and for the upbringing of children. So it could be said that men have always assumed the right to speak and have themselves heard. They could write their own narratives and expect them to be taken seriously by historians.

## Language/ethics

Some men are more entitled to speak than others, and relations of class, power and authority make a difference to who is entitled to speak and who is expected to listen and show deference. The social movements of the 1970s questioned traditional relationships of authority and deference and helped to frame new visions of democracy that were shaped around implicit challenges to Kantian notions of the rational self, freedom and autonomy that had been largely framed within masculinist terms within a liberal moral culture. In *Kant, Respect and Injustice: The Limits of Liberal Moral Theory* (1986) I was attempting to explore different notions of respect, equality and justice which had been framed through traditions of sexual politics that had questioned disembodied conceptions of the rational self framed within liberal moral and political theory. I showed connections with liberal masculinities and ways in which they had often been shaped through traditions of Kantian rationalism. I also suggested, though this was harder to sustain, how Kantian ethics had been framed through secularised Christian traditions and their particular visions of 'the human' as a rational self.[11]

The categorical distinction that Kant had made between 'reason' and 'nature' was made clear through his dualistic vision of 'human nature', which was ready to identify the 'human' with a reason and rationality that was radically split from a 'nature' that was identified as 'animal' and so as a threat to the very status of 'the human'. This duality also helped to frame Kant's vision of autonomy and freedom that was part of a paradoxical inheritance in the women's movement. At one level there was a reclaiming of bodies, and so a challenge to disembodied conceptions of self that had framed a Kantian modernity, in the women's health movement's insistence on our bodies, our selves. This frames feminism as a challenge to modernity, and so disturbs a postmodernism that would suggest that feminism exists as yet another grand narrative of modernity organised around the emancipation of the category 'woman'.[12] This has often featured as an attempt to displace feminism as a discourse of modernity, rather than as a fundamental philosophical challenge to the terms of a rationalist modernity. But, at another level, freedom and autonomy were framed within liberal feminism around rationalist traditions that were often tacitly fearful of bodies and their diverse pleasures. Freedom within traditions of liberal feminism often became a matter of rational choice.

In *Kant, Respect and Injustice* I also tried to frame issues around visibility and silence. I had been moved by feminist concerns with visibility and, though I probably could not have articulated it at the time, this was connected to a sense of Jewish invisibility – a sense that 'safety' somehow lies in maintaining a sense of invisibility. As a child who wanted to join CND and the Aldermaston marches in the late 1950s, I was made to feel that visibility as Jews was dangerous. This was communicated by my refugee family, who had themselves been forced to flee continental Europe as Hitler took power. They did not really want to talk about themselves as refugees because they did not want to threaten the possibilities of their children gaining a sense of belonging they knew, because of their accents, they could not achieve themselves.[13]

Of course, people are marked in different ways, and somehow it seemed easier to relate to issues around masculinity, which, after all, reflected a more general concern, than talk openly about Jewish identities that were still shamed. At some level there might also have been an unspoken recognition of ways in which Jewish masculinities had been feminised. At least, this might explain the larger number of men with Jewish backgrounds who took significant positions within different countries in these early men's movements. A sense of marginality possibly allows a sense of how masculinities are not somehow given by nature, but rather are socially and historically constructed, because you sense a tension between the masculinities you might experience in families and the masculinities you aspire to identify with in school. As boys from refugee backgrounds, we learnt to watch other boys to identify what was expected of us and so to make it easier for us to become 'like everyone else'.

But there was also the relief that came for many men with feminism, which allowed men to share more emotionally within relationships. It helped to question a fear of intimacy that often characterised diverse masculinities and which became a central theme in my writing at the time. There was a sense that you did not have to perform a traditional masculine identity and that women expected more contact, intimacy and sharing in heterosexual relationships. As women voiced what they needed to, men often felt challenged in their traditional expectations of relationships. But this opened up a reflective space in which to explore and experiment tensions between how we felt as men and the masculinities through which we felt obliged to judge ourselves. There was a questioning of traditional terms of judgement, and a recognition that men could not change through will alone, but that there were complex processes of change that would inevitably take time to be explored. There was an awareness that masculinities did not simply need to be deconstructed as relationships of patriarchal culture, but also needed to be re-visioned and transformed. But there is also a sense that the more awareness we develop in this way the more attuned our senses might be to the historical tensions in men's lives that we are researching. We might be more sceptical of the language in which men present themselves in the historical record and more able to discern tensions between different levels or layers of experience.[14]

For a while there were few spaces in which this critical work in relation to men and masculinities could be explored. There were new feminist publishers, but they had their own priorities for publishing women's writing. Somehow these concerns were not recognised within traditional academic disciplines until the mid-1980s, and for many people gender continued to mean women and feminist writings. There were some early writings about men's relationships with feminism, but it was not till the mid-1980s that Routledge published *Rediscovering Masculinity: Reason, Language and Sexuality* (Seidler, 1989). This recognised that men often assumed the authority to speak about themselves and also, too often, felt entitled to speak for others. Often men found it harder to listen, and it took time for them to realise the importance of learning *how* to listen to themselves as well as to others. But there was also a recognition of the way men learn to rationalise and intellectualise their experience so that they are constantly presenting a certain image of themselves and concealing or hiding aspects of their emotional lives which they might judge harshly. Often men carry a harsh critical voice that they turn upon themselves as much as they turn it on others.

If a man felt sad, he would often not recognise this feeling himself, or would seek to dismiss it before it emerged into consciousness. Since many emotions are regarded as signs of weakness, they are disciplined and regulated before they can be allowed to threaten male identities. Often men can find it hard to acknowledge illness, particularly chronic conditions that can be experienced as signs of weakness. Men often feel that, with time, they will make a recovery and so become 'normal' again, and so can find it difficult to pace themselves or make the necessary changes in their lives. Sometimes men will conceal what they are feeling from others, even from those closest to them, because they want to be strong and supportive to their partners. They can feel locked into their role as fathers or as providers, and, even if they have questioned these roles intellectually, they can find themselves unable to really share themselves emotionally. At some level, having grown up to be independent and self-sufficient, they can find it hard to really feel that others can be there for them. Unconsciously they might feel that if they show themselves to be 'weak' they will be rejected because they will have shown themselves to be 'useless'.

Of course, these feelings might be inflected quite differently in different cultural settings, and historically men will be confronting diverse masculinities and ways of affirming their male identities. But what was striking in the early men's movements was a break with the privatisation of male experience and the sense that men could *support* each other as they explored their inherited masculinities. The tension between men and masculinities was vital for giving permission to transcend traditional boundaries and so to validate experience even when it meant challenging a moralism that often legislated how men should feel. Within a rationalist culture men learn to frame their experience, at least in public, so that it accords with the ideals they have set themselves. What goes on privately is quite another matter. In the 1990s we saw a redrawing of lines between public and private spheres which meant that the notion 'the personal is political' became a rhetoric with limited substance.

As R.W. Connell's work became significant, particularly in the later text *Masculinities* (1995), there was a shift in theoretical framework that threatened to lose the tension between men and masculinities.[15] This might also relate to reasons why historians have refused, at least for a while, an easy pluralisation of masculinities because they maintain in their work a tension between 'men' and diverse historically framed 'masculinities'. But it is also through drawing a sharp distinction between the 'therapeutic' and the 'political' that Connell re-inscribes a break between 'the personal' and the 'political' that comes to be displaced and somehow devalued and identified with an earlier sexual politics that was associated in Britain with *Achilles Heel*.

There is also an assumption that men cannot really change and that men gain privileges through their masculinities. But there is also a tension in the ways Connell frames relationships of power that suggests an implicit rationalist universalism. Sometimes this is marked in a tension within his own work between the theoretical frameworks and the empirical chapters that draw directly upon ethnographic work. Often there is a difficulty in relating them, and a tendency to miss the tensions and contradictions in men's experience in relation to dominant masculinities and to frame them as almost illustrative of particular masculinities.[16]

Though Connell is critical of post-structuralist traditions and the ways in which they tacitly rely upon distinctions between nature and culture, so shaping identities within the discursive spheres of culture alone, there is a tendency in his work to draw upon a hierarchy of power that makes it difficult to appreciate the significance of cultural and historical traditions. At some level masculinities remain part of the problem and find no space to be part of the solution, for masculinities themselves are framed as relationships of power. There is a tacit echoing of radical feminist theories and how they have conceptualised male experience. There is also a danger that a theory of hegemonic masculinities is allowed to provide a 'theoretical framework' coming from the anglophone world that can then be applied, if slightly amended, to different cultural contexts.

## Difference/s

In the closing discussion for the conference 'What is Masculinity?' there was some concern about the theoretical validity of notions of 'hegemonic masculinity' and the kind of grand narratives it can sustain. John Tosh, who in the opening plenary shared his suspicions of a 'cultural turn' in historical studies that may mean displacing concerns with structural violence and relationships of power, would seek to defend Connell's work as a way of maintaining a focus upon relationships of power.

Other people seemed more wary, and sought to think more in terms of dominant masculinities and how issues cluster differently within different historical settings. In fact, John Tosh himself talked well about how patriarchal analysis seems to be significant in studies of early modern Europe, where the household remains a critical centre for production and where the household provides crucial metaphors for the body politic. He notes that a patriarchal analysis seems to have been abandoned, or is seen to be less significant, in studies of the nineteenth and twentieth centuries, when production comes to be removed from households and there is a more abstract role for the family.

Alexandra Shepard, who had given a plenary address on 'The Uses and Abuses of Masculinity as a Category in Early Modern Europe', raised some different concerns in the closing discussion about the place of masculinities and gender in historical research. She asked whether 'it was always present; and if so, how did it make itself felt', and were there not generic concerns to do with 'the human' that were somehow in danger of being lost? She was concerned with questioning the generic character of masculinity, so that to 'be human' was to be 'masculine', for women have in different ways been regarded as 'closer to nature' and therefore 'less than human' within a dominant Christian culture that has defined 'the human' in radical contrast to 'the animal'.

It was through an exclusion of bodies that are so often identified with sexualities and the 'sins of the flesh' that 'the human' was to be affirmed through its identification with 'the spiritual self'. The body was to be disavowed, and a dominant Christian anti-Semitism was framed through the rejection of 'Carnal Israel', as Daniel Boyarin has explored.[17] There is a fear of the body and its desires, which can so easily seem out of control, and the identification of male identities with notions of self-mastery that have been given secularised forms within an Enlightenment modernity. There is a fear of what nature might reveal and a need to control.

What was striking in the Birkbeck conference was the attempt to bring different historical periods into dialogue with each other around particular themes.

This could be disturbing, because it took historians out of their comfort zones, which are usually framed through conversations with people working within a similar time period. Though historians will insist that their understandings always depend upon context and that you have to be wary of introducing terms and language that are not referred to by people themselves, it was the resonances across these differences that were telling. This seemed to say something about the significance of masculinity as a historical theme, especially when there was an awareness of the tensions between men and the masculinity they were often struggling with and so a resistance to reading these men through established masculinities.

It was the care historians showed in their use of sources, as well as the variety of sources they would draw upon, that was impressive. But it also left me thinking about whether there were also certain 'resonances' that might echo across time because these papers were framed within the cultural assumptions of a dominant Christian tradition. As emerged in my conversation with John Tosh, religion is often regarded as the 'context' – a kind of background – against which these historical narratives take place. But often the theologies are left implicit and their significance, as Walter Benjamin recognised, is often not appreciated.[18]

In a Western world post-9/11, where we are obliged to rethink relationships with Islam and the Islamic world, we need to explore new historical ways of thinking across differences. This means a different kind of self-awareness of the ways in which religious traditions and beliefs make themselves felt in these diverse historical narratives. In a session chaired by Ruth Mazo Karras entitled 'Paradigms and Nomenclature ll', the opening paper, by Katherine Lewis, entitled '"A girl came in here, but I see a man!" Sanctity and masculinity in lives and cults of medieval saints', drew attention to the heroic struggle to preserve virginity that defined a Christian sexual ethic and set it apart from paganism. The ideal of virginity was something that men could be expected to defend, and Lewis shares the tale of a knight who changes clothes with a woman who had been forced into prostitution as a way of rescuing her from this terrible fate. She also draws attention to the gendering of miracles and the superiority of male bodies that can withstand pain, particularly high-class men such as knights. It is through self-mastery that they affirm their male identities. But this makes it difficult to acknowledge impotence, which is so often blamed on the female bodies that are more usually the objects of medical discourses of the time.

The idea that male bodies can prove their manliness through showing that they can endure pain, and the implicit contrast between 'hard' male bodies over which men have 'mastery' and the 'soft' bodies of women, is an idea that seems to be reconfigured in different historical periods. This is linked with the threat from a femininity that is identified with softness to the virile bodies of 'real' men. Potency becomes a sign of virility, so that childlessness renders men incomplete if they have not been able to father children. They might feel obliged to see other ways of affirming their masculinities and so prove themselves to be 'manly' and properly 'virile'. But, as Lewis points out, men are less likely to visit shrines to seek help, or, if they do, they will be more likely to go to local shrines that they can visit more privately. Given that there are quite different expectations associated with different social orders in the Middle Ages, there are different ways in which masculinities are affirmed and rank established. But there is an ideal of balance or moderation, a middling path between extremes of behaviour that men are supposed to aspire to and affirm in their relationships with others. In this way manliness comes to be identified with a historically framed vision of maturity in contrast to boyhood or ideas of effeminacy.

Though there were marked differences, there were also resonances with Jennifer Jordan's paper ' "To make a man without reason": examining manhood in early modern England', focusing upon a transition across social order between boyhood and manhood that was marked by a ceremony around the wearing of breeches. This was a moment when childish behaviours could be left behind and different expectations around manhood and manly behaviours framed. Though there was no explicit language relating to masculinity, there were assumptions about the naturalness of gender categories, even if not everyone could conform to them.

Even if religion often played a different part in people's lives, there was still a sense that people were living in Christian societies that were shaped through an identification between 'the human' and 'the spiritual' that involved a denigration of bodies assumed to be 'animal' and so disturbed by the 'sins of the flesh'. It was a *shared grammar* in relation to bodies, sexualities and emotional life that accounted for the resonances across historical periods. But gender remains a relational term; it is framed not only in relation to women, but also for men in relation to themselves and the need to deal with the anxieties of masculinities that can never be taken for granted. Notions of 'self-mastery' are often framed in heterosexual terms to involve a denial of emotions that might be too easily identified as 'queer' and so experienced as a threat to heterosexual masculinities.

Often the records that remain from the early modern period concern advice books that often survived across generations and seem to have been used over long periods of time. These conduct books not only instruct boys in relation to the importance of piety and devotion but also help to structure the advice that fathers have the authority to pass on to their sons. They seek advice about how to achieve a balanced life that allows young men to have self-mastery, to select an appropriate wife to their station and to set up an independent household. Most of this advice follows from a literary culture of the ruling classes, so it is difficult to know how widespread their influence might have been within cultures that were framed around relationships of authority and deference. Young men from different backgrounds could be expected to emulate the behaviours of older men and so make a transition from dependent boyhood to independent and self-sufficient manhood. But at some level this produced its own silences, as diverse desires emerged and young people often learnt to keep their fears to themselves and behave appropriately in the company of adults. It was difficult to know whom they could confide in, because there was a fear of 'losing face' in front of others. Boys are used to different cultures of banter, but these are often invoked as ways of controlling emotions and fears that might otherwise leak out and *threaten* an identity they feel they need to sustain in front of others.

Though framed in different terms and through different symbols, rituals and practices, the final paper in the session, by Heather Ellis, entitled ' "Boys, semi-men and bearded scholars": The importance of maturity in the construction of Oxford "men" in the early Victorian period', shared a struggle about competing masculinities, even if the narratives of the time talked in Mathew Arnold's terms about achieving 'manliness' and 'moral and intellectual maturity'. There was a sense that a different curriculum was needed in Oxford, since boys were coming to the university older and so might be more susceptible to 'moral vice' and 'moral weakness'. These young men needed to be challenged through the introduction of competitive examinations that would sharpen their fear of failure and so motivate them to hard work and manly emulation. They would learn self-discipline and self-mastery that would help them prepare for leadership positions in society. They would inherit a sense of social responsibility, and, if they felt compassion for others, it would not be 'merely subjective' and 'emotional' but intellectually grounded within reason. Learning from the experience of Rugby, Arnold was to become a critical figure in the reform of Oxford education and the introduction of logic as a means to train 'sharp' minds.

As I listened with interest to the details of the discussion, I was interested in the framework that was being accepted and the terms within which historical narratives seem to be produced. There is an admirable respect for sources and for context, but also a narrowing of concerns that can be made visible. I realised that the introduction of logic and competitive examinations had shaped my own experience at Oxford in the mid-1960s and so was very much part of my own history of the present. There was a clarity of thought that was supposedly achieved through giving centrality to philosophical logic, in which I took a special paper, and a notion of 'intellectual rigour' that was thankfully being questioned in the 1960s through the writings of the later Wittgenstein that was being taught by Elizabeth Anscombe at Oxford at the time. This was an influence that challenged the narrowness of the terms of the 'examples' that we would draw upon to clarify the logic of a particular concept. The terms of 'analytic philosophy' or 'conceptual analysis' as Oxford Philosophy had been partly prepared by the rationalism of Arnold and Mill in the early nineteenth century.

But, if this was a tradition that was being challenged by Wittgenstein's influence, it had been challenged in a different way by John Stuart Mill's *Autobiography* (1873), in which he questioned the terms of the education that had been provided for him by his father. This was a text that I learnt about later, but it questioned the dryness of a particular form of intellectual education and the vision of sharpness of mind. If there is value in the ability to discern fine distinctions, which is true, there is also a limit to the philosophy of mind and the kind of self-mastery it frames. Wittgenstein challenged these modes of thinking, and so, implicitly, the visions of male superiority that they also embodied. Too often self-mastery is framed as an issue of 'mind' over 'matter', as if emotions were a sign of weakness, so that 'giving in' to emotions is deemed a threat to self-mastery.[19]

Though there were competing Tractarian traditions in Oxford in the early nineteenth century, represented by John Henry Newman and others who sought to defend the place of Christian theologies in the curriculum, there were also certain shared class assumptions about masculinities that were framed through the discussions around 'muscular Christianity' and the dangers of a certain kind of aesthetic education. This is not a field I know well, though I recall discussions I had with Irving Spitzberg, a postgraduate student in the 1960s, supervised by Isaiah Berlin, who was working on a thesis contrasting the theories of education in Mill and Newman. What is at issue is not a particular curriculum, but the different visions of moral education and how they sustain a particular philosophical culture in the West that too often assumes the superiority of a white European masculinity.

## Experience/s

Walter Benjamin aimed to make philosophy embrace the totality of experience. As Andrew Benjamin and Peter Osborne write in their introduction to *Walter Benjamin's Philosophy: Destruction and Experience* (1993), 'he sought, thereby, to render experience philosophical: the experience of truth. It was in the breadth of this ambition that he parted company with the predominantly neo-Kantian philosophy of his day and came to ally his work to literature. In a context in which institutionalised philosophy had given up the claim to totality of its tradition, Benjamin remained true to that tradition by rejecting its institutional form and philosophising 'directly' out of the objects of cultural experience. 'The object of philosophical criticism', he wrote in 1925, 'is to show that the function of artistic forms is...to make historical content...into a philosophical truth'.[20]

As Benjamin and Osborne go on to emphasise, 'For Benjamin, "destruction" always meant the destruction of some false or deceptive form of experience as the productive condition of the construction of a new relation to the object' (p. xi). So it is that, in *The Origins of German Drama*, allegory is seen to destroy the deceptive totality of the symbol, wrenching it out of context and placing it in a new, transparently constructed, configuration of meaning. So it can be helpful to recognise that there are different configurations relating to masculinities which are more or less significant in different historical periods but might well be shaped through a dominant Christian tradition that only becomes visible as we learn to think both inside and outside historical context. There are meanings at play, legitimating particular forms of male superiority in relationships, which sometimes are rendered more visible through being taken out of context or else put alongside other historical periods, allowing a dialogue of resonances to take place.

As Benjamin and Osborne point out, 'In Benjamin's own work, montage destroys the continuity of narratives as the conditions for a new construction of history; while now-time destroys the experience of history as progress, replacing it with the apocalyptic doublet of catastrophe and redemption. It is the destructive element that "guarantees the authenticity of dialectical thought". The destructive character is "the consciousness of historical man"' (p. xi). They go on to recognise that crucial to instances of destruction is 'Benjamin's understanding of the temporality of the present as the moment of destruction. It is through his interest in time that Benjamin's theory of experience is connected up to his philosophy of history. Above all, this interest is an interest in the present as the site of historical experience...The fundamental question that it addresses is the question of the character of the present' (p. xii).

For Benjamin the present is both the moment and site of the actuality of the present. The past is contingent upon the action of the present. As he explores much later in the famous 'Theses on the Philosophy of History' (in *Illuminations*, thesis V), 'every image of the past that is not recognised by the present as one of its own threatens to disappear irretrievably.' As he goes on to say, 'In every era the attempt must be made anew to wrest tradition away from a conformism that is about to overpower it.'[21] This is a danger also present in historical research that seeks a sense of security through 'staying within the context' of the narratives that are invoked to make sense of gender relations in a specific historical period.

It can be important to recognise that it was the questions posed to men by the women's movements in the 1970s that made masculinity 'visible' in the present. If it has achieved a certain currency, this is partly due to men's recognition of the transformative power of rethinking what they had taken as their 'personal' and 'individual' experience through exploring the tensions between their experience as men and the cultural masculinities with which they were being implicitly disciplined. This is not to say that the insecurities that were helping to frame a 'crisis of masculinity' in Western postmodern consumer cultures can be discovered in the past, but, as with women's history, they allowed histories to be 'opened up' as new questions were directed to the past that had previously been unavailable. As Benjamin recognises, the past has been made available in different ways, and relationships of patriarchal power, violence and abuse have been named in previously unrecognised ways. But this also brings history and philosophy into a different kind of relationship with each other, challenging some post-structuralist and postmodern views that too often enforce a cultural turn that produces its own blindness in relation to the workings of structural relationships of power and violence that were central to Benjamin's engagement with the historical shapings of Western culture through a grasp of its implicit theologies of time and redemption.

As Benjamin and Osborne recognise, to speak of Benjamin 'the philosopher' should not be mistaken for a disciplinary claim. They are aware that 'if Adorno is misleading when he maintains that Benjamin "chose to remain completely outside the manifest tradition of philosophy," he is nonetheless right to emphasise the distance of his thought from philosophy in its institutionalised, academic form. In this sense, Benjamin's is indeed a "philosophy directed against philosophy"... However... it is not thereby to be sought at its margins. Rather, it occupies another space altogether' (p. x). A different kind of challenge to philosophy that might echo some of Benjamin's themes, but opens up quite different concerns, is the resonance between Wittgenstein and certain themes within feminist philosophy and practice.[22]

There is a different validation of experience, and an acknowledgement of its different layers or levels, that also engages with questions made possible through Freud and post-analytical psychotherapies that engage in different ways possible relationships between the 'personal' and the 'political'. Some of these connections are made possible through a different kind of revolutionary moment following the events in Paris in May 1968 and the narratives of oppression and liberation that were to be shaped in their wake.

Adapting the terms of Benjamin's own work on translation in 'The Task of the Translator' (1923) (*Illuminations*, p. 81), Benjamin and Osborne argue for their 'philosophical' reading of Benjamin, recognising that 'philosophy must expand and deepen its conception of itself if it is to recognise itself in Benjamin's writings'. Something similar might be said about philosophy after Wittgenstein and after feminism and queer politics. But there might also need to be a different kind of dialogue between philosophy and history in light of the new histories that have been made possible through the social movements of the 1970s and 80s. Not only have new questions been framed, but there are questions about historiographies and the implicit masculinist assumptions that help to shape historical practices in the present. Engaging with Benjamin's notions of 'the now' (*Jetztzeit*) calls for a different history of the present from those encouraged by Foucault, though there might be helpful discussions between them.

There might be no single history of men and masculinities because of the complexity of the interrelations that are alive in different historical moments, but there are historical studies that engage critically with histories of men and masculinities that work to queer relationships between present and past. This calls for new forms of interdisciplinarity and so for a more serious engagement with the theoretical writings that have emerged to make tensions between men and diverse cultural masculinities visible in the present, so opening up a new kind of dialogue between history, social theory and philosophy.

As different issues emerge in the present, particularly after 9/11, there is an awareness that we also need to rethink relationships between the secular and the religious, and the different kinds of masculinities that are fostered through a resistance that seems to easily mutate into a hatred of the West. A different kind of history of the present becomes necessary, as I have tried to explore in *Urban Fears and Global Terrors: Citizenship, Multicultures and Belongings* (London: Routledge, 2007), in which we have to frame different ways of thinking relationships between men and masculinities that allow for cultural diversity and religious tradition.[23] We are engaging with forms of precarious belongings, as different historical narratives come together in the present, framing challenging questions to historical traditions that have been largely framed as narratives of the nation state.

## Notes

1. Some of the papers from this Bradford conference and some of the discussions they provoked have been published by Jeff Hearn and David Morgan (eds), *Men, Masculinities and Social Theory* (London, 1990). For a sense of the later development of Jeff Hearn's work see, for instance, *Men in the Public Eye* (London, 1992) and *The Violences of Men* (London, 1998). For a sense of David Morgan's work see *Discovering Men* (London, 1992). The conference was initially framed through a presentation of work by Harry Brod and Michael Kimmel that had been done in the United States, where men more readily identified themselves as 'male feminists', while in the UK we were inclined to think in terms of the critical study of men and masculinities. For Brod's work, see his edited collection (which had just been published and was offered as a possible text), H. Brod (ed.), *The Making of Masculinities: The New Men's Studies* (Boston, 1987), and Michael Kimmel (ed.), *Changing Men: New Directions in Research on Men and Masculinity* (Newbury Park CA, 1987).
2. Initially it was through role theory that psychology as a discipline had learnt to think and research the nature of gender relations, and it was largely through questioning some of the disciplinary assumptions in psychology that the first collection of work was gathered by Joseph H. Pleck and Jack Sawyer (eds), *Men and Masculinity* (Englewood Cliffs, 1974). I share some of my own experience of my time in Boston and the intensities of the political and cultural movements largely stimulated through

the anti-Vietnam war movement, as well as the beginnings of reflections on men and masculinities that move across disciplinary borders, in Victor J. Seidler, *Rediscovering Masculinity: Reason, Language and Sexuality* (London, 1987).

3. There are different historical traditions, and it might well have been that there was a different historical awareness in the ways in which feminisms developed in the UK and in the USA, though historians were critical in both movements. For a sense of the development of Sheila Rowbotham's work, see *Woman's Consciousness, Man's World* (Harmondsworth, 1972); *Hidden from History* (London, 1973); and her collection of essays *Dreams and Dilemmas* (London, 1983).

4. For an illuminating biography of Edward Carpenter and the cultural and political movements of which he was a part, see Sheila Rowbotham, *Edward Carpenter* (London, 2009). For work that largely focuses upon the histories of men and masculinities in Britain, see M. Roper and J. Tosh (eds), *Manful Assertions: Masculinities in Britain since 1800* (London, 1991). For some interesting work on the social history of men and masculinities in the United States, see Michael Kimmel, *Manhood in America: A Cultural History* (New York, 1996).

5. The ways in which dominant masculinities are framed through an Enlightenment vision of modernity is a theme explored in Victor J. Seidler, *Unreasonable Men: Masculinity and Social Theory* (London, 1993). It is also a theme in Arthur Brittan, *Masculinity and Power* (Oxford, 1989). Before his untimely death Arthur Brittan had been planning to write a book that would focus upon the relationship between masculinities and modernity.

6. It is surprising that some of the collections that bring together the work on men and masculinities tend to be focused around an implicit anti-sexist men's politics, while tending to displace the writing within *Achilles Heel* that could question this tendency of work and maintain a different sense of the polarity, with writings framed around notions of men's liberation. For a sense of the writing within *Achilles Heel*, including some specifically historical writing by Paul Atkinson and others, see Victor J.J. Seider (ed.), *The Achilles Heel Reader: Men, Sexual Politics and Socialism* (London, 1991) and *Men, Sex and Relationships: Writings from Achilles Heel* (London, 1992). Most of this writing was collected from the early years of the journal, but it continued late into the 1980s, and some of this later work is available on the Internet.

7. The way in which a dominant masculinity can leave men in an externalised relationship with their own experience is something that is difficult to illuminate within post-structuralist traditions that find it hard to value the interior emotional lives of subjects as anything other than an internalisation of external structures. Possibly this helps account for the resistance to post-structuralisms that otherwise offered significant insights into the fragmentation and fluidity of identities. Issues around the relationship between language, power and experience were a theme in Victor J. Seidler, *Rediscovering Masculinity: Reason, Language and Sexuality* (London, 1987).

8. For an interesting collection that cut across the boundaries of 'straight' and 'gay' masculinities and which drew upon work from *Achilles Heel*, see Andy Metcalf and Martin Humphries (eds), *The Sexuality of Men* (London, 1985).

9. For a sense of Laing's work and the significance of thinking about the complex relations between reason and madness within the wider counterculture of the 1970s, see, for instance, R.D. Laing, *The Divided Self* (Harmondsworth, 1966); *The Politics of Experience* (Harmondsworth, 1967); and the later *The Voice of Experience* (Harmondsworth, 1983). For a helpful engagement with the anti-psychiatry

movement, see, for instance, A. Collier, *R.D. Laing: The Philosophy and Politics of Psychotherapy* (Brighton, 1977).
10. An interesting collection that helps to frame a sense of the tensions as feminist insights came to be cast within post-structuralist terms is Judith Butler and Joan Scott (eds), *Feminists Theorize the Political* (New York, 1992). See also Linda Nicholson and Steven Seidman (eds), *Social Postmodernism: Beyond Identity Politics* (Cambridge, 1996).
11. In exploring how a tradition of Kantian ethics, and the ways in which it helped frame secular notions of modernity, carried implicit masculinist assumptions in relation to a notion of the rational self that came to be universalised within a dominant secularised Christian tradition, I was showing how gender, ethics, language and power were related to each other within particular academic disciplinary practices. See Victor J. Seidler, *Kant, Respect and Injustice: The Limits of Liberal Moral Theory* (London, 1986).
12. For some helpful and illuminating discussions of the relationship of feminisms to postmodernities see, for instance, Linda Nicholson (ed.), *Feminism/Postmodernism* (New York, 1990).
13. I have shared some of these memories of cultural and family displacement that trace back to the Holocaust and the ways they are communicated trans-generationally in Victor J. Seidler, *Shadows of the Shoah: Jewish Identity and Belonging* (Oxford, 2000).
14. I have attempted to explore different levels or layers of men's experience and the tensions with cultural masculinities they are brought up to identify with in Victor J. Seidler, *Man Enough: Embodying Masculinities* (London, 2000).
15. For a sense of the development of Connell's work over time, see, for instance, R.W. Connell, *Which Way is Up? Essays on Sex, Class and Culture* (London, 1983); *Gender and Power: Society, the Person and Sexual Politics* (Cambridge, 1987); and *Masculinities* (Cambridge, 1995 and 2006).
16. For a critical engagement with Connell's work and some of the literature on 'hegemonic masculinities' regarding the difficulties it creates for effectively researching the changes in men's lives across diverse globalised cultures, see Victor J. Seidler, *Transforming Masculinities: Men, Cultures, Bodies, Power, Sex and Love* (London, 2007).
17. For a sense of the work that Daniel Boyarin has done to shift the terms of discussion about the relationship of a dominant Christian tradition and its traditions of contempt for 'Carnal Israel', which came to be identified with a rejected body that was associated with sexuality and the 'sins of the flesh', see Daniel Boyarin, *Carnal Israel: Reading Sex in Talmudic Judaism* (Berkeley, 1993) and *A Radical Jew: Paul and the Politics of Identity* (Berkeley,1994). These are themes that I have also attempted to explore in Victor J. Seidler, *Jewish Philosophy and Western Culture* (London, 2008).
18. For a helpful introduction to Walter Benjamin's thinking about history and theory, see, for instance, Howard Caygill, *Walter Benjamin: The Colour of Experience* (London, 1998). See also Andrew Benjamin and Peter Osborne (eds), *Walter Benjamin's Philosophy: The Destruction of Experience* (London, 1994).
19. For an illuminating intellectual biography that helps us think connections between Wittgenstein's life and the developments in his philosophical work, see, for instance, Ray Monk, *Wittgenstein* (London, 1980). See also Norman Malcolm, *Ludwig Wittgenstein: A Memoir* (Oxford, 1958) and *Nothing is Hidden* (Oxford, 1986). For an interesting engagement with John Stuart Mill's work, see Kwame Anthony Appiah, *The Ethics of Identity* (Princeton NJ, 2005); Alan Ryan, *The Philosophy of John*

*Stuart Mill*, rev. edn (Basingstoke, 1987); Wendy Donner, *The Liberal Self: John Stuart Mill's Moral and Political Philosophy* (Ithaca, 1992); and Fred Berger, *Happiness, Justice and Freedom: The Moral and Political Philosophy of John Stuart Mill* (Berkeley, 1984).
20. W. Benjamin, *The Origins of German Tragic Drama* (London, 1977), p. 182.
21. Walter Benjamin's seminal reflections on 'Theses on the philosophy of history' are to be found in Hannah Arendt (ed.), *Illuminations*, trans. H. Zohn (London, 1973).
22. Some of the resonances between Wittgenstein's later work and insights made available through feminism and sexual politics are explored in *Unreasonable men: Masculinity and Social Theory* (London, 1993).
23. I have explored some of the ways in which histories make themselves 'present', and how this relates to particular cultural and religious traditions and the ways in which they help to shape particular masculinities, in Victor J. Seidler, *Urban Fears and Global terrors: Citizenship, Multicultures and Belongings after 7/7* (London, 2007). See also Tahir Abbas (ed.), *Islamic Political Radicalism* (Edinburgh, 2007).

# Index

Abu-Lughod, Lila, 36, 53, 134
*Achilles Heel*, 13, 18, 32, 219, 434, 435, 441
Activism, 22, 39, 136
Adolescence, 3, 9, 22, 51, 62, 70, 78, 108, 148, 158, 174, 190, 194, 195, 198, 200, 202, 204, 205, 207, 209, 211, 212, 213, 215, 218, 226, 228, 229, 230, 234, 236, 238, 245, 246, 250, 253, 254, 255, 271, 287, 298, 308, 317, 323, 329, 331, 332, 334, 336, 338, 343, 351, 374, 397; *see also* Boys; Childhood/Children; Girls
Aesthete, 267, 383
Africa, 27, 116, 133, 134, 136, 190, 360, 421, 422, 430
Age/life stage, 4, 9, 10, 23, 27, 45, 50, 51, 60, 62, 66, 78, 90, 103, 107, 108, 109, 110, 113, 114, 119, 120, 121, 128, 134, 150, 158, 176, 180, 181, 191, 192–202, 203, 207, 209, 215, 217, 218, 220, 221, 222, 224, 226–45, 246, 247, 248, 250, 251, 252, 253, 263–79, 288, 290, 291, 293, 324, 330, 338, 352, 380, 398, 406; *see also* Adolescence; Boys; Children; Maturity; Old Age
Agency, 6, 9, 18, 21, 31, 44, 47, 49, 57, 118, 119, 120, 121, 123, 124, 130, 132, 133, 134, 136, 137, 162, 178, 287, 327, 402, 423
AIDS, 318
Alcoholism, 141, 330; *see also* Drinking
Alexander the Great, 98, 100, 103
Amussen, Susan, 246, 257n, 258n
Androgyny, 42
Anglicanism, 152, 290, 292, 301, 302, 391, 392, 393, 395, 407, 408; *see also* Christianity; Religion
Anthropology, 6, 35–56, 71, 125, 136, 191; *see also* Bourdieu, Pierre; Geertz, Clifford; *Habitus*; Lévi-Strauss, Claude; Rite of Passage; Rituals; van Gennep, Arnold
Anti-psychiatry movement, 316, 435; *see also* Laing, R. D.

Anti-sexism, 19, 20, 21, 30, 32; *see also* Activism; Feminism
Apprentices, 202, 229, 396, 399
Ariès, Philippe, 246, 258
Aristophanes, 101, 198, 200, 211, 220, 224
Aristotle, 102, 103, 195, 198, 200, 202, 221, 222, 228, 277
Arithmetic, 249, 252, 256
Arnold, Matthew, 272–3, 445; *see also* Rugby (school)
Arnold, Thomas, 263, 268, 272, 278, 280, 282
Asceticism, 10, 84, 85, 86, 129, 294–6, 298; *see also* Celibacy; Sexuality
Asia, 56, 97, 111, 135, 422
Athens, 7, 9, 34, 97–114, 189–226, 279
Athleticism, 129, 200, 215, 216, 217, 221, 267, 314
Augustine of Hippo, 82, 129
Australia, 112, 345, 421
Autobiography, 29, 170, 182, 246, 288, 344, 414

Bailey, Joanne, 8, 31, 34, 167, 279, 323
Ballads, 173, 185, 253; *see also* Songs
Bastardy, 167, 171, 182, 226, 232, 236, 237, 239
Bayly, C. A., 128, 136n
Benin, 114–16, 128, 133
Benjamin, Walter, 443, 446
Bennett, Judith M., 120, 123n, 126, 134, 136n, 142, 162n, 242n, 243n
Bible, 292, 371, 373, 375, 376, 378, 379, 381, 386, 387, 395, 403
Biology, 8, 43, 44, 46, 76, 167, 227, 249, 385, 386
Birkbeck, University of London, 13, 17, 31, 71, 437
Birmingham, 29, 290, 404, 412
Bly, Robert, 21, 32n, 39
Bonding, 20, 60, 118, 209, 355, 359, 416; *see also* Homosociality; Rituals
Bourdieu, Pierre, 1, 2, 14, 38, 54, 71, 74, 142, 143, 144, 159, 162; *see also* Anthropology; *Habitus*

453

454  *Index*

Boys, 1, 9, 49, 83, 158, 191, 192, 193, 194, 195, 198, 200, 201, 202, 205, 207, 209, 212, 213, 215, 217, 218, 220n, 221n, 223n, 224n, 228, 246, 247, 250, 251, 253, 255, 256, 257, 264, 266, 267, 269, 270, 273, 276, 277, 285, 312, 313, 323, 329, 330, 333, 336, 343, 351, 357, 358, 359, 362, 363, 439, 444, 445; *see also* Adolescence; Childhood/Children; Family; Fathers; Mothers
Bradford, 13, 17, 433, 450
Braudel, Fernand, 8, 144, 163n, 189
Britain, 8, 12, 17, 18, 19, 21, 24, 27, 263, 266, 267, 277, 278, 286, 290, 294, 305, 375, 390, 391, 392, 396, 415, 417, 434, 435, 441
British Columbia, 330, 344, 345
British Sociological Association, 14, 17, 433
Brod, Harry, 74n, 218n, 437, 450n
Brothels, 12, 210, 236, 355, 359, 362, 413–33; *see also* Prostitutes
Bruges, 230, 233, 238
Buddhism, 124, 135, 376; *see also* Religion
Butler, Judith, 43, 55n, 134n, 451n

Calais, 226, 230, 233, 234, 238, 422
Calvinism, 402; *see also* Christianity; Protestantism; Religion
Cambridge, 10, 70, 120, 267, 270, 285, 288
Canada, 11, 12, 323–46, 365, 389–411, 430
Canning, Kathleen, 24, 33n, 119
Canterbury, 250, 295
Capitalism, 12, 42, 45, 124, 136, 142, 265, 376, 404
Carlyle, Thomas, 152, 290
Carter, Philip, 173, 185n, 317, 322n
Castration, 62
Catholicism, 128, 130, 155, 275, 286, 287, 290, 298, 300, 397; *see also* Christianity; Religion
Celibacy, 60, 62, 70, 72, 77, 81, 82, 83, 86, 94, 121, 137, 242, 289, 290, 417; *see also* Asceticism; Sexuality
Chakrabarty, Dipesh, 125, 126, 128, 136n
Charity, 80, 176, 249, 276, 298
Charlemagne, 76, 78, 80, 83, 90
Chester, 236, 243
Child Oblation, 83, 92

Childhood/children, 1, 3, 27, 28, 29, 30, 45, 64, 83, 98, 102, 106, 107, 110, 148, 153, 158, 167–186, 194, 198, 202, 222, 224, 227, 228, 229, 236, 237, 239, 240, 246–59, 264, 274, 275, 303, 306, 323–44, 363, 389–412, 417, 419, 436, 438, 439, 444; *see also* Adolescence; Boys; Girls; Families
China, 6, 37, 44, 48, 49, 50, 55, 56, 111, 124, 128, 130, 131, 132, 134, 135, 136, 137, 422
Chivalry, 3, 63, 65, 68, 69, 443
Chodorow, Nancy, 49
Christianity, 10, 12, 66, 79, 81, 82, 84, 128, 129, 145, 147, 151, 152, 156, 159, 249, 274, 276, 287, 288, 297, 328, 371, 375, 376, 377, 378, 379, 382, 383, 385, 386, 393, 396, 398, 400, 401, 403, 406, 438, 442, 443, 444, 446, 447; *see also* Calvinism; Catholicism; God; Methodism; Muscular Christianity; Presbyterianism; Protestantism; Religion
Christie, Nancy, 12, 168, 324, 389
Cicero, 277
Citizens, 100–11, 189, 191, 192, 194, 200, 202, 210, 213, 218, 222, 230, 305, 326, 391, 405, 406
Civility, 161, 248
Clark, Anna, 22, 32n, 34n
Class/social status, 4, 7, 8, 10, 11, 13, 19, 23, 24, 27, 29–30, 45, 58, 60, 82, 83, 105–6, 116, 121–2, 129–30, 132, 139–40, 142–5, 153–4, 156, 158–9, 167–9, 171, 173–4, 176–80, 190, 192, 202, 209–11, 218, 228–9, 231–2, 246, 249, 263–8, 286–7, 289, 291–3, 295, 297–8, 305–8, 311, 312, 314, 315, 317–18, 326, 327, 330, 342, 350–1, 353, 354, 355, 357, 358, 359, 360, 362, 363, 392–3, 396, 397, 399, 402, 404, 406, 407, 418, 419, 435, 436, 443
Classification, 36, 47, 49, 62, 117, 246, 417, 418
Clergy, 3, 62, 67, 69, 70, 72, 78, 81, 83, 84, 86, 91, 93, 129, 130, 131, 137, 151, 270, 289, 299, 357, 373, 391, 405; *see also* Papacy; Religion

Clifford, James, 36, 53n
Clothing, 28, 69, 134, 148, 156, 158, 200, 203, 215, 216, 234, 235, 250, 251, 253, 260, 287, 301, 312, 349, 353, 362, 443
Cobbett, William, 29, 178, 179
Codes of masculinity, 4, 9, 20, 22, 143, 145, 149, 153, 157, 170, 174, 180, 308, 372, 373, 374, 414, 419, 423, 424; *see also* Gentlemanliness; Hegemonic masculinity; Heroes; Honour; Independence, ideal of; Internalization; Muscular Christianity; Self-control; Stereotypes
Cohen, David, 191, 202
Cohen, Deborah, 304, 311, 319n
Cold War, 125, 326, 345
Coleridge, Samuel Taylor, 270, 273
Collini, Stefan, 71n, 266, 280n
Colonial, 4, 8, 23, 25, 26, 27, 28, 38, 39, 40, 46, 51, 116, 133, 136n, 324, 390, 391, 392, 393, 394, 397, 420, 422, 423; *see also* Race
Conduct literature, 2, 5, 10, 141, 145, 159, 162, 246, 247, 248, 249, 254, 255, 259, 414, 444
Confucianism, 48, 49, 131, 133; *see also* Religion
Connell, R. W., 7, 8, 17, 20, 25, 32, 33, 45, 46, 47, 55n, 60, 72, 101, 110, 111n, 113n, 118, 122, 126, 127, 133n, 136n, 139, 140, 142, 143, 145, 152, 160n, 163n, 181n, 184, 187, 219n, 258, 262, 265, 279, 280, 415, 430n, 441, 442
Constructivism, 44, 48, 60
Consumerism, 324, 326, 448; *see also* Capitalism
Cook, Matt, 11, 34n, 286, 318n, 319n, 322n
Cooper, Kate, 82, 92n, 129, 137n
Counter-culture, 21, 433
Crete, 192, 205, 222
Crisis (of masculinity), 11, 119, 326, 327, 328, 335, 338, 342, 343, 344, 413, 448
Cuckoldry, 76, 78, 79, 81
Culture, 1, 2, 4, 5, 6, 8, 9, 11, 12, 18, 20, 22, 23, 24, 25, 27, 28, 29, 30, 31, 35, 36, 37, 38, 39, 41, 42, 43, 44, 45, 46, 49, 50, 51, 57, 58, 60, 61, 63, 66, 70, 97, 98, 99, 100, 118, 119, 121, 123, 124, 125, 126, 127, 128, 132, 139, 141, 144, 149, 152, 154, 159, 160, 169, 170, 172, 173, 174, 177, 179, 181, 209, 263, 264, 266, 273, 286, 304, 305, 306, 308, 313, 317, 318, 350, 373, 377, 381, 389, 390, 391, 392, 393, 394, 396, 397, 407, 413, 414, 433, 437, 441, 442, 443, 446, 447, 448, 449

Daughters, 106, 172, 174, 175, 176, 213, 229, 231, 247–8, 251, 252, 329, 331, 332–4, 340, 341, 372; *see also* Children; Families; Fathers; Girls; Mothers
Davidoff, Leonore, 22, 29, 32n, 33n, 34n, 183n, 184n, 319n
Davidson, James, 200
Davis, Natalie Zemon, 20, 117
Deane, Anthony C., 285, 299n
Dearden, Basil, 307
Demosthenes, 103, 277
Deslandes, Paul, 267, 280n, 286, 299n
Devon, 148, 150, 151, 152, 163, 164
Diaries, 11, 12, 27, 145, 169, 171, 176, 177, 246, 247, 249, 251, 252, 255, 256, 257, 261, 295, 297, 302, 303, 308, 309, 310, 312, 313, 314, 315, 318, 321, 326, 341, 344, 370, 394, 397, 398, 402, 410, 414, 427
Dickens, Thomas, 27
Dieppe, 422
Dierks, Konstantin, 22, 32n
Disgrace, 78, 94, 211, 230
Divorce, 30; *see also* Marriage
Dollimore, Jonathan, 306, 319n
Domesticity, 10, 11, 24, 29, 139, 161, 168, 169, 173, 184, 286, 299, 303, 306, 310, 319, 345, 392, 394, 401, 407, 408, 411; *see also* Family; Household
Douglas, Lord Alfred, 378
Dover, Kenneth, 191
Drama, 1, 99, 100–8, 198, 313
Drinking, 157, 174, 201, 236, 254, 295, 350, 354, 355, 356, 359, 361, 362, 367, 399; *see also* Alcoholism
Duty, 10, 12, 31, 146, 155, 180, 249, 276, 331, 394, 395, 399, 417
Dyer, Richard, 313, 321n

East India, 158
Education, 1, 3, 11, 20, 22, 25, 29, 30, 102, 130, 150, 155, 189, 194, 198, 202, 209, 210, 218, 249, 253, 263–83, 325, 330, 332, 334, 342, 343, 344, 434, 439; *see also* Arnold, Thomas; Rugby (school)
Effeminacy, 45, 80, 179, 264, 267, 269, 271, 279, 308, 311, 318, 327; *see also* Emasculation
Egypt, 98, 99, 134, 422, 426, 429
Ellis, Havelock, 321n, 374
Emasculation, 7, 11, 43, 50, 60, 62, 70, 82, 230, 269, 327, 350, 363; *see also* Effeminacy
Emigration, 25, 27, 28, 34
Emotions, 19, 69, 100, 167, 168, 172, 174, 176, 177, 178, 179, 180, 193, 207, 246, 249, 251, 252, 255, 256, 270, 286, 307, 315, 316, 317, 328, 400, 437, 439, 440, 444, 445, 446; *see also* Love; Tenderness
England, 8, 26, 27, 31, 32, 34, 62, 64, 66, 70, 71, 72, 73, 74, 91, 140–65, 167–86, 227–43, 245–62, 266, 267, 268, 272, 279, 288, 290, 291, 298, 299, 300, 301, 304, 318, 320, 322, 331, 390, 391, 392, 393, 408, 409, 412, 426, 428, 429, 444
Enlightenment, the, 44, 49, 162, 442
Erotic, 200, 204, 211, 215, 216, 220, 373, 374, 383, 385, 386, 388, 419; *see also* Love; Sexuality
Ethnicity, 4, 5, 7, 102, 103, 104, 105, 106, 109, 110, 121, 126, 181, 278, 425; *see also* Race
Eton, 149
Eurocentrism, 124, 125, 127, 135
Evangelicalism, 139, 169, 288, 397, 399, 401, 402, 403, 406; *see also* Christianity; Religion

Family, 7, 9, 10, 11, 12, 19, 20, 22, 24, 28, 29, 30, 48, 78, 82, 83, 98, 102, 105, 106, 107, 110, 121, 127, 130, 132, 145, 146, 147, 148, 149, 150, 151, 152, 153, 154, 156, 157, 158, 159, 167–86, 189, 212, 213, 226–44, 245, 252, 253, 256, 286, 298, 304, 305, 306, 308, 309, 312, 314, 315, 316, 317, 323–48, 351, 358, 360, 374, 384, 385, 389–412, 419, 435, 438, 439, 442; *see also* Children; Daughters; Fathers; Mothers; Sons
Fathers, 1, 3, 8, 9, 11, 12, 25, 28, 29, 30, 31, 83, 105, 149, 167–86, 213, 218, 224, 227, 231, 232, 239, 247, 249, 253, 255, 256, 279, 316, 323–44, 351, 389–412, 440, 444; *see also* Boys; Children; Family; Mothers
Fathers, Financial responsibilities of, 19, 171, 176, 178, 180, 232, 237, 339, 391, 395, 400, 401, 402, 404, 407, 438
Femininity, 4, 13, 20, 55, 86, 118, 119, 122, 142, 167, 191, 213, 264, 265, 267, 280, 436, 443
Feminisation, 43, 192, 286
Feminism, 1, 13, 17, 20, 21, 28, 36, 38–41, 44, 48, 49, 52, 54, 59, 92, 117, 118, 120, 123, 125, 133, 134, 135, 162, 189, 263, 265, 280, 406, 423, 433, 437, 438, 439, 440, 441, 448
Filene, Peter G., 18, 32n, 364n
Films, 307, 327, 363
Finn, Margot, 311, 320n
First World War, 3, 12, 161, 220, 326, 413–31
Flagellation, 272
Fletcher, Anthony, 74n, 161n, 182n, 249, 258n, 259n, 279n, 322n
Foppishness, 139
Foucault, Michel, 2, 24, 44, 45, 55n, 190, 218n, 219n, 220n, 280n, 300n, 435, 449
Foyster, Elizabeth, 34n, 141, 181n, 246, 247, 250, 258n
France, 12, 24, 33, 54, 76, 95, 148, 155, 182, 186, 243, 268, 269, 278, 322, 390, 394, 397, 408, 410, 412, 413, 414, 416, 417, 422, 425, 426, 428, 429, 431
Francis of Assisi (Saint), 10, 285–303
Freud, Sigmund, 44, 55n, 316, 321n, 448; *see also* Psychoanalysis

Gambling, 157, 230, 239, 288, 350, 354, 355, 359, 362, 399
Gangster, 41, 331

Geertz, Clifford, 24, 33, 45, 54, 163; *see also* Anthropology
Gellner, Ernest, 131, 137n
Geneva, 146, 147, 160, 163
Gentlemanliness, 8, 26, 142, 144, 146, 149, 154, 157–60, 173, 248, 416
Germany, 22, 37, 76, 116, 140, 419, 447
Gift-exchange, 205, 207, 215; *see also* Anthropology; Bonding; Rituals
Gilmore, David, 44, 55n, 60, 72n, 74n
Girls, 41, 104, 201, 229, 256, 330, 332, 334, 338, 420–1; *see also* Children; Daughters
God, 3, 12, 65, 67, 68, 69, 77, 79, 84, 85, 115, 116, 121, 129, 130, 157, 172, 176, 232, 237, 248, 249, 252, 255, 287, 290, 291, 292, 293, 379, 389, 390, 391, 392, 393, 394, 395, 398, 399, 400, 401, 402, 403, 404; *see also* Christianity; Religion
Goldberg, Jeremy, 73n, 230, 240n, 242n, 243n
Gramsci, Antonio, 7, 45, 55n, 121, 136n, 143, 159
Gregory, Jeremy, 140, 144, 409n

*Habitus*, 38, 142, 143, 144, 153, 155; *see also* Anthropology; Bourdieu, Pierre
Haggard, H. Rider, 5, 26
Hagiography, 68, 77, 85, 130, 287, 288, 296
Hall, Catherine, 26, 32n, 33n, 127, 133n, 184n, 319n
Hall, Stuart, 266, 317, 322n
Halliwell, Kenneth, 303, 319
Halperin, David, 190
Hanawalt, Barbara H., 227, 229, 240n, 241n, 243n
Harvey, Karen, 25, 32n, 33n, 71n, 170, 278n, 279n, 280n, 319n
Heather Ellis, 10, 34n, 263, 278n, 280n, 282n, 324, 445
Hegemonic masculinity, 8, 20, 32, 33, 37, 45, 46, 96, 101, 110, 118, 119–22, 132, 139, 144, 415, 426, 442
Henry IV, king of England, 115, 122, 132, 134
Heroes, 5, 11, 64, 65, 89, 102, 104, 174, 316, 336, 349, 357, 361, 363
Heterosexuality, *see* Sexuality (heterosexuality)

Himmbelfarb, Gertrude, 289, 301n
Holter, Øystein Gullvåg, 265, 280
Holy man, in late antiquity, 78, 127, 129, 132
Homophobia, 375
Homosexuality, *see* Sexuality (homosexuality)
Homosociality, 3, 10, 20, 22, 51, 103, 106, 209, 372, 405, 415, 416, 421, 423
Honour, 1, 2, 5, 7, 8, 9, 39, 62, 63, 64, 65, 66, 67, 68, 69, 70, 77, 79, 84, 140, 142, 144, 145, 146, 148, 149, 154, 159, 247, 250, 254, 356, 357, 358, 372, 380
Hornsey, Richard, 311, 320n
Houlbrook, Matt, 34n, 313, 319n, 320n
Houlbrooke, Ralph, 246, 249, 258n
Household, 2, 3, 19, 28, 30, 98, 100, 103, 105, 106, 110, 141, 146, 156, 168, 169, 177, 180, 192, 230, 234, 237, 243, 389–407, 438, 442, 444; *see also* Family; Fathers, financial responsibilities of
Hufton, Olwen, 22, 32n
Hume, David, 131
Husbands, 1, 3, 27, 77, 78, 85, 173, 256, 327, 328, 344, 395, 397, 405; *see also* Family; Household; Wives
Hypermasculinity, 9, 227

Iconic masculinity, 8, 26, 42, 114–38, 350
Immaturity, 10, 247, 256, 266, 275
Imperialism, 9, 26, 33, 53, 55, 140, 189
Impotence, 63, 64, 66, 73, 129, 443
Independence, ideal of, 8, 27, 130, 142, 149, 151, 153, 154, 168, 173, 178, 179, 180, 194, 202, 218, 245, 246, 269, 339, 399, 440, 445
India, 6, 33, 49, 54, 124, 135, 157, 158, 422, 429
Industrialization, 19, 124–5, 140, 142, 287, 291, 327, 358, 390, 392, 398, 404, 406
Insults, 39, 50, 104, 211
Internalization, 143, 144, 159, 394, 397; *see also* Codes of masculinity; Hegemonic masculinity
Ireland, 27, 148, 368, 428
Islam, 55, 124, 128, 130, 131, 227, 443; *see also* Religion

458  Index

Japan, 12, 37, 48, 54, 56, 111, 124, 136, 294, 370–87
Jarman, Derek, 317
Jews, 130, 439
Jordan, Jennie, 444
*Journal of British Studies*, 19, 25, 141

Karras, Ruth Mazo, 59, 60, 72n, 73n, 74n, 182n, 183n, 236, 240n, 241n, 242n, 243n, 264, 265, 279n, 280n, 443
Kimmel, Michael, 19, 22, 25, 32n, 54n, 227, 350, 364n, 450n
Kingsley, Charles, 273, 399

Laing, R. D., 316
Laqueur, Thomas, 44, 55n
Laslett, Peter, 28, 34n, 251, 260n
Legislation, 1, 78, 200, 202, 305, 317, 359, 374
Letters, 1, 2, 9, 12, 26, 27, 30, 77, 81, 115, 139–66, 170, 171, 175, 176, 177, 178, 185, 192, 226–42, 271, 273, 293, 310, 312, 314, 315, 358, 364, 368, 370, 376, 378, 383, 386, 391, 394, 395, 400, 401, 403, 407, 413, 414, 429
Lévi-Strauss, Claude, 317, 342; *see also* Anthropology
Lewis, Katherine, 72n, 443
Leyser, Conrad, 82, 129
Libertines, 139, 187
Linda Pollock, 246, 258n
Locke, John, 146, 392, 395, 406–7
London, 10, 19, 70, 139, 140, 141, 156, 158, 229, 230, 238, 251, 285–301, 303–22, 378, 398, 400, 421, 449
Love, 20, 35, 77, 83, 109, 172, 174, 175, 180, 184, 207, 209, 226, 233, 235, 238, 288, 290, 296, 307, 309, 313, 315, 331, 333, 335, 361, 374, 375, 382, 383, 385, 397; *see also* Emotions; Erotic; Sexuality; Tenderness

Macedonia, 99, 100, 102, 221
Marcus, Sharon, 304, 310, 319n
Marriage, 63, 78, 81, 82, 84, 85, 98, 100, 102, 103, 104, 106, 107, 108, 130, 147, 151, 168, 171, 174, 177, 191, 209, 215, 226, 228, 229, 231, 232, 233, 238, 245, 294, 331, 332, 339, 354, 374, 397, 398, 399, 400, 401, 402, 415, 436, 438; *see also* Husbands; Wives
Marxism, 45, 46, 54, 55, 121, 125, 127, 133, 135, 136, 265, 435
Masculinity, *see* Bonding; Codes of Masculinity; Crisis (of masculinity); Effeminacy; Emasculation; Gentlemanliness; Hegemonic masculinity; Heroes; Homosociality; Honour; Hypermasculinity; Iconic masculinity; Independence, ideal of; Internalization; Muscular Christianity; Patriarchy; Self-control; Stereotypes; Strength; Tenderness; Virility/*Virilitas*
Masturbation, 199, 230
Maturity, 10, 59, 107, 110, 113, 168, 200, 213, 215, 227, 252, 253, 257, 263, 264, 266, 267, 268, 269, 270, 271, 272, 273, 275, 277, 278, 282, 324, 417, 444, 445
Medical ideas, 49, 64, 178, 186, 227, 229, 246, 256, 293, 374, 383, 414, 443
Mediterranean, 37, 70, 74, 98, 126, 163, 189, 190, 191, 219
Melanesian, 42, 43
Methodism, 393–4, 399, 404; *see also* Christianity; Religion
Mexico, 41, 349, 356, 360, 361, 362, 364, 368
Michael Roper, 25, 32n, 33n, 170, 280n
Military, 60, 62, 63, 66, 69, 74, 78, 84, 88, 90, 128, 140, 213, 222, 371, 407, 414, 415, 425; *see also* First World War; Violence
Mill, John Stuart, 446
Milne-Smith, Amy, 286, 299n
Misogyny, 80, 81, 82, 84, 130, 313
Missionaries, 26, 27, 290, 336, 391, 406
Monasticism, 83, 92, 93, 289–300
Morgan, David, 14n, 184n, 433, 450n
Mort, Frank, 414, 426n
Mothers, 3, 8, 83, 167, 172, 173, 182, 249, 344, 390, 404, 412; *see also* Children; Family; Fathers; Household
Muscular Christianity, 145, 152, 273, 446

National identity, 3, 13, 4, 124, 308, 371, 373
Nelson, Janet, 81, 83
New Men, 18, 183, 219, 407, 450

New Zealand, 26, 27, 33, 421, 430
Newfoundland, 335, 342, 344, 430
Newman, John Henry, 271, 273, 275, 282n, 446
Newsome, David, 32n, 273, 281n
Newspapers (and Periodicals), 32, 161, 172, 173, 174, 175, 176, 180, 185, 219, 255, 262, 269, 270, 276, 281, 293, 294, 301, 302, 311, 313, 319, 321, 328, 340, 345, 352, 354, 358, 360, 361, 362, 365, 367, 368, 414
Nova Scotia, 336, 344
Novels, 27, 28, 171, 286, 307, 314, 327, 370–88

Old age, 9, 64, 107–9, 148, 246
Ontario, 332, 334, 336, 340, 341, 344, 346, 389, 402, 407, 408
Ortner, Sherry, 45, 56n, 123
Orton, Joe, 11, 303–22
Osborne, John, 303, 318
Oxford, 10, 150, 151, 193, 235, 247, 263–83, 285, 286, 287, 288, 289, 291, 292, 293, 295, 296, 297, 298, 324, 445, 446
Oxford House, 275, 285–99

Paintings, 172, 312
Papacy, 81, 82, 115, 116, 128, 134
Papua New Guinea, 41, 42, 54
Paris, 71, 74, 87, 219, 300, 418, 448
Patriarchy, 1, 4, 9, 12, 18, 19, 20, 21, 27, 28, 30, 32, 38, 45, 46, 49, 74, 86, 87, 101, 117, 119, 122, 123, 124, 132, 134, 139, 141, 142, 143, 144, 145, 154, 156, 160, 168, 173, 174, 177, 180, 189, 190, 224, 227, 240, 245, 246, 248, 254, 257, 258, 264, 323, 327, 328, 329, 358, 375, 390, 392, 393, 394, 395, 396, 397, 398, 401, 402, 403, 404, 405, 406, 407, 408, 409, 410, 415, 422, 423, 424, 437, 440, 442, 448
Plato, 131, 194, 198, 202, 204, 210, 223, 224
Poetry, 116, 132, 171, 193, 209, 274, 288, 296, 333
Politeness, 8, 139, 140, 141, 145, 147, 154, 155, 162, 237
Prayers, 83, 248, 252, 394, 395, 396, 397, 398, 403, 406

Presbyterianism, 387, 394, 395, 402, 403, 410; see also Christianity; Religion
Prostitutes, 73, 103, 108, 209, 239, 242, 266, 280, 413–31
Protestantism, 10, 139, 258, 290, 292, 298, 324, 386, 390, 398, 405, 406, 407, 408, 412; see also Christianity; Religion
Psychoanalysis, 1, 44, 46, 23, 72, 306; see also Freud, Sigmund
Psychology, 44–5, 48, 57
Puberty, 62, 200, 221, 227, 229, 241

Queer, 11, 21, 32, 34, 36, 41, 53, 54, 104, 300, 303–22, 444, 448, 449; see also Sexuality (homosexuality)

Race, 4, 23, 26, 45–7, 119, 121, 190, 263–4, 327, 350, 351, 356, 360–2, 383–4, 422–3, 436, 446; see also Ethnicity
Rape, 99, 108, 191; see also Violence
Reisman, David, 327, 345n
Religion, 4, 10, 12, 23, 80, 128, 131, 139, 150, 153, 169, 285, 286, 287, 290, 292, 354, 389–412, 443, 444; see also Anglicanism; Bible; Buddhism; Calvinism; Catholicism; Christianity; Confucianism; Evangelicalism; God; Holy Man, in late antiquity; Islam; Methodism; Missionaries; Monasticism; Muscular Christianity; Presbyterianism; Protestantism
Republicanism, 12, 390, 393, 397
Riley, Denise, 119
Rite of passage, 48, 60, 205, 209, 250, 251, 253, 415; see also Anthropology; Rituals; van Gennep, Arnold
Rituals, 20, 29, 40, 42, 43, 48, 51, 116, 128, 205, 207, 235, 324, 337, 350, 355, 356, 373, 391, 394, 395, 416, 445; see also Anthropology; Rite of passage
Roosevelt, Teddy, 349–50, 356, 363
Rotundo, Anthony, 19, 32n, 364n, 367n
Rouen, 418, 422
Rousseau, Jean-Jacques, 174
Rowbotham, Sheila, 21, 32n, 434
Rugby (school), 150, 151, 263–82, 445

Rutherdale, Robert, 2, 11, 34n, 170, 279n, 346n

Said, Edward, 26, 41, 53n
Scotland, 27, 299, 389, 391, 395
Scott, Joan Wallach, 4, 14n, 24, 25, 33n, 71n, 117, 119, 133n, 134n, 451n
Scouting, 329; *see also* Muscular Christianity
Second World War, 10, 184, 304, 325, 326, 336, 338, 426; *see also* First World War; Violence
Sedgwick, Eve Kosofsky, 304, 319
Self-control, 7, 8, 105, 108, 109, 110, 129, 142, 147, 148, 156, 168, 179, 180, 190, 254, 255, 270, 271, 352, 353, 358, 359, 389, 390, 392, 395, 398, 399, 406, 421, 442, 443, 444, 445, 446
Sermons, 5, 68, 77, 150, 151, 172, 249, 274, 395
Servants, 3, 98, 152, 230, 234, 235, 251, 254, 266, 289, 341, 389, 391, 396, 397, 398, 401, 406
Sexuality, 4, 7, 9, 10, 11, 12, 19, 23, 26, 37, 40, 42, 45, 50, 51, 59, 60, 61, 62, 63, 64, 66, 69, 70, 77, 80, 82, 84, 85, 86, 103, 105, 108, 110, 117, 118, 119, 121, 126, 129, 139, 140, 141, 144, 147, 172, 189, 190, 191, 192, 194, 198, 215, 217, 226, 229, 230, 233, 234, 235, 236, 237, 238, 247, 256, 263, 264, 287, 294, 304, 305, 306, 307, 308, 311, 316, 317, 324, 331, 333, 334, 372, 373, 374, 375, 383, 389, 397, 399, 414, 415, 416, 417, 418, 420, 421, 422, 434, 436, 437, 438, 441, 443
 heterosexuality, 13, 21, 60, 86, 87, 126, 139, 304, 306, 308, 309, 323, 374, 383, 385, 400, 413, 414, 415, 425, 435, 436, 439, 444; *see also* Marriage
 homosexuality, 11, 19, 21, 24, 31, 32, 45, 48, 156, 192, 200, 209, 212, 220, 221, 279, 287, 294, 300, 303–23, 372, 374, 375, 379, 435; *see also* Erotic; Queer
Shame, 39, 64, 65, 66, 68, 69, 70, 147, 157, 189, 203, 416
Shapiro, Alan, 194, 207

Shepard, Alexandra, 32n, 33n, 34n, 71n, 74n, 134n, 141, 160n, 161n, 163n, 170, 182n, 183n, 184n, 185n, 187n, 246, 254, 257n, 258n, 262n, 264, 265, 266, 278n, 279n, 280n, 319n, 442
Shepherd, Simon, 305, 309, 319n, 321n
Sinfield, Alan, 317, 319, 320, 322
Slavery, 7, 26, 98, 103, 104, 105, 106, 110, 191
Sobriety, 249, 359; *see also* Alcoholism; Drinking
Socrates, 204, 210
Songs, 27, 69, 173, 192, 210, 211, 215, 223, 298; *see also* Ballads
Sons, 26, 65, 84, 106, 107, 146, 150, 153, 154, 156, 157, 158, 175, 176, 177, 210, 226, 229, 230, 232, 236, 238, 247, 248, 249, 251, 252, 254, 255, 256, 269, 288, 316, 330, 334, 336, 337, 338, 339, 350, 356, 357, 391, 399, 400, 403, 437; *see also* Boys; Children; Family; Fathers; Mothers
Spivak, Gayatri Chakravorty, 6, 37, 54n, 134n
Sport, 22, 157, 207, 216, 228, 267, 329, 330, 336, 337, 338, 358
Stearns, Peter, 18, 19, 23, 32n, 124, 133n, 135n, 364n, 365n, 367n
Steedman, Carolyn, 24, 33n, 306, 319n
Stereotypes, 8, 9, 11, 19, 22, 23, 29, 41, 42, 50, 86, 142, 143, 145, 149, 153, 154, 155, 156, 157, 158, 159, 160, 189, 190, 191, 287; *see also* Codes of masculinity; Hegemonic masculinity
Stone, Lawrence, 246, 258n, 281n, 408n
Strathern, Marilyn, 36, 38, 42, 43, 44, 47, 52, 53n, 54n, 55n, 134n
Strength, 4, 7, 27, 62, 63, 66, 69, 70, 78, 79, 80, 93, 213, 246, 252, 256, 358, 363, 386
Suicide, 12, 172, 370, 371, 372, 375, 380, 381, 419

Teenagers, 217, 229; *see also* Adolescents; Boys; Girls
Television, 11, 327
Tenderness, 171–80, 185, 270, 323, 334
Thompson, E. P., 22

Tokyo, 372, 377, 385, 386, 387
Toronto, 32, 328, 331, 332, 333, 339, 391, 399, 402, 404
Tosh, John, 4, 6, 17, 32n, 33n, 34n, 44, 55n, 71n, 118, 123, 127, 133n, 141, 152, 160n, 161n, 162n, 179, 182n, 183n, 184n, 187n, 219n, 266, 277, 278n, 280n, 281n, 286, 299n, 304, 318n, 319n, 324, 325, 345n, 390, 398, 399, 407n, 408n, 410n, 412n, 415, 426n, 428n, 429n, 430n, 442, 443
Toynbee, Arnold, 292
Trial records, 63, 76, 145, 171, 179, 357, 366, 394

United States, 12, 13, 24, 135, 327, 336, 351, 360, 361, 364, 384, 388, 390, 433, 450
University, 10, 60, 64, 253, 263–83, 285, 286, 287, 297, 341, 445

van Gennep, Arnold, 228, 241n
Vickery, Amanda, 141, 162n
Violence, 8, 9, 50, 62, 66, 68, 69, 70, 104, 108, 121, 126, 139, 140, 158, 174, 175, 189, 193, 200, 205, 207, 236, 350, 355, 356, 357, 358, 359, 360, 362, 376, 420, 421, 423, 442, 448; *see also* First World War; Second World War; Warriors
Virility/*virilitas*, 1, 2, 4, 64, 73, 74, 76, 79, 80, 88, 89, 90, 168, 174, 220, 444

Warriors, 3, 4, 14, 50, 51, 84, 121, 127, 129, 131, 132, 192, 205, 220
Wayne, John, 349
Webb, Beatrice, 292, 301
Weber, Max, 131, 139, 386n
Weeks, Jeffrey, 32n, 316, 321n

Weil, Rachel, 392, 409n
White, Edmund, 316, 321n
Wiesner-Hanks, Merry, 123, 133n, 135n
Williams, Barrie, 296, 302n
Williams, Kenneth, 311, 320
Williams, Raymond, 45, 55n
Wittgenstein, Ludwig, 437, 445, 446, 448
Wives, 1, 3, 9, 26, 28, 30, 76, 77, 78, 79, 84, 85, 103, 106, 110, 114, 121, 130, 156, 171, 172, 176, 226, 229, 230, 231, 232, 238, 256, 294, 307, 328, 337, 338, 339, 341, 352, 359, 370, 380, 381, 382, 385, 389, 396, 397, 398, 400, 401, 402, 405, 416, 418, 419, 420, 438, 444; *see also* Husbands; Marriage; Women
Women, 3, 4, 7, 9, 20, 21, 22, 24, 25, 26, 32, 37, 38, 41, 50, 56, 59, 60, 62, 63, 64, 66, 73, 76, 80, 81, 82, 83, 86, 87, 90, 92, 95, 99, 102, 103, 108, 111, 117, 118, 119, 120, 121, 122, 123, 124, 130, 132, 134, 135, 137, 140, 141, 143, 144, 146, 162, 163, 184, 190, 191, 202, 209, 213, 215, 221, 227, 234, 236, 245, 246, 263, 264, 265, 266, 280, 286, 294, 300, 304, 306, 319, 323, 326, 342, 350, 351, 355, 358, 363, 374, 390, 391, 393, 394, 395, 396, 397, 401, 405, 406, 413, 414, 417, 418, 420, 421, 422, 423, 434, 435, 437, 438, 439, 440, 442, 443, 444, 447, 448; *see also* Girls; Mothers; Wives
Women's History, 20, 21, 22, 59, 92, 117, 118, 119, 120, 132, 141, 227, 300, 434, 448
Würzbach, Natascha, 253, 261n

Zinserr, Judith P., 120, 123, 126, 133n, 134n

Printed in Great Britain
by Amazon